MILLER'S
ANTIQUES
PRICE GUIDE
1982
(Volume III)

Compiled and Edited by

Martin and Judith Miller

Assistant Editor

Stuart Brunger B.A.

mJm

PUBLICATIONS LTD.
Pugin's Hall
Finchden Manor
Tenterden
Kent
telephone 058 06 2234

Acknowledgements

The publishers would like to acknowledge the great assistance given by our consultant editors

PORCELAIN: **Gordon Lang,** *Sotheby, King and Chasemore, Station Road, Pulborough, Sussex.*

Mrs. P. Lycett, *Market Bosworth Antiques, 5-7 Market Place, Market Bosworth, Nuneaton, Warwickshire.*

FURNITURE: **Richard Davidson,** *Richard Davidson Antiques, Lombard Street, Petworth, Sussex.*

CLOCKS & WATCHES: **Mr. Symonds,** *Kingston Antiques, 138 London Road, Kingston, Surrey.*

BAROMETERS: **Nigel Coleman,** *Nigel Coleman Antiques, High Street, Brasted, Kent.*

SCIENTIFIC & MEDICAL INSTRUMENTS: **Arthur Middleton,** *Arthur Middleton Ltd., 12 New Row, Covent Garden, London, W.C.2.*

GLASS: **Wing Cdr. R. G. Thomas,** *Somervale Antiques, 6 Radstock Road, Midsomer Norton, Bath, Avon.*

Gordon Lang, *Sotheby, King and Chasemore, Station Road, Pulborough, Sussex.*

SILVER & SILVER PLATE: **Eileen Goodway,** *Sotheby Parke Bernet & Co., 34 & 35 New Bond Street, London, W.1.*

ART NOUVEAU & ART DECO: **Gordon Lang,** *Sotheby, King and Chasemore, Station Road, Pulborough, Sussex.*

TOYS & DOLLS: **A. Morris,** *Sotheby, King and Chasemore, Station Road, Pulborough, Sussex.*

TREEN: **Anthony Foster,** *A. & E. Foster, 'Little Heysham', Naphill, Nr. High Wycombe, Bucks.*

TOOLS: **Richard Maude,** *Richard Maude Tools, 6 Malbrook Road, Putney, London, S.W.15.*

PINE & KITCHENALIA: **Ann Lingard,** *Rope Walk Antiques, Rye, Sussex.*

RADIOS: **J. Powell,** *York House Antiques, 37 High Street, Seal, Nr. Sevenoaks, Kent.*

EDITORIAL

Stuart Barton, Jackie White, Sheila Blackshields, Joan Bower, Samantha Irvine, Frances Page.

PHOTOGRAPHY

Peter Mould, *Brickwall, Northiam, Sussex.*
Ian Pooley, *Century Studios, Tenterden, Kent.*

Printed in Great Britain by Robert MacLehose and Company Limited Printers to the University of Glasgow

Introduction

The compilation of an annual reference work such as Miller's is a fascinating task. Not only does it involve months of photography, and research to produce the many thousands of illustrations which form each year's 'pool', it also demands constant reappraisal of the antiques trade to ensure that each section of the book is balanced in a way that is appropriate to the market at the time of going to press.

In this edition, which contains over one hundred pages more than last year's, extra space has been devoted to such subjects as drinking glasses and fans, while Oriental porcelain, Arts Nouveau and Deco, tools and treen have each been expanded to form their own, new, sections. Although, within the overall context of the antiques trade, each of these subjects represents only a small proportion, the current growth of the collectables market has been such as to suggest that there it is here the additional space can be best employed.

The late 1960s and '70s were undoubtedly boom years for the antiques trade. Indeed, conditions were such that anyone possessed of a buccaneering spirit and the price of a gallon of petrol could reasonably expect to make a good living as an 'antiques dealer' — and many did. Alongside — and often in cahoots with — these cowboys and cowgirls, the High Street and up-market sections of the trade also thrived as never before. Inevitably, some people grew greedy and, finding that they could make handsome profits from the sale of inferior stocks, lowered their trading standards accordingly. Those who preferred to maintain high professional standards found they were having to pay increasingly high prices for quality goods, tying up large amounts of capital in the process; which was fine while the boom lasted.

But then came the recession.

Although the past couple of years has, regrettably, spelled disaster for numbers of responsible dealers, many of whom found themselves caught up in the liquidity problems inherent in such a situation, it can be argued that, in the longer term, the recession will be seen to have a beneficial cleansing effect on the trade as a whole. When money is scarce, buyers tend to spend more carefully and set a premium on quality. Hitherto overpriced, inferior goods have to be turned over quickly at realistic prices in order to provide cashflow and showroom space for more merchantable goods. Complacent dealers are forced to adopt more outward-looking attitudes in order to survive and, perhaps most importantly, the get-rich-quick brigade moves on.

MARKET IMPROVING

It is against this background that the public, awakened to the pleasure and value of antiques during the boom years, is pursuing its interest with new discrimination. At last, many dealers — and particularly those who have adapted their marketing methods to prevailing conditions — are reporting a steady, if gradual, improvement in trade. The collectables market, in particular,

is showing clear signs of recovery, and the phenomenal demand for each new edition of Miller's indicates that public interest in antiques is still very much alive and growing.

The compilation of Miller's involves a great deal of contact and consultation with individuals at all levels of the antiques trade, and although there are still some pundits and a very few antiques dealers who sniff disparagingly at the mention of the words 'price guide', by far the majority of professionals heartily endorse the publication of a responsibly undertaken work which adds to the generally available fund of knowledge and information. Of course, no book can adequately substitute for years of experience in handling and assessing age, quality and value of antiques — but only a fool would imagine that this is what price guides are about, and only an arrogant fool would condemn price guides out of hand on such a charge. **The professionals who use Miller's — and their numbers run into the thousands, from general dealers to insurance assessors to cataloguers for the nation's leading auction houses — are agreed that no other publication so conveniently complements their acquired knowledge and experience.** The ten thousand or so illustrations in this, the third edition of Miller's, have been selected with this in mind, and everyone who has all three editions now has a reference system containing in the region of 24,000 photographs of different items described and valued.

NEW TRENDS

Purists may be alarmed to find that this edition contains some examples of late — and in the case of toys, particularly, very late — objects, and will doubtless object to the inclusion in an antiques reference book of, for example, an electrically powered toy robot made in Japan in the late 1960s (valued at £80–100). It is, however, an indication of the changing nature of the collectables market that such objects are now being recognised as worthy of preservation in their pristine state and no longer are required to wait out the passing of generations before being transferred from toybox to showcase.

Although this is a small example, it is indicative of two definite trends which seem likely to have an effect upon the trade within the foreseeable future. The first and simplest of these is the perfectly logical, profit-based desire to predict the 'antiques of the future' from among the artefacts of today. The second is involved with the changing social attitudes of our time, and the widespread desire to understand and preserve any and every aspect of ordinary living. Where in the past the task of documenting the age was considered to lie within the exclusive province of aesthetes and scholars (who saw it their duty to record and preserve only the 'best' products of their time; those which represented its highest aspirations and greatest achievements), it is now widely held that it is among everyday objects that the truth of the matter lies, and that a seventeenth century wooden bowl may tell more about its times than St. Paul's Cathedral, and that a toy robot is as valid a contemporary social document as a Makepeace cabinet.

This is not to say that there is likely to be a lessening of demand for objects finely made of prime materials, but that there is a growing *additional* market for things of little or no intrinsic worth whose interest and value lie outside themselves in the inferences which may be drawn from them concerning the people who might have owned them and the circumstances which might have caused them to have been made. Such motives will be incomprehensible to those collectors whose constant aim is to improve the intrinsic value of their collections, and it is not difficult to understand their sense of incredulity when they discover that what was a cheap, mass produced toy just a few years ago has acquired a value perhaps greater than that of a delicate Worcester bowl made by a craftsman over two hundred years ago.

CONTACT WITH THE TRADE

But the question of 'rightness' of values crops up all the time, and is by no means confined to such comparisons as this. In the course of a year, Miller's editorial staff spend a great deal of time discussing values with dealers, collectors and professional valuers all over the country. Dealer A, not having consulted the code letters under each photograph will say: 'Where do you get your oak prices — I wish I could buy it that cheaply'. Dealer B, less than fifty miles away will swear that no-one would ever pay such high prices for oak — not in his part of the country, anyway, while Cataloguer C, bless him, had to be convinced that a particular piece catalogued by him had sold at auction, within his estimate, for so little!

Messrs. A, B and C will then go on to say that they are perfectly happy with the illustrations, descriptions, data boxes — and even the valuations throughout the remainder of the book. **The fact is that any given set of valuations tends to appear high to a buyer and low to a seller.** Although mistakes are possible, every care is taken to ensure that all information contained in Miller's is as accurate and reliable as it can be. No item, description or valuation is included without having been considered by at least one, and often two or three, independent experts.

By these means, the immediate pressures of the market place are set aside and reasonable valuations arrived at by competent observers of — rather than participants in — the contest. Miller's, by its nature, is concerned with generalities — and *only* with generalities. **It does not pretend, or even aspire, to stand as a substitute for professional expertise in the assessment of the precise worth of any particular item, but by illustrating such a wide variety of particular items and suggesting average values it will provide a worthwhile starting point for collectors and will prove to be an invaluable aide-memoire for even the most experienced professional.**

Key to Illustrations

Each illustration and descriptive caption is accompanied by a letter-code. By reference to the following list of Auctioneers and Dealers, the source of any item may be immediately determined. In no way does this constitute or imply a contract or binding offer on the part of any of our contributors to supply or sell the goods illustrated, or similar articles, at the prices stated.

A	Aldridges, 130-132 Walcot St., Bath, Avon. Tel: 0225 62830/9
AA	Abbey Antiques, 54 High Street, Glastonbury, Somerset. Tel: 0458 31694
AAS	Ashby De-La-Zouch Auction Sales, 58 Market Street, Ashby De-La-Zouch, Leicestershire LE6 9BD. Tel: 0530 412766
AD	Andrew Dando, 4 Wood Street, Queen Square, Bath, Avon. Tel: 0225 22702
ADH	Alonzo Dawes and Hoddell, Six Ways, Clevedon, Avon. Tel: 0272 876011
AEF	A & E Foster, 'Little Heysham', Naphill, Nr. High Wycombe, Bucks. Tel: 024 024 2024
AG	Anderson and Garland, Market Street, Newcastle-upon-Tyne NE1 6XA. Tel: 0632 26271
AGr	Andrew Grant, 59/60 Foregate Street, Worcester, Worcs. Tel: 0905 52310
AK	Anthea Knowles, P.O. Box 287, London N1 1EV. Tel: 01-607 4026
AL	Ann Lingard, Rope Walk Antiques, Rye, Sussex. Tel: 3486
AM	Arthur Middleton Ltd., 12 New Row, Covent Garden, London, W.C.2. Tel: 01-836 7042 or 7062
B	Boardman Fine Art Auctioneers, Station Road Corner, Haverhill, Suffolk CB9 0EY. Tel: 0440 3784
BC	Boulton and Cooper Ltd., St. Michael's House, Malton, North Yorkshire
BHW	Butler and Hatch Waterman, High St., Tenterden, Kent TN30 6HU. Tel: 058 06 3233
BK	Bruton Knowles & Co., Albion Chambers, 55 Barton Street, Gloucester. Tel: 045 221267
BM	Bishop (Marlow) Ltd., 8 and 10 West Street, Marlow, Bucks. Tel: 062 84 3936
Bon	Bonhams, Montpelier Street, London, S.W.7. Tel: 01-584 9161
Brit	Britannia, Stands 101/59, Grays Antique Market, 58 Davies Street, London, W.1
BS	Banks and Silvers, 66 Foregate Street, Worcester, Worcs. Tel: 0905 23456
BTH	Bay Tree House Antiques, 24 West Street, Alresford, Hants. Tel: 096 273 3958
BW	Burtenshaw Walker, 66 High Street, Lewes, Sussex BN7 1XG1. Tel: 079 16 4225
BY	Bygones, (O. Dodgson), Charing, Kent. Tel: 2494
C	Christie Manson & Woods Ltd., 8 King Street, London SW1Y 6QT. Tel: 01-839 9060
Cas	Casterbridge Antiques (Ian Beards), Stands D13, 14, 18, 19, Grays Mews, 1–7 Davies Mews, London, W.1
CC	Chez Chalon (Furniture) Ltd., 10 Church Street, Crewkerne, Somerset. Tel: 0460 72920
CD	Clifford Dann and Partners, The Auction Galleries, 20/21 High Street, Lewes, Sussex. Tel: 079 16 77022
CDC	Capes Dunn & Co., 38 Charles Street, Manchester
CEd	Christie's & Edmistons Ltd., 164–166 Bath Street, Glasgow G2 4TG. Tel: 041-332 8134/7
CH	Charnwood Antiques, 65 Sparrow Hill, Loughborough, Leics. Tel: 0509 31750
Ch	Churchmans, 53 High Street, Steyning, West Sussex. Tel: 0903 813815
CKK	Coles, Knapp and Kennedy, Palace Pound, Ross-on-Wye, Hereford. Tel: 0989 2225/6/7
Cl.A	Close Antiques, 19 Little Minster Street, Winchester, Hants. Tel: 0962 64763
CR	Carl Ridley, Stand J22, Grays Mews, 1–7 Davies Mews, London, W.1
CrA	Crispin Antiques, 10 The Broadway, Amersham, Bucks.
CS	Constance Stobo, 31 Holland St., London W8 4LX. Tel: 01-937 6282
CSK	Christie's South Kensington, 85 Old Brompton Road, London S.W.7. Tel: 01-581 2231
DA	Dee and Atkinson, The Exchange, Driffield, East Yorkshire YO25 YLJ. Tel: 0377 43151
DDM	Dickinson, Davy & Markham, 10 Wrawby St., Brigg, South Humberside, DN20 8JH. Tel: 0652 53666
DEB	David E. Burrows, 4 High Street, Quorn, Leicester. Tel: 0509 42191
DLJ	Douglas L. January & Partners, Rothsay House, 122 & 124 High Street, Newmarket CB8 8JP

DO	Dodo Old Advertising, 185 Westbourne Grove, London, W.11. Tel: 01-229 3132
DSH	Dacre Son and Hartley, 1–5 The Grove, Ilkley, Yorkshire. Tel: 0943 600655
DWB	Dreweatt Watson & Barton, Donnington Priory, Donnington, Newbury, Berks. Tel: 0635 31234
EA	Exquisite Antiques, 78 High Street, Tunbridge Wells, Kent. Tel: 27755
EAN	Edward A. Nowell, 21/23 Market Place, Wells, Somerset. Tel: 0749 72415
EBB	Edwards Bigwood and Bewlay, The Old School, Tiddington, Stratford-upon-Avon CV37 7AW. Tel: 0789 69415
EE	Eatons of Eton, 62/63 High Street, Eton, Bucks. Tel: 075 35 60337
EEW	Eldon E. Worrall, 15 Seel Street, Liverpool L1 4AU. Tel: 051-0709 2950
ELR	Eadon, Lockwood and Riddle, 2 St. James' Street, Sheffield S1 1XJ. Tel: 0742 71277
F	Fabrique, 208 Clarendon Park Road, Leicester, Leics. Tel: 0533 707217
FA	Foley Antiques, Stand 124, Grays Antique Market, 58 Davies Street, London, W.1
G	Patrick and Susan Gould, Stand L17, Grays Mews Antique Market, 1–7 Davies Mews, London, W.1. Tel: 01-408 0129
GAK	G. A. Key, Aylsham, Norfolk. Tel: 026 373 3195
GBT	Gribble, Booth and Taylor, West Street, Axminster, Devon. Tel: 0297 32323
GC	Geering and Colyer, Hawkhurst, Kent. Tel: 3181
GKH	G. K. Hadfield, Blackbrook House, Tickow Lane, Shepshed, Leicester, Leics. LE12 9E7. Tel: 050 95 3014
GO	Golden Oldies Antiques, Stands 17, 61 & 62, Great Western Antiques Centre, Bartlett Street, Bath, Avon
GT	Garrod Turner, 50 St. Nicholas Street, Ipswich, Suffolk. Tel: 0473 54664
Gs	Greystoke Antiques, Swan Yard, Off Cheap Street, Sherborne, Dorset. Tel: 093 581 2833
GW	Gina Wilmshurst, Sandhill Barn Antiques, Washington, Sussex
HA	Hadlow Antiques, 1 The Pantiles, Tunbridge Wells, Kent. Tel: 0892 29858
HFM	Hothersall, Forest, McKenna & Son, Bank Salerooms, Clitheroe, Lancs. Tel: 0200 25446
HSS	Henry Spencer & Sons, 20 The Square, Retford, Notts. Tel: 0777 706767
HyD	Hy. Duke & Son, 40 South Street, Dorchester, Dorset. Tel: 0305 5080
JC	Julian Chanter Antiques, 15 East Street, Blandford Forum, Dorset. Tel: 0258 52525
J.Cr	J. Crotty & Son Ltd., 74 New King's Rd., Parsons Green, London, S.W.6. Tel: 01-385 1789
JF	John Francis, Thomas Jones & Sons, King Street, Carmarthen. Tel: 0267 33456
JGM	John G. Morris Ltd., Market Square, Petworth, Sussex GU28 0AH. Tel: 0798 42305
JH	Jonathan Horne, 66b/c Kensington Church Street, London W8 4BY. Tel: 01-221 5658
JHB	John H. Raby and Son, The Estate Office, 21 St. Mary's Road, Bradford. Tel: 0274 491121
JHS	John Hogbin & Son, 53 High Street, Tenterden, Kent. Tel: 058 06 2241
KA	Kingston Antiques, 138 London Road, Kingston, Surrey
KNG	K. Norton Grant, Stand 176, Grays Antique Market, 58 Davies Street, London, W.1
L	Lawrences, South Street, Crewkerne, Somerset. Tel: 0460 73041
LAC	Leicester Antiques Centre Ltd., 16–26 Oxford Street, Leicester, Leics.
Lan	Langlois, 10 Waterloo Street, Jersey, Channel Isles. Tel: 0534 22441
LEX	L'Exposition (Marilyn Mellins), Stand C29/32, Grays in the Mews, Davies Mews, London W.1. Tel: 01-493 7862
LL	Lowe of Loughborough, 37–40 Church Gate, Loughborough, Leics. Tel: 0509 212554, 217876
LMT	Laurence and Martin Taylor, 63 High Street, Honiton, Devon
LT	Louis Taylor & Sons, Percy Street, Hanley, Stoke-on-Trent. Tel: 0782 260222
M	Morphets of Harrogate, The Mart, 4 & 6 Albert Street, Harrogate, Yorks. HG1 1JL. Tel: 0423 502282
MA	Morgan Antiques, 22 Oppidons Road, London, N.W.3. Tel: 01-722 8287
MAI	Moore Allen and Innocent, 33 Castle Street, Cirencester, Glos. Tel: 0285 2862
MAT	Matsell Antiques Ltd., 1–3 High Street, Quorn, Leicester. Tel: 0509 414218
Max	Maxey & Son, 1–3 South Brink, Wisbech, Cambridgeshire PE13 1JA. Tel: 0945 3123/4
MB	Market Bosworth Antiques, Market Bosworth, Nuneaton, Warwickshire CV13 0LF. Tel: 0455 290316
McH	MacHumble Antiques, 11 Queen Street, Bath, Avon. Tel: 0225 62751
McMB	McCartney, Morris & Barker, Corve Street, Ludlow, Shropshire. Tel: 0584 2636
Mlms	Mallams, 24 St. Michaels Street, Oxford. Tel: 0865 41358
MM	Mark Maynard, Hawkhurst, Kent
MMB	Messenger May Baverstock, 93 High Street, Godalming, Surrey. Tel: 048 68 23567
MS	Mary Salter, East Street, Lewes, Sussex
MT	Melvyn Traub, 148–149 Grays Antique Market, 58 Davies Street, London, W.1. Tel: 01-493 0560
N	Neales of Nottingham, 192 Mansfield Road, Nottingham. Tel: 0602 53511
NC	Nigel Coleman Antiques, High Street, Brasted, Kent. Tel: 0959 64042
NCr	Nigel Cracknell Antiques Ltd., Cavendish House, 138 High Street, Marlborough, Wiltshire. Tel: 0672 52912
NWH	Norman Wright & Hodgkinson, 1 Abbey Road, Bourne, Lincs. Tel: 077 82 2567
O	Olivers, 23/24 Market Hill, Sudbury, Suffolk. Tel: 0787 72247
OA	Odiham Antiques, 45 High Street, Odiham. Hants. Tel: 025 671 3344
OB	The Old Bakery Antiques, St. David's Bridge, Cranbrook, Kent
OL	Outhwaite & Litherland, 'Kingsway Galleries', Fontenoy Street, Liverpool L3 2BE. Tel: 051 236 6561
OT	Osmond Tricks & Son, Regent Street Auction Rooms, Clifton, Bristol. Tel: 0272 37201 or 30810
P	Phillips Auctioneers, Blenstock House, 7 Blenheim Street, London W1Y 0AS. Tel: 01-629 6602
PAM	Petworth Antiques Market, East Street, Petworth, West Sussex.
PC	Pine Cellars, 38 Jewry Street, Winchester, Hampshire. Tel: 0962 67014
PCF	Pine and Country Furniture, North Street, Worthing, Sussex
PD	Pine and Design, Haywards Heath Road, Balcombe, Sussex
Pe	Pearsons, Pinewood Auction Rooms, Kings Road, Fleet, Hants.
PF	Paul Fewings Ltd., 38 South Street, Titchfield, Nr. Fareham, Hants.
PJ	Phillips and Jollys, 1 Old King Street, Bath, Avon. Tel: 0225 310609/310709
PK	Phillips, Station Road, Knowle, Solihull, W. Midlands B93 0HT. Tel: 056 45 6151
PM	Peter McAskie, Stand D11–12, Grays Mews, 1–7 Davies Mews, London, W.1.
PO	Pine Oast, Burwash, Sussex
PS	Phillips, Bold Place, Chester, Cheshire. Tel: 0244 313936
PSH	J. R. Parkinson Son & Hamer, 14 Bolton Street, Bury, Lancashire
PW	Peter Wilson, Market Street, Nantwich, Cheshire. Tel: 0270 63878/9
PWC	Parsons, Welch and Cowell, 129 High Street, Sevenoaks, Kent. Tel: 51211/4
RBB	Russell Baldwin & Bright, Ryelands Road, Leominster, Hereford. Tel: 3897

9

RD	Richard Davidson Antiques, Lombard Street, Petworth, Sussex. Tel: 0798 42508		Hoton, Nr. Loughborough, Leics. LE12 5SF. Tel: 0509 880208
RDv	Robert Dove & Partners, Dover House, Wolsey St., Ipswich, Suffolk. Tel: 0473 55137	**SV**	Sutton Valence Antiques, Sutton Valence, Kent. Tel: Maidstone 843333
RG	Rowland Gorringe & Co., 15 North Street, Lewes, Sussex. Tel: 079 16 2503/ 2382	**SW**	Swetenhams, 5 St. Werburgh St., Chester. Tel: 0244 315333 (now Phillips)
		TJ	Tobias Jellinek, 18 Chepstow Corner, Chepstow Villas, London, W.2. Tel: 01-727 5980
RJG	R. J. Garwood, 55 Mill Street, Ludlow, Shropshire. Tel: 0584 3242	**TNM**	Thomas N. Miller, 18–22 Gallowgate, Newcastle-upon-Tyne. Tel: 0632 25617
RM	Richard Maude, 6 Malbrook Road, Putney, London, S.W.15. Tel: 01-788 2991	**Tr**	Tom Tribe, Bridge Street, Sturminster Newton, Dorset. Tel: 0258 72311
RMcT	Robert McTear & Co., Royal Exchange Salerooms, 6 North Court, St. Vincent Place, Glasgow. Tel: 041-248 6263/8	**TW**	Thomas Watson & Son, Northumberland Street, Darlington, Co. Durham DL3 7HJ. Tel: 0325 62555
S	Sotheby, Parke Bernet and Co., 34–35 New Bond Street, London W1A 2AA. Tel: 01-493 8080	**V**	Vidler & Co., Auction & Estate Offices, Cinque Ports St., Rye, Sussex. Tel: 2124
SAL	Salmagundi, 63 Charlton Street, Maidstone, Kent. Tel: 26859	**VC**	Vintage Cameras Ltd., 254 & 256 Kirkdale, Sydenham, London SE26 4NL. Tel: 01-778 5841
SB	Sotheby's Belgravia, 19 Motcomb Street, London SW1X 8LB. Tel: 01-235 4311	**VV**	Vanderpump & Wellbelove, Chattel Auctioneers, 6 Station Road, Reading RG1 1JY. Tel: 0734 53211
SBA	Sotheby Beresford Adams, Booth Mansions, Watergate Street, Chester, Cheshire. Tel: 0244 315531	**W**	Wylton Antiques, The Old Rectory, Burrough on the Hill, Melton Mowbray, Leics. LE14 2JQ. Tel: 066477 321
SBe	Sotheby Bearne, Rainbow, Torquay, Devon. Tel: 0803 26277	**WA**	Wilberry Antiques, 32 Crawford Street, London, W.1. Tel: 01-724 0606
SKC	Sotheby. King & Chasemore, Station Road, Pulborough, Sussex. Tel: 07982 3831	**WHB**	William H. Brown, 31 St. Peters Hill, Grantham, Lincs. NG31 6QF. Tel: 0476 66363
SM	Susan March, Swigs Hole Farm, Horsmonden, Kent	**WHL**	W. H. Lane & Son, Central Auction Rooms, Penzance, Cornwall TR18 2QT. Tel: 0736 2286
Som	Somervale Antiques, 6 Radstock Road, Midsomer Norton, Bath, Avon BA3 2AJ. Tel: 0761 412686	**Win**	Wingett and Son, 24/25 Chester Street, Wrexham, Clwyd. Tel: 0978 53553
SR	Samuel Rains and Son, Trinity House, Northenden Road, Sale Moor, Manchester M33 2PP. Tel: 061-962 9237	**WR**	Whytock and Reid, Sunbury House, Belford Mews, Edinburgh, Scotland
SS	Sheila Smith Antiques, 10A Queen Street, Bath, Avon. Tel: 0225 60568	**WW**	Woolley and Wallis, The Castle Auction Mart, Castle Street, Salisbury, Wilts. Tel: 0722 27405
SSP	Stanley Stripped Pine, Hayne Barn, Saltwood, Hythe, Kent. Tel: 06793 2137	**WY**	Wyatt and Son, 59 East St., Chichester, Sussex. Tel: 0243 787548 or 786581
ST	Stable Antiques, 14 Loughborough Rd.,	**YHA**	York House Antiques, 37 High Street, Seal, Kent

---

The Publishers would also like to thank the following auction houses for their important contributions:—

Noel D. Abel, 32 Norwich Road, Watton, Norfolk.
Allen and May, 18 Bridge Street, Andover, Hampshire.
Apthorpes, St. Nicholas Street, Diss, Norfolk.
Richard Baker & Thompson, 9 Hamilton Street, Birkenhead, Merseyside.
Biddle and Webb, Fine Art Auction Galleries, Five Ways, Edgbaston, Birmingham.
Sheldon Bosley & Partners, Moreton-in-Marsh, Glos.
Bracketts, 27–29 High Street, Tunbridge Wells, Kent.
Buckell & Ballard, 49 Parsons Street, Banbury, Oxfordshire OX16 8PF.
Button Menhenitt & Mutton Ltd., Belmont Auction Rooms, Wadebridge, Cornwall.
Chancellor & Co., 31 High Street, Ascot, Berkshire.
H. C. Chapman and Son, The Auction Mart, North Street, Scarborough.
Clarke Gammon, 45 High Street, Guildford, Surrey.
Fellows & Sons, Bedford House, 88 Hagley Road, Edgbaston, Birmingham.
Fox and Sons, Cranbury Salerooms, 1 Cranberry Terrace, Southampton, Hants.
John German, Ralph Pay, 131A High Street, Burton-on-Trent.
J. M. Gilding, 2 New Walk, Leicester LE1 6TF.
Graves, Son and Pilcher, 71 Church Road, Hove, East Sussex.
Hall Wateridge and Owen, Welsh Bridge, Shrewsbury, Salop.
Harrods Estate Offices, Arundel Terrace, London, S.W.13.
Giles Haywood, The Auction House, St. Johns Road, Stourbridge, West Midlands.
Edgar Horn Auction Galleries, South Street, Eastbourne, Sussex.

Jacobs and Hunt, Lavant Street, Petersfield, Hants.
James and Lister Lea, 11 Newhall Street, Birmingham B3 3PF.
Jones and Llewelyn, 21 New Road, Llandeilo, Dyfed.
J. David King, 14 St. John Street, Keswick, Cumbria.
Lacy Scott, Fine Art Dept., Angel Hill, Bury St. Edmunds, Suffolk.
Laidlaws, Crown Court Saleroom, Wakefield, Yorkshire.
Landles, Kings Lynn, Norfolk.
Philip Laney & Jolly, 12a Worcester Road, Malvern.
J. G. Lear and Son, 46 Foregate Street, Worcester.
W. H. Lee & Co., 21 Castle Street, Hertford, Herts SG14 1HJ.
Locke and England, 1 and 2 Euston Place, Leamington Spa CV32 4LW.
R. Longstaff & Co., Sheep Market, Spalding, Lincs.
Thomas Love & Sons Ltd., 12 St. John's Place, Perth PH1 5TS.
Frank R. Marshall & Co., Knutsford Auction Salerooms, Church Hill, Knutsford, Cheshire.
Martin & Pole, The Auctioneers Offices, 5A & 7 Broad Street, Wokingham, Berks.
Thomas Mawer & Son, 63 Monks Road, Lincoln.
May, Whetter and Grose, Cornubia Hall, Par, Cornwall.
Meads, St. Nicholas Road, Brighton, Sussex BN1 3LP.
E. P. Messenger & Son, Pevensey House Salerooms, Manorsfield Road, Bicester, Oxon.
Nock, Deighton & Son, 10 Broad Street, Ludlow, Shropshire.
D. M. Nesbit & Co., 7 Clarendon Road, Southsea, Hants. PO5 2ED.
E. J. Pallot, 75 Albert Street, Rugby, Warwickshire.
M. Philip H. Scott, 'East View',

Langthorne, Bedale, North Yorkshire.
Phillips inc. Brooks, 39 Park End Street, Oxford.
Phillips in Scotland, 98 Sauchiehall Street, Glasgow G2 3DQ.
Robert Pugh, 114 Walter Road, Swansea, West Glamorgan.
Rendells, 13 Market Street, Newton Abbot, Devon.
Rippon Boswell & Co., The Arcade, South Kensington Station, London SW7 2NA.
Tyrone R. Roberts, Watton Road, Swaffham, Norfolk.
Sandhoe Luce Panes, The Estate Offices, Wotton-under-Edge, Glos.
Simmons and Lawrence, 32 Bell Street, Henley-on-Thames, Oxon.
Smith-Woolley and Perry, 24/26 Dover Road, Folkestone, Kent.
Spear & Sons, Wickham Market, Nr. Woodbridge, Suffolk.
Specialised Postcard Auctions, 24 Watford Road, Wembley, Middlesex.
Stanilands, William H. Brown, 28 Netherhall Road, Doncaster.
Surrey Antique Auctions, 10 Windsor Street, Chertsey, Surrey.
G. Tarn Bainbridge & Son, Montrose, Tayside.
James Thompson, 64 Main Street, Kirkby Lonsdale, South Westmorland, Cumbria.
Turner, Rudge & Turner, 29 High Street, East Grinstead, West Sussex.
Walker, Barnett and Hill, 3–5 Waterloo Road, Wolverhampton.
Watson Bull and Porter, 79/81 Regent Street, Shanklin, Isle of Wight.
Watsons, Water Lane Salerooms, Bishops Stortford, Herts.
Weller and Dufty Ltd., 141 Bromsgrove Street, Birmingham B5 6RQ.
P. F. Windibank, 18–20 Reigate Road, Dorking, Surrey.
Wright-Manley, 56 High Street, Nantwich, Cheshire.

CONTENTS

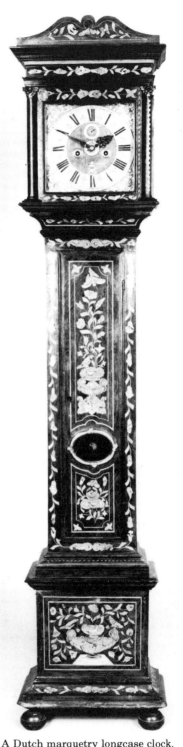

A Dutch marquetry longcase clock,
the movement with five latched
pillars, anchor escapement, pull
wind alarm and outside countwheel
Dutch strike on two bells, 11 in.
square dial with latched feet, the
matted centre with central alarm
disc, subsidiary seconds, ringed
winding holes and apertures for
calendar and weekday with planet,
silvered chapter-ring signed Jacob
Hasius Amsterdam, 7 ft. 1 in. high.
£3,000-4,000   C

A MEISSEN FIGURE OF A KESTREL (SPERBER) FEEDING ON ITS KILL
Modelled by J. J. Kaendler, circa 1740-45

The kestrel naturalistically modelled in brown, black and iron red feather markings, with yellow beak and claws, perched on a gnarled tree stump devouring a dead bird held in his claws — *28 cm high*

While every care has been exercised in the compilation of this guide, neither the authors or publishers accept any liability for any financial or other loss incurred by reliance placed on the information contained in Millers Price Guide.

PORCELAIN & POTTERY

Porcelain, pottery, earthenware and stoneware have been combined under subject categories in this section to aid identification. Hence if one is looking for a plate one looks at the plate section and then under factory in alphabetical order (sometimes the order may change slightly for lay-out purposes.) The only exceptions to this are Oriental and Antiquities which are separated at the end of the section.

Porcelain was discovered by the Chinese in the T'ang dynasty. By the end of the 17th C. it had become a European obsession to discover the secret. Johann Böttger at Meissen discovered the formula for hard paste porcelain in the early years of the 18th C. By 1770 the secret had spread to Vienna, Strasbourg, Frankenthal and Nymphenburg. In France, Vincennes and Sevres first produced soft-paste porcelain in 1745-72. Soft-paste porcelain was produced at most of the 18th C. English and Welsh factories; Derby, Chelsea, Bow, Coalport, Swansea and Worcester.

The distinction between hard and soft paste is:

Hard paste (or true porcelain) — *fired at a higher temperature than soft paste; cold feel to the touch; chip is flint or glass like; hard, glittery glaze.*

Soft paste (or artificial) — *file will cut easily into soft paste (not a test to be recommended!); chip is granular; warmer feeling to the touch; less stable in the kiln, figures in particular were difficult to fire; soft glaze — liable to crazing; the early soft paste was prone to discolouration.*

Bone China — achieved by Josiah Spode in 1796.

Much of the early English porcelain was a direct copy of the popular imported Chinese ware. The English however did not have the potting skills of the Chinese.

MARKET TRENDS

Due to the recent recession, prices of many items have remained quite static. Condition is of vital importance when dealing with porcelain. Pieces which are cracked, chipped, restored or merely very common have not been selling. Slight damage on figures is acceptable but in the case of wares, only if the piece is very rare.

English pottery and porcelain in mint condition has always been a favourite with British collectors. Chelsea and Worcester are still firm favourites. Bow has always been underpriced and although has seen some improvement, still seems comparatively inexpensive. Excellent condition and a rare design fetch premium prices with Worcester. Caughley is, at long last, recovering from being thought of as second-rate Worcester and prices for good hand-painted pieces have risen considerably. Wedgwood, a great favourite with Americans, tends to fluctuate with the strength and weakness of the dollar. Doulton seems to have increased in popularity once again — with endless Hannah Barlow vases, ewers and jugs fetching ever increasing prices.

A rare pair of Belleek figures of 'Belgian Hawkers', heightened in pink lustre (damaged), 17 cm., printed dog and harp mark, 1863-91. **£700-770** *SB*

A Berlin group of Arithmetic from the set of the Sciences, modelled by W. C. Meyer (minor damage), blue sceptre mark and impressed T, c. 1765, 30.5 cm. high. **£600-700** *C*

A Berlin figure of a fruit seller, sceptre in underglaze blue, printed orb and KPM, 21.8 cm., late 19th C. **£90-110** *SB*

A pair of Bow white figures of Kitty Clive and Henry Woodward, in the roles of 'The Fine Lady' and 'The Fine Gentleman' (restored), c. 1750, 25.5 cm. and 26.5 cm. high. **£1,200-1,400** *C*

A pair of Berlin figures of Malabar musicians, modelled by F. E. Meyer in bright colour, blue sceptre marks, c. 1765-70, 23 cm. high, some damage. **£1,300-1,500** *C*

A biscuit figure of Shakespeare (one of a pair with Milton), c. 1785, 9½ in. high. **£165-185,** model made in colour **£250-300** *AD*

A pair of Bow musicians, c. 1765, 6 in. high. £1,200-1,500 *BM*

A Bow figure of Earth, modelled as a lady, in puce, yellow, blue and gilding (restoration, chips, lacks crown), 27 cm. high, c. 1760. £230-300 *C*

A Bow figure of a nun, damaged (should be reading a book), c. 1760, 6 in. high. £450-600 *MB*

A Bow figure, c. 1765, 6 in. high, slight firing crack (anchor and dagger and Worcester mark). £520-600 *MB*

BOW FIGURES

- the earliest Bow figures have plain bases
- in the mid 1750's some rococo bases appeared; these became more popular
- by 1760 C & S scroll decoration was in great demand as were large shell bases
- the large shell bases can be thought of as a trademark of Bow, although many other factories copied successful features
- very little Bow is marked
- anchor and dagger mark added by James Giles when he painted a piece at the factory
- figures with an underglaze blue crescent *tend* to be Bow (although this was a Worcester mark, it was often copied by Bow and other lesser factories)

A Bow figure of a bagpiper, in black, pink and puce (minor restoration), 25.5 cm. high, c. 1758. £400-480 *C*

A Bow figure of a lady, c. 1760-1775, 10 in. high (slight damage to bocage). £500-560 *MB*

A Capodimonte (Carlo III) white group of La Dichiarazione, modelled by Giuseppe Gricci (his head restored, restoration to rockwork), c. 1750, 14 cm. high. £600-700 *C*

A Chantilly figure of a gardener (his fore-arms restored), c. 1740, 16 cm. high. £950-1,100 *C*

A pair of Chelsea figures of a gallant and companion, wearing puce and green and richly gilt flowered clothes (chips, other minor damages), gold anchor marks, c. 1770, 28 cm. high. £1,300-1,500 *C*

A Chelsea figure of a pedlar, gold anchor period, c. 1765, 7½ in. high. **£300-350**   *AD*

A Chelsea Derby figure of Neptune, 10 in. high, c. 1775. Perfect **£350-400**, restored arm **£280-320**   *AD*

A pair of continental coloured biscuit figures (damaged), 60 cm., moulded initials, late 19th C. **£235-265**   *SB*

A pair of Chelsea Derby figures holding baskets, c. 1790 (restored), 5¼ in. high. **£250-280**   *AD*

A Chelsea Derby figure group (with some restoration to bagpipes), c. 1780. **£295-325**   *B.M*

A Chelsea figure of a Muse, emblematic of Smell, her dress painted in puce and gilding, with scattered floral sprigs, with a blue-green cloak lined in yellow, chipped, gold anchor mark, c. 1765, 25.5 cm. **£500-800**   *SKC*

A pair of 19th C. Continental figures, man 10 in. high. **£160-180**   *SV*

CHELSEA POINTS TO NOTE

- marks usually very small and not in prominent position
- paste varies from white to greenish when seen by transmitted light
- look out for 'moons' caused by frit in the kiln, also seen by transmitted light
- three spur marks often found on the base, left by kiln supports (not to be confused with Derby pad marks)
- glaze on early pieces is reasonably opaque, this later becomes clearer and more glassy, then thicker, when it tends to craze

A pair of Continental groups, probably Austrian, painted arrow mark and incised numerals, 42 cm., c. 1900. **£350-400**   *SB*

A pair of continental figures, probably Bohemian, intended for use as scent flasks, one with a gilt stopper, chips, 36 cm., mid-19th C. **£200-260**   *SBe*

A pair of Continental coloured biscuit figures (chips), 52 cm., c. 1900. **£220-280**   *SB*

15

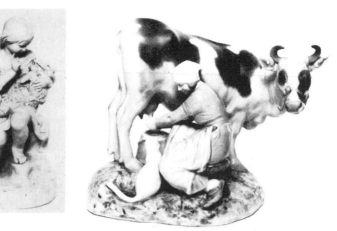

A Copeland Parian Figure of 'Go To Sleep', after an original by J. Durham, moulded signature, and made for the Art Union of London, 44.5 cm., impressed mark and date code for 1884. **£200-250** *SB*

A Bing & Grondahl Copenhagen group, after the original model by Alex Locher, incised signature, coloured in soft underglaze blue and brown, 23 cm., printed green castle Danmark, painted 2017 SI-K, B & G, 20th C. **£155-175** *SB*

A Derby figure of Justice, in pink, turquoise, red and gilt (sword lacking), Wm. Duesbury & Co., 28.5 cm. high, c. 1765. **£350-420** *C*

A Derby figure group 'Cupids bird nesting' (one wing repaired), c. 1760, 11½ in. **£380-460** *MB*

Two Derby white dry-edge figures, emblematic of Summer and Winter (minor chips), Andrew Planche period, c. 1755, about 11.5 cm. high. **£500-560** *C*

A Derby figure of Diana, in pink-lined pale yellow dress (minor chipping), Wm. Duesbury & Co., 26.5 cm. high, c. 1765. **£210-260** *C*

A Derby figure of Minerva, in puce, green and yellow (minute chips), Wm. Duesbury & Co., 34.5 cm. high, c. 1765. **£350-420** *C*

A pair of Derby figures of Mars and Minerva, c. 1760, 14 in. high. **£1,250-1,500** pr. *MB*

A Derby pair 'The Ranelagh Figures', c. 1760, 10 in. high. **£750-800** *AD*

A Derby bisque Cupid with dog, c. 1760-70, 4¾ in. high. **£330-370** *MB*

A pair of Derby figures, 'The Piping Shepherd and Shepherdess', unrestored and mint, 10 in. high, c. 1770. **£950-1,050** *MB*

A Derby figure group 'Mars paying homage to Diana', c. 1770, 13 in. high. **£450-520** *MB*

A Derby bisque Cupid with falcon, c. 1760-70, 5 in. high. **£330-370** *MB*

A pair of Derby figures of a monk and nun, reading books, the pages inscribed 'Spes mea in Deo' and 'Omnia Gloria' (chipped and restored), W. Duesbury & Co., c. 1770, 14.5 cm. and 13.5 cm. high. **£400-490** *C*

A Derby figure of Shepherd girl, pre Chelsea-Derby, c. 1765, unusual peacock motif on dress (head restored), 8 in. high, perfect. **£250-320** *AD*

A Derby figure of Brittania, c. 1770, 13½ in. high. **£480-540** *MB*

DERBY

- by the end of 18th C. the Derby factory concentrated on highly ornamental, lavish pieces
- Derby's numerous decorators specialised in birds, fruit, English flowers and landscapes
- decorators of note: William 'Quaker' Pegg; Moses Webster; William Billingsley, famous for his flower painting; Robert Brewer, famous for his landscapes (named views being particularly collectable); Thomas Steele, decorated with fruit; Richard Dodson with birds
- gilders of note include Thomas Till (gilder's numeral 33)
- vases were one speciality of the factory, particularly during the Regency period
- the factory specialised in highly decorative and 'grand' pieces for the nobility until its closure in 1848

A pair of Bloor Derby figures of a Swiss or Austrian couple, marked c. 1825, 6 in. high. **£300-330** pair *AD*

A Derby figure, c. 1775, 8½ in. high. **£500-570** *MB*

A Derby comic figure with dog, c. 1775, 6 in. high. **£420-480** *MB*

A pair of Derby figures, c. 1780, 5½ in. high. **£600-650** *B.M*

A pair of Derby figures of children, c. 1830-40 (good quality), marked Bloor Derby, 5½ in. high. **£260-285** pair *AD*

A pair of Stevenson Hancock Derby figures, 'The Gardeners', 5 in. high, c. 1862. **£185-200** *BY*

A rare Derby figure of Napoleon, c. 1840, 8½ in. (slight chip to base). **£400-465** *MB*

A pair of Derby Mansion House dwarfs, the hats with advertisements (chips and minor restoration), 17 and 17.7 cm., incised No. 277, mid-19th C. **£480-550** *SB*

A Bloor Derby figure, marked, 4¼ in. high. **£230-250** *MB*

A Bloor Derby figure inscribed 'Prodigious', marked c. 1825, 6¾ in. high. **£160-185** *AD*

A Bloor Derby figure with rare mark, 6 in. wide (with damage to bocage). **£110-140**; perfect **£175-200** *MB*

A Doccia white figure of the Farnese 'Hercules', slight damage, c. 1760, 14 cm. high. **£150-250** *C*

A Doccia figure of Paris holding a golden apple (damage to staff and repair to his jacket), c. 1760, 13 cm. high. **£300-350** *C*

DOCCIA

- factory started by Carlo Ginori, near Florence in 1735
- hybrid hard-paste porcelain of greyish-white appearance
- body liable to firecracks
- often decorated with mythological, religious and hunting subjects
- used strong enamel colours
- from 1757-1791 the factory was directed by Lorenzo Ginori, glaze and body improved considerably

- figures often in white and sometimes decorated with an iron-red colour exclusive to the factory
- porcelain often confused with Capodimonte, although Doccia is hard paste and Capodimonte soft paste
- around 1770 figures covered in a white tin-glaze, often firecracked
- factory still exists

A Royal Crown Derby silver lustre figure, 'Wings', c. 1920, 8 in. **£140-160** *CS*

A Doulton salt-glaze stoneware figure of a Boer War soldier, after John Broad, 30.5 cm., impressed mark, incised initials, c. 1900. **£200-260** *SB*

A Royal Doulton figure group, 'The love letter' HN.2149, 8 by 5 in. **£110-170** *RMcT*

'A Saucy Nymph', a Royal Doulton figure, modelled as a naked child, circle mark, lion and crown, HN 1539. **£110-160** *P*

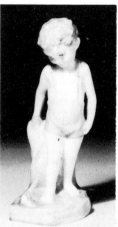

A Royal Doulton figure 'A Victorian Lady', H.N. 728, 7¾ in., 1934. **£145-165** *MT*

A Royal Doulton figure of 'Mantilla', HN.2712, 12 in. **£140-200** *RMcT*

'Do you wonder where Fairies are that Folks declare have Vanished', a Royal Doulton figure, 13 cm. high, circle mark, lion and crown, HN 1544. **£110-160** *P*

A Royal Doulton figure of a young girl, 'Celia', H.N. 1727, 11½ in. high. **£230-290** *SR*

A Royal Doulton figure of 'Carmen', HN.2545, 12 in. **£110-160** *RMcT*

'Coppelia', a Royal Doulton figure based on the mechanical doll in the ballet Coppelia by Delibes, 18.50 cm. high, circle mark, lion and crown, HN 2115. **£220-280** *P*

A Royal Doulton figure of 'A La Mode', HN.2544, 12½ in. **£100-150** *RMcT*

A Royal Doulton figure of 'Boudoir', HN.2542, 12 in. **£150-200** *RMcT*

'A Victorian Lady', a Royal
Doulton figure, in green and
purple plume, 20.50 cm. high,
circle mark, lion and crown,
HN 1452. **£190-250** *P*

A Royal Doulton miniature
figure, 'Sweet Anne', M.27, 4 i
£110-125 *MT*

'Chloe', a Royal Doulton figure
modelled as a girl, in mauve and
pink, 14.50 cm. high, circle
mark, lion and crown, HN 1479
and date code for 1932. **£110-
160** *P*

'Symphony', a Royal Doulton
figure of a young lady, in yellow
and brown, 13.50 cm. high,
circle mark, lion and crown,
HN 2287. **£120-180** *P*

A Royal Doulton figure
'Pantalettes', H.N. 362, 8 in.,
1933. **£320-340** *MT*

'Boy with a Turban', a Royal
Doulton model of a young
Middle Eastern prince, 9 cm.
high, circle mark, lion and
crown, HN 1210, and date code
for 1930. **£200-260** *P*

A Royal Doulton figure 'Miss
Demure', H.N. 1402, 7 in., 1932,
£150-160 *MT*

A Royal Doulton figure 'Lady
Charmian', H.N. 1949, 8 in.,
1940. **£200-225** *MT*

A Royal Doulton figure of 'The
Bather', after a model by L.
Harradine, 27 cm., printed lion
and circle, painted title,
HN 687, date code for 1927.
£160-190 *SB*

A Royal Doulton group
'Scotties', designed by Leslie
Harradine, title and pattern no.
'1281' in red enamel, 14 cm.,
1930's. **£360-430** *SKC*

A Royal Doulton figure 'Shy
Anne', H.N. 65, 7¾ in., before
1927. **£590-620** *MT*

A Royal Doulton figure 'Biddy', H.N. 1445, 5½ in., 1931. **£130-145**   *MT*

A Royal Doulton figure 'Veronica', H.N. 1517, 8 in., 1935. **£300-330**   *MT*

A Royal Doulton figure of 'Elisa', HN.2543, 11½ in. **£110-160**   *RMcT*

A Royal Dux group of lovers, after Hampel, inscribed, in tones of rose-red, green and beige, 47 cm., applied and impressed pink triangle mark, impressed shape number 1559, c. 1910. **£180-220**   *SB*

A pair of Royal Dux busts, in pastel shades of green, rose and beige (minor chips), applied pink triangle mark, impressed shape numbers 235 and 236, 29 cm., c. 1910. **£220-300**   *SB*

A pair of Royal Dux figures, in pale colours, applied pink triangle and impressed numerals, early 20th C., height 54 cms. **£460-520**   *SBe*

A pair of Dresden figures of a gallant and a lady, chips, 50.5 and 49 cm., crossed swords in underglaze blue, one incised Petit, late 19th C. **£700-800**   *SB*

A Royal Dux camel group in green, pink and brown, the details gilt, 59.5 cm., impressed and applied pink triangle, impressed shape number 1706, c. 1910. **£415-475**   *SB*

A Royal Dux figure of 'Diana', on a rocky base forming a vase, 32 cm., applied and impressed pink triangle, impressed 461, c. 1910. **£180-220**   *SB*

A late 19th C. Royal Dux figure of Middle Eastern girl, 'JMX 6808' stamped inside base (base repaired and small chips), 26½ in. high. **£160-230**   *DWB*

A Frankenthal Chinoiserie group, modelled by Karl Gottlieb Luck (some restoration work), blue crowned interlaced CT mark, c. 1765, 22.5 cm. high. **£1,700-2,000**   *C*

A Frankenthal group of singing children, modelled by Adam Bauer, painted in pastel colours (some damage), blue crowned interlaced CT mark over 71, paints mark G.H., c. 1771. **£1,100-1,400** *C*

A French group, after Meissen originals, 42 cm., crossed swords and star in underglaze blue, late 19th C. **£255-285** *SB*

A Frankenthal pastoral group, modelled by J. W. Lanz (some damage and repair work), blue lion rampant mark, 1756-59, 22 cm. high. **£1,500-1,800** *C*

FRANKENTHAL

- Paul A. Hannong started producing porcelain in Frankenthal in 1755, under the patronage of the Elector Carl Theodor
- high quality porcelain produced under modellmeister J. W. Lanz, who favoured striped gilt grounds and green and crimson
- K. G. Luck and his brother or cousin J. F. Luck came to Frankenthal from Meissen in 1758
- K. G. Luck's work tends to be quite fussy and often on grassy mounds, with rococo edges picked out in gilding
- in the late 18th C. a fine range of figures produced by J. P. Melchior and A. Bauer
- Frankenthal utility ware is noted for the quality of the painting

A Frankenthal group of children, modelled by Adam Bauer (some damage), blue crowned interlaced CT mark over 72, c. 1772, 15.5 cm. wide. **£890-1,000** *C*

FURSTENBERG

- factory founded in 1747 but it was not until Johann Benckgraff arrived from Hochst in 1753 that porcelain was produced here
- principal modeller at this period was Simon Feilner
- enamelling technique was not perfected at this factory until the early 1760's, and underglaze blue remained of poor quality until the late 1760's
- the body remained of a yellow tinge until the 1770's and the glaze tended to speck
- it was these imperfections which encouraged the use of high-relief rococo scrollwork
- other modellers of note are A. C. Luplau, J. C. Rombrich and Desoches
- the factory passed into private ownership in 1859 and still exists today

A Furstenberg figure of a young boy, in puce, orange, pink and yellow, blue F mark and impressed NO3, 14.5 cm. high, c. 1760. **£930-1,100** *C*

A pair of French biscuit figures, painted in pale colours, late 19th C. (slight damage), height 48.5 cm. **£460-550** *SBe*

A Furstenberg white figure of Mezzetin, modelled by Simon Feilner (wrist repaired), incised Ff/O, 1753/54, 19.5 cm. high. **£1,200-1,450** *C*

A French 'Chelsea' arbour group, modelled as a shepherd teaching a shepherdess to play a pipe, chips, gilt anchor, 22.5 cm., c. 1900. **£190-230** *SBe*

A Ginori white figure of a Nymph emblematic of Summer, (Doccia) slight damage, c. 1760, 12.3 cm. high. **£150-200** *C*

A pair of German pottery figures, with coloured and turquoise detailing beneath a crackled glaze, marked Meissen, 26 cm. high. **£200-300** *P*

A German earthenware Arab after the original model by Kaffsack, signed, stamped mark, c. 1800, 86 cm. **£300-400** *SB*

A Goldschneider earthenware group of flamenco dancers, after Lorenzl, moulded signature, 46 cm., printed marks, 20th C. **£240-300** *SBe*

A 19th C. German porcelain figure of Europa and the Bull, 7½ in. high, 7 in. wide. **£230-280** *PWC*

An early Hochst group of a peasant and companion, modelled by Simon Feilner (restored), c. 1753, impressed 2H and inscribed GS in manganese, 23 cm. high. **£2,700-2,900** *C*

A Hochst figure of a girl, modelled by J. P. Melchior (her right arm repaired), blue wheel mark and incised W 74 No. 88, c. 1770, 11.5 cm. high. **£480-580** *C*

A Hochst group of a Chinese boy and a girl, modelled by J. P. Melchior (minor chips), c. 1775, 17 cm. high. **£2,700-3,000** *C*

A rare Leeds figure, c. 1780, 13 in. high. **£300-340** *MB*

A Liverpool figure of La Nourrice, after the Chelsea original, in purple, blue, brown and yellow (restored), incised 2 mark, 1755/1760, 15 cm. high. **£580-680**   *C*

A Ludwigsburg figure of a butcher (broken through waist), blue interlaced C mark, impressed numbers and iron-red painter's mark of Sausenhofer, c. 1765, 12 cm. high. **£440-500**   *C*

A Limbach figure of a woman, emblematic of Winter, in white, brown and puce (minor chips), purple LB monogram on base, 18 cm. high, c. 1780. **£550-700**   *C*

A Limbach figure of a young man, in red, purple and black (his left hand missing), purple LB monogram on base, 17 cm. high, c. 1780. **£300-400**   *C*

A Ludwigsburg figure of a peasant woman (small chip), blue interlaced C mark, impressed numbers and iron-red painter's mark of Sausenhofer, c. 1765, 12.5 cm. high. **£800-900**   *C*

A Ludwigsburg figure of a young gentleman, in pink, iron-red and yellow (restored), blue interlaced C mark at back, c. 1770, 11 cm. high. **£520-620**   *C*

A Ludwigsburg figure of a woman (some restoration work), traces of interlaced C mark, impressed numbers and iron-red painter's mark of Sausenhofer, 12.5 cm. high. **£550-650**   *C*

A fine Meissen figure of a shepherd, after model by J. Kaendler, 11 in. high. **£500-600**   *Cr.A*

A Meissen group of a peasant, in black, blue and brown, blue crossed swords mark under the base, c. 1745, 16 cm. high. **£1,000-1,200**   *C*

MEISSEN

- late 19th C. figures often disregarded and treated disparagingly by dealers
- due to the increased demand and high prices of pieces from 1720-1760, later pieces are becoming much more collectable
- the same is true for many of the other great 18th C. factories and is an area where collectors can often find bargains
- late 19th C. Meissen pieces often marked with blue crossed swords in underglaze blue

---

A fine Meissen figure of a shepherdess, after model by J. J. Kaendler, 12 in. high. **£550-650**   *Cr.A*

A Meissen figure of a tinker, modelled by J. J. Kändler and from the first Cris de Paris series (slight restorations), blue crossed swords mark at back, c. 1745, 19 cm. high. **£1,000-1,200** *C*

A Meissen figure of a youth, modelled by J. J. Kändler, in black, yellow, lilac and buff (minute chips), blue crossed swords mark at back, c. 1742. **£1,600-1,800** *C*

A Meissen figure of Chinese lovers, modelled by Kändler, Meyer and Reinicke, in white, cream and pink (damaged and restored), c. 1745, 13 cm. wide. **£1,650-1,850** *C*

A Meissen figure of a Polish lady modelled by P. Reinicke, in yellow, pink and turquoise (slight restoration), c. 1750, 16 cm. high. **£780-880** *C*

A Meissen figure of a sawyer, modelled by J. J. Kändler and P. Reinicke (slight restorations), c. 1745, 13 cm. high. **£780-900** *C*

A Meissen figure of Apollo (some chips), blue crossed swords mark under the base, c. 1747, 27 cm. high. **£300-400** *C*

A Meissen figure of a dancing Chinese woman, by P. Reinicke (some restoration), blue crossed swords mark, c. 1745, 17 cm. high. **£1,300-1,500** *C*

A Meissen figure of a young girl in green, pink, black and yellow (restored), blue crossed swords mark, c. 1750, 13.5 cm. **£430-530** *C*

A Meissen figure of a Pole, modelled by P. Reinicke, in pink, turquoise and yellow (restored), blue crossed swords mark at back, c. 1745, 15 cm. high. **£950-1,200** *C*

A Meissen figure of a Chinese gentleman, by P. Reinicke (base restored), blue crossed swords mark at back, c. 1745, 15.5 cm. high. **£600-800** *C*

A Meissen figure of a young woman dancing, on later ormolu scroll base (both arms repaired), 15 cm. high, c. 1750. **£400-500** *C*

A Meissen figure of a gardener (hat chipped, watering can damaged), traces of blue crossed swords mark, c. 1750, 11 cm. high. **£320-380** *C*

A Meissen group of a peasant woman and children, decorated in shades of pink, buff and brown (chipped), blue crossed swords mark at back, c. 1750, 24 cm. high. **£1,100-1,400**   *C*

A Meissen figure of a Cupid, painted in green, pink, iron-red and yellow (one wing restored), blue crossed swords marks at back, c. 1755, 9 cm. high. **£330-380**   *C*

A pair of Meissen figures of a gardener and companion, modelled by P. Reinicke (some chips and restoration), blue crossed swords marks, c. 1750, 12 cm. high. **£1,300-1,400**   *C*

A Meissen figure of a grapeseller, in black, yellow, white and turquoise, blue crossed swords mark at back, c. 1745, 19 cm. high. **£1,600-1,900**   *C*

A Meissen figure of Juno, on Louis XV ormolu scroll base (peacock's crown and her left arm restored), blue crossed swords mark, c. 1755, 17.5 cm. high overall. **£700-800**   *C*

A Meissen figure of a Bulgarian lady, modelled by J. J. Kandler and P. Reinicke, in pink, white, yellow and puce (chips to ribbon), blue crossed swords mark at back, c. 1750, 23 cm. high. **£1,450-1,650**   *C*

A pair of 18th C. Meissen figures of a gardener and companion, crossed swords mark in underglaze blue (some restoration), 5½ in. **£730-950**   *WW*

A Meissen group of Asia, from a set of the Continents, modelled by Kändler and Eberlein, blue crossed swords mark under the base (chipped), c. 1750, 24 cm. wide. **£1,550-2,000**   *C*

A Meissen figure of a Tartar, modelled by J. J. Kandler and P. Reinicke, in pink, lilac, white and yellow (chipped), blue crossed swords mark at back, c. 1750, 21 cm. high. **£3,400-3,800**   *C*

An 18th C. Meissen recumbent Sphinx, 3 in. high. **£120-150** *MB*

An outside-decorated Meissen crinoline group, after an original model by J. J. Kaendler, 16.6 cm., crossed swords in underglaze blue, incised model number 604, R painted in red, 18th C. and later. **£180-210** *SB*

A Meissen figure of 'Sight' from the set of 5 senses, mark in underglaze blue, late 19th C., height 14 cm. **£330-400** *SBe*

A Meissen group 'The Apple Pickers', c. 1830, 11 in. high. **£700-750** *Cr.A.*

A pair of Meissen figures of Gardeners, 16.5 and 18 cm., crossed swords in underglaze blue, incised F69, late 19th C. **£575-675** *SB*

An outside-decorated Meissen group of a children's band, minor damage, cancelled crossed swords in underglaze blue, incised 2489, 14 cm., late 19th C. **£170-250** *SBe*

A Meissen group of Polyhymnia (chips), 23.5 cm., cancelled crossed swords in underglaze blue, incised E27, late 19th C. **£320-380** *SB*

A Meissen figure of a young woman, cross swords mark, 19 cm., late 19th C. **£300-350** *SBe*

A Meissen group of 'Lessons in Love', bookstand damaged, 29 cm., crossed swords in underglaze blue, incised F74, mid-19th C. **£1,000-1,200** *SB*

A Meissen group of Putti, 13 cm., crossed swords in underglaze blue, incised 2903, late 19th C. **£230-270** *SB*

A Meissen group 'Allegorical of the Arts', swords mark in underglaze-blue, incised numerals (some damage), 7¾ in. (19.7 cm.), late 19th C. **£270-330** *SBA*

A Meissen monkey band, after originals by J. J. Kändler, in brightly coloured court costume, crossed swords mark in underglaze blue (slight damage), 13 to 18.2 cm., late 19th C. **£3,800-4,500** *SBe*

A Meissen group emblematic of 'The Arts', 20.3 cm., crossed swords in underglaze blue, incised N4, late 19th C. **£240-270** *SB*

A Meissen outside-decorated musical group, restored, 37 cm., cancelled crossed swords in underglaze blue, incised C59, late 19th C. **£660-800** *SB*

A Meissen figure of a girl, c. 1860, 5 in. high. **£470-500** *Cr.A*

A Meissen festive group, in bright colours, painted marks and impressed numerals (slight damage), height 47 cm., late 19th C. **£780-880** *SBe*

A Meissen group of The Three Graces, in blue, pink and yellow (chips), 41 cm., cancelled crossed swords in underglaze blue, incised H71, late 19th C. **£1,200-1,400** *SB*

A Meissen figure of 'Smell' from a set of the senses (chips), 13.5 cm., crossed swords in underglaze blue, incised G3, late 19th C. **£300-350** *SB*

A pair of Meissen figures of cupids, 17.5 cm., crossed swords in underglaze blue, incised L 102 and impressed L 101, early 20th C. **£280-320** *SB*

A Meissen group of lovers, crossed swords in underglaze blue, incised 35, late 19th C. **£240-300** *SB*

MEISSEN

- in 1709, J. F. Bottger produced a white hard-paste porcelain
- wares often decorated by outside decorators (hausmaler)
- in 1720, kilnmaster Stozel came back to Meissen bringing with him J. G. Herold

- from this time Meissen was supreme in enamelling hard-paste porcelain
- crossed swords factory mark started in 1723
- many port scenes painted by C.F. Herold
- finest Meissen figures modelled by J. J. Kändler from 1731

- cut-flower decoration (schnittblumen) often associated with J. G. Klinger
- from 1755 the rococo style became very popular, especially as a base for figures
- this period saw softer colours used with a great deal of gilding

A Meissen group of bubble-blowers, gilt-scroll-edged base (minor chips), 14.5 cm., crossed swords in underglaze blue, incised P122, late 19th C. **£340-380**   *SB*

A Meissen figure of Atalanta, 29.3 cm., crossed swords in underglaze blue, incised Q100, early 20th C. **£300-340**   *SB*

A Meissen figure of a classical maiden, 46 cm., crossed swords in underglaze blue, incised M193, late 19th C. **£600-800**   *SB*

A Meissen musical group (minor damage), 18 cm., crossed swords in underglaze blue, incised D4-8. **£600-700**   *SB*

A Meissen figure of The Merchants Wife, in 18th century taste, brightly coloured overall with gilt details, 17 cm., underglaze blue crossed swords, impressed numerals, 20th C. **£160-190**   *SB*

A Meissen figure of a 'Paris Crier', gilt-scroll-edged base, 14.5 cm., crossed swords in underglaze blue, incised No. 24, c. 1900. **£200-250**   *SB*

An early 19th C. pair of figures probably Minton (finger and hat repaired). **£150-170** pair   *B.M*

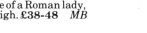

A Paris 'Mermaid' salt (minor chip), 19 cm., c. 1840. **£80-130**   *SB*

A Neale figure of a Roman lady, c. 1795, 5 in. high. **£38-48**   *MB*

A Neale figure of 'A Harvester', c. 1790, 6½ in. high. **£55-65**   *MB*

An Ottweiler figure of a girl, in bright colours (the much fire-cracked base repaired, probably in the factory), c. 1770, 23 cm. high. **£1,800-2,300**   *C*

A Portobello group of boy with dog, c. 1830, 4 in. wide. **£70-80**   *AD*

A pair of Paris biscuit porcelain groups, coloured and gilt, 24 cm., c. 1870. **£350-400**   *SB*

A Rockingham figure of a Russian pilgrim, in black hat, green jacket, striped trousers and pale yellow shoes (restored), incised griffin mark and No.37, 1826-1830, 16.5 cm. high. **£300-360**   *C*

A Potschappel 12-piece monkey band, of Meissen inspiration, initials mark in underglaze blue, 13 cm. to 16.5 cm., late 19th C. **£400-500**   *SB*

A good Ridgway, Bates & Co., Parian group of Cupid and Psyche, after F. Gibson, R.A., made for the Art Union of London, 49 cm., impressed mark and sculptor's name, 1858. **£280-330**   *SB*

A Rockingham figure of Napoleon, in black hat, green coat with gilt decorations and epaulettes, white waistcoat, pale yellow breeches and black boots (extensive restoration), incised No. 42, 1826-1830, 20 cm. high. **£280-350**   *C*

A Pratt pedestal figure group, c. 1810 (left arm restored), 5½ in. **£55-60**   *MB*

A fine pair of Samson figures, c. 1870, 9 in. high. **£400-500** *LAC*

A Portobello fisherwoman, c. 1825, 8 in. **£200-250**   *AD*

A pair of Samson figures of continents, after Derby originals, 26 and 27 cm., crowned gilt BB monograms, late 19th C. **£170-200**   *SB*

A Sevres white biscuit group of pastoral lovers (Corydon et Lisette ou La Mauseuse de Raisins), modelled by Falconet after Boucher (restored), c. 1755, 22.5 cm. high. **£750-900** *C*

A French biscuit de Sevres bust of Louis XV, after Gois, inscribed on the back Gois 1770, 25¼ in. (64 cm.) high. **£570-700** *C*

A Sevres white biscuit group of pastoral lovers (Le Lecon de Flageolet), modelled by Falconet after Boucher (damaged and restored), c. 1755, 23 cm. high. **£700-900** *C*

A Sevres biscuit figure of a nymph, modelled by Bachelier, incised script B to top of base, 30 cm. high, c. 1755. **£200-300** *C*

A Staffordshire theatrical figure of an unidentified girl, with a musician holding a guitar, 10 in. high. **£65-75** *WA*

A Staffordshire figure of a 'Highland lover and his lass', with dark underglaze blue jackets, 9½ in. high. **£45-55** *WA*

A Staffordshire group of 'Auld Lang Syne', with blue underglaze jackets and colourful waistcoats, 7 in. high. **£75-85** *WA*

A Staffordshire group of St. George, with underglaze blue tunic and orange cape, slaying a green dragon, 7½ in. high. **£80-90** *WA*

A rare Staffordshire figure of Lord Nelson, in underglaze blue jacket and yellow breeches, 8 in. high. **£180-200** *WA*

A pair of Staffordshire figures, c. 1830, 3¾ in. high. **£145-165** pair *AD*

A Ralph Wood 'St. George and the dragon' figure group, in typical blue and green underglaze colours, c. 1770 (some repair). **£1,100-1,350** *AD*

A porcellaneous pair of Staffordshire figures of 'Elijah and the raven' and 'The Widow of Zarephath', c. 1825, 10½ in. high. **£170-220** *WA*

A pair of Ralph Wood figures, 'Apollo and Venus', c. 1770, 8½ in. **£1,200-1,800** pair *JH*

A pair of Staffordshire porcelain dogs, with little girl, c. 1830, 5 in. long. **£100-120** pair *AD*

A Staffordshire figure of a Scottish hunter, with horn and gun and underglaze blue jacket, 12½ in. high. **£45-65** *WA*

A square base Staffordshire figure group 'Pastime', c. 1790, 7 in. high. **£85-95** *DEB*

A Staffordshire Neale & Co. figure of Apollo, impressed Apollo, c. 1810, 6 in. high. **£150-175** *AD*

A Ralph Wood Vicar and Moses, impressed pattern No. 62, 1790, 10 in. high (damage to back of chair). **£360-400**, perfect **£650-700** *MB*

A Staffordshire figure group of Charity, c. 1820, 7¾ in. **£38-42** *MB*

A pair of Staffordshire furniture rests of John Wesley, c. 1830, 5 in. high. **£170-190** pair *AD*

A Staffordshire figure 'Mate', 9 in., c. 1820. **£80-100** *MB*

A pair of Staffordshire figures of Victoria and Albert, mainly white and gilt, c. 1845, 11 in. high. £230-250   WA

A Staffordshire figure group, 'Vy Sarah you'r drunk', 5 in. high, c. 1830-40. £150-170 AD

A Staffordshire figure of a small boy with mouse in cage, c. 1830-40, 4 in. high. £150-165 AD

A Staffordshire figure of a young boy, c. 1840, 6¼ in. high. £100-110   AD

A Staffordshire figure of a young boy in uniform, c. 1840, 7 in. high. £100-110   AD

A Staffordshire figure of Prince Albert, c. 1840, 8 in. high. £150-175   AD

A rare colourful Staffordshire figure of Romeo and Juliet, c. 1845, 11½ in. high. £380-400 WA

Figures of Queen Victoria and Prince Albert, in blue, pink and green, 15.5 cm. and 16 cm., c. 1840. £120-160   SB

A Staffordshire figure of 'The Pot Boy', inscribed 'I wish as there was a hact O' Parliment to make people find their own Pots', c. 1830-40, 9 in. high. £220-250   AD

A pair of Staffordshire horses and jockeys, mid-19th C., 9 in. £145-160   Cl.A

A Staffordshire figure of 'Fortune Teler' in white and gilt, very finely moulded, c. 1850. £75-85   WA

33

A Staffordshire group of Chang and Eng Bunker, 1811-74, born of Chinese parents in Siam, they appeared in Barnum's Circus. They married English girls, Chang had 10 children, Eng had 9, c. 1850. **£100-120** WA

A mid-19th C. Staffordshire group of 'Burns and Highland Mary', 7 in. high. **£50-60** Cl.A

A Staffordshire group of Lorenzo and Jessica from The Merchant of Venice, c. 1850. **£65-75** WA

A Staffordshire figure of Daniel in the lions' den, in white and gilt, c. 1855, 11 in. high. **£80-100** WA

A Staffordshire group of Victoria and Albert holding the Princess Royal, c. 1850, 7½ in. high. **£230-250** WA

A Staffordshire figure of Rayleyn, George Gordon Cumming 'The Lion Slayer', c. 1855, 17 in. high. **£75-85** WA

A fine Staffordshire alpha figure of Uncle Tom and Eva, c. 1852, 9 in. high. **£100-120** WA

A pair of Staffordshire figures of 'Sir Colin Campbell 1792-1863' and 'Sir Henry Havelock 1795-1857', in white and gilt and with orange hats and saddle clothes, 9½ in. high. **£140-160** pair WA

An unusual vividly coloured Staffordshire group 'The Rivals', c. 1860, 12 in. high. **£85-95** WA

A Staffordshire figure of Joseph Paxton the gardener, 1801-65, c. 1860, 9 in. high. **£90-100** WA

A Staffordshire penholder of a gardener and his wife, with dark underglaze blue jacket, c. 1860, 6½ in. high. **£30-35** *WA*

A Staffordshire figure of David Garrick as Richard III, c. 1860, 9½ in. high. **£65-75** *WA*

A Staffordshire figure of a Highland huntsman with pheasant, hare and dog, c. 1860, 15 in. high. **£75-95** *WA*

A Staffordshire figure of Red Riding Hood and the wolf, c. 1880, 14½ in. high. **£130-150** WA

A Staffordshire figure of King John signing the Magna Carta, with multi-colour overglaze, c. 1860, 12 in. high. **£120-140** WA

A Staffordshire figure of a young girl with fawn, c. 1880, 14 in. high. **£50-60** *WA*

A rare Sampson Smith Staffordshire figure of Daniel O'Connell, with underglaze blue jacket, c. 1875, 16 in. high. **£220-240** *WA*

A pair of Staffordshire spill holders of the game keeper and his wife, c. 1890, 11 in. high. **£120-140** *WA*

A 19th C. Staffordshire group 'Tenderness', some damage, 6 in. high. **£100-120** *SV*

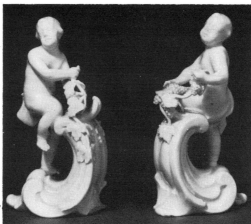

A pair of Sunderland Dixon Austin lustre figures, from the The Four Seasons Set, 'Winter' and 'Autumn', unmarked, c. 1825. 9 in. **£600-660**   *CS*

A pair of Vienna white glazed figures of Putti, emblematic of Autumn and Winter, shield mark in underglaze-blue, impressed workman's mark H, c. 1760-70, 12 cm. **£88-100**   *P*

A Talavera Maiolica group of The Virgin and Child, painted in cobalt blue, manganese, green, ochre and yellow, 60 cm., mid-18th C. **£200-250**   *SKC*

A pair of Volkstedt groups of lovers, 21.5 and 22 cm., hayfork marks in blue, late 19th C. **£200-230**   *SB*

VIENNA

- du Paquier opened the factory in 1719 with the help of Stolzel and Hunger from Meissen
- it was taken over by Empress Maria Theresa in 1744. This began the 'State Period' from 1744-1784. The style of this period is Baroque, with scrollwork and lattice-like gilding
- excellent figure modelling was undertaken by J. J. Niedmayer from 1747-1784
- Sorgenthal became director of the factory from 1784-1805, which was its greatest period
- the factory finally closed in 1864

A Vienna group of a young woman (minute chips), impressed E marks, c. 1775, 14.5 cm. high. **£650-750**   *C*

A Vincennes white figure of a Calliope, after the Meissen original by J. J. Kandler (chips), 1747-52, 20 cm. high. **£480-550**   *C*

A Volkstedt figure of a fruit seller, chips, 23 cm., crossed swords and initials mark, c. 1900. **£70-120**   *SB*

The Balloon Seller, a Charles Vyse earthenware figure, painted CV monogram, Chelsea, 22 cm., dated 1922. **£220-260**   *SB*

A Walton figure the 'Widow of Zarephath', signed, restored, 10 in., c. 1820. **£80-90**   *MB*

A Weesp white sweetmeat figure of a putto, blue crossed swords and dots mark, c. 1765, 11 cm. high. **£1,000-1,400** *C*

A large Wedgwood black basalt bust of Mercury, from the Antique, 47 cm., impressed mark, late 19th C. **£330-380** *SB*

A pair of Royal Worcester parian busts of young maidens, impressed marks, 36 cm., mid 19th C. **£300-360** *SBe*

A rare Whieldon ware figure, c. 1745, 6½ in. **£650-950** *JH*

A pair or Royal Worcester Hadley figures (The Holbien figures), c. 1880, 8½ in. high. **£600-640** pair *MB*

A Royal Worcester figure, c. 1880, 8½ in. high. **£280-320** *MB*

A pair of Royal Worcester figures of a Huntsman and a Fisher-girl, in pastel 'Raphaelesque' glazes (minor chips), 43 cm., impressed crowned circle mark, c. 1865. **£480-550** *SB*

SOME ROYAL WORCESTER ARTISTS AND THEIR SPECIALITIES

C. Baldwyn	– *birds, particularly swans*	R. Rushton	– *landscapes*
		R. Sebright	– *fruit and flowers*
George Johnson	– *exotic birds*	H. Price	– *fruit*
James Stinton	– *game birds*	J. Stanley	– *hunting scenes*
John Stinton	– *highland cattle*		
		E. Barker	– *sheep*
Harry Stinton	– *highland cattle (more vivid colours than father)*	Kitty Blake	– *blackberries & autumnal leaves*

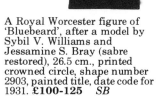

A Royal Worcester 'Shot Enamels' figure of a moorish slave, after a model by James Hadley, moulded signature, coloured in ochre, green and grey-blue (hair cracks), 61 cm., printed Shot Enamels mark, shape number 1744, Rd. No. 233559, date code for 1898. **£300-400** *SB*

A pair of Royal Worcester 'New Large Grecian Water-Carriers', 52 cm., printed crowned circle mark, shape number 125 and date code for 1912. **£500-550** *SB*

A Royal Worcester figure of 'Bluebeard', after a model by Sybil V. Williams and Jessamine S. Bray (sabre restored), 26.5 cm., printed crowned circle, shape number 2903, painted title, date code for 1931. **£100-125** *SB*

A pair of Bow sheep, picked out in purple or brown (slight damage), height 8.6 cm., mid-18th C. £150-180   *SBe*

A Yorkshire pottery group of longcase clock and figures, c. 1825, 9 in. high. £330-370 *AD*

A Burmantofts Faience figure of a monkey, in bright turquoise, 6 in. £60-70   *Brit*

A Royal Worcester figure of 'Fatima', after a model by Sybil V. Williams and Jessamine S. Bray, 25.5 cm., printed crowned circle, shape number 2904, painted title, date code for 1932. £150-175   *SB*

A Royal Doulton 'Flambe' model of a tiger, 35 cm. long, circle mark lion and crown and 'flambe'. £100-150   *P*

A Derby pug, c. 1780, 3 in. high. £350-400   *MB*

A Dutch Delft polychrome figure of a parrot (beak restored, glaze chips), c. 1725, 21 cm. high. £500-650   *C*

A Derby sheep, c. 1770, 3½ in. high. £220-280   *MB*

A Derby figure of a peacock, painted in gold and green, mark in underglaze blue of Sampson Hancock, height 17.6 cm., c. 1859. £160-190   *SBe*

A pair of Derby figures of a recumbent stag and hind, in russet, pink and yellow (restoration), Wm. Duesbury & Co., c. 1765, about 17 cm. wide. £550-650   *C*

An early 20th C. Royal Dux group of two game dogs, in a subdued palette, impressed and applied pink triangle, impressed 2429, printed mark, 45 cm. £150-200   *C*

A rare English porcelain yellow, brown and black mottled figure of a recumbent cat, 3 in. long. **£260-320** *PK*

A pair of French models of terriers, coloured in black or brown, 17 and 18 cm., crossed arrows in underglaze blue, late 19th C. **£170-230** *SB*

An early Martinware bird, coloured olive, blue and brown, incised on the removable head, R. W. Martin, London and Southall, and dated 14.9.81, also dated on chest (cracked), 25 cm. high. **£200-300** *P*

A Martin Brothers stoneware model of a wild cat, the body painted dark brown, blue and grey, inscribed on the base 'R.W. Martin London Southall 2.82' (damaged), length 11.2 cm. **£340-400** *SBe*

MARTINWARE

- name given to stoneware made at Southall and Fulham by the Martin brothers
- made between 1873 and 1914
- normally stamped or incised e.g.
  R. W. Martin, Fulham 1873-1874
- 'Brothers' or 'Bros' was added to signature mark after 1879

A Martin Brothers bird, in a royal-blue glaze, the beak and claws brown, 19 cm., the head and base signed and dated 10.1913. **£950-1,100** *SB*

A Martin Brothers bird, in a runny aubergine glaze with inky-blue and olive (chip and restoration), 28.5 cm., signed and dated 20.7.1905. **£1,000-1,200** *SB*

A Martin Brothers bird with detachable head (chips, beak restored), 26.3 cm., the head signed and dated 7.1892, the base marked R.W. Martin, London & Southall, 2.9.1881. **£440-540** *SB*

A Meissen figure of a dog (repaired), 6.5 cm. wide, c. 1745. **£300-400** *C*

A Meissen figure of a whippet (restorations to tail), c. 1750, 5 cm. wide. **£300-360** *C*

A Meissen figure of a sitting bear, modelled by J. J. Kändler, and painted in shades of black and brown (lacks ring on collar), c. 1745, 10 cm. high. **£950-1,100** *C*

A Meissen figure of a hen, painted in grey, ochre and red (beak repaired), traces of blue crossed swords mark, 9 cm. wide, c. 1740. **£800-1,000** *C*

A Meissen miniature figure of a seated cat, with pale brown fur markings (tail chipped, ears repaired), 4 cm. high, c. 1750. **£180-250** *C*

A Meissen figure of a parrot by J. J. Kändler, in grey, black and orange (one wing chipped, minor chips to base), traces of blue crossed swords marks, 19 cm., c. 1745. **£3,700-4,000**   *C*

A pair of Meissen figures of hares, painted brown, grey and ochre (repaired and chipped), blue crossed swords marks, 16 cm. and 15 cm. high, c. 1750. **£3,000-3,600**   *C*

A Meissen figure of a Magpie, 21 in. high (slight restoration on tail and beak). **£470-500** (not restored) **£700-800**   *MB*

A Meissen figure of a Danish hound, modelled by J. J. Kändler, wearing a brown collar edged in yellow with puce rosette, seated on an iron-red cushion (repair to one ear), Pressnummer 50 twice, c. 1745, 11 cm. high. **£650-850**   *C*

A Meissen figure of a turkey with chicks, in brown, ochre, red and blue, blue crossed swords mark at back, 11 cm. wide, c. 1755. **£700-850**   *C*

A Meissen figure of a thrush, painted ochre and brown (chipped and repaired), blue crossed swords mark at back, 16 cm. high, c. 1745. **£1,000-1,500**   *C*

A pair of Minton poodles, on cushion bases, c. 1840. **£200-210**   *AD*

A Meissen cat feeding her young, c. 1765, 10½ in. high. **£900-1,000**   *Cr.A*

A Meissen figure of a parrot, with red, green, blue and yellow plumage, chips, 32 cm., crossed swords in underglaze blue, incised 63, late 19th C. **£300-350**   *SB*

A Newcastle sheep, c. 1800, 6 in. long. **£130-150**   *AD*

PORCELAIN & POTTERY

A Pratt sheep, c. 1800, 3 in. long.
£60-70   AD

A Pratt sheep with spotted
decoration, c. 1810, 3¾ in. long.
£50-60   AD

A Nymphenburg figure
of a parrot, modelled by
Dominicus Auliczek, in
green, yellow, red, blue
and gilt (chips),
impressed Bavarian
shield mark and ID,
15.5 cm. high, c. 1765.
£1,800-2,100   C

A pair of porcellanous
models of leopards, on
a green rocky base with
a gilt-line border (one
base with hair crack),
impressed 256, c. 1830.
£200-300   SB

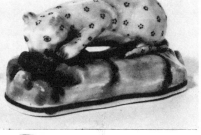

A saltglaze agateware figure of
a seated cat (restored), c. 1755,
12 cm. high. £100-150
If perfect £600-900   C

A Schwarzburger Werkstatten
fur Porzellankunst model of a
cheetah, with moulded
modeller's monogram A.St., 40
cm., impressed running fox
mark and shape number U1221,
early 20th C. £180-220   SB

A rare Portobello horse, c. 1810.
£780-820   CS

A Sitzendorf Bolognese hound,
c. 1860, 8 in. high. £150-175
MB

A Ralph Wood Sen. group of
birds, with interesting 'birds'
painted on, obviously by
children, c. 1770, 7 in. high.
£500-580   AD

A Staffordshire porcelain figure
of a leopard, pale yellow
rockwork base, 5 in. long. £150-
190   PK

A pair of Staffordshire deer
penholders, in perfect
condition, 4½ in. long. £60-
70   WA

A Staffordshire porcelain dog, c. 1825, 4 in. high. **£110-125** *AD*

A Staffordshire porcelain reclining stag, c. 1825, 5 in. (restored). **£50-60** *AD*

A late 18th C. Ralph Wood figure of a sheep (base restored), 6½ in. wide. **£80-90** *MB*

A late 18th C. Ralph Wood underglaze colour figure of a doe, some damage, 6½ in. wide. **£145-165**; perfect **£380-450** *MB*

A Staffordshire porcelain dog, c. 1825, 3¼ in. **£60-75** *AD*

A Staffordshire 'Country Piece' bird, following colours and design of earlier Whieldon pieces but without quality and lightness, 3½ in. high, c. 1800. **£75-85** *AD*

A Staffordshire porcelain dog, c. 1825, with floral base, 5 in. long. **£100-110** *AD*

A pair of Staffordshire porcelain reclining sheep, with applied coloured flowers, c. 1830. **£110-120** pair *AD*

One of a pair of Staffordshire porcelain cat groups, after Rockingham originals, c. 1830. **£300-340** pair *AD*

A pair of Staffordshire dalmatians, c. 1845, 5¼ in. **£95-105** *CS*

A pair of Staffordshire poodles, c. 1860, 8 in. **£80-90** *CS*

One of a pair of Staffordshire dog groups, after Rockingham originals, c. 1830. **£300-340** pair *AD*

An unusual Staffordshire figure of a black and white spaniel with a puppy, sitting on a bright orange cushion, c. 1850, 6½ in. high. **£70-75** *WA*

A pair of black and white
Staffordshire King Charles
spaniels, c. 1860, 6 in. high.
£70-80 *WA*

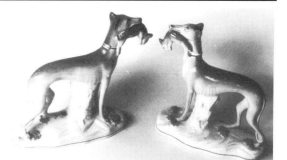

A pair of Staffordshire
greyhounds, very finely
moulded, c. 1860, 7½ in. high.
£90-110 pair *WA*

A fine colourful Staffordshire
parrot, c. 1870, 9 in. high. **£60-
70** *WA*

One of a pair of Staffordshire
red and white cow and calf
spillholders, c. 1870, 11 in. high.
£120-140 pair *WA*

One of a pair of Staffordshire
modelled greyhounds, on green
and brown mound bases, 8 in.
high. **£150-190** the pair *CSK*

A group of a man, a cow and a
dog, in green and ochre,
possibly Yorkshire, 5½ in. high.
£400-500 *CSK*

A Royal Worcester Group of
Princess Grace and Foal, after
the original model by Doris
Lindner, 26., printed crowned
circle, title and facsimile
signature, number 330 of an
edition limited to 750, dated
1970, certificate and stand.
£300-350 *SB*

A pair of Staffordshire spill
vase figures of lions, on gilt-
lined bases, 7 in. high. **£200-
250** *CSK*

A pair of Staffordshire well
coloured spill vase groups of
dogs chasing stags, with gilt-
lined bases, 11½ in. high. **£90-
120** *CSK*

A pair of Staffordshire well
coloured groups of lions seated
with lambs at their feet, with
gilt-lined bases, 10½ in. high.
£550-650 *CSK*

A very rare Staffordshire
peacock, with impressed mark
'Sandland', c. 1901, 11½ in.
high. **£75-85** *WA*

43

A Yorkshire cow group, c. 1800, 5½ in. **£340-380** *CS*

A small Welsh pottery cow creamer, probably Llanelli, 5½ in., c. 1825. **£150-165** *CS*

A Portobello hobbled cow creamer, c. 1810, 5½ in. **£260-290** *CS*

A Portobello cow creamer, in typical crude red and black decoration (restored), c. 1820, 5¼ in. high. **£120-150** *AD*

A Pratt cow creamer, in ochre and deep blue, c. 1795, 4 in. high. **£250-275** *AD*

A Staffordshire pearlware cow-creamer group, with brown hide (tail restored), c. 1780, 16.5 cm. wide. **£160-190** *C*

An unusual Staffordshire spillholder of a hunting group, 7½ in. high. **£75-85** *WA*

A Staffordshire spill holder of recumbent lion and serpent in a tree, c. 1860, 12 in. high. **£60-70** *WA*

A Whieldon cow-creamer group, lightly spotted in manganese, enriched in ochre (damaged and restored), c. 1775, 18 cm. wide. **£260-300** *C*

A Staffordshire milkmaid and cow spillholder, c. 1860, 8½ in. high. **£55-65** *WA*

A Martin Brothers stoneware 'Grotesque' tooth-pick holder of armadillo type, in pink, grey and brown tones, 14 cm., incised R.W. Martin & Bros, London & Southall, dated 13-37. **£150-180** *SB*

A third period Belleek table centre piece, 12 in. **£500-550** *MT*

A Dresden centrepiece, with pierced bowl, brightly coloured and with gilt details, 40 cm., painted crossed swords and AR monogram, late 19th C. £275-315 *SB*

A Bloor Derby Centrepiece inscribed G IV R coloured in turquoise and gilding (chips), 15 cm., painted iron-red Bloor Derby and crown, c. 1825. £150-200 *SB*

A Meissen centrepiece, in pink, turquoise and gilding, erased crossed swords mark, 49 cm., c. 1860-70. £850-950 *SKC*

A Meissen centrepiece, on four scrolled feet, in pastel shades with gilt details, 43 cm., crossed swords in underglaze blue, incised W174, late 19th C. £1,100-1,300 *SB*

A Royal Dux centrepiece, in brown, green and pink, applied pink triangle mark, printed circular mark, impressed shape number 710, 43 cm., c. 1910. £450-550 *SB*

A Meissen-style centre-piece, painted mark in underglaze blue, late 19th C., height 67½ cm. £500-600 *SBe*

A Minton part-Parian six-light candelabrum-centrepiece, the details in turquoise enamel and gilding (damaged), 56.5 cm., impressed mark, c. 1860-65. £520-620 *SB*

A Minton 'Majolica' Centrepiece, in ochre, green and blue glazes, 29 cm., impressed mark, shape number 784 and date code for 1876. £160-220 *SB*

A Sitzendorf centre-piece, with pierced flared circular bowl, coloured and with gilt details, 54.5 cm., crossed parallel lines in underglaze blue, late 19th C. £250-300 *SB*

45

A Plaue centrepiece, the whole coloured in a soft palette, chips, printed shield mark, 30.5 cm., late 19th C. **£240-300** *SBe*

A Belleek tulip vase, 1st period, 9 in. **£570-600** *Cr.A*

A Baron, Barnstaple small vase, c. 1930, 4 in. high. **£20-25** *Brit*

A Plaue centrepiece, minor chips, 40.5 cm., crossed parallel lines in underglaze blue, late 19th C. **£300-350** *SB*

A pair of Fulham stoneware vases, probably by C. J. C. Bailey, 35 cm., c. 1875. **£130-170** *SB*

A pair of Berlin vases, painted with figures from classical history, sceptre mark in underglaze blue, and subject titles in red, 18¾ in. **£630-700** *L*

A second period Belleek vase, 'The Prince Arthur Vase', 11 in. **£320-350** *MT*

A First Period Belleek open lily vase, with buds, with Exhibition mark, 9 in. diam. **£400-500** *MT*

A Royal Bonn vase, on ground shading from deep lilac through apple-green to lemon yellow, 92 cm., printed mark, painted numerals, c. 1900. , **£500-600** *SB*

Left
A Royal Bonn vase, indistinctly signed, 27 cm., printed mark, c. 1910. **£175-225** *SB*

A Berlin vase, painted with views of the Royal Palace in Berlin, and the Palace of Sanssouci, with gilded detail, 67.5 cm., printed marks in underglaze-blue and red enamel. **£4,400-4,600** *P*

A pair of Brannam Barum ware vases, in cream, chestnut, blue and green on a blue ground (chips), incised C. H. Brannam, Barum, 53.5 cm., dated 1897. **£90-110** *SB*

A Bretby Art Potters large vase, c. 1880, 27 in. high. **£100-120** *MB*

A pair of Coalport 'New Poperee' vases and covers, with deep encrustations of flowers amongst turquoise and gilt foliate decoration, 29 cm. **£440-500** *P*

A Caltagirone vase, in blue, yellow and green (repair to neck), 17th C., 23 cm. high. **£260-320** *C*

A Carltonware lustre vase, hand-painted, 5½ in. high. **£30-40** *Brit*

A pair of Coalport pink-ground vases and covers, in 18th C. Sevres style (chipped, slightly rubbed), 21.5 cm., CBD gilt mark, 1851-61. **£270-330** *SB*

A Chelsea vase, finely painted with flowers within gilt rims (slight chip to foot), c. 1758, 20.5 cm. high. **£580-680** *C*

A Coalport vase and cover, the ovoid body painted against a royal-blue ground, 25 cm., printed crown mark, painted titled and numbered V5327/s/s161, c. 1910. **£320-380** *SB*

A Coalport vase on pink ground with hand painted landscape, c. 1875, 6¼ in. high. **£170-200** *MB*

A pair of Coalport vases, in Sevres style, each painted against a vivid azure-blue ground (hair cracks in foot), 27.3 cm., CBD mark in gilding, c. 1855. **£300-350** *SB*

A Faience Manufactory Aluminia Copenhagen vase, painted by Arth. Boesen., signed, in brown and blue-grey, 28 cm., printed Dahl-Jensens, 164/111, c. 1930. **£225-275** *SB*

A pair of Dutch Delft blue and white octagonal vases and covers, in gold and red colours (minor chips) blue AC marks, 39 cm. high, c. 1760 **£500-620** *C*

A Dutch Delft vase, painted in blue, yellow and green (minor glaze chips), 25.5 cm. high, c. 1690. **£700-850** *C*

A De Morgan bottle-vase, painted by Fred Passenger in Isnik taste, in turquoise, blue, mauve, crimson and green (restored), 58.7 cm. impressed Merton Abbey oval mark, painted FP, c. 1882-88. **£1,800-2,300** *SB*

A garniture of 3 Dutch Delft blue and white vases and 2 covers (chips, one with a hair crack), blue, 5 marks, 37-43.5 cm. high, c. 1765. **£700-850** *C*

A buff stoneware vase, by Hans Coper, the interior in a brown glaze, impressed oval mark, 27 cm. high. **£1,100-1,300** *C*

A Derby flared flower vase and pierced cover, painted in the manner of Jockey Hill, inscribed on the base 'Both Views on the Dove, Derbyshire' (base of one handled restored) inscribed and crown, crossed batons and D marks in blue, Duesbury & Kean, 1795-1800 11 cm. high. **£500-600** *C*

A pair of Derby crested Campana vases, painted by Thomas Steel against green ground, printed crowned circle mark, Robert Bloor & Co., 29 cm. high, c. 1830. **£2,700-3,000** *C*

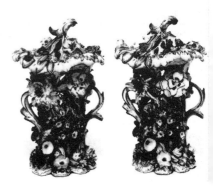

A vase, by Fred Passenger, painted in Isnik style, inscribed 'W. De Morgan, Fulham' and the artist's monogram 'F.P.', 40 cm., c. 1890. **£420-480** *SKC*

A Pair of Derby Pierced and Floral-Encrusted vases and covers, coloured in pastel shades with gilt details (chips), 19 cm., one with printed crowned D, c. 1830. **£190-230** *SB*

A pair of Royal Crown Derby vases and covers, each painted by W. Mosley, signed, 18 cm., printed crowned initials, numbered 1019/5152, indistinct date code, c. 1910. **£350-400** *SB*

A pair of Royal Crown Derby vases, each painted by A. Gregory, signed, against a royal-blue ground, one restored, 16.5 cm., printed crowned initials mark and date code for 1914. **£300-350** *SB*

A Crown Devon lustreware small vase, 5 in. high. **£10-20** Brit

A pair of Doulton stoneware vases, painted by Florence Barlow, the necks incised by Frank Butler, impressed Lambeth mark, incised artist's monograms and 667, 22 cm., dated 1889. **£320-350** *SB*

A pair of Doulton stoneware vases, decorated in pate-sur-pate technique by Florence E. Barlow, 'F.E.B.' and 'A.E.B.' (assistants) monograms, florette mark, 24.5 cm., dated '1885'. **£450-550** *SKC*

A pair of large Doulton Lambeth vases, by Florence Barlow, height 17¾ in. **£420-480** *LT*

DOULTON

- factory at Doulton in Lambeth from c. 1815
- main figure in rise of Doulton was Henry Doulton, who began his apprenticeship in 1835
- from 1862 Doulton produced decorated stoneware
- artists signed their work, either with initials or monogram
- most celebrated decorative artists:
  Hannah B. Barlow (c. 1872-1906)
  Florence Barlow (c. 1873-1909)
  Arthur Barlow (c. 1872-1879) — Arthur worked for only eight years and hence his work is rare
- George Tinworth (working 1866-1913)
- Eliza Simmance (c. 1873-1928) — had particular influence on the Art Nouveau movement
- Frank A. Butler (c. 1873-1911)
- Frances E. Lee (c. 1875-1890)
- Edith D. Lupton (c. 1876-1889)
- Mark V. Marshall (1876-1912)
- Florence C. Roberts (c. 1879-1930)

A Doulton Lambeth vase, with incised decoration of deer, by Hannah Barlow, 16 in. high. **£350-450** *LT*

A Doulton Lambeth vase, decorated in pate-sur-pate by Florence Barlow, 32.50 cm. high, rosette mark and England, incised F.E.B. in monogram, numbered 773 and L.R. 265 as assistant. **£220-280** *P*

A pair of Doulton stoneware vases, decorated by Hannah and Lucy Barlow, in ochre and royal blue, 26 cm., impressed rosette mark, incised artists monograms, 108 and 83, dated 1883. **£320-360** *SB*

A Doulton Lambeth vase, impressed 1881, by Hannah Barlow, 8½ in. high. **£250-280** *Brit*

A pair of Doulton stoneware vases, each decorated by Hannah Barlow and Frank Butler, in green, blue, brown and grey, 26.8 cm., impressed Lambeth mark, incised artist monograms and 82, c. 1885. **£360-430** *SB*

A Doulton stoneware vase, body incised by Hannah Barlow with quatrefoil panels, the overall royal-blue ground incised by Emily Stormer, 35.5 cm., impressed Lambeth mark, England, incised artists monograms and MA, c. 1891. **£580-650** *SB*

A pair of Doulton stoneware vases, decorated by Hannah Barlow and Florence Roberts, base chips, 32.5 cm., impressed Lambeth mark, England, numerals, incised artists monograms, 77 and BN for Bessie Newbury, c. 1895. **£280-300** *SB*

A Doulton stoneware vase, incised by Hannah Barlow, 20.5 cm., impressed Lambeth mark, England, incised artist's monogram, initials for Florence C. Roberts and numerals, c. 1900. **£160-200** *SB*

A Doulton Lambeth vase, with incised panel of horses, by Hannah B. Barlow and Francis E. Lee, height 12¼ in. **£350-400** *LT*

An unusual Doulton stoneware bottle vase, the body incised and impressed by Frank Butler, in blue, brown and olive, 16.8 cm., impressed Lambeth mark, incised artists monogram, V.E.X.E.C. and G.P., c. 1880. **£260-320** *SB*

A Doulton vase, decorated in a brown mottled glaze, the neck incised by Hannah Barlow, height impressed and incised marks, late 19th C. **£430-500** *SBe*

A Doulton Lambeth vase, decorated in heavy relief, by John Broad, height 11½ in. **270-330** *LT*

A pair of Doulton Lambeth vases, with blue motifs, by Frank A. Butler, height 11¾ in. **£350-400** *LT*

A Doulton Lambeth vase, with applied decoration on blue ground, by Frank A. Butler, height 11½ in. **£150-200** *LT*

A Doulton Lambeth vase, with incised decorated panel, by Hannah B. Barlow, assistant Annie Contle, height 14½ in. **£300-360** *LT*

A Doulton Lambeth artist's piece by Louise Edwards, dated 1880 and signed, 13 in. high. **£200-240** *CH*

A pair of Doulton Lambeth vases, with applied floral decoration, by Francis E. Lee and Mary Ann Thompson, height 12 in. **£230-290** *LT*

A Doulton stoneware pate-sur-pate vase, painted by Frances E. Lee, with celadon green ground, 25.4 cm., impressed Lambeth mark, incised 104, artists initials, DB monogram, assistants initials for Mary Aitken, dated 1884. **£120-150** *SB*

A Doulton Lambeth vase, Edith D. Lupton, assistant Mary Aitken, height 11 in. **£100-120** *LT*

A pair of Doulton stoneware vases, decorated by Edith Lupton, 25 cm., impressed Lambeth mark, incised artist's initials, 512 and 513, dated 1877. **£440-520** *SB*

A pair of Doulton stoneware vases, incised and carved by Edith Lupton, minor base chip, 17.8 cm., impressed Doulton Lambeth mark, incised 288, artists initials, c. 1891. **£170-210** *SB*

A Doulton Lambeth piece, by Edith Lupton, impressed 1880, 3½ in. high. **£40-45** *Brit*

A pair of Doulton vases, decorated by Francis E. Lee, one with rim chips, 23.7 cm., impressed Lambeth mark, incised artist's initials, 465, and LA for Elizabeth Adams, dated 1886. **£130-170** *SB*

A Royal Doulton vase, by Mark
V. Marshall, c. 1909, 8 in. high.
£140-160   *Brit*

A Doulton Lambeth vase, with
applied floral decorations on
cane ground, by Mark V.
Marshall, assistant probably
Mary Aitken, height 15 in.
£220-280   *LT*

A Doulton Lambeth vase, 9¼ in.
high. **£110-150**   *Brit*

A Royal Doulton vase, painted
by Mark V. Marshall, 39 cm.
high, circle mark, lion and
crown, incised M.V.M. 108.
£220-280   *P*

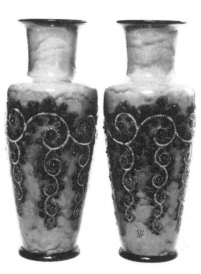

A Doulton stoneware vase,
decorated by Eliza Simmance,
in pale blue, pink and olive, 34.4
cm., impressed Lambeth mark,
Art Union of London, 6142,
incised artists monogram,
909R, c. 1895. **£140-180**   *SB*

A pair of large Doulton
stoneware vases, incised by
George Tinworth, signed, 40
cm., impressed Lambeth mark,
incised initials for Rosina
Brown, dated 1880. **£200-
240**   *SB*

A pair of Doulton Lambeth
vases, decorated by George
Tinworth, 23 cm. high, circular
mark, dated 1878, artist's
monogram and assistant's
mark HH monogram. **£200-
260**   *P*

A pair of Doulton and Slaters
silicon vases, with pate-sur-pate
panels, by Edith L. Lupton,
height 10½ in. **£380-430**   *LT*

A pair of Royal Doulton vases,
each painted by E. Wood,
signed, 15 cm., printed lion,
crown and circle mark, c. 1910.
£260-350   *SB*

A Doulton stoneware vase, by
Emily E. Stormer, blue and
olive green on a buff ground,
impressed marks, late 19th C.
£100-120   *SBe*

A Royal Doulton small vase, post 1921, 4½ in. high. £30-35 and two small bowls in similar style. £25-30   *Brit*

A pair of Royal Doulton vases, 'Dickensware Series', 8 in., c. 1910. £140-160   *MT*

A Doulton Burslem small vase, with yellow ground, 5½ in. high. £40-50   *Brit*

A pair of late 19th C. Dresden pot-pourri vases and covers, on bleu-de-roi ground with tooled-gilt handles, necks reduced, 29.5 cm., crowned D in underglaze blue. £250-350   *SB*

A pair of large Dresden vases and covers (one cover damaged), 53 cm., late 19th C. £400-460   *SB*

A Frankenthal Rococo two-handled pot-pourri vase and cover (minor damage), blue lion rampant mark, 1756-59, 27 cm. high. £1,800-2,200   *C*

An early Bernard Leach stoneware vase, impressed seal in script and St. Ives mark, 25.5 cm., c. 1930. £700-900   *SB*

A pair of English porcelain Campana vases, painted with baskets of garden flowers, with wide gilt line rims (one with restoration), 38.6 cm. high, c. 1820. £2,900-3,200   *C*

A pottery vase by Hart and Moist, 8 in. high. £20-25   *Brit*

A Sicilian tin glaze earthenware vase, dated 1784, 9 in. high. £150-220   *JC*

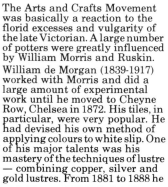

THE ARTIST POTTERS

The Arts and Crafts Movement was basically a reaction to the florid excesses and vulgarity of the late Victorian. A large number of potters were greatly influenced by William Morris and Ruskin.

William de Morgan (1839-1917) worked with Morris and did a large amount of experimental work until he moved to Cheyne Row, Chelsea in 1872. His tiles, in particular, were very popular. He had devised his own method of applying colours to white slip. One of his major talents was his mastery of the techniques of lustre — combining copper, silver and gold lustres. From 1881 to 1888 he

worked at Merton Abbey, Wimbledon, where he also used to great effect the Persian colours of red, blue and green. He moved back to Fulham in 1888 and mainly concentrated on writing novels. The factory closed in 1911.

The Della Robbia Company Ltd. was set up in 1894 by Harold Rathbone at Birkenhead, Merseyside. Most of the wares produced under Rathbone's direction were inspired by the Renaissance movement. The factory made both decorative, often highly abstract, based on geometric shapes, and architectural wares.

The doyen of the Studio Pottery movement was undoubtedly Bernard Leach (1887-1979). He had a studio workshop at St. Ives in Cornwall. He was greatly influenced by the philosophy and styles of the Orient. Bernard Leach's ware has always been held in high regard by collectors and prices soared after his death in 1979. After recent publicity of fakes of his work from enterprising potters in Her Majesty's Custody it will be interesting to see how prices will react.

An early Bernard Leach stoneware vase, in blue beneath a clear greyish green glaze, impressed seal mark in script, St. Ives mark, 16 cm., c. 1930. **£350-450** *SB*

A Longwy Primavera crackle glazed earthenware vase, in deep blue, turquoise, black and cream, 31 cm., printed factory mark, 1920's. **£220-280** *SB*

A Leeds undecorated finger vase, c. 1780, 8 in. high. **£45-50** *AD*

A Martin Brothers vase, in brown against a pale green glaze, 13.5 cm., signed and dated 6-97. **£280-330** *SB*

A Leeds vase with 'The Gardener', c. 1790, 8 in. high. **£280-300** *MB*

A Martin Brothers stoneware vase, in brown, white, blue and green, with three angular handles, 27.5 cm., incised R.W. Martin & Bros, London & Southall, dated 21.3.84. **£150-270** *SB*

A Martin Brothers stoneware vase, painted in brown and cream against a buff ground, 24.8 cm., incised R.W. Martin & Bros, London & Southall, dated 24.11.84. **£225-255** *SB*

A Martin Brothers vase, in olive, blue and shades of brown, 23.5 cm., affixed exhibition label signed and dated 9-1892. **£650-800** *SB*

A Martin Brothers vase, in greens, browns and white against a biscuit-coloured ground, 25.50 cm. high. incised R. W. Martin & Bros. London & Southall 4—1887. **£120-200** *P*

A Martin Brothers gourd vase, in an olive-grey glaze (hair cracks), 44 cm., signed and dated 1910. **£180-220** *SB*

A Maw & Co. earthenware vase, designed by Walter Crane, in ruby on a cream ground, 21.6 cm., with original paper label inscribed 'A18697 Ruby Lustre Vase Diver', 1880's. **£800-1,000** *SB*

A Martin Brothers vase, in shades of brown, olive and washy blue, 24 cm., signed and dated 3-1904. **£190-230** *SB*

A pair of Meissen pot-pourri vases and covers, painted against a deep-blue ground (one finial restored), crossed swords in underglaze blue, incised G59, 29 cm., mid-19th C. **£1,300-1,500** *SB*

A pair of Meissen basketwork double-gourd vases and covers (slight chips to foliage, one finial riveted), c. 1745, 37.5 cm. high. **£3,400-3,800** *C*

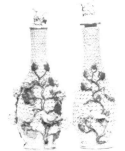

A Meissen Augustus Rex small chinoiserie vase, painted by J. E. Stadler (restored), blue AR monogram mark, c. 1728, 16 cm. high. **£750-950** *C*

A pair of Meissen 'schneeballen' vases and covers, underglaze mark in blue, 34 cm. high, late 19th C. **£350-400** *SBe*

A Meissen vase and cover, converted to a vase from a coffee-pot and with later ormolu finial, handles and foot (the cover repaired), blue crossed swords mark, Pressnummer 24, Gilder's mark G, the porcelain, c. 1745, 24.5 cm. high. **£550-650** *C*

A pair of Meissen vases and covers (damaged), crossed swords in underglaze blue, incised A6H, 14 cm., late 19th C. **£280-350** *SB*

A late Meissen vase-figure group, crossed swords mark in blue, 32 cm. **£620-750** *P*

A pair of Meissen vases, with flowers within gilt-scroll borders on a deep-blue ground, crossed swords in underglaze blue, 13.5 cm., early 20th C. **£170-210** *SB*

Two Meissen vases, ovoid body on a gilt fluted circular foot, one painted with flowers, the other with flowers and a gilt Jubilee inscription and a coat-of-arms, 26.5 cm., crossed swords in underglaze blue, c. 1907. **£550-650** *SB*

A Meissen vase, painted in orange, foot-rim chip, crossed swords in underglaze blue, 34.8 cm., early 20th C. **£110-160** *SBe*

A pair of apple-green-ground vases, probably Minton (one handle chipped), 25.5 cm., c. 1830. **£300-380**   *SB*

A Minton 'Cloisonne' vase, enamelled gilding against a turquoise and white ground (gilding worn), 20.5 cm., impressed Minton, 1398 and date code for 1869. **£80-120** *SB*

A pair of Mintons Ltd. vases, in turquoise, ochre and cream, 7 in. tall. **£50-60** pair   *Brit*

A pair of Minton 'Cloisonne' vases and covers, enamelled and gilt on a pink ground (covers restored), 23 cm., impressed Minton, E and date code for 1869. **£120-160**   *SB*

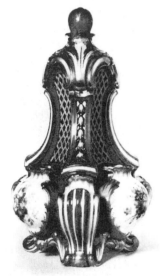

A Minton 'Rothschild' pot-pourri vase and cover, in 18th C. Sevres style (cover restored), 40.5 cm., high, painted ermine mark, c. 1870. **£360-420**   *SB*

A Minton porcelain 'Cloisonne' vase, with a crackled turquoise ground, 20 cm., impressed Minton and '0821', c. 1870. **£60-90**   *SB*

A Minton Ltd. vase, on deep red ground, 7½ in. high. **£30-40** *Brit*

A Mintons vase, 8½ in. high. **£30-35**   *Brit*

A pair of Minton vases, painted by Aaron Green (damaged and repaired), 55.6 cm., impressed Minton, 1640 and date code for 1871, signed and dated 1872. **£450-550**   *SB*

A pair of Minton pate sur pate porcelain vases, 11½ in. **£400-500**   *WW*

A pair of Moorcroft vases, 9 in. high. **£110-125**   *Brit*

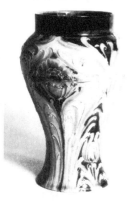

A Moorcroft Macintyre vase, coloured in blue and sage green, 24.2 cm., printed florian mark, painted W. Moorcroft des. in green, c. 1898. **£370-430** *SB*

A Moorcroft Macintyre vase, coloured in blue and sage green, 20.4 cm., printed florian mark, painted W. Moorcroft des. B.160 in green, c. 1898. **£330-390** *SB*

A Moorcroft Florian ware MacIntyre vase, 7 in. high. **£250-285** *Cr.A*

A Moorcroft vase, made for Liberty and Co., in yellow and blue against an olive-green ground, signed in green W. Moorcroft des., 30.50 cm. high. **£160-220** *P*

A Moorcroft Florian MacIntyre ware vase, c. 1880, 7 in. high. **£200-220** *Cr.A*

An unusual early Moorcroft Florian vase, in primrose, green and blue, 30.5 cm., printed Florian mark, painted W. Moorcroft des in green, c. 1898. **£360-460** *SB*

A Moorcroft 'Claremont' vase, in reds, yellows and olive greens against a blue and olive green ground, impressed marks and signed W. Moorcroft, 32 cm. high. **£250-310** *P*

A Moorcroft Macintyre florianware vase, in olive and shades of blue, 20.5 cm., painted W. Moorcroft des. in green, printed florian mark, Rd. No. 360576, c. 1900. **£220-280** *SB*

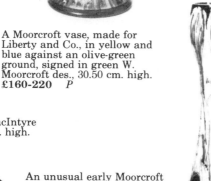

A Macintyre vase, decorated in relief picked out in coloured glaze, printed Macintyre mark in sepia, signed 'W. Moorcroft' in green, 8¼ in. 1900's. **£130-170** *SBA*

A Moorcroft large vase, c. 1900, 7 in. high. **£50-60** *Cr.A*

A Moorcroft Macintyre Florian vase, white, grey-green and blue, 23 cm., printed Macintyre mark and green painted W.M.des., c. 1903. **£110-160** *SB*

A Moorcroft Macintyre florianware vase, decorated with the 'Brown Cornflower' pattern, 20.5 cm., printed Macintyre mark in sepia, painted signature in green, printed retailer's mark for Riggs & Son, Glasgow, c. 1898. **£220-260** *SB*

A Moorcroft Macintyre 'Hesperian Ware' vase in royal blue, mauve and sky-blue (neck restored), 43 cm., painted W. Moorcroft des in green, printed Osler retailer's mark, Hesperian Ware, c. 1902. **£400-450** *SB*

One of a pair of large Moorcroft vases in deep rose, plum, green and beige ground (crack), 27 cm., painted signature in green and dated 1914. **£440-500** the pair *SB*

A large Moorcroft vase, in apricot, deep rose, mauve and olive green against a green ground, 51.2 cm., painted signature in green and dated 1911. **£620-730** *SB*

A William Staite Murray stoneware vase, in rust and black (restoration to rim), 43.5 cm., impressed pentagon and M., c. 1930. **£180-220** *SB*

A pair of Paris Cornucopia vases, with beaded ornament in gold and gilt on a maroon ground, the white centres painted in colours, on white marble bases with ormolu borders, 12½ in., first half 19th C. **£320-400** *L*

A William Staite Murray stoneware vase, in black and iron-red, 26 cm., impressed pentagon and M., c. 1930. **£100-130** *SB*

A Moorcroft 'Hazledene' vase, in olive, bottle green, brown, orange, yellow and peach, 21 cm., painted signature in blue, impressed Moorcroft, Made in England, c. 1925. **£380-430** *SB*

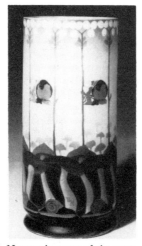

A Norwegian porcelain vase, painted in pale colours, factory marks 'Porsgrund Norde' and signed Th.H. in monogram, 30.5 cm. **£200-260** *P*

A pair of Paris vases, each elongated ovoid body colourfully painted, the rim an foot gilt, 43 cm., mid 19th C. **£300-350** *SB*

A pair of Directoire Ormolu and Paris porcelain tripod vases and covers, the porcelain marked with interlaced L's below a crown (one cover damaged), 13 in. (33 cm.) high. **£650-750** *C*

A pair of Paris vases, 33.8 cm., c. 1850 **£235-265** *SB*

A pair of large Paris vases and stands, 82.5 cm., late 19th C. £680-750   *SB*

A Pilkington's Royal Lancastrian lustre vase, the burgundy ground painted in slate lustre (minor chips to foot), impressed Bees mark, indistinct painted marks, 27 cm. high. £240-300   *C*

A pair of Paris vases, painted by W. Mussill, signed, with landscapes and wild flowers, on a pale-blue ground, 43 cm. high, c. 1865. £400-600   *SB*

Pilkington Lancastrian lustre vase, painted by William Walter Mycock, 19.50 cm. high, Bees mark, date code for 1913, and signed with artist's monogram. £160-220   *P*

A Pilkington Lancastrian lustre vase, painted by William Salter Mycock, 20.50 cm. high, impressed Bees mark, date code for 1910, and artist's monogram. £100-140   *P*

A Pilkington's Lancastrian Vase, decorated by Gordon M. Forsyth in gold, crimson and cream (base chips), 29.2 cm., impressed bees mark, England, 2626, painted artists initials and tree design, date code for 1907. £155-175   *SB*

A Pilkington's Royal Lancastrian vase, designed by C. E. Cundall, artists lustre monogram, impressed marks, 19 cm. high. £120-200   *C*

> **Make the most of Miller's**
> Look for the code letters in italic type following each caption.
> Check these against the list of contributors on page 12 to identify the source of any illustration
> Remember — valuations may vary according to locality; use of the codes can allow this to be taken into account.

A Royal Lancastrian small vase, 4½ in. £30-40   *Brit*

Pilkington 'Royal Lancastrian' lustre vase, painted in ruby and silver lustre Richard Joyce, against a turquoise and brown ground, impressed factory marks, 21.50 cm. high. £200-260   *P*

A Royal Lancastrian lustre vase, painted by William Salter Mycock, in golden and ruby tones against a powder-blue ground, 26 cm. high, impressed factory marks and artist's monogram. £450-550   *P*

A Pilkington's Royal Lancastrian vase, in a 'broken ruby' glaze, impressed marks P in a rosette, Royal Lancastrian England and pattern no. 3115, 16¼ in. £210-260   *L*

A pair of Potschappel pot-pourri vases and covers, each with lobed and ribbed body, chips, late 19th C., 15 cm., cross and T in underglaze blue. £100-130   *SB*

A Pratt finger vase, in ochre and blue, c. 1800 (restored on one finger), restoration halves value, 7½ in. **£50-55**   *AD*

A Sevres-pattern ormolu-mounted vase and cover, painted by H. Desprez, on a bleu-nouveau ground, 100.5 cm. high. **£2,500-3,000**   *C*

A Reissner Stellmacher and Kessel earthenware 'Amphora' vase, printed factory mark, 20 cm., c. 1900. **£420-520**   *SB*

A Lucye Rie stoneware vase, in stone-grey and mottled celadon glaze, artist's monogram, 35.5 cm. high. **£650-750**   *C*

A Rockingham flared cylindrical vase, painted in bright colours by John Randall, within gilt line rims, the reverse with stylised gilt foliage (rim cracked), C1.3 in red, c. 1830, 20 cm. high. **£200-250**   *C*

A Ruskin high-fired vase, in lavender, mauve, emerald and olive-green, 24.5 cm., impressed Ruskin pottery, West Smethwick, original paper label, dated 1906. **£150-200**   *SB*

A Rockingham hexagonal baluster vase and domed cover, painted in blue, pink, iron-red and green (finial damaged, cracks to vase), 1826-1830, 48.5 cm. high. **£650-730**   *C*

A Ruskin high fired vase, minor hair crack to rim, 24 cm., impressed marks, dated 1922. **£170-220**   *SB*

A Ruskin 'Highfired' vase, in sage-green on a streaked lilac and puce ground, impressed Ruskin England, 39.5 cm. high. **£320-380**   *C*

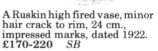

A Sevres stoneware vase, decorated by Charles Pihan, 44 cm., painted artist's signature, printed Sevres oval mark, dated 1917. **£260-320**   *SB*

A pair of 'Sevres' bleu-celeste-ground vases, 40.3 cm., painted interlaced 'L's', late 19th C. **£390-450**   *SB*

A Sevres Bleu Nouveau vase and domed cover, painted en grisaille with Cupid and his trophies in two shaped rectangular panels (long firing crack in body, finial and foot bolted). c. 1770, 35.5 cm. high. **£380-440**   *C*

A pair of Sevres bleu nouveau vases a oreilles (the upper parts restored), blue interlaced L marks enclosing the date letter for 1764, 18 cm. high. £440-540   *C*

A Champleve-mounted 'Sevres' vase, painted by Armand, signed, with gilt-bronze handles, on onyx base, 46.5 cm., late 19th C. £320-380   *SB*

A pair of gilt-metal-mounted 'Sevres' vases and covers, each bucket-shaped body painted within tooled gilt borders, against a bleu-de-roi ground, one cover rim repaired, 61.5 cm., mid 19th C. £2,400-2,600   *SB*

A pair of 'Sevres' gilt-metal-mounted pot-pourri vases and covers, painted interlaced L's, 36 cm., late 19th C. £380-460   *SB*

A pair of 'Sevres' pate-sur-pate vases, decorated by Marc Louis Solon, signed in monogram (chipped), 35 cm., incised numerals, printed crowned N mark and date code for 1865. £650-750   *SB*

A pair of 'Sevres' bleu-celeste-ground vases, gilding slightly rubbed, painted interlaced L's, 48.5 cm., late 19th C. £500-700   *SBe*

A pair of ormolu mounted 'Sevres Style' vases and covers, covers inscribed in blue enamel 'masselotte miroy' and various numerals, 11½ in. (29.2 cm.), late 19th C. £590-690   *SBA*

A gilt-metal-mounted 'Sevres' vase and cover, painted by Garnier, signed, enclosed by gilt arabesque and diaper borders reserved on a bleu-de-roi ground, 41 cm., painted interlaced L's, Bleu de Sèvres, Paris, France, c. 1900. £200-250   *SB*

A pair of 'Sevres' covered vases, painted by Dumas, signed, 37 cm., late 19th C. £420-500   *SB*

A Sicilian vase, painted in colours (base cracked, rim chipped), probably Palermo, c. 1580, 29 cm. high. £550-650   *C*

A porcelain baluster vase, with gilt scroll and foliage borders and gilt dentil rim (roof repaired), probably Spode, c. 1820, 16.5 cm. high. **£140-180** *C*

A pair of Spode blue-ground spill vases, script marks and pattern no. 3226, 11 cm. high, c. 1820. **£200-250** *C*

A Staffordshire saltglaze blue-ground vase, painted in colours with Oriental figures, c. 1755, 11 cm. high. **£440-500** *C*

A Spode Copeland vase, signed K. Macgill, 7 in. high. **£35-40** *Brit*

A Ralph Wood tree vase, with sheep, in typical colours, c. 1770, 7½ in. high. **£300-330** *AD*

A Stockelsdorf baluster reticulated vase (minor glaze chips), c. 1755, 23 cm. high. **£1,000-1,100** *C*

A Venice vase (cracked, rim repaired), c. 1580, 23 cm. high. **£1,000-1,200** *C*

A pair of 'Vienna' vases and covers, 26.5 cm., shield mark, 2nd half 19th C. **£380-450** *SKC*

A pair of Vienna vases and covers, on square plinths, decorated with named scenes and Kauffman scenes, signed, 18 in. overall. **£840-980** *WW*

A Vienna vase and cover, on deep blue ground with gilding, c. 1860, 12 in. **£500-600** *Cr.A*

A pair of 'Vienna' vases and covers, each painted by K. Weh, signed, 43 cm., painted 'Austrian' shield mark and titles in blue enamel, about 1870-80. **£700-800** *SB*

A Vienna vase, the shoulders/neck in a bleu de roi glaze heightened with gold borders, mark in underglaze blue, late 19th C., height 21.8 cm. **£190-230**   *SBe*

A pair of 'Vienna' claret ground vases and covers, 58.5 cm., shield marks in underglaze blue, late 19th C. **£740-840** *SKC*

A Villeroy and Boch glazed earthenware vase, in blue and pink/beige against a blue/grey ground, stencilled factory monogram, 41 cm., c. 1910. **£110-160**   *SB*

A 'Vienna' vase and cover, with two mythological scenes, shield in underglaze blue, painted titles, 37 cm., late 19th C. **£300-360**   *SBe*

A Walton tree vase, c. 1820, signed, 5½ in. high. **£70-80** *MB*

A pair of Vincennes bleu lapis campana vases (vases parseval), blue interlaced L marks enclosing the date letter for 1755 and painter's mark Y, 9 cm. high. **£1,200-1,400**   *C*

A Wedgwood encaustic-decorated black basalt vase, painted with Dionysius and Maenad in red, black and white enamel, impressed and moustache marks, c. 1815, 30 cm. high. **£800-900**   *C*

A Wedgwood black basalt encaustic-decorated vase, painted with classical gods and goddesses, impressed mark and Z, c. 1800, 28.5 cm. high. **£1,000-1,200**   *C*

A late 19th C. Wedgwood blue basalt copy of the Portland vase, 11 in. **£450-550**   *Lan*

A Wedgwood black basalt encaustic-decorated krater vase, decorated in red and white, impressed mark, c. 1810, 33 cm. wide. **£400-460**   *C*

A Wedgwood fairyland lustre vase, of square section, decorated with the 'Dana' pattern of 'Castle on a Road', 19.2 cm., printed urn mark, Z5125, 1920's. **£450-500**   *SB*

A pair of Wedgwood vases, each decorated probably by Harry Barnard, 36 cm., impressed Wedgwood, incised shape number, c. 1900. **£190-250** *SB*

One of a pair of Wedgwood fairyland lustre vases, decorated with 'Butterfly Women', 15 cm., printed urn mark, Z4968, 1920's. **£600-680** pr. *SB*

A Wedgwood fairyland lustre vase, decorated with the 'Candlemas' design, the rim and foot with 'Flaming Wheel' borders, 17.6 cm., printed urn mark, Z5157, 1920's. **£380-450** *SB*

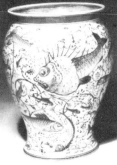

A Wedgwood fairyland lustre 'Florentine' vase, decorated with the 'Goblins' pattern, 17.5 cm., printed urn mark, incised shape number 3281, 1924-1929 **£900-1,100** *SB*

A Wedgwood vase, painted by Alfred Powell, in underglaze-blue and copper lustre, 32.50 cm. high, impressed 'Wedgwood', signed in monogram and having a 'Cotswold Tradition Exhibition' label, 1925. **£390-470** *P*

A Wedgwood fairyland lustre vase, decorated with 'Imps on a Bridge' design, crack in base, printed mark, Z5462 in red, 3451 incised, 12 in., c. 1923. **£320-380** *SBA*

A pair of Helena Wolfsohn bottle vases and covers, 33 cm AR monogram in underglaze blue, late 19th C. **£135-165** *SB*

A Michael Cardew Winchcombe Pottery vase, painted in brown on a honey ground, impressed MC seal and Winchcombe mark, 32 cm., 1926-29. **£300-350** *SB*

One of a pair of Chamberlain's Worcester spill vases, 12.5 cm. inscribed 'Ceres' and 'Bacchante', Chamberlain's Worcester manufacturers to their Royal Highnesses The Prince of Wales and Duke of Cumberland, c. 1807-10. **£350-400** the pair *SKC*

A pair of Helena Wolfsohn vases, with gilt scroll borders and pink scale pattern, 17.5 cm., AR monogram in underglaze blue, late 19th C. **£115-150** *SB*

Royal Worcester vase
y Stinton, 6 in. high.
290-325 *MB*

A Flight, Barr and Barr
Worcester vase, impressed
mark and inscribed Flight Barr
and Barr, Royal Porcelain
Works Worcester (small chip),
6½ in. high. **£330-400**   *DWB*

A Flight Barr and Barr vase, c.
1813-40, 3½ in. high. **£400-
480**   *MB*

A Royal Worcester globular
vase, 1876, 3½ in. high. **£65-
75**   *MB*

A Worcester royal-blue ground
vase, painted in the manner of
Enoch Doe, on a pale-blue
ground with gilt scrolling, 23.5
cm., mid 19th C. **£180-230**
SB

A pair of unusual Royal
Worcester vases, each
decorated in the Japanese taste,
28.6 cm., printed and impressed
crowned circle, date code for
1878. **£200-250**   *SB*

A Royal Worcester pierced vase,
in mauve and green, with
enamel 'jewelling' and gilding
(chips), 20 cm., printed crowned
circle and indistinct date code,
c. 1880. **£250-300**   *SB*

A Royal Worcester apricot-
ground vase, the whole with gilt
details, 33 cm., printed crowned
circle, shape number 1133, Rd.
No. 41796, date code for 1888.
£130-160   *SB*

A Royal Worcester 'lobed' vase,
of Persian inspiration, 42 cm.,
printed and impressed crowned
circle marks, shape number
1061, indistinct date code, c.
1885. **£200-250**   *SB*

A pair of Royal Worcester
vases, each printed and painted
by W. Powell, signed, 43.5 cm.,
printed crowned circle,
numbered 229/H 50.74, date
code for 1910. **£1,000-1,200**
SB

A Royal Worcester vase with cover, by Harry Davis, 8½ in. high, 1903. **£700-750** *MT*

A pair of Royal Worcester vases, 29 cm., printed crowned circle, Rd. No. 45756, shape number 1445 and date code for 1892. **£200-250** *SB*

A Royal Worcester vase, with apricot ground, shape 1507, 1896, 8½ in. **£180-240** *MB*

A Royal Worcester vase, painted by W. Powell, signed (one handle cracked), 19.5 cm., printed crowned circle, painted numerals, date code for 1905. **£150-200** *SB*

A pair of Royal Worcester vases and covers, each painted by Baldwyn, signed, against an azure-blue ground (one cover damaged), 24 cm., printed crowned circle, shape number 1937, Rd. No. 298665, date code for 1899. **£1,100-1,400** *SB*

A Royal Worcester vase, painted by John Stinton, signed, 31.8 cm., printed crowned circle, shape number 1969, date code for 1907. **£6–750** *SB*

A pair of Royal Worcester globular vases, 1909, 3¼ in. **£110-120** *MB*

A Royal Worcester vase, painted by C. H. C. Baldwin, signed (neck restored), 30.3 cm., printed crowned circle mark, Rd. No. 442799, shape number 2336, date code for 1906. **£200-250** *SB*

A Royal Worcester spill vase, pattern 283, 4½ in. high, 1908. **£65-75** *MB*

A Royal Worcester vase and cover, painted by H. Stinton, signed, 36.8 cm., printed crowned circle, shape number 1957, date code for 1905. **£1,000-1,200** *SB*

A Royal Worcester pot pourri vase and covers, painted and signed by J. Stinton, purple printed mark including date code for 1919, 13¼ in. **£850-1,000** *SBA*

A Zsolnay lustre vase, 11 cm. high, raised spires and Zsolnay Pecs mark. **£140-195**   *P*

Royal Worcester
ase, painted by R.
ebright, signed, 29.8
n., printed crowned
rcle, shape number
368, date code for
937. **£800-900** *SB*

A Royal Worcester vase, painted by J. Stinton, signed, 33.6 cm., printed crowned circle, shape number 1911, and date code for 1918. **£450-500**   *SB*

A Royal Worcester vase, painted by Kitty Blake, 9 in., 1930. **£250-300**   *MT*

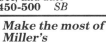

Make the most of Miller's

When buying or selling, it must always be remembered that prices can be greatly affected by the condition of any piece.
Unless otherwise stated, all goods shown in Miller's are of good merchantable quality, and the valuations given reflect this fact.
Pieces offered for sale in exceptionally fine condition or in poor condition may reasonably be expected to be priced considerably higher or lower respectively than the estimates given herein.

A Caffaggiolo circular pedestal bowl (rim repair cracked), c. 1530, 32 cm. diam. **£1,500-1,700**   *C*

pair of Zsolnay Pecs vases, in
hades of pink, brown and
reen on a bottle-green gilt
llular ground, 42.5 cm.,
rinted blue spire mark,
npressed Z W Pecs and
umerals, late 19th C. **£340-**
90   *SB*

A Chantilly Kakiemon deep bowl, with shaped cinquefoil rim (chipped), c. 1735. **£380-460**   *C*

A Berlin fruit bowl, with gilt scroll rim, sceptre in underglaze blue, printed orb and KPM, late 19th C. **£160-230**   *SB*

A Bretby bowl, c. 1925, 8 in. high. **£30-35**   *Brit*

A Roses Coalport small blue and white bowl, c. 1780, 4 in. diam. **£11-15**   *BY*

A bowl by Carter Stabler,
Adams Ltd., Poole, 7½ in. diam.
£20-25   *Brit*

A 17th C. Le Croisic faience bowl, in ochre and blue, 30.5 cm. **£130-180**   *SBe*

A Bristol polychrome Delft bowl, 7½ in. diam. **£600-650**   *Cl.A*

A Derby cache-pot, painted in the manner of Jockey Hill with 'Near Breadsall, Derbyshire' against a pale yellow ground, crown, crossed batons and D mark in blue, Wm. Duesbury & Co., 7.5 cm. high, c. 1790. **£480-580**　*C*

A Lambeth blue and white bowl, inscription inside 'One bowl more and then', 10 in. diam. **£230-270**　*Cl.A*

A Royal Doulton bowl, 5 in high. **£30-40**　*Brit*

A Doulton Lambeth bowl (with chips to rim), 7½ in. high. **£70-80**　*Brit*

A Royal Doulton 'Chang' bowl, by Harry Nixon, hair cracks, 31 cm., painted Chang script mark, England, Noke and HN initials, c. 1920. **£120-150**　*SB*

A Leeds bowl, c. 1785, 9¾ in. diam. **£140-150**　*AD*

A Longton Hall cabbage leaf-moulded bowl, the centre painted by 'The Castle Painter' (minute rim chips, crack to base), c. 1755, 21.5 cm. diam. **£900-1,000**　*C*

A Frankfurt Faience shaving-bowl, with pierced drainer, in manganese, green and yellow (cracked, glaze chips), manganese S mark, c. 1720, 30.5 cm. wide. **£300-350**　*C*

A Lowestoft 'Dolls House' pattern bowl, c. 1775, 6 in. diam. **£105-135**　*CH*

A Liverpool blue and white bowl (minute rim chip), Philip Christian's factory, c. 1765, 19.5 cm. diam. **£100-130**　*C*

A Lowestoft blue and white patty pan with painted butterfly, no glaze inside, 3⅜ in. diam., c. 1770. **£65-75**　*BY*

A Mason's patent ironstone china large punch bowl, printed in colours, 14¼ in., impressed mark. **£60-100**　*L*

A Lowestoft polychrome bowl, c. 1790, 4 in. diam. **£85-95**　*CH*

A Meissen circular bowl, brilliantly painted by A. F. von Löwenfinck, blue crossed swords mark, slight damage, 1730-35, 21 cm. diam. £1,600-1,900   C

A Meissen Hausmalerei slop-bowl, painted in underglaze-blue and colours in the manner of Ferner (in half and repaired), blue crossed swords and dot mark within a double circle, Pressnummer 3, c. 1730, 18 cm. wide. £450-550   C

A Meissen bowl, from the Roter Drachen service, painted in iron-red and orange and enriched in gilding, blue crossed swords mark, 22 cm. wide, c. 1735. £600-700   C

A Morris ware bowl, 9½ in. £70-80   Brit

A Moorcroft bowl, in deep blue, 6½ in. £90-100   Brit

A Moorcroft Florian ware small bowl, 4 in. diam. £70-80   Brit

A Moorcroft powder bowl and cover, early 20th C. £70-80   LAC

A Moorcroft bowl, decorated with the 'Claremont' design, 18 cm., painted W. Moorcroft in green, impressed Moorcroft, Burslem, dated 1914. £300-370   SB

An early 19th C. Spode bowl, 6¼ in. wide. £60-70   SV

A Sunderland lustre bowl, with ships and verse, c. 1850, 11 in. diam. £100-125   AD

A Talavera shallow bowl, in green, manganese and yellow, late 17th C., with wood stand, 35 cm. diam. £200-250   C

A cachepot and stand, with copper lustre transfer printed decoration, probably Sunderland, c. 1840, 7 in. diam. £110-130   CS

Right

A Charles Vyse bowl, the ochre and brown glaze decorated in black on an aubergine ground, incised CV initials, 24 cm., dated 1930. £90-110   SB

Left

A Tournai 'Drageoire' or sweetmeat bowl, painted with sprays of flowers, iron-red castle mark, 15 cm. high, c. 1760. £200-280   C

An Urbino Istoriato shallow bowl, painted with Christ (rim cracked), the reverse inscribed Christo libaro la figlia da la cananea, 31 cm. diam., c. 1560. **£2,300-2,600** *C*

A Vincennes cache-pot, with unfinished decoration (the base drilled), blue interlaced L enclosing a dot mark, 1750-53, 12.5 cm. diam. **£350-400** *C*

A Wedgwood flame fairyland lustre bowl, decorated with the 'Running Figures' pattern and the 'Bird in a Hoop' pattern, 21.3 cm., printed urn mark, Z5360, 1920's. **£700-800** *SB*

A Wedgwood fairyland lustre bowl, decorated with the 'Woodland Elves VIII, Boxing Match' pattern and the 'Castle on a Road' pattern, 28.5 cm., printed urn mark, Z5125, 1920's, wood stand. **£800-900** *SB*

FAIRYLAND LUSTRE

- The Wedgwood factory had been experiencing serious financial difficulties during the closing years of the 19th C.
- Daisy Makeig-Jones helped bring about a total reversal with the introduction of her 'Fairyland Lustre'
- the patterns for 'The First Ten Lustre Decorations' Z4823 were published in October 1914
- the butterflies of the First Series tended to be of the 'solid' variety, which were normally printed in gold
- the butterflies of the Second Series were 'open' and were filled with various colours
- in 1917 perhaps the most successful of Daisy's natural lustre subjects — The Hummingbird, was perfected
- the 'Fairy' lustre subjects now command high prices at auction, particularly the more unusual lustre colour combinations

A Wedgwood Fairyland Lustre Bowl, interior decorated with 'Woodland Elves V', the gilt design incorporating five MJ monograms (cracked), 10¾ in., 27.5 cm., printed urn mark, Z4968, 1920's. **£180-240** *SB*

Two Wedgwood Fairyland Lustre Bowls, decorated with 'Leap-frogging Elves' 14 cm., printed urn mark, Z4968, 1920's. **£320-400** *SB*

A Wedgwood fairyland lustre bowl, decorated with the 'Ship and Mermaid' pattern and the 'Fiddler in Tree' version of the 'Woodland Elves VI', 21.2 cm., printed urn mark, Z4968, 1920's. **£500-600** *SB*

A Wedgwood Fairyland Lustr punch bowl, decorated with th 'Woodland Bridge', 'Poplar Trees' patterns, 27.8 cm., printed urn mark, 24968, 1920's **£850-1,050** *SB*

A Wedgwood Flame Fairylan Lustre bowl, decorated with 'Poplar Trees' and 'Elves and Bell Branch' patterns, 23.4 cm printed urn mark, 25360, 1920' **£500-700** *SB*

A Wedgwood fairyland lust bowl, the interior with the 'F in a Hoop' pattern, the exte with the 'Gargoyles' patter 19.5 cm., printed urn mark, Z4968, 1920's. **£430-470**

A Wedgwood fairyland lustr bowl, the interior with the 'Feather Hat' variation of th 'Woodland Elves' pattern, th exterior with the 'Poplar Tre pattern, 24.4 cm., printed ur mark, Z4968, 1920's. **£550-620** *SB*

A Worcester blue and white 'Blue Rock or Cannonball' pattern bowl, 4¾ in. **£60-75** *CH*

WORCESTER PORCELAIN DATES	
1751-1783	First Period
1751-1774	Dr. Wall Period
1776-1793	Davis/Flight or Middle Period
1783-1793	Flight Period
1793-1807	Flight and Barr Period
1807-1813	Barr, Flight and Barr
1813-1840	Flight, Barr and Barr
1840-1852	Chamberlain and Company
1852-1862	Kerr and Binns (W.H. Kerr & Company)
1862	Royal Worcester Porcelain Company

A 1st period Worcester polychrome bowl with script W mark, c. 1765, 6¼ in. diam. **£45-50** *MB*

A Worcester bowl, 'Sampan' pattern, c. 1765, 6 in. wide. **£95-105** *CH*

A 1st period blue and white Worcester bowl, c. 1765, hand painted, 4 in. diameter. **£30-35** *MB*

1st period Worcester 'Chinese Figures' bowl, c. 1768, 5 in. diam. **£180-200** *CH*

A 1st period Worcester blue and white 'Long Eliza' pattern bowl, c. 1770, 4 in. diam. **£120-150** *CH*

A Worcester blue and white 'La Terre' and 'Child and Toy' pattern bowl, c. 1785, 4½ in. wide **£65-80** *CH*

Worcester bowl, c. 1775, 6¼ in. diam. **£95-115** *CH*

A Worcester (Flight, Barr and Barr) square salad bowl, from the Stowe Service, impressed mark, c. 1813, 27.5 cm. wide. **£1,600-1,750** *C*

A Worcester artichoke holder, with blue and white transfer-printed 3 flower pattern, 3½ in. diam., c. 1780. **£50-60** *BY*

A Royal Worcester small bowl, 1909, 3 in. diam. **£40-50** *MB*

A Doccia oval quatrefoil sugar-basin and cover, moulded in relief and enriched in pink and gold, c. 1755, 11 cm. wide. **£350-430** *C*

A Royal Worcester bowl, painted by Barker, 8 in. diam., 1923. **£600-650** *MT*

A Davenport pink lustre sucrier, 4¼ in., c. 1850. **£16-20** *BY*

A Meissen sugar basin and cover, blue crossed swords mark, Pressnummer 10, each piece with a 7 in sepia, 10 cm. diam., c. 1745. **£1,150-1,400** *C*

A Sevres bleu celeste sugar-bowl and cover, painted and enriched with gilding (finial restuck), blue interlaced L mark and letter N for 1766, 9 cm. high. **£250-350** *C*

A Worcester blue and white sucrier and cover, c. 1765, 5 in. high. **£315-400** *CH*

A Meissen yellow-ground quatrefoil sugar-box and cover (chipped and restored), blue crossed swords, dot and K.P.M. marks, Pressnummer 26, c. 1765, 12.5 cm. wide. **£900-1,100** *C*

A Newhall hard paste sugar basin, pattern no. 122, c. 1785, 5 in. diam. **£45-50** *BTH*

A Wedgwood transfer creamware sucrier and cover, c. 1810, 3¼ in. high. **£50-65** *B.M*

A Coalport pot pourri jar and cover, profusely painted and gilded on a deep blue ground, printed mark, late 19th C., 33 cm. **£360-390** *SBe*

A Moorcroft, MacIntyre tobacco jar and cover, made for Fribourg and Treyer, with arms of Westminster, 4 in. high, c. 1880. **£270-300** *Cr.A*

A Meissen sugar-bowl and cover, blue crossed swords ar gilt 22 marks, the base with Pressnummer 10, c. 1742, 11 cm diam. **£1,900-2,200** *C*

A Vincennes sugar-basin and cover, painted in the Meissen style (minute rim chip), c. 1750 11.5 cm. diam. **£200-250** *C*

A Worcester sugar bowl and cover, with small chips to finial iron-red painter's mark to cover and base, 11.5 cm. wide, c. 1770 **£450-550** *C*

An Electroplate-mounted Doulton stoneware biscuit barrel and cover, incised by Hannah Barlow, restored, 21.3 cm., impressed Doulton Lambeth mark, incised artists monogram, dated 1879. **£360-430** *SB*

A Lancastrian jar, decorated by Gordon Forsyth, on a rich indigo blue background, device for Forsyth beneath bird, Pilkington's mark impressed above XII and England, 1912, 3¾ in. **£110-140** *SBA*

A pair of Mennecy silver-mounted cylindrical pomade-pots and covers, painted with bouquets of flowers (chipped and repaired), 16 cm. high, c. 1750. **£950-1,200** *C*

A Pilkington's Lancastrian jar and cover, decorated by Richard Joyce in gold lustre, 13 cm., impressed bees mark, painted artist's monogram and shell date motif for 1913. **£220-300** *SB*

A Lancastrian jar, decorated by Gwladys Rodgers in gold, yellow and green lustres, signature device for Rodgers, impressed trade mark above X111, England and 279, 1913, 3 in. **£88-100** *SBA*

A Spode pearlware pot pourri and covers, printed and over-enamelled in vivid colours, on a ruby ground, enamelled pattern number '3009' in red, 23.5 cm., c. 1820. **£170-200** *SKC*

A Pilkington's Royal Lancastrian Jar and Cover, painted by Richard Joyce, 20 cm., impressed rosette mark, Royal Lancastrian England, 2930, painted monogram and fish, c. 1915. **£300-350** *SB*

A Royal Worcester pot-pourri vase and cover, 20.5 cm., printed crowned circle, shape number 1194, date code for 1890. **£330-360** *SB*

A Baltic faience tureen and cover, painted with flowers within moulded blue feuille-de-choux (minor chips), Stralsund or Eckernfarde, 38 cm. wide, c. 1770. **£1,200-1,400** *C*

A Spode pot and cover, pattern no. 967, c. 1826. **£135-160** *MB*

A fine Royal Worcester pot pourri jar, with two covers, 10 in. **£280-340** *RMcT*

D

An early Derby tureen and cover, patch marks (cover cracked), 21 cm. wide, 21 cm. high, c. 1758-60. **£100-130** *SKC*

An ironstone tureen and cover, decorated in the Chinese manner, late 19th C., 33 cm. **£280-320** *SBe*

A Dresden tureen, cover and stand, painted with brightly coloured flowers, stand, 23 cm., painted crossed swords in blue, late 19th C. **£100-125** *SB*

A Mason's ironstone tureen and cover, Stoke-on-Trent, c. 1840, 12 in. wide. **£175-200** *LAC*

A Pesaro creamware documentary dated tureen and cover, in the Sevres style (cover handle restored, cracked), inscribed Pesaro, Callegari e Casali, Ottobre 1786, 29.5 cm. wide. **£1,500-1,800** *C*

A Meissen soup tureen and cover, painted within gilt Laub-und-Bandelwerk cartouches (damaged and repaired), traces of blue crossed swords mark, 34 cm. wide, c. 1740. **£1,000-1,200** *C*

A Staffordshire dish of a greater crested grebe on nest with seven chicks, with muted pink and grey figuration, c. 1850, 6 in. high. **£180-200** *WA*

A Chamberlain's Worcester muffin warmer and domed cover, from the Nelson service, with the Admiral's crest (damaged and restored); the cover with script mark, 1802/5, 26 cm. wide. **£460-570** *C*

A Sevres two-handled ecuelle, cover and stand, on a pink oeil de-perdrix ground (restoration to finial), blue interlaced L marks with a dot below, c. 1770. **£650-750** *C*

A Staffordshire dish of hen on nest, with soft grey colouring, c. 1860, 7 in. high. **£110-120** *WA*

A Barr, Flight and Barr sauce tureen and cover, each piece transfer printed in black, impressed marks, early 19th C., height 18 cm. **£80-100** *SBe*

A Derby comport, painted by John Brewer, 'Heliathus Multiflorus', blue mark, c. 1795, 12 in. wide. **£280-320** *CH*

A pair of Meissen comports, painted mark in underglaze blue (slight damage), height 30 cm. **£750-820** *SBe*

A Sevres-style gilt metal-mounted comport, gros bleu ground enriched with gold, 27 cm., late 19th C. **£360-420** *SBe*

A Moorcroft Macintyre florianware bonbonniere and cover, gilt details, painted W. Moorcroft in green, printed sepia mark, c. 1905. **£180-220** *SB*

A late 19th C. Potschappel comport, by Carl Thieme, 12 in. high. **£350-450** *LAC*

A pair of Moorcroft Macintyre Florian ware bonbonnieres, in aquamarine and gilt against a sage-green ground, printed sepia mark, Rd. No. 404017, painted W M des in green, 19 cm., c. 1903. **£330-380** *SB*

A Meissen sweetmeat dish, modelled by J. J. Kändler (minor chips), traces of blue crossed swords mark on base, Pressnummer 26, 29.5 cm. high, c. 1745. **£1,500-1,800** *C*

A pair of Bevington comports, painted mark in underglaze blue, late 19th C., height 28.5 cm. **£300-330** *SBe*

A Faenza (Ferniani) circular basket, painted in bright colours, c. 1760, 20 cm. diam. **£220-260** *C*

A Bow shell sweetmeat dish, painted with bouquets of flowers in bright colours, 11.5 cm. high, c. 1755-60. **£330-400** *SKC*

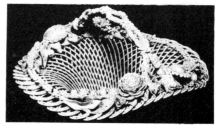

A Ludwigsburg circular basket, blue crowned interlaced C mark, impressed IP 2, painter's mark K, and incised repairer's marks, c. 1765, 15 cm. diam. **£350-400** *C*

A Belleek basket, the whole with a creamy glaze (chips), 27 cm., impressed ribbon mark, c. 1900. **£220-280** *SB*

A basket of Rockingham type, painted in the shallow well with a view of Byland Abbey, Yorks, 23 cm., painted title, c. 1830. **£160-220**   *SB*

A Meissen basket, painted in polychrome colours with bouquets of flowers, 33 cm., over handles, underglaze blue crossed swords, incised A57, late 19th C. **£250-320**   *SB*

A Worcester polychrome basket with English flowers, c. 1770, 8 in. diam. **£500-560**   *MB*

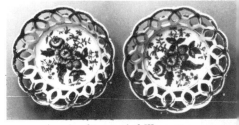

A Rockingham octagonal miniature basket, the centre with the floral initial V, puce mark and C1.3 in gold, c. 1837, 10 cm. wide. **£500-560**   *C*

A pair of 1st period Worcester baskets with the 'Pine Cone' pattern, c. 1775, 6 in. diam. **£520-600** pr.   *CH*

ROCKINGHAM

- porcelain factory opened c. 1826 and closed in 1842
- potters of the Brameld family
- bone china appears softer than contemporaries
- tended to use green, grey and puce
- known for rococo style of decoration, frequently with excellent quality flower painting
- the glaze had a tendency to irregular fine crazing
- of a smoky ivory/oatmeal colour
- large number of erroneous attributions made to the Rockingham factory

A Bassano Faience tureen-stand, painted with bouquets of flowers in colours (minor glaze chips), c. 1760, 37 cm. wide. **£280-350**   *C*

A good Royal Worcester sweetmeat, 20 cm., printed and impressed crowned circle marks, impressed registration mark and shape number 896, date code for 1883. **£440-500**   *SB*

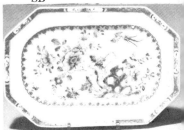

A pair of Bow famille-rose dishes, painted with a phoenix in flight among pink and iron-red chrysanthemums (minute rim chips), 27.5 cm. wide, c. 1753. **£280-350**   *C*

CASTELLI

Francesco Grue, a well-known maiolica painter, established the first Neapolitan factory in the later half of the 17th C. His initials are found on pieces of the 1640's and 1650's. This led to the typical Castelli style, which was dominated by rural landscapes, and figures inspired by the baroque decorators of the Roman and Bolognese schools. This style was continued by Grue's sons, particularly Carlantonio and Liborio, who specialised in the miniature. Also involved in the school were members of the Gentile factory and later, the Capelletti and the Fuina.

A Castelli armorial dish, painted probably by Liborio Grue (minor rim chips), c. 1740, 28.8 cm. diam. **£1,100-1,300**   *C*

An early Castelli dish (the rim drilled for suspension), 1660/1680, 46.5 cm. wide. **£800-1,000**   *C*

A Chantilly dish, rim edged in brown, painted in Kakiemon style, red hunting horn mark, 13 cm. **£200-250**   *P*

CHANTILLY

- factory founded in 1725 by the Prince de Conde
- up to the 1750's, milk white opaque tin-glaze
- beautiful white finish, inspired by Japanese porcelain
- Kakiemon style is most typical of early Chantilly wares
- in the mid 18th C. European floral styles introduced
- 1750's, transparent lead glaze introduced to compete with Vincennes
- tended then to copy Meissen and Vincennes designs
- from 1755-1780 many floral designs produced often in one colour, like the 'Chantilly sprig' which was then copied by other factories e.g. Caughley
- the factory had basically ceased by the end of the century

A Chantilly Kakiemon lobed decafoil dish, iron-red hunting horn mark, c. 1730, 11.5 cm. diam. **£400-480**   *C*

A Chelsea leaf dish, c. 1752-56, red anchor, 11 in. long. **£500-560**   *MB*

A Chelsea dish, a firing crack to the rim disguised by a leaf, red anchor mark, c. 1755, 34.5 cm. wide. **£280-340**   *C*

A Chelsea gold anchor dish with fruit and vegetable decoration, c. 1760. **£340-400**   *CH*

A late 17th C. Frankfurt faience in glazed dish, painted in manganese and yellow, slight glaze chipping, 33.5 cm. diam. **£340-400**   *SBe*

A Daniel green-ground crested dish, with the crest of the Earls of Shrewsbury, within a gilt gadrooned rim, 42 cm. wide, c. 1827. **£460-560**   *C*

A Davenport miniature dish, 5⅛ in. diam., c. 1870. **£11-14**   *BY*

A Bristol Delft blue and white dish (small piece missing from rim and cracked), c. 1730, 35 cm. diam. **£200-250**   *C*

A mid 18th C. Dutch Delft 'Peacock' pattern dish, painted in blue, with yellow-edged rim, 13¾ in., M.Q.2. mark in blue. **£200-300**   *L*

A Bristol delft blue and white dish, Lime Kiln Lane, c. 1735, width 33 cm. **£135-160**   *SBe*

A pair of Dutch Delft blue and white peacock pattern dishes, with yellow rims (rim chips), c. 1720, 35 cm. diam. **£350-420** *C*

A Liverpool Delft polychrome large dish, c. 1750's. **£450-650** *JH*

A Derby dish with a Billingsley Rose, puce marked, 8½ in. **£140-160** *MB*

A Bristol Delft polychrome large dish, c. 1740. **£800-1,200** *JH*

A Derby spoon tray, with carmine mark, 6 in. wide. **£160-180** *CH*

A De Morgan lustre dish, painted in ruby and salmon pink, details in gold and silver lustre (hair crack), 36.2 cm., impressed 20, early 20th C. **£330-400** *SB*

A Derby quatrefoil dish, the centre painted in sepia by Zachariah Boreman, crown, crossed batons and D mark and pattern No. 66 in puce, and gilder's No. 3, Wm. Duesbury & Co. c. 1785, 24.5 cm. wide. **£670-770** *C*

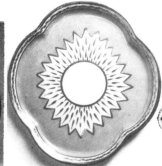

A rare yellow ground Derby teapot stand, c. 1790, with puce mark, 5¼ in. wide. **£165-185** *CH*

A pair of Derby fluted quatrefoil dishes, the centres painted in sepia by Zachariah Boreman, crown, crossed batons and D marks and pattern No. 43 in puce, Wm. Duesbury & Co., c. 1785, 25 cm. wide. **£760-840** *C*

A Doccia white and gold leaf dish, c. 1820. **£40-50** *BY*

A Derby saucer dish with dark blue ground and gilding, 'View in Oxfordshire', c. 1820, 8½ in. wide. **£245-285** *MB*

A Frankenthal dish, with pierced border (repaired), blue crowned CT mark and 86, 30 cm. diam. **£650-780** *C*

A South Italian Maiolica dish (cracked, chipped), c. 1650, 41 m. diam. **£1,000-1,200** *C*

A Bernard Leach Stoneware 'Pilgrim' dish, heavily potted with a Khaki glaze, 32 cm., impressed BL mark in block letters and St. Ives seal, c. 1965. **£800-900** *SB*

A pair of Furstenberg pierced dishes, each painted with flowers, and with gilt borders, F in underglaze blue, 27.7 cm., late 19th C. **£390-450** *SBe*

A Longton Hall leaf-moulded ish, painted with a flower-pray and an insect, the nderside with a firing crack isguised by a green leaf, c. 755, 30.5 cm. wide. **£330-00** *C*

A Kloster Veilsdorf shaped Quatrefoil spoon-tray, with gilt rim, blue CV mark, c. 1770, 18.5 cm. **£330-400** *C*

A Lowestoft blue and white pickle dish, c. 1770. **£65-75** *BY*

A Meissen saucer dish, painted n Kakiemon style, within a hocolate brown rim, crossed words mark in underglaze lue, 22 cm. **£700-800** *P*

A Meissen saucer dish with Dulong moulded border, 25 cm., crossed swords mark in blue and impressed 21. **£520-650** *P*

A Meissen Kakiemon decafoil shaped saucer-dish, blue crossed swords mark, c. 1730, 12 cm. diam. **£550-650** *C*

A Meissen chinoiserie plain ircular dish, the centre painted y C. F. Herold, the reverse with cattered indianische Blumen broken in numerous pieces and epaired), blue crossed swords ark and inscribed H4, c. 1734, 7 cm. diam. **£1,450-1,650** *C*

A Meissen saucer-dish from the Red Dragon service (chip to foot rim), blue crossed swords mark, Pressnummer 11 and K.H.C.W. inventory mark in puce, 1735-40, 19 cm. diam. **£450-520** *C*

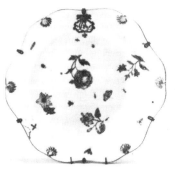

A Meissen Schmetterling-pattern lobed and fluted saucer-dish, painted in the Kakiemon style, blue crossed swords mark and Pressnummer 23, c. 1738, 22 cm. diam. **£880-1,000** *C*

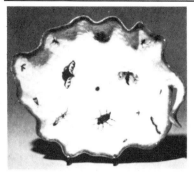

A pair of Meissen leaf-dishes, moulded with veins (minute chips to one handle), blue crossed swords marks, c. 1755, 26 cm. wide. **£580-700**   *C*

A pair of Meissen ornithological circular dishes, moulded Neubrandenstein Ozier borders (one with minor rim chip), blue crossed swords marks and Pressnummer 36, c. 1745, 25 cm. diam. **£1,250-1,400**   *C*

Two Meissen pink Feuille-De-Choux saucer-dishes, with pink scaled rims, blue crossed swords mark and Pressnummer 22, c. 1755, 23.5 cm. diam. **£250-320**   *C*

A Meissen dish, painted in bright colours, crossed swords mark in underglaze blue, 30 cm., c. 1760-70. **£660-760**   *SKC*

A Meissen blue and white onion pattern dish, c. 1880, 7½ in. wide. **£45-50**   *Cr.A*

A Montelupo dish, painted in yellow, ochre and green (chips to underside of rim), 32 cm. diam., 17th C. **£700-820**   *C*

A Puente del Arzobispo dish, painted in green, blue manganese and ochre (rim chips, drilled), c. 1650, 35.5 cm. diam. **£350-400**   *C*

A Nantgarw lobed oval dish, from the MacIntosh service, painted with a yellow and blue long-tailed bird within a gilt dentil rim, impressed Nant-Garw C.W. mark, c. 1820, 29.5 cm. wide. **£1,100-1,200**   *C*

A Spode 'Stone china' dish, patt. no. 2053, 7½ in. diam., c. 1813. **£36-40**   *BY*

A Strasbourg dish, painted with sprays of flowers (minute chips), blue 26H mark, 44.5 cm. diam., c. 1765. **£990-1,200**   *C*

A Netherland tin-glazed dish, painted in manganese, blue and yellow, late 17th C., 30 cm. **£440-500**   *P*

A Sevres dish, blue interlaced L mark enclosing the date letter for 1792, painter's mark of Fumez, 20.5 cm. wide. **£210-300**   *C*

An Urbino Istoriato crespina (rim restoration, chips, foot damaged), c. 1540, 16 cm. diam. £1,500-1,800 *C*

A pair of Swansea cushion-shaped dishes, painted by William Pollard, the borders moulded with C-scrolls and trailing flowers, gilt line rims, iron-red stencil mark, c. 1820, 20.5 cm. wide. £1,200-1,400 *C*

An Urbino Istoriato crespina (restored, foot damaged), c. 1550, 22.5 cm. diam. £600-700 *C*

An Urbino Istoriato dish, painted with Pan and Apollo, inscribed Apollo et le Dio pano (the rim repaired), c. 1560, 44.5 cm. diam. £1,800-2,000 *C*

A fluted crespina, in ochre, green and blue, painted with the initials S.P.Q.R. (foot rim chipped), Urbino or Castel Durante, c. 1560, 21 cm. diam. £800-900 *C*

A Venice Istoriato dish, painted with the Sacrifice of Isaac (repaired and chipped), c. 1550, 25 cm. diam. £1,000-1,200 *C*

A Venice Istoriato dish, painted with Moses (rim glaze chips), the reverse inscribed 'moise', 30.5 cm. diam., c. 1550. £3,000-3,300 *C*

A 19th C. Vienna dish, on pink ground with gilding and pierced rim, 9½ in. wide. £100-115 *SV*

An Urbino Istoriato trefoil dish, painted with the rape of Ganymede (repaired), 46 cm. wide, c. 1579. £3,000-3,400 *C*

A Wedgwood fairyland lustre dish, with the 'Fairy Gondola' design on a mother of pearl ground, with humming birds, chipped, hair crack, 33 cm., printed urn mark, Z4968, 1920's. £280-350 *SB*

A late First Period Worcester gros bleu dish, with scalloped rim, with English flowers, 9 in. diam. £300-400 *MB*

One of a pair of Wedgwood moonlight shell dishes, c. 1810, 10 in. long. £280-320 pair *CS*

A Wedgwood dish, painted in silver lustre by Therese Lessore, impressed 'Wedgwood' and signed by artist in monogram, 31 cm. diam. £150-200 *P*

A first period Worcester leaf-shape dish, transfer-printed with swans, 8½ in. **£270-350** *L*

A 1st period Worcester saucer dish, with gros bleu and English flowers, 7½ in. wide. **£350-390**   *MB*

A 1st period Worcester blue and white pickle dish, with workman's mark. **£175-210** *MB*

A Worcester gros bleu cushion dish, with English flowers, c. 1765, 10 in. wide. **£450-525** *MB*

A Worcester blue and white stand for a finger bowl (rim chipped), painter's mark, c. 1755, 14.5 cm. diam. **£280-340**   *C*

A Worcester blue and white shell dish with bird, with workman's mark, c. 1756. **£300-340**   *MB*

A 1st period Worcester scalloped dish, cornflower pattern, c. 1765, script W mark, 7 in. diam. **£150-165**   *MB*

A Worcester blue and white spoon tray, c. 1770, 6½ in. wide. **£180-200**   *MB*

A 1st period Worcester polychrome teapot stand, 'Campagnie des Indes' pattern, c. 1770. **£220-250**   *MB*

A Worcester blue and white cress dish with printed pine cone pattern, c. 1770. **£170-190**   *MB*

A blue scale Worcester dish with English flowers, c. 1770, 8¾ in. wide. **£350-400**   *MB*

A Worcester white and gilt dish c. 1780, 8 in. wide. **£38-48**   *ME*

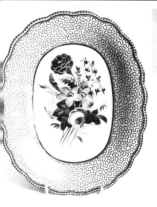

A pair of Worcester (Barr, Flight and Barr), cushion-shaped dishes, with a circular gilt husk-pattern cartouche reserved on a marbled grey ground within gilt line rims, one with script mark, both with incised B marks, c. 1805, 25.5 cm. wide. £440-500   *C*

A lustre saucer dish, c. 1830, 7½ in. £20-24   *CH*

Chamberlain Worcester footed dish, with vermicular pattern border, 10½ in., c. 1814. £40-50   *BY*

A fluted hexagonal spoon tray, painted in Imari style, 15.5 cm. wide, c. 1770. £300-360   *C*

A pair of saltglaze leaf pickle dishes, c. 1755. £200-240 pair   *JH*

One of 12 Berlin plates, blue sceptre mark to each piece, 24.5 cm. high, c. 1795. £2,200-2,500 for 12   *C*

A Bow plate, painted in Compagnie-des-Indes 'famille-rose' palette, c. 1755. £50-70   *SKC*

A Bow blue and white plate, painted in a bright tone, within diaper-pattern rim, c. 1752, 22 cm. diam. £240-300   *C*

BOW PORCELAIN

- probably the first porcelain factory in England
- established c. 1747
- very similar body to early Lowestoft
- painter's numerals sometimes in footrings — another confusion with Lowestoft
- body heavy for its size and very porous, prone to discolourations
- translucency poor
- tended to warp in the kiln
- could make plates (most English factories had problems with plates, even Worcester) but thickly potted and heavy in weight
- after 1765 quality markedly deteriorated
- not much Bow can be authenticated after the end of the 1760's
- factory closed in 1776

One of a pair of Bow blue and white plates, painted with the 'Golfer and Caddy' pattern (crack to centre, and rim chips), blue 6 marks, c. 1760, 17.5 cm. diam. £330-360 pair   *C*

A Castelli tondo, painted in the Grue workshop with the capture of Jesus Christ, 21.5 cm. diam., c. 1750. £1,400-1,600   *C*

Caughley blue and white plate, hand painted, impressed Salopian mark, 8 in. diam., c. 1785-95. £75-85   *BY*

A red anchor Chelsea botanical plate, c. 1752-56, 8½ in. wide. **£270-300** *MB*

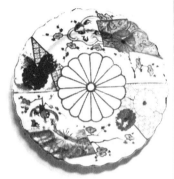

A Chelsea Derby plate, in early Chinese Imari style, slightly rubbed, c. 1770. **£90-130** *MB*

A pair of Chelsea plates, with shaped gilt rims, gold anchor marks, c. 1763, 22 cm. diam. **£600-700** *C*

CHELSEA 1745-1770

- Chelsea was certainly the wealthy man's factory and produced a high percentage of non-useful wares
- the finest figures were produced from 1750-1770, especially from 1750-1756
- *TRIANGLE PERIOD 1745-1749*
  - wares scarce and costly
  - many based on silver prototypes
  - many left undecorated
  - if decorated generally in Kakiemon and Chinese style
  - body comparatively thick, slightly chalky with 'glassy' glaze
- *RAISED ANCHOR PERIOD 1749-1752*
  - paste now improved
  - shapes still derived from silver, although Meissen influence noticeable
  - mostly restrained decoration, either Kakiemon or sparse floral work (often to cover flaws)
  - most collectable ware of this period was fable decoration by J. H. O'Neale
- *RED ANCHOR PERIOD 1752-1756*
  - this period mainly influenced by Meissen
  - glaze now slightly opaque
  - paste smoother with few flaws
  - the figures unsurpassed by any other English factory
  - on useful wares, fine flower and botanical painting
  - Chelsea 'toys' are rare and very expensive
- *GOLD ANCHOR PERIOD 1757-1769*
  - Chelsea's rococo period, with rich gilding and characteristic mazarine blue
  - quite florid in style
  - influenced by Sevres
  - elaborate bocage greatly favoured on figures
  - has thick glaze which tends to craze

A Chelsea brown anchor plate, with fruit and moth decoration, c. 1760, 8 in. wide. **£350-400** *CH*

A Coalport plate, with overhang 2 mark, c. 1810, 8½ in. **£68-75** *CH*

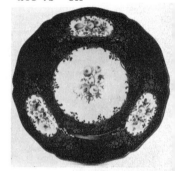

A pair of English china plates printed retailer's mark for Daniell, probably Coalport, width 25.5 cm., early 19th C. **£200-230** *SBe*

A Coalport plate, from the service presented to Tsar Nicholas I of Russia by Queen Victoria, raised gilt decoration on blue ground, printed mark of the retailers A. B. & R. P. Daniell, 25 cm. **£550-650** *P*

One of 6 Coalport (John Rose) armorial dinner plates, the centres with the arms and motto 'Libertas' rims, 24 cm. diam., c. 1810. **£500-600** for six *C*

A Coalport plate with hand painted flowers, c. 1815, 9¼ in. diam. **£130-150** *MB*

A Coalport hand-painted plate, c. 1850, 9½ in. diam. £135-165   *MB*

DELFT

- golden age of Delft from 1650-1750
- development really started at the beginning of the 17th C. with the arrival in Holland of two shiploads of Chinese porcelain
- in England there were three main centres, London, Liverpool and Bristol, although a small factory did exist in Wincanton for a few years c. 1750's
- English delftware tends to have less of a high shine and fine body in comparison to Dutch Delft
- not really until after 1750 that floral decorations gained popularity
- in 18th C. religious subjects are rare

A Bristol blue and white Delft plate, 8 in. £250-300   *JH*

A Bristol Delft polychrome blue dash charger of Duke of Marlborough, damaged, c. 1690-1700, 13 in. £1,200-1,500   *Cl.A*

A late 17th C. English Delft blue and white plate, in the Ming style, 8¼ in. £330-500   *JH*

A Bristol Adam & Eve polychrome blue dash charger (damaged), c. 1700, 13½ in. £580-650   *Cl.A*

A blue and white Delft plate, the centre with the monogram AR (chips to rim), probably Bristol, c. 1710, 22.5 cm. diam. £900-1,200   *C*

A Bristol Delft polychrome blue-dash charger (cracked across and riveted), c. 1710, 34 cm. diam. £480-540   *C*

An early 18th C. Delft blue charger, with painting of Queen Anne, 13¾ in. £2,200-3,000   *JH*

A Bristol Delft polychrome plate, c. 1715, 13 in. £380-420   *Cl.A*

A Bristol polychrome Delft plate, c. 1720, 8 in. £600-800   *JH*

An early 18th C. Bristol polychrome Delft plate with cockerel, from the 'The Farmyard Series', 8 in., c. 1720. £700-900   *JH*

A Bristol Delft blue and white inscribed and dated plate, the border with the initials HL and date 1727, the reverse with a flower-spray (damaged), 21 cm. diam. **£2,000-2,500**   *C*

A Bristol Delft blue and white plate, 14 in., c. 1760, restored **£50-75**; perfect **£90-130**   *JC*

A Bristol blue and white Delft plate date 1722, 9 in. **£600-800**   *JH*

A mid 18th C. Bristol Delft plate, painted in the style of John Bowen, 9 in. **£190-220**   *Cl.A*

A Bristol Delft blue and white plate, c. 1760, 8¾ in., restored **£10-15**; perfect **£50-65**   *JC*

A Dutch Delft plate, dated 1677, 8¾ in. diam. **£350-380**   *Cl.A*

A late 18th C. Delft blue and white plate, probably Dutch, 9¼ in. diam. **£27-30**   *Gs*

An English Delft polychrome plate, possibly Bristol (damaged), early 18th C., c. 1720, 9 in. **£60-70**   *Cl.A*

An English Delft plate, painted in muted colours, late 18th C., 34 cm. **£190-220**   *SBe*

A Lambeth Delft plate, painted in blue, green and manganese, 9 in. **£140-200**   *L*

A Lambeth Delft polychrome Royalist plate, painted in blue, green and iron-red, with a crowned monarch and the initials GR (cracked and chipped), c. 1714, 21.5 cm. diam. **£1,500-1,700**   *C*

An English Delft blue and white plate, probably Lambeth, c. 1720, 13 in. **£115-135**   *Cl.A*

A Liverpool Delft blue and white plate, mid-18th C., 13 in. diam. **£150-170**   *Cl.A*

A Liverpool polychrome Delft plate, in Fazackerly colours, mid-18th C., 12 in. **£210-230** *Cl.A*

A Liverpool Delft plate, mid-18th C., 13½ in. diam., slight damage **£180-200,** perfect **£200-300**   *Cl.A*

A Liverpool Delft plate, c. 1780, 9 in. wide. **£120-150**   *MB*

A mid 18th C. Liverpool Delft plate, in Fazackerly colours, 9 in. wide. **£120-160**   *MB*

A Liverpool Delft plate, c. 1760, 12 in. wide. **£120-140**   *MB*

A rare London Delft blue and white plate, dated 1690, 8½ in. **£1,900-2,200**   *Cl.A*

A Wincanton Delft polychrome plate, mid-18th C., 9 in. **£125-150**   *Cl.A*

A William de Morgan lustre charger, painted in ruby copper (rim chip), 52 cm., Fulham period, 1888-1907. **£450-530** *SB*

A Derby botanical plate, the centre painted in the manner of William Pegg with 'Creeping Cereus' (rim cracked), blue crown, crossed batons and D marks and inscription, Duesbury & Kean, 1795-1800, 21.5 cm. diam. **£240-270**   *C*

One of a pair of Derby plates, painted with exotic birds (slight rim chips), red anchor marks, Wm. Duesbury & Co., about 20.5 cm. diam., c. 1758. **£440-540** the pair   *C*

A Derby plate with a painted scene of Lake of Albano, Italy, c. 1780, lime green ground, 8½ in. **£300-320**   *MB*

A Derby plate, with Swiss landscape, c. 1810-20, 9 in. wide. **£220-280** *MB*

A Derby botanical plate, painted with a specimen of Amaryllis Reticulata, 9¼ in., named in blue and crowned batons and D mark and pattern No. 115 in blue. **£150-250** *L*

A Derby botanical deep plate, in the style of 'Quaker' Pegg, outlined with gilt, 10¼ in., named in blue and crowned batons and D mark and pattern No. 216 in blue. **£150-250** *L*

A Derby plate (with view 'Near Bakewell'), c. 1820, with unusual turquoise border. **£150-190** *MB*

A Derby plate, by Zachariah Boreman, view near Mosley Moor, c. 1782-1800, 8½ in. wide. **£540-600** *MB*

A Derby plate, painted by Moses Webster, 1821-25, 9 in. diam. **£115-135** *CH*

> ### Make the most of Miller's
> *Every care has been taken to ensure the accuracy of descriptions and estimated valuations.*
> *Where an attribution is made within inverted commas (e.g. 'Chippendale') or is followed by the word 'style' (e.g. early Georgian style) it is intended to convey that, in the opinion of the publishers, the piece concerned is a later —*
> *though probably still antique — reproduction of the style so designated.*
> *Unless otherwise stated, any description which refers to 'a set' or 'a pair' includes a valuation for the entire set or the pair, even though the illustration may show only a single item.*

A Derby plate, 'A Gudgeon', by Tatlow, 9 in. diam., c. 1820. **£350-400** *MB*

A Duesbury Derby plate, with a view in Lancashire, c. 1826, 8½ in. wide, black marked. **£270-300** *MB*

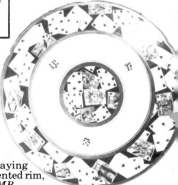

A Derby plate, with an Italian scene, c. 1820, 9 in. wide. **£270-310** *MB*

A Derby plate with playing cards, 8½ in. wide, indented rim, c. 1810. **£350-400** *MB*

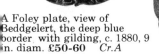

A Crown Derby large plate, 1882, 11½ in. wide. **£55-65** *CH*

A Doccia blue and white plate, the centre transfer-printed and painted (small crack), c. 1752, 22.5 cm. diam. **£400-500** *C*

A pair of Faenza (Ferniani) plates, painted in bright colours, with chocolate rims (minor glaze chips), c. 1760, 26.5 cm. diam. **£200-250** *C*

A Foley plate, view of Beddgelert, the deep blue border with gilding, c. 1880, 9 in. diam. **£50-60** *Cr.A*

A pair of Frankenthal ornithological plates, with lobed Ozier borders and painted in colours, with gilt rims, blue crowned CT marks, AB monograms, c. 1775, 23 cm. diam. **£820-920** *C*

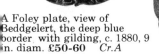

A Royal Doulton plate, painted by J. H. Plant, signed, with a view of La Madonna de Sasso, Lago Maggiore, 26.5 cm., printed lion, crown and circle, painted title, impressed date code for May, 1910. **£90-140** *SB*

A Russian pottery plate (Kuznetsoff factory), with blue background, late 19th C., c. 1890. **£18-24** *BY*

A 16th C. Hispana-Moresque lustre ware plate, covered in birds, restored, 16 in. wide. **£150-200** *JC*
if perfect. **£700-1,100**

A Marseilles plate (minor rim chips), c. 1765, probably Robert, 25 cm. diam. **£350-400** *C*

A Royal Doulton plate, painted by F. Harper, signed, reserved on a royal-blue ground printed with gilt, the shaped rim also gilt, 26 cm., printed lion, crown and circle, painted DD2421 and H3415, impressed date code for June, 1920. **£130-160** *SB*

A Chaffer's Liverpool small plate, after a Kang H'si original, painted in underglaze blue with the 'Jumping Boy' pattern, pseudo Chinese mark, 12 cm. **£300-360** *P*

A pair of Marseilles (Veuve Perrin) plates, painted with orientals after Pillement, one with VP mark, c. 1770, 24 cm. diam. **£550-650**   *C*

A Meissen dessert plate, enamelled in tones of green, 26 cm., academic mark in blue. **£420-500**   *P*

A Mason's table and flower-pot pattern plate, c. 1813, 10½ in. **£18-22**   *MB*

A Meissen Hausmalerei plate, painted by J. F. Mayer von Pressnitz, 1730-40, 21.5 cm. diam. **£1,100-1,300**   *C*

A pair of Meissen ornithological plates, blue crossed swords marks, Pressnummer 8 and incised 58/2, 23.5 cm. diam. **£500-600**   *C*

A Meissen Hausmalerei plate, painted by J. F. Mayer von Pressnitz, blue crossed swords mark, and Pressnummer 22, 1735-40, 21.5 cm. diam. **£1,700-1,900**   *C*

A Meissen plate, painted in the manner of Klinger, with Ozier moulded border and gilt rim (crack to well), blue crossed swords mark, Pressnummer 16, c. 1745, 22.5 cm. diam. **£320-360**   *C*

A pair of Meissen brocade-pattern plates, with waved gilt rims, blue crossed swords and star mark, Pressnummer 12, c. 1735, 23.5 cm. diam. **£1,000-1,100**   *C*

A Meissen plate, the centre painted in the manner of Klinger with Ombrierte holzschnitt Blumen, the border moulded with Brühlsches Allerlei and edged with gilt lines, blue crossed swords mark and Pressnummer 21, c. 1744, 26 cm. diam. **£1,100-1,300**   *C*

A Meissen cabinet plate, painted after Raphael, 24.1 cm., crossed swords in underglaze blue, early 19th C. **£200-250** *SB*

A Meissen plate, Marcolini period, 1774-1814, 9½ in. diam. **£68-78**   *CH*

A Meissen blue and white plate, from the Kinder a la Raphael series, blue crossed swords and dot marks, 23.5 cm. diam., c. 1765. **£400-500**   *C*

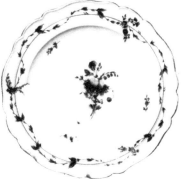

One of a pair of Meissen (Marcolini) plates, one painted with 'Les Albanois d'Athenes', blue crossed swords and star marks and Pressnummer 54, 24 cm. diam., c. 1790. **£1,000-1,200** the pair   *C*

One of 16 Meissen (Marcolini) soup plates, blue crossed swords, star and 95 marks, 22.5 cm. diam., c. 1775. **£1,400-1,600** for 16   *C*

One of 12 Meissen (Marcolini) plates, painted with flower-sprays, with gilt rims, blue crossed swords and star marks, various Pressnummern, 24 cm. diam., c. 1790. **£1,000-1,200** for 12   *C*

A Meissen cabinet plate, 24 cm., crossed swords in underglaze blue, early 19th C. **£330-380** *SB*

pair of Meissen (Marcolini) ates, blue crossed swords and r marks and Pressnummer , 24 cm. diam., c. 1790. ,100-1,400   *C*

A Meissen plate, with pierced rim, c. 1860, 9½ in. diam. **£200-250**; for lesser quality. **£130-250**   *Cr.A*

A late 19th C. pair of outside decorated Meissen cabinet plates, with blue and gilt lattice pierced rims, 20.3 cm, cancelled crossed swords in underglaze blue. **£300-350** pair   *SB*

A Mettlach stoneware charger, decorated by R. Chevenin, impressed factory mark, numbered 2541, incised artist's signature, 40.5 cm., c. 1900. **£500-600**   *SB*

An outside decorated Meissen late, painted with 'The riumph of Venus', cancelled rossed swords in underglaze lue, painted title, 22.4 cm., late 9th C. **£170-240**   *SBe*

A Milan Faience plate, painted in colours, c. 1760, 27.5 cm. diam. **£750-800**   *C*

A set of five Meissen dessert plates, with pierced borders, 23.8 cm., underglaze blue crossed swords, incised 38 and impressed numerals, early 20th C. **£710-770**   *SB*

A Minton plate, with puce cupid, possibly by T. Kirkby, c. 1870, 10 in. wide. **£50-60**   *MB*

One of a set of 10 Minton turquoise-ground dessert plates, painted with various scenes, 23 cm., painted pattern number A6802, impressed marks, and date code for 1860. **£200-240** set   *SB*

A Mintons Art Pottery Studio wall plate, in the style of W. S Coleman, 42.5 cm., printed mark, painted initials E.M. an No. 8, impressed mark and dat code for 1874. **£250-350**   *SB*

A pair of Nantgarw London-decorated plates, with a C-scroll and flower wreath border within shaped gilt dentil rim, impressed Nantgarw C.W. mark, c. 1820, 25 cm. diam. **£1,200-1,350**   *C*

A Nantgarw plate, the border with trailing garden flowers within a lobed moulded feuille-de-choux border and gilt dentil rim, impressed Nant-Garw C.W. mark, c. 1820, 23.5 cm. diam. **£450-550**   *C*

A Pearlware black transfe printed plate, c. 1810, 10 ir wide. **£35-45**   *MB*

A Rockingham plate, c. 1830-37, 'To the King' mark, 9 in. wide. **£175-195**   *MB*

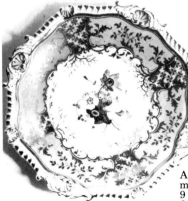

A Rockingham plate, puce marked, decorated by Baguley, 9 in. wide, c. 1842. **£300-370** *MB*

A Rockingham plate, painted by Edwin Steele, red mark, c. 1826, 9 in. wide. **£750-820** *MB*

A Pratt plate, with turquoise rim, c. 1860, 8½ in. wide. **£120 150**   *MB*

A blue and white transfer plat by John Rogers and sons, 'Country House Series', c. 1814 36, 9¾ in. diam. **£25-28**   *Gs*

A blue and white transfer plate by John & William Ridgway, foreground taken from view of Lacey House, Middlesex, c. 1820, 9¾ in. diam. **£35-40** *Gs*

An Enoch Wood blue and white transfer plate, early 19th C., 10 in. **£135-155** *Cl.A*

RIDGWAY

- one of the most important factories manufacturing English bone china
- most of the early Ridgway porcelain, from 1808-1830 is unmarked
- the quality of the early porcelain is excellent, brilliant white and with no crazing in the glaze
- in 1830 the partnership between John and William Ridgway was dissolved; John continued to produce quality porcelain
- there were many skilled flower painters employed at the Cauldon Place works including George Hancock, Thomas Brentnall, Joseph Bancroft
- the development of the Ridgway factory is as follows:—

  John Ridgway & Company 1830-1855

  John Ridgway, Bates & Company 1856-1858

  Bates, Brown-Westhead & Moore 1859-1861

  Brown-Westhead, Moore & Co. 1862-1905

  Cauldon Ltd. 1906-1920

  Cauldon Potteries Ltd. 1920-1962

A Ridgway miniature plate, with one Chinaman on bridge, 3⅞ in. diam., c. 1830. **£10-13** *BY*

A Spode stone china plate pattern no. 2148, c. 1815. **£16-18** *Gs*

A pair of 'Sevres' plates, later painted with a putto within a bleu-céleste-ground rim and gilt oeil-de-perdrix border, 26 cm., painted interlaced L's, the porcelain late 18th C., the decoration mid 19th C. **£290-320** *SB*

A pair of Sevres plates, with gilt-dash and dentil rims, blue interlaced L marks enclosing the date letter for 1792, 24 cm. diam. **£400-460** *C*

One of a pair of spode Copeland and Garret plates, replacement for a Chinese Armorial Service, c. 1833-47, 8 in. diam. **£30-35** pair *Gs*

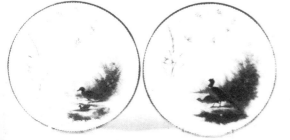

Two of a set of 12 Staffordshire dessert plates, painted with various game birds (one chipped), 22.7 cm., c. 1900. **£160-220** set *SB*

Three Strasburg shaped circular soup-plates (rim chips), blue H/37 marks, c. 1765, 24.5 cm. diam. **£500-560** *C*

A Swansea plate, painted with a bouquet of flowers, with gilt dentate rim, 9¼ in. **£300-400** *L*

A Swansea plate, painted in the centre with a bouquet of flowers and richly gilt with feuille de choux panels, London decorated, 8¼ in. **£200-300** *L*

An unmarked Swansea plate, 'Parakeet' pattern, 7 in. **£160-185** *B.M*

A Swansea plate, 8 in. diam., c. 1814-1822 impressed mark. **£180-190** *MB*

An Urbino Istoriato circular tazza (cracked), workshop of Orazio Fontana, 23.5 cm. diam., c. 1550. **£1,100-1,400** *C*

A Swansea plate, with a cruciform-moulded border and moulded white bead rim (minor rim repairs), c. 1815, 21.5 cm. diam. **£150-170** *C*

A Vienna plate, with deep claret ground, 1798, 8 in. **£155-175** *MB*

A 'Vienna' plate, the polychrome panelled rim enriched with gilt scrolls, 24.7 cm., shield in underglaze blue, painted title, late 19th C. **£200-250** *SB*

An Urbino Istoriato plate, painted with Hercules (repaired), inscribed on the reverse Ercole e Dionira, c. 1550, 24 cm. diam. **£600-800** *C* perfect. **£4,000-6,000**

A pair of Wedgwood porcelain plates, with rare red mark, c. 1812-22, 8½ in. diam. **£220-260** pair *B.M*

A Dresden-decorated 'Vienna' plate, with gilt-ground rim, 24 cm., shield in underglaze blue, mid 19th C. **£170-220** *SB*

A Whieldon plate with typical underglaze colours of brown and green, c. 1750, 9½ in. **£100-120** *AD*

scale blue Dr. Wall Worcester calloped plate, with English owers, c. 1760-70, 8½ in. **£330-60** *MB*

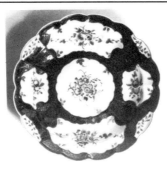

A Dr. Wall Worcester scale blue plate, with English flowers, c. 1765, 7½ in. wide. **£300-340** *MB*

A Worcester Dr. Wall scale blue plate, with birds, 8 in. wide. **£500-560** *MB*

A Dr. Wall Worcester plate, cale blue with oriental flowers, . 1770. **£200-230** *MB*

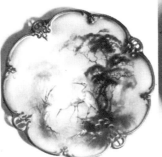

A Royal Worcester James Hadley plate, painted and signed by Powell, 8½ in. **£200-220** *MB*

A Worcester fable plate, by Duvivier, c. 1770, 8 in. wide. **£540-600** *MB*

pair of Royal Worcester binet plates, painted by H. avis, signed, shape No. 1120, te codes 1907, 22 cm. **£600-00** *P*

> ## WORCESTER PATTERNS
>
> - most valuable standard type of decoration is birds, particularly if painted by James Giles
> - this is followed by English flowers
> - then Continental flowers
> - and finally the rather stylised Oriental flowers
> - it cannot be stressed strongly enough with Worcester that any rim rubbing or wear will greatly reduce the value, often by as much as a half

A 1st period Worcester scalloped plate, with apple green border and English flowers, 9 in. wide, c. 1775. **£235-265** *MB*

A Worcester 'Blind Earl' polychrome plate, c. 1760, 7½ in. diam. **£300-330** *MB*

A Worcester polychrome scalloped rim plate, with English flowers, c. 1770, 7½ in. diam. **£155-185** *CH*

A First Period Worcester plate with cerulean blue border, c. 1760-65, 7½ in. diam. **£160-200** *MB*

A Worcester blue and white plate with pine cone pattern, 8¼ in. diam., c. 1780, slight chip. **£50-60; perfect £100-130** *BY*

A polychrome 1st period Worcester plate, with English flowers and birds, c. 1775, 9 in. wide. **£380-440** *MB*

A Worcester plate with black transfer print of 'The Ruins' with gold border, c. 1780, 8 i. diam. **£90-110** *MB*

A Worcester plate, a black transfer print by Hancock, c. 1780, 9 in. diam. **£140-160** *MB*

A late 18th C. Staffordshire serving plate, with chinoiser decoration, 14 in. wide, c. 178 **£85-95** *DEB*

A Worcester 'Bishop Sumner' pattern plate, c. 1780, 8¾ in. diam. **£120-180** *CH*

A pair of Flight, Barr & Barr plates, with shaped rims, decorated within a gilt seaweed border, 7¾ in. diam. **£290-350** *MMB*

A Worcester Flight, Barr and Barr armorial plate, c. 1825, c deep burgundy ground, 8½ in **£140-160** *MB*

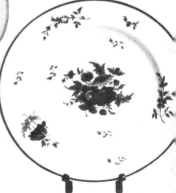

A Worcester polychrome plate, with English flowers (copy of alte osier border of Meissen), c. 1780, 8¾ in. wide. **£120-145** *MB*

A Chamberlain Worcester pla (mark 155 New Bond st.), 8½ diam. **£32-40** *BY*

A set of 6 Royal Worcester dessert plates, the centres painted by Richard Sebright, all signed, date marks for 1926-30, 23 cm. **£1,550-1,800** *P*

A Worcester Flight, Barr and Barr plate for the Imaum of Muscat, scene of Prince Regent entering Muscat Cove, pale lime green ground, gadroon border, 1836, 10½ in. **£220-240** *MB*

A set of six Royal Worcester dessert plates, each painted by *. Lockyer, signed, with ripening fruits within shaped gilt rim, 22.5 cm., printed crowned circle, retailers mark for Maple, date code for 1933. **720-820** *SB*

An English blue and white transfer plate, 9¾ in. **£30-35** *Cl.A*

A black transfer decorated 'Leeds type' plate, c. 1780, 9¾ in. diam. **£70-75** *AD*

An English blue and white transfer plate, mid-19th C., 10 in. **£25-30** *Cl.A*

A blue and white transfer plate by Jones and Son, 'British History Series, Signing of Magna Carta', c. 1826-28, 10 in. diam. **£40-44** *Gs*

An English blue and white plate, by Hamilton, mid-19th C., 10 in. **£25-30** *Cl.A*

An English blue and white dishet, 15 in. wide. **£85-95** *Cl.A*

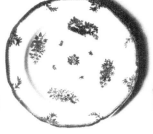

A blue and white transfer plate 'Floral Pattern' by John Turner, c. 1810-15, 7 in. diam. **£16-18** *Gs*

A blue and white transfer printed plate 'The Grazing Rabbits' pattern, c. 1820, 10 in. diam. **£35-38** *Gs*

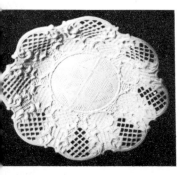

An 18th C. saltglaze plate, 8½ in. **£85-95** *Cl.A*

A child's pottery plate, c. 1850, 6¼ in. **£15-17** *Gs*

A miniature blue and white plate by Alcock, 5⅛ in., c. 1840. **£15-20** *BY*

E

A 19th C. pottery children's plate, 7½ in. diam. **£35-40** *Cl.A*

A David Methven & Son, Scotland, miniature blue and white plate, 5¾ in. diam., c. 1860. **£8-10**   *BY*

A 19th C. pottery plate, 6 in. diam. **£35-40**   *Cl.A*

A Coalport part dessert service, painted with bouquets of flowers, 19 pieces, some damaged, some with the Society of Arts marks, c. 1820. **£1,200-1,500**   *C*

A Coalport (John Rose) sea-green ground part dessert service, 40 pieces, some damaged, restored or replaced, c. 1810. **£2,900-3,200**   *C*

A Coalport service with 91 pieces, c. 1820. **£1,800-2,000** *B.M*

A Davenport 'Stone China' dessert service, printed in the Chinese manner, comprising a low comport, 8 dishes and 17 plates, printed mark, early 19th C. **£440-500**   *SBe*

A 9-piece Coalport dessert service, each piece printed and painted by P. Simpson, signed, 22.4 cm., printed mark, title and retailer's mark for Harrods, London, painted pattern number 9192/A, early 20th C. **£200-250**   *SB*

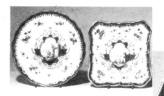

A late Meissen part dessert service, painted in the manner of J. G. Herold, comprising: two shaped square dishes and 16 plates (one with rim chip). **£2,000-2,500**   *C*

A Derby blue-ground topographical part dessert service, paint in the manner of Luc with named views, 2 pieces (damaged), crown, crossed bator and D marks in iron red, Robert Bloor & C c. 1820. **£2,300-2,600**   *C*

A Furstenberg dessert service, each rim lightly moulded and ilt, comprising; nine plates nd an oval two handled bowl, late; 21 cm., crowned F in nderglaze blue, c. 1900. **£250-00**   *SB*

A Sevres part dinner-service, 69 pieces, some damaged, blue interlaced L marks and First Republic marks with date letters for 1793, painter's mark of Chulot and others. **£1,600-2,100**   *C*

A Booth's Worcester 16-piece dessert service, each piece printed and painted in 18th C. style in the manner of James Giles (bowl damaged), plate: 23 cm., one oval dish with impressed mark, c. 1910. **£220-250**   *SB*

A Sevres dessert-service, 22 ieces, some with blue nterlaced L marks enclosing he date letter for 1770 and arious painters' marks. **£880-,100**   *C*

A Staffordshire 96 piece dinner service, each piece painted with naturalistically coloured floral sprays (numerous pieces damaged), dinner plate: 26.5 cm., 1835. **£600-700**   *SB*

A 16-piece Royal Worcester 'shell' dessert service, printed and painted with flowering branches on a cream ground, the details gilt (minor chips), plate: 21.5 cm., printed crowned circle, shape numbers 1146 and 1197, date codes for 1897 and 1902. **£350-400**   *SB*

A Bow toy tea and coffee ervice, painted in underglaze lue, comprising: teapot, sugar asin, 2 tea bowls, 4 coffee cups nd saucers. **£2,000-2,200**   *L*

8 Coalport (John Rose) custard cups and covers on a tray, one a Derby (Samson Hancock) replacement (one handle riveted), the tray 40 cm. wide, c. 1810. **£550-700**   *C*

An outside-decorated Meissen chocolate set, some wear and damage, cancelled crossed swords in underglaze blue, saucer 12.5 cm., c. 1900. **£170-220**   *SBe*

A Leeds Pottery yellow ground tea service, comprising teapot and cover, sucrier and cover, milk jug, 6 tea cups, 6 saucers, impressed mark, late 18th/early 19th C. **£125-155**   *SBe*

A Royal Doulton 'Dickensware'
teaset (of same character), c.
1910. **£120-140**   *MT*

A Newhall 70-piece part tea and
coffee service, painted in an
Imari palette with the Tobacco
Leaf Pattern, damaged, pattern
no. 274, c. 1800. **£1,400-
1,600**   *C*

A Newhall tea service, with
vertical fluting, painted with
gilt wheat-ears and loop border
enriched with mauve details,
painted Mark N 89, 73 pieces.
£800-1,200   *RBB*

An outside-decorated Sevres
chocolate set, 12 pieces, minor
damage, tray: 45 cm., various
printed and painted marks,
some cancelled, incised Le 31-5,
date codes for 1840 and 1842.
£650-800   *SB*

A Paris porcelain tea-service in
the Empire style, comprising: a
teapot and cover, hot water jug
and cover, milk jug, sugar-bowl,
slop bowl, and 8 cups and
saucers (restored). **£1,450-
1,650**   *C*

An early 19th C. Spode Japan
pattern tea service, 31 pieces,
pattern no. 1823, capital mark
in red. **£550-650**   *PWC*

Right
A pair of Berlin cups and
saucers, sceptre in underglaze
blue, printed orb and KPM, 15.8
cm., early 20th C. **£240-320**
SBe

A Chamberlain's Worcester gold-ground crested
part coffee service, with a crest within the motto
'Nos Pascit Deus', 26 pieces, some damaged and
repaired, the plates and cover with script mark, c.
1815. **£880-980**   *C*

Right
A Caughley blue
and white teabowl
and saucer, S.
marked, c. 1785.
£40-46   *CH*

Caughley painted blue and white 'Long Eliza' pattern teabowl and saucer. £125-145 *MB*

A Capodimonte (Carlo III) teacup and saucer, painted within gilt rims, blue fleur-de-lys marks and incised Po and O, c. 1760. £1,700-2,100 *C*

A Caughley printed teabowl and saucer, c. 1785. £50-55 *MB*

Chelsea Derby teabowl and saucer, c. 1780. £170-200 *MB*

A Coalport tea cup and saucer, interesting Coalport improved feltspar porcelain mark, c. 1825. £27-30 *MB*

A Chantilly Kakiemon octagonal teabowl and saucer, chocolate mock Chinese seal mark within a circle, c. 1735. £360-420 *C*

A Coalport (John Rose) gold-ground two-handled cup, cover and stand (chips to rim of cover), the stand 14.5 cm. diam., c. 1805. £200-600 *C*

A Coalport cup and saucer, jewelled and gilded, painted 'ampersand' mark, c. 1870. £180-220 *SBe*

COALPORT (Rose & Co.)

- factory began in the early 1790's and is still in existence today
- purchased the Caughley works in 1799 and ran them until 1814
- produced hard-paste porcelain certainly after 1800, before then produced soapstone porcelain, this was quite similar to Caughley but does not have the yellow-brown translucency
- in this period the highly decorated Japan wares have great quality as do some of the flower painted examples
- in around 1811 firm taken over by John Rose, William Clarke and Charles Maddison
- in 1820 a new leadless glaze was invented and they also began to use Billingsley's fritt paste
- in terms of translucency and whiteness Coalport certainly competed with Swansea and Nantgarw
- after 1820 CD, CD monogram, C. Dale, Coalbrookdale and Coalport were all marks used, before this date the marks tend to vary and much was unmarked
- from 1830-1850 the 'raised flower' was the most popular decoration
- in 1840's and 1850's Coalport perfected many fine ground colours: maroon, green and pink. These often rivalled Sevres

A Davenport teacup and saucer, c. 1840. **£45-50**   *Cr. A*

An unusual Coalport small cup and saucer with yellow, green and gilt decoration, c. 1920. **£60-80**   *MB*

A Derby coffee can and saucer, with dark blue ground, with matching Scottish scenes. **£345-395**   *MB*

A Derby cup and saucer by Zachariah Boreman, pattern 86, c. 1770, puce mark. **£720-800** *MB*

A Derby teabowl and saucer with puce mark, 1782-1800. **£45-50**   *CH*

A Derby powdered-purple ground octagonal coffee-cup and saucer, the saucer in bla and gold, blue enamel crosse swords and gilt 29 marks, c. 1780. **£1,500-2,000**   *C*

A Derby cup and saucer, with hand painted flowers, c. 1780-1810, blue marked. **£170-200** *MB*

A Derby cup and saucer with dark blue ground and gilding, with matching Derbyshire scenes, c. 1810-20. **£325-380** *MB*

A late 19th C. Dresden cup and saucer, on pink ground. **£40-50**   *SV*

A Doccia teabowl and saucer, decorated alla Sassonia, c. 1750, **£530-630**   *C*

A Hilditch porcelain cup and saucer, pattern no. 379, c. 1825. **£14-18**   *BTH*

A Derby coffee can and saucer on dark blue ground with gilding and rare flower. Gilders saucer; Munday Simpson; coffee cup: Thomas Till, c. 1810-20. **£500-560**   *MB*

pair of Liverpool blue and hite teabowls and saucers, riched in overglaze iron-red d gold, William Ball's ctory, c. 1760. **£280-320**   *C*

A Liverpool blue and white teabowl and saucer, William Ball's factory, c. 1760. **£300-350**   *C*

A Leeds teabowl and saucer, with Dutch decoration, c. 1785. **£50-55**   *AD*

Liverpool blue and white eabowl and saucer painted ith 'Fisherman pattern', with rinted border, c. 1780. **£40-5**   *MB*

A blue and white transfer teabowl and saucer probably Mason, Wolfe and Lacock, c. 1790-1800. **£40-44**   *Gs*

A pair of Meissen teabowls and saucers, painted in Eisenrot (one saucer riveted, the other with haircrack), Gilder's marks 26, c. 1725. **£600-700**   *C*

A pair of Meissen white teabowls and saucers (minor chips to foot rims of saucers), blue crossed swords marks, c. 1735. **£250-300**   *C*

Meissen Kakiemon bucket-haped teabowl and cinquefoil aucer, both pieces with aduceus marks, c. 1730. **£1,300-1,500**   *C*

A Meissen beaker and trembleuse saucer, with pierced gallery, painted in colours with Indianische Blumen (chipped and restored), blue crossed swords marks, c. 1730. **£350-420**   *C*

A pair of Meissen teabowls and a saucer, blue crossed swords and snow-flake marks, 1735-40. **£650-750**   *C*

A pair of Meissen teabowls and saucers, blue crossed swords and gilt 52L mark, the saucers with Pressnummer 2, c. 1740. **£1,550-1,750** *C*

A pair of Meissen teabowls and saucers, blue crossed swords and gilt snow-flake marks, 1735-40. **£1,500-1,700** *C*

A pair of Meissen coffee-cups and saucers, blue crossed swords and gilt 52 marks, the saucers with Pressnummern, 1740. **£1,900-2,200** *C*

A Meissen coffee-cup and saucer, blue crossed swords and gilt 52 marks, c. 1740. **£700-900** *C*

A Meissen coffee-cup and saucer, blue crossed swords marks and Gilders 43, c. 1740. **£650-750** *C*

A pair of Meissen yellow-ground quatrefoil teacups and saucers, with gilt scroll borders (restored), blue crossed swords marks and gilt G, c. 1742. **£1,000-1,200** *C*

A Meissen teacup and saucer, with hand-painted flowers, c. 1760. **£350-450** *Cr.A*

A pair of Meissen teacups and saucers, blue crossed swords marks and gilt 22, various Pressnummern, c. 1742. **£1,900-2,200** *C*

A Meissen teacup and saucer, c. 1765. **£560-630** *Cr.A*

A 1st period Minton cup and saucer, Patt. 305, c. 1809. **£38-48** *CH*

Minton teacup and saucer,
1850. **£30-40** *CH*

Newhall hard paste tea bowl
nd saucer, pattern no. 421, c.
790. **£40-45** *BTH*

Newhall cup and saucer,
attern 421, c. 1805. **£38-45**
H

Newhall cup and saucer,
attern no. 1677, c. 1815. **£35-**
0   *BTH*

NEWHALL

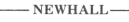

- Newhall was the second Staffordshire pottery to successfully make porcelain, Longton Hall being the first (although Neale may have been making porcelain)
- the usual date for the commencement of the factory is 1782, however then it was known as Hollins, Warburton & Company
- they used the Cookworthy method of making a class of porcelain known as hybrid hard-paste
- porcelain is a greyish colour to transmitted light and is seldom crazed
- Duvivier, who had worked at Derby and Worcester, also painted at New Hall from 1782-1790 — because of the rarity of attributable pieces one wonders if some of his work at New Hall has been wrongly attributed to another factory
- very few pre-1790 wares had a pattern number
- around 1812 a new bone-china body was introduced and the factory was by this time known as New Hall
- after 1820 the bone-china wares seemed to lose some quality and the factory closed in 1835
- New Hall, above all other 18th C. English factories, has seen what can only be called an explosion in price in the last year. This has probably been caused by the disparaging attitude of many porcelain dealers to the more ordinary Newhall wares in the past and hence their underpricing

A Newhall hard paste tea bowl
and saucer, pattern no. 191, c.
1790. **£40-45** *BTH*

A Newhall teabowl and saucer,
pattern 172, c. 1795. **£35-40**
CH

A Newhall trio, patt. 1153, c.
1810. **£42-50** *BY*

A Newhall teacup and saucer,
pattern 446, 1795-1810, with
workman's mark. **£45-52** *CH*

A Ridgway cup and saucer, c.
1820. **£40-46** *Gs*

105

A St. Cloud blanc-de-Chine pattern white beaker, cover and Trembleuse saucer (short hairline crack in cover), c. 1730. **£190-260**　*C*

ST. CLOUD

- factory produced wares from late 17th C. to the 1770's
- pieces heavily potted
- glaze thick and clear, frequently showing pitting
- body has yellowish tone
- until mid 1730's pieces mainly decorated in underglaze blue
- also specialised in pieces influenced by the blanc-de-Chine wares
- after mid 1730's polychrome wares produced

A pair of St. Cloud white artichoke-moulded coffee-cup and Trembleuse saucers, c. 1730. **£280-350**　*C*

A Sevres small coffee-cup and saucer (small chip), blue interlaced L marks, double F's for 1783 and unidentified painter's mark. **£290-390**　*C*

A Sevres apple-green-ground coffee-cup and saucer, blue interlaced L marks enclosing the date letter R for 1770. **£280-380**　*C*

A Sevres bleu nouveau cup and saucer, painted with lovers (the cup cracked), c. 1770. **£150-210**　*C*

A Spode new stone coffee can and saucer, c. 1815. **£45-50**　*CH*

A Swansea porcelain cup and saucer, with red, green and gilt motifs on a banana colour ground. **£150-200**　*GC*

A Worcester powder blue teabowl and saucer, with European flowers, 1760-70. **£280-320**　*CH*

A Weesp teabowl and saucer (minor rim chips, saucer cracked), blue crossed swords and three dot marks, 1765-1770, 16 cm. high. **£350-400**　*C*

A Worcester blue and white 'Gilly Flower' cup and saucer. **£115-135**　*CH*

106

1st period Worcester blue and white teabowl and saucer painted, c. 1765. **£90-100**   *MB*

A Worcester fluted coffee cup and saucer, with 'Prunus Root' pattern, c. 1756-58, with workman's mark. **£240-280**   *CH*

A Worcester teabowl and saucer with black transfer print 'The Ruins' by Hancock, c. 1765. **£60-70**   *MB*

Worcester blue and white teabowl and saucer with 'Three Flowers' pattern, c. 1765. **£55-65**   *CH*

A Worcester polychrome 'Japan pattern' cup and saucer, c. 1765. **£230-280**   *CH*

A Worcester painted 'Blue Rock' teabowl and saucer, c. 1765. **£90-100**   *CH*

Worcester cup and saucer, with gros bleu border and bird in centre, c. 1765. **£420-490**   *MB*

A Worcester blue and white Fruit and Flowers pattern teabowl and saucer, c. 1770. **£68-75**   *CH*

Worcester teabowl and saucer with turquoise and gilt border, c. 1770. **£90-105**   *MB*

A First Period Worcester teacup and saucer, with 'Marriage Pattern' (note arrow through flowers), c. 1770. **£450-500**   *MB*

A 1st period Worcester teacup and saucer, with turquoise border, c. 1770. **£180-210**   *MB*

A Worcester polychrome
teabowl and saucer, with bird, c.
1770. **£180-210**   *MB*

A Worcester puce-ground coffee-
cup and saucer, painted in the
atelier of James Giles, within
gilt line rims, blue crossed
swords and 9 mark, c. 1775.
£1,300-1,500   *C*

A Worcester blue scale tea bowl
and saucer, with English
flowers, c. 1770. **£225-250**
MB

A Worcester teabowl
and saucer, painted in
the famille-rose style, c
1768. **£150-180**   *MI*

A Flight Barr & Barr teacup
and saucer, on apricot ground
with gilding, c. 1814. **£50-60**
BY

A Worcester blue and white trio,
'Immortelle' pattern, c. 1780.
£145-165   *CH*

A Flight, Davis trio, 1780. **£60**
75   *MB*

A Royal Worcester demi-tasse,
painted and signed by Harry
Stinton, 1924. **£150-165**   *MT*

A Copenhagen shaped
chocolate-pot and cover,
painted with leopards, and
enriched with gilding, blue
wave mark, c. 1780, with
contemporary gilt-metal
mounts and ebony handle, 19
cm. high. **£710-850**   *C*

A Derby yellow ground bucket
shaped chocolate cup, cover and
Trembleuse saucer, painted by
James Banford (the finial a
replacement), crown, crossed
batons and D marks and
pattern No. 201, in puce, Wm.
Duesbury & Co., c. 1795, the
saucer 16.3 cm wide, **£2,000-**
2,300   *C*

A Berlin trembleuse cup and
cover, c. 1850. **£230-250**   *Cr.A*

A Chaffers Liverpool blue and white saucer, 4¾ in. diam., c. 1760. **£70-80** *BY*

A Worcester blue and white saucer, workman's mark, 5¾ in. diam., c. 1768. **£75-85** *BY*

A Du Paquier Trembleuse saucer, painted in red, green, puce and blue, with gilt rim (minor rim chip), moulded mock Chinese seal mark, c. 1725. **£1,300-1,600** *C*

One of a pair of Meissen chinoiserie saucers, painted with a Laub-und-Bandelwerk and Bottger-lustre cartouches (one with minute rim chip), gilt 24 marks, c. 1724 **£900-1,000** the pair   *C*

A Worcester blue and white saucer with fruit pattern, with blue rim, transfer print, 5 in. diam., c. 1780-90. **£25-30;** teabowl and saucer **£45-60** *BY*

A Zurich saucer, with gilt rim, blue Z mark above a dot, c. 1770. **£200-250** *C*

A Newhall cup, pattern 186. **£22-25** *CH*

A Duesbury Derby coffee can. **£30-35** *BY*

A pair of Bristol coffee cans, each painted in gold, underglaze mark in blue, c. 1775, height 7 cm. **£300-360** *SBe*

A Meissen Kakiemon cup (minor restoration to handle), blue crossed swords mark, c. 1735. **£340-380** *C*

A Newhall coffee can, Imari pattern patt. no. 446, c. 1795 (pre bone china). **£40-50** *BY*

A Spode coffee can, with later handle, c. 1805. **£45-50** *BY*

A Spode coffee can, with gilding, c. 1820. **£32-40**　*BY*

(l) A Worcester polychrome coffee cup, c. 1770. **£35-45** *CH*

(m) A Worcester polychrome coffee cup, c. 1770. **£40-50** *CH*

(r) A Worcester polychrome coffee cup, c. 1775. **£40-50** *CH*

A Martin Barr Worcester coffee can, the feathers painted by George Baxter. **£300-350** *MB*

A Worcester blue and white coffee can, with 'The Fence Pattern', c. 1770, 2½ in. high. **£95-105**　*CH*

A Chamberlain's Worcester coffee can, c. 1800. **£27-30**　*Gs*

A black printed and painted porcelain teabowl, c. 1800-10. **£10-14**　*Gs*

A Chaffers Liverpool moulded blue and white teabowl, c. 1768. **£30-35**　*BY*

A Vezzi white and gold teabowl, c. 1725. **£1,100-1,400**　*C*

A blue transfer feeding cup, possibly Copeland and Garrett, c. 1846, 6 in. wide. **£28-30**　*Gs*

An English blue transfer feeding cup, factory unknown, 8 in. wide, c. 1830-40. **£28-30** *Gs*

A Worcester Flight, Barr & Barr cabinet cup, on cobalt blue ground, with moth handle, c. 1820. **£200-240**　*MB*

A Bow bell-shaped mug, 14.5 cm. high, c. 1760. **£440-520**　*C*

A Beswick, England, sentimental mug, 'Parting is such sweet sorrow', 4½ in. **£10-15**　*Brit*

A Caughley blue and white tankard, c. 1775, 5½ in. high. **£215-245**　*CH*

A Leeds hand painted tankard, with oriental figures (possibly Rhodes), c. 1785, 4¾ in. £110-125   AD

An early Doulton Lambeth tankard, incised by Hannah Barlow, 12.5 cm. high, silver collar with hallmarks for 1873, oval mark dated 1873 and monogram HBB 715. £240-300   P

An Erfurt Faience tankard, painted in colours on powdered-manganese grounds (two hair cracks from rim), blue E mark, c. 1740, 20 cm. high. £400-480   C

A Pennington's Liverpool blue and white mug, c. 1778-80, 3 in. high. £85-95   CH

A Chaffer's Liverpool mug, c. 1760, 3¾ in. high. £195-215   CH

A Liverpool small mug, printed with quail, c. 1775, 2¾ in. £50-60   MB

A Wedgwood blue jasper ware tankard, with unusual backstamp, silver rims by Elkington, 1910, 4¾ in. high. £65-75   BTH

A Prattware mug, 4 in. high. £80-120   MB

A Liverpool small mug, painted with cannonball pattern, c. 1780. £110-130   MB

A 1st period blue and white Worcester tankard with the 'Plantation' pattern, c. 1765, 4½ in. high. £188-200   CH

A 1st period Worcester polychrome small mug, with English flowers, 3 in. tall. £240-280   MB

A First Period Worcester blue and white mug, with the 'Plantation' pattern, 3½ in. £125-145   MB

A 1st period Worcester blue and white bellied mug, c. 1765, 5 in. high. £260-290 *MB*

A Worcester black transfer mug by Hancock, with chip, 3½ in. high. £150-175; perfect £200-250 *MB*

A Worcester tapering mug, with a deep blue transfer print, crescent mark in underglaze blue, 14 cm., late 18th C. £150-180 *SBe*

A Meissen chinoiserie octagonal beaker, painted by J. G. Herold beneath a band of gilt Laub-und-Bandelwerk, the interior with a spray of flowers (minute rim chips), blue crossed swords mark within a double circle, c. 1730. £550-650 *C*

A Royal Worcester pierced and double-walled goblet, 19 cm., printed and impressed crowned circle marks, date code for 1875. £300-400 *SB*

A Dr. Wall Worcester scale blue tankard with English flowers, 3½ in. high. £850-930 *MB*

A Worcester polychrome mug, with Long Eliza pattern, c. 1770, 5 in. high. £460-500 *MB*

A Grainger's Worcester hand-painted mug, with 'A present from a friend', c. 1820, 4 in. high. £210-240 *MB*

A Doulton beaker, by Jessie Bowditch, 5½ in. impressed 1880. £55-65 *Brit*

A Worcester mug by R. Hancock with black transfer print, 'The Fishing Lesson', 4½ in. high, c 1770. £110-140 *MB*

A Worcester blue and white small tankard, with fence pattern, 2¼ in. high, 2¾ in. diam., c. 1780. £55-65 *BY*

A mid-19th C. child's pottery mug, 2¾ in. high. £16-18 *G.*

A Capodimonte beaker, painted in soft colours, fleur-de-lys mark in underglaze blue, incised n, 6.5 cm. £520-620 *P*

A Nottingham stoneware loving cup, dated 1846, 5 in. £55-65 *Cl.A*

A silver lustre resist loving cup, probably Leeds, c. 1815, 5 in. £50-70   *CS*

A Meissen goldchinesen beaker, the interior entirely gilt (rim chips), c. 1725, 8 cm. high. £550-750   *C* if perfect £1,000-1,200

A Doulton Lambeth three-handled Loving Cup, with incised decoration on buff ground, by Hannah B. Barlow, height 7 in. £420-480   *LT*

A silver mounted Doulton 'Rowing' tyg, applied with reliefs after designs by John Broad, 17 cm., impressed Lambeth mark, incised HH, dated 1882, the rim with maker's mark for London 1881. £240-300   *SB*

A Doulton silver mounted tyg, by Florence E. Barlow, decorated in naturalistic colours, impressed marks and monogram, height 16 cm., c. 1895. £200-260   *SBe*

A Moorcroft Macintyre Florian-ware tyg, in green and blue, the interior similarly decorated, printed Florian ware mark, painted W. Moorcroft des., 25.3 cm., c. 1898. £350-400   *SB*

An Annaberg portrait tankard, with pewter foot rim and hinged cover, the cover dated 1684 (minute rim chip), 23.5 cm. high, mid-17th C. £2,000-2,300   *C*

A Bayreuth blue and white Faience tankard, with pewter foot-rim and cover (cracked), c. 1740, 28.5 cm. high. £300-350   *C*

An Attenburg pale-grey stoneware tankard, with pewter footrim and cover with ball thumbpiece, c. 1740, 26.5 cm. high. £600-700   *C*

A Bayreuth blue and white tankard, with hinged pewter cover and footrim, painted with The Immaculate Conception, blue B.F.S. mark of Frankel and Schreck, 1745-47, 26 cm. high. £1,200-1,400   *C*

A mid-German faience tankard, painted in pale colours and permanganate, the pewter cover inscribed, dated 1775 (glaze chipped in parts), total height 22 cm. £300-360   *SBe*

A Crailsheim Faience tankard, painted in colours, with pewter cover and foot rim (base cracked, pewter thumbpiece missing), c. 1790, 17.5 cm. high. £250-300   *C*

A Dutch Delft blue and white
tankard, with pewter foot rim
and cover with ball thumb-piece
(chipped), 26.5 cm. high, c. 1700.
£600-720   *C*

A German stoneware mug,
modelled in the manner of
Kreussen with the twelve
apostles with pewter cover, 7½
in., 17th C. **£550-650**   *L*

An Erfurt tankard, with late
hinged pewter cover and
mounts, blue underlined V
mark, 26.5 cm. high, c. 1760.
£300-380   *C*

A pair of South German faience
tankards, painted in
polychrome, the pewter covers
with ball billets, 8¾ in. (one
tankard damaged), 18th C.
£500-600   *L*

A large 'Naples' tankard and
cover, 20 in. high, crowned N
mark on base. **£220-290**   *SR*

A Raeren stoneware tankard,
moulded with the arms of
Austria, the initials K.L.W. and
dated '93, with hinged pewter
cover and thumbpiece
(restored), c. 1693, 29 cm. high.
£300-350   *C*

A Kreussen stoneware apostl
tankard, painted in bright
enamel colours, late 17th C., 1
cm. high. **£2,000-2,300**   *C*

A Raeren brown stoneware
schnelle, bearing a coat-of-arms
and dated 1586 (chipped and
cracked), 25.5 cm. high, 16th C.
£880-1,000   *C*

A Schwarza 'Naples' tankard
and cover, the body moulded in
high relief, 30 cm. high, printed
crowned 'N' and Schwarza
marks, late 19th C. **£100-150**
SB

A Doulton Lambeth metal-
mounted stoneware flagon,
decorated by Frank Butler, with
incised foliage on a blue ground
impressed marks, artist's mark
and dated 1880, 30.5 cm. **£240**
280   *SBe*

A late 17th C. Caltagirone bottle, painted in green, yellow and manganese, on a blue ground, 23.5 cm. high. £300-00   C

A Worcester blue and white bottle, painter's mark, c. 1758, 26 cm. high. £450-520   C

A Staffordshire saltglaze bottle (some moulding missing), c. 1750, 22.5 cm. high. £300-340   C

'Girl in a Swing' triple scent bottle, in brown, pale yellow and purple (slight chips, restored), 7.5 cm. high, c. 1751. £1,000-,300   C

A Derby scent bottle, with hand-painted flowers on sky blue ground, c. 1810-1820, 5¼ in. high. £170-200   MB

'Girl in a Swing' Factory

This was probably a small factory closely associated with the Chelsea factory. It was possibly only in existence for about 7-8 years in the late 1740's/early 1750's. Very few useful pieces have yet been attributed to the factory whose products are extremely rare and always expensive.

A 'Girl in a Swing' scent-bottle and stopper, its plumage enriched in puce, brown and yellow with white enamel and gilt collar inscribed 'Charmante', the base with gold mount, 1751-1754, 6 cm. high, £3,300-3,600   C

A Meissen scent-bottle, modelled as a young woman holding a pug-dog, its head forming the stopper, 8 cm., c. 1745. £800-1,000   C

A Dutch Delft spirit-barrel, modelled as a seated toper, in manganese, yellow and blue (chips), 36 cm. high, bronze spout, c. 1760. £300-400   C

A Flight Barr and Barr scent bottle, c. 1815, 4 in. high. £500-580   MB

A pair of Royal Doulton 'Kingsware' spirit flasks, depicting Horatio Nelson, made for Dewars Whisky, circle mark, lion and crown, 21.5 cm. high. £160-220   P

A Martin Brothers 'John
Barley-Corn' spirit flask,
incised Southall Potteries, Rd.
No. 559677, 18 cm., c. 1900.
£500-560 *SB*

A Royal Doulton 'Kingsware'
spirit flask, entitled 'The Pipe
Major', made for Dewars
Whisky, circle mark, lion and
crown, 21.5 cm. high. **£80-
120** *P*

A Royal Doulton 'Kingsware'
spirit flask, depicting the
Dickensian character Tony
Weller, made for Dewars
Whisky, circle mark, lion and
crown, 19.5 cm. high. **£80-
120** *P*

A Westerwald stoneware
square flask, with pewter
mounts and screw cover (min
chips to base), c. 1650, 18 cm
high. **£1,800-2,200** *C*

A pair of Mintons yellow-
ground earthenware
moonflasks, of Isnik
inspiration, in turquoise, claret,
blue and olive (restored), 29.2
cm., printed Mintons Art
Pottery mark, impressed 1348,
Mintons, 1871-74. **£150-200**
SB

A Westerwald stoneware
square flask, with incised and
moulded decoration, pewter
mount and screw cover, c. 1680,
25 cm. high. **£750-850** *C*

A pair of Minton 'Cloisonne'
moonflasks, on turquoise
ground (hair cracks), 32.1 cm
impressed Mintons, 166,
indistinct date code, c. 1870.
£450-550 *SB*

Left

A pair of Mintons turquoise-
ground moonflasks (hair
crack), 27 cm., c. 1870. **£150-
200** *SB*

A Royal Worcester 'Japonaise'
porcelain pilgrim bottle, the
whole heightened in bronze,
gold and shades of brown, puce
printed mark and date '1874',
32.5 cm. **£360-420** *SKC*

A Mintons Pate-Sur-Pate
Moonflask, deep-olive-green
body decorated in white, 25.4
cm., impressed and printed
marks, moulded shape number,
c. 1900. **£300-380** *SB*

A Minton moon flask, painte
in bright enamels on a
turquoise ground, details in
gold, mid-19th C., height 30.5
cm. **£240-280** *SBe*

Caffaggiolo dated armorial armacy ewer (panel at back paired), marked under each ndle, 38 cm. high, 1541. ₹,000-3,500   *C*

Caltagirone waisted barello, painted in blue, en, ochre and manganese ips to base, base drilled), late th C., 28 cm. high. **£300-** 0   *C*

APOTHECARY JARS

- wide range of items produced by the potteries for pharmacists include apothecaries' jars, bleeding bowls, feeding cups, mixing implements etc.
- apothecary jars used from the Middle Ages, often beautifully decorated
- from 1650-1700 the angel design predominated
- from 1700 to late 1770's mainly bird designs
- after 1780 cherub design the most popular
- before 1650's the name of contents was omitted
- in England from 1570's-1650's the jars were decorated with coloured lines
- from 1650's, the English fashion was for a white pottery background with blue decoration
- this was overtaken by Wedgwood creamware after the 1760's

A Caltagirone waisted albarello, in yellow, green, ochre and blue (minor chip to foot), 17th C., 30.5 cm. high. **£350-400**   *C*

A Castel Durante pharmacy bottle, for A. D. VIOLE (neck repaired, foot chipped), 25 cm. high, c. 1585. **£440-520**   *C*

A Castelli wet-drug jar for Sirop: Rosato: Soluti:, in blue, yellow and manganese (base chipped), c. 1720, 24 cm. high. **£80-120.**   *C*

A Castel Durante dated pharmacy-jar, the date 1574 to one handle (cracked, chips, to neck and foot), 32 cm. high. **£2,000-2,300**   *C*

Castel Durante waisted barello, painted with Juno inor rim restoration, foot rim ound, base drilled), 20 cm. gh, c. 1575. **£1,300-1,500**

A Castelli wet-drug jar for Sirop; Rosato: Soluti:, painted in yellow, blue and green (repair to rim, chips to base), c. 1680, 22.5 cm. high. **£300-350**   *C*

A Castelli pharmacy vase for 'a de. cram icna' (neck repaired), 42 cm. high, c. 1720. **£850-1,000**   *C*

Deruta wet-drug jar, for O. ardino (minor glaze chips), 23 . high, c. 1560. **£1,500-** 700   *C*

A Faenza albarello, for 'Dia prums. So', in blue, green and yellow, 15 cm. high, c. 1530. **£1,200-1,400**   *C*

117

A Faenza armorial wet-drug jar for Hiperic : Usuale (spout and foot rim chipped), c. 1740, 22.5 cm. high. **£350-420**   *C*

A Faenza small waisted albarello, for Pill. Masticis named in Gothic script (restored), 15.5 cm. high, c. 154 **£500-650**   *C*

A Faenza A Quartieri waisted albarello, in yellow, ochre and green on a blue ground (minor restorations), 18.5 cm. high, c. 1590. **£600-800**   *C*

A wet-drug jar, for Mela Violato, the reverse painted with a blue B, probably Montelupo, 23 cm. high, c. 1560. **£500-700**   *C*

A Sicilian waisted albarello painted in blue, green and yellow (minor chips), probal Palermo, 26 cm. high, c. 158 **£500-700**   *C*

An Italian majolica drug jar from Savona, 6¾ in. high, late 17th C. **£180-220**   *JC*

A Sicilian albarello (rim chips and cracks), 24.5 cm. high, 17th C. **£270-350**   *C*

An Urbino waisted albarello, for LOH.D.PINO. (cracked through and repaired, later metal rim mount), 20 cm. diam., c. 1565. **£550-670**   *C*

A pair of Venice blue and white albarelli, for dia Calamit and H. D. Avolto, named in Gothic script (one cracked, minute chips), 22 cm. high, c. 1600. **£800-1,000**   *C*

A pair of Urbino waisted pharmacy jugs (one with minor crack and repair, glaze chips), 19 cm. high, c. 1590. **£1,500-1,700**   *C*

A Venice Berrettino blue and white pharmacy-ewer (foot chipped, minor glaze chips), c. 1580, 35.5 cm. diam. **£1,100-1,300**   *C*

Four Victorian chemist's pottery jars, and with gold name panels on a green groune 9 in. **£125-170**   *Hy.D*

Dutch Delft tobacco jar,
nted in cobalt oxide, fitted
electricity, slight damage, 27
., c. 1790. **£200-250**
perfect **£300-450** *SKC*

A Doulton stoneware 'Squash'
pot, decorated by Frank Butler,
13 cm., impressed Lambeth
mark, incised artist's
monogram and 637, c. 1885.
£240-300 *SB*

A Delft tobacco jar, the base
inscribed 'A and P.V.M.V.8, De
Griekshe A factory, fitted for
electricity, slight damage, 28
cm., c. 1790. **£200-250** if perfect
£300-450 *SKC*

A pair of small Doulton ewers, 5
in. high. **£60-70** *SV*

Left
A Doulton Lambeth,
ewer, by Florence B.
Barlow, impressed
1877, 10 in. high. **£140-
170** *Brit*

arge Cantagalli majolica
er, in Renaissance taste, well
nted after Benozzo Gozzili,
t damaged, 71.5 cm., painted
kerel mark, late 19th C.,
nised wood stand. **£260-
0** *SB*

A Doulton Lambeth ewer, with
verse, 7 in. high. **£100-130**
Brit

Right
A silver-mounted Doulton
stoneware Carafe, decorated by
George Tinworth, signed, in
brown and royal blue, with
hinged lid and thumbpiece, 26
cm., impressed Doulton oval
mark, dated 1874, the mount
with marks for London, 1874.
£130-160 *SB*

Doulton ewer, by Hannah
arlow, 10¾ in. **£300-320**
r.A

A pair of good Doulton Burslem
ewers, each painted by C. N.
Wright, signed, with gilt
decoration, 35 cm., printed and
impressed marks, c. 1890.
£400-460 *SB*

A Martin ware ewer, in blue-
grey and dark brown, incised
Martin, London & Southall, 24
cm. high. **£110-180** *P*

A Meissen Ewer symbolic of water, after the original mode by J. J. Kaendler, 62.5 cm., crossed swords in underglaze blue, incised numerals, mid 19th C. **£500-600**   *SB*

A Mettlach pewter-mounted ewer and cover, decorated after Warth, moulded signature, 50.5 cm., impressed mark and 1690, c. 1910. **£440-530**   *SBe*

A Mettlach stoneware ewer, in the form of an ammorite, impressed mark, late 19th C., 40 cm. **£150-200**   *SBe*

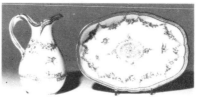

A Wedgwood jasper ewer, in black and white, c. 1880, 6½ in. high. **£45-55**   *Cr.A*

A Sevres ewer and basin (broc roussel), blue crowned interlaced L marks and the date letter q for 1769, the basin 26 cm. wide. **£660-800**   *C*

A Nuremberg enghalskrug, with hinged pewter cover an thumb-piece, 27.5 cm. high, c 1735. **£1,300-1,550**   *C*

A Worcester blue and white ewer, c. 1780, 6 in. high. **£170-190**   *MB*

A Worcester blue and white painted Ewer in 'Immortelle' pattern, c 1780, 5½ in. high. **£195-215**   *CH*

A Royal Worcester ewer, with pale cream ground, Shape 1094, 1892, 6½ in. **£100-120**   *MB*

Left
A Bow blue and white fluted oval sauceboat (minute chip to lip), blue X mark, c. 1760, 15 cm. wide. **£130-170**   *C*

Two salt glaze ewers 'scratch blue', c. 1750, 6½ in. high. **£100-150**   *MB*

Right
A Bow blue and white sauceboat, the interior with a diaper-pattern rim (lip chip), c. 1752, 18 cm. wide. **£130-170**   *C*

A rare painted Caughley blue and white sauceboat, in mint condition. £100-115   *MB*

Derby blue and white oval auceboat (slight crack to base nd handle), Wm. Duesbury & o., c. 1768. £150-190   *C*

A Derby creamer, puce mark, 1782-1800, 2¾ in. high. £95-105   *CH*

A Lowestoft sparrow beak jug, c. 1770, 3¼ in. high. £200-220   *MB*

Derby blue and white shell-oulded sauceboat, Wm. uesbury & Co., c. 1770, 14.5 n. wide. £190-240   *C*

A Liverpool blue and white fluted sauceboat (lip chips), William Ball's factory, c. 1760. £240-300   *C*

A Liverpool blue and white sauceboat painted with a fisherman, c. 1780. £70-80 *MB*

A Derby milk jug, with two gilt cartouches containing crests against a yellow ground, crown, crossed batons and D mark in puce, Duesbury & Kean, 13.5 cm. wide, c. 1800. £560-700   *C*

A Liverpool blue and white mask-jug, printed with bouquets of flowers (crack to rim), Seth Pennington's factory, c. 1780, 14 cm. high. £90-120   *C*

A Lowestoft blue and white spirally-moulded butter boat, c. 1785, 10 cm. wide. £200-250 *C*

A Meissen Kakiemon milk jug, of fluted form (restored), blue crossed swords mark, c. 1735, 16 cm. high. £400-480   *C*

Meissen Kakiemon cream-jug ninute chip to rim), blue rossed swords mark, c. 1735, 5 cm. high. £225-275   *C*

A Newhall creamer, pattern 171, 1787-95, 4¼ in. high. £65-75   *CH*

A Newhall cream jug, pattern 195, c. 1790-1805, 4½ in. high. **£62-70** *CH*

A Meissen cream jug, painted with merchants and trading vessels within quatrefoil Laub-und-Bandelwerk cartouches divided by sprays of Indianische Blumen (spout chipped), c. 1738, 11 cm. high. **£450-500** *C*

A Whieldon cabbage-leaf moulded creamboat, in tones of green and aubergine with ochre rim (minute chips to rim), c. 1765, 12 cm. wide. **£600-660** *C*

A 1st period Worcester sparrow beak jug with hand-painted English flowers, c. 1765, 3½ in. high. **£200-230** *MB*

A Worcester polychrome 'Lamprey' jug, 3¼ in. high. **£260-290** *MB*

A Worcester blue and white sparrow beak jug, some repair with European landscape, 3⅝ in. high. **£40-50** repaired; **£120-140** perfect *BY*

A Worcester blue and white milk-jug, painted with the 'Eloping Bride' pattern, blue Oriental character mark, c. 1768, 10 cm. high. **£680-780** *C*

A 1st period blue and white Worcester sauce boat, c. 1768, 6½ in. wide. **£110-125** *CH*

A 1st period Worcester sparrow beak jug, with hand-painted English flowers, c. 1765, 3¾ in. high. **£220-250** *MB*

A Worcester blue and white sparrow beak jug, c. 1765, 3¼ in. high. **£160-180** *MB*

A documentary Bristol blue and white hexagonal cream-boat, with moulded trailing C-scrolls the interior rim painted with trailing foliage from a stylised shell, incised X mark and 'Bristol' in relief, Benjamin Lund's Factory, c. 1750, 11 cm. wide. **£13,000-14,500** *C*

pair of Worcester blue and
hite sauceboats with Chinese
enes, c. 1770, 6 in. long. £350-
00 pr.   *CH*

Right
A Worcester blue and white
sauceboat, c. 1770, 6 in. wide.
£165-185   *CH*

A Worcester blue and white
sparrow beak jug, c. 1775, 4¼ in.
high. £110-140   *CH*

A Worcester spirally-moulded
milk-jug, the interior with iron-
red and gilt loop and dot-
pattern rim, c. 1770, 8.5 cm.
high. £380-430   *C*

. Worcester blue and white
parrow beak jug, c. 1775, 3½ in
igh. £85-95   *CH*

A Baron, Barnstaple jug, 1932,
5 in. high. £25-30   *Brit*

A Baron Barnstaple jug, 7 in.
high. £30-40   *Brit*

Berlin porcelain jug, in
aeren style, well painted on a
own ground, 35 cm., sceptre in
derglaze blue, incised marks
d numeral, c. 1870. £300-
0   *SB*

A Berlin jug, painted in sepia
with a musical trio, within gilt
dentillated and moulded
borders, underglaze blue
sceptre and printed red orb
mark, 50 cm., c. 1880. £290-
350   *SBe*

A C. H. Brannan-ware
puffin bird jug, 1898, 10
in. high. £80-90   *Brit*

Liverpool Delftware puzzle
g, 'What tho I'm common and
ell known to almost everyone
Town. My hunch to sixpence
you will, that if you drink you
me do spill', 7¾ in. c. 1770.
400-700   *JH*

A silver-mounted Doulton
stoneware jug, coloured in blue,
brown and green, 27.3 cm.,
impressed oval mark, dated
1876, the rim with marks for
Atkin Brothers, Sheffield, 1875.
£85-100   *SB*

A Roses Coalport blue and
white jug, pine cone pattern, 7½
in. high, c. 1840. £65-75   *BY*

A Doulton Lambeth lemonade jug, decorated in pate-sur-pate, by Florence Barlow, 24 cm. high, rosette mark and England, incised F.E.B. in monogram, numbered 884. **£170-250**   *P*

An electroplate-mounted Doulton stoneware covered jug, decorated by Mary Mitchell, in blue on the buff ground, impressed mark, incised artist's monogram and 245, 20.5 cm., dated 1880. **£330-380**   *SB*

An early Doulton stoneware jug, incised by Hannah Barlow 19 cm., impressed Lambeth mark, incised artist's monogram and assistant's initials M.T., for Mary Ann Thomson, dated 1875. **£220-280**   *SB*

A rare Carrara-ware jug, painted in sepia camaieu by Hannah Barlow, green printed Carrara mark, artist's and assistant's monograms 'H.B.B. and M.D.', c. 1887-90, 20 cm. **£240-280**   *SKC*

A Crown Ducal jug, signed Charlotte Rhead, 7½ in. high. **£35-40**   *Brit*

'The Clown', a rare Doulton character jug, 16 cm. high, circle mark, lion and crown. **£320-400**   *P*

A colour transfer printed jug by Jonathan Lowe, Cheltham, c. 1841-62, 5½ in. high. **£40-44** *Gs*

A Leeds pink resist jug of fine quality, c. 1815, 6¾ in. **£280-300**   *CS*

A Pennington barrel shape jug (damaged), 4 in., c. 1790. **£30-35**   *BY*

An Italian majolica jug, from Savona, late 17th C., 6 in. high **£100-150**   *JC*

A James Kent Ltd. jug, 'W Rose', 7 in. **£14-18**   *Brit*

Martin Brothers stoneware
ce jug, covered in an ochre
aze (minor spout chip), 20.5
m., incised R.W. Martin &
rothers, London & Southall,
ated 5-1899. **£1,250-1,450**
B

A late Martin Brothers face jug,
22.5 cm., incised R.W. Martin
Bros., c. 1915. **£200-260**   *SB*

A Masons ironstone jug, c. 1825,
6½ in. high. **£50-55**   *Gs*

A set of majolica monkey jugs,
robably Minton, c. 1880, 11 in.
igh, 9 in. high, 8 in. high.
200-230   *WA*

A Mason's ironstone jug in
Oriental pattern, c. 1835, 6½ in.
high. **£60-70**   *MB*

A Portobello jug with religious
scenes, Mary, Joseph and
Christ and Peter and cockerel, c.
1830 (chip to rim), 8 in. high.
£50-55   *AD*

Pratt jug, with typical
olours: ochre yellow and deep
ue, c. 1810, 6 in. high. **£100-**
15   *AD*

A 19th C. Prattware jug, 6½ in.
high. **£65-75**   *SV*

A Pratt jug, modelled with bust
portraits of Admiral Duncan
and Captain Tarrop, in brown,
ochre, green and blue, 5½ in.
£120-150   *L*

Prattware jug, c. 1850, 9½ in.
igh. **£75-85**   *MB*

A Saltglaze Bacchus mask jug,
3¾ in. high, c. 1790. **£36-40**
BY

A Raeren dated brown
stoneware jug, with an
inscription, dated 1598 (foot
and neck chipped), 24.5 cm.
high. **£900-1,100**   *C*

125

A slipware puzzle jug, West Country pottery, dated 1790, inscribed with a rhyme, 7½ in. **£200-300** *JC*

A Westerwald stoneware jar, in blue and manganese glaze, chip to rim, after 1714, 12 in. high. **£200-300 if perfect £300-400** *JC*

A Siegburg beige stoneware jug with a later silver mounted neck, c. 1650, 15 cm. high. **£900-1,100** *C*

A Staffordshire gravelware jug, c. 1800, 6½ in. high. **£120-145** *AD*

A Staffordshire silver lustre jug, with slip decoration, c. 1825, 6½ in. **£210-240** *CS*

A lead glaze slipware puzzle jug, 7 in., dated 1880. **£65-75** *JC*

A mid-19th C. Sunderland lustre jug, 7¼ in. high. **£200-250** *LAC*

A Sunderland lustre jug, transfer printed with a view of the iron bridge, and a verse entitled 'The Sailors tear', early 19th C., 21 cm. **£50-60** *SBe*

A Sunderland lustre jug by Dixon & Co., with the ship Northumberland, 7 in. high, chip restored on spout, c. 182 **£80-90** perfect **£110-120** *C*

A late 19th C. Verwood pottery earthenware jug, 11 in. high. **£10-15** *JC*

A late 19th C. Verwood pottery two-handled earthenware jug, 10 in. **£10-15** *JC*

A blue and white mask lipped jug, by John Turner, 'The Village Pattern', c. 1806, 5 in. high. **£60-65** *Gs*

Two Victorian pink lustre jugs, 3½ in. high. **£25-30**; 4¾ in. high **£35-40** *SV*

A Victorian pink lustre large jug, 6½ in. high. **£90-100** *SV*

A Victorian gold lustre jug, with heavy moulding, 6 in. high. **£60-70** *SV*

A Wedgwood jug, 6½ in. high. **£80-90** *LAC*

A Westerwald or Raeren stoneware jug, moulded with a medallion of William and Queen Mary, the coat-of-arms Orange-Nassau, and a Dutch inscription, dated 1691 (crack to handle), 18 cm. high. **£800-1,100** *C*

A Westerwald or Raeren toneware jug, incised with flowers on a manganese ground (base cracked), c. 1700, 21 cm. high. **£350-400** *C*

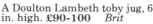

A Doulton Lambeth toby jug, 6 in. high. **£90-100** *Brit*

A Westerwald stoneware jug, moulded with the crowned initials RAR on blue ground, with manganese neck, c. 1710, 18 cm. high. **£350-400** *C*

A Michael Cardew Winchcombe Pottery earthenware cider jar, in toffee against the honey ground, flakes, impressed monogram and Winchcombe Pottery seal, 24.5 cm., 1926-39. **£130-170** *SB*

Davenport Toby jug marked, restoration to hat, 9¾ in., c. 36-60. **£90-100** *CS*

Pratt pipe of Martha Gunn, c. 85, 5 in. **£150-180** *JH*

A Prattware Yorkshire Toby Jug, c. 1790, 10 in. **£200-280** *JH*

A Ralph Wood type Toby Jug, with attractive running glazes, c. 1770. **£400-500** *JH*

127

A Rhenish Bellarmine, c. 1600, 9½ in. **£1,000-1,500** *JH*

A Whieldon-type Toby Jug, with unusual deep base, pipe held in reverse, c. 1760, 10 in. **£550-650** *JH*

An 18th C. Yorkshire toby jug, 10 in. high. **£210-240** *Cl.A*

A saltglaze stoneware bellarmine, late 17th C./early 18th C., 18 in. high. **£180-250** *JC*

A German stoneware jug, with three oval medallions of coats of arms, one with the initials G.K., another with H.E.V., with pewter handle, cover and foot rim, 11 in. (28 cm.), 16th-17th C. **£400-450** *L*

A silver-mounted Doulton stoneware lemonade jug, in royal blue and olive ground, 23.2 cm., impressed Lambeth marks, dated 1878, the rim with marks, for Birmingham, 1878. **£70-100** *SB*

An Electroplate-mounted Doulton stoneware lemonade jug, body incised by Hannah Barlow on a buff ground in sage-green and brown, with hinged lid with thumbpiece, 25.5 cm., impressed Lambeth mark, incised artists initials, Jn, dated 1881, damaged. **£180-220** if perfect **£300-400** *SB*

A Meissen hot-milk jug, painted with Watteauesque figures in wooded landscapes, blue crossed swords and dot marks, c. 1765, 15.5 cm. high. **£650-750** *C*

A Meissen 'Famille-Verte' octagonal pear-shaped jug and cover (the upper part restored), caduceus mark in blue, c. 1728, 15 cm. high. **£450-550** *C*

A Meissen Hausmalerei hot-milk jug and cover, moulded with flutes and painted in the manner of Ferner (spout restored), blue crossed swords and star marks and incised 4 and 47, c. 1740, 15.5 cm. high. **£300-400** *C*

A Linthorpe Pottery claret jug with electroplated mount, designed by Christopher Dresser, 24.5 cm., impressed mark Linthorpe 1517, mount stamped with maker's marks of James Dixon & Sons and numbered F5669, c. 1885. **£250-350** *SB*

A pear-shaped milk jug and cover, painted in Imari style, 13 cm. high, c. 1770. **£460-570**   *C*

A Sevres jug and cover, painted in colours, blue interlaced L mark, date letter for 1764 and unidentified painter's mark, 13.5 cm. high. **£180-260** *C*

A Weesp hot-milk jug and cover (repair to finial), c. 1760, 16 cm. high. **£600-650** *C*

Ludwigsburg ornithological coffee-pot, on three feet, painted bright colours (replacement cover, one foot restored), blue crowned interlaced C mark and impressed IS/11/R, c. 1770, overall height 24 cm. **£520-620** *C*

A Davenport blue and white coffee pot, c. 1820, 10½ in. high. **£150-160** *Gs*

A Bottger porcelain Hausmalerei pear-shaped coffee-pot, painted by Johann Dannhöfer with Chinese figures (spout chipped, cover chipped and with minor restoration), the porcelain c. 1725, the decoration almost contemporary, 19 cm. high. **£5,000-6,000** *C*

A Kloster Veilsdorf ornithological coffee-pot and cover (minor chips under rim of cover), blue CV mark, c. 1770, 22 cm. high. **£1,200-1,500** *C*

A Meissen chinoiserie coffee-pot and cover, painted in the manner of C. F. Herold (with restoration), blue crossed swords mark, each piece with gilder's number 77, c. 1725, 20 cm. high. **£2,100-2,500** *C*

A Meissen yellow-ground quatrefoil coffee-pot and cover (the handle restored), blue crossed swords mark, c. 1742, 23.5 cm. high. **£650-730** *C*

A Staffordshire glazed redware miniature coffee-pot and cover, c. 1755, 16.5 cm. high. **£220-260** *C*

A Staffordshire salt glaze coffee pot, enamelled in brilliant tones of pink, green and yellow, cane-covered metal handle, 6½ in. **£55-100**   *L*

A Weesp pear-shaped coffee-pot (minute chip to rim and foot rim), c. 1760, 18 cm. high. **£650-800**   *C*

A Worcester blue and whit coffee-pot and cover (minut chip to spout), blue crescen mark, c. 1765, 21.5 cm. hig **£400-460**   *C*

A Worcester coffee pot and cover, crescent mark, 18.7 cm., late 18th C. **£150-180**   *SBe*

A black printed miniature pottery coffee pot, c. 1825-35, 5¼ in. high. **£40-44**   *Gs*

A Caughley Mansfield patter small teapot, printed in underglaze blue, 5 in. **£130-200**   *WW*

A Davenport teapot, of Lichfield Cathedral, c. 1860, 4¼ in. high. **£200-230**   *MB*

A creamware teapot by Cockpit Hill, Derby, with rust coloured flowers, c. 1765, 5 in. high. **£200-245**   *Gs*

A Gardner factory teapot, in deep blue, with flowers, c. 189 **£35-40**   *BY*

A Hochst teapot, iron-red wheel mark, c. 1755, 18 cm. wide. **£1,400-1,600**   *C*

A Leeds creamware tea pot and cover, painted by David Rhodes, in red and black, 5 in. **£85-120**   *L*

A faience teapot and cover, probably Hochst, painted in soft colours with chinoiserie figures, marked H in black, cm. **£2,000-2,200**   *P*

Staffordshire saltglaze
olychrome Jacobite teapot and
ver, moulded and coloured
ith a half-length figure of the
oung Pretender (rim cracked),
1745, 12.5 cm. high. **£330-**
0   C

TEAPOTS

- the first mention of tea in England is in the late 1650's
- it was very much a luxury item and was originally served from silver pots
- many imported Chinese teapots started arriving at the beginning of the 18th C.
- the early Chinese teapots were either octagonal or globular
- the Continental factories, led by Meissen, were the first to produce tea and coffee pots
- initially these were straight copies of the Chinese
- then the rococo designers and individual decorators began creating their own styles

- the globular teapot was popular until the mid 1760's
- Worcester tends to be the English factory which perfected the making of teawares
- silver being very expensive and European porcelain difficult to obtain meant that the English factories had tremendous demand for teawares
- the beginning of the 19th C. saw the introduction of the 'oval' shape of teapot and an increase in the number of factories producing teawares of many different forms
- in the 19th C. many novelty and amusing shapes were introduced

Left
An early Meissen chinoiserie teapot, painted in the workshop of J. G. Herold, puce crossed swords mark and gilder's number 28, c. 1725, 15 cm. wide.
£1,300-1,500   C

A Newhall teapot and stand, pattern 425. **£185-200   CH**

Left
A Meissen Hausmalerei teapot, moulded with flutes and painted in the manner of Ferner (cover restored, spout reduced), blue crossed swords and double dot mark, Pressnummer 19, c. 1740. **£250-350   C**

A Sadler pottery teapot, 10 in. wide. **£60-80   Brit**

Meissen teapot and
lacement silver gilt cover, in
e manner of C. F. Herold, in
senrot with gilt Laub-und-
ndelwerk, the scroll spout
th mask head terminal (the
dy restored), blue crossed
ords and K.P.M. marks,
lder's mark 26, c. 1725, 16.5
. wide. **£900-1,100   C**

A Staffordshire treacle ware teapot, 10½ in. high, c. 1870. **£75-85   LAC**

A Staffordshire Littler blue teapot, c. 1750, 3¾ in. **£500-600   JH**

A Staffordshire saltglaze polychrome teapot and cover (chips to spout), c. 1755, 15.5 cm. wide. **£350-400   C**

An 18th C. English tin glazed teapot, decorated in underglaze blue T.S.L. and dated 1750, height 7¼ in. (restored). **£100-120   WHL**

131

A Wedgwood black jasper ware teapot, c. 1880. £45-55   *Cr.A*

A Measham ware barge teapot, made for Mr. G. Bird in Church Grisley (sic) (actually Gresley) dated c. 1900. £140-160   *WA*

A miniature Whieldon teapot and cover, splashed in manganese (finial restored), 1750, 14 cm. wide. £330-390 *C*

A Barr Worcester teapot and stand, incised B, 1792-1800. £135-145   *CH*

A Royal Worcester 'Aesthetic' teapot (repaired and damaged), 15.8 cm., printed mark, registration mark for 1881, 'Budge' impressed 'T2R', date code for 1882. £160-200   *SB*

A Whieldon ware teapot, c. 1755, 4 in. £250-350   *JF*

Left
A Worcester blue and white teapot and cover, painted with the 'cannonball' scene (slight chip to rim), 15 cm., late 18th C. £120-160   *SBe*
Right
A 1st period Worcester polychrome teapot (slight chip on spout), 5 in. high. £175-200   *MB*

Left
A Worcester polychrome teapot, c. 1775, 5 in. £315-350 *CH*

Right
A 1st period Worcester blue and white 'Mansfield Pattern' teapot, c. 1770, 4¾ in. high. £325-365   *CH*

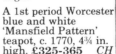

Left
A 1st period Worcester polychrome teapot, c. 1765, 5 in. high. £375-400   *MB*

A Worcester polychrome teapot c. 1775, 6 in. £285-325   *CH*

A Royal Worcester tea kettle and cover, in green, yellow bronze and gold, impressed marks, late 19th C. **£150-200** *SBe*

A Meissen miniature teapot, c. 1840, 4 in. high. **£125-150** *LAC*

l) A Coalport miniature teapot, 1¾ in., c. 1795, perfect. **£100-130** *LAC*

r) A Coalport miniature teapot, c. 1915, 1¾ in. **£15-20** *LAC*

(l) A Meissen miniature teapot, c. 1780 (white and gold), 2 in. high. **£300-340** *LAC*

(r) A Duesbury Derbyshire miniature teapot, c. 1795-1825, 2¼ in. **£75-85** *LAC*

A salt glaze teapot and cover, enamelled in the Chinese manner, late 18th C. **£250-280** *SBe*

(l) An Oriental miniature teapot, c. 1900, 2¾ in. **£20-23** *LAC*

(r) An Oriental miniature teapot, c. 1900, 2¾ in. **£28-32** *LAC*

A Meissen white hexagonal baluster teacaddy, c. 1725, 12 cm. high. **£450-550** *C*

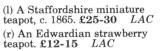

(l) A Staffordshire miniature teapot, c. 1865. **£25-30** *LAC*

(r) An Edwardian strawberry teapot. **£12-15** *LAC*

(l) A Royal Worcester miniature teapot, 1898. **£60-70** *LAC*

(r) An Imari miniature teapot, c. 1900. **£13-18** *LAC*

A rare William Reid Liverpool tea caddy and cover, in the form of a boy's head, painted with washes of underglaze blue, 13 cm. **£1,000-1,300** *P*

A Wedgwood black transfer printed tea caddy and cover, marked, c. 1780-90, 5¼ in. high. **£100-115** *AD*

A Worcester blue and white teapoy, c. 1768, 5 in. high. **£110-135**   *CH*

A 1st period Worcester polychrome painted teapoy, c. 1770, 5¼ in. **£135-155**   *CH*

A 1st period Worcester 'dry blue' teapoy, 5¼ in. **£125-150**   *CH*

A 1st period Worcester teapoy with cover, c. 1775, 6¼ in. **£23..285**   *CH*

A Worcester blue and white caddy (without lid), with fence pattern, 4⅜ in. high, c. 1780. **£40-50;** with lid **£120-140** *BY*

A Dresden clockcase, with 4 figures representative of the seasons, damaged, crossed swords in underglaze blue, 40 cm., late 19th C. **£240-300** *SBe*

A 'Sevres' gilt-bronze-mounted clock case, with a bleu-céleste ground and gilt enrichment, 38 cm., the dial indistinctly signed mid 19th C., gilt wood stand. **£300-350**   *SB*

A Dresden clock case, applied with four putti emblematic of the seasons, chips, 46 cm., shield in underglaze blue, late 19th C. **£400-460**   *SB*

A decorative late Meissen cloc.. the movement contained in a.. case of square section, painte.. in blue, picked out in gilt, crossed swords mark in blue, .. cm. **£1,150-1,300**   *P*

A Meissen clock case, with circular enamelled dial and movement contained in a drum-form body with gilt details, minor damage, 28.5 cm., crossed swords in underglaze blue, incised D68, the dial inscribed 'Examd. by Lund & Brockley', c. 1880. **£900-950** *SB*

Left
A Meissen clock case, with enamelled dial and movement set in an architectural pedestal, some restoration, 39 cm., crossed swords in underglaze blue, incised 1668, c. 1880. **£1,100-1,400**   *SB*

Left
A Meissen rococo clock and stand, the dial indicating the phases of the moon, date and seconds, blue crossed swords mark, 35 cm. high, c. 1760. **£2,200-2,500**   *C*

A pair of First Period Belleek candlesticks, 8 in. £300-350 *Cr.A*

A candlestick by Carter, Stabler, Adams Ltd., Poole, 5 in. high. £60-70   *Brit*

A pair of Bow candlestick-groups, emblematic of summer and autumn, enriched with puce and gilding (nozzles cracked), anchor and dagger marks in iron-red, c. 1765, 26 cm. high. £750-900   *C*

A pair of continental four-light andelabra, chips and repairs, R monogram in underglaze lue, 49 cm., late 19th C. £280-30 *SBe*

A rare Clarice Cliff pottery candlestick, designed by Laura Knight, A.R.A., painted in green, pink and yellow with gilt detailing, facsimile signature and factory marks, 11 cm. high. £150-215   *P*

A pair of late 19th C. Copeland candlesticks, in Imari palette, 5½ in. high. £70-80   *SV*

A pair of Chelsea-Derby candelabra, for two lights each, 10¼ and 10½ in. £690-800   *L*

A pair of Chelsea candlestick-figures emblematic of the four seasons, spring and summer as ladies, autumn and winter as gentlemen (minor chips, the nozzles later replacements), gold anchor marks, c. 1765, 27.5 cm. high. £1,000-1,200   *C*

A pair of Doulton Lambeth candlesticks, by Frances E. Lee, 1876, 6 in. high. £255-275 pair *Brit*

A Doulton Lambeth candlestick, by Frank Butler, impressed 1873, 6½ in. high. £150-175   *Brit*

One of a pair of Derby chamber candlesticks (chipped and restored), Wm. Duesbury & Co., 13 cm. wide, c. 1765. £280-360 the pair   *C*

A pair of Doulton stoneware candlesticks, by Mary Ann Thompson, minor restoration, 18.5 cm., impressed Lambeth mark, incised artist's monogram, dated 1879. **£170-220** *SB*

A pair of Doulton stoneware candlesticks, decorated by Francis E. Lee, chip restored, 16 cm., impressed Lambeth mark, incised artist's initials, 601, 602 and FC, dated 1876 with silver nozzles, Thomas Wilkinson, Birmingham, 1876. **£200-260** *SB*

A pair of Doulton Lambeth candlesticks, by Eliza Atkins, 7 in. high, 1881. **£350-380** pair *Brit*

A pair of Royal Doulton candlesticks 'Shakespeare Series', 6½ in., c. 1915. **£75-85** *MT*

A Dresden 4 light candelabrum, minor chips, cross and initials mark in underglaze blue, 50 cm., c. 1900. **£150-210** *SBe*

A Martin Brothers chamber candlestick, in olive and brown against a pale blue glaze, 11 cm., signed and dated 6-189. **£200-260** *SB*

A pair of Meissen rococo candlesticks, edged in green and pink, blue crossed swords and dot marks, 25 cm. high, c 1765. **£880-1,100** *C*

A pair of Meissen candlesticks (damaged), crossed swords in underglaze blue, 13.5 cm., late 19th C. **£190-230** *SB*

A Meissen blue and white onion pattern chamber stick, c. 1860. **£100-120** *Cr.A*

A pair of Meissen candelabra, 22.5 cm., crossed swords in underglaze blue, incised 1153 and 1160, late 19th C. **£600-680** *SB*

A pair of Meissen-style 3 branch candelabra, each with the figure of Diana, AR monogram in underglaze blue, late 19th C., height 30 cm. **£370-420** *SBe*

A Meissen 'Bottger Steinzeug' candlestick, moulded in Art Deco taste, incised crossed swords, A1017, impressed marks, 25.5 cm., c. 1930. **£190-240** *SB*

A pair of Minton candlestick figures, on circular rocaille moulded bases, 21.5 cm., about 1835-36. **£700-850** *SKC*

A candlestick by Myatt Pottery, Bilston, Staffordshire, 9 in. high. **£30-40** *Brit*

A Royal Worcester Cricklite, fitted with Clarks Cricklites, with shot silk decoration, impressed Cricklite on base (in perfect condition), 35½ in. high, 1880. **£1,050-1,150** *MB*

A Burmantoft's faience jardiniere and stand, hair crack to jardiniere, 95.5 cm. overall, impressed marks, painted numerals, c. 1885. **£330-380** *SB*

Two very early English lead glazed earthenware candlesticks, late 16th C./early 17th C. **£100-150** each *JC*

A Coalport (John Rose) bombe flower-pot and pierced cover, lightly enriched in gilding, c. 1810, 29 cm. wide. **£200-230** *C*

A pair of Continental glazed earthenware pedestals, probably French, some damage, 98 cm., late 19th C. **£400-460** *SB*

A pair of Derby flared flower-pots and two-handled stands, painted in the manner of Richard Dodson, crown, crossed batons and D marks in iron-red, Robert Bloor & Co., c. 1815, about 19 cm. high. **£650-730** *C*

A Derby bough-pot and pierced cover of bombe form, painted in the manner of Jockey Hill with 'Near Wirksworth, Derbyshire' (cracked round side), crown, crossed batons and D mark and inscribed in blue, Duesbury & Kean, 1795-1800, 19 cm wide. **£200-250** *C*

A pair of Derby yellow ground flared flower-pots, painted in the manner of George Robertson with 'At Panmure in Angushire, Scotland', and 'Near Inverness, Scotland', crown, crossed batons and D marks in blue, Duesbury & Kean, c. 1800, 13 cm. high. **£670-750**　*C*

A Doulton small flower pot, by Edith Lupton, 1879, 3½ in. high. **£25-30**　*Brit*

A Derby D-shaped bough pot, painted in the manner of William Billingsley, on a yellow ground, crown, crossed batons and D marks in puce, Duesbury & Kean, 1796-1800, 24.5 cm. wide. **£450-550**　*C*

A Derby D-shaped bough pot, painted in lavender blue and gilt, crown, crossed batons and D mark in puce, Duesbury & Kean, 1796-1800, 24 cm. wide. **£220-260**　*C*

A Lambeth Doulton salt glazed stoneware jardiniere on stand, with incised Art Nouveau stylised design, signed by Mark V. Marshall, 1879-1912, height 50 in. **£600-700**　*JF*

A Doulton stoneware jardiniere painted by Florence Barlow, the green ground incised by Emily Stormer, impressed marks, incised artist's monogram, 23 cm., c. 1885. **£280-320**　*SB*

A jardiniere with tray, possibly Minton, c. 1860, 8 in. high. **£65-75**　*Cr.A*

A Doulton stoneware jardiniere, body incised by Hannah Barlow, impressed Lambeth mark, incised artist's monogram for Hannah Barlow and Emily E. Stormer, 1890, height 38 cm. **£400-450**　*SBe*

One of a pair of Mintons majolica jardinieres and stands, in transparent green, brown, lilac and yellow glazes, 86.5 cm., about 1870 (repaired footrim). **£550-650** the pair *SKC*

A pair of Dresden yellow-ground cassolettes, fitted with reversible cover forming a lid or nozzle, the details gilt, 27.5 cm., sceptre in underglaze blue, late 19th C. **£280-320**　*SB*

A Dresden small jardiniere, c. 1850, 5 in. high. **£75-85**　*Cr.A*

A rare Newcastle pink lustre
ough pot, without cover, 9 in.
vide, c. 1820. **£110-130** *CS*

A pair of Potschappel
jardinieres, with gilded rim,
painted in underglaze blue
(slight damage), width 30 cm.
£240-330 *SBe*

A pair of demi-lune bough pots,
the central reserves painted
landscapes 'Near Canterbury',
and a 'View near Pinxton,
Derbyshire', probably
decorated at Pinxton (one
cracked), 24 cm. wide, 17.5 cm.
high, c. 1795-1800. **£400-460**
SKC

A Sceaux divided tulipiere (one
foot repaired, chips), pink fleur-
de-lys mark, 21 cm. wide, c.
1760. **£650-780** *C*

A Staffordshire earthenware
ardiniere and stand, chip to
ase, 114 cm., the jardiniere
noulded 'Vulcan', c. 1900.
£300-380 *SB*

A pair of 19th C. Paris porcelain
jardinieres, with hand painted
coloured panels in gilt
cartouches against a royal blue
ground (one with cracks), 15 in.
diam. **£580-700** *WW*

A Spode blue and white tower
pattern jardiniere, or fish bowl,
height 36 in. **£400-470** *JF*

A Wedgwood mustard jasper
vare jardiniere, c. 1880, 7¼ in.
igh. **£135-150** *Cr.A*

An Edwardian English
jardiniere and stand,
unmarked, 35 in., c. 1910. **£190-
210** *MT*

A Wedgwood majolica pedestal,
63 cm., impressed marks,
painted numerals, indistinct
date code for 1899?, and a
Burmantoft's Faience
jardiniere, rim chip, 37 cm.,
impressed marks, c. 1895.
£220-260 *SB*

A pottery Majolicaware
jardiniere and stand, in enamel
colours on a cobalt blue ground,
height 38 in. **£340-400** *JF*

A Royal Worcester jardiniere,
signed A. Hood, transfer mark
R/W England, 7 in. high. **£180-
250** *PW*

One of a pair of Worcester (Barr) flower pots
and stands, the stands incised 13, 17.5 cm.
high, c. 1805. **£500-600** the pair *C*

139

One of a pair of Berlin two-handled seaux a glaces, covers and one liner (damaged), blue sceptre mark to each piece, 23.5 cm. high, c. 1795. **£400-500** the pair. *C*

A pair of 19th C. Continental 2-handled wine coolers, decorated with interior scenes, height 14½ in. **£550-650**   *RG*

A matt and glazed Parian ice pail and cover, by Robert Williams Armstrong, registration design marks for 1868 and early Belleek mark of hound, tower and harp and Belleek, 47 cm. **£1,600-1,800** *SKC*

A pair of Derby lime-green ground bucket-shaped ice-pails, covers and liners from the Animal Service, painted by John Brewer (one base with crack to rim, one finial restored), crown, crossed batons and D marks and pattern No. 268 in puce, Duesbury & Kean, 1795-1800, 25 cm. high. **£880-980**   *C*

A pair of Worcester (Barr) ice pails, covers and liners, painted in the manner of Thomas Baxter against an orange ground, richly gilt, incised B marks, 36 cm. high, c. 1800. **£5,300-5,900**   *C*

A Theodor Deck faience double inkwell and stand, pots and base marked Th. Deck., 38 cm. across. **£130-180**   *P*

A Meissen yellow-ground gilt bronze-mounted inkstand, with chinoiserie scenes, reduced, 31 cm., underglaze blue crossed swords, mid 19th C. **£270-330**   *SB*

A Derby ink-well, painted with blue, iron-red and gilt scrolling foliage, iron-red crown, crossed batons and D mark, Robert Bloor & Co., c. 1820, 10 cm. high. **£220-260**   *C*

A Rockingham rectangular bombe desk-set, painted with bouquets of garden flowers (restored), puce marks and CL4 in iron-red, c. 1835, 23.5 cm. wide. **£500-600**   *C*

A Swansea cylindrical ink-well, with gilt line rims, resting on three paw feet, containing a later well, c. 1820, 8 cm. diam. **£320-360**   *C*

A Directoire Ormolu and Sevres porcelain encrier, the porcelain with interlaced L mark and date letter D for 1756, 10¾ in. (27 cm.) wide. **£800-900**   *C*

Chamberlains Worcester
tandish, maroon with a panel
epicting the city of Worcester,
etails in gold, width 21.6 cm.,
arly 19th C. **£170-200** *SBe*

A 19th C. porcelain inkstand,
painted in blue, maroon and gilt
(small chip). **£100-150** *PWC*

A pottery inkwell, 3½ in. (9 cm.)
high. **£40-50** *SB*

Berlin plaque, painted with
ith, impressed mark and
umerals, late 19th C., 31.5 by
.5 cm. **£800-880** *SBe*

BERLIN

- factory started in 1751 and
  was bought by Frederick the
  Great in 1763
- from 1763-1918 it was known
  as Königliche Porzellan-
  manufaktur (K.P.M.) which
  means 'Royal Porcelain
  Factory'
- many finely painted pieces —
  particularly plates and
  plaques
- from 1800-1823 the mark was
  a sceptre in red or blue
- from 1823 a Prussian
  crowned eagle mark was
  sometimes used
- after 1832 the mark of the orb
  and KPM used
- from 1837 the sceptre and
  KPM were impressed

A Berlin plaque, painted with a
portrait of Prince Albert, dated
9th Feb, '70, 26.8 by 17 cm.,
impressed KPM and sceptre,
1870. **£200-240** *SB*

Berlin religious plaque,
mpressed 'K.P.M.', 20 by 33
n., late 19th C. **£850-950**
KC

A Berlin plaque painted by L. (?)
Enfs, signed, 15.5 by 11.6 cm.,
impressed KPM and sceptre,
late 19th C., framed. **£550-
650** *SB*

A Castelli rectangular plaque,
25 cm. wide, gilt frame, c. 1750.
£1,100-1,300 *C*

A Burmantofts faience wall
plaque, 61.8 cm., impressed
Burmantofts Faience England
and 1131, c. 1895. **£120-190**
SB

Castelli plaque, painted in the
rue workshop, 25.5 cm. wide,
lt frame, c. 1750. **£1,200-
400** *C*

A Castelli rectangular plaque,
painted with a woman and
companion with cows, 23 cm.
wide, gilt frame, c. 1750.
£1,100-1,400 *C*

141

A Della Robbia plaque, artist impressed W, and painted HJ, diam. 18½ in. **£200-260**   *OL*

A Continental plaque, probab Berlin, framed 7½ by 5½ in., 1840. **£700-750**   *Cr.A*

A Delft ware plaque, with lightly scrolled raised rim, painted in tones of blue, 57 cm., late 19th C. **£110-140**   *SB*

A Derby circular plaque, painted by Jockey Hill, Duesbury & Kean, 1795-1800, giltwood frame, 14.5 cm. diam. **£950-1,050**   *C*

A Doccia plaque, with portrait busts of Empress Maria Theresa and Franz I, 12.5 cm. high, c. 1745-50. **£950-1,100** *C*

A pair of Doulton faience plaques, painted with Titani caressing the ass's head of Bottom, or Oberon, each 7¾ b 10½ in. **£700-800**   *MMB*

A Dresden plaque, painted with the Madonna and child, impressed numerals, 16 by 11.7 cm., late 19th C., framed. **£160-210**   *SBe*

A terracotta relief panel, incised H. Doulton & Co., Lambeth, G. Tinworth and monogram, in original frame, 32 by 15 cm., c. 1875-81. **£150-200**   *SB*

A late 19th C. Dresden plaqu painted with 'The Three Fates painted initials L.C.M.K., 22 l 14.7 cm., giltwood frame. **£26** 320   *SBe*

A pair of French plaques, each in a gold coloured frame under a convex glass, overall diam. 41.5 cm., late 19th C. **£280-320** *SBe*

A pair of Furstenberg biscuit plaques, modelled by J. C. Rombrich with busts of King George III and Queen Sophia Charlotte (minor damage), gol script F marks, c. 1785, 11.5 cm high. **£700-850**   *C*

Meissen rectangular plaque, ted in the style of Perugino, y 41 cm., crossed swords in erglaze blue, late 19th C., ned. **£200-240** *SB*

A Martin Brothers stoneware wall plaque, in brown, blue and cream against a buff ground, 25.5 cm., incised R.W. Martin & Brothers, London & Southall, dated 10-1887. **£250-300** *SB*

A Mettlach circular plaque, decorated after Stahl, moulded signature, in diaphanous white relief against a grey-green ground, 46.8 cm., impressed mark and 2443, c. 1910. **£450-650** *SB*

Mintons earthenware plaque, nted by E. Moira, signed, pressed Mintons, painted ailer's mark for T. Goode & ., London, dated 1875, ginal wood frame, 40.5 by .3 cm. **£230-270** *SB*

A rare Pratt plaque 'The Last One In' after W. Mulready, c. 1860. **£260-290** *MB*

A Pratt plaque, of typical colours: ochre yellow and deep blue, 10 in. high, c. 1810. **£250-280** *AD*

Siena plaque, framed, 16 cm. ., c. 1680. **£500-600** *C*

A pair of Siena plaques, painted with figures in river landscapes (one broken in two and repaired), 17.5 cm. diam., c. 1740. **£990-1,200** *C*

care Sunderland lustre plaque Queen Charlotte, c. 1815, 5 in. gh. **£260-285** *AD*

A pair of 'Vienna' circular wall plaques, painted by Josef Lang, signed, on a gilt ground, 35.8 and 37 cm., painted shield and title, impressed mark obliterated, late 19th C. **£1,100-1,300** *SB*

A 'Sevres' oval plaque, painted with a scene of 18th C. rustic lovers, on bleu-celeste ground, 38.5 cm., late 19th C., framed. **£280-360** *SBe*

A Vinovo plaque, painted with a mountainous wooded river landscape, black V mark above D.G., c. 1800, giltwood frame, 19 by 24 cm. wide. **£410-520** *C*

A set of Copeland yellow ground tiles, each transfer printed and painted, rim chip, 15.2 cm., impressed Copeland Fresco, c. 1878. **£330-400** *SB*

A Bristol manganese Delft tile with goat, c. 1750's. **£60-90** *JH*

A pair of Dutch Delft framed tile pictures, painted in manganese (four tiles cracked, glaze chips), c. 1750, each about 39 cm. high. **£900-1,100** *C*

A continental tile panel, consisting twelve Delft ware tiles, in bright colours 53 by 39.5 cm., late 19th C. set in a wood mount and frame. **£225-275** *SB*

ENGLISH DELFTWARE TILES

- Tinglazed tiles were produced from the late 16th C./early 17th C.
- English delftware tiles mainly produced in 18th C.
- main centres London, Bristol and Liverpool, although a factory at Wincanton was open for a few years in the mid 18th C.
- the London production in the 18th C. was mainly from Lambeth
- a factory at Brislington was set up in the mid 17th C. which lasted until c. 1750
- in 1683 Edward Ward set up a pottery in Bristol — this lasted until 1780's
- in 1712 a pottery was started in Liverpool; in 1750 there was a large quantity of delft produced but by the 1770's the popularity of the new porcelain and creamware caused the factories to close
- up to c. 1740 most English delftware closely followed Dutch designs and styles
- English delftware is always duller than Dutch Delft
- 'Chinese' decoration was always popular from the very early days of delft
- by 1740 the English potters had perfected a very high quality of Chinese motifs
- after 1740 a more English style of landscape painting evolved
- 'botanical' flowers very rare on English delftware — the flower painting tends to be very stylised
- religious subjects very popular on tiles

A large and rare Royal Worcester circular wall pla painted by H. Davis, sign 40.5 cm., printed crowned c mark, date code for 1906. **£1,000-1,200** *SB*

An 18th C. Dutch Delft blue a white tile. **£20-25** *Cl.A*

An 18th C. Bristol blue and white Delft tile. **£18-22** *Cl.*

A Lambeth blue and white De tile. **£25-30** *JH*

A Lambeth blue and white d tile, c. 1750's. **£15-20** *J.H*

A Liverpool blue and white
Delft tile, powdered blue. £30-
35   *JH*

An 18th C. Liverpool Sadler &
Green printed Aesop's Fable
tile. £55-65   *Cl.A*

n 18th C. Liverpool Delft blue
nd white tile. £14-18   *Cl.A*

An 18th C. Liverpool
olychrome Delft tile,
'azackerly colours. £95-105
Cl.A

A Liverpool woodblock
transfer-printed tile, 1757.
£200-250   *JH*

A Liverpool polychrome Delft
tile with bird, c. 1760's. £120-
160   *JH*

A Liverpool Delft tile, transfer
rinted in black with 'Man
ancing to the Bagpipes' (slight
im chip), signed J. Sadler,
iverpool, c. 1760, 12.5 cm. wide.
70-100   *C*

A Liverpool Delft tile, transfer
printed in black with a rustic
couple with garlands of flowers
under a tree (minute rim
flaking), signed Sadler Liverp.
1, c. 1760, 12.5 cm. wide. £50-
100   *C*

A Liverpool polychrome Delft
tile with figures, c. 1760's.
£200-240   *JH*

Liverpool Delft tile, transfer-
rinted in black with
hinoiserie scene, woman with
macaw and child, by John
adler, c. 1760, 12.5 cm. wide.
55-70   *C*

***Make the most of
Miller's***

*When buying or selling, it
must always be remembered
that prices can be greatly
affected by the condition of
any piece.
Unless otherwise stated, all
goods shown in Miller's are
of good merchantable
quality, and the valuations
given reflect this fact.
Pieces offered for sale in
exceptionally fine condition
or in poor condition may
reasonably be expected to be
priced considerably higher
or lower respectively than
the estimates given herein.*

A set of 6 painted nursery
rhyme tiles, with illustrations
adapted from 'The Baby's
Bouquet' by Walter Crane
(minor chips), 15.3 cm., moulded
marks 'Minton Hollins & Co.,
Patent Tile Works Stoke-on-
Trent', painted monogram
'MN', c. 1870. £350-450   *SB*

A plate to commemorate Queen
Victoria's 'Glorious reign of 60
years', 1897, 6½ in. **£45-50**
Brit

BRITISH COMMEMORATIVE POTTERY

- the earliest wares available to collectors tend to be the blue-dash chargers of the late 17th C.
- since the Lipski collection sale English delftware has been fetching much higher prices — blue and white pieces however, do not seem to have increased at the same rate
- there has always been a strong royalist or political theme on chargers
- of the blue dash chargers the 'Royals' tend to be more valuable than, say, the Duke of Marlborough and the late delft dishes with Queen Anne or George I are very sought after
- delft has rarely come through

- the last 200 years without some damage and this does not severely affect value, the rarity of the subject being the most vital point
- electioneering plates of the mid 18th C. were in limited supply and are hence much in demand
- the end of the century saw a great increase in naval and military items
- the 19th C. saw an absolute glut of 'royal' items, particularly of Victoria
- these should only be bought in good condition
- Jubilee items tend to be at a premium as American collectors have always sought them out

A plate to commemorate Queen
Victoria's Diamond Jubilee,
1897, 7 in. **£65-70**   *Brit*

A plate to commemorate the
death of Gladstone, died May
19th, 1898, 8½ in. **£30-35**   *Brit*

A Foley china plate to
commemorate the death of
Queen Victoria, 9 in. **£55-60**
Brit

A rare pair of 'Caroline' plates,
16.3 cm., c. 1821. **£250-320**
SB

A plate to commemorate the
death of King Edward VII, died
May 6th, 1910, 10 in. wide. **£50-60**   *Brit*

A Wedgwood plate to
commemorate the coronation o
George V, June 22nd, 1911, 10
in. **£50-60**   *Brit*

A plate to commemorate the
Coronation of King George VI
and Queen Elizabeth, May
12th, 1937, 10½ in. **£70-80**
Brit

A Paragon china baby plate
commemorate 'Our Empire's
Little Princess' April 21st, 192
8½ in. wide. **£50-60**   *Brit*

A commemorative tin glaze jug,
with masonic emblems, dated
1778 (chipped), 7½ in. **£180-210**   *MB*

A Sidney Smith, Battle of Acre 799 commemorative Parian ug, 6 in. **£65-70** *Brit*

A pink lustreware jug to ommemorate the death of King ieorge IV, c. 1830's, 7 in. **£200-85** *Brit*

An Aynsley & Co. inscribed and lated jug, the cerise-ground oody reserved with a panel of a gilt inscription, 22.5 cm., 1861. **£100-120** *SB*

A mid-19th C. Sunderland commemorative jug, 6 in. **£250-320** *LAC*

A rare 'Caroline' and 'Brougham' jug, transfer-printed in blue, restored, 14 cm., c. 1820. **£200-260** *SB*

A rare Sunderland 'Coal Trade' jug, printed and painted, inscribed 'Sunderland Coal Trade' and 'Alexr. & Margaret McDonald', 17.2 cm., c. 1820. **£90-120** *SB*

A Van Amberg commemorative jug, c. 1840, 6½ in. high. **£90-95** *Gs*

A W. E. Gladstone jug, made by Hackney & Co., Longton, 1868, 5 in. high. **£45-50** *Brit*

A Cheetham and Robinson Commemorative Jug, for the coronation of William IV and Adelaide, transfer-printed in lilac, some damage, 18.5 cm., c. 1831. **£200-250** *SB*

A late 18th C. Pratt ware commemorative jug, 6½ in. **£100-150** *SBA*

A 'Caroline Green-Bag' batprinted jug, the reverse with a verse and inscribed 'Long Live Caroline, Queen of England', the shoulder and rim in copper lustre, loop handle, slight wear, 12 cm., c. 1820. **£220-280** *SB*

A Commemorative and Reform jug made on the occasion of the Coronation of William IV and Adelaide, transfer-printed in puce, 17.5 cm., c. 1831. **£200-250** *SB*

A commemorative jug, Queen Victoria's 60 years reign, late 1890's, 6 in. tall. **£35-40** *Brit*

A Doulton Lambeth stoneware jug, commemorating Victoria's diamond jubilee, with a motto, 19.50 cm. high, Doulton, Lambeth, England. **£110-160** *P*

A J. & M. P. Bell 'Victoria' commemorative jug, 8 in. tall **£35-40** *Brit*

A coloured Jubilee mug 1887, 3½ in. **£45-50** *Brit*

A Roosevelt small jug, made by Thorley, 3 in. **£35-40** *Brit*

A H.R.H. Prince of Wales jug, 5 in. **£25-30** *Brit*

A mug to commemorate the 60 years reign of Queen Victoria, 3½ in. **£35-40** *Brit*

A Victoria Diamond Jubilee mug, late 1890's, 3½ in. **£35-40** *Brit*

A souvenir mug of Queen Victoria 1837-1897, Empress of India, 4 in. **£65-70** *Brit*

A Victoria Diamond Jubilee mug, late 1890's, 3 in. **£45-50** *Brit*

A commemorative mug on the Coronation of King George VI and Queen Elizabeth, May 12th, 1937, 3¼ in. **£65-70** *Brit*

A mug to commemorate Queen Victoria's Diamond Jubilee Year, 1897, 3¼ in. **£35-40** *Brit*

A Coronation memorial mug of King Edward VII and Queen Alexandra, 1902, 3 in. **£35-40** *Brit*

A Winston Churchill mug, 4 in.
£25-30   *Brit*

A mug to commemorate the
Coronation of King George V
and Queen Mary, June 22nd,
1911, 3 in. £30-35   *Brit*

A mug to commemorate the
visit of George V and Queen
Mary to Stoke-on-Trent. April
22nd and 23rd 1913, 3 in. £45-
50   *Brit*

A rare Copeland
commemorative tyg, marking
the termination of the Boer War
(rim restored), 15.5 cm., printed
Copeland, edition de luxe, No.
44 of 100, T. Goode & Co., South
Audley Street, London, c. 1902.
£250-300   *SB*

A shaving mug to
commemorate the coronation of
King George VI and Queen
Elizabeth, 1937, 4 in. £24-30
Brit

A Victoria 60 glorious years
commemorative beaker, 1897, 4
in. £35-40   *Brit*

A Blairs commemorative small
vase, 3 in. £15-20   *Brit*

A large Staffordshire 'Prize-
Fighters' loving cup, printed in
black and naively coloured,
interior restored, 18 cm., c. 1840.
£250-300   *SB*

A MacIntyre ashtray, with
inscription 'A gentleman in
kharki', and poem by R. Kipling
on reverse, 5 in. wide. £25-30
Brit

A Denby and Codnor Park
stoneware reform flask of
'Daniel O'Connell Esq.' holding
an unfurled scroll, impressed
Denby and Codnor Park,
Bournes Potteries, Derbyshire,
8 in., c. 1833-61. **£110-160**
Bon

A commemorative bowl, Queen
Victoria's 60 glorious years, 6
in. tall. £35-40   *Brit*

A 'Hitler's Terror' bulldog, c.
1940's, 6 in. £35-40   *Brit*

Two Victorian fairings; l. 'The Last in bed to put out the light' £30-45; r. 'An Awkward Interruption'. £40-60   *LAC*

'Pluck' and 'The Decided Smash', two fairings, titled in black script, minor chip, 13.5 cm., impressed 3352 and incised 3553, c. 1900. £60-90   *SB*

Two Victorian fairings; l. 'Who is coming?'. £40-60; r. 'Three o'clock in the morning'. £30-50   *LAC*

A pig-fairing: a spill-vase group of two baby pigs seated beneath an umbrella. £30-80   *CSK*

'Kiss Me Quick' and 'Takin The Cream', titled in black script, the second restored, and 8.8 cm., the first incise 2665, c. 1900. £40-60   *SB*

A car with two 'piggies', 5 in. wide. £30-40   *Brit*

Miller's Antiques Price Guide builds up year by year to form the most comprehensive photo-reference system available. The first three volumes contain over 20,000 completely different photographs.

'Lor! Three Legs! I'll charge 2d.!', titled in black script, 11 cm., incised 3313, c. 1900. £60-80   *SB*

'Who is Coming?' and 'Sarah Young Man', both titled in black script, the second damaged, 9 cm., the first with printed mark, the second incised 2877, c. 1910. £50-70   *SB*

A pair of 19th C. fairings, 'Tug of War' and 'Spoils of War', restored. £55-65   *CS* if perfect. £150-200

'Favourable Opportunity', a Conta & Boehm fairing, title in black script, 8.6 cm. c. 189 £50-70   *SB*

Arctic Expedition, a small pot lid, with double line border (rim crazed). £450-500 *SB*

Great Exhibition 1851 (opening ceremony), a large lid. £220-260 *SB*

Polar Bears, a small pot lid, with gilt line border, painted in black, blue and green. £270-320 *SB*

Bear Hunting, a small pot lid, retailers inscription Ross & Sons, gilt line border. £320-380 *SB*

Harriet Beecher Stowe, a rare large lid with a well-defined print. £1,200-1,500 *SB*

Interior View of The Crystal Palace, a large pot lid. £320-400 *SB*

Exhibition Buildings 1851, a large pot lid. £440-540 *SB*

'Albert Edward, Prince of Wales and Princess Alexandra, on their marriage in 1863': a medium lid with floral border. £120-150 *CSK*

Dublin Industrial Exhibition 1853, a large pot lid. £160-180 *SB*

A Pratt pot lid 'Contrast', c. 1860. £53-65 *MB*

'Queen Victoria and the Prince Consort': a large lid with blue acorn leaf border and base. £120-150 *CSK*

Pegwell Bay (S. Banger Shrimp Sauce Manufacturer), a rare large pot lid, with a clear print. £580-680 *SB*

Belle Vue Tavern (with Tatnell's Cart), a rare large pot lid, with a clear print. £600-720 *SB*

The Late Duke of Wellington, a large pot lid, without sash, marbled border. £180-220 *SB*

A False Move, an unusual large pot lid. **£150-200** *SB*

Alma, a large lid with additional leaf and formal borders, retailer's mark for Robert Feast, 15 & 16, Pavement, Finsbury Square, London. **£800-900** *SB*

Queen Victoria On Balcony, large pot lid of the first versio (rim stained). **£110-130** *S*

A Pratt pot lid of 'Two Allied Generals, Lord Raglan and General Canrobert', c. 1860. **£78-88** *MB*

'Contrast' a medium lid. **£50-70** *SKC*

'I see you my boy'; medium lid. **£45-55** *SBA*

'Cattle and ruins'; a large lid with additional fancy border. **£35-45** *CSK*

'Tam o'Shanter and Souter Johnny'; medium lid. **£70-80** *SBA*

'A letter from the Diggings'; medium lid with line and dotted border. **£35-45** *SKC*

'The Wolf and the Lamb'; a medium lid with line and dot border. **£35-45** *CSK*

'Old Jack'; a small lid with double-line border. **£130-160** *CSK*

'Ann Hathaway's Cottage'; medium lid, pearl dot border. **£35-45** *SBA*

'The Village Wakes'; a small lid with fancy border. **£100-120** *SBA*

'The Parish Beadle'; small lid. **£80-100** *SBA*

'The Enthusiast'; a medium lid. **£35-45** *SKC*

'Blind man's Buff'; a small lid with registration mark and title. **£110-150** *CSK*

'The bull fight'; a late large lid with decorative border. **£45-65** *SBA*

'Dangerous Skating'; a small lid. **£45-65** *SBA*

'Alas! poor Bruin'; a small lid with lantern on the end of the inn sign (produced by the Pratt factory, c. 1850). **£50-70** *CSK*

'Bears at school'; a small lid with frame (Pratt factory). **£50-70** *CSK*

A Staffordshire pot lid and pot, 'Hide and Seek', No. 255, 4 in. (pot damaged). **£30-40** *WHL*

A Pratt pot lid and base with verse and titled 'Our Home'. **£280-310** *MB*

A small black and white lid, showing hounds hunting bears. **£140-160** *SBA*

A small black and white lid, 'Genuine Russian Bears Grease'; key fret border. **£45-65** *SBA*

'Shooting Bears'; small lid. **£70-90** *SBA*

'Royal Harbour, Ramsgate'; a large lid with base. **£20-30** *SKC*

'New Jetty and Pier, Margate'; large lid (probably produced by the Cauldon factory, c. 1850-60). **£50-70** *SBA*

'Grand International Buildings of 1851'; with double line border. **£50-70** *SBA*

'Philadelphia Exhibition 1876'; medium lid. **£50-70** *SBA*

'England's Pride'; a medium lid with black background. **£95-125** *CSK*

'Wellington' (with clasped hands); a large lid with additional laurel leaf border and red berries. **£140-170** *CSK*

The Outs, a small pot lid. **£90 120** *SB*

'A Gay Dog'; small lid, pot li rim damaged. **£900-1,000** *SBA*

'The Late Duke of Wellington' large lid, with sash, marbled border. **£70-100** *SBA*

'Dr. Johnson'; a medium lid with line and dot border. **£25-35** *CSK*

'The Late Prince Consort'; a medium lid with laurel leaf anc berry border. **£30-50** *CSK*

'Tria Juncta in Uno'; Three united in one, large lid. **£200-230** *SBA*

'Allied Generals'; large lid, with laurel leaf border. **£60-80** *SBA*

'Osborne House'; large lid. **£50 70** *SBA*

'Strathfieldsay'; a large lid. **£50-75** *SBA*

'Embarking for the East'; medium lid. **£50-70** *CSK*

'Meeting of Garibaldi and Victor Emmanuel'; a medium lid with double-line border. **£25-45** *CSK*

'War'; a medium lid, signed J. Austin, with line and dot border. **£35-45** *CSK*

(l) An Arcadian crested piano.
£5-10 *Brit*

(r) A Sylvan crested golf ball.
£10-15 *Brit*

(l) An Arcadian map of the Isle
of Wight. £10-15 *Brit*

(r) A crested tennis racket. £5-
10 *Brit*

(l) A crested soldier. £20-25
Brit

(r) A Carlton crested grenade.
£10-15 *Brit*

CRESTED WARE

- from the late 19th C. to World War II, souvenir shops had a vast display of crested china, bearing the crest of the town
- damage is important on crested ware, therefore avoid any rubbing, chips, cracks or faded crests
- many famous names had followed the enterprising W. H. Goss in producing these small, inexpensive presents, Arcadian, Swan, Crescent, Carlton, Clifton, Shelley, Podmore, Grafton, Willow, etc.
- after George Jones and Sons Ltd. bought W. H. Goss Ltd., they continued to use the Goss mark and moulds but usually included the word 'England'
- 'theme' collecting is very popular, 'military', 'historical', 'buildings' or coat-of-arms of a specific town

(l) An Arcadian crested boater.
£10-15 *Brit*

(r) A Carlton crested cap. £10-
15 *Brit*

(l) A Carlton china crested lion.
£15-20 *Brit*

(r) A Clifton crested model of
colonial hat. £12-15 *Brit*

Right
An Arcadian souvenir mug,
with cats, 3 in. high. £15-20
Brit

(l) A small crested pipe and
stand. £5-8 *Brit*

(r) An Arcadian china crested
model of British aerial torpedo.
£15-20 *Brit*

St. Nicholas Chapel,
Ilfracombe, grey roof, beige
walls, terracotta and green
details, unglazed, 7.2 cm.,
printed goshawk and title, early
20th C. £110-160 *SB*

(l) An Arcadian crested
model of gunner and
machine gun. £25-
30 *Brit*

(r) An Alexandra china
crested plane, 6 in.
long. £23-28 *Brit*

Goss Oven, grey roof,
terracotta brickwork,
green details, arms of
Blackpool, 7.6 cm.
printed goshawk and
title, early 20th C.
£140-180 *SB*

The Old Smithy, Gullane, a rare
model, red, beige and black
(minor chip), 7.2 cm., printed
goshawk and title, early 20th C.
£130-190 if perfect £500-600
SB

(tl) Dove Cottage, Grasmere, grey-tiled roof, green foliage and brown details, unglazed, 10 cm., printed goshawk and title, early 20th C. **£380-450** *SB*

(tr) Prince Llewellyn's House, Beddgelert, grey roof, beige walls, blue and terracotta details, unglazed, 6 cm., printed goshawk and title, early 20th C. **£160-200** *SB*

(bl) Old Maid's Cottage, Lee, straw-coloured roof, green creeper, pale-blue and terracotta details, unglazed, 7.4 cm., printed goshawk and title, early 20th C. **£80-100** *SB*

(br) Ann Hathaway's Cottage and Shakespeare's House, both with typical colours, both unglazed, 6.4 and 7.7 cm., both with printed goshawk and title, early 20th C. **£160-190** *SB*

Doctor Samuel Johnson's House, Lichfield, red-tiled roof, beige walls, brown details, unglazed, 7.5 cm., printed goshawk and title, early 20th C. **£140-180** *SB*

Cat-and-Fiddle Inn, Buxton, unglazed, 6.7 cm., printed goshawk mark and title, early 20th C. **£200-250** *SB*

A Meissen model of a town house, in iron-red, buff and white (chipped), c. 1748, 18 cm. high. **£2,000-2,200** *C*

A rare Prattware church pastille burner, with open door, c. 1790, 9 in. **£385-415** *CS*

A Yorkshire pastille burner with detachable roof, c. 1810, slight restoration to roof, 4½ in. **£250-270** *CS*

A pastille burner, in the form of a lodge (chips), 13 cm., mid-19th C. **£170-200** *SB*

A pastille burner and cover, in the form of a blue-walled cottage, the details gilt (hair cracks), 14 cm., mid-19th C. **£290-330** *SB*

A good pastille burner and cover, probably Coalport (minor chips), 11.5 cm., c. 1830 **£400-450** *SB*

pastille burner, in the form of rustic cottage (minor amage), 11.2 cm., c. 1830. **280-340** *SB*

A Staffordshire cottage, with pierced windows, c. 1830-40, 4 in. high. **£80-100** *AD*

A Staffordshire cottage, with good painting and detail, c. 1830-40, 4¾ in. high. **£130-140** *AD*

A Staffordshire money bank, 7¾ in. high, c. 1840. **£325-375** *AD*

A Staffordshire cottage, with good number and condition of flowers, 6¾ in., c. 1835. **£120-150** *AD*

A Staffordshire cottage moneybank, with plain back, 5 in. **£40-50** *AD*

A Staffordshire cottage, with detachable roof, 5 in. high (cracks on base), c. 1830. **£145-165** *AD*

STAFFORDSHIRE COTTAGES

- often taken to be Rockingham although no marked piece has been found
- peak of popularity 1810-1840
- later examples tend to be of much poorer quality
- condition is very important as is rarity of subject
- the cottages are more valuable if;
  - they are completely decorated all the way round
  - they have more pieces, flowers, sheep, dogs etc.
  - they have pierced windows and detachable roofs
- if damaged;
  - crack on base, not too bad
  - slight damage to flowers, acceptable
  - severe damage to flowers can halve value

A Staffordshire cottage, in green, orange, gilt and white with multi-coloured bocage, c. 1850, 7½ in. high. **£85-95** *WA*

A Staffordshire cottage with figure and sheep (chimney restuck), 4 in. high. **£110-125** *AD*

A Staffordshire cottage, with pierced windows, 6½ in., c. 1860. **£40-50** *CS*

A Staffordshire cottage, with pierced windows, c. 1840, 5 in. high. **£130-145**   *AD*

A good and rare Staffordshire cottage, with detachable roof and good decoration (with eggs in nests under eaves), c. 1830, 5½ in. **£200-230**   *AD*

A Staffordshire cottage, wit applied flowers, c. 1830-40, 5 **£75-85**   *AD*

A Staffordshire cottage, mid-19th C. **£45-50**   *Cl.A*

One of a pair of Staffordshire cottages, c. 1830-40, 4½ in. high. **£200-230** pair   *AD*

A Staffordshire Russian fortress of Sebastapol in t Crimea, c. 1854, 10 in. hig **£110-130**   *WA*

A Chelsea chicken box and cover, in yellow, grey and iron-red (small restoration to rims and tail), red anchor period, c. 1755, 9.5 cm. wide. **£1,700-1,850**   *C*

A Staffordshire castle with piercing, c. 1830-40, 3½ in. high. **£95-105**   *AD*

A Frankfurt spice box, of tin glazed earthenware, the side painted in blue with a Chine river scene, 11¼ in. numeral mark 6 or 9, late 17th C. **£23 300**   *L*

A Meissen pate-sur-pate box and cover, on yellow ground, c. 1860, 4 in. diam. **£330-360** *Cr.A*

A 'Sevres' box, the gilt-metal cover painted by Delys, sign painted interlaced L's, printe pseudo Chateau des Tuilerie mark, 14.5 cm., late 19th C. **£360-440**   *SB*

A Copenhagen snuff-box and cover, modelled as the head of a dog, 6.5 cm. wide, c. 1793. **£380-500**   *C*

A blue and white transfer bourdalou, 'The Bridge and Pagoda pattern', by Thomas and John Curry, c. 1818. **£100-115**   *Gs*

A large Doulton font, by Lily Partington, impressed 1931, 5½ in. high. **£120-140**   *Brit*

A Doulton font, by Florrie Jones, 3 in. high. **£40-50**   *Brit*

A Meissen shaped cinquefoil spittoon, painted with scattered deutsche Blumen, the rim gilt (chips to leaves), blue crossed swords mark, c. 1745, 13 cm. high. **£620-750**   *C*

A Meissen tray, 43.5 cm., crossed swords mark in blue and impressed 54. **£650-800** *P*

A rare Staffordshire garniture by Obadiah Sherratt of Turkish and travelling musicians, 9 in. at tallest (small amount of damage), c. 1810. **£900-1,000**   *MB*

A Du Paquier 'schwarzlot' shaped oval bourdalou (extensively repaired), c. 1725, 21.5 cm. wide. **£1,000-1,200** *C*

A Vincennes bourdalou, painted in the Meissen style (hair crack and rim chips), c. 1750, 21 cm. wide. **£380-450** *C*

A Vincennes circular chamberpot (pot de chambre rond), the sides painted in the Meissen style, the rim gilt (extensively cracked, rim chip repaired), elaborate interlaced L mark, 1750-53, 20 cm. wide. **£100-115**   *C*

A Minton-style garden seat, unmarked, c. 1850-60. **£180-190**   *MT*

A 19th C. blue and white china foot bath, 18 by 14 in. **£400-480**   *BW*

A Coalport claret-ground racing trophy and cover, inscribed 'Pains Lane Races Sept. 27th, 1853', the cover gilt with a band of trailing vine, 29 cm. high. **£980-1,080**   *C*

A 'Vienna' oval tray, painted by Berger, signed, shield in underglaze blue, painted title 'Amor auf Reisen', further inscribed Rob. Pilz, Wein, 42.8 cm., late 19th C. **£280-330** *SBe*

A late 19th C. Majolica jardiniere stand, in shades of green, brown and ochre, 53 cm. **£200-250**   *SBe*

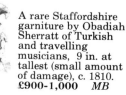

A Brown-Westhead & Moore
majolica garden seat,
impressed Brown-Westhead,
Moore & Co., 18¾ in., late 19th
C. **£88-100**   *SBA*

A Meissen outside-decorated
oval tray, 44 cm. over handles,
cancelled crossed swords in
underglaze blue, late 19th C.
£160-200   *SB*

A Royal Worcester lotus flo
holder, 27 cm., impressed a
printed crowned circle,
decorator's monogram for
James Callowhill, shape
number 765, date cyphers f
1880 and 1881. **£200-250**

A pair of Minton majolica
garden seats, in blue, ochre,
brown and green (one with
chipped foot), 46.2 cm.,
impressed Minton and date
code for 1861. **£600-750**   *SB*

A Doulton stoneware posy
holder, modelled by George
Tinworth, minor chips to wings,
13 cm., impressed Lambeth
mark, dated 1878. **£320-400**
SB

A Chelsea thimble, painted
with the inscription 'Pour Ma
Belle', the indented rim
enriched in green and gilt, c.
1760, in hinged silver-gilt
filigree case, c. 1700, 2 cm. high.
£1,300-1,400   *C*

A Meissen needle case, pain
with Watteau figures, with g
mounts, 10 cm. high, c. 176
£800-1,000   *C*

A Furstenberg gold-mounted
etui, painted with sprays of
single flowers and fruit (cover
cracked), 11 cm. long, c. 1760.
£120-190   *C*

A Staffordshire cradle in green
glaze, of Ralph Wood type, c.
1800. **£140-160**   *AD*

A pair of Liverpool Delft
polychrome wall pockets, c.
1760-70. **£600-900** pair   *JH*

A 1940's terracotta wall mask of
Rita Hayworth, 13 in. high.
£25-30   *LEX*

An unusual Doulton Burslem wall pocket, probably designed by C. J. Noke, 30 cm. across, rosette and crown mark. £140-200 *P*

A Royal Doulton miniature face mask, 7 cm. high, Royal Doulton, England, HN 1612. £90-140 *P*

An unusual Clarice Cliff wall mask, heightened in colours, printed marks. £80-120 *P*

A Royal Doulton ashtray, in glazed blue, 4½ in. diam. £20-25 *Brit*

A Royal Doulton ashtray, specially designed for Wright's Coal Tar Soap, 6 in. long. £40-50 *Brit*

A Royal Doulton Lambeth ashtray titled 'Silver Seal Port', 5 in. diam. £140-150 *Brit*

A Doulton painted student's lamp, on dark blue ground, with gilding, signed J. H. Plant, 20½ in. high. £300-350 *SV*

A Doulton stoneware oil-lamp base, incised by Mark V. Marshall in royal blue, green and brown, with gilt metal supports and base, 38 cm., impressed Lambeth mark, incised J and artists initials, RB and KH, dated 1884, with liner. £180-220 *SB*

A pair of gilt-bronze-mounted porcelain lamps, painted on a pale blue ground, fitted for electricity, the mounts English, the vases 71 cm., c. 1880. £950-1,100 *SB*

Eighteen Meissen knife and fork handles, with sprays of Deutsche Blumen above an Ozier band and gilt monogram J.F., all have gilt metal blades and forks, the porcelain, c. 1745, 8.5-9 cm. long. £800-900 *C*

A Meissen chinoiserie small bell, painted in the manner of C. F. Herold, blue crossed swords mark, 1735-40, with wooden clapper, 11 cm. high. £2,600-3,200 *C*

A pair of Mintons 'Henri Deux' salts, by Charles Toft, signed (minor chips), 13 cm., inlaid 'Mintons' and 'C. Toft', c. 1875. £370-450 *SB*

A Staffordshire watchholder 'The Welsh Legend of Beddgelert', c. 1810, 10 in. high. £80-100 *WA*

Two 18th C. Pratt Bonbonnieres, c. 1780 (screw tops missing), 3 in. **£140-160** each   *CS*

A Yorkshire pottery clock, in Pratt style — late and crudely decorated, c. 1825, 8 in. high. **£120-140**   *AD*

A Caughley blue and whit asparagus server, with 'Fisherman' pattern, c. 17 **£48-54**   *CH*

A Zsolnay Pecs umbrella stand (restored), 54 cm., printed spire mark, c. 1880. **£350-420**   *SB*

A rare set of 3 Castleford obelisks, painted in colours on all four faces with musical trophies and river scenes, 8¾ and 11¼ in. **£850-1,050**   *L*

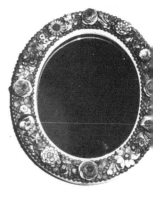

A Meissen mirror frame, c. 18 13 in. high. **£500-560**   *LA*

A Staffordshire stirrup cup, c. 1860. **£75-85**   *LAC*

A George Tinworth Doulton 'Monkey' bibelot, entitled 'Sa Travelling', signed with monogram, 18 cm., incised Doulton's Ltd., Lambeth, and FJ, initials for Florrie Jones, 1890. **£770-900**   *SB*

A Royal Crown Derby miniature watering can, decorated with an Imari pattern, printed marks including date code for 1917, 3 in. **£210-260**   *SBA*

One of a pair of Clarice Cliff 'Bizarre' porcelain bookends, modelled as a country cottage in greens, orange, blue and black, printed factory marks, 13.5 cm. high. **£70-130** the pair   *P*

A hand-painted Coalport shoe, c. 1895, 6 in. long. **£200-230** *MB*

A Yorkshire Iron, c. 1820, 2½ i high. **£25-30**   *CS*

SOME ENGLISH PORCELAIN MARKS

PILKINGTON'S

P

c. 1897-1904

Printed 1904-5, impressed 1905-1914

Impressed c. 1914-38

1948-1957

LONGTON HALL

Most pieces unmarked. Painted in Underglaze blue c. 1749-55

CHELSEA

Incised triangle c. 1745-50

Raised anchor c. 1749-52

Red anchor c. 1752-56

Gold anchor c. 1756-69

CAUGHLEY

SALOPIAN
Impressed name mark c. 1775-80

S So Sx
Painted or printed 'S' marks c. 1775-95

C C
Printed and painted 'C' mark c. 1775-90

BOW

Most Bow porcelain is unmarked.

Early incised marks c. 1750

Painted anchor and dagger marks c. 1760-76

For more information see: 'Encyclopaedia of British Pottery and Porcelain Marks' by Geoffrey A. Godden.

WORCESTER

Blue c. 1755-90

hand painted in blue c. 1755-75

printed or painted in blue c. 1755-70

C
Flight

blue painted c. 1783-88

blue painted c. 1783-92

Flight·

FLIGHT
painted c. 1783-92

BFB
Barr, Flight & Barr c. 1807-1813

FBB
Flight, Barr & Barr c. 1813-40

Kerr & Binns c. 1852-62

arked wares have to be treated with caution as many factories in the 18th C. copied more
ccessful factory marks. Closer attention should be paid to the body, glaze and shape in order
ascertain the factory. The mark should only be used as a final check. Many recent discoveries
ve changed previously held beliefs, e.g. the disguised numeral mark, once held to be
ughley and now known to be Worcester. It is also true that a large number of 18th C. wares
re unmarked.

DERBY

Chelsea-Derby 1769-84

Incised mark c. 1770-80

Painted mark c. 1770-82

Painted mark c. 1782-1825

Printed mark c. 1820-40

Printed mark in red c. 1825-40

Printed mark in red c. 1830-48

King Street Factory 1861-1935

CHINESE PORCELAIN

The Chinese had perfected the techniques of porcelain making during the T'ang dynasty (A.D. 618-906). The potters of the Sung dynasty (A.D. 960-1279) made exquisite pieces for the Imperial Court. In the Yuan dynasty (1280-1368) underglaze painting had been developed.

The Ming dynasty was established in 1368 by Chu Yuang-chang (Hung-wu). By this time the potters had developed a beautiful translucent porcelain. The body of the early wares often burnt a pale orange colour at the base and the glazes were slightly greyish in

tone. In the 15th C. the glazes were much thicker and this sometimes allowed the blue to merge slightly which gives a wonderful deep colour to this class of porcelain. By this time much porcelain was being exported.

By the end of the 15th C. in the reign of Ch'eng-hua the first enamel decorated porcelain was produced.

The late Ming period from the Emperors Hung-chih to Wan-li, saw the greatest expansion of export ware. The later Ming wares have a deep purplish-blue hue (although this tends to look rather

watered down) and often have sand from the saggers on the fo⌐ rims.

The later Chinese wares tended t⌐ be mass produced for export, ofte⌐ to specific demands from the traders. It should be noted that Chinese potters frequently used the marks of earlier dynasties o⌐ their wares. This was not the wor⌐ of a faker. The Chinese believe⌐ they should venerate the skills ⌐ previous generations and when piece was done in a particular style the mark of the Emperor wh⌐ was reigning at that time was added.

A blue and white 'Rotterdam Riot' Plate, encircled Chenghua six-character mark, Kangxi, c. 1690-5, 8 in. diam. **£750-900** *C*

One of a pair of Chinese Imari plates, painted in underglaze-blue, iron-red and gilt, after 'La Dame au Parasol' by Cornelius Pronk (cracked, some rim restoration), early Qianlong, 9¼ in. diam. **£700-900** pair   *C*

One of a pair of 'famille ros⌐ armorial plates (one with ri⌐ chip) Qianlong, c. 1740, 9 in. diam. **£480-580** pair   *C*

Six Chinese Imari plates, painted in underglaze blue, iron-red and gilt (one cracked, three chipped), early 18th C., 10½ in. (27.5 cm.) diam. **£450-550**   *C*

An armorial plate, painted in 'famille rose' enamels and gilding with the arms of Mordaunt, Qianlong, 23 cm. diam. **£200-250**   *SKC*

A pair of European subject Imari plates, the reverse of e⌐ with peony and chrysanthemum sprays, ea⌐ with spur marks, Arita in Hi⌐ Province, 26 cm. diam., c. 1⌐ **£520-600**   *SKC*

A famille rose plate, common design, c. 1765, 9 in. diam. **£80-90**   *AD*

A famille rose plate, of good quality, in rare pattern, 9 in. diam. (perfect), c. 1760. **£160-180**   *AD*

One of a pair of famille ros⌐ plates of good quality, unus⌐ design, 9 in. diam. (perfect), 1760. **£330-380** pair   *AD*

18th C. famille rose Chinese
te, c. 1780, 17 in. £250-
0   *DEB*

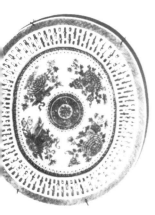

hinese export blue and
ite 'Fitzhugh' pattern
ketwork plate, 9 in., c. 1790.
-48   *DEB*

19th C. Imari plate, with
alloped rim, 8¾ in. diam. £40-
0   *SV*

n Imari plaque, 24 in. diam.
280-330   *DSH*

A set of early Canton plates,
comprising 11 dinner plates, 6
soup plates, 6 side plates and an
extra dinner plate: 25 cm.,
Jiaqing. £600-700   *C*

A 19th C. Imari plate, slight
rubbing, 8½ in. diam. £30-35
SV

A pair of Japanese blue and
white plates, 40.5 cm., painted
mark, c. 1900. £120-150   *SB*

One of a pair of early 19th C.
Cantonese plates (one rim chip),
10 in. diam. £180-200 the
pair   *SV*

A 19th C. Imari charger, 18 in.
diam. £220-240   *SV*

A 19th C. Imari plate, with
lobed rim, 8½ in. diam. £30-
35   *SV*

In this section Chinese and
Japanese porcelain have been
combined under subject
heading e.g. plates, bowls etc.
to aid quick identification.

A 19th C. Imari plate, with
slight damage, 8 in. diam. £12-
15   *SV*

163

Two blue and white saucer-dishes, with central hunting scenes (one foot rim pierced), encircled Chenghua six-character marks, Kangxi, 7¾ in. (20 cm.) diam. **£600-800**   *C*

An Annamese blue and white dish, the reverse with petal-shaped lappets issuing from the foot (cracked and chipped), 15th C., 14¾ in. (37.5 cm.) diam. **£350-500**   *C*

A late Ming blue and white Kraak porcelain dish (minor chips), Wanli, 20 in. (51 cm.) diam. **£1,300-1,500**   *C*

A Swatow blue and white deep dish (cracked and chipped), 17th C., 16¾ in. (41.5 cm.) diam. **£450-500**   *C*

An Arita blue and white saucer dish, early 18th C., 37.9 cm. diam. **£700-900**   *C*

A blue and white saucer di 33.7 cm., K'ang Hsi. **£120-150**   *SKC*

A pair of large Arita blue and white dishes, late 17th C., 41.7 cm. diam. **£1,000-1,200**   *C*

A Kakiemon deep dish painted in iron-red, blue and turquoise enamels and gilt within a chocolate rim (restored), late 17th/early 18th C., 24.4 cm. wide. **£950-1,200**   *C*

A Celadon saucer-dish, in se translucent pale bluish-gree glaze (foot-ring chipped), 18 C., 7½ in. (9.5 cm.) diam. **£25-350**   *C*

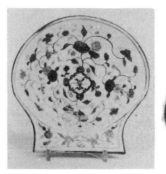

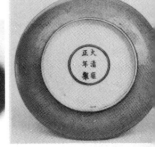

A pair of Chinese Imari sweetmeat-dishes, (fritted, one repaired), early 18th C., 7¾ in. (19.5 cm.) wide. **£150-200**   *C*

A Chinese Mandarin period spoon tray, c. 1780, 5 in. wide. **£50-60**   *AD*

A yellow-glazed saucer-dish, encircled Yongzheng six-character mark and possibly the period, 5¼ in. (13.5 cm.) diam. **£400-500**   *C*

Japanese circular dish,
corated in underglaze blue,
n-red and gold, 18½ in., 19th
£140-200   *L*

A Chinese dish, in the shape of
a fan, decorated in 'famille-rose'
enamels, underglaze blue and
gold, 10¼ in., Ch'ien Lung. **£80-
120**   *L*

One of a pair of 19th C. Satsuma
leaf dishes, on gilt ground, 9¾
in. wide. **£220-250** the pair
SV

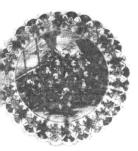

Japanese earthenware dish,
) cm., painted mark, 1870's.
180-220   *SB*

A pair of armorial dishes,
painted in 'famille rose'
enamels with the Arms of Byam
impaling Nichols, within a gilt
border, Qianlong, 26 cm. wide.
£330-360   *SKC*

An iron-red dish, 40.5 cm.,
enriched with gilding,
Daoguang. **£100-130**   *SB*

n Imari dish, 62 cm., late 19th
. **£540-600**   *SB*

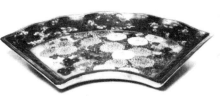

A Taizan earthenware dish,
64.5 cm., painted dai Nihon
Taizan sei, c. 1900. **£300-350**
SB

A large Hichozan Shinpo blue
and white dish, 67.5 cm.,
painted dai Nihon, Hichozan
Shinpo tsukuru, late 19th C.
£180-220   *SB*

A Fukugawa dish, painted and
ilt, 47 cm., painted Fukawa
sukuru and other mark, c. 1900.
160-200   *SB*

A pair of Kraak Porselein
bowls, Wan-li (Wanli), 13.8 cm.
£230-270   *SBe*

A Fukugawa Imari dish,
painted and gilt, 38 cm., painted
Fukugawa sei and leaf mark,
underglaze seal, c. 1900. **£120-
160**   *SB*

A Ming Celadon tripod
jardiniere, in a crackled semi-
translucent pale bluish-green
glaze (cracked, base firing crack
repaired), with metal liner,
16/17th C., 11¼ in. (28.5 cm.)
diam. **£440-540**   *C*

A Qing blue and white tripod cylindrical brush-pot (feet fritted), Kangxi, 7¾ in. (19.5 cm.) diam. **£350-450**   *C*

A large blue and white fish bowl, in cobalt underglaze blue, Kangxi, 55 cm. wide and 49 cm. deep. **£2,700-2,900**   *SKC*

A blue and white Monteith (slightly chipped), encircled z (made to order) mark, Kangx 12¾ in. (32.5 cm.) diam. **£1,20** **1,400**   *C*

A blue and yellow bowl (cracked and chipped), encircled Kangxi six-character mark, 5½ in. (14 cm.) diam. **£200-250**   *C*

A Chinese Imari Jardiniere, with three short pyramidal feet (chipped), early 18th C., 11½ in. (29 cm.) wide. **£350-450**   *C*

A large Chinese exportwa jardiniere, painted on a p ground, 40 cm., mid-19th **£460-520**   *SKC*

A 19th C. Oriental bowl, 7 in. diam. **£120-135**   *SV*

A blue and white censer, Kangxi, inscribed with a collector's mark zhan ding xiang, 9½ in. (24 cm.) diam. **£300-350**   *C*

A 19th C. Imari bowl and saucer, with interior blue r saucer, 6½ in. diam. **£45-5** *SV*

A 19th C. Imari bowl, 5¼ in. diam. **£30-35**   *SV*

A pair of famille rose jardinieres (chipped, one handle replaced), Yongzheng/early Qianlong, 10¼ in. (26.5 cm.) wide. **£1,700-** **1,900**   *C*

A Canton bowl, 47 cm., Daoguang. **£1,200-1,400**

A 19th C. Imari bowl, 4¼ in. diam. **£30-35**   *SV*

An Imari bowl, the inside painted, enamelled and gilt, 19th C., 13⅜ in. **£220-300**   *L*

A Satsuma bowl, 4¼ in. **£3** **400**   *L*

A pair of Famille-Rose Jardinieres and stands, 19 cm., Guangxu. £250-300 *SB*

A 19th C. Japanese Satsuma bowl, 9⅛ in. diam. £90-100 *SV*

Satsuma tall bowl, with erted lip, 4 in. high. £430-
0 *L*

A Famille-Rose fish bowl, the exterior with dragons amongst flowers on a yellow ground, the interior with fish amongst water weed, 46.5 cm., Guangxu. **£850-950** *SB*

An Imari bowl, painted and gilt, 30.5 cm., late 19th C. **£240-290** *SB*

lue and white Jardiniere, 36 ., Guangxu. £500-560 *SB*

A Gyokuzan earthenware bowl, gilt Gyokuzan, 11 cm., late 19th C. **£220-300** *SB*

famille rose' semi-eggshell e bowl painted en grisaille, interior with a band of puce lis-pattern at the rim, ngzheng. 4½ in. (11.5 cm.) m. £400-500 *C*

A pair of Japanese polychrome jardinieres, each brightly painted, 36 cm., c. 1900. **£280-320** *SB*

A Japanese jardiniere, 37.5 cm., late 19th/early 20th C. **£190-240** *SBe*

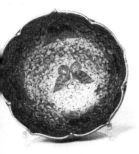

Shinzan earthenware bowl, ainted and gilt, 12.5 cm., gilt hinzan tsukuru and mon, c. 900. **£70-100** *SB*

A Shoji Hamada stoneware bowl, in dark brown and grey, 19.5 cm., c. 1930, with invoice. **£450-500** *SB*

A Fukugawa Imari fish bowl, 42 cm., painted Fuji-yama mark, c. 1900. **£260-320** *SB*

good famille-rose bowl, ainted mark, Hongxian, 17 n. **£400-450** *SB*

A pair of Celadon-glazed Jardinieres with bracket feet (one slightly cracked), 7½ in. (19.5 cm.) square. **£200-250** *C*

A Canton tureen, cover and stand, moulded bat and cash mark, 15.5 cm. overall, c. 1820-40. **£240-280**   *SKC*

An early 19th C. Chinese vegetable dish and cover, decorated in underglaze blue, 11 in. **£200-250**   *WW*

An Eastern Market Canton tureen, cover and stand, gilt with panels of calligraphy, on a blue ground, Guangxu, 41 cm. **£450-550**   *SB*

A Canton export porcelain tureen, cover and stand, decorated in famille rose enamels. **£520-600**   *WW*

An export tureen and cov Jiaqing, 35 cm. wide, c. 1 **£570-650**   *SKC*

A garniture of 5 famille ver vases, comprising: two beak vases (the necks repaired), 1 in. (40 cm.) high, and three baluster vases (damaged), w covers, 17¾ in. (45 cm.) high Kangxi. **£4,400-5,000**   *C*

A garniture of 3 ormolu-mounted Chinese blue and white porcelain vases, decorated with stylised flov and foliage, the porcelain Kangxi, 10¼ in. (26 cm.), an in. (30.5 cm.) high. **£550-65** *C*

A glazed grey stoneware bottle, in greyish-white glaze (chipped), probably c. 10th C., 11¾ in. (30 cm.) high. **£220-280**   *C*

A famille verte vase, Kangxi, with wood cover, 11½ in. (29 cm.) high. **£440-500**   *C*

A Doucai vase (cracked), encircled Chenghua six-character mark, Kangxi, 14 in. (36 cm.) high. **£330-400**   *C*

Two blue and white Yanyan vases, (fritted, one base chipped), Kangxi, 18 in. (46 cm.) high. **£1,600-1,800**   *C*

A Robins-egg blue-glazed v impressed Qianlong six-character seal mark, with v stand, 9¼ in. (23.5 cm.) hig **£320-400**   *C*

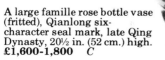

A large famille rose bottle vase (fritted), Qianlong six-character seal mark, late Qing Dynasty, 20½ in. (52 cm.) high. **£1,600-1,800**   *C*

A Takuzan Satsuma vase, gilt Takuzan ga, painted mon, 30 cm., mid 19th-19th C. **£230-300**   *SB*

pair of Satsuma small vases,
inted and gilt, 4½ in. **£450-**
20   *L*

A pair of Satsuma vases,
painted and gilt, on four bracket
feet, 4¾ in. **£310-350**   *L*

A pair of Satsuma spherical
vases, painted and gilt, 3½ in.
£350-400   *L*

A pair of Satsuma vases, 4⅝ in.
£280-320   *L*

A pair of 19th C. Satsuma
vases, 7½ in. high. **£100-120**
SV

A pair of Satsuma vases and
stands, 12¼ in. **£280-320**   *L*

A 19th C. Japanese Satsuma
vase, with inner lid and cover, 6
in. high, on wood stand. **£225-
260**   *SV*

pair of Satsuma
ases, 4¾ in. **£380-
20**   *L*

19th C. Imari vase,
½ in. high. **£65-70**
V

A pair of 'famille rose'
oviform vases, with Buddhistic
lion handles, the celadon-
ground exteriors with bands of
blue enamel and gilt stylised
'shou' characters (one restored),
35 in. (89 cm.) high. **£1,100-
1,400**   *C*

An Imari vase, with decoration
on blue ground, height 36 in.
£780-880   *LT*

A pair of lozenge section Imari
vases, in underglaze blue, iron-
red and gilding, 42 cm. **£300-
360**   *SKC*

Satsuma vase, the body
ickly enamelled, 25.5 cm., mid
9th C. **£110-150**   *SB*

A pair of Imari vases, 19th C.,
18½ in. **£570-640**   *L*

A 19th C. Imari large vase, 10½ in. high. **£420-460**   *SV*

A 19th C. Oriental vase, 10½ in. high. **£70-80**   *SV*

A Canton vase, brightly enamelle Daoguang, 60.5 c **£370-420**   *SB*

A Chinese blue and white spill vase (slight restoration) Kangxi, 5½ in. high. **£30-40** *SV*

A pair of 19th C. Oriental vases, with green background, 8 in. high. **£90-100**   *SV*

A pair of 19th C. Famille rose verte Oriental vases, one with rim chip, 10 in. high. **£160-180**   *SV*

A pair of 19th C. Kutani spil vases, with orange ground, c 1830, 7 in. high. **£40-50**   *S*

A pair of Cantonese bottle vases, each with six character marks, 15 in. **£400-450**   *PWC*

A mid 19th C. Kinkozan earthenware vase, in gilding green and blue enamelling with the 'Seven Sages of the Bamboo Grove', painted mark, Kin-ko-zan, 47.5 cm. **£400-500**   *SKC*

A Famille-Verte vase, with powder-blue ground, 85 cm., mark and period of Daoguang, with wood stand. **£900-1,050**   *SB*

A pair of celadon ground Canton vases, painted in underglaze blue, gilding an 'famille rose' enamels, 62 cm 1840/50. **£1,200-1,400**   *S*

A Baigyokuzan early Satsuma vase, painted Baigyokuzan, 24.5 cm., mid-19th C. **£220-260**   *SB*

An ormolu-mounted Chinese porcelain vase, decorated with a flambe red and purple glaze, mid-19th C., 21¾ in. (55 cm.) high. **£700-800**   *C*

A Meigyoku Satsuma va painted and gilt, painte Satsuma yaki, Meigyoki Satsuma mon and paint mark, 25 cm., mid-19th C **£800-900**   *SB*

A Transitional blue and white globular vase, c. 1640, 14 in. (35.5 cm.) high. £900-1,100 C

... famille-rose vase, Guangxu, 5.5 cm. £340-400 SB

A famille-verte vase, fitted for electricity, painted mark of Yongzheng, Tonghzi period, 45.5 cm. £200-250 SB

A famille-verte vase, fitted for electricity, Tonghzi, 45.5 cm. £250-300 SB

... Canton vase, with pierced ...nd enamelled decoration, ...mpressed mark, Guangxu, 44 ...n. £450-520 SB

A pair of Imari double-gourd vases, painted on an inky-blue ground, 29 cm., painted mark, c. 1880. £220-260 SB

A pair of Flambe vases, each with a sang-de-boeuf glaze, Guangxu, 57 cm. £330-430 SB

A pair of Canton vases, each painted and gilt, Guangxu, 33 cm. £440-500 SB

...pair of Canton vases, ... cm., Guangxu. ...50-400 SB

...pair of Japanese ...ses, 34.5 cm., painted ...rk, c. 1880. £450- ...0 SB

A pair of Rouleau vases, the powder-blue ground decorated in gilt and 'Famille-Verte' panels of figures, 35 cm., Guangxu. £400-480 SB

A Japanese earthenware vase of hexagonal section, 22 cm., late 19th C. **£200-230** *SB*

A pair of Imari vases, with a squat octagonal body, 28 cm., late 19th C. **£260-320** *SB*

A Kyoto earthenware vase, painted and gilt on a broca ground, 46 cm., painted mai 1880's. **£270-330** *SB*

A pair of Japanese earthenware vases, painted and gilt on a diaper ground, 40 cm., late 19th C. **£700-900** *SB*

A pair of Hichozan Shinpo vases, each body moulded in relief, 48 cm., painted dai Nihon Hichozan Shinpo tsukuru and Satsuma mon, late 19th C. **£620-700** *SB*

A pair of enamelled vases, painted with panels of schol; on a blue ground, 43 cm., la 19th C. **£460-550** *SB*

A pair of Kutani vases (restoration to handles), 43 cm., late 19th C. **£500-580** *SBe*

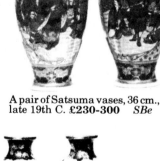

A pair of Satsuma vases, 36 cm., late 19th C. **£230-300** *SBe*

A pair of Canton vases, each body thickly enamelled, heig 38.5 cm., late 19th C. a.f. **£18** **220** *SBe*

A Kutani vase, painted with numerous panels, on a diaper ground, 64 cm., c. 1900. **£320-380** *SB*

A pair of Yabu Meizan earthenware vases, each enamelled and gilt, gilt Yabu Meizan, 30.5 cm., c. 1900. **£950-1,050** *SB*

A pair of Taizan earthenwai vases, each painted and gilt an orange ground, 31 cm., painted dai Nihon, Taizan s impressed Taizan, c. 1900. **£150-200** *SB*

A pair of Japanese earthenware vases, each painted and gilt, 18.5 cm., gilt mark, c. 1900. **£350-400** *SB*

A Kinkozan earthenware vase, 28.5 cm., gilt dai Nihon Kinkozan tsukuru, c. 1900. **£500-600** *SB*

A pair of Famille Rose vases, reserved on a pink graviata ground (some restoration), 17½ in. (44 cm.) high. **£250-350** *C*

A pair of Taizan earthenware vases, 24.5 cm., painted dai Nihon Taizan sei, c. 1900. £160-200 *SB*

A pair of Japanese earthenware vases, each painted and gilt, 9.5 cm., c. 1900. **£150-200** *SB*

A pair of Chinese vases, of square tapering form, decorated in 'famille-verte' enamels with the Flowers of the Seasons, 18¾ in. **£490-550** *L*

. pair of Fukugawa Imari ottle vases, 31 cm., painted ukugawa sei and leaf mark. 260-300 *SB*

A pair of Imari vases, 29.5 cm., c. 1900. **£220-300** *SB*

A pair of greenish-white-glazed funerary jars, with crackled translucent glazes, Southern Song Dynasty, 20 in. (51 cm.) high. **£700-800** *C*

A small transitional olychrome jar, painted on the ides in iron-red, green, yellow nd black enamels, 13.5 cm., nid-17th C. **£150-180** *SKC*

Unless otherwise stated, any description which refers to 'a set' or 'a pair' includes a valuation for the entire set or the pair, even though the illustration may only show a single item.

Two Qing blue and white baluster jars, with emblems on the necks (one with base chip repaired), Kangxi, 12¾ in. (32 cm.) high. **£800-1,000** *C*

A Cizhou baluster jar (the rim reduced, neck cracked), Song/Yuan Dynasty, 8 in. (20 cm.) high. **£450-600** *C*

A blue and white jar, Tian mark, Kangxi, 4 in. (10 cm.) high. £390-450 *C*

A large Arita baluster jar (slight glaze cracks around shoulder), early 18th C., with carved wood cover, 51 cm. high. £600-800 *C*

A Qing blue and white moonflask, Yongzheng six-character seal mark, 14 in. (36 cm.) high. £1,000-1,200 *C*

A pair of Qing blue and whit oviform jars and covers, probably Kangxi, 6¼ in. (16 cm.) high. 260-320 *C*

A Chinese 'Famille-Rose' garniture, comprising 3 vases and covers, 2 beakers, of octagonal section, Ch'ien Lung, 21 and 17¾ in. £5,000-6,000 *L*

A pair of Imari jars and covers (both covers slightly damaged) late 17th/early 18th C., 49 cm. high. £1,300-1,600 *C*

A pair of blue and white vases and covers (chipped), Kangxi, 18 in. (46 cm.) high. £1,100-1,300 *C*

A pair of 19th C. Imari lidde vases (slight chip), 9½ in. hig £260-290 *SV*

An Imari jar, late 17th/early 18th C., 30.8 cm. high. £570-700 *C*

A large Imari baluster jar and cover (cover damaged), late 17th/early 18th C., 63.4 cm. high. £1,000-1,200 *C*

A large Imari baluster jar and cover (restored), late 17th/early 18th C., 58.3 cm. high. £550-700 *C*

A pair of large Imari baluster jars and covers, late 17th/early 18th C., 67.5 cm. high. £4,000-4,600 *C*

A Satsuma koro and pierced cover, on three elephant-head feet (one foot repaired slight restorations), signed Nippon Jozan Ishi below a blue Shimazu mon, 19th C., 40.3 cm high. £800-1,000 *C*

blue and white baluster vase with related cover, painted with 'qilin' (cover chip restored and inor crack), ransitional/early Kangxi, 35 n. high. **£300-400**   *C*

A pair of Imari vases and covers, 34 cm., painted mark, early 19th C. **£260-320**   *SB*

A globular bottle vase, painted in underglaze blue and copper-red (rim fritted), Qianlong six-character seal mark, late in the period, 12 in. (30.5 cm.) high. **£900-1,100**   *C*

A Meigyokuzan Satsuma vase and cover, the ribbed body hickly enamelled and gilt, 28 cm., painted Satsuma Meigyokuzan tsukuru and mon, mid 19th C. **£650-750**   *SB*

A pair of famille-rose jars and covers, in bright enamel colours on a powder blue ground, 43 cm., mid-19th C. **£520-600** *SBe*

A Japanese earthenware koro and cover in the form of a rope-tied bag, 38 cm., gilt mark, 1880's. **£240-280**   *SB*

A pair of Imari vases and covers, the domed covers with lion finials, 40 cm., painted mark, late 19th C. **£280-320** *SB*

A pair of Japanese vases, covers and liners, both painted and gilt, 23.5 cm., gilt mark, late 19th C. **£200-250**   *SB*

A pair of Imari vases and covers, 41 cm., late 19th C. **£440-540**   *SB*

A pair of blue and white jars nd covers, 40 cm., Guangxu. **£300-350**   *SB*

A pair of Japanese earthenware koro and covers, on three mask and tongue legs, 39 cm., c. 1900. **£330-380**   *SB*

A pair of Satsuma ovoid vases and covers, 4¾ in. **£370-420** *L*

A large Imari vase and cover, 66 cm. **£400-460** *SKC*

A Kyoto octagonal box and cover (cover with small crack), signed on the base Kinkozan zo and on the side Takao, late 19th C., 25.8 cm. wide. **£750-900**   *C*

A pair of Qing blue and wh hexagonal garden seats (on repaired), 19½ in. (49.5 cm.) high. **£650-800**   *C*

A pair of blue and white octagonal garden seats (one with minor damage), Qianlong, 19 in. (48.5 cm.) high. **£1,500-1,700**   *C*

A pair of blue and white garde seats, with pierced top and sides, 48 cm., Guangxu. **£780 880**   *SB*

A pair of Cantonese garden stools, 18 in. high. **£270-330**   *AG*

A Canton garden seat, with studded and painted body, 48.5 cm., Daoguang. **£750-880**   *SB*

A Ming Celadon censer and cover, modelled as a seated duck, the detachable right wing forming the cover, bluish-green glaze (chipped), 16th/early 17th C., 8 in. (20 cm.) high. **£880-1,000**   *C*

A pair of green, ochre and brown glazed figures, impressed Qianlong six-character seal marks, woo stands, 16¼ in. (41 cm.) hi **£450-600**   *C*

A Compagnie-des-Indes spaniel, the hairwork rendered en grisaille, Qianlong, c. 1750-70. **£750-850**   *SKC*

A pair of famille-rose figures of Phoenix, 47.5 cm., late 19th C. **£600-700**   *SB*

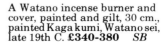

A Watano incense burner and cover, painted and gilt, 30 cm., painted Kaga kumi, Watano sei, late 19th C. **£340-380**   *SB*

An Ao-Kutani group, the details painted in iron-red, coloured enamels and gilt, late 19th C., 44 cm. high. **£500-650**   *C*

Two glazed biscuit figures of dignitaries, decorated in gree ochre and blue, 52 cm., and 4 cm., Guangxu. **£100-200**

A Chinese yellow glazed
Buddhistic lion, 11½ in. high.
£75-100 *GC*

A Japanese earthenware figure
of a young woman, 15.5 cm., c.
1900. **£100-130** *SB*

turquoise-glazed group
extremities restored), with
ood stand, 13½ in. (35 cm.)
igh. **£250-300** *C*

A good Chinese Mandarin
period mug, with 'Mandarin
pattern', c. 1780, 5¾ in. high
(price varies with condition).
£200-230 *AD*

pair of figures of cockerels in
white, red, yellow and ochre
one chipped), 15 in. (38 cm.)
igh. **£700-770** *C*

A famille rose teabowl and
saucer, of average quality, c.
1765. **£60-68** *AD*

A Chinese blue and white
tankard, of rare shape, c. 1785,
6½ in. high. **£130-150** *AD*

A mid-18th C. Chinese
porcelain teapot, with the arms
of Denison impaling Sykes, in
gold and enamels, Ch'ien Lung,
7¾ in. wide, 5½ in. high. **£150-
220** *DSH*

Two Chinese mugs, decorated
in 'famille-rose' enamels, 5¼ in.
and 5⅞ in., Ch'ien Lung. **£250-
300** *L*

JAPANESE ART PERIODS

**PREHISTORY AND
PROTOHISTORY**
c. 7,000 B.C. Jomon culture; first
recorded pottery with simple
design.
c. 300 B.C. Yayoi culture; bronzes
and more sophisticated pottery.
1st to 4th C. A.D. Haniwa culture.
Bronzes and distinctive red
pottery.
A.D. 220; first influence from
Korea.
ASUKA PERIOD — 552-645
HAHUKO PERIOD — 672-685

NARA PERIOD — 710-794
HEIAN PERIOD — 794-1185
KAMAKURA PERIOD — 1185-
1333
**MUROMACHI (AHIKAGA)
PERIOD** — 1338-1573
MOMOYAMA PERIOD — 1573-
1615
1598: Immigrant Korean potters
begin kilns at Kyushu, producing
the first glazed pottery.
EDO (TOKUGAWA) PERIOD
— 1615-1867

1616: First porcelain made by
Ninsei (1596-1666)
1661-1673: Great age of porcelain;
Arita, Nabeshima, Kutani and
Kakiemon.
1716-1736: Popularity of
lacquering and netsuke as art
forms.
MEIJI PERIOD — (1868-1912)
Strong influence of Western
cultures developing and growing.
Japanese art appears to decline in
many respects. Much trading with
the West.

A Korean grey pottery baluster jar, with areas of ashglaze, Silla Dynasty, with fitted box, 6½ in. (16.5 cm.) wide. **£240-300** *C*

A Chinese teapot, copy of a Lowestoft pattern, c. 1775, 5½ in. **£120-130** *AD*

A Famille Rose pear-shaped ewer, with moulded shell-scroll spout (some restoration, spout chipped and small body crack), Qianlong, 9 in. (30.5 cm.) high. **£230-270** *C*

A pair of giltmetal and Japanese Imari porcelain candelabra, with vase bodies, 18th C. (one nozzle missing), 36½ in. (93 cm.) high. **£3,000-3,500** *C*

A set of four good Famille-Rose panels, 37.5 by 24.5 cm., framed, painted mark, Guangxu. **£1,000-1,300** *SB*

A Ming Celadon stand, in widely cracked semi-translucent olive glaze (some restoration), 16th/17th C., 72 in (8.5 cm.) high. **£300-350** *C*

A Celadon tripod censer, under a widely crackled semi-translucent olive glaze (one handle restored, extended firing cracks), Qing Dynasty, with wood cover, 9½ in. (24 cm.) wide. **£600-660** *C*

A celadon ground umbrella stand, modelled with two bronzed dragons, incised mark Tonghzi, 63 cm. **£110-140** *SB*

A Famille Rose desk set, painted in underglaze-blue and iron-red with gilt foliage at the border, all with turquoise interiors, Jiaqing four-character seal marks, wood stand for the vase, from 3¼ in. (8.5 cm.), to ¾ in. (2 cm.) high. **£400-500** *C*

Chinese dynasties and marks

Earlier Dynasties

Shang Yin, c. 1532-1027 B.C.
Western Zhou (Chou) 1027-770 B.C.
Spring and Autumn Annals 770-480 B.C.
Warring States 484-221 B.C.
Qin (Ch'in) 221-206 B.C.
Western Han 206 B.C.-24 A.D.
Eastern Han 25-220
Three Kingdoms 221-265
Six Dynasties 265-589
Wei 386-557

Sui 589-617
Tang (T'ang) 618-906
Five Dynasties 907-960
Liao 907-1125
Sung 960-1280
Chin 1115-1260
Yüan 1280-1368

Ming Dynasty

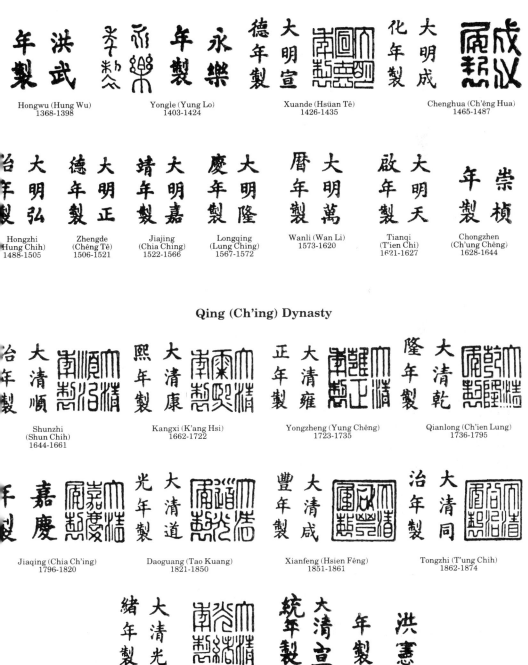

Hongwu (Hung Wu)
1368-1398

Yongle (Yung Lo)
1403-1424

Xuande (Hsüan Tê)
1426-1435

Chenghua (Ch'êng Hua)
1465-1487

Hongzhi
(Hung Chih)
1488-1505

Zhengde
(Chêng Tê)
1506-1521

Jiajing
(Chia Ching)
1522-1566

Longqing
(Lung Ching)
1567-1572

Wanli (Wan Li)
1573-1620

Tianqi
(T'ien Chi)
1621-1627

Chongzhen
(Ch'ung Chêng)
1628-1644

Qing (Ch'ing) Dynasty

Shunzhi
(Shun Chih)
1644-1661

Kangxi (K'ang Hsi)
1662-1722

Yongzheng (Yung Chêng)
1723-1735

Qianlong (Ch'ien Lung)
1736-1795

Jiaqing (Chia Ch'ing)
1796-1820

Daoguang (Tao Kuang)
1821-1850

Xianfeng (Hsien Fêng)
1851-1861

Tongzhi (T'ung Chih)
1862-1874

Guangxu (Kuang Hsü)
1875-1908

Xuantong
(Hsüan T'ung)
1909-1911

Hongxian
(Hung Hsien)
1916

179

ANTIQUITIES —
POTTERY

It comes as a great surprise when one is used to seeing quite modern 'antiques' sell for many hundreds, if not thousands of pounds, to find that much pottery which can be as much as 5,000 years old still sells very cheaply. This is standard throughout the field of antiquities and certainly refutes the claim that the older something is, the more desirable it is.

This is one of the few areas of collecting which one can say, with some confidence, that a price explosion is bound to happen. These pieces of ancient pottery seem to fulfil so many of the demands of collectors; they are old — extremely old; they are hand made; they are of great social and historical interest. Yet they remain, comparatively, a specialist area, without the devout band of followers which other much more modern fields demand. Because much ancient pottery was

for a functional rather than pur decorative purpose, it was made large quantities. However it is s quite amazing how much has survived. It may simply be the a of some of these artefacts whic lessens their relevance to collectors. Possibly the pottery Bernard Leach 'means' somethi to such collectors because it is reflection of a reasonably rece past whereas the potters of Enkomi in Cyprus in 1300 B.C. virtually of another world.

There are obviously fakes arou particularly of the more valua decorated pieces. Some of the fakes are easy to detect, being made of modern materials. So however are made by experts a if in doubt a new collector woul well advised to buy from a reputable dealer and visit Muse collections. The British Museu has an excellent collection of antiquities along with some interesting fakes.

An Islamic underglaze blue Ewer, painted with panels of stylised birds divided by calligraphic cartouches and floral roundels, an Arabic inscription band of benedictions below (restored), 12th C. Syria, 8 in. (20 cm.) high. **£800-1,000**   *C*

A late Apulian red-figure Bell-Krater, by the Como Painter, 10½ in. (26.5 cm.) high, late 4th C. B.C. **£880-1,000**   *C*

An Apulian red-figure bell-krater, by the Zagreb painter, 11½ in. high, 4th C. B.C. **£550-700**   *C*

An Apulian red-figure Volut Krater, related to the Deri Group, 17½ in. (44.5 cm.) hig 4th C. B.C. **£900-1,100**   *C*

An Apulian red-figure Hydria, in the manner of the Darius/Underworld Painter (the base hollow), 14 in. (35.5 cm.) high, late 4th C. B.C. **£880-980**   *C*

A Campanian redfigure bell-krater, by the APZ painter, 12½ in. high, 320-330 B.C. **£550-700**   *C*

An Etruscan black-figure Amphora (worn), 8¾ in. hig mid-6th C. **£400-480**   *C*

180

An Attic black-figure neck
Amphora, 11¼ in. (28.5 cm.)
igh, c. 520 B.C. **£2,500-
,700**   *C*

A Roman red burnished pottery
pedestal bowl (repaired), 7⅜ in.
diam., late 1st C. B.C. **£500-
600**   *C*

An Apulian red-figure Pelike,
from the workshop of the
Underworld Painter, 13½ in.
(34.4 cm.) high, 4th C. B.C.
£720-820   *C*

An Attic black-figure amphora,
9 in. high, c. 520 B.C. **£1,000-
1,300**   *C*

An Attic black-figure Kalpis
(repaired with minor
restoration), 13 in. (33 cm.) high,
late 6th C. B.C. **£2,200-
2,400**   *C*

A Corinthian Skyphos
(repaired and restored), 10 in.
(25.5 cm.) diam., early 6th C.
B.C. **£500-600**   *C*

n Apulian red-figure pelike, by
e Bologna 497 painter (rim
ightly chipped), 10¾ in. high,
th C. B.C. **£400-500**   *C*

An Attic black-figured
Skyphos, with incised detail,
10¾ in. (27.3 cm.) diam. across
handles, late 6th C. B.C. **£600-
700**   *C*

n Attic black-figured Skyphos
minor restoration), 9¼ in. (23.5
m.) diam. across handles, late
th C. B.C. **£770-870**   *C*

An Attic black-glazed Skyphos
(repaired with minor
restoration), 8½ in. (21.6 cm.)
diam. across handles, late 6th
C. B.C. **£660-760**   *C*

An Attic black-figure Siana
cup, 13 in. (35 cm.) diam. across
handles, 4½ in. (14 cm.) high, c.
560 B.C. **£2,100-2,300**   *C*

A Cypriot geometric white
painted ware Oinochoe, 16 in.
(40.5 cm.) high, 850-750 B.C.
£1,300-1,700   *C*

181

An Egyptian blue glazed Frit blue crown fragment, on perspex stand, 5¼ in. (13.4 cm.) high, Dynasty XVIII, probably Amarna. £800-900   C

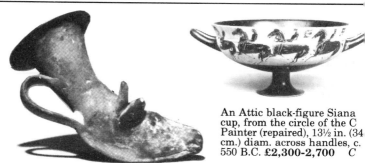

An Attic black-figure Siana cup, from the circle of the C Painter (repaired), 13½ in. (34 cm.) diam. across handles, c. 550 B.C. £2,300-2,700   C

An Apulian pottery rhyton, in the form of a cow's head, 7¾ in. long, 4th C. B.C. £240-300   C

A turquoise glazed Frit amulet of Isis (feet missing), 2½ in. (6.5 cm.) on perspex stand, Late Period. £300-330   C

An Egyptian limestone sculptor's model of a king's head, wearing a nemes-crown, on metal stand, Ptolemaic, c. 3rd C. B.C. £360-400   C

An Egyptian white glazed Frit Ushabti of Penrenu, with hieroglyphs in dark brown glaze: 'Cause to shine the Osiric Penrenu, justified'; and another similar in green glaze, 5 in. (12.7 cm.) high, Dynasty XIX. £880-1,000   C

A blue glazed Frit Ushabti, hieroglyphs in dark purple glaze, made for the Chief of the Double Granaries, Djedkhonsiuefankh, 4¼ in. (11.1 cm.) high, Dynasty XXI. £440-500   C

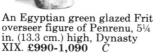

(r) A 1st C. Alexandrian oil lamp, with two burner holes, 2¾ in. wide. £24-30   FA

(l) A Hellenistic 1st C. BC oil lamp, 2¾ in. wide. £12-15   FA

An Egyptian green glazed Frit overseer figure of Penrenu, 5¼ in. (13.3 cm.) high, Dynasty XIX. £990-1,090   C

A 26th Dynasty Egyptian Ushabti, with worn turquoise glaze, 4½ in. tall. £250-280 FA

An Egypto-Roman 1st C. BC terracotta dog, 2½ in. high. £40-50   FA

A 26th Dynasty Egyptian Ushabti, with worn turquoise glaze, 8 in. high. £620-720 FA

SOFAS AND SETTEES

sociable pieces of furniture 'sofa' comes from the Egyptian word 'sopha' and was a cushioned throne; 'settee' is derived from 'settle': as 18th C, progressed the sofa became more popular — the settee being relegated to the hall

curving lines of Queen Anne and George I periods used to good effect with the settee — most had cabriole legs ending in hoof, pad, claw-and-ball or paw feet

marquetry decoration on walnut can often indicate Dutch origin

- Italian settees often very long — to seat six to eight people
- at beginning of George II period mahogany began to replace walnut and by 1750's was to overtake walnut virtually completely
- style also changed — the vase-shaped splats becoming more linear and delicate into the 'ribbed' backs of the Chippendale-style
- the legs and feet remained virtually the same until the 1760's when vertical square legs became the vogue

- the 'Chinese Chippendale' style became one of the most popular form of settees
- as the 18th C. progressed padded 'camel' backs became very popular
- the French canapé was designed to seat 3 people and was often covered in specially designed tapestries
- sofas in the 19th C. were made of mahogany, rosewood or satinwood and sometimes painted or gilded
- the French Empire style had enormous impact on 19th C. England

A late 17th C. oak settee with carved and panelled back, 68 in. wide. **£220-280**   *DSH*

A rare 2 ft. 6 in. early 17th C. box settle. **£1,500-1,800**   *PW*

n elm bacon settle, of lovely ape, c. 1800, 77 in. high. ,050-1,150   *W*

A Victorian oak Gothic style settle, the seat with hinged lid, 72 in. wide. **£250-290**   *CEd*

A carved oak panelled settle, mainly 17th C., 57 in. wide. **£160-230**   *L*

late 17th C. carved oak settle, in. wide, 60 in. high. **£1,600-850**   *TJ*

An early 18th C. elm bacon settle, the back with single cupboard below four short drawers, solid seat, with cupboard below, 56 in. wide, c. 1720. **£620-750**   *SKC*

n unusual bronze-mounted ench, the seat supported on ronze winged griffin nonopodia, mid-19th C. 191 cm. ide; 107 cm. high. **£2,400-,600**   *C*

An early 20th C. oak monk's bench and rug chest, 42 in. wide. **£320-380**   *PSH*

A 19th C. French 'Duchesse' suite. **£290-350**   *CDC*

A transitional beechwood canape, covered in blue velvet, 50 in. (127 cm.) wide. **£1,600-1,800**   *C*

─── FRENCH FURNITURE ───

- France had started, during the High Renaissance of the late 16th C., to move away from the strong Italian influence
- The reign of Louis XIV saw a period of great expansion of the industry. Colbert and Fouquet, his two senior Ministers, were great patrons of the arts. In 1662 Colbert set up the Gobelins factory to produce furniture for the Sun King; based on the classical concepts but with strong baroque adornment. Furniture was also made in the galleries of the Louvre by André Charles Boulle (or Buhl). He created two major decorative forms; inlaying on tortoiseshell ground, and use of bronze mounts, now known as ormolu
- Some great French cabinet-makers of the subsequent periods:—
  - Regence — Poitou and Cressant
  - Louis XV — Messonier (1695-1750)
    — Pineau (1684-1754)
    — Van Risenburgh
- from 1742 the cabinet-maker's guild instructed
- that each piece should be stamped by the maker
- if it was up to standard 'J.M.E.' (juré des menuisiers-ébenistes) was added after the name
- cabinet-makers to the King and foreign cabinet-makers did not have to stamp their work
- the main styles of this time Louis XV — rococo, Transitional, Louis XVI — neo-classical
- Louis XVI's main cabinet-maker was Riesener
- Jacob and family were some of the few cabinet-makers to survive the revolution and prosper in the Directoire
- the sons formed a partnership called Jacob Freres in 1796
- this was changed to Jacob Desmalter in 1803 and prospered in the Empire period
- the 19th C. saw the creation of a large number of factories and workshops
- this culminated in the Art Nouveau styles of Gallé, Majorelle and Vallin

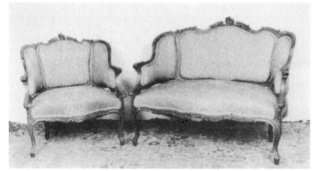

A three-piece French Edwardian style boudoir suite, upholstered in wine coloured damask. **£560-700**   *DLJ*

A Louis XV walnut canape, covered in brown velvet, 80 in. (203 cm.) wide. **£2,800-3,000**   *C*

A 'Louis XVI' giltwood canape, upholstered in contemporary Aubusson tapestry after Boucher, 52½ in. wide, mid-19th C. **£550-650**   *SB*

An Adam style painted satinwood sofa, with striped sage green upholstery, 75 in. wide. **£460-580**   *L*

A Louis XV giltwood canape, covered in pale green silk, 69 in. (175 cm.) wide. **£1,100-1,500**   *C*

An early Louis XV giltwood marquise, stamped Falconet, 32½ in. (83 cm.) wide. **£1,600-1,800**   *C*

A mid-Georgian red walnut sofa, possibly Irish, 78 in. (19 cm.) wide. **£1,500-1,700**   *C*

walnut double chair-back
ttee, on cabriole legs with
roll feet on later castors, 67
., c. 1850. **£330-400**   *SB*

A Victorian walnut-framed
parlour suite, a set of 6 dining
chairs, a chaise longue, an open
armchair and a lady's chair, c.
1860. **£2,200-2,500** the suite
SBe

An American mahogany sofa,
in the manner of John Belter,
mid 19th C., 61 in. (155 cm.)
wide. **£350-450**   *C*

A mahogany settee, with
sprung serpentine seat, 84½ in.
wide, c. 1860. **£300-360**   *SB*

A walnut chaise longue, late
1850's. **£440-550**   *SB*

A walnut settee, 72 in. (183 cm.)
wide, mid-19th C. **£480-540**
SBA

A Victorian chaise longue,
upholstered in green damask
brocade, c. 1860. **£775-875**
LL

large William IV mahogany
haise longue. **£210-260**
DM

A rosewood settee, 65 in. long, c.
1850. **£300-400**   *SB*

One of a pair of Regency
ebonised and gilded sofas, 83 in.
(211 cm.) wide. **£1,900-2,100**
pair   *C*

A Regency painted sofa,
upholstered in beige striped
woven cloth, 76 in. wide. **£160-
190**   *S*

A rosewood chaise longue, 73
in., c. 1840. **£670-800**   *SB*

A parcel gilt centre settee, 89 in. wide approx., c. 1880. **£460-560** *SB*

An ebonised conversation settee, c. 1870. **£300-360** *SB*

A pair of giltwood banquett with padded arms, one stamp SE, c. 1830, 103½ in. (263 cn wide. **£1,800-2,200** *C*

A laminated and plywood chaise longue, made by Heal's after a design by Marcel Brener, 140 cm. high, 1930's. **£600-700** *SB*

A George Walton oak chair-back settee, each tall splat pierced with a heart through the seat to a solid heart below, c. 1900. **£900-1,000** *SB*

A George III giltwood wind seat, 59 in. wide. **£990-1,20** *C*

A mid-Victorian ebonised sociable, with three serpentine sprung seats, covered in pink dralon, 137 cm. wide. **£330-400** *HSS*

A Queen Anne walnut wing armchair, legs and underframe restored, c. 1710. **£1,000-1,300** *S*

A George I walnut wing armchair, on cabriole legs a pad feet. **£900-1,200** *C*

A mahogany framed 3-seater settee, with studded stuffover seat, 5 ft. 7 in. wide. **£370-420** *V*

Left
A pair of Louis XV beechwood bergeres, covered in brown velvet. **£4,400-4,800** *C*

A George I style walnut wing armchair, upholstered in green velvet, mid-19th C. **£360-420** *SBA*

An early Georgian walnut wi armchair (restored). **£890-990** *C*

George III armchair, covered
nailed tan hide, c. 1770.
50-850   *SKC*

A Louis XV grey-painted
bergere J. Boucauld, stamped I.
Boucauld. **£3,000-3,300**   *C*

A Queen Anne walnut wing
armchair, upholstered in 17th
C. Dutch tapestry, complete
with loose cover. **£1,700-
1,900**   *Win*

air of Louis XV beechwood
geres, stamped C. V. Bara.
500-6,000   *C*

A William and Mary wing
armchair, upholstered in
scalloped green Renaissance
pattern velvet, some
restorations. **£570-680**   *S*

A Victorian lady's crinoline
chair, with rosewood show-
frame, upholstered in tapestry.
£180-250   *WY*

late George III mahogany
rmchair, covered in nailed
reen hide, c. 1800. **£520-580**
KC

A William IV mahogany
library armchair, covered with
button-upholstered leather,
19th C. **£450-550**   *SBA*

A mahogany armchair, c. 1860.
£330-400   *SB*

Victorian mahogany easy
air. **£260-320**   *A*

A Victorian lady's chair,
having a carved rosewood show
frame. **£350-430**   *WY*

An Edwardian upholstered tub
chair. **£70-120**   *Max*

187

A Flemish walnut open
armchair, covered in
contemporary gros and petit
point needlework, 17th C.
£1,250-1,350   *C*

A pair of walnut armcha
Scandinavian or German
restored, covered in red le
c. 1680. **£1,100-1,300** th
pair   *S*

A George III mahogany
Gainsborough armchair,
covered in worn deep red
leather, c. 1780. **£1,200-
1,400**   *SKC*

One of a set of 4 Louis XV
beechwood fauteuils,
upholstered in contemporary
gros point needlework. **£4,000-
4,800** the set   *C*

A 19th C. oak high back ha
chair, upholstered in embos
velvet. **£200-250**   *DA*

One of a suite of 6 giltwood
drawing room chairs, with
drop-in seats, early 19th C.
£2,200-2,600 the set   *SB*

One of a set of 4 George III
painted armchairs, c. 1775.
£2400-2,800 the set   *S*

A pair of Italian giltwood
armchairs, c. 1790. **£1,450-
1,600**   *SKC*

A pair of Louis XV walnut
fauteuils by J. B. Tilliard,
stamped Tilliard. **£5,000-
5,600**   *C*

A Louis XV giltwood armchair,
with sprung serpentine seat, c.
1880. **£160-220**   *SB*

A pair of Louis XVI grey
painted fauteuils, stampe
Nadal. **£1,300-1,500**

suite of Austrian neo-
ssical white-painted and
ded seat furniture,
mprising a pair of fauteuils, a
ir of stools, and a canape, late
th C., the stools 24 in. (61 cm.)
de, the canape 55 in. (140 cm.)
de. **£1,550-1,750**   *C*

A pair of early Louis XV walnut
fauteuils, covered in tan
leather, possibly German.
£2,600-2,900   *C*

Two Louis XV beechwood
fauteuils, covered in grey
velvet. **£1,700-1,900**   *C*

George III mahogany open
rmchair, covered in green silk.
680-750   *C*

A Victorian mahogany
armchair. **£380-420**   *A*

One of a set of 4 Venetian Lacca
Povera fauteuils, with padded
backs and upholstered seats,
the cream-painted frames
outlined in blue and decorated.
£800-1,000 set   *C*

One of a pair of walnut
chauffeuses, 34 in. (86.4 cm.)
wide, 1850's. **£660-760** pr.
SB

One of a pair of Regency
mahogany bergeres, in the
manner of Gillows. **£1,500-
1,700** the pair   *C*

n Empire mahogany
mchair, with brass mounts,
gs with brass claw feet. **£330-
0** *MMB*

A pair of Empire mahogany
fauteuils, covered in yellow
velvet. **£1,700-1,900**   *C*

A William IV
mahogany library
rocking chair, with a
button-upholstered
leather back, c. 1835.
£440-540   *SB*

189

A Victorian walnut lady's arm chair, with ceramic castors, upholstered in pale green dralon. **£550-650** *L*

A William IV mahogany library armchair, by C. Munro, Johnstone & Jeanes, 67 New Bond Street, London, c. 1835. **£550-650** *SB*

A walnut salon chair, mid-1 C. **£320-400** *SBA*

A cow-horn armchair, c. 1900. **£140-200** *SB*

A large Bugatti throne armchair, inlaid with pewter and applied with beaten copp recovered in dark brown leather, 100 cm., c. 1900. **£52 620** *SB*

A late Victorian saloon chair. **£240-255** *LAC*

A William and Mary oak open armchair, the panelled back carved, dated 1692. **£700-800** *C*

A 17th C. oak open armchair, inlaid with marquetry. **£460-560** *P*

A pair of Mills and Backhou 'Gothic' oak armchairs, and Christopher Pratt and Sons o 'Gothic' armchair in the sam manner, mid-19th C. **£220-2** the pair *SBA*

Two Chinese carved hardwood chairs, each solid serpentine seat carved with a mon, Guangxu. **£250-300** *SB*

An antique oak armchair, in Elizabethan style. **£200-30** *EBB*

early oak armchair, c. 1670
th restoration). **£200-240**
AT

A dark oak wainscot chair and
companion chair, height 58½
in. **£420-520**   *OL*

A carved oak panel back arm
chair (restorations), mainly
17th C. **£200-250**   *L*

late 17th C. English turned
rmchair. **£370-420**   *SBA*

A Chinese carved hardwood
armchair, 20th C. **£240-280**
SB

A walnut 'Renaissance'
armchair, French, mid-19th C.
£300-400   *SB*

red lacquer armchair, in the
hinese style, late 19th C.
530-630   *SB*

An oak armchair, the back with
a brass-studded leather
armorial shield, on lion
monopodia feet, 19th C. **£700-
900**   *C*

A carved framed high-back
elbow chair, of Charles II style.
£230-300   *WY*

191

A 17th C. walnut corner elbow
chair, the slip-in seat covered in
leather-cloth, c. 1680 (restored),
probably Dutch. **£330-400**
SKC

One of a pair of late 17th C.
Venetian walnut open
armchairs, backs and seats in
brass studded red velvet. **£630-
730 pr.** *DWB*

A George I mahogany 'Writing'
chair. **£460-560** *Bon*

A George II mahogany
commode corner chair, c. 1740.
£700-800 *EAN*

A George II fruitwood corner
commode, with a drop-in seat.
£150-200 *SBe*

A George I oak corner elbow
chair, c. 1735. **£420-490** *SKC*

An 18th C. oak elbow cha
with padded lift-out seat,
having a drawer in the ba
£290-360 *WY*

A pair of miniature corn
chairs (one chair damag
19th C. **£200-270** *SBe*

A fine George II red wal
elbow chair, c. 1750. **£66
725** *B.M*

A mahogany elbow chair, c.
1770. **£365-395** *W*

A late Georgian mahogany
Chippendale-style chair. **£225-
275** *E.E*

An early George III mahoga
open armchair. **£1,000-
1,200** *C*

George III mahogany open
mchair. £990-1,200   C

One of a pair of George III
mahogany open armchairs.
£3,500-3,900 the pair   C

A George III beechwood open
armchair. £600-700   C

George III mahogany ladder-
ack armchair, with slip-in
eat, c. 1760. £300-350   SKC

A Chippendale elm and oak
armchair, with padded seat, c.
1770, 37 in. high. £195-220
OB

An early George III beechwood
'Cockpen' open armchair, with
drop-in caned seat. £1,700-
2,000   C

ne of a set of 5 'George III
epplewhite' mahogany
rmchairs, each with a shield
ack, 1880's. £420-520 the
et   SB

A 'Sheraton' mahogany
armchair, c. 1800. £125-150
LL

One mahogany Hepplewhite
elbow chair with camel back, c.
1790. £320-375   W

A Regency sabre leg mahogany
elbow chair, c. 1825. £185-
200   LL

A Sheraton period elbow chair,
c. 1790. £375-400   B.M

I   193

A mahogany Regency sabre leg elbow chair, c. 1830. **£145-165** *LL*

One of a pair of late Regency mahogany elbow chairs, with panelled bar backs, out-curving arms and dip seat. **£320-400** the pair *L*

A fine and unusual set of Regency mahogany elbow chairs, c. 1810, 35 in. high **£4,800-5,500** *JGM*

An Edwardian inlaid elbow chair. **£65-75** *ST*

One of a set of 6 ebonised beechwood 'Rossetti' chairs, by Morris and Company, including a pair of armchairs, late 19th C. **£200-260** the set *SB*

An elm Mendlesham chair **£150-210** *GT*

One of a set of 4 mahogany armchairs, early 20th C. **£350-400** set *SB*

A decorative high-backed mahogany arm chair, with moquette seat and scrolled moquette back with spindles, late Victorian, 54 in. high. **£160-240** *EEW*

A pair of Chinese red lacqu open armchairs, bearing Kangxi six-character mark (partly relacquered), 19th C. **£1,400-1,600** *C*

An Egyptian export parquetry armchair, the apron and legs forming mehrabs, c. 1900. **£120-150** *SB*

One of a pair of elbow chairs, satinwood veneered and ebonised, having slip-in seats. 220-310 pair *P*

An Edwardian mahogany framed elbow chair, on cabriole front supports. **£100-150** *WY*

An 18th C. yew wood Windsor chair. **£300-350** *MMB*

yew wood smoker's chair. 210-250 *MAT*

A good yew wood Windsor chair, c. 1800. **£250-280** *MAT*

An 18th C. yew-wood Windsor chair, with bow, spindle and splat back. **£330-390** *A*

An 18th C. yew wood Windsor chair. **£330-390** *MMB*

An 18th C. elm, beech and yew framed Windsor arm chair, with later squab seat. **£230-270** *WHL*

WINDSOR CHAIRS

- unknown before 1720's
- basically Georgian tavern and coffee house chairs
- earliest examples have comb backs, plainly turned splayed legs, no stretchers
- cabriole legs suggest a date between 1740-1770
- hooped back introduced c. 1740

- wheel splat introduced c. 1790
- Gothic Windsors, recognised by the carving of their splats and their pointed-arch backs, made c. 1760-1800
- some better quality Windsors stained black or japanned black or green; these are more valuable in original

- condition — do not strip them
- most desirable wood is yew, followed by elm
- some mahogany Windsors were made for the gentry, these are always of good quality
- curved stretchers, carved and well proportioned backs add value

A Windsor chair, with part ye
back, 35 in. high, c. 1800. **£19**
215   *SV*

A yew wood Windsor chair, c.
1800. **£220-260**   *MAT*

An elm Windsor armchair, c.
1825. **£125-150**   *LL*

A beech and elm Windsor chair,
c. 1840. **£125-150**   *LL*

An elm Windsor chair, c. 1850.
£160-180   *LL*

An elm and ash Windsor cha
with crinoline stretcher, c. 185
£150-175   *DEB*

An elm and ash Windsor ch
c. 1850. **£100-120**   *DEB*

A mixed set of 5 Lancashire
spindle back dining chairs,
including one elbow chair, 19th
C. **£550-670**   *L*

A country elm and ash Windsor
chair, c. 1900. Set of 6 **£150-**
175, pair **£30-40**   *DEB*

ne of a set of 8 oak dining
hairs, including a pair of
rmchairs, in the late 17th C.
tyle of Daniel Marot, Flemish,
1920. **£1,500-1,700** the set
B

An oak and elm Derbyshire side
chair, mid-17th C. **£90-150**
SBA

A set of 6 Charles II chairs, with
cane seats and carved
stretchers. **£3,500-3,900**
NCr

A Charles II oak chair, c. 1680,
7 in. high. **£155-180**   *OB*

An early oak chair (with
restoration), 17th C., 37 in. high.
£68-88   *OB*

A rare pair of William and Mary
walnut side chairs, late 17th C.
£350-500 the pair   *SBA*

A late 17th C. oak chair, 39 in.
high. **£155-175**   *OB*

An oak chair, 18th C., 44½ in.
high. **£130-160**   *PAM*

One of a set of eight Charles II
style walnut dining chairs,
including two armchairs, early
20th C. **£780-900** the set
SBA

One of a pair of early 18th C.
oak single chairs, c. 1710, 40½
in. high. **£400-500** the pair
JGM

One of a harlequin set of 6 17th
C. Lancashire chairs. **£3,500-
4,000** the set   *NCr*

A 17th C. oak side chair. £16
185   *TJ*

A set of 8 walnut dining chairs,
in the Marot style, the seats
with needlework squab
cushions. **£5,500-6,000**   *C*

Left
A Queen Anne period walnu
chair with rush seat, c. 1710
£245-285   *LL*

One of a set of 6 George I style
walnut dining chairs, with slip
in seats on carved cabriole legs
with ball and claw feet. **£620-
750** the set   *L*

One of a set of 6 early Georgian
oak dining chairs. **£1,900-
2,200** the set   *C*

One of a set of 6 George I-sty
carved walnut cane-back
dining chairs, c. 1910. **£2,00
2,300** the set   *SKC*

One of a set of 4 Dutch elm and
marquetry dining chairs, the
arched backs inlaid with floral
marquetry, with drop-in seats.
£2,200-2,500 the set   *C*

A set of 6 walnut chairs, with
padded leather drop-in seats,
19th C., 39 in. high. **£550-575**
for 6; **£50-65** for 2; **£25-30** for
1   *SV*

A set of 5 George II walnut
fiddleback dining chairs.
£1,000-1,300 the set   *B.W*

A Queen Anne/George I eln
and fruitwood dining chair,
1710. Set of 6 **£2,000-2,30
single £150-175   *DEB*

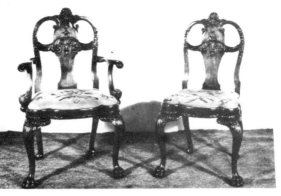

pair of Chinese padouk
asional chairs, richly inlaid
h mother of pearl, inset with
rble circular panels. £350-
0   AG

A carved walnut 9-piece dining
suite, comprising 2 elbow and 6
single chairs, with matching
table, 87 by 43 in., with plate
glass top. £1,600-2,000
DSH

A set of 4 18th C. Dutch walnut
and marquetry dining chairs.
£870-1,000   DWB

One of a set of 4 18th C.
marquetry inlaid walnut
standard chairs, the drop-in
seats covered in needlework
tapestry. £1,100-1,400 the
set   RG

A set of 8 Dutch walnut and
marquetry dining chairs, with
serpentine drop-in seats, late
18th C., and two open
armchairs similar. £7,000-
8,000   C

ne of a pair of walnut dining
airs, with pierced double
luster splats, early 18th C.
150-550 the pair   C

A set of seven Georgian style
oak dining chairs, including an
armchair, 19th C. £650-850
the set   L

set of 5 Victorian
ippendale-style chairs, 4
thout arms, 37 in. high
prox. £625 for 5   SV

One of a set of 4 Portuguese
rosewood dining chairs, mid
18th C. £2,500-3,000 set   CA

A set of reproduction
mahogany Chippendale chairs,
comprising 6 single and 2 arms,
loose seats upholstered in
rexine, late 19th C. £1,700-
2,000 the set   PW

One of a set of 8 'George II' mahogany dining chairs, including a pair of armchairs, 1880's. **£1,100-1,500** the set *SB*

A Victorian copy of a Georgian Chippendale chair, c. 1890. Set of 6 **£1,200-1,400**, single **£75-85** *DEB*

A set of six mahogany dining chairs, including a pair of armchairs, c. 1880. **£500-580** *SB*

One of a set of 6 early Geo red walnut dining chairs, drop-in floral needlework c. 1735. **£2,500-2,700** se

One of a set of 4 Chippendale-style Victorian dining chairs. **£350-425** set *E.E*

One of a set of 6 19th C. mahogany Chippendale-style chairs (4 singles, 2 carvers). **£800-890** set *E.E*

One of a set of four 'George II' mahogany chairs, including two armchairs. **£490-600** the set *SB*

One of a set of 10 'George II' mahogany chairs, including two armchairs. **£2,000-2,500** the set *SB*

A set of 8 Victorian Chippendale design mahogany dining chairs. **£1,500-1,800** *PWC*

A set of 8 mahogany reproduction Chippendale-sty chairs, including two arm. **£900-1,100** *RMcT*

e of a set of 10 'George II' oak
ing chairs, 1880's. **£800-**
0 the set   *SB*

One of a set of 4 Chippendale
mahogany chairs, c. 1765.
£4,200-4,700 the set   *SKC*

A set of eight 'George III'
mahogany dining chairs, mid-
20th C. **£600-800** the set   *SB*

ne of a set of 6 Chippendale-
yle carved mahogany chairs,
1890. **£770-850** the set
KC

A set of 6 Georgian period
provincial mahogany side
chairs, and a pair of later
matching carver armchairs.
£1,150-1,400 set   *WW*

One of a set of 8 George III
mahogany dining chairs,
including a pair of armchairs,
one armchair with slight
variations. **£4,000-4,300** the
set   *C*

A pair of Sheraton mahogany
armchairs, c. 1800. **£400-500**
the pair   *SKC*

A single mahogany side chair
with interlaced splat, c. 1775.
£140-160   *EAN*

A set of six early George III
provincial walnut dining
chairs, c. 1760. **£1,850-2,050**
set   *EAN*

Ten 18th C. Chippendale mahogany ladder-back dining chairs. **£2,700-2,900** *B*

An elm country Chippendale ladder-back chair, c. 1760. Set of 6 **£600-700**, pair **£150-175** *DEB*

One of a set of eight 19th C Chippendale-style ladderba chairs, 6 single and 2 arms. **£1,600-1,800** set *B.M*

One of a set of 6 Irish Georgian fruitwood dining chairs, with drop-in seats. **£880-1,080** set *C*

A walnut country Chippendale ladder-back chair, c. 1760. Set of 6 **£1,500-1,750**, pair **£250-300** *DEB*

A 'Chippendale' side chair, 1780. **£65-75** *LL*

A set of four George III mahogany dining chairs, c. 1870. **£220-290** *SB*

A set of 12 19th C. Chippendale style mahogany ladder-back chairs, comprising 10 standards and 2 carvers, c. 1880. **£2,500-3,000** the set *SKC*

A George II walnut dining chair, c. 1750. **£145-165** *L.*

One of a set of 8 Georgian style mahogany dining chairs, the slip-in seats covered with needlework on sage green ground. **£770-900** set *L*

Two of a set of 6 carved mahogany chairs, by Marsh, Jones, Cribb & Co., dated 1900. **£900-1,200** set *DSH*

Left
A pair of late 18th C. Hepplewhite hoop-back chairs. **£250-300** pair *W*

Same two matching chairs, plus 6 19th C. chairs. **£1,800-2,000** *W*

One of a pair of painted satinwood Adam style side chairs, the shield backs centred by Prince of Wales feathers. £300-400 the pair   *L*

ne of a set of 9 'George III' ahogany dining chairs, cluding a pair of armchairs, rly 20th C. £550-700 the t   *SB*

A set of 6 George III mahogany dining chairs, with leather upholstered seats. £1,600-1,800   *C*

One of a set of 4 George III mahogany dining chairs, the oose seat in floral pattern green apestry. £400-480 the set *CDC*

One of a set of 6 Hepplewhite mahogany single chairs, 35 in. high. £1,700-2,100 the set *JGM*

One of a pair of Hepplewhite mahogany dining chairs, c. 1780. £380-430 pair *EAN*

Two of a set of 6 Hepplewhite style and period mahogany side chairs, stuffed over seats covered in wine coloured velvet. £600-700 set   *WW*

Miller's Antiques Price Guide builds up year by year to form the most comprehensive photo-reference system available. The first three volumes contain over 20,000 completely different photographs.

A country cherrywood Hepplewhite dining chair, c. 1790 with wheat-ear back splat. Set of 6 £600-680, pair £120-140, single £35-45   *DEB*

Two of a set of 8 George III mahogany chairs of Hepplewhite design, c. 1795, restored. £1,700-2,000 the set   *SKC*

One of a set of 4 of Hepplewhite mahogany chairs, c. 1790 (re-upholstered). £725-800 set *LL*

One of a pair of 'Hepplewhite' chairs, c. 1780. £180-200 pair *MAT*

Two of a set of 16 early 19th C. Hepplewhite-style dining chairs, 14 singles, 2 arms (restored). £4,300-4,700 set *Win*

A pair of Hepplewhite c. mahogany shield-back c the backs with Prince of feathers, the stuffed sea covered in damask, c. 17 £1,000-1,300 *SKC*

A pair of George III mahogany dining chairs, with drop-in seats. £120-160 the pair *Hy.D*

One of 6 country spindle ba dining chairs, with rush sea nearly matching, 19th C. £66 760 the six *L*

An 18th C. Hepplewhite single dining chair, one of a set of four. £370-420 *CDC*

One of a set of 3 early George III mahogany 'Cockpen' chairs, and an open armchair and dining chair similar, the legs with later additions. £1,500-1,700 the five *C*

A set of 5 George III mahogany 'Bamboo' chairs, including a pair of open armchairs. £3,800-4,200 the set *C*

A set of three 'bamboo' spi back chairs, c. 1800, £130 180 *LL*

A country Sheraton oak chair, c. 1790-1800, with later upholstered seat. Set of 6 £450-520, pair £65-80 *DEB*

One of a pair of elm spindle back chairs, c. 1800. £85-95 pr. *LL*

A set of 4 Lancashire spindle back single chairs, with rush woven seats. £400-450 *PSH*

One of a set of 6 beechwood dining chairs, on cabriole legs with later block feet, Low Countries, mid 18th C. £1,600-1,900 the set *C*

A set of four George III style mahogany dining chairs, re-railed, late 19th C. £400-600 the set *SBA*

One of a set of 4 'Sheraton' dining chairs, in gold style brocade, c. 1800. £785-850 set *LL*

A pair of 'Sheraton' mahogany armchairs, c. 1800. £400-500 the pair *SKC*

One of a set of 4 'Sheraton' mahogany dining chairs, c. 1790. £750-850 the set *LL*

One of a set of 5 mahogany dining chairs of Sheraton style, including one carver. £370-420 set *Y*

One of a set of 6 late George III mahogany rail-back chairs, c. 1795. £880-1,000 the set *SKC*

A George III mahogany chair, with drop-in seat, c. 1800, 35 in. high. £45-65 *OB*

One of a set of 4 late Georgian fruitwood framed dining chairs. £230-270 set *WY*

Make the most of Miller's
Every care has been taken to ensure the accuracy of descriptions and estimated valuations.
Where an attribution is made within inverted commas (e.g.

'Chippendale') or is followed by the word 'style' (e.g. early Georgian style) it is intended to convey that, in the opinion of the publishers, the piece concerned is a later — though probably still antique — reproduction of the style

so designated.
Unless otherwise stated, any description which refers to 'a set' or 'a pair' includes a valuation for the entire set or the pair, even though the illustration may show only a single item.

A set of 8 Regency mahogany dining chairs, including a pair of armchairs, one re-railed and with later front legs. **£1,900-2,200** *C*

One of a set of 6 Regency mahogany railback chairs, c. 1810. **£800-1,000** the set *SKC*

One of a set of 6 George III mahogany side chairs, with chequered inlay and stuff-ov seats. **£1,300-1,500** the set

A pair of Regency mahogany dining chairs, with sabre legs. **£130-170** *Max*

A set of 8 Regency mahogany dining chairs, on moulded sabre legs. **£1,300-1,600** *PS*

A Regency mahogany sabre le dining chair, c. 1810. Set of 6 **£900-1,000**, pair **£150-175** *DEB*

A set of 6 Regency mahogany sabre leg dining chairs. **£850-1,100** *BW*

One of a set of 6 Regency mahogany-framed dining chairs. **£1,150-1,350** set *SBe*

Two of a set of 12 Regency mahogany dining chairs, including a pair of armchairs, with drop-in leather seats. **£5,800-6,300** the set *C*

One of a set of 4 Regency mahogany dining chairs, wi drop-in-seats, c. 1805. **£390-430** the set *N*

One of a set of 9 Regency mahogany dining chairs, in the manner of Gillows, the caned seats on sabre legs. £2,500-2,800 the set   *C*

Two of a set of 8 Regency mahogany sabre leg chairs, fitted Trafalgar seats, comprising 6 standards and 2 carvers, c. 1815. £1,400-1,600 the set   *SKC*

ie of a set of 6 Regency t brass inlaid sabre-leg airs, four with Trafalgar edlework seat covers, c. 1810. ,000-2,300 the set   *SKC*

set of 6 19th C. mahogany abre leg side chairs, with uttoned leather seats. £1,500-,800   *WW*

A set of 6 Regency single chairs, 33½ in. high. £1,800-2,200 *JGM*

A set of six Regency ebonised dining chairs, early 19th C., drop-in seats lacking. £1,200-1,600 the set   *SBA*

ne of a set of four Regency lack and gilt lacquered chairs, onsisting 3 single and an bow chair. £500-600 the et   *DWB*

One of a set of 6 Regency simulated rosewood dining chairs, with brass inlay. £1,100-1,300 set   *Hy.D*

A set of six late Regency mahogany dining chairs, early 19th C. £700-900 the set *SBA*

A set of 6 Regency mahogany dining chairs, the canework seats with loose squab cushion. **£800-950** *CDC*

Two of a set of 6 Regency mahogany rail-back chairs, comprising 4 standards and 2 carvers, c. 1810. **£1,100-1,400** the set *SKC*

Two of a set of 8 Regency mahogany rail-back chairs, with stuffed horsehair seats, comprising 6 standards and 2 carvers, c. 1810. **£2,000-2,400** the set *SKC*

A set of 8 late Regency mahogany dining chairs, stuffed-over seats covered in red simulated leather with brocade loose covers. **£2,150-2,500** *CDC*

Two of a set of 18 William IV mahogany dining chairs, including two elbow chairs, with slip in blue velvetine seats, c. 1835. **£3,500-4,000** set   *L*

One of a set of 5 Regency mahogany dining chairs, with non-matching upholstery. **£480-550** set   *L*

One of a set of 12 William I faded mahogany dining chai the pegged seat in floral upholstery, c. 1835 (faults **£2,400-2,600** set   *L*

One of a set of 6 Regency mahogany dining chairs, c. 1820. **£1,100-1,300** the set   *L*

One of a set of 7 George IV mahogany dining chairs, including an armchair, c. 1825. **£1,700-2,000** the set   *S*

A set of 10 George IV mahogan railback chairs, comprising 8 standards and 2 carvers, c. 1825. **£2,200-2,500**   *SKC*

Three of a set of 8 William IV mahogany dining chairs, including 2 elbow chairs. £1,800-2,200 set   *PWC*

A set of 7 William IV oak dining chairs. £850-1,050   *C*

of a set of 8 Victorian
ogany dining chairs, with 2
ers and 6 standards,
lstered in green patterned
rial. £1,200-1,600 the
Mlms

One of a pair of early Victorian mahogany chairs. £150-175 pair   *E.E*

One of a set of 4 Regency rosewood chairs. £350-450 set   *E.E*

ne of a set of 6 mahogany
ictorian balloon back dining
airs, c. 1880. Set of 6 £450-
0, a pair £60-80   *DEB*

One of a set of 6 carved mahogany dining chairs, 1840's. £580-650   *SB*

One of a set of 8 William IV simulated rosewood dining chairs. £700-850 the set   *L*

One of a set of 6 early Victorian mahogany dining chairs. £150-220 the set   *DSH*

art of an oak drawing-room
uite comprising an armchair, a
w chair and a set of 6
Regency' side chairs, 1880's
330-390 suite   *SB*

One of a set of 6 Victorian dining chairs. £400-450 the set   *MAT*

One of a set of 6 Victorian balloon back dining chairs. £350-400 set   *MAT*

A set of 6 Victorian walnut chairs, 37 in. high approx. **£850-925** for 6; **£100-130** for 2; **£45-50** for 1   *SV*

One of a set of 6 Victorian walnut balloon-back dining chairs, with stuffed-over serpentine seats, c. 1860. **£700-800** the set   *N*

One of a set of 4 Victorian walnut oval-back dining cha c. 1860. **£550-650** the set

One of a set of 6 walnut balloon back chairs, 1840's. **£700-770** set   *SB*

One of a set of 6 rosewood chairs, c. 1850. **£590-650** set *SB*

One of a pair of Victoriar walnut balloon-back chai **£200-225** pair   *E.E*

Two of 6 Victorian walnut dining chairs. **£950-1,300** the set   *BW*

A set of four walnut balloon-back chairs, with stuffed serpentine seat, c. 1860. **£310-380**   *SB*

CHAIRS

- check seat rails are the same, with equal patination
- top rail should never over-hang sides
- carving should not be flat
- if stretchers low, chair could have been cut down
- the height from floor to seat should be 1 ft. 6 in.

One of a set of 4 mid-Victori carved walnut dining chairs **£400-460** set   *DSH*

A set of six Victorian carved rosewood balloon-back chairs, c. 1855. **£800-1,000** the set *SKC*

e of a set of 6 walnut chairs, 855. **£690-800** the set   *SB*

A set of four rosewood Salon chairs, mid-19th C. **£450-650** the set   *SBA*

of a set of 5 rosewood side rs, 1840's. **£500-550** set

One of a set of 6 Victorian walnut chairs. **£650-725** set *E.E*

Two of a set of 6 19th C. walnut framed salon chairs, with tapestry panels and seats. **£380-430** set   *WHL*

inlaid rosewood chair, with holstered seat, 19th C., 30 in. ;h. **£35-56**   *SV*

One of a set of 20 early Victorian mahogany side chairs, 1840's. **£2,900-3,300** set   *L*

Miller's is a price GUIDE Not a price LIST.
The price ranges given reflect the average price a purchaser should pay for similar items. Condition, rarity of design or pattern, size, colour, pedigree, restoration and many other factors must be taken into account when assessing values.

A set of eight oak, ash and elm Mendlesham chairs, including a pair of armchairs, each with a ladder back, 1880-1900. **£500-600** the set   *SB*

One of a set of 6 oak dining chairs, with a balustrade top-rail above stuffed leather seats, c. 1880. **£340-400** the set *SB*

Two of a set of 8 Victorian oak Pugin style dining chairs, including two armchairs, bearing the label of G. M. & H. J. Story, cabinet makers. **£330-420** the set *CEd*

One of a set of six mahog dining chairs, mid-19th C **£600-700** the set *SBA*

A set of six oak dining chairs, each with a button-upholstered back and seat, c. 1860. **£270-350** *SB*

A set of six mahogany dining chairs, c. 1840. **£350-420** *SB*

One of a set of 4 carved ebo side chairs, with drop-in se and brass castors. **£1,100-1,300** set *PWC*

One of a set of six walnut side chairs, c. 1880. **£500-600** the set *L*

A set of six walnut side chairs, c. 1860. **£400-580** the set *SB*

One of a set of 6 walnut side chairs, mid 19th C. **£600-700** set *SB*

One of a set of 8 Victorian chairs. **£475-550** set *MA*

An 18th C. ladder back chair.
£75-95 *TJ*

A Marion and Co. 'Rustic' oak side chair, late 19th C., stamped verso Marion & Co. **£120-150** *SBA*

ne of a set of 8 late Victorian arolean style dining chairs. **,050-1,200** the set *Ch*

An elm and ash country ladder-back chair, with American influence, c. 1740, set of 6. **£750-850**, pair **£125-150**, single **£45-50** *DEB*

An elm and ash country ladder-back chair, c. 1760. Set of 6 **£650-750**, pair **£100-120**, single **£35-45** *DEB*

elm and ash slat-k chair, c. 1880. Set £120-140, pair 0-40 *DEB*

A set of 4 chairs, with rushwork seats, c. 1820-30, 33 in. high. **£220-280** for 4 *SV*

An Edwardian set of four chairs with inlay. **£125-135** *LAC*

One of a set of 4 Edwardian dining chairs (re-upholstered), in excellent condition. **£250-300** set *LL*

One of a set of 4 Edwardian walnut dining chairs. **£285-300** set *LL*

One of a set of 8 19th C. oak Black Forest styled chairs, with two carving chairs. **£1,900-2,200** the set. *RDv*

A set of six Edwardian chairs, 4 singles, 2 carvers, with inlay. £525-595   *LAC*

ENGLISH CHAIRS

- c. 1630 backs of chairs were like panelled sides from a coffer
- early 17th C. chairs very square and made of oak
- in Charles II period principal wood walnut — such chairs tend to break as walnut splits easily and is relatively soft
- chairs have carved top rails, often with a crown, the stretcher will then be similarly carved, the legs are either turned or plain and simple spirals — sometimes called barley sugar twists; the caning in the backs is usually rectangular — any chair with oval caning is highly desirable
- by the end of the 17th C. backs were covered in needlework, the cabriole leg made its appearance, now stretchers have subtle curves
- the beginning of the 18th C. — the Queen Anne spoon back chair — with upright shaped splat, plain cabriole front legs, pad feet

- George I — carved knees a ball and claw feet, solid splats were walnut or veneered, often in burr walnut
- William Kent — introduced heavy carved mouldings — greatly influenced by Italia baroque
- from this time on chairs became lighter in design through the work mainly o Chippendale and Hepplewhite
- splats now pierced, legs square or tapered
- the square legs were also much cheaper than the cabriole legs, so they appealed to the large and growing middle class
- many of the designs came from France
- Hepplewhite, in particular, developed the chair with tapered legs, no stretchers and very plain splats
- during the 19th C. the taste was once again for heavier more substantial furniture

A high quality Victorian occasional chair, c. 1850. £285-300   *LL*

A Collinson and Lock mahogany chair, stamped Collinson & Lock. £120-180 P

A set of three 'Hepplewh chairs. £120-145 set   *I*

A Victorian mini slipper chair in gold velvet, c. 1850, 27 in. high. £275-300   *LL*

A pair of Louis XV beechwood chaises. £1,000-1,200   *C*

A late Victorian walnut lad chair, with petit point upholstery, c. 1880. £125-150   *DEB*

George II carved mahogany
d upholstered occasional
air, covered in brocade, c.
55. **£500-600** *SKC*

An Anglo-Indian hardwood
side chair, with a padded drop-
in seat, probably North India or
Burma, c. 1870. **£160-200** *SB*

A pair of Louis XV stained
beechwood chaises, by L.
Cordier, covered in rust-
coloured velvet, one stamped L.
Cordier. **£850-950** *C*

A rosewood nursing chair, mid-
9th C. **£250-300** *SBA*

One of a set of 6 Austrian white-
painted and gilded chairs, with
detachable cartouche-shaped
padded backs and serpentine
drop-in seats covered in red
damask, mid 18th C., later
supports. **£2,600-2,800** the
set *C*

One of a set of 6 George II
mahogany chairs (lacking
upholstery). **£3,500-4,200**
set *C*

William IV mahogany prie-
u chair, with original
adwork cover, on porcelain
tors, 43 in. high. **£80-110**
M

Venetian walnut fauteuil de
ndole, lined in ribbed cloth,
e back centred by an inlaid
ariot, crossbanded
roughout (faults), 18th C.
,100-1,300 *L*

A Regency mahogany
metamorphic library bergere,
converting to library steps with
four felt-lined treads, on sabre
legs. **£1,500-1,800** *C*

An American rosewood nursing
chair, in the manner of John
Belter, the seat-rail carved with
foliage on cabriole legs, mid-
19th C. **£200-300** *C*

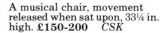

A musical chair, movement
released when sat upon, 33¼ in.
high. **£150-200** *CSK*

A Prie-dieu chair with original tapestry, c. 1860. £125-150 *LL*

A country ladder-back nursing elm and ash rocking chair, c. 1760. £85-95   *DEB*

A Regency mahogany libra chair/steps. £900-1,100 *DWB*

One of a pair of Victorian hall chairs. £40-45 pr.   *LAC*

A pair of oak hall chairs, 19th C., 34 in. high. £33-45   *SV*

A cast-iron hall chair, number 43, possibly French, 1850's. £200-250   *SB*

A pair of Regency mahoga hall chairs, c. 1820. £200-220   *W*

A George III mahogany child's chair and stand. £120-170 *Max*

CHAIRS

Elizabethan Chairs
oak

Charles II and William and Mary
walnut and veneers, elaborate carving.

Queen Anne
cabriole legs (often carved with a shell at the knee) at first stretchers, later disappeared, hooped back and vase or fiddle-shaped splat introduced, winged armchair introduced.

George I
mahogany began to be used around 1720, but not in large quantities until 1730-35, many good chairs made in walnut.

'Chippendale' Chairs
noted for fine mahogany chairs, beautiful back splats, with curving uprights, usually measures 3 ft. 1 in. to 3 ft. 2½ in. from back to floor, main types, 'ribband' back, Gothic back, fret back, perforated ladder-back, rococo back.

Robert Adam
oval, heart or lyre-shaped backs, legs tapered, turned or fluted, often made of beech, classical motifs, known as paterae often applied.

George Hepplewhite
shield-backs, often with an enclosed central splat, often decorated with 'Prince of Wales' feathers, wheat ear, classical urn or flowers, seats usually square, legs generally straight, tapered, often with spade foot, revival of the cabriole — a very graceful example was called 'French Hepplewhite'.

Sheraton
lighter, plainer, more square, much painted decoration, known for cane-work, disliked marquetry.

* In the provinces these chairs copied in cheaper more available woods — oak, birch, yew, elm, ash . . .

* The ladder-backs and spindle-backs were made in large quantities by 18th C. country cabinet makers.

* Thomas Hope's 'X'-back chair greatly influenced Regency cabinet makers.

* Balloon-backs introduced about 1830 — very popular until early 1870's, usually made in rosewood, mahogany or walnut.

* Victorian spoon-back was a revival of the Queen Anne chair.

An Edwardian mahogany child's chair, with original upholstery, 28 in. high. £30-50 *PAM*

An 18th C. yew-wood spindle and bow back child's elbow chair, 22 in. high. £170-230 *A*

A child's 18th C. yew wood tall Windsor chair, with cow horn stretcher. £600-700 *MMB*

An oak child's chair, c. 1800, 29½ in. high. £150-175 *A.E.F.*

A mahogany child's rocking chair, c. 1770, 23½ in. high. £420-480 *EAN*

A rare Charles II walnut child's arm chair. £1,800-2,100 *NCr*

An elm and ash child's school chair, c. 1880. £35-40 *DEB*

STOOLS

- until the middle of the 17th C. stools were virtually the only form of seat for one person
- many 17th C. 'joint' or 'joyned' stools have been reproduced
- look for good patination, colour and carving on oak examples. Yew-wood examples with good turning are highly desirable
- by the end of the 17th C. the chair was taking over and the

oak stool became less popular, walnut stealing the show from about 1670
- stools now tend to follow the style of chairs of the period, they also tend to be upholstered
- many Queen Anne stools have stretchers
- these have usually disappeared by George I
- when mahogany was introduced from 1730-1740,

stools became simpler, the cabriole leg being replaced with the straight leg, often with stretchers
- mid 18th C. the 'drop-in' seat became fashionable
- some stools made from chairs (this can increase the value of the chair twenty times)
- check for hessian under the seat — never used until 1840 (often conceals some alterations)

A 17th C. oak joint stool, c. 1660, 18 in. wide by 11 in. deep by 21 in. high. £280-350 *JGM*

A late 17th C. yew wood joint stool, 22 in. wide. £400-600 *SBA*

A joined oak stool, varnished, 1 ft. by 6 in. by 11 in. £150-175 *L*

A 17th C. oak joint stool, 22 in. high. **£500-580** *TJ*

A joined oak box stool. **£250-300** *L*

An early 17th C. oak joint stool, 23 in. high. **£750-850** *TJ*

One of a pair of George I walnut stools, on cabriole legs, with shells and padfeet, c. 1720, 16 in. high. **£2,250-2,500** pair *EAN*

A George I cabriole leg stool, c. 1720 (legs restored), 17 in. high. **£400-480** *EAN*

A 17th C. oak joint stool, 23 in. high. **£500-600** *TJ*

One of a pair of George I walnut stools, with differing needlework-upholstered drop-in seats, 21 in. (53.5 cm.) wide. **£1,600-1,800** pr. *C*

A Victorian stool. **£60-70** *MAT*

A pair of Louis XV beechwood tabourets, with differently-upholstered nailed serpentine seats, 17¾ in. (45 cm.) wide. **£2,500-3,000** *C*

A George I walnut stool, c. 1730. **£350-400** *DEB*

An Adam style painted satinwood dressing stool with stuff-over sage green seat. **£80-130** *L*

A Victorian carved walnut stool, the seat covered in yellow damask, 2 ft. wide, c. 1850. **£420-500** *SKC*

A Chinese rosewood and marble stool, 48 cm., Guangxu. **£180-220** *SB*

One of a pair of footstools, c. 1840. **£70-78** pair   *Gs*

A Regency green-painted X-frame stool, with lion masks holding brass ring handles, 34½ in. wide. **£550-650**   *C*

A mid-Victorian mahogany footstool, with original beadwork cover and on 3 bun feet, 11½ in. diam. **£20-40** *PAM*

A carved wood and gilt Gesso Baroque-style foot-stool, 17½ in. square, Italian, mid-19th C. **£80-100**   *SBA*

A Victorian walnut duet stool, c. 1850, 44 in. wide. **£225-250** *DEB*

A parquetry inlaid walnut footstool, with original tapestry cover, mid-Victorian, 48 in. long. **£120-140**   *PAM*

An Italian iron and brass faldistorio, the seat covered with red velvet, late 16th C., 25 in. wide, 33½ in. high. **£700-850**   *C*

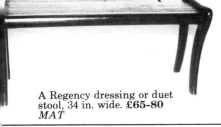

A Regency dressing or duet stool, 34 in. wide. **£65-80** *MAT*

A gilt mahogany stool in French Louis XV style, the rectangular padded seat with serpentine aprons boldly carved with marguerites, with cabriole legs, 34 by 86 in.; 150 by 300 cm., mid-19th C. **£200-300**   *SB*

DINING TABLES

- in mediaeval times the dining table was a board supported by trestles
- the first 'joined' tables appeared during the reign of Henry VIII
- Elizabethan tables were notable for the rich carving on bulbous legs
- the Elizabethan table also frequently had a draw leaf
- this table was common throughout the reigns of James I, Charles I and Charles II
- around this time the refectory table was introduced — fakes and reproductions abound
- prior to the early 18th C. the 'dining room' had often contained the bed and was a total living room. In Georgian England the elegant dining room and table was an essential part of the house
- walnut was a problem on large areas so oak was used until c. 1715; then came the advent of mahogany c. 1725-30
- as the 18th C. progressed — so did the length of the dining tables
- the 18th C. tables often had detachable ends and in the late 1780's cabinet makers introduced the D-end design
- late 18th C. pedestal tables gained popularity, having one, two or three pedestals
- the centre pillar dining table appeared around 1800

An oak refectory table, partly early 17th C., some carving done in 19th C., 34 by 121 by 34 in. **£3,000-4,000**   *SBA*

An oak refectory table, 2 ft. 5½ in. high by 7 ft. 9¼ in. wide. **£4,500-5,000**   *L*

A joined oak dining table, part
17th C., 6 ft. ½ in. long, 2 ft. 7 in.
wide. **£400-500**   *L*

A 17th C. oak refectory table
107 by 33 in., some restoration
£1,800-2,100   *SKC*

A fine cherrywood refectory
table, 17th C., German or Swiss,
102 in. (259 cm.) wide. **£2,000-
2,500**   *C*

An oak dining table, with plank
top, late 17th C., 99 in. (252 cm.)
wide. **£2,000-2,500**   *C*

An oak refectory table, with
quadruple plank top, 17th C.,
110 in. wide. **£2,700-3,000**   *C*

A 17th C. Flemish oak drawleaf
refectory table, 2 ft. 5 in. by 4 ft.
1 in., extending to 6 ft. 11 in.
£1,200-1,400   *SKC*

A 17th C. oak refectory table, 72
in. wide by 29½ in. deep by 29½
in. high, c. 1670. **£1,300-
1,600**   *RD*

An elm centre or dining table,
65½ by 29 in., 1900-20. **£350-
500**   *S*

A country oak farmhouse table,
one leaf deficient, George III, 7
ft. 10 in. (239 cm.) long, 2 ft. 7 in.
(79 cm.) wide. **£770-870**   *L*

*The price ranges given
reflect the average price a
purchaser should pay for
similar items. Condition,
rarity of design or pattern,
size, colour, pedigree,
restoration and many other
factors must be taken into
account when assessing
values.*

*Miller's Antiques Price Guide
builds up year by year to
form the most comprehensive
photo-reference system
available. The first three
volumes contain over 20,000
completely different
photographs.*

A late 17th C. oak drawleaf
dining table, 37 by 72 in.
extending to 118 in. **£1800-
2,000**   *DWB*

A mid 16th C. Tudor refectory
table, 31½ by 125½ by 32 in.
£1,500-2,500   *SBA*

A William IV mahogany dining table, the gateleg centre section fitted with two flaps, restored, mid-19th C. **£750-1,000** *SBA*

A rare George III Richard Brown patent extending mahogany dining table, extending to accommodate three leaves. **£2,750-3,250** *SBA*

A Regency mahogany triple pedestal dining table, including two extra leaves, 3.59 by 1.35 m. fully extended. **£2,200-2,500** *P*

A William IV mahogany extending dining table, 4 ft. 7 in. (140 cm.) by 4 ft. 5½ in. (136 cm.) extending to 10 ft. (306 cm.), c. 1835. **£1,500-1,700** *SKC*

A Regency mahogany dining table, with telescopic underframe, 5 additional leaves, 158 in. long (extended) by 59 in. wide by 29 in. high. **£1,500-1,800** *L*

A figured mahogany dining table, the patent construction with telescopic extending action, with standing leaf case containing seven leaves, leaf faults, first half 19th C., 18 ft. 4 in. extended. **£2,500-2,900** *L*

A George III mahogany four pillar dining table with brass toe castors, late 18th C. **£12,000-15,000** *SBA*

A George III style mahogany three-pillar dining table, with two leaves, 20th C. **£1,000-1,200** *SBA*

A late Regency mahogany twin pillar dining table, with two additional leaves, 1830's, 10 ft. long (extended) by 4 ft. 4 in. wide. **£1,800-2,100** *L*

A George IV mahogany triple pillar dining table, with 2 loose leaves, 11 ft. 2 in. by 4 ft. 6 in. **£4,600-5,000** *MMB*

Right
A large 17th C. oak gateleg table, fitted with a drawer. **£1,600-1,900** *NCr*

Left
A 17th C. oak gate-leg table, with later oval top, fitted two frieze drawers, 3 ft. (91.5 cm.) wide, c. 1660. **£330-400** *SKC*

A mid-17th C. gate-leg table, with pearwood top, 2 ft. 5 in. wide. **£650-750**   *SKC*

A late 17th C. oak gate-leg table, 3 ft. 5 in. by 1 ft. 3 in., extending to 3 ft. 9 in. **£400-480**   *SKC*

A late 17th C. oak gate leg table, **£300-380**   *RD*

A Chippendale mahogany Pembroke dining table, 62 by 51 in. **£2,500-2,900**   *M*

A mid-18th C. mahogany dining table, 3 ft. 7 in. **£300-390**   *WHL*

A George II red walnut flap top dining table, on leather covered brass roller casters, 4 ft. 1 in. by 5 ft. **£1,400-1,600**   *WW*

A George III mahogany drop-leaf dining table, 4 ft. 3 in. (130 cm.) by 4 ft. 4½ in. (133 cm.) fully extended, c. 1770. **£330-400** *SKC*

A mid-18th C. mahogany oval twin-flapped dining table, 48 by 54 in. **£450-550**   *WHL*

A Regency crossbanded mahogany snap-top breakfast table, the top having brass inlay and applied brass decoration to frieze, 41 in. **£1,200-1,600**   *BW*

A rare padouk-wood colonial gateleg dining table, possibly Portuguese Colonial, mid-18th C. **£2,000-2,500**   *SBA*

An early Victorian rosewood dining table, c. 1850, 45 in. **£340-420**   *L*

A Victorian rosewood tip up top breakfast table, 3 ft. 9 in. **£500-550**   *AG*

A George IV mahogany breakfast table, the tip-up top cross-banded and inlaid with brass, with brass feet and casters, 48 in. diam., c. 1825. **£800-1,000**   *SBe*

A 19th C. mahogany dining table, the support turned in the form of four pillars, 62 in. **£500-600**   *PWC*

A walnut centre table, the
quarter-veneered tip-top inlaid
with boxwood stringing and
foliage, 27½ by 53½ in., c. 1870.
£420-520   *SB*

A Victorian walnut centre
table, the top inlaid in coloured
woods, mother of pearl and
ivory, 56 in. £850-950   *A*

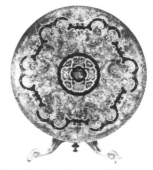

A walnut and marquetry
circular breakfast table, 57¼ in.
diam. £2,300-2,600   *SB*

mahogany breakfast table, of
Georgian design the top with
rosewood crossbanding, legs
ending in brass toes and
castors, part George III, 4 ft. 8
in. long, 2 ft 11 in. wide. £300-
350   *L*

A Victorian walnut circular tip
up top breakfast table, richly
inlaid in coloured woods, 4 ft. 4
in. £1,300-1,500   *AG*

A George III mahogany and
satinwood inlaid breakfast
table, crossbanded in rosewood,
tulipwood and satinwood, with
brass paw cappings and
castors, 1.48 by 1.17 m. £2,700-
3,000   *P*

George III mahogany
breakfast table, late 18th/early
19th C. £1,200-1,400   *SBA*

A Collinson & Lock mahogany
centre table, 46½ in. diam.,
stamped 'Collinson & Lock
London 6387', 1870's. £180-
240   *SB*

A 19th C. Italian marble and
Roman mosaic table top, 57.5
cm. diam. £1,400-1,800   *P*

19th C. continental
marquetry centre table, the
amboyna centre panel inlaid
and with brass edging, the
frieze with drawer, 3 ft. 9½ in.
wide (extended), 1 ft. 11 in. deep,
ft. 5½ in. high. £450-520   *L*

An octagonal rosewood centre
table, 28½ by 38½ in., c. 1880.
£220-280   *SB*

A rosewood centre table, with a
circular marble inset top,
Guangxu, 82 cm. £370-420
SB

A Victorian oak pedestal breakfast table. **£500-600** *Max*

A Regency mahogany breakfast table, 51 in. diam. **£1,200-1,500** *C*

A George IV rosewood tilt-top pedestal table, with brass paw feet finials, 4 ft. ½ in. (124 cm.) diam., c. 1825. **£570-630** *SKC*

A rosewood breakfast table, 29 by 48 in., c. 1840. **£320-390** *SB*

A rosewood oval breakfast table, late 1830's, 64 in. (162.5 cm.) wide. **£580-700** *SB*

A very fine Victorian loo table, c. 1880. **£460-500** *MAT*

An early Victorian walnut and marquetry centre table, with circular tip-up top inlaid in stained and engraved woods, 42 in. (109 cm.) diam. **£2,200-2,400** *C*

A fine and rare early Victorian marquetry centre table, by E. H. Baldock of Hanway Street, London, for Louis Philippe of France, 1845, 46 in. **£3,800-4,400** *JGM*

A Regency rosewood centre table, the tip-up top with ormolu border, 51½ in. (131 cm.) diam. **£1,000-1,100** *C*

A Victorian marquetry centre table, the top inlaid with kingwood, satinwood, ebony and harewood on a burr walnut ground, c. 1860, 4 ft. 9 in. (145 cm.) diam. **£2,600-3,200** *L*

A rosewood dining table, the circular top crossbanded with bird's-eye maple, c. 1850, 53 in. diam. **£750-900** *SBe*

A William IV mahogany breakfast table, 31 by 47 in. (by 120 cm.), c. 1835. **£480-550** *SB*

A pollard oak centre table, the crossbanded top inlaid with ebonised lines, mid-19th C., 72 in. (183 cm.) wide. £2,500-3,000   C

A walnut 'Renaissance' centre table, Italian, mid-19th C., 31 by 3 by 37 in. (79 by 134.5 by 94 m.). £800-880   SB

A Biedermeier cherrywood centre table, with quartered mirror-figured circular top, and a single drawer, 40 in. (105.5 cm.) diam. £1,000-1,200   C

A Victorian oak library table, he leather-lined top with ebonised border, the frieze with 4 drawers divided by false drawers, 58 in. wide. £680-800   C

A late Victorian drum table, having 4 drawers with brass drop handles, with red tooled leather top, 54 in. £450-550   BW

A 'George I' giltwood centre table, with a polychrome marble top, c. 1850, 30¼ by 46½ in. (77 by 118 cm.). £400-480   SB

A Regency mahogany library table, the leather-lined top fitted with 6 drawers, 46½ in. (118 cm.) wide. £1,900-2,100   C

A satinwood drum-top library table, the 48 in. dia. top with an inset green leather surface, reconstructed out of some 18th C. pieces. £800-1,000   SBA

A George IV mahogany library table, the frieze with 3 drawers divided by segmental drawers, 72 in. (183 cm.) diam. £1,300-1,500   C

Miller's Antiques Price Guide builds up year by year to form the most comprehensive photo-reference system available. The first three volumes contain over 20,000 completely different photographs.

rosewood library table, 1830-0, 48 in. wide. £300-380   L

A George III mahogany library table, with two frieze drawers flanked by two dummies, modified, 60 in. wide, 28½ in. high, 37 in. deep extended. £620-740   L

A late Regency mahogany library table, 36 in. wide by 21 in. deep by 29 in. high. £460-580   L

A mahogany library table, of George II design, with alternate real and dummy frieze drawers, 51 in. £680-780   Hy.D

SOFA TABLES

- examples with low stretchers tend to be later
- an elegant feminine writing table, usually with two shallow drawers
- either had two vertical supports or a central pillar
- many fine examples made in mahogany with satinwood or rosewood stringing and crossbanding
- rosewood examples can be of exceptional quality
- examples with stretchers tend to be later
- lyre end supports, particularly with a brass strip, are likely to increase value
- many sofa tables have been made from old cheval mirrors
- long drawers are undesirable but many have been cut down

A George III faded rosewood sofa table, the top crossbande with satinwood, 66 in. (168 cm. wide open. £2,600-2,900   C

A mahogany sofa table, 5 ft. 3 in. £790-900   RMcT

A Regency rosewood sofa table, with boxwood stringing to top, 39 by 30 in. £1,150-1,400 BW

A mahogany sofa table of excellent colour, with nice high stretcher, c. 1805, 55 in. wide, 27 in. deep, 28 in. high. £1,650-1,750   W

A Regency pollard oak sofa table, 57½ in. (146 cm.) wide, open. £3,000-3,500   C

A 19th C. Regency style Cocobolo sofa table, with brass lion head and ring handles, cappings and castors, 155 cm. max. £770-900   PJ

A Regency rosewood sofa table crossbanded with burr maple, 59½ in. wide. £900-1,200   C

A Georgian mahogany sofa table, on reeded sabre legs with brass claw castors, faults, 60 in. wide, 28 in. high, 25 in. deep. £600-700   L

A Regency rosewood sofa table, crossbanded with maplewood outlined by ebony and boxwood lines, 65 in. wide. £3,000-3,300   C

A George III mahogany sofa table crossbanded with rosewood, inscribed ink '... Dr. Habbnig 63 in. wide, open. £1,500-1,800   C

A late Regency rosewood sofa table, with two drawers, on quadruped supports with brass paw terminals and castors, 36 in., opening to 58 in. £600-650   DWB

A rosewood sofa tabl c. 1820, 61½ in. wide b 27 in. high by 26 in. deep. £1,500-1,600 W

mahogany Pembroke table, c.
60, 30 in. high by 41 in.
tended. £375-425 *LL*

PEMBROKE TABLES

- became popular in the mid to late 18th C., possibly designed and ordered by Henry Herbert, the Earl of Pembroke (1693–1751)
- on early examples the legs were square which are by far the most desirable
- later tables had turned legs
- rounded flaps and marquetry again increase desirability
- satinwood was greatly favoured, particularly with much crossbanding and inlay
- the Edwardians made many fine Pembroke tables which have appeared wrongly catalogued at auction
- many 18th C. Pembroke tables have chamfering on the insides of the legs

A Chippendale mahogany
Pembroke table, fitted with a
drawer, 2 ft. (61 cm.) wide, c.
1770. £440-500 *SKC*

George III satinwood
embroke table, the top
ossbanded with rosewood and
laid with amboyna, 37½ in.
5 cm.) wide, open. £1,400-
,600 *C*

A Sheraton mahogany
Pembroke table, with a single
long drawer and opposing
dummy, crossbanded in
rosewood and lined in boxwood
and ebony, George III, 2 ft. 8 in.
long. £900-1,100 *RD*

A late 18th C. mahogany
Pembroke table on castors, 38
in. extended, 27½ in. high.
£370-430 *NC*

mahogany Pembroke table,
ossbanded with satinwood
nd some ebony stringing, c.
790, 29 in. high by 3 ft. 9 in.
ide extended. £685-750 *LL*

A George III mahogany
Pembroke table, with
satinwood stringing, 2 ft. 7½ in.
(80 cm.) wide, c. 1800. £300-
350 *SKC*

A Georgian mahogany supper
Pembroke table, with four sabre
legs ending in lion's paw brass
castors, 3 ft. 11 in. extended, 3 ft
6 in. wide. £260-350 *L*

A serpentine mahogany
Pembroke table, of Sheraton
design, reduced, mainly 19th C.,
30 in. wide. £500-600 *L*

A George III mahogany
'Butterfly-leaved' Pembroke
table, drawer to frieze, 2 ft. 6 in.
(76 cm.) wide, c. 1790. £420-
460 *SKC*

A Regency mahogany pedestal Pembroke table, with two rule jointed leaves, 36 in. **£220-320**   *PSH*

A George III mahogany Pembroke table, crossbanded with satinwood and fitted with two drawers, 41 in. wide, open. **£850-1,000**   *C*

A George III mahogany Pembroke table, with satinwood crossbanding an line inlay, 39 in. extended. **£390-470**   *L*

A small late 18th C. mahogany Pembroke table, c. 1790, 25 in. wide (open) by 16 in. deep by 29 in. high. **£650-790**   *JGM*

A Victorian Sutherland table, 26 in. high, top 23 by 29 in. **£100-125**   *E.E*

A mahogany Sutherland tab brass feet and castors, 30 in. high, 35 in. deep, 6 in. wide (closed) 40 in. wide (open), c. 1850. **£200-250**   *PAM*

A late 19th C. walnut Sutherland table, with inlay, 24 in. deep, 24½ in. high, 6 in. wide (closed), 27 in. wide (open). **£130-160**   *PAM*

An ormolu-mounted kingwood table a ecrire, with leather-lined kidney-shaped top, gallery incorporating an inkwell and pen-holder, signed F. Linke Paris, 30 in. (76 cm.) wide. **£2,800-3,200**   *C*

A contre-partie boulle writin table, of Louis XV design w cloth-lined top, 34 in. (86.5 cr wide. **£1,100-1,300**   *C*

A Louis XV tulipwood and palisander table a ecrire, stamped H. Hansen JME, 19½ in. (49.5 cm.) wide. **£6,800-7,300**   *C*

A Transitional tulipwood and parquetry table a ecrire, the leather-lined top fitted with a leather-lined slide and a drawer, the sabots not matching, stamped G. Dester JME, 22½ in. (57 cm) wide. **£4,400-5,000**   *C*

A French kingwood table a ecrire, in the Louis XVI manne crossbanded in harewood an rosewood, 19th C., possibly Napoleon III, 2 ft. 10 in. high, ft. 1 in. wide, 1 ft. 4 in. deep. **£750-850**   *L*

A 'Louis XV' kingwood serpentine writing table, applied with painted porcelain plaques, 30 by 38½ in., the base stamped E.H.B. with a marque au feu, c. 1850. **£680-780** *SB*

A Louis XV tulipwood and marquetry table a ecrire, 15½ in. (42 cm.) wide. **£5,500-6,000** *C*

kingwood ormolu-mounted ble a ecrire, top and stretcher laid with jugs and vases, 24 . (61 cm.) wide. **£1,400-600** *C*

POINTS TO NOTE ON 'FAKES'

- can't satisfactorily fake patination — but watch heavily applied wax polishes
- can't get modern brass to look like 18th C. brass — 18th C. brass had a higher copper content, which gives it a softer feel and a more subtle colour
- can't get realistic looking patches of discolouration round heads of nails and screws
- can't authentically fake herring-bone inlay — usually on fakes it is completely flat, which is an obvious giveaway, as after a period of time with changes in temperature and humidity the inlay lifts in places. This effect is extremely difficult for a restorer to perfect

Mid-Victorian tulipwood riting-table, the serpentine ather-lined top inlaid with crolling, finished with iltmetal border, 55½ in. (141 m.) wide. **£1,350-1,500** *C*

A Louis XVI amaranth and marquetry table a ecrire, with a divided drawer on the right and a leather-lined slide on the left, 34 in. (86 cm.) wide. **£5,500-6,000** *C*

n early Louis XV kingwood able a ecrire, enclosing two dded compartments and fitted ith a drawer each side, 32¼ in. 2 cm.) wide. **£3,500-4,000**

A late 18th C. Dutch marquetry inlaid mahogany writing table, with two drawers and two false drawers, having ornate brass plate handles and brass feet, 3 ft. 8 in. **£1,200-1,500** *WW*

An Austrian rococo white-painted and gilded writing-table, fitted with a leather-lined slide and drawer, mid-18th C., 38 in. (96.5 cm.) wide. **£1,300-1,500** *C*

A mahogany writing table by Gillow & Co., the superstructure nset with a painted panel, tamped L 107000 Gillow and Co., 43¾ by 42 in., c. 1880. **£220-280** *SB*

A Regency rosewood writing table, the top inlaid with brass lines with two drawers, 60 in. (152.5 cm.) wide. **£2,000-2,200** *C*

An early Victorian oak writing table, inlaid with ebony, 107 cm. wide. **£550-650** *Bon*

An oak and pollard oak writing table, the top inset with a writing surface, the frieze with two drawers, 30 by 48 in., c. 1870. **£240-300**   *SB*

A joined oak inlaid writing table, late 17th/18th C., 2 ft. 7½ in. wide, 1 ft. 7½ in. deep, 2 ft. 5 in. high. **£250-350**   *L*

A Regency pollard elm writi table, the top crossbanded w rosewood, 40 in. wide. **£750 850**   *C*

A Regency mahogany writing table, rosewood crossbanded and boxwood line inlaid, two drawers and two false drawers with brass ring handles, 41 by 28½ in. **£1,600-1,900**   *DWB*

A Regency mahogany writing table, 2 ft. 11 in. (89 cm.) wide. **£110-130**   *L*

A Sheraton writing table, in rosewood, crossbanded in satinwood and partridge woo ebony and boxwood stringin ivory handles, drawer with adjustable reading/writing slide, c. 1795-1800, 18 in. wide 22 in. deep by 48 in. high. **£2,200-2,500**   *RD*

A small Sheraton period writing table, in mahogany with ebony line inlay, with 2 drawers and 2 false drawers, having brass sabots, 3 ft. **£1,950-2,200**   *WW*

A William and Mary walnut side table, with crossbanded top on later turned feet, 37½ in. (95 cm.) wide. **£1,150-1,300**   *C*

One of a pair of Charles II grained side tables, with later simulated Portor marble tops, the grained decoration of later date, 27¼ in. wide, 34 in. high. **£2,200-2,500** the pair   *C*

A 17th C. German oak serving table, the two-plank top above a deep frieze, 58 in. long. **£1,100-1,500**   *B*

A Lignum Vitae side table, with moulded rectangular top inlaid with oyster roundels, on later turned feet, 17th C., 35 in. (89 cm.) wide. **£2,600-3,200**   *C*

17th C. oak and walnut table, e top a replacement, probably ench, 29 in. wide by 22 in. ep by 28 in. high. **£280-0** *RD*

A Regence polished oak side table, with breche d'Aleps marble top, the frame with later back-rail and supports, 72 in. (183 cm.) wide. **£4,000-4,500** *C*

A rare George II two drawer side table, in yew-wood, in original condition throughout, c. 1740, 30 in. wide by 20 in. deep by 28 in. high. **£3,300-3,700** *RD*

A pair of North Italian giltwood side tables, with breccia marble tops, mid-18th C. (reduced), 43 in. (109 cm.) wide. **£3,300-3,800** *C*

An early 18th C. oak side table, c. 1710, 30 in. wide by 20 in. deep by 28 in. high. **£620-730** *JGM*

George II mahogany side ble, with drawer, c. 1750, 29½ . wide by 19 in. deep by 28 in. gh. **£470-570** *JGM*

An 18th C. mahogany side table, c. 1760, 34 in. wide by 21 in. deep by 28 in. high. **£280-340** *JGM*

early 19th C. Dutch ahogany and floral arquetry side table with grey arble top, mirror back and atform base, 35 in. **£660-0** *DWB*

A George II giltwood side table, with Portor marble top, the frieze with later moulded border, 46½ in. (118 cm.) wide. **£1,200-1,400** *C*

A George III mahogany serving-table, with semi-elliptical top, the frieze crossbanded with rosewood, 81½ in. wide. **£2,000-2,300** *C*

George III mahogany drop-af side table, with frieze rawer and with brass handle, 1780, 36 in. wide, 27 in. high. **330-380** *OB*

Miller's is a price GUIDE Not a price LIST.

The price ranges given reflect the average price a purchaser should pay for similar items. Condition, rarity of design or pattern, size, colour, pedigree, restoration and many other factors must be taken into account when assessing values.

A George III painted side table, 47 in. wide. **£880-1,080** *C*

A mid-Georgian red walnut side table, in the manner of John Channon, with moulded brass borders, possibly Irish, cut down, later back legs, 69½ in. wide. **£2,200-2,500**   *C*

An Edwardian satinwood sidetable, crossbanded in tulipwood with marquetry inlay, 52 in. **£450-600**   *BW*

A Dutch marquetry occasio table, the frieze enclosed by doors, 2 ft. 4½ in. wide. **£3 480**   *GC*

One of a pair of Regency mahogany side tables, 72 in. (183.5 cm.) wide. **£2,100-2,300** the pair   *C*

A mahogany side table, 19 in. deep by 30 in. wide, 27½ in. high. **£200-240**   *PAM*

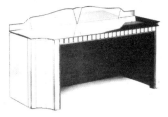

A 1930's mirror glass side table, in shades of peach and pink, 79 cm. high, 157 by 51 cm., 1930's. **£200-270**   *SB*

A George III oak-grained side table, with marble top, the grained decoration of later date, possibly cut down, the top not fitting, 58½ in. wide. **£1,600-1,900**   *C*

A Bugatti side table, vellum covered and applied with beaten copper, body inlaid wi pewter, 64 cm., the top with painted facsimile signature 'Bugatti', c. 1900. **£820-920** *SB*

A Victorian parquetry occasional table, the crossbanded top inlaid with circles and stars, on entwined spiral column, 17½ in. long. **£220-290**   *L*

A pair of carved pine eagle side tables of George II style, each with a verde antico marble top, 2 ft. 11 in. high by 3 ft. 6½ in. wide, 20th C. **£800-1,000**   *S*

A Victorian parquetry occasional table, inlaid with chain link design, on entwined spiral column, 17½ in. long. **£270-330**   *L*

A kingwood occasional tabl applied with gilt-bronze mounts, 29 by 17½ in., c. 18 **£460-560**   *SB*

osewood and Boulle
asional table, inlaid with
ry, pewter, cut-brass and
ther of pearl on a brass
uid column, 30¼ in., c. 1840.
0-540   *SB*

A red lacquer table, the top
elaborately carved with
interlocking octagonal panels,
18th C. (some damage), 41 in.
square, 33 in. high. **£3,400-
3,800**   *C*

An early George III yew-wood
occasional table, 22½ in. wide.
£600-700   *C*

A Victorian mahogany table,
with frieze drawer, 30 in. high,
33 in. wide. **£150-185**   *SV*

An antique mahogany
occasional table, with three
bands of inlay and central shell
inlay, 27 in. **£250-320**   *RBB*

all rare late 18th C.
gany screen table, with
al castors, c. 1780, 18 in.
by 12 in. deep by 48 in.
£650-750   *JGM*

A walnut reading table, the
hinged velvet-lined top with an
easel support, with a drawer
and candle-slide, 31 in. (78.5
cm.) wide. **£1,200-1,400**   *C*

A Regency stained beech wine
table, with brass ball feet, 1 ft. 6
in. (43 cm.) wide, c. 1810. **£340-
400**   *SKC*

A late Regency ebony and
ebonised table, with brass
inlay, 20½ in. high, 17 in. top.
£650-700   *NC*

Villiam IV marble and
ined oak centre table, with a
mond inlay of various
rbles and semi-precious
nes, including bluejohn and
lachite, on a simulated
rble base, 34 by 32 in. (86 by
cm.), c. 1835. **£300-390**   *SB*

A William and Mary walnut
and seaweed marquetry
occasional table, inlaid with
foliage, the frieze with two long
and four short drawers, early
1900's, 27 by 32½ in. (69 by 82.5
cm.). **£350-420**   *SB*

A late 17th C. oak credence
table, with folding semi-circular
top, opening to reveal a frieze
compartment (in need of
restoration), 3 ft. 3 in. (99 cm.)
diam. **£770-870**   *L*

A Regency mahogany
architect's table, the frieze
fitted on each side with five
small drawers, 45 in. wide.
£2,000-2,200   *C*

A mid-Georgian mahogany
architect's table, the hinged
flap each side enclosing four
short drawers, 38 in. wide.
£900-1,200   *C*

A cast-iron hall table, the t
inset with tiles, adapted fr
two standard umbrella sta
31 by 44 in., 1850's. **£440-54**
SB

A mid-Georgian mahogany
architect's table, with a drawer
with baize-lined slide, 38¼ in.
(97 cm.) wide. **£1,300-1,600**
C

An extensively inlaid tip-top
table, with tripod base and with
brass feet, early Victorian, 28
by 36 by 25 in. **£500-600**   *SV*

A mid-Georgian walnut
architect's table, the
rectangular easel top with br
candle-slides and a well-fitt
drawer, 36 in. wide. **£1,100**
1,400   *C*

A late 18th C. mahogany tripod
table, c. 1790, 29¼ in. high by 15
in. deep by 19 in. wide. **£300-**
385   *JGM*

A William IV mahogany tip-top
table, c. 1835, 28 in. high, top
19½ by 30 in. **£150-175**   *E.E*

A mahogany lamp table, c.
1825, 28 in. high by 18 in. width
by 15 in. depth. **£70-85**   *LL*

A mahogany snap-top tabl
with tripod base, c. 1850, 27
high, 20 in. wide. **£68-98**

A Regency stained beech wine
table, with brass ball feet, 1 ft. 6
in. (43 cm.) wide, c. 1810. **£340-**
400   *SKC*

Left
A rosewood tripod table, in the
Chippendale style, with floral
needlework cover, the label
inscribed '. . . Le Duc de
Nemours' and with stencilled
monogram and inventory
number 15433, 23 in. diam., mid
19th C. **£800-1,100**   *C*

A Regency lacquered birdc
wine table (lacquer rubbed)
in. high. **£335-395**   *E.E*

A dished-top oak table, with tripod base, c. 1790, 27 in. high, 26 in. diam. **£135-155** *OB*

A Chippendale design mahogany snap top table, 24 in. diam. **£500-580** *M*

A tripod table, with painted decoration. **£180-230** *LMT*

mid-19th C. ebonised papier che snap-top table, with aid mother of pearl and nted flower decoration, 28 in. le. **£160-220** *DSH*

Regency oak pedestal table, tip-up top inlaid in various ods, bearing a label inscribed Marshall Maker', 29½ in. m. **£500-600** *C*

An Empire bronze and ormolu centre table, with Portor marble top, 34½ in. (88 cm.) diam. **£4,000-5,000** *C*

A 19th C. walnut and inlay parquetry occasional table, 61 cm. diam., c. 1855. **£100-130** *SKC*

An 18th C. mahogany pedestal table, with shaped scallop top. **£620-750** *PW*

callop-top birdcage tea table, 750 (restored), 28 in. wide by in. high. **£525-600** *LL*

A mahogany tripod table, with twisted rope stem, c. 1760. **£225-260** *DEB*

18th C. mahogany tripod ble, c. 1760, 34 in. diam., 28 in. gh. **£380-430** *RD*

A George III Irish mahogany pedestal table, diam. 37½ in., 1760. **£500-600** *SBe*

A 'George III' mahogany table, 27½ by 34 in., c. 1880. **£320-400**   *SB*

A walnut and elm wine ta (top cracked), c. 1790, 29 i high, 22 in. diam. **£135-1** *OB*

A mahogany tripod table with dish top, c. 1780 (with repaired top), 21 in. diam., 28 in. high. **£325-375**   *W*

A Chinese Chippendale design tea or china table, 29 by 22 in. **£320-400**   *RBB*

A Georgian games and t table, 36 in. wide. **£840-** *Win*

A George III style mahogany silver table, 27 by 33 in., 20th C. **£450-500**   *SBA*

A pair of Sheraton figured mahogany tea tables, George III, 3 ft. (92 cm.) wide, 1 ft. 6 in. (46 cm.) deep. **£3,300-3,600** *L*

A Georgian mahogany tea table, 33 in. wide. **£240-300** *L*

A mahogany D shape tea t of Sheraton design, the figu top with boxwood edging a satinwood line inlay. **£230** 300   *L*

A 'Sheraton' mahogany tea table, figured folding top with boxwood lines (restored), 19th C., 3 ft. (92 cm.) wide. **£230-270**   *L*

A George II walnut tea-table, with folding top, the border re-carved, 32¼ in. (82 cm.) wide. **£800-880**   *C*

A Sheraton mahogany an inlaid tea table, the fold-o top above a drawer. **£270-** 320   *RMcT*

Regency mahogany circular table, 37 in. wide. **£390-**
0   *L*

A John Kendall & Co. rosewood tea or games table, bearing a printed label John Kendall & Co., workman's name written in ink Curtis 33753, 1840's, 36½ in. (92.7 cm.) wide. **£340-400**   *SB*

A Victorian rosewood fold-over tea table, 3 ft. wide. **£300-**
370   *VV*

William IV mahogany tea le, 3 ft. (92 cm.) wide. **£240-**
0   *L*

A mahogany card table, c. 1790, 28½ in. high, 35 in. wide, 17 in. deep. **£600-700**   *W*

A kingwood and rosewood serpentine card table, enclosing a crossbanded quarter veneered interior, 30 by 34 in. **£550-**
650   *SB*

sewood card table, c. 1800, 1. high by 35½ in. wide. **£250-1,350**   *NC*

rare George II concertina tion mahogany card table, th candle stands and counter ntainers, the frieze with a awer. **£1,500-1,750**   *NCr*

A French Hepplewhite design mahogany card table, with baize lined moulded edge twin flap top, 3 ft., 19th C. **£600-**
750   *WW*

George III satinwood card-ble, the baize-lined top ssbanded with rosewood and inted, 36 in. wide. **£1,800-**
000   *C*

A 19th C. walnut serpentine card table, with ormolu mounts and tulipwood banding, 35 in. **£540-670**   *O*

A pair of walnut and marquetry card tables, opening to reveal a circular baize-lined surface, with gilt-metal mouldings and mounts, 30 by 34½ in., mid-19th C. **£1,800-2,200**   *SB*

A rosewood card table, crossbanded with satinwood and inlaid boxwood stringing. **£650-750** *NC*

A Boulle serpentine card table, the interior with a playing surface, with gilt-bronze mounts, 31 by 37 in., c. 1870. **£680-780** *SB*

A Victorian rosewood card table, on cabriole legs with s[feet, 33 in. **£190-250** *GA*

A Louis-Philippe tulipwood and marquetry card-table, with baize-lined swivelling top, ormolu-mounted, 35 in. wide. **£2,700-3,000** *C*

A William IV rosewood folding top card table, 36 in. **£280-330** *A*

A rosewood card table, with swivelling top, late 1830's, 36 (91.5 cm.) wide. **£220-300**

A rosewood card table, the swivel top enclosing a well, 30 by 36 in., c. 1840. **£300-380** *SB*

A Victorian rosewood card table, 36 in. **£250-350** *A*

A Victorian walnut card ta[the serpentine folding top w baize lined interior, c. 1850, [(92 cm.) wide. **£460-550**

A George III mahogany turn over top table, with maple and kingwood crossbanded borders, on four brass cap feet, 3 ft. 3 in. **£1,000-1,100** *AG*

A serpentine rosewood card table, c. 1855, 30½ by 36 in. (77.5 by 91.5 cm.). **£350-420** *SB*

A George IV mahogany ca[table, the top crossbanded [rosewood, 2 ft. 5½ in. high [ft. 1¾ in. wide, c. 1820. **£64[** **760** *S*

A 19th C. Sheraton design card table, the top inlaid with satinwood, 30 in. wide. **£480-580**   *M*

mahogany envelope card ...e, inlaid with boxwood ...nging, 30½ by 22 in. (77.5 by ...m.), c. 1910. **£260-320**   *SB*

A satinwood marquetry envelope card table, with under tier. **£650-800**   *DLJ*

A thuya and porcelain-mounted card table, the interior with a red baize lining and gilt tooled leather banding above a well, 30 by 36 in., 1870's. **£600-750**   *SB*

...Edwardian rosewood ...eered envelope fold top card ...e, fitted with one drawer, ... cm. **£300-380**   *OT*

A rosewood envelope card table, each flap inlaid with ivory and beechwood, with a drawer, c. 1910, 29 by 21¾ in. (73.5 by 55 cm.). **£310-360**   *SB*

A Queen Anne black and gilt lacquered triple top games table, inlaid with mother of pearl (restored), 31½ in. **£760-900**   *DWB*

...riple top games table, c. 1755, ...½ in. high. **£1,450-1,550**

A George II red walnut games table, with triangular triple flap, baize-lined and fitted with counter-wells, with two swivelling drawers, 36½ in. wide. **£2,400-2,800**   *C*

...ne quality George II ...ogany triple top card, tea ... writing table, on pad feet, c. ...0, 29 by 29 in. open, 28 in. ...h. **£1,800-2,200**   *JGM*

A Dutch walnut games table, c. 1750, 29 in. wide. **£1,300-1,500**   *B.M*

A George III mahogany games table, with two fold-over flaps, 2 ft. 9 in. (84 cm.) wide, c. 1780. **£1,100-1,300**   *SKC*

A Regency larchwood games table, the top crossbanded with rosewood, enclosing a backgammon well, 38 in. wide. **£2,000-2,500**   *C*

A mid Victorian walnut games/sewing table, enclosing chess, backgammon and score boards in ebony, kingwood and maple, above a tapering sewing box, 67 cm. wide. **£550-650** *HSS*

A Regency rosewood games table, inlaid with a chess-boa enclosing a backgammon w 34 in. wide. **£1,300-1,500**

A Dutch mahogany and marquetry games table, inlaid for chess and draughts, the frieze with two hinged drawers, 36 in. **£600-700**   *Hy.D*

An early 19th C. late Regency/William IV rosewood games table, with fitted drawers, 31 in. wide by 28 in. high. **£2,000-2,250**   *NC*

An 18th C. games table wi backgammon, cribbage, 30 high. **£1,800-2,000**   *B.M*

A rosewood games table, c. 1830, 28 in. high. **£485-525** *B.M*

A mahogany games table/dumb waiter, the folding top lined in blue baize, rising to form a two tier dumb waiter, c. 1850, 3 ft. 4 in. (102 cm.) wide. **£390-450**   *L*

A William IV rosewood ga table, top 24½ in. wide by 29 high. **£1,300-1,400**   *NC*

A Victorian games tables with folding top, 28 in. high. **£150-180**   *MAT*

An early 19th C. Dutch yewwood and marquetry inlaid games table, 24 in. **£1,300-1,600**   *DWB*

A Sheraton satinwood w table, 30 in. high. **£1,20 1,400**   *EAN*

Regency mahogany games
le, inlaid with ebony
nging, width 31½ in., c. 1810.
50-560   *SBe*

A George III mahogany and
kingwood banded work table,
with a pleated silk well, 2 ft. 6 in.
high by 1 ft. 6 in. wide, c. 1790.
£660-760   *SKC*

A Regency rosewood lady's
Davenport work table, 1 ft. 2½
in. (37 cm.) wide, by 2 ft. 8 in. (81
cm.) high, c. 1815 (restored).
£550-620   *SKC*

A 19th C. William IV
rosewood work table
with fitted drawer, 38
in. high. **£450-500**
NC

A rosewood work table, with
fitted interior including
compartments for cottons and
needles, 28½ by 20 in., mid-19th
C. **£360-420**   *SBA*

te 18th C. workbox
crossbanding
laced bag), 29 in.
by 20 in. wide by
in. deep. **£350-**
 W

A fine Regency lady's
work table, with fully
fitted interior, c. 1830,
31 in. high. **£350-
450**   *ST*

An Edwardian satinwood work
table, with hinged top enclosing
a fitted interior, 28½ by 15½ in.,
early 20th C. **£320-360**   *SBA*

A walnut combined
games and work
table. **£700-800**
SBA

burr-walnut work table, the
side with two pierced fretwork
mpartments and a silk-lined
ll, late 1850's, 28½ by 24¼ in.
2.5 by 61.5 cm.). **£450-550**

A lady's burr walnut oval
worktable, with fitted interior,
25 by 17 in. **£370-420**   *A*

A Victorian walnut
games/sewing table, inlaid in
satinwood and tulipwood, with
sliding sewing compartment,
26¾ in. wide. **£550-660**   *O*

L

A Regency mahogany work table, 34 in. high. **£500-590** *WR*

A rosewood work table with inlaid brass, c. 1830, 29 in. high. **£500-560**   *B.M*

A George III mahogany work table, crossbanded and strung with boxwood, fitted with compartments and a removable tray, 2 ft. 6¾ in. by 1 ft. 8 in., c. 1795. **£700-800**   *S*

A 19th C. marquetry needlework table, 21 in. wide, 28 in. high. **£400-475**   *E.E*

An early 19th C. Anglo-Indian ebony work box, 33 in. high. **£380-450**   *WR*

A George III Sheraton ladies rosewood and inlaid work table, with fitted interior, decorated in boxwood patterned inlay and crossbanding. **£460-520**   *B*

A Victorian French ebonised and marquetry work table, 18 in. **£350-450**   *Hy.D*

An unusual Louis XV kingwood and tulipwood table a ouvrage, the mirror-backed hinged lid enclosing a material-lined interior, 19¼ in. (49 cm.) wide. **£3,000-3,200**   *C*

A 'Sheraton' sewing box (in need of restoration), c. 1790, in. wide, 28 in. high. **£300-350**   *MAT*

A lady's 19th C. French rosewood inlaid sewing tabl with mirrored interior and sliding sewing box below, 2 **£700-900**   *MMB*

A 19th C. French marquetry and parquetry tricoteuse, in la Louis XVI style, 76 cm. long. **£1,100-1,300**   *HSS*

A Louis XV provincial fruitwood table de nuit, 17 in. (43 cm.) wide. **£500-600**   *C*

A Louis XV giltwood console table, with breche violette marble top, stamped SMR MC LES 175, and branded with a salamander below a crown, 36 in. (91.5 cm.) wide. **£1,500-1,700**   *C*

A Louis XV fruitwood table en chiffoniere, stamped J. F. JME, 15 in. (38 cm.) wide. **£1,000-1,100**   *C*

A German walnut worktable, of globe form, the domed cover swivelling to reveal a fitted interior, 21 in. wide. **£1,400-1,600**   *C*

An oak console table, with a serpentine white marble top, possibly Danish or Swedish, mid-19th C. **£300-360**   *SB*

A nest of four J. & J. Kohn bentwood tables, possibly designed by Josef Hoffman, 74.5 cm. height of largest table, c. 1905. **£280-360**   *SB*

A pair of giltwood console tables, with bowed Portor marble tops, winged griffin monopodia, c. 1820, 33½ in. (85 cm.) wide. **£550-750**   *C*

A Victorian satinwood and marquetry console table, bearing the label of Howard and Sons, 25, 26, 27 Berner Street, lacking rail back, 72 in. wide. **£650-750**   *C*

A pair of William IV parcel-gilt mahogany pier tables, with marble tops, with a paper stamp D. J. McLauchlan, 3 Printing House Sq., Blackfriars, London, 37½ by 61 in., c. 1835. **£1,250-1,500**   *SB*

A nest of four mahogany coffee tables, 19 in. **£310-400**   *WY*

A 19th C. mahogany quartetto of tables, from 22 in. wide. **250-320**   *Mlms*

A nest of mahogany and satinwood inlaid tea tables, each with simulated bamboo spindle legs, 20 in. wide. **£600-800**   *Mlms*

A set of fine Sheraton satinwood quartetto tables, crossbanded in tulipwood and outlined in ebony, 65 cm. wide. **£2,300-2,600**   *P*

An early 19th C. mahogany butler's tray. **£300-350**   *W*

A quartetto of tables, each with a cockbeaded and thuyawood inlaid top contained by a rosewood banding, the largest 27 by 19½ in., early 20th C. **£500-600**   *SBA*

A mahogany butler's tray, c. 1780. **£450-500**   *LAC*

A mid-17th C. oak monk's table, the adjustable back hinged for use as a table, c. 1640. **£520-620**   *SKC*

A Victorian oak butler's tray and stand, 27 in. wide by 17 in. deep by 29½ in. high. **£40-50**   *PAM*

A Victorian coaching table, 35 in. wide. **£135-150**   *MAT*

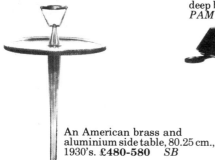

An American brass and aluminium side table, 80.25 cm., 1930's. **£480-580**   *SB*

A mahogany reading table, the rectangular top with two adjustable flaps and two adjustable candle stands, late 1830's, 32¾ by 41¾ in. (83 by 106 cm.). **£350-420**   *SB*

An oak cricket table, c. 1760. **£120-150**   *DEB*

A Queen Anne walnut and feather banded lowboy, with crossbanded and quarter veneered top, 2 ft. 3½ in. high by 2 ft. 6 in. wide, c. 1710. **£2,600-3,000**   *SKC*

LOWBOYS

- has four, or six, turned legs with stretchers in late 17th C. and early 18th C.
- has cabriole legs without stretchers after c. 1730
- if Queen Anne the veneer will be quartered, with herringbone inlay round the edges
- old veneers can be quite thick, later veneers were thin
- the best tend to have cabriole legs, although a good example with square tapered legs if of good colour and 'right' can command a high price

A George I walnut lowboy, with quartered and crossbanded to and boxwood stringing, 34 in. wide, 20 in. deep, 28 in. high, c. 1730. **£900-1,000**   *DEB*

n early Georgian mahogany wboy, the drawers with oak nings and pierced brass plate andles. **£550-700** *L*

A George I oak lowboy, fitted with three frieze drawers, 30½ in. wide, c. 1730. **£770-900** *SKC*

An early Georgian oak lowboy, 31 in. wide by 18½ in. deep by 29 in. high. **£700-830** *L*

Georgian oak lowboy, with ne inlay, 30 in. wide. **£500-00** *L*

A George II walnut lowboy, 29 by 34 in., mid-18th C. **£500-600** *SBA*

A mahogany lowboy, c. 1750. **£1,400-1,600** *NC*

n 18th C. lacquered lowboy, th single drawer, 28½ by 21 **£350-430** *BW*

FRENCH FURNITURE PERIODS

1610-1643 Louis XIII
1643-1715 Louis XIV
1715-1723 Regence
1723-1774 Louis XV
1774-1793 Louis XVI
DIRECTOIRE
1793-1795   Revolution
1795-1799   Directoire
1799-1804   Consulate
1804-1815 Empire
RESTORATION
1815-1824   Restoration
1824-1830   Charles X
LOUIS-PHILIPPE
1830-1848   Louis-Philippe
1848-1852   2nd Republic
1852-1870 Napoleon III
1871-1940 3rd Republic

An 18th C. continental oak lowboy, the drawer with brass escutcheon and pear drop handles, 29 in. wide. **£240-300** *L*

French Louis XV style uartered kingwood bureau at with navy-blue leather-ned top, a painted porcelain al plaque to the centre of each de, with ormolu knee-mounts d sabots, 3 ft. 10 in. by 2 ft. 4 **£1,100-1,300** *CDC*

A Louis XV kingwood bureau plat, the serpentine leather-lined top with moulded brass border, probably remounted, 51½ in. (131 cm.) wide. **£9,000-10,000** *C*

A Louis XV kingwood bureau plat, with leather-lined top and ormolu handles and angles, on cabriole legs ending in sabots, 45 in. (114.5 cm.) wide. **£3,000-3,500** *C*

245

A kingwood and marquetry bureau plat, of Louis XV sty with ormolu-bordered serpentine top profusely inla the frieze with a drawer, mi 19th C., 55 in. (140 cm.) wid **£3,800-4,300** *C*

A Serpentine marquetry bureau plat, the top with brass edge, the frieze with single drawer, with ormolu mounts, mid 19th C., 3 ft. 4 in. wide, 1 ft. 9 in. deep. **£1,350-1,500** *L*

A walnut serpentine writing desk, with a leather writing surface above three frieze drawers, with gilt-bronze mounts, 1850's, 29½ by 53½ in. (75 by 136 cm.). **£1,300-1,600** *SB*

A giltmetal-mounted walnut bureau plat, with serpentine leather-lined top, 50 in. (127 cm.) wide. **£2,000-2,300** *C*

A Serpentine marquetry bureau plat, the top profusely inlaid with panels of scrolling leaves, with a single frieze drawer, edges in satinwood (faults), 3 ft. 9 in. wide, 2 ft. 5 in. deep. **£460-550** *L*

A kingwood serpentine burea plat, with two frieze drawers, 29¾ by 46½ in., c. 1870. **£66 760** *SB*

A stained hardwood Bonheur-du-Jour, with panels of ivory flowers, 135 by 106 cm., early 20th C. **£360-420** *SB*

A rosewood lady's writing desk, inlaid with satinwood stringing, 2 ft. 10½ in. (88 cm.) high by 2 ft. 3 in. (68.5 cm.) wide, c. 1890. **£750-850** *SKC*

One of a pair of rosewood and tulipwood bonheurs du jour, giltmetal-mounted, with rococo handles and plaques, 49 in. wide. **£2,600-4,000** the pair *C*

A 19th C. French kingwood cabinet, with ormolu mounts and inset with Sevres panels, 2 ft. 7 in. wide. **£1,500-1,700** *MMB*

A fine George III West Indian satinwood bonheur-du-jour, attributed to Gillows of Lancaster, the frieze drawer fitted with a writing section and concealed pen and ink drawer, c. 1795, width 25 in. **£3,800-5,000** *SBe*

rosewood crossbanded onheur-du-jour, 44½ by 33 in., id-19th C. **£550-650** *SB*

A kingwood bonheur-du-jour, the cupboard doors with 'Sevres' portrait plaques, with gilt-bronze mounts, crossbanded with rosewood, 47½ by 20 in., Swedish or Russian, c. 1860. **£1,600-1,800** *SB*

A German giltmetal-mounted walnut and Dresden porcelain Bonheur du Jour, mounted with plaques of Watteauesque lovers, mid-19th C., 41 in. (105 cm.) wide. **£6,500-7,500** *C*

A Boulle bonheur du jour, cabinet back with 2 doors and 2 drawers, the base with drawer and pull-out slide, ormolu mounted, 6 ft. 3 in. high by 2 ft. 8 in. wide. **£580-700** *RMcT*

porcelain-mounted uyawood writing desk, the rror back flanked by pboards above a pull-out iting drawer, 60 by 53½ in., 70's. **£1,650-1,900** *SB*

A 19th C. French porcelain mounted thuyawood and ebonised writing desk, with a pull-out writing drawer enclosed by two open shelves, 48 in. wide by 56 in. high. **£1,200-1,500** *EBB*

A Victorian satinwood and marquetry bonheur du jour, by Holland & Sons, the mirror-backed centre crossbanded with amaranth, 53½ in. (136 cm.) wide. **£2,000-2,300** *C*

19th C. figured walnut avenport (one of the drawers ith label of Druce & Co.), with ull-out writing slab and secret ising stationery rack, 22 in. ide. **£1,900-2,200** *Pe*

DAVENPORTS

- the first Davenport was made by the firm of Gillow for Captain Davenport in the late 18th C.
- a very distinctive piece of furniture with a sloping lid and a gallery of either brass or wood, also having real drawers, usually four, on one side and dummy on the other
- in the early 19th C. sometimes misspelt 'Devonport'
- split into two main styles: the elegant Regency and the flamboyant or even florid Victorian
- some very high quality mid 19th C. examples in burr walnut with good carving — these are now commanding high prices

A walnut harlequin davenport, the fitted interior with two drawers and a well, 37 by 23 in., c. 1860. **£800-1,000** *SB*

A walnut harlequin davenport, enclosing a pull-out writing surface and 2 short drawers, above 4 real opposing 4 dummy drawers, 36½ by 23 in., c. 1860. **£600-720** *SB*

A mid-19th C. Irish yew wood and marquetry davenport, the interior with small drawers and pigeon holes, 29 in. wide. **£3,600-4,000** *PWC*

A Victorian walnut davenpo the superstructure with a ris stationery compartment, th bowed front enclosing two sh drawers and an adjustable writing slide, c. 1860, 23 in. wide. **£1,000-1,200** *SBe*

A mid-Victorian carved oak davenport, with boxed stationery compartment, sliding front with fitted interior and 2 side cupboards, 28 in. wide. **£440-540** *DSH*

A Victorian walnut davenport, with raised rear stationery compartment, and fitted four side drawers and four dummy drawers, 53 cm. wide, c. 1855. **£330-400** *SKC*

A papier mache desk and stan set with shells depicting Windsor Castle, the stand wi a shell impressed chessboard finely decorated overall, c. 18! 24 in. wide. **£1,600-1,900**

A walnut davenport, the leather writing slope enclosing a fitted interior, with 4 real and 4 dummy drawers, 21¼ in., c. 1870. **£500-600** *SB*

A Victorian walnut davenport fitted with a maple wood interior, the side door enclosing 4 small drawers, 2 ft. **£600-800** *MMB*

An early Victorian rosewood davenport, fitted with a pen an ink drawer above four drawe 2 ft. 2¾ in. (68 cm.) wide. **£57** **630** *SKC*

A William IV rosewood davenport, the top sliding forward on the lower part which contains a slide and three drawers, 2 ft. 10 in. high by 1 ft. 8½ in. wide, c. 1835. **£900-1,200** *S*

A walnut davenport, enclosing a fitted interior above four real opposing four dummy drawers, 21¼ in. wide, 1850's. **£340-400** *SB*

walnut and marquetry
avenport, enclosing a fitted
interior, 36 by 22½ in., 1860's.
500-600   SB

A rosewood davenport writing
desk, with sliding top. £770-
900   DLJ

A walnut and marquetry
davenport, inlaid with boxwood
with a fitted interior, stamped
JAS. Shoolbred & Co., 31 by 22
in., c. 1870. £400-500   SB

late George III mahogany
avenport, with a swivelling
p, 2 ft. 10 in. high by 1 ft. 5½ in.
ide, early 19th C. £2,000-
,500   S

An early 19th C. child's
davenport, in crossbanded
mahogany, 17 in. wide by 20 in.
high. £450-550   A

A small Georgian mahogany
davenport, with revolving
sloping top, 4 drawers and 4
dummy drawers, 14 in. wide.
£1,600-1,800   PWC

Damascus parquetry writing
esk, the frieze containing three
rawers, 79 by 118 cm., c. 1900.
280-320   SB

An Edwardian mahogany
lady's writing desk, 3 ft. 1 in. (94
cm.) high by 3 ft. 4 in. (101.5 cm.)
wide, c. 1910. £570-620   SKC

A mahogany Carlton House
desk, of Regency design with
leather-lined writing surface,
inlaid with chequered lines, 48
in. wide. £1,400-1,600   C

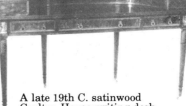

A Regency style
Cocobolo Carlton
House desk, the stage
top fitted with eight
short drawers, 152 cm.
wide. £1,500-1,800
PJ

A late 19th C. satinwood
Carlton House writing desk,
painted with flowers, 51 in.
(varnish discoloured). £1,500-
1,700   DWB

An Art Nouveau writing desk, the top with leaded glass panels and baluster rails, 3 ft. 6 in. **£500-600** *RMcT*

A Regence bureau Mazarin, veneered in calamander and inlaid with floral marquetry, with a later panel of tooled hide, ormolu mounted, 1.7 by 8.6 m. **£14,000-17,000** *P*

An Italian walnut and floral marquetry kneehole writing desk, with brass drop handles ft. 2 in. wide, 1 ft. 11 in. deep **£1,300-1,600** *Mlms*

A late 17th C. Dutch red walnut kneehole writing table, with rising top, fitted four short bow-fronted drawers with cupboard to recess, 47 in. wide, c. 1690. **£2,000-2,500** *SKC*

An unusual walnut bureau Mazarin, on later turned feet, mid-17th C., 45 in. (114 cm.) wide; 33 in. (84 cm.) high. **£8,000-8,800** *C*

A mahogany and floral inlai kneehole writing table, crossbanded in pearwood, no with plate-glass top, 2 ft. 6 in (76 cm.) high by 4 ft. 2¾ in. (12 cm.) wide, c. 1890. **£2,100-2,600** *SKC*

A mid-Georgian mahogany kneehole desk, 40½ in. (103 cm.) wide. **£850-950** *C*

One of a pair of 19th C. oak davenport styled writing desks, 53 in. **£1,900-2,200** the pair *RDu*

A George II walnut, crossbanded and featherstr kneehole desk, with pierced brass escutcheons and key plates, 78 cm. **£1,400-1,60** *P*

A mahogany pedestal desk, 121 cm. wide, c. 1760, with some alteration. **£440-540** *Bon*

> **Miller's Antiques Price Guide builds up year by year to form the most comprehensive photo-reference system available. The first three volumes contain over 20,000 completely different photographs.**

A mahogany kneehole desk, c. 1790, 31½ in. high. **£2,000-2,200** *NC*

A George III mahogany kneehole desk, with 8 variou sized drawers surrounding th central cupboard, 34½ in. wid **£900-1,200** *C*

mahogany kneehole desk,
th brass line inlay and
ndles, 2 ft. 6 in. by 1 ft. 6 in.,
th C. **£1,300-1,500**   *AG*

A Modernist rosewood desk,
attributed to Victor Champion,
75 cm. high, 154 by 79 cm.,
1930's. **£650-750**   *SB*

A 'George I' yellow lacquered
knee-hole desk, the recess with
an arched cupboard, gilded and
painted with chinoiseries, late
19th C., 31 by 33½ in. (79 by 85
cm.). **£250-400**   *SB*

William IV rosewood pedestal
sk, the leather inset top with
ree frieze drawers, 2 ft. 6 in.
6 cm.) high x 3 ft. 3 in. (99 cm.)
de, c. 1835. **£750-850**   *SKC*

A mahogany pedestal desk,
stamped T. Wilson, 68 Great
Queen Street, London, handles
replaced and escutcheons inlaid
at a later date, 30 by 65½ by 41
in., mid-19th C. **£2,000-
2,300**   *SB*

A mahogany pedestal desk, the
top inset with a writing surface,
31 by 53½ in., c. 1870. **£560-
660**   *SB*

Victorian mahogany
edestal desk, the nests of
rawers with side locking
ilasters, the front with a
entral false drawer, 4 ft. **£630-
00**   *WW*

A Georgian mahogany
partners' desk, crossbanded
and line inlaid in ebony, 56 in.
wide by 38 in. deep by 31 in.
high. **£2,400-2,800**   *L*

A George III
mahogany partners'
desk, with leather-lined
top, stamped H. Mawer
& Stephenson, 65½ in.
(166 cm.) wide. **£4,400-
5,000**   *C*

'George III' mahogany
artners' desk, with a leather-
ined rectangular top, 31 by 60
y 37½ in., c. 1900. **£1,300-
,600**   *SB*

A mahogany partners' desk, c.
1790, 37 in. deep, 66 in. wide, 29
in. high. **£3,000-4,000**   *W*

A mahogany partners' desk,
with 6 frieze drawers and 6
pedestal drawers, with
opposing cupboard doors, 60 in.
wide, 30 in. high, 41½ in. deep.
£1,100-1,300   *L*

George III mahogany
artners' desk, with 3 frieze
awers and 3 drawers in each
destal, 30½ by 63 by 47 in.,
te 18th/early 19th C. **£2,000-
400**   *SBA*

A mahogany partners' desk, 30
by 60 by 41 in., early 19th C., but
with later locks and
restorations. **£1,400-1,600**
SBA

251

An early 19th C. mahogany architect's kneehole desk, with 8 small drawers to one side, and cupboards on the other, 5 ft. wide. **£2,300-2,700** *B*

A George III mahogany library desk, the leather-lined top with two easels, one side with 9 drawers, the other with 6 drawers and an adapted cupboard door, 55½ in. wide. **£3,600-4,000** *C*

A mahogany kneehole desk, with tambour top, and brass furnishings, 52 in. wide, 29½ i deep, 41 in. high. **£540-590** *SW*

A Victorian walnut cylinder desk, enclosing small drawers, pigeon holes and a pull-out slide with adjustable writing slope, 4 ft. 2 in. **£1,000-1,200** *PWC*

An inlaid roll-top bureau, with fitted interior, 3 ft. 7 in. wide. **£700-800** *VV*

A mahogany architect's pedestal desk, with inset leath lined top on adjustable doub ratchet, and an adjustable central writing slope, stampe Graygoose, 57 Great Queens Street, 19th C. **£3,200-3,800** *AG*

A George III Tambour top writing desk, the interior with lined writing slide, pigeonholes and small drawers, 3 ft. 3½ in. (100 cm.) wide, c. 1800. **£800-1,000** *SKC*

A mahogany lady's cylinder top desk, finely painted, signed L. Lebrum, with fitted interior, pull-out slide, and marble top with ormolu gallery. **£2,100-2,500** *SW*

A mahogany cylinder burea by Edwards and Roberts, with pierced gilt brass gallery, th cylinder fall enclosing fitted interior, 54 in. wide. **£1,500-1,800** *PWC*

A George III satinwood bonheur-du-jour, crossbanded in rosewood, the tambour shutter enclosing a leather lined writing-surface, pigeonholes and drawers, 30 in. wide. **£3,700-4,100** *C*

A small French bonheur-du-jour, with galleried marble to 2 ft. 2 in. **£720-820** *MMB*

kingwood and marquetry linder bureau, the roll top closing a fitted interior and a iting slide, 42 by 29 in., 70's. **£680-780** *SB*

A mahogany bureau a cylindre, ormolu-mounted, verde antico marble top, the solid cylinder enclosing a leather-lined slide, 35½ in. wide, mid-19th C. **£800-1,000** *C*

A 19th C. mahogany bonheur du jour, with Vernis Martin panel of figures in a garden, signed 'B. Diste', 2 ft. 6 in. **£440-550** *WHL*

ate 19th C. rosewood and inwood inlaid bureau de ne, the interior fitted with eon holes, enclosed by a inder fall front, 30 in. wide. 50-450 *Mlms*

A satinwood cylinder bureau, the top and drawer opening together to reveal a fitted interior with a secret spring-operated drawer, c. 1910, 41½ by 33 in. (105.5 by 84 cm.). **£1,000-1,200** *SB*

A Victorian rosewood and floral marquetry bureau de dame, the fall front enclosing a fitted interior with a well, with gilt metal mounts, width 30 in. **£400-480** *JF*

German rosewood and boulle inder bureau, inlaid with olling foliage and strapwork ghtened with coloured amel and mother of pearl, d-19th C., 48 in. (122 cm.) le. **£1,500-2,000** *C*

A French ormolu-mounted kingwood and tulipwood secretaire, of Louis XVI style, with breccia marble top, the fall-flap enclosing drawers above a spring-operated drawer, 19th C., 25 in. (63.5 cm.) wide. **£2,200-2,800** *C*

A Louis XV style marquetry bonheur du jour, rosewood and boxwood strung and ormolu-mounted, 27 in. wide. **£900-1,100** *CEd*

Louis XV tulipwood and arquetry miniature bureau de ame, enclosing a fitted terior, the lock stamped Ferry Luneville, 21¼ in. (54 cm.) ide. **£1,300-1,500** *C*

A kingwood lady's bureau, the fall painted with lovers in the Vernis Martin style, with fitted interior, brass mounted, French, 3 ft. 1½ in. high by 2 ft. 10½ in. wide, c. 1865. **£750-850** *SKC*

An ebonised and Ormolu-mounted bureau de dame, decorated with Sevres-style plaques, the fall revealing fitted interior, French, 3 ft. 1 in. high by 2 ft. 1 in. wide, c. 1860. **£680-750** *SKC*

A mahogany bureau on stand, in the George I style, the writing slope enclosing a concave fitted interior, drawers with chequered inlay, above a long drawer, 19th C., 29½ in. wide. **£440-500** *L*

A small George II red waln bureau on stand, enclosing pigeon-holes and 3 drawers, apron with a slide, 56 cm. wi **£1,200-1,500** *P*

A William and Mary style walnut and featherbanded bureau, the fall revealing a stepped and fitted interior, 3 ft. ½ in. high by 1 ft. 10 in. wide, c. 1880. **£900-1,050** *SKC*

A George I walnut bureau, in two parts, the sloping flap crossbanded with oak enclosing a fitted interior and a well, 37½ in. wide. **£1,600-1,900** *C*

An antique George I style crossbanded walnut lady's bureau, with fitted interior and well, 24 in. **£470-570** *BW*

An Italian provincial chestnut bureau, enclosing a shaped stepped interior, sunken well, restorations, 36 in. wide, 39½ in. high, 19 in. deep. **£540-650** *L*

BUREAUX

- around mid 17th C. bureaux on stand were popular, initially in oak then in walnut
- note the quality and proportion of the cabriole legs — good carving is another plus factor
- always more valuable if containing an *original* stepped interior and well
- from about 1680 most bureaux made from walnut, many with beautiful marquetry and inlay
- from about 1740 mahogany became the most favoured wood, although walnut was still used
- the 'key' size for a bureau is 3 ft. 2 in., as the width diminishes so the price increases dramatically
- original patination, colour and original brass handles are obviously important features for assessing any piece of furniture, but these are crucial when valuing bureaux and chests

---

A George I solid walnut bure having shaped and stepped interior, 42 in. wide. **£650-820** *BS*

A late 18th C. French Provincial walnut bureau, th fall with carved panel enclosi stepped fittings and a centra well, 37½ in. **£1,600-2,000** *DWB*

An Italian fruitwood bureau, with crossbanded sloping flap enclosing a fitted interior, 40 in. (102 cm.) wide. **£1,200-1,500** *C*

An inlaid Georgian mahogany bureau, with knob handles, ivory escutcheons and fitted interior, 40 in. £700-780   *BW*

A small Queen Anne walnut bureau, with stepped interior, well and secret drawers, herring-bone inlay throughout. £3,900-4,250   *NCr*

A small early 18th C. figured walnut bureau, fall reveals fitted interior (reconstructed) with well, original brass fittings, Queen Anne/George I, c. 1710-20, 28 in. wide, 17 in. deep by 37 in. high. £5,200-6,000   *RD*

An early Georgian oak bureau, the writing slope enclosing a shaped and stepped interior, with sunken well, early 18th C., in. wide. £500-600   *L*

A George I walnut bureau, with fall front, fitted interior with pigeon holes and drawers, the drawers with brass ring handles, and oval escutcheons, 29 in. wide. £2,100-2,600 *DSH*

An 18th C. mahogany slope front bureau, with a fitted interior (some restoration), 2 ft. 11¼ in. £790-890   *WHL*

A George I walnut and feather banded bureau, the fall revealing a fitted interior, on later shaped bracket feet, c. 25. £1,500-1,700   *SKC*

A Georgian oak bureau, enclosing a fitted interior, with pierced plate brass handles and escutcheons, 39 in. wide at top by 20 in. deep by 40½ in. high. £440-540   *L*

A Georgian oak bureau, enclosing a fitted interior, over four graduated long drawers, 36 in. wide at top. £500-600   *L*

A good George I walnut bureau, the sloping front crossbanded and featherstrung enclosing a fitted interior, 91 cm. wide. £2,200-2,500   *P*

A Georgian oak bureau, the writing slope enclosing a fitted interior, with sunken well, 3 ft. 3 in. wide, 3 ft. 5 in. high, 1 ft. 10 in. deep. £440-500   *L*

255

A Georgian mahogany bureau, the crossbanded writing fall enclosing a fitted interior, 3 ft. 1½ in. (96 cm.) wide, 1 ft. 9½ in. (55 cm.) deep. **£520-680**   *L*

A George III mahogany bureau, enclosing a fitted interior, centred by a cupboard concealing drawers and pigeon holes, 38½ in. wide at top. **£380-450**   *L*

A George III mahogany bureau, the crossbanded writing slope enclosing a fitted interior, with brass handles and ivory escutcheons, 42 in. wide. **£770-900**   *L*

A small figured mahogany bureau, the satinwood crossbanded writing slope enclosing a fitted interior centred by a cupboard, late 19th C., 30 in. wide by 18 in. deep by 40 in. high. **£550-670**   *L*

A Georgian mahogany bureau, the fall enclosing well fitted interior, 42 in. wide, 44 in. high. **£580-700**   *TW*

A Georgian mahogany bureau, enclosing a fitted interior, the drawers with oak linings and stamped brass oval handles, c. 1770, 46 in. wide. **£330-400**   *L*

A Georgian mahogany bureau, the figured writing slope enclosing an arrangement of 11 drawers and pigeon holes, 38 in. wide. **£550-670**   *L*

A mahogany bureau, c. 1785. **£1,000-1,100**   *NC*

A George II walnut bureau v crossbanding, c. 1740, 39 in wide. **£2,200-2,400**   *B.M*

A mid-18th C. oak bureau, w a sloping fall front enclosin fitted interior, 36 in. wide. **£400-500**   *SBe*

A Georgian mahogany burea enclosing a well fitted interio with a mirrored central door George III, 3 ft. 5 in. wide. **£1,200-1,500**   *L*

A walnut and chevron-band bureau, the fall revealing a stepped and fitted interior w well, 3 ft. 3 in. (99 cm.) high b ft. 9 in. (84 cm.) wide, c. 186(**£2,900-3,400**   *SKC*

antique mahogany bureau,
id interior fittings, the
wers with brass handles, 3
½ in. wide. **£760-900** *AG*

A small Edwardian mahogany
bureau, satinwood and
harewood inlaid, 30 in. wide,
16½ in. deep, 33½ in. high.
£150-190 *PAM*

A William and Mary walnut
bureau, in two parts, the
crossbanded flap enclosing a
fitted interior with a well, on
later turned feet, 40 in. wide.
£2,100-2,400 *C*

Queen Anne oak bureau, the
l flap enclosing a fitted
erior with well, 2 ft. 9 in.
de. **£700-800** *SKC*

A Georgian mahogany bureau,
in two parts with brass loop
handles and escutcheons, with
fitted stepped interior and well,
35 in. **£850-1,050** *BW*

A continental oak bureau,
enclosing an interior of
drawers, pigeon-holes, central
cupboard and well, veneered in
walnut and inlaid with
stringing, 3 ft. 4 in. wide, c. 1750.
£1,000-1,200 *SKC*

ate 19th/early 20th C. roll
oak bureau, enclosing fitted
rior, 49 in. wide. **£950-**
00 *Win*

A Dutch walnut and parquetry
cylinder bureau, the cylinder
bearing signature 'N. Solts
Fecit', 3 ft. 7½ in. high by 3 ft. 5½
in. wide, c. 1785. **£1,500-**
1,700 *SKC*

An 18th C. Italian walnut and
marquetry bureau, the sloping
front enclosing a well and
shallow drawers, 1.30 m.
£3,300-4,000 *P*

A Queen Anne black and gold
lacquer bureau, in two parts,
flap enclosing a fitted interior
including a well, 34½ in. (88 cm.)
wide. **£3,500-3,700** *C*

An 18th C. Dutch burr walnut,
oak and marquetry bureau, in
two sections, the sloping fall
enclosing a fitted interior with a
well, 1.33 m. **£3,800-4,200** *P*

An 18th C. South German walnut bureau, with boxwood inlay and angle crossbanding, enclosing a simple interior of small drawers with original brass handles, 45 in. wide. **£2,200-2,600** *B*

A Sinhalese padouk bureau, in panelled wood and with a fitted interior, with brass mounts and handles, 3 ft. 7½ in. high by 3 ft. 5 in. wide, mid 18th C. **£1,200-1,400** *S*

A Dutch mahogany bureau, two parts, the fall revealing fitted interior with well, 3 ft. in. wide, c. 1780. **£1,900-2,200** *SKC*

An early 18th C. Dutch marquetry bureau, interior of many serpentine-fronted drawers, secret drawers, document slides flanking a central drawer with internal drawer, the double bombe front with four long drawers. **£4,400-5,000** *B*

A Dutch walnut and marquetry bombe bureau, possibly the base of a bureau-cabinet, 47½ in. (121 cm.) wide. **£1,900-2,100** *C*

An 18th C. Dutch floral marquetry bureau, with fall front enclosing drawers, pig holes and cupboards, 38 in. wide. **£2,800-3,500** *Lan*

A Dutch marquetry bombe bureau, the folding writing slope enclosing a shaped and stepped interior with a sunken well, some late inlays, 18th C. 46 in. wide by 22 in. deep by 40 in. high. **£3,000-3,500** *L*

A mid-Georgian oak chest, with quarter-column angles, on later bracket feet, 32 in. (81 cm.) wide. **£1,300-1,500** *C*

A late 18th C. walnut and flor marquetry bombé bureau, th drawers with neo-Classical brass handles, width 48 in. **£3,200-3,600** *JF*

A Jacobean oak chest of 3 long drawers, on bun feet, 37¾ in. **£550-700** *O*

A Charles II oak chest, 40 by 42 in. (102 by 107 cm.), mid-late 17th C. **£700-900** *SBA*

A Jacobean oak chest, of sma proportions, having a secret drawer concealed within the freize, 17th C., 36 in. wide, 38 in high, 22 in. deep. **£520-620**

Jacobean oak chest, drawers fronted by walnut panelling, t. 11 in. wide. **£720-820** C

A Restoration Stuart oak chest, fitted with frieze drawer, inlaid with mother of pearl and bone, enclosing three long drawers, 42 in. wide, c. 1660. **£720-830** SKC

A Cromwellian oak chest, in two sections, inlaid with ivory and mother of pearl, 1.10 m. wide. **£680-780** P

Charles II walnut chest of awers, the cushion fronted awers with moulded ecoration, and original andles on bun feet, c. 1660-70, in. wide by 24 in. deep by 37½ . high. **£1,000-1,200** RD

A Jacobean walnut chest of four long graduated drawers, 40 in. wide, c. 1660. **£880-1,000** SKC

A Stuart oak chest of four long drawers, 35 in. wide, c. 1660. **£460-560** SKC

9th C. oak Jacobean style est, 40 in. **£360-420** BW

An antique oak chest, of 17th C. style, having engraved brass loop handles, on ball feet, 3 ft. 6 in. **£550-650** WY

A James II oak chest, with brass floral paterae, enclosing two short and three long drawers, 115 cm. wide. **£550-650** Bon

walnut inlaid chest, ossbanded, with brass rolling axe-drop handles, on ter bun feet, early 18th C., 36 . wide by 21 in. deep by 35 in. gh. **£440-550** L

A William and Mary walnut and marquetry chest, 95 cm. wide. **£2,700-3,000** P

An oak and walnut chest of drawers, wrong escutcheons, with base restored, c. 1690-1700, 23½ in. deep, 40 in. high, 41 in. wide. **£700-800** W

A William and Mary walnut chest, of good colour (not original handles or feet), c. 1690, 31 in. high, 33 in. carcase, 35 in. top, 21 in. deep. **£3,500-4,000**   *B.M*

A William and Mary chest of drawers, oyster veneered and inlaid. **£2,500-3,000**   *NCr*

A small Georgian mahoga chest, with rococo brass handles and escutcheons. **£680-800**   *L*

A small Georgian figured mahogany chest, with brushing slide, four long drawers with oak linings and brass rosette handles, 35 in. wide by 19 in. deep by 34 in. high. **£570-700**   *L*

CHESTS

- if a chest has three short drawers one would suspect that it started life as the top of a tallboy
- up to c. 1660 drawers had bearers attached to the side which ran in deep grooves on the side
- after c. 1670 bottom runners, usually made of oak, appeared
- early 17th C. drawers were nailed together
- c. 1680–90 walnut came to be used more and more along with the bracket foot
- in the mahogany period from around c. 1740, the square shape gave way to the bow front, serpentine, etc.
- satinwood appeared in chests c. 1780–90
- 19th C. saw a gradual increase in size and decrease in quality as more and more chests were made to satisfy growing demand — many different woods, such as pine, mahogany, rosewood and walnut were used

---

A George II oak chest of drawers, 24 in. carcass wid 28 in. high, 12 in. deep, c. 1 **£500-600**   *LAC*

A Georgian mahogany chest, with satinwood crossbanding and fitted handles, bears impressed mark E. James to top right hand drawer, 44 in. wide by 20 in. deep by 40½ in. high. **£200-270**   *L*

A Georgian mahogany chest drawers, the drawers with co beaded edges, 4 ft. wide, 1 ft in. deep, 3 ft. 8½ in. high. **£2(250**   *L*

A Georgian mahogany chest of drawers, the top drawer having sliding writing surface enclosing fitted interior, 36 in. **£430-550**   *BW*

A Georgian mahogany chest of drawers, of small proportions, with brushing slide and four graduated long drawers, 2 ft. 8½ in. high, 2 ft. 6 in. wide, 1 ft. 6½ in. deep. **£660-760**   *L*

An early Georgian walnut bachelor chest of drawers, w a brushing slide, 30 in. **£3,6 4,000**   *BW*

Georgian mahogany chest of
ur long graduated drawers,
th brass bail handles and
cutcheons, 2 ft. 7 in. wide.
80-580   *GC*

A walnut chest, of 2 short and 3
feather crossbanded long
drawers, 3 ft. 1 in. wide, 21 in.
deep, 36 in. high. **£260-300**   *V*

A Mid-Georgian padoukwood
and olivewood chest, with
crossbanded top, on ogee
bracket feet, 33½ in. (85 cm.)
wide. **£1,000-1,300**   *C*

George III fruitwood chest,
corated with green lines, 42
wide. **£900-1,100**   *C*

A late George II/early George
III chest of drawers, 54½ in.
high by 42 in. wide. **£950-
1,000**   *NC*

A George III mahogany and
crossbanded small chest, 2 ft. 9
in. (84 cm.) high by 2 ft. 7½ in.
(80 cm.) wide, c. 1770. **£550-
620**   *SKC*

n eight drawer mahogany
est of drawers, c. 1780, 38½ in.
de by 18½ in. deep by 41½ in.
gh. **£475-520**   *LL*

A mahogany chest of drawers
with brushing slide, c. 1770, 29
in. wide carcass, 17 in. deep, 31
in. high. **£575-650**   *DEB*

A mahogany chest of drawers
(possibly top of a tallboy), early
19th C., 41 in. wide by 21 in.
deep by 37 in. high. **£200-
240**   *PAM*

ate 18th C. cherrywood chest,
9 in. wide. **£440-500**
C

A Dutch late 18th C. mahogany
and marquetry commode, with
gilt brass handles and keyhole
plates, 52 in. wide. **£800-880**
PWC

A Victorian bird's-eye maple
shaped front chest, with
rosewood banding and
stringing, 3 ft. 2½ in. (98 cm.)
high by 3 ft. 2½ in. (98 cm.) wide,
c. 1845. **£440-500**   *SKC*

A small mahogany chest of drawers, 19th C., 2 ft. 8 in. (81 cm.) high, 2 ft. 7½ in. (80 cm.) wide, 1 ft. 5½ in. (45 cm.) deep. **£880-1,000** *L*

A small 18th C. bow-fronted mahogany chest of drawers, c. 1780, 31 in. wide by 20 in. deep by 32 in. high. **£900-1,100** *JGM*

A small Georgian mahogan bow front chest of drawers, satinwood crossbanded, the drawers with stamped oval brass handles, 34½ in. wide 18 in. deep by 36 in. high. **£46 580** *L*

A small Georgian mahogany bowfront chest of drawers, the top with crossbanding and chequered line inlay, 2 ft. 10 in. wide, 1 ft. 7 in. deep, 2 ft. 8 in. wide. **£1,000-1,100** *L*

A mahogany bow-fronted chest, c. 1800, 32½ in. high by 35 in. wide. **£900-1,000** *NC*

A Georgian figured mahogany bow-front chest of small proportions, with crossbanded top and boxwood lines, 2 ft. 9 in. wide. **£500-600** *L*

A Regency mahogany chest of drawers, reeded, pillar corners, palm leaf motif, 35¼ in. high by 36¼ in. wide. **£1,000-1,100** *NC*

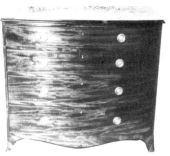

An early 19th C. mahogany chest (handles not original), 34 in. high by 38½ in. wide. **£550-600** *NC*

A bow-fronted mahogany che of drawers, c. 1820, 41½ in. hig by 43 in. wide. **£275-300** *L*

A George II mahogany commode, with gilt metal pierced escutcheons and handle pulls, 1.16 m. **£6,300-6,600** *P*

A small N. Country serpentine chest of drawers with canted fluted corners, with brushing slide, oak lined, c. 1770, 33 in. wide, 29 in. high, 17 in. deep. **£1,350-1,500** *DEB*

A fruitwood chest, with bras bordered serpentine top, late 18th C., German or Swedish, 46½ in. (118 cm.) wide. **£1,20(1,400** *C*

George III mahogany
rpentine chest of four long
awers, 3 ft. ½ in. high by 3 ft. 7
. wide, c. 1770. **£1,000-**
300   *S*

A Georgian mahogany
serpentine-fronted commode,
47½ in. wide, 36 in. high. **£600-**
675   *E.E*

A George III mahogany
serpentine chest, with 4 long
drawers, the upper drawer with
a brushing slide, 41 in. wide.
£1,900-2,100   *C*

Serpentine figured
hogany chest of drawers,
er handles, 19th C., 3 ft. 7 in.
de, 2 ft. 1 in. deep, 2 ft. 9½ in.
zh. **£660-760**   *L*

A serpentine fronted mahogany
dressing chest, crossbanded
and with chequered inlay, brass
swan's neck handles (replacing
knobs), 37 in. wide, early 19th C.
£990-1,300   *PW*

A fine elm serpentine-fronted
chest with slide, original
brasses, inlaid mahogany, 47
in. wide, 43 in. high. **£4,000-**
4,500   *B.M*

Transitional mahogany and
arquetry commode, with grey
arble top, 3 drawers in the
ieze and 2 long drawers,
ounted with gilt-metal guttae,
utch, 50 in. wide. **£2,000-**
300   *C*

A Transitional amaranth and
marquetry commode, with
breakfront grey marble top and
fitted with two drawers sans
traverse, 45 in. (114 cm.) wide.
£2,200-2,500   *C*

A Louis XVI mahogany
commode by Bernard III Van
Risenburgh with lobed Carrara
marble top, stamped BVRB
JME, 46½ in. (118 cm.) wide.
£2,500-3,000   *C*

n Italian rosewood and
arquetry commode, in the
aggiolini style with verde
tico marble top, frieze drawer
laid with grottesche, late 18th
, 49 in. (124.5 cm.) wide.
,000-3,500   *C*

An Italian walnut chest, with
crossbanded top, late 18th C.,
51½ in. (131 cm.) wide. **£800-**
1,000   *C*

A giltmetal-mounted
marquetry commode, after the
model by J. H. Riesener, the
frieze fitted with a drawer above
two long drawers sans traverse,
65½ in. wide. **£1,600-1,800**
C

A fruitwood commode fitted
with three panelled drawers,
mounted with giltmetal
handles, late 18th C. German or
Swedish, 49 in. (124.5 cm.) wide.
£1,500-1,700 *C*

A mid-18th C. oak serpentine-
fronted commode, French, 2 ft. 9
in. wide. **£590-650** *SKC*

A small Continental serpenti
walnut commode, with cross
banded top, 36 in. **£1,450-
1,700** *MMB*

A French 18th C. walnut
parquetry commode, of
serpentine block-fronted form,
the top crossbanded and
geometrically inlaid, with frieze
brushing side, 3 ft. 6 in. wide, 2
ft. 6 in. deep, 2 ft. 9½ in. high.
£2,600-2,800 *L*

A Liege oak commode, with
moulded serpentine top, mid-
18th C., 56 in. (142 cm.) wide.
£3,500-4,000 *C*

A South German stained bu
maple and marquetry chest,
crossbanded with plumwood
bordered with fruitwood and
inlaid with an architectural
capriccio, with giltmetal
handles and lockplates, on la
turned feet, mid-18th C., 42 i
wide. **£8,000-10,000** *C*

An early Louis XV rosewood
commode, with mottled black
and white marble top, 51½ in.
(131 cm.) wide. **£6,300-7,000**
C

A scarlet Boulle serpentine
commode, 63 in. (160 cm.) wide.
£5,000-6,000 *C*

A kingwood bombe commode,
with marble top, two short and
two long drawers, and with
giltmetal fittings, 56 in. wide,
mid 18th C. **£1,800-2,200** *C*

A French marquetry bombe
front commode, veneered in
rosewood and kingwood, wi
ormolu handles, mounts an
sabots, and a marble top
(repaired), 4 ft. 2½ in. wide.
£2,700-3,300 *GC*

A Swiss walnut serpentine
chest, with crossbanded top,
inlaid with arabesque
marquetry, on later turned feet,
mid-18th C., 35½ in.(90 cm.)
wide. **£2,300-2,600** *C*

An 18th C. Swiss walnut
commode, of serpentine outline,
crossbanded and quartered,
1.42 m. wide. **£800-1,000** *P*

An Italian walnut and
marquetry chest, the serpentir
top crossbanded with rosewoo
the sides each with a cupboar
door, on later turned feet, earl
18th C., 79½ in. (202 cm.) wide
44 in. (112 cm.) high, 29 in. (7
cm.) deep. **£5,500-6,000** *C*

Dutch Colonial walnut
commode, with crossbanded
serpentine top, inlaid with
chequered line borders, 18th C.,
½ in. (123 cm.) wide. **£1,500-**
900 *C*

A marquetry commode, with
three long drawers, 31 by 36½
in., Dutch, mid-19th C., inlaid, c.
1880. **£790-900** *SB*

A 19th C. Dutch marquetry
chest, 3 ft. 3 in. high by 3 ft. 1½
in. wide, c. 1840. **£900-1,100**
SKC

Louis XV kingwood
commode, with later serpentine
verde antico marble top, 38 in.
.5 cm.) wide. **£2,400-**
800 *C*

An ormolu-mounted marquetry
commode, of Louis XV design,
with serpentine red and white
marble top, fitted with two
drawers sans traverse, 44½ in.
wide. **£1,700-1,900** *C*

A Dutch ironwood bombe
commode, 39½ in. wide. **£800-**
950 *C*

Louis XV kingwood and
floral marquetry bombe
commode, with serpentine
portor marble top and fitted
with two drawers sans traverse,
in. (112 cm.) wide. **£8,000-**
,000 *C*

A serpentine parquetry
commode, with two long
drawers, 31 by 27¾ in., probably
Dutch, c. 1880. **£590-690** *SB*

A Louis XV kingwood and
tulipwood commode, with
moulded serpentine rosso
Levanto marble top,
remounted, stamped J. B. Galet
JME, 32 in. (81 cm.) wide.
£2,800-3,200 *C*

gilt-bronze mounted walnut
bombe commode, attributed to
athaus Funk, with serpentine
ottled pink marble top,
anded twice EO, 38 in. (96
n.) wide. **£8,500-9,500** *C*

A mahogany commode, with a
cushion drawer above two long
drawers and an ogee drawer,
34¼ by 39½, North German,
1840's. **£660-760** *SB*

An Austrian walnut chest of
drawers, with 4 panelled
crossbanded drawers, the sides
inlaid with the Imperial eagle,
26 in. wide, early 18th C.
£1,300-1,500 *C*

A continental carved and inlaid chest, 23 in. wide by 35 in. high. **£570-700** *L*

An Anglo-Indian solid padouk chest, 35½ by 50 in., mid-19th C. **£220-280** *SB*

An early Victorian walnut Wellington chest, with 8 drawers, 24 in. **£480-600**

An elm brass-bound military chest, in two parts, Bramah type locks, stamped Store (one replaced), mid-19th C., 41¼ by 37½ in. (104.8 by 95.3 cm.). **£500-600** *SB*

A mahogany stained military chest, with sunken brass handles and brass corner pieces and edges, mid-19th C., 40 in. wide by 22 in. deep by 38 in. high. **£300-380** *L*

A mahogany military chest, i two parts, with brass mounts and handles, 40 by 36 in., mi 19th C. **£370-430** *SB*

A mahogany campaign chest in two parts, with brass mounts and flush-fitting brass handles, mid 19th C., 44 by 39 in. (112 by 99 cm.). **£300-350** *SB*

One of a 'pair' of early 19th C. Regency teak campaign chests, 37 in. wide by 30 in. high. **£2,000-2,100** the pair *NC*

A campaign chest, c. 1800, w flat swan neck handles, 32 high by 28 in. wide. **£1,300 1,400** *NC*

COFFERS

- in mediaeval England a coffer was a portable trunk for clothes and valuables, it was usually a hollowed out tree-trunk covered with leather
- even in the 13th C. some were carved
- by the 16th-17th C. many more had carved and even inlaid decorations on the panels, and sometimes even the top
- the quality and originality of carving is one of the main points of value, with, of course, the normal importance of colour and patination
- this last year has been a difficult time for oak, and particularly coffers — in fact, there was a joke in the trade that coffers had reached three figures again! However, that now seems to have stabilised and the old adage still holds true, if it's good quality, original, and of good colour it has held its value

An oak coffer, 16th C., 41½ (105.5 cm.) wide. **£700-900**

A very rare 16th C. oak chest, 26 in. high, 57 in. long, 17 in. deep. **£2,500-3,250** *TJ*

An oak coffer, 15th/16th C., 72 in. wide. **£770-870** *C*

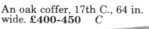

A Charles II carved oak coffer, 4 ft. 4 in. wide. **£240-300** *SKC*

walnut coffer, with iron rrying-handles, 17th C., 58 in. 47 cm.) wide. **£700-900** *C*

An oak coffer, 17th C., 64 in. wide. **£400-450** *C*

A Charles II oak coffer, carved and with the initials M.N., c. 1670, 50 by 19½ by 30 in. **£350-380** *OB*

A carved oak coffer, with floral marquetry panels, 17th C., 66½ in. wide by 26 in. deep by 33 in. high. **£570-700** *L*

n oak coffer, early 17th C., 46½ . (118 cm.) wide. **£300-500**

A massive 16th C. German oak muniments chest, the front carved in deep relief with a scene of Jesus throwing the money-changers out of the Temple, 71 in. wide. **£700-790** *B*

A late 17th C. French walnut coffer, raised on later turned supports, 48 in. wide, c. 1670. **£440-540** *SKC*

Stuart oak coffer, the front th two drawers to the base, d bearing the initials 'E.W.' d later date of 1722, 4 ft. 6 in., 1670. **£580-660** *SKC*

CARVING

- if original should always be proud of the piece
- flat or incised carving would have been added later and virtually always detracts from the value of a piece
- Victorian carving is almost always quite flat as they had become more sparing with timber

An oak coffer, 18th C., 60 in. (125.5 cm.) wide. **£250-350** *C*

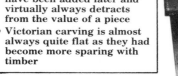

oak coffer, with lock, 17th 44 by 20 by 27 in. **£350-0** *OB*

An oak coffer, 17th C., 41 by 14 by 19 in. **£320-350** *OB*

A mid-17th C. oak coffer, inscribed 'H.B.A.R., 1744', 3 ft. 10 in. wide. **£460-520** *SKC*

An Adige cedarwood chest, in. wide, mid-17th C. **£440-540** *SKC*

A Moorish walnut chest, inlaid with mother of pearl roundels and fans, 49 in. wide. **£280-350** *CEd*

A Dutch colonial Padoukwood chest, the hinged lid mounted with pierced brass lockplates, angles and brass studs, 55 in. wide, 17th C. **£1,200-1,500** *C*

A George II walnut coffer-on-stand, the moulded crossbanded and quartered lid inlaid, 49½ in. wide. **£1,500-1,800** *C*

An early 17th C. Flemish oak coffer, 43 by 22 in. **£210-300** *BW*

An Eastern Colonial 19th C. hardwood chest, profusely mounted and studded in brass, with three base drawers, 46 in. wide. **£350-400** *PWC*

A 16th/17th C. oak ark, with three-plank lid, 41 in. wide. **£800-900** *SBe*

A Flemish brass and leather covered coffer, enclosing a hessian-lined interior, 17th C., 55 in. wide. **£480-520** *C*

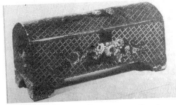

A Florentine antique rug chest painted with trelliswork and flowers, 4 ft. 11 in. long. **£500-600** *AG*

A Spanish embossed leather trunk, with wrought-iron loc plate, 17th C., 39 in. wide. **£50-620** *C*

A late 16th C. oak grain ark chest, 51 in. wide by 42 in. high. **£600-650** *LAC*

An oak ark, of peg construction, late 15th/early 16th C., 53 in. wide. **£600-700** *C*

An oak chest, interior fitted with two drawers and candlebox, 36 in. wide by 20 deep by 12 in. high. **£60-80** *PAM*

An 18th C. oak dower or mule chest, with lift-up top enclosing candle box and two small drawers, and four short drawers, 63 in. long. **£240-300** *SR*

A small food hutch, extensively carved and on turned legs and stretchers. **£1,500-2,000** *NCr*

n early 18th C. oak mule chest, ith brass handles and scutcheons, 4 ft. 5 in. by 1 ft. 11 . by 2 ft. 10 in. **£220-260** *LR*

A mid-18th C. oak dower chest, of small dimensions, with rising top, 2 ft. 7 in. (79 cm.) wide, c. 1740 (reduced). **£450-520** *SKC*

Make the most of Miller's

Look for the code letters in italic type following each caption.
Check these against the list of contributors on page 10 to identify the source of any illustration.
Remember — valuations may vary according to locality; use of the codes can allow this to be taken into account.

A mahogany Lancashire mule chest, c. 1790, 68 in. wide, 40 in. high, 22 in. deep. **£475-550** *DEB*

A 19th C. Japanese lacquer cabinet, inset with 25 cloisonne enamel panels, 3 ft. wide. **£1,650-1,800** *MMB*

A cabinet, fitted with a drawer below 2 hinged doors enclosing 6 drawers, decorated in gold and red hiramakie, engraved kanagu (some damage), 19th C., height 73 cm. **£2,400-2,800** *C*

A Dutch marquetry cabinet, nlaid overall with vases of lowers, rococo scrolls, birds nd insects, 3 ft. 3 in. wide, 1 ft. ½ in. deep. **£880-1,000** *L*

A fine Louis XV kingwood parquetry meuble d'Appui, with moulded breccia marble top, 36¾ in. (93 cm.) wide. **£6,000-6,500** *C*

A 17th C. Italian walnut cabinet, 38 by 33½ in. high. **£2,250-2,500** *DWB*

An 18th C. walnut buffet, French, 3 ft. 4 in. wide. **£550-650** *SKC*

A 1930's pale wood cocktail cabinet, the fall-front with mirrored interior, 138.5 cm. **£270-330** *SB*

A Chilean low cupboard, the interior fitted with one long drawer, 50½ in. wide, 18th/19th C. **£600-700** *SKC*

A Victorian walnut music cabinet, inlaid with satinwood stringing and with brass gallery, 26 in. wide. **£350-460** *O*

A 17th C. Swiss walnut and marquetry table cabinet, dated 1671, having a rising top, 31 cm. wide. **£380-460** *P*

An early 19th C. mahogany music cabinet, with two short drawers and two adjustable shelves enclosed by doors, 73 cm. **£400-500** *OT*

A Chinese export lacquer table cabinet, 18½ in. (47 cm.), late 18th/early 19th C. **£500-600** *C*

An 18th C. South German walnut and satinwood table cabinet, having a rising top, the doors enclosing six drawers and a central compartment, 49 cm. wide. **£800-1,000** *P*

An Oriental lacquer cabinet, with 6 short drawers and 1 long drawer, 19th C., 8½ by 15 by 1 in. **£90-110** *SV*

An Edwardian coal cabinet, 16 in. wide, 15 in. deep, 24 in. high. **£120-140** *ST*

A Jacobean oak spice cabinet, with four long panelled drawers, 15½ in. wide, c. 1660. **£520-620** *SKC*

A pair of George III mahogany and satinwood inlaid sideboard pedestals and urns, with zinc lined cisterns, height 1.94 m., 50 cm. wide. **£3,000-3,600** *P*

A pair of 'George III' mahogany side cabinets, c. 1910, 44½ by 1 in. (114 by 31 cm.). **£185-215** *SB*

A Majorelle Art Nouveau mahogany cabinet, with naturalistic bronze mounts, 125 m. height, 30 cm. width, 39 cm. depth, stamped 'L. Majorelle a Nancy', c. 1900. **£550-650**

An 18th C., tray top commode, 29 in. high by 19½ in. wide. **£450-500**   *NC*

An 18th C. mahogany bedside commode, 20 in. wide, 32 in. high. **£290-390**   *WR*

An ormolu-mounted ebonised and scarlet Boulle dwarf cabinet, mid-19th C., 34 in. (86 m.) wide. **£600-800**   *C*

A George III mahogany commode, in the manner of John Cobb, inlaid with satinwood crossbanded with kingwood, the top possibly of later date, 45¼ in. wide, 35 in. high, 22 in. deep. **£6,000-6,500**   *C*

A pair of Biedermeier walnut commodes, top and doors inlaid with brass lines, on later block feet, 30 in. (76 cm.) wide. **£1,100-1,400**   *C*

A walnut and marquetry side cabinet, with gilt-bronze foliate mounts, 43¾ by 30 in. (111 by 76 m.), 1850's. **£500-600**   *SB*

A satinwood and painted small cupboard, with rosewood crossbanded doors, 66½ by 55 in., 1840-60. **£360-430**   *SB*

A marquetry pedestal cabinet, with Siena marble top, the angles mounted with free-standing reeded columns, mid-19th C., 33 in. (84 cm.) wide. **£1,600-1,800**   *C*

A pair of inlaid walnut side cabinets, the doors now with a velvet-lined trellis, c. 1860, 42½ by 33 in. (107.3 by 84 cm.). **£750-950**   *SB*

A walnut side cabinet, in well-figured wood, with a pair of doors applied with heavily craqueleur paintings, now with a fitted interior, 1860's, 36 by 65 in. (91.5 by 165 cm.). **£450-550**   *SB*

A late William IV rosewood side cabinet, the frieze with three drawers, 37 by 81½ by 20½ in., late 1830's. **£520-640**   *SB*

An early 19th C. mahogany credenza, 7 ft. wide, 19 in. deep 39 in. high. **£1,350-1,450** *SW*

A side cabinet, of bowed outline, crossbanded and inlaid with mahogany and satinwood, c. 1890, width 62 in. **£1,600-2,000**   *SBe*

A Victorian walnut credenza, crossbanded and marquetry inlaid, ormolu-mounted, 6 ft. 1 in. wide. **£1,300-1,600**   *GC*

An Edwardian satinwood credenza, by Edwards and Roberts, the doors with painte oval scenes, with Adam style marquetry decoration and brasswork, 75 in. **£2,800-3,300**   *BW*

A walnut side cabinet, the door with an oval blue jasper plaque, 44½ by 69 in. (113 by 175 cm.), c. 1860. **£1,200-1,400**   *SB*

A Victorian walnut side cabinet, the 2 cupboard doors filled with fretwork foliage on a giltwood ground, between 2 glazed cupboard doors, stamped Seddon London 36483, 73½ in. wide. **£900-1,100**   *C*

A walnut side cabinet, crossbanded in kingwood with panels of burr-chestnut, 41 by 72¼ in., c. 1870. **£660-760**   *SE*

A walnut side cabinet, with a mirrored centre cupboard, 39 by 65 in., c. 1870. **£660-800**   *SB*

A Victorian ebonised pier cabinet, with amboyna and boxwood inlaid frieze and bas c. 1870, 62 in. wide. **£350-420** *L*

A walnut side cabinet, the 'D' shaped top above the central cupboard door inlaid with a kingwood border, 42 by 58 in., c. 1870. **£850-1,050**   *SB*

A Victorian walnut credenza, inlaid with satinwood and Ormolu mounts, 3 ft. 6 in. (107 cm.) high by 5 ft. (153 cm.) wide, c. 1855. **£900-990**   *SKC*

A 19th C. walnut and ormolu credenza, inlaid with satinwoo and crossbanded with rosewood, set with Sevres ble celeste romantic plaques, 78 in wide. **£1,950-2,200**   *M*

9th C. ebonised and inlaid
molu-mounted credenza
maged), 5 ft. 2 in. wide.
80-580   *VV*

A walnut and marquetry
ormolu mounted credenza, 3 ft.
9 in. (114 cm.) high by 6 ft. 6 in.
(198 cm.) wide, c. 1865. **£1,900-
2,100**   *SKC*

A Victorian walnut and floral
marquetry ormolu-mounted-
credenza, 77 in. wide (glass to
l.h. door broken). **£2,700-
3,200**   *DLJ*

pair of ormolu-mounted
ngwood pedestal vitrine
binets, with moulded bowed
ccia marble tops, 28½ in. (72
.) wide. **£3,400-4,000**   *C*

A Victorian ebonised and inlaid
breakfront credenza, inset with
Sevres porcelain panels, 3 ft. 6
in. high, 5 ft. 6 in. long. **£750-
950**   *AG*

A 19th C. inlaid breakfront
walnut credenza, with ormolu
mounts, 5 ft. 9 in. wide. **£750-
900**   *VV*

alnut and marquetry side
inet, applied with gilt-
nze mounts, the back cut for
ting rails, 37 by 46 in.,
0's. **£750-900**   *SB*

A Victorian ebonised and floral
marquetry breakfront side
cabinet, the whole with ormolu
mounts and brass stringing
lines, width 65 in. **£330-380**
JF

A French First Consulate
mahogany side cabinet, with
marble top, and brass fittings,
on bracket feet, 4 ft., c. 1805.
£1,100-1,500   *WW*

ouis XV kingwood bas
rmoire, with two glazed
rs, mounted with later
rced foliate plaques, borders
d angles, 44¾ in. (114 cm.)
le. **£900-1,100**   *C*

A bone-inlaid ebonised wood
side cabinet, c. 1870, 43½ by 70
in. (110.5 by 178 cm.). **£140-
180**   *SB*

An Edwardian inlaid rosewood
display cabinet, 40 by 30 by 13
in. **£130-160**   *SV*

French 19th C. satinwood and tulipwood banded pedestal china display cabinet, mounted with ormolu beading and three oval painted porcelain portrait medallions, 2 ft. 6 in. wide by 3 ft. 11 in. high. **£400-480** *CDC*

A 19th C. rosewood and veneered chiffonier, with serpentine front, fitted with two glazed doors, 3 ft. 6 in. **£230-300** *WHL*

A rosewood chiffonier, the marbled shelf above three fitte shelves, first half 19th C., 33 i wide. **£300-360** *L*

A Boulle side cabinet, the top inlaid after Jean Berain, with a brass moulding and with gilt bronze mounts, the top 18th C., made up mid-19th C., 43 by 48 by 16¾ in. (109 by 122 by 42.5 cm.). **£600-660** *SB*

A George III mahogany sideboard, the bowed top inla with boxwood and ebony line 54½ in. wide. **£1,800-2,100** *C*

SIDEBOARDS

- the sideboard, as opposed to the side table, was initially designed by Robert Adam probably in the 1770's
- all 18th C. sideboards have six legs
- although most sideboards of the 18th C. had square tapering legs, some still retained turned legs, although most of these are Victorian
- handles; started with circular plates with rings suspended from top, 1790's ovals became the vogue, in the Regency period they retained these shapes but also the 'Lion's mask and ring' handle: after 1800 the central drawer often had no handles
- all 18th C. sideboards had tops made from a single piece of timber, the Victorians often made tops with two or three pieces of wood
- again the narrower the better, especially if under 4 ft., however, restorers have been known to cut down larger sideboards
- sideboards tended to become ugly and ungainly after 1850

An antique mahogany sideboard inlaid fleur de lys, flowers in medallions and boxwood stringings, the drawers with brass handles, 6 ft. 7 in. wide. **£1,300-1,500** *AG*

A George III Sheraton mahogany bow-front sideboard, of small proportions, the crossbanded and line inlaid top above three drawers, 41 in. wide, 36 in. high, 24 in. deep. **£1,300-1,600** *L*

A George III mahogany bowfront sideboard, 3 ft. 9 in. wide, 35 in. high. **£1,000-1,400** *WR*

A George III mahogany a tulipwood crossbanded der lune sideboard, with circul bands of tulipwood, 183 cm wide. **£2,100-2,300** *Bon*

George III mahogany bow-
nted sideboard, crossbanded
th rosewood, 71¾ in. wide.
,600-2,000   *C*

A George III
mahogany bow-
front sideboard, one
centre drawer and
one concealed
drawer flanked by
two cupboards,
satinwood-banded
and with floral
inlay (not original
condition). **£450-
550**   *WY*

mahogany serpentine
deboard, of Sheraton design,
ossbanded and line inlaid in
tinwood, 19th C., 5 ft. ½ in.
54 cm.) wide. **£800-880**   *L*

A George III mahogany and
inlaid serpentine sideboard,
with a crossbanded top on
square tapered legs terminating
in spade feet, 1.86 m. **£1,300-
1,700**   *P*

An 18th C. Sheraton mahogany
bow-fronted sideboard, fitted
centre drawer and two cellaret
drawers, crossbanded in
tulipwood and satinwood, 54 in.
wide. **£1,700-2,100**   *SB*

Regency mahogany
akfront sideboard, the front
aid with stringing, fitted
th a baize slide, with brass
ndles, 74 in. **£1,400-1,600**

*Miller's is a price GUIDE Not
a price LIST.*

*The price ranges given
reflect the average price a
purchaser should pay for
similar items. Condition,
rarity of design or pattern,
size, colour, pedigree,
restoration and many other
factors must be taken into
account when assessing
values.*

A George III style mahogany
sideboard, crossbanded in
satinwood and inlaid with
boxwood lines throughout, 52
by 77 in., 19th C. **£300-350**
SBA

William IV mahogany
deboard, 65 in. wide, 44 in.
gh. **£580-650**   *WR*

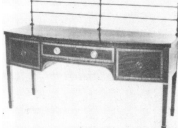

A George III style
mahogany sideboard,
33 by 59 in., early 20th
C. **£300-350**   *SBA*

A mahogany
sunken centre
pedestal sideboard,
with mirror back,
second half 19th C.,
78 in. wide. **£400-
500**   *EEW*

A Regency mahogany
sideboard, with four drawers
surrounding the central arched
drawer, 50½ in. wide. **£1,900-
2,100**   *C*

A mahogany and satinwood sideboard, probably made by William Morris & Co., applied with damask, the cupboard doors inset with painted canvas panels, 65¼ by 63¼ in., 1900-10. **£190-230** *SB*

A late Victorian pollard oak sideboard, by Thomas Turner, Manchester, 8 ft. 3 in., by 8 ft. 3 in. **£1,400-1,700** *CDC*

A marquetry and kingwood dressing table, enclosing a mirror-lined and burr-satin birch interior, with gilt-bronze mounts, 28¾ by 21 in., 1860's. **£300-360** *SB*

A George III mahogany dressing table, c. 1800, 18 in. deep, 30 in. high, 53 in. overall width. **£675-775** *WR*

A George III satinwood dressing table, the twin-flap t enclosing a divided and fitte interior surrounding a mirro 28 in. wide. **£1,500-1,800**

An oak and gilt-bronze mounted centre dressing table, flanked by two drawers each with a velvet-lined slide, 29½ by 36¼ in., closed, c. 1860. **£480-580** *SB*

A Regency birchwood and rosewood dressing-table, with crossbanded top, two drawers and one false drawer, 46 in. wide. **£750-850** *C*

A George III satinwood dressing-table, the central ea flap flanked by lidded compartments, 37½ in. wide **£1,600-1,800** *C*

A George III faded mahogany dressing table, crossbanded with rosewood, 46¼ in. (117.5 cm.) wide. **£1,300-1,500** *C*

A George III inlaid mahogany dressing table, with hinged top enclosing 12 compartments, the 6 drawers with brass handles and side drawer fitted with a bidet, 3 ft. 5½ in. **£1,250-1,450** *AG*

A Georgian mahogany dressing table, with pull up mirror, and brass cup castors 1810, 50 in. **£740-900** *L*

'late George II' mahogany essing table, the drawers c-lined, 42 in., 1880's. **£380-** 0   *SB*

A kingwood dressing table, the single frieze drawer with two oval 'Sevres' porcelain plaques, 58 by 29 in., c. 1870. **£990-1,100**   *SB*

A Louis XV tulipwood table de toilette, with three flaps, the central backed by a mirror, 35¼ in. (89.5 cm.) wide. **£3,000-3,300**   *C*

An early 19th C. mahogany shaped front kneehole dressing table (one handle missing), 29 in. high, 63 in. wide, 21 in. deep. **£300-380**   *WR*

Dutch marquetry dressing est, brass-mounted, 5 ft. 9 in. 75 cm.) by 3 ft. 2½ in. (98 cm.), 1815. **£850-950**   *SKC*

An American rosewood chest of drawers, with white marble top, stamped 'J & J W Meeks N214 Vesey St. New York', 37 in. (94 cm.) wide. **£350-500**   *C*

Maple & Co. satin walnut essing table, the swing mirror carved frame, mounted with drawers, and a frieze drawer, in. wide. **£360-500**   *McMB*

A Liberty oak dressing table, the mirror plate below three stylised pewter flowerheads, bearing an enamel label Liberty & Co., London, 62½ by 38 in., c. 1900. **£150-200**   *SB*

A George III mahogany dressing and toilet table, 3 ft. 2 in. high by 2 ft. 4 in. wide, c. 1790. **£710-840**   *S*

An oak four-post bed, the headboard inlaid with marquetry panels, partly 17th C., with box-spring and mattress, 64½ in. (164 cm.) wide. **£2,500-3,000** *C*

An Elizabethan oak full-tester bed (with some later restoration), 55 in. wide, c. 1600. **£2,300-2,800**   *B*

277

A George III four poster bed, with a mahogany tester and two reeded baluster posts, length 80 in., width 64 in., c. 1790. **£1,600-1,800** *SBe*

A Chinese hardwood canopy bed, with a solid platform, the upper canopy formed by a lattice framework, Guangxu. **£400-450** *SB*

A grey-painted lit a la Polonnaise, late 18th C., Frenc or Italian, 78 in. (198 cm.) wide **£1,200-1,500** *C*

An ormolu-mounted kingwood and marquetry bed, inlaid with 'BVRB' style floral marquetry, the ormolu stamped F. Linke, box-spring and mattress, damask cover, 68 in. (173 cm.) wide, 90 in. (229 cm.) long. **£2,000-2,200** *C*

A Burmese 19th C. palki, with iron pole supports, 169 cm. **£700-850** *PJ*

A 17th C. oak cradle, the canopy, back and sides carve with tulip and lunettes, 42 in. long. **£600-750** *McMB*

DRESSERS

Dressers to be 'good' should be of good colour, with a nice chunky feel about them. It also helps, as many restorers will tell you, if it looks old. Dressers are often very hard to date, as with all country pieces, they were made over long periods of time and were not influenced by the demands of fashion to any great extent.

An oak cradle, Dutch or German, 17th C., 38½ in. (98 cm.) wide. **£700-800** *C*

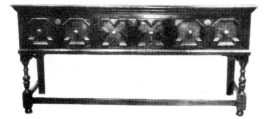

A Stuart oak serving table with four deep drawers with fielded panel fronts, 7 ft. 8 in. wide. **£500-600** *CDC*

A 17th C. dresser base, with three drawers, 6 ft. long, 2 ft. 10 in. high. **£2,500-3,000** *NCr*

A Jacobean oak dresser, on later turned supports, 5 ft. 10 in wide, c. 1670. **£1,050-1,200** *SKC*

An oak low dresser, with 3 geometrically panelled drawers, 17th C., 84½ in. wide. **£3,800-4,100**   *C*

An oak low dresser, 18th C., 72 in. wide. **£1,100-1,300**   *C*

A country oak dresser base, with later handles, 5 ft. 2½ in. (159 cm.) wide. **£390-480**   *L*

A fine George II oak backless dresser, with cockbeaded drawers and pierced brass handles, 77½ in. wide, c. 1730. **£2,200-2,500**   *N*

A George I oak dresser, with later 19th C. brass handles and lockplates, 5 ft. 11 in. long. **£980-1,100**   *OB*

Georgian oak dresser base, h mahogany crossbanding, h plate brass handles and tcheons, steel locks, c. 1800, n. long by 20 in. deep by 35 high. **£3,000-3,500**   *L*

An antique oak dresser base, with pot board, 57 in. wide by 19 in. deep, 32 in. high. **£2,100-2,400**   *SW*

18th C. oak dresser, the ree centre drawers with brass p handles, on bracket pports, 5 ft. 9 in. **£850-000**   *WY*

A mid-18th C. oak dresser, 69 by 58 in. **£600-720**   *SBe*

An early 18th C. oak dresser, 57 in. wide, c. 1730. **£2,200-2,600**   *SKC*

An early 18th C. Montgomeryshire oak dresser, of good original colour and patination, 8 ft. wide. **£3,400-4,000**   *B*

A small Georgian oak cottage dresser, with good patina, early 19th C., 57 in. long by 16 in. deep by 66 in. high. **£1,250-1,500**   *L*

joined oak high dresser, 5 ft. 5 wide, 6 ft. 8 in. high. **£900-100**   *L*

A late Georgian dresser, with moulded cornice, 63½ in. (161 cm.) wide, 81½ in. (202 cm.) high. **£1,000-1,500** *C*

An 18th C. enclosed dresser, crossbanded in mahogany with brass drop handles, 7 ft. 1 in. wide. **£1,200-1,500** *PWC*

An oak Welsh dresser, carve with the letters A.M.O.W.B., 1 cm. wide, early 18th C. with some alteration. **£990-1,100** *Bon*

A late 18th C. oak dresser, with three frieze drawers above two panelled cupboards, 4 ft. 10 in. wide, c. 1780. **£1,100-1,300** *SKC*

A Georgian oak high dresser, 5 ft. 11 in. (181 cm.) wide, 1 ft. 5 in. (44 cm.) deep, 6 ft. 6 in. (198 cm.) high. **£800-900** *L*

Miller's Antiques Price Guide builds up year by year to form the most comprehensive photo-reference system available. The first three volumes contain over 20,000 completely different photographs.

A late 18th C. oak dresser, 4 ft. in. wide, c. 1790. **£1,100-1,300** *SKC*

A late Georgian oak dresser, fitted five drawers and pot board underneath, on bracket feet, 5 ft. 5 in. long, 6 ft. 5½ in. high. **£1,300-1,600** *RBB*

A Regency rosewood secretaire, in the manner of S. Jamar, the hinged fall-flap inlaid with cut-brass, with fitted interior, 31 in. wide. **£1,000-1,200** *C*

An unusual mother pearl inlaid polychrome lacquer secretaire-on-stand, enclosing a fitted interior, Dutch of N German, 49½ in. wi late 17th C. **£2,000- 2,500** *C*

A Regency calamanderwood chiffonier, the top with three shelves supported on brass colonnettes, on sabre legs, 39 in. (99 cm.) wide. **£900-1,100** *C*

harles X mahogany
etaire a abattant, with
et marble top, the fall-flap
osing a fitted interior, with
cupboard doors below, 39½
ide. **£500-700**   *C*

A late 19th C. French walnut
and floral marquetry bow-front
Secretaire A Abattant, the fall
front enclosing drawers and
cupboard, 1 ft. 9½ in. (54 cm.)
wide. **£1,000-1,200**   *SKC*

A giltmetal-
mounted kingwood
and marquetry
secretaire a
abattant, with
rectangular verde
antico marble top,
33 in. (83.5 cm.)
wide. **£1,300-
1,800**   *C*

An ormolu-mounted kingwood
and marquetry secretaire a
abbatant, with a marble top,
frieze drawer, concave and
convex secretaire and a pair of
cupboards below, now fitted as
a cocktail cabinet, c. 1860, 55 by
43½ in. (140 by 110.5 cm.).
£1,100-1,400   *SB*

9th C. German walnut
cretaire A Abattant, with
ze drawer, the fall revealing
tted interior, 5 ft. 1 in. high
3 ft. 7¾ in. wide, c. 1850.
70-870   *SKC*

An early 18th C. walnut
escritoire, with arabesque
marquetry panels, top fitted
with a cushion drawer with fall
flap and fitted interior, 5 ft. 4 in.
£2,250-2,600   *MMB*

A William III burr-
elm secretaire, the
fall-front enclosing
a fitted interior, 5 ft.
8 in. high by 3 ft. 8½
in. wide, c. 1700,
later handles and
bun feet. **£4,200-
4,600**   *S*

A walnut William and Mary
escritoire (not original feet or
handles), with cushion top and
beautiful interior, 69 in. high, 19
in. deep, 42 in. wide. **£3,000-
3.500**   *B.M*

ecretaire a abattant, in
ard oak, the fall front
osing pigeon holes and
wers, length 41½ in., width
n., height 62½ in. **£680-
   OL**

A Japanese black and gilt
lacquer writing desk, with fitted
interior, 167.5 by 77.5 cm., on a
later stand, 1880's. **£1,500-
2,000**   *SB*

A Victorian rosewood secretaire
Wellington chest, with a
simulated double drawer drop
front enclosing stationery
compartments, 2 ft. 3 in. wide,
20 in. deep, 48 in. high. **£450-
550**   *V*

A mulberry veneered bureau cabinet, of Queen Anne design, with fitted interior, the doors having bevelled mirror glass, 41 in. wide. **£6,800-7,500** *M*

A Dutch burr-walnut bureau cabinet, enclosing a fitted interior and a well, 7 ft. 4 in. high by 4 ft. wide, c. 1740, distressed. **£4,000-5,000** *S*

A mid-18th C. British Color walnut bureau cabinet, with secret drawers and with a reversible games slide below with later brass handles, 38 99 in. high. **£3,500-4,200** *DWB*

A small George I figured walnut bureau cabinet, the bureau with stepped interior of small walnut fronted drawers beneath pigeon holes, early 18th C., 2 ft. 1½ in. wide by 6 ft. 5½ in high. **£3,000-3,500** *B*

A George II mahogany and burr-yewwood secretaire cabinet, in the manner of William Hallett, with fitted interior, 1.10 m. wide. **£8,000-10,000** *P*

A rare George III mahogany estate bureau cabinet, crossbanded in tulipwood, enclosing a fitted interior, wi cast brass ring handles, 47 i wide by 22½ in. deep by 75 i high. **£1,000-1,200** *L*

A mid-18th C. style oak bureau cabinet, the fall flap enclosing an interior fitted with cupboards, drawers and pigeon-holes, 41½ in. wide, restored. **£1,100-1,300** *SKC*

A Queen Anne walnut bureau cabinet, crossbanded and inlaid with yew-wood lines, enclosing a fitted interior, 6 ft. 11 in. high by 3 ft. wide, c. 1710. **£5,000-7,000** *S*

A William and Mary Queen Anne period figured walnut cabinet with fitted top and secretaire drawers, c. 1690-17 20 in. deep by 80 in. high by in. wide. **£7,800-8,300** *R*

orth Italian olivewood
au cabinet, enclosing an
ior of drawers, pigeon-
s and a well, 6 ft. 7 in. high
ft. 6½ in. wide, early 18th C.
,000-12,000 S

A rare late 17th C. William and
Mary oak bureau bookcase, of
small proportion, with fitted
interior. Now raised upon
bracket feet, 27 in. wide.
£2,900-3,200 *B*

A George III mahogany bureau
bookcase, the fall flap reveals a
fitted interior, with original
open plate brass handles,
escutcheons and carrying
handles, 3 ft. 5 in. **£2,200-
2,500** *WW*

A South German
walnut bureau
cabinet, veneered
with panels of
figured walnut,
outlined with
boxwood, ebony
and oak bandings,
mid-18th C., height
83 in., width 45 in.
£3,200-3,700
SBe

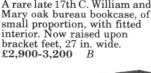

ate 18th C. inlaid mahogany
eau bookcase, the bureau
erior well fitted, width 42 in.
100-1,400 *LT*

A Queen Anne walnut bureau-
cabinet, enclosing a fitted
interior including a well, 43 in.
(109 cm.) wide, 81 in. (206 cm.)
high. **£8,000-9,000** *C*

A Queen Anne
walnut bureau
cabinet, enclosing a
fitted interior of
drawers, pigeon-
holes and a well, 6
ft. 6 in. high by 2 ft.
2½ in. wide, 1710,
upper part restored.
£7,000-8,000 *S*

A Queen Anne style
walnutwood bureau-bookcase,
the superstructure cabinet with
mirror panel, the base with
writing compartment enclosed
by fall flap, 1 ft. 11 in. wide, 7 ft.
high. **£1,900-2,400** *CDC*

Left
An early Georgian style walnut
bureau bookcase, the cupboard
in recess with sunray inlaid
door, 3 ft. wide, 6 ft. 6 in. high.
£3,500-4,000 *RBB*

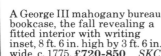

A George III mahogany bureau
bookcase, the fall revealing a
fitted interior with writing
inset, 8 ft. 6 in. high by 3 ft. 6 in.
wide, c. 1775. **£720-850** *SKC*

An 18th C. mahogany bureau
bookcase, with two mirrored
doors, a fitted interior and four
drawers. **£3,500-3,750** *NCr*

A George II mahogany bureau
cabinet, enclosing a fitted
interior, 7 ft. 4 in. high by 3 ft. 6
in. wide, c. 1750, pediment
possibly later. **£2,000-2,300**
S

A Georgian mahogany bureau/bookcase, with a well fitted interior, 43 in. wide. **£2,800-3,200** *B*

A mahogany bureau bookcase, the fall quartered and strung with satinwood, with crossbanded glazing bars, c. 1800, 45 in. wide by 90½ in. high. **£3,500-4,000** *NC*

A 19th C. mahogany burea bookcase, the lower part w writing slope enclosing an arrangement of small draw and pigeon holes, later han and top, 111 cm. **£1,100-1.400** *OT*

An Edwardian inlaid mahogany bureau bookcase, with brass handles, 6 ft. 8 in. high, 3 ft. wide. **£580-700** *AG*

A George III-style mahogany bureau bookcase, the fitted interior with baize inset, decorated with satinwood, chevron stringing and crossbanding, 7 ft. 2½ in. high by 3 ft. 8 in. wide, c. 1850. **£2,500-2,800** *SKC*

A crossbanded mahogany cylinder bureau bookcase, the cylinder crossbanded in rosewood, enclosing a fitted interior, first half 19th C., 7 ft. 7 in. high, 3 ft. 10 in. wide, 2 ft. 2 in. deep. **£1,000-1,100** *L*

A late 18th C. oak burea bookcase, the flap enclos fitted interior. **£650-750** *SKC*

An Edwardian mahogany and satinwood chevron banded bureau bookcase, with fitted interior, 7 ft. 2 in. (219 cm.) high by 3 ft. 4 in. (102 cm.) wide, c. 1910. **£860-950** *SKC*

A palisander bureau-cabinet, the sloping flap enclosing a well-fitted interior, 18th C., 48 in. wide. **£3,500-4,000** *C*

A bureau-cabinet, the panelled flap enclosing a fitted interior including a well, mid 18th C., probably German, 50 in. (127 cm.) wide, 97 in. (246.5 cm.) high. **£3,300-3,600** *C*

satinwood and kingwood
nded bureau bookcase on
nd, the fall with marquetry
ne of lovers, with fitted
erior, 7 ft. 1½ in. high by 2 ft.
in. wide, c. 1880. £1,600-
00   *SKC*

An Edwardian mahogany
bureau bookcase, with
satinwood crossbanding and
boxwood and ebony stringing,
36 in. **£790-850**   *Hy.D*

A George III mahogany
secretaire bookcase, the fitted
writing drawer with satinwood
veneered interior, 7 ft. 8 in. (234
cm.) high by 3 ft. 11 in. (120 cm.)
wide, c. 1800. **£1,500-1,600**
SKC

Georgian mahogany
retaire bookcase, in the
eraton style, the fitted
wer with crossbanded front,
in. **£3,600-4,300**   *BW*

A Georgian mahogany
secretaire bookcase, the
secretaire drawer enclosing a
fitted interior, the cupboard
door enclosing a pair of
drawers, 7 ft. 9 in. high, 4 ft. 2 in.
wide. **£1,450-1,650**   *L*

A late George III satinwood
secretaire cabinet, with a well-
fitted secretaire drawer, 46 in.
wide. **£3,300-3,700**   *C*

George III mahogany
eakfront secretaire bookcase,
e drawers with brass handles,
in. wide. **£5,800-6,500**   *JF*

A Georgian mahogany
secretaire bookcase, the
secretaire drawer crossbanded
and lined with boxwood,
enclosing a fitted interior, 7 ft. 9
in. high, 3 ft. 8½ in. wide, 1 ft. 11
in. deep. **£1900-2,300**   *L*

A late Georgian figured
mahogany breakfront
secretaire bookcase, two short
dummy drawers, enclosing
fitted interior, 8 ft. 1 in. high, 7
ft. wide, 2 ft. 1 in. deep. **£4,800-
5,500**   *L*

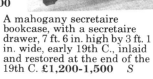

A Regency mahogany secretaire-cabinet, 45¼ in. (115 cm.) wide. **£2,200-2,500** *C*

A William IV mahogany secretaire bookcase, the fitted drawer containing rising writing slope with brushing slide, 30 in. **£1,050-1,400** *BW*

A mahogany secretaire bookcase, with a secretaire drawer, 7 ft. 6 in. high by 3 ft. 1 in. wide, early 19th C., inlaid and restored at the end of the 19th C. **£1,200-1,500** *S*

A 19th C. mahogan secretaire bookcase, with fitted interior a brass drop handles, in. wide. **£990-1,10** *PWC*

A Georgian crossbanded mahogany bookcase, the doors enclosing shelves above pigeon holes, 3 ft. 4½ in. (103 cm.) wide. **£680-780** *L*

An oak bookcase, early 18th C., the glazing panels of later date, 45½ in. (116 cm.) wide. **£1,800-2,200** *C*

A George I-style walnut bookcase, crossbanded and outlined with feather bandin (re-constructed from 18th C. pieces), height 74 in., width in. **£840-990** *SBe*

A pair of Regency 2 ft. 6½ in. bookcases, with ebony inlay, the cupboards with brass grille doors, 8 ft. 8 in. high. **£1,850-2,000** *AG*

A Regency mahogany breakfront bookcase, 86 in. wide. **£3,300-3,600** *C*

A 19th C. walnut and marquetry bookcase, with floral inlay and brass embellishments, width 51 in. **£2,250-2,400** *LT*

A mahogany inlaid bookcase, banded in satinwood and line inlaid throughout, late 19th C., 3 ft. 1 in. wide, 1 ft. 5 in. deep, 6 ft. 11 in. high. **£600-700** *L*

A mid-19th C. Flemish oa bookcase, 5 ft. 6 in., c. 186 **£600-750** *SKC*

George III fiddle back
mahogany cabinet on chest, the
cabinet with silk lined interior
and two glass shelves, the base
with gilt brass swan neck
handles, 3 ft. £2,100-2,400
W

BREAKFRONT BOOKCASES

- originally bookshelves in libraries were fixtures
- freestanding bookcases were developed in the 17th C. and perfected in the 18th C.
- bookcases were made for the rich and have always been collectable
- again the smaller a bookcase is the more desirable it is; one should also always check height as many bookcases were made for higher ceilings than present room heights allow
- it is vital to remember the 18th C. love of proportion — if the groove for the first shelf is six inches from the bottom, the groove for the top shelf will be six inches from the top
- many breakfront bookcases started life as breakfront wardrobes
- tell-tale signs can be seen where about 8-10 inches have been cut off the depth

A Georgian style breakfront
bookcase (reconstructed), 8 ft.
1½ in. (247 cm.) wide, 7 ft. 3 in.
(221 cm.) high. £1,000-1,150
L

A Victorian oak breakfront
bookcase, 6 ft. 4 in. by 3 ft.
£600-700   ELR

19th C. satinwood and
marquetry breakfront library
bookcase, 2.56 m. wide. £5,500-
000   P

A double domed breakfront
mahogany bookcase, by Gillow
of Lancaster (cornice missing),
raised on carved ogee feet, 8 ft. 8
in. wide, 7 ft. 2 in. high. £3,800-
4,300   PS

A late Victorian break-fronted
bookcase, in the manner of
Pugin, 9 ft. 4 in. (285 cm.) wide,
c. 1880. £1,300-1,500   SKC

ne of a pair of walnut
ookcases, enclosing mirrored
teriors, 58 in. wide, 90 in.
gh. £3,300-3,600 the pair

An 'Art Nouveau' oak corner
bookcase, with copper
strapwork hinges, 87 by 307 in.,
c. 1900. £620-720   SB

A 'George III' mahogany breakfront bookcase, 100 by 77½ in.
(254 by 197 cm.), c. 1900.
£2,200-2,500   SB

A kingwood and tulipwood bibliotheque basse, with breccia marble top and a frieze drawer above two cupboard doors filled with silk-backed wire mesh, 37 in. (94 cm.) wide. **£650-750**   *C*

A pair of mahogany bookcases, 87½ by 60 in., late 19th C. **£650-750**   *SBA*

A pair of Louis XVI mahogan bookcases, in the style Anglais each with two full-length glaze cupboard doors, stamped G. Jacob, 52 in. (132 cm.) wide, 8 in. (216 cm.) high. **£7,800-8,500**   *C*

One of a pair of Regency rosewood and parcel-gilt dwarf bookcases, with white marble top, 54 in. wide. **£1,900-2,200** the pair   *C*

A Regency cabinet inlaid with ebony with fold-over writing surface, 30 in. wide by 51 in. high. **£2,300-2,400**   *NC*

A 19th C. rosewood bookstan the rectangular top having a leather inset, the 3 shelves i each flank faced with leather books, 1 ft. 7 in. by 1 ft. 4 in., 3 in. high. **£800-950**   *V*

A mahogany bookcase, c. 1800, 31 in. high, 17 in. deep, 24 in. wide. **£525-600**   *B.M*

A late Victorian satinwood display cabinet, marquetry inlaid overall, height 80 in., width 40 in., c. 1900. **£800-900**   *SBe*

A Regency painted open bookcase, fitted brass carry handles, 3 ft. 9 in. (114 cm.) h by 1 ft. 5¾ in. (45 cm.) wide 1810. **£220-280**   *SKC*

A small mahogany display cabinet, formerly with a superstructure, 46¾ by 36 by 14¾ in., 1890's. **£450-520**   *SB*

mahogany and
rquetry display
pinet, c. 1900, 59
27½ in. (150 by 70.
.). £800-900

A mahogany vitrine cabinet,
ormolu-mounted, with inset
Breccia marble top, the frieze
mounted with a plaque after
Clodion, 28½ in. wide. £1,000-
1,300   C

A 19th C. French kingwood and
ormolu vitrine, with marble top,
32 in. wide. £1,100-1,500   M

A late Victorian mahogany
display cabinet, outlined with
boxwood stringing and painted
with panels of floral swags, c.
1900, height 63½., width 30 in.
£530-630   SBe

nahogany vitrine, applied
h gilt-bronze acanthus and
sk mounts, 64½ by 28 in. (164
71 cm.), c. 1900. £850-
00   SB

An Edwardian mahogany
serpentine-fronted display
cabinet, 6 ft. (182 cm.) high by 5
ft. 9 in. (176 cm.) wide, c. 1910,
fitted for electric light. £1,500-
1,700   SKC

An Edwardian display cabinet.
£300-340   LAC

An Art Nouveau mahogany
display cabinet, inlaid in
stained fruitwoods, 107 cm.
across. £580-700   P

Edwardian mahogany
na cabinet, with box string,
rquetry and crossband
ay. £350-430   GAK

An Art Nouveau marquetry
cabinet, 76½ by 50 in., bearing a
label John Taylor & Son
Edinburgh Ltd., Cabinet
Makers, Edinburgh, numbered
B 995, c. 1905. £830-930   SB

An Edwardian carved
rosewood and inlaid display
cabinet, 64 in. high, 45 in. wide.
£460-560   DSH

A kingwood and Vernis Martin vitrine, 78¾ by 38¾ in., c. 1900. **£1,250-1,500** *SB*

An Art Nouveau cabinet, in inlaid mahogany, length 47 in., width 14 in., height 69 in. **£500-620** *OL*

A giltmetal-mounted rosewood vitrine cabinet, the lower part inset with a Vernis Martin panel of a gallant and two companions, the sides decorated with woodland landscapes, 45 in. (112.5 cm.) wide. **£2,600-3,000** *C*

A Louis XV-style vitrine, the central bowed glazed door wit a Vernis Martin pane below, c. 1880, height 85 in., width 43 in. **£1,350-1,500** *SBe*

A kingwood marquetry and Vernis Martin serpentine bombe vitrine, with gilt-bronze foliate mounts, 78 by 39 in., early 20th C. **£1,700-2,100** *SB*

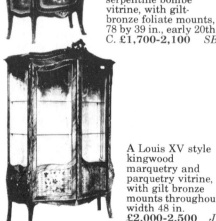

A Louis XV style kingwood marquetry and parquetry vitrine, with gilt bronze mounts throughout, width 48 in. **£2,000-2,500** *JF*

A French kingwood and ormolu-mounted vitrine, wit Vernis Martin-style painted panels, 6 ft. 10¾ in. high by 4 1½ in. wide, c. 1890. **£1,500-1,800** *SKC*

A Louis XV-style kingwood vitrine, the central serpentine glazed door with a Vernis Martin panel, enclosing a velvet lined shelved interior, early 20th C., 74 by 42 in. **£1,600-2,000** *SBe*

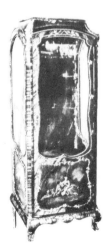

A mahogany display cabinet, 81 by 39¼ in., probably Portuguese, c. 1900. **£550-650** *SB*

A late 19th C. walnut china cabinet, painted with a pastoral scene of 18th C. lovers, ormolu mounted, 25½ in. wide, 5 ft. 5½ in. high. **£660-800** *BK*

A walnut display cabinet, of William & Mary design, 39 in. **£750-850** *Hy.D*

A 19th C. ormolu mounted kingwood china cabinet, 3 ft. in. wide, 4 ft. 8½ in. high. **£1,650-2,100** *BK*

An 18th C. Dutch marquetry vitrine with original brasswork, profusely decorated in a floral marquetry on a walnut background, 90 in. high by 61 in. wide. **£3,600-4,000** *B*

A Dutch walnut display cabinet, with arched moulded cornice, on cabriole legs headed by foliage and claw-and-ball feet, 90 in. (229 cm.) wide. **£3,000-3,500** *C*

early 18th C. Dutch parcel ony and satin hardwood rine, 57 in. wide. **£2,900- 300** *B*

A mahogany display cabinet, with a painted solid lower panel, 70 by 53 in. (178 by 135 cm.), c. 1890. **£570-650** *SB*

A Dutch walnut and marquetry display cabinet, the base with two drawers, on hexagonal tapering legs, 80 in. (203 cm.) wide, 78 in. (198 cm.) high. **£4,000-4,500** *C*

dwardian mahogany and quetry display cabinet, d with satinwood and ood lines, 78 by 37 in., 20th C. **£980-1,200**

An Edwardian inlaid mahogany display cabinet, 48 in. wide, 70 in. high. **£390- 460** *TW*

One of a pair of early 19th C. mahogany display cabinets, with brass lion head and ring handles, 165 cm. wide. **£4,200- 4,600** the pair *PJ*

18th C. Dutch marquetry d walnut shaped cabinet, the se with two secret frieze awers, 5 ft. **£3,400-3,700** W

A mahogany inlaid display cabinet, on a two drawer stand, 4 ft. 8 in. wide by 6 ft. 5 in. high. **£550-650** *RMcT*

An Edwardian mahogany display cabinet by Edwards and Roberts, the drawers with brass handles, 7 ft. 4 in. high, 4 ft. 4 in. wide. **£2,050-2,450** *AG*

A Dutch oak and marquetry display cabinet, 59 in. (150 cm.) wide. **£5,000-7,000** *C*

A Dutch inlaid mahogany display cabinet, the drawers with brass handles, 8 ft 2 in. high, 6 ft. 10 in. wide, 19th C. **£1,900-2,200** *AG*

A Dutch floral marquetry display-cabinet, the base wi two shaped panelled cupbo doors, 64 in. (163 cm.) wide, in. (224 cm.) high. **£4,000-4,500** *C*

A Louis XV style mahogany and kingwood dwarf vitrine, ormolu-mounted and inlaid, stamped G. Durand, 42 in. wide. **£2,300-2,600** *CEd*

One of a pair of mid-Georgian mahogany display-cabinets, 51 in. wide. **£3,300-3,600** the pair *C*

One of a pair of late 19th C. walnut and zebrawood display cabinets, with ormolu mounts and brass beading, 28 in. wide. **£1,100-1,400** the pair *Mlms*

A Victorian ebonised display cabinet, with gilt metal and Sevres style mounts and outlined with bra banding, c. 1880, height 72 in., wid 29 in. **£440-540** *SBe*

One of a pair of mahogany display cabinets, 59 by 26 in., c. 1880. **£1,100-1,300** the pair *SB*

An Edwardian mahogany display cabinet, two drawers in the frieze with brass knob handles, 5 ft. 9 in. high, 34½ in. wide. **£820-900** *AG*

A Chinese ebonised display cabinet, 199 by 105 cm., Guangxu. **£350-400** *SB*

A Regency rosewood displa cabinet, the table base wit baize-lined flap, the whole inlaid with boxwood lines, 4 wide. **£2,000-2,300** *C*

A Dutch marquetry display cabinet, the cupboard doors inlaid and engraved with scenes of courtship, framed by ormolu borders, c. 1830, 66 in. (169 cm.) wide, 93 in. (236 cm.) high. **£2,300-2,600**   *C*

small early 19th C. French ngwood and rosewood rossbanded vitrine commode, f serpentine form, 28 in. wide, 3 in. high. **£1,200-1,500**   *B*

A satinwood and parquetry side cabinet, inlaid with geometric patterns and panelling, 74 by 55 in., c. 1900. **£900-1,100**   *SB*

walnut side cabinet, the upboard doors painted with gures after Burne-Jones, 92 by 8 in., late 1870's. **£500-600** ;B

A Japanese stained hardwood display cabinet, with sliding doors, a cupboard door and two drawers, 98 by 71 cm., c. 1900. **£150-200**   *SB*

A Victorian inlaid rosewood side cabinet, 48 in. wide. **£250-300**   *PSH*

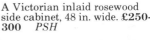

n inlaid display cabinet, robably German, c. 1900/05. **270-310**   *SB*

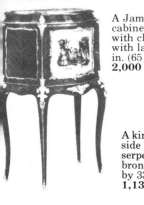

A James I black japanned cabinet on stand, doors painted with chinoiserie landscapes, with later ebonised stand, 25½ in. (65 cm.) wide. **£1,000-2,000**   *C*

An Antwerp inlaid ebony cabinet with 2 long, 4 short and 1 deep drawer, mounted with red tortoiseshell, on later stand, width 28 in., c. 1670. **£570-650**   *SBe*

A kingwood and Vernis Martin side cabinet, with a brocatelle serpentine marble top and gilt-bronze mounts throughout, 50¼ by 33½ in., c. 1900. **£930-1,130**   *SB*

A pair of George II black and gold lacquer display cabinets on stands, mounted with gilt-brass angles, 23 in. wide, 51 in. high. **£1,600-1,900**   *C*

A scarlet and gold lacquer cabinet-on-stand, of Charles II design, enclosing various-sized drawers, 46 in. wide. **£3,200-3,500** *C*

A Spanish walnut vargueno, 4 ft. 6½ in. high by 3 ft. 3½ in. wide, late 16th/early 17th C. **£1,600-1,800** *S*

A Flemish ebony and tortoiseshell cabinet-on-stan drawers inset with a panel o Italian silk and silver threa embroidery of flowers, 17th 44 in. (112 cm.) wide. **£7,000 7,500** *C*

A German rosewood cabinet-on-stand, inlaid in pewter, the central cupboard door inlaid with a figure emblematic of Monarchy and inscribed 'Monarchia', 17th C., 51½ in. (131 cm.) wide. **£3,300-3,600** *C*

An electrotype-mounted oak cigar cabinet enclosing cigar trays, sides with cupboard doors, 58 by 30 in., possibly Danish, c. 1870. **£490-590** *SB*

A 17th C. South German waln cabinet, with pictorial inlay buildings, 26½ in., later stan **£1,600-2,000** *DWB*

A lacquer cabinet on stand, the two doors enclosing shelves and drawers, 61.5 cm., late 19th C. **£470-520** *SB*

A French parquetry table de nuit, with frieze drawer and fall flap, 21 in. (53 cm.) wide. **£1,200-1,500** *C*

A Dutch oak cabinet o stand, inlaid with lea marquetry and enclosing slotted adjustable shelves, la 18th C., 68 in. high b 37 in. wide by 14 in. deep. **£200-260** *L*

A small Japanese parquetry cupboard, two doors each enclosing six small drawers, 115 cm. by 75 cm., c. 1900. **£275-325** *SB*

A George III mahogany collector's cabinet, with lift-up top and an arrangement of small drawers, 21 in., on a later stand with a drawer. **£290-350** *Hy.D*

A Georgian mahogan cabinet, fitted with tw panelled doors over tw short and one long drawer, 30½ in. high, 2 in. wide. **£400-480** *MAI*

Charles II oak chest-on-
and, with 2 short and 3 long
nelled and coffered drawers,
e stand with 2 drawers, 40 in.
de. **£900-980**   *C*

Queen Anne design walnut
eneered and herringbone
ossbanded chest on stand, 3
. 3 in. by 5 ft. 1 in. by 1 ft. 11 in.
2,000-2,300   *OT*

A walnut chest on stand, in the
Queen Anne manner, with
crossbanded top, 2 ft. 8 in. wide,
1 ft. 8 in. deep, 3 ft. 8 in. high.
£600-700   *L*

An early 18th C. burr elm chest,
on later stand, decorated with
crossbanding, 3 ft. 2 in. (97 cm.)
wide, c. 1720. **£1,100-1,400**
SKC

A Queen Anne walnut chest, on
later stand, 3 ft. 3 in. (99 cm.)
wide. **£600-700**   *SKC*

A Queen Anne walnut chest on
stand, decorated with
crossbanding, 3 ft. (92 cm.)
wide. **£1,500-1,700**   *SKC*

BEADING

- 18th C. beading was all done
  out of the one piece of wood
  — hence the grain always
  runs true
- with Victorian and Edwardian
  beading, the beads were
  glued on

An oak chest on stand,
crossbanded in fruitwood, with
brass steel locks and pierced
brass late handles and
escutcheons, early 18th C., 62
in. high by 41 in. wide. **£1,100-
1,500**   *L*

An early 18th C. oak chest on
stand, 3 ft. 3 in. wide. **£550-
650**   *SKC*

n 18th C. inlaid walnut chest,
n later stand, with swan-neck
andles, 44 in. **£700-850**   *BW*

A Queen Anne oyster-veneered
kingwood chest on stand, the
stand originally with taller
legs, 3 ft. 8½ in. high by 3 ft. 3 in.
wide, c. 1700. **£3,000-4,000**   *S*

An early 18th C. walnut chest on stand, the drawers with contemporary pear drop brass handles on 6 compressed bun feet. **£650-800** *BC*

A George I walnut tallboy top herringbone banded and inlaid on later base with bun feet, 41 in. **£500-600** *DWB*

An early Georgian black and gold lacquer chest-on-stand, redecorated, 39 in. (99 cm.) wid **£1,900-2,200** *C*

An early 18th C. crossbanded walnut chest of three long and three short drawers, with brass bail handles and escutcheons, 3 ft. 4 in. wide. **£680-800** *GC*

A mid-18th C. oak chest on stand, with mahogany crossbanding, 43 in. wide. **£450-600** *SBe*

A mid-Georgian oak chest-on stand, width 46 in. **£550-700** *JF*

An oak chest on stand, with axe drop brass handles, the base with spiral supports (faults), mainly 17th C., 54 in. high by 45 in. wide. **£420-500** *L*

An antique walnutwood bow-fronted tallboy, 3 ft. 2 in. wide, ft. 11 in. high. **£760-900** *CDC*

An early George I walnut tallboy, the drawers with crossbandings and featherbanding and original brass plate handles, with brushing slide, c. 1720, 71 in. high by 41½ in. wide by 20½ in. deep. **£5,500-6,300** *L*

A Georgian mahogany tallboy, the drawers with oak linings and later brass plate handles, with a brushing slide, 46 in. wide by 78 in. high by 22 in. deep. **£550-680** *L*

A George I burr walnut tallboy, the base with a fitted secretaire drawer, 42 in. (107 cm.) wide. **£4,400-4,800** *C*

George III mahogany tallboy, ith satinwood and harewood hequered frieze, the drawers ith oval stamped brass andles, 44 in. wide by 70 in. igh by 19½ in. deep. **£440-50** *L*

A Georgian inlaid mahogany tallboy, with brass loop handles, 42 in. **£850-1,050** *BW*

A George I walnut tallboy, with a brushing-slide, 42½ in. wide. **£3,000-3,300** *C*

Make the most of Miller's

When buying or selling, it must always be remembered that prices can be greatly affected by the condition of any piece.
Unless otherwise stated, all goods shown in Miller's are of good merchantable quality, and the valuations given reflect this fact.
Pieces offered for sale in exceptionally fine condition or in poor condition may reasonably be expected to be priced considerably higher or lower respectively than the estimates given herein.

mid-Georgian amaranth lboy, the frieze inlaid with rr-yew, the base with a ushing slide, 43 in. (109 cm.) de. **£1,600-1,800** *C*

A mahogany chest-on-chest, original handles, fluted frieze with paterae, 1760-1770, 69½ in. high by 41¾ in. wide. **£1,100-1,200** *NC*

A Chippendale mahogany tallboy, with rococo gilt brass handles and escutcheons, 41½ in. wide by 75 in. high by 22 in. deep. **£680-800** *L*

George III mahogany tallboy, ith moulded beaded and entilled cornice, the frieze arved with anthemions, 48 in. 22 cm.) wide. **£700-900** *C*

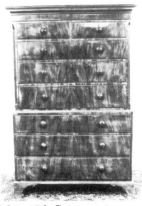

A late 18th C. two part mahogany veneered tallboy, on bracket feet, 3 ft. 9 in. (later handles). **£400-480** *WHL*

A George III mahogany tallboy, 6 ft. 11½ in. (182 cm.) high by 3 ft. 7½ in. (111 cm.) wide, c. 1770. **£870-950** *SKC*

A George III mahogany tallboy, 40 in. wide by 72 in. high by 20 in. deep. £620-800   *L*

An 18th C. burr elm tallboy, the drawers crossbanded. £4,000-4,350   *NCr*

A walnut chest-upon-chest, with feather crossbanded drawers, having brass bail handles and escutcheons, 3 ft in. wide, 1 ft. 10 in. deep, 71 i high. £460-560   *V*

A small mahogany tallboy chest, late Sheraton period, having brass ring handles, on splay bracket feet, 3 ft. 3 in. £650-750   *WW*

An early 19th C. Queen Anne style walnut chest on chest, 41 in. wide. £1,400-1,700   *Lan*

An early 19th C. Dutch marquetry tall chest, of six drawers, with brass ring handles, on turned feet, 3 ft. 4 in. £1,200-1,500   *WW*

PATINATION

- the patination on different woods varies considerably but the same piece of wood will basically colour to the same extent (always allowing for bleaching by sunlight etc.
- dirt and grease from handling are important guides (especially under drawer handles, on chair arms etc.)
- on pieces with carving or crevices, dirt will have accumulated, giving dark patches
- by repolishing a piece of furniture and removing evidence of patination, a dealer can conceal replacement or conversion

A 19th C. Dutch marquetry and mahogany tall chest, inlaid with satinwood floral sprays, 5 ft. ¼ in. high by 3 ft. 3¾ in. wide, c. 1835. £1,150-1,300   *SKC*

A Queen Anne walnut cabinet on chest, crossbanded and strung with ebony lines, 1.06 m. £2,500-3,000   *P*

A Georgian mahogany tallboy, with brass swan-neck handles and architectural cornice, 42 in. £1,000-1,300   *BW*

A Dutch oak and ebony cupboard, 68 in. wide, mid-17th C. £2,400-2,800   *SKC*

mid-18th C. German walnut cupboard, the base containing a single drawer, on massive bun feet, 2.2 m. wide. £3,500-4,200　P

A 17th C. Dutch oak and ebony cupboard, of small proportion, 59 in. wide by 58 in. high. £1,600-1,900　B

A Flemish oak cupboard, with frieze drawer above two arcaded panelled cupboard doors, 57 in. wide. £900-1,000　C

A George III oak cupboard, 6 ft. 9½ in. (207 cm.) by 5 ft. (152 cm.) wide, c. 1770. £400-480　SKC

A Venetian burr-walnut cabinet, with crossbanded cupboard doors enclosing 10 various-sized drawers, mounted with bronze handles, 44 in. wide, 77½ in. high. £4,000-5,000　C

A 16th C. Gothic oak cupboard, with single long door with fretted Gothic decoration, 58 in. wide, 62 in. high. £1,150-1,500　B

A 17th C. North German oak cupboard, raised upon sledge feet, 62 in. wide. £1,750-2,000　B

A 17th C. Dutch oak cupboard, raised upon heavy bun feet, 65 by 77 in. £1,900-2,200　B

An early 18th C. German baroque cupboard, decorated in parcel ebony on a hardwood background, 73 in. wide, 82 in. high. £1,950-2,300　B

A 17th C. English oak cupboard, of Dutch influence, with hardwood inlay, 55 in. wide. £1,050-1,350　B

An 18th C. North Country oak bread and cheese cupboard, 42 in. wide. £660-860　B

A George III mahogany breakfront wardrobe, 84 in. wide by 97 in. high by 18½ in. deep. £1,400-1,700   *L*

A Georgian mahogany breakfront wardrobe cupboard, the doors enclosing sliding trays, 8 ft. 1 in. wide. £900-1,100   *PWC*

A small 17th C. North Germa[oak and parquetry cupboard with drawer, raised upon thr[flat bun feet, 73 in. high by 62 [wide. £1,850-2,100   *B*

An oak wardrobe, in the Arts and Crafts style, with bronzed fittings, 78 in. high. £100-150   *CSK*

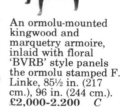

An ormolu-mounted kingwood and marquetry armoire, inlaid with floral 'BVRB' style panels the ormolu stamped F. Linke, 85½ in. (217 cm.), 96 in. (244 cm.). £2,000-2.200   *C*

A giltmetal-mounted tulipwood armoire, 37 in. (94.5 cm.) wide. £800-1,000   *C*

A Biedermeier mahogany armoire, the base with a draw[36 in. wide, 67½ in. high. £75[900   *C*

A 17th C. Aumbrey extensively carved, 6 ft. wide, 7 ft. 6 in. tall. £1,400-1,700   *LMT*

An 18th C. Normandy oak armoire, 54 in. wide, 86 in. high. £900-1,200   *B*

A Dutch colonial ebony and amaranth armoire, on hexagonal tapering legs, 44 in. wide, late 17th C. £700-850   *C*

A French carved oak armoire with brass escutcheons and hinges, 62 in. £880-1,000   *Hy.D*

A Continental armoire, the doors inlaid with ovals and with chevron chequer banding overall, 7 ft. high, 4 ft. 8 in. wide, 1 ft. 11½ in. deep. £900-1,000   *L*

17th C. German walnut ide-schrank, with five wers, 84 in. wide, 91 in. high. ,000-3,500 *B*

An 18th C. Flemish armoire, constructed of fruitwood, 68 in. wide, 78 in. high. **£2,300-2,600** *B*

A Louis XV Normandy oak armoire, 156 cm. wide. **£1,500-1,650** *Bon*

good small 17th C. Dutch oak eldenkast. The bun feet pports now missing, 57 in. de. **£5,500-6,000** *B*

A Flemish walnut armoire, the base with a long drawer, late 17th/early 18th C., 73 in. wide. **£1,400-1,600** *C*

A North German oak armoire, on bun feet, 64 in. wide, 19th C. **£500-620** *SKC*

Make the most of Miller's

Every care has been taken to ensure the accuracy of descriptions and estimated valuations.

Where an attribution is made within inverted commas (e.g. 'Chippendale') or is followed

by the word 'style' (e.g. early Georgian style) it is intended to convey that, in the opinion of the publishers, the piece concerned is a later — though probably still antique — reproduction of the style so designated.

Dutch walnut and marquetry noire, the bombe base with ree long drawers with neo-ssical giltmetal handles, 64½ (160 cm.) wide. **£3,400-00** *C*

A 17th C. Dutch oak beeldenkast cupboard, the lower part with shallow frieze drawers and with two shallow drawers to the base, 83 in. high by 65 in. wide. **£3,700-4,200** *B*

An 18th C. Dutch floral marquetry armoire, fitted with three long drawers, on claw and ball feet, 69 in. wide. **£4,700-5,100** *PK*

A Dutch padoukwood armoire,
76½ in. wide, late 18th C.
£1,500-1,700 *C*

A George III mahogany linen
press, with satinwood banding,
the doors enclosing a fitted
interior of shelves and four
drawers, 52 in. wide by 81 in.
high by 24 in. deep. **£450-
550** *L*

A Dutch mahogany armoire,
70½ in. wide, late 18th C. lat
back. **£1,200-1,500** *C*

A Georgian mahogany linen
press, with panelled and
crossbanded doors edged with
chequer banding, 6 ft. 6 in. high.
4 ft. 7 in. wide, 2 ft. 2 in. deep.
£460-550 *L*

An early George III mahogany
clothes press, bearing a label,
tracing its descent to 'Jane
Fowler — June 1920', 50 in.
wide. **£1,500-1,800** *C*

A Georgian oak press cupb
50 in. wide, 70 in. high ap
£500-600 *L*

A Georgian oak clothes press,
with two short dummy drawers
above two short and two long
drawers, George III, 4 ft. 3 in.
wide, 6 ft. 5 in. high, 1 ft. 9½ in.
deep. **£460-560** *L*

A late Georgian Welsh oak
linen press, in two stages, width
50 in. **£650-800** *JF*

A Regency mahogany linen
press, inlaid with ebony lin
panelled doors enclosing fi
sliding linen shelves, c. 182
ft. 3 in. high, 4 ft. 1 in. wide,
9½ in. deep. **£400-480** *L*

mahogany linen press, 19th
48 by 74 in. high. £400-
0 *L*

A mid-19th C. mahogany linen
press, profusely inlaid with
floral and other marquetry,
fitted with sliding trays
enclosed by two panelled doors,
4 ft. £850-1,000 *WY*

A 19th C. Padouk linen press, 39
in. wide by 59½ in. high.
£1,000-£1,100 *NC*

lemish oak and ebony press,
C., 71½ in. (182 cm.) wide,
in. (222 cm.) high. £2,500-
00 *C*

A dark oak press cupboard,
having double panelled doors, 2
dummy drawers and 4 real
drawers below, length 53 in.,
width 20 in., height 66 in. £450-
550 *OL*

A Flemish carved oak press,
with two pairs of cupboard
doors with original steel locks,
on flat bun feet, 64 in. wide by 70
in. high by 26 in. deep. £3,400-
4,000 *L*

Velsh oak press cupboard
wrdd deuddarn), late 18th
4 ft. 9 in. wide, 6 ft. 1½ in.
, 1 ft. 11 in. deep. £800-
00 *L*

A 17th C. oak press,
with later top and
gadrooned frieze, some
recarving, 58½ in. (147
cm.) wide. £800-950
C

th C. German oak schrank,
ower part with two drawers
ve two doors, raised upon
e large ball feet, 54 in. wide
6 in. high. £3,200-3,600

A 17th C. North
German walnut and
oak schrank, with
central date 1661, 63 in.
wide, 64 in. high.
£2,700-3,300 *B*

A 17th C. Dutch oak and ebony kast, the lower part with a shallow drawer, 53 in. wide, 82 in. high. **£2,200-2,800** *B*

A 19th C. North European oak buffet, 54 in. wide. **£3,300-3,700** *B*

A late 18th C. Normandy buffet, 4 ft. 7 in. wide, c. 1780. **£1,200-1,500** *SKC*

An 18th C. German oak baroqu schrank, cross-grain decoratio and ebony moulding, 62 in. wide. **£1,700-2,000** *B*

An antique Flemish oak side cupboard, 1.20 m. wide. **£1,800-2,100** *P*

A James I oak food cupboar fitted with a pair of pierced panelled doors enclosing a lir lined interior, 48 in. wide, c. 1620. **£550-660** *SKC*

A mid-17th C. oak parlour cupboard, with original carving and turned handles, 61½ in. wide. **£1,800-2,100** *N*

A late 17th C. oak hall cupboard, the frieze bearing inscription 'T.E.H., 1731', 4 11 in. wide. **£720-830** *SK*

A 17th C. carved oak court cupboard, enclosed by a pair of panel doors, 1.53 m. **£990-1,200** *P*

An early 17th C. court cupboard, with geometric box and holly inlay and lunette carving, 5 ft. 6 in. high, 5 ft. 1 in. long. **£2,500-2,750** *NC*

oak court cupboard, 17th C., 2 in. wide. **£2,200-2,500**

te George III grained oak cabinet, the upper part ed to fit a recess, orated, 54½ in. wide. 0-700   C

A Welsh oak tridarn with two gothic-panelled cupboard doors flanking a fall-flap enclosing three drawers, on later turned feet, 56½ in. (144 cm.) wide, 81½ in. (207 cm.) high. **£2,800-3,200**   C

An oak tri-darn, with 3 drawers and 4 cupboards, length 53 in., height 81 in. **£1,400-1,700** OL

A German mid-19th C. ebonised and marquetry cabinet, inlaid with ivory, 5 ft. wide. **£2,800-3,200**   PK

lipwood parquetry and quetry music cabinet, the e drawer and two sliding our cupboard doors above further cupboard doors, 58 in., c. 1870. **£960-1,100**

A Chinese hardwood cabinet, the cupboard doors mounted with ivory and mother of pearl, 36 in. (91 cm.) wide. **£1,300-1,600** C

A Charles II oak chest, the cornice fitted with a long drawer inlaid in bone and mother of pearl, 48 in. (121 cm.) wide. **£700-900**   C

An 18th C. oak deudarn, 54 in. wide, 72 in. high. **£1,600-1,800**   B

A George III black and gold lacquer encoignure, the 'nashje' top with ormolu border, 25½ in. (55 cm.) wide. **£2,000-2,300** *C*

A pair of Louis XV rosewood encoignures, with breche d'Aleps marble tops, possibly German, 30½ in. (77.5 cm.) wide. **£4,000-4,500** *C*

A good painted satinwood Sheraton Revival standing corner cabinet, 26 in. wide, 74 in. high, late 19th C. **£1,000-1,300** *N*

One of a pair of amaranth marquetry encoigneurs, ormolu-mounted, with Carr marble tops, crossbanded v tulipwood, 24½ in. wide, m 19th C. **£1,500-1,700** the pair *C*

A Chippendale period (plum pudding) mahogany bow fronted corner cupboard, c. 1760. **£400-500** *DEB*

A fine quality inlaid oak corner cupboard, c. 1800, 44 in. high (Sheraton period). **£450-550** *W*

A Queen Anne walnut and feather-banded hanging corner cupboard, 3 ft. 8 in. (112 cm.) by 3 ft. (92 cm.), c. 1710. **£900-1,200** *SKC*

An oak two-door corner cupboard, c. 1750, 41 in. high 33 in. wide. **£265-300** *LL*

A Flemish oak hanging display cabinet, inlaid with ebony, fitted for electricity, 26 in. wide. **£600-700** *C*

An oak corner cupboard, c. 1790, 43½ in. high by 31 in. wide. **£175-200** *LL*

An oak and mahogany cor cupboard, door enclosing 2 shelves with a short drawe under, 2 ft. 11 in. wide, 20 i deep, 45 in. high. **£110-140**

A Victorian walnut veneered corner display cabinet, with marble top, 3 ft. 8 in. £850-1,100   *WW*

n Austrian white-painted and lded standing corner cabinet, ith a damask-lined interior, id-18th C., 46 in. (117 cm.) ide, 92 in. (234 cm.) high. ,400-1,600   *C*

A Georgian mahogany corner cabinet, 40 in. wide by 82 in. high. £1,100-1,400   *L*

A 'George III' mahogany corner cabinet on stand, inlaid throughout with satinwood banding and shellwork, late 19th C. £420-520   *SB*

ahogany corner cabinet, ssbanded with satinwood, 89 34 in., late 19th C. £900-00   *SB*

A 17th C. oak corner cupboard, with five shelves, 31 in. wide, 50 in. high. £900-1,000   *TJ*

An 18th C. mahogany two tier corner cabinet, width 43 in. £1,500-1,700   *LT*

An Edwardian mahogany double corner cupboard, 28 in. wide, 6 ft. 6 in. high. £780-900   *AG*

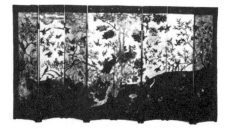

A painted leather six-leaf screen, 18th C., each leaf 21 in. wide, 80 in. high. £1,100-1,300   *C*

e of an unusual pair of ivory marquetry tall corner inets, 94½ by 33 in., North ian, mid-19th C. £6,500-00 the pair   *SB*

A Chinese coromandel lacquer 8-leaf low screen, incised and decorated in colours, 18th C., each leaf 11½ in. (29 cm.) wide, 46¼ in. (117.5 cm.) high. £1,600-1,750   *C*

A three-fold leather-panelled screen, 151 by 56 cm. each fold, 1870's. **£250-500**   *SB*

A Japanese four fold lacquer and ivory screen, 189 by 252 cm., late 19th C. **£480-550** *SB*

A lacquer, ivory and mother o pearl three-fold screen, 172 by 183 cm. open, late 19th C. **£130 160**   *SB*

An ivory bone and lacquer two fold screen, each fold 144 by 67 cm., c. 1900. **£480-550**   *SB*

A satinwood four-fold screen, each fold with a painted oval glazed panel, above a silk brocade panel in 18th C. style, c. 1900, 70¼ by 16 in. (178.5 by 40.5 cm.). **£450-550**   *SB*

A Japanese mother of pearl an ivory inlaid two fold screen, each fold 192 by 87 cm., c. 1900 **£520-620**   *SB*

A parcel gilt three-fold screen, each panel with six mirrored panels, each fold 58 by 23½ in., c. 1900. **£380-430**   *SB*

An embroidered silk four-fold screen, each fold 200 by 72 cm., c. 1900. **£560-620**   *SB*

A pair of oak-framed panels, 104 by 36 in. **£100-150**   *SBe*

A rosewood four-fold scr each fold inset with 5 b panels, each fold 229 by cm., early 20th C. **£380** *SB*

A mahogany fire-screen, 19th C., 37 in. high. **£50-70**   *SV*

A four-leaf wood tabl screen, each leaf with three pale green bowenite panels embellished in serpentine, agate, amethyst, quartz, lapis-lazuli and coral (one panel cracked), 48.5 cm. high. **£350- 400**   *C*

Galle marquetry fire screen, id with 'bois de satine', ewood, elm and maple, ned in mahogany, signed in rquetry 'Galle', 100 cm. high. 70-250 *P*

An Edwardian Sheraton rosewood screen, inlaid with boxwood and ivory in the Kauffman manner, the Berlinwork oval panel illustrating a castle scene. **£500-600** *BC*

An early 19th C. lacquered pole screen. **£145-160** *EAN*

A giltwood screen, well carved with deities, Tonghzi, 112 cm. **£410-490** *SB*

pair of William IV pole reens. **£200-230** *WHL*

A Regency rosewood polescreen, 56 in. high. **£95-105** *E.E*

An ivory table screen, 17.5 cm., with wood stand, c. 1880. **£170-220** *SB*

A George II mahogany pole screen, c. 1740. **£430-470** *EAN*

MIRRORS

mirror plate could not be made in large pieces until the late 18th C.

William and Mary, Queen Anne and early Georgian mirrors were often made in 2 or 3 pieces — the joins were usually hidden by astragal bars

if these have been removed, notches can be seen in the sides

early mirrors were blown — hence the glass tended to be thinner at one end, which was always set at the top of the frame

early glass is always generally thinner than its modern equivalent

to measure the thickness of a piece of mirror glass — take a pointed object, place it on the mirror, note the distance between the point and its image

old mirror glasses have a darker reflective quality

often the backing has broken down in places, giving non-reflective spots

An ivory two-leaf table screen, inlaid in Shibayama style (piece of inlay missing), signed on a rectangular red tablet, Shibayama, late 19th C., each leaf 24.6 by 13.9 cm. **£1,300-1,600** *C*

A Queen Anne style walnut toilet mirror, 28 by 16 in., early 20th C. **£300-400** *SBA*

A 19th C. mahogany dressing table mirror, with brass inlay, with original label, c. 1820.
£260-285   *B.M*

A William and Mary lacquered toilet mirror, c. 1690, 33 in. high.
£950-1,050   *EAN*

An 18th C. Dutch marquet and walnut toilet mirror, t fall revealing small drawe ft. 6 in. (46 cm.) wide, c. 17
£400-460   *SKC*

A satinwood 3 drawer box mirror, 20 in. wide, c. 1820.
£235-255   *AD*

A box-base swing toilet mir mahogany with inlay, mid-1 C., 21 in. high, 19 in. wide.
£100-130   *PAM*

A mid-19th C. carved mirror, c. 1850. **£360-390**   *EAN*

A French giltwood toilet-mirror, mid-19th C., 31 in. (79 cm.) wide.
£500-700   *C*

A giltwood and plas mirror, Italian, mid 19th C., 68½ by 33¼ (174 by 84.5 cm.). **£4(** **450**   *SB*

A cheval mirror, c. 1820, 57 in. high. **£550-590**   *EAN*

A walnut toilet glass, c. 1750, 19½ in. high. **£130-160**   *EAN*

A walnut dressing mirror, c. 1740, 18 in. high. **£165-185** *LL*

Carolean cushion wall
rror, the frame burr walnut
aid with boxwood, 27 by 31½
£280-350   *AGr*

A carved oak overmantel,
initialled HMI, the sides with
porcelain stands, 56 by 61¼ in.
(142.3 by 155.5 cm.). **£360-
420**   *SB*

A Queen Anne verre eglomise
mirror, the border decorated in
scarlet, gold and mother of
pearl, with later easel support,
22½ by 19 in. **£770-850**   *C*

Regency gilt mirror, 35 in.
de, 43 in. high. **£300-350**
R

A Regency carved ebony
mirror, c. 1820, 14 in. **£50-
100**   *JC*

A George III walnut and gilt
framed landscape mirror, with
18th C. North Italian school oil
on canvas, 3 ft. 4 in. (102 cm.)
high by 4 ft. 10 in. (147.5 cm.)
wide, c. 1770. **£1,200-1,400**
SKC

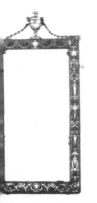

A Regency gilt overmantel
mirror, 63 in. wide, 21 in. high.
£180-220   *WR*

Verre Eglomise mirror, with
angular plate, 44 by 21½ in.
0-1,200   *C*

A Regency gilt convex mirror,
42 in. high. **£200-285**   *WR*

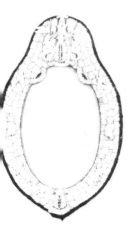

ivory and bone Dieppe
rror, 33¼ by 22 in., c. 1880.
60-560   *SB*

A Regency convex wall mirror,
in gilt ball and cavetto frame, 90
cm. **£130-200**   *PJ*

A moulded and engraved glass
mirror, 52 by 34 in., Venetian,
mid-19th C. **£680-800**   *SB*

A George II giltwood mirror, with later ogee-arched rectangular plate, 49½ by 27¼ in. **£1,900-2,300** *C*

A Florentine giltwood mirror, with later rectangular plate, early 18th C., 58 by 46 in. (147 by 117 cm.). **£1,100-1,300** *C*

A pair of engraved glass mirrors, Venetian, 15½ in. 1870. **£280-360** *SB*

A George III carved gilt wood rococo wall mirror. **£1,700-2,000** *M*

A George II giltwood mirror, with later plate, 64 by 33 in. **£1,800-2,000** *C*

A George III mahogany and parcel-gilt framed wall mirror, of Chippendale design, 3 ft. 3 in. high by 1 ft. 8 in. wide, c. 1760. **£700-830** *SKC*

A George II parcel gilt a mahogany wall mirror. **£1,600-2,000** *M*

A rococo revival giltwood mirror, mid-19th C., 85 by 76 in. (216 by 193 cm.). **£400-480** *SB*

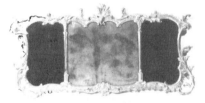

An early George III giltwood overmantel, with later shaped triple plate, 27½ by 54 in. **£1,100-1,300** *C*

A George III giltwood mirror with later rectangular plate, by 27½ in. (132 by 70 cm.). **£1,200-1,400** *C*

A Continental 19th C. carved giltwood framed wall mirror, overall 63 by 45 in. **£330-400** *PWC*

A giltwood mirror, 43 by 32 in., Italian, 1870's. **£300-340** *SB*

George II-style carved and
ilt gesso wall mirror, 4 ft. 2½
a. (128 cm.) by 1 ft. 9 in. (53 cm.),
1850. **£440-500**   *SKC*

A 'George II' giltwood pier
mirror, with a bevelled
mirror plate, 62 by 38¼ in.,
1880's. **£340-400**   *SB*

An early Victorian burr-walnut
music Canterbury, 1 ft. 11 in. (58
cm.) high by 1 ft. 8 in. (51 cm.)
wide, c. 1850. **£600-660**   *SKC*

A Regency mahogany
4-division music
Canterbury, 19 by 14
in. **£500-680**   *SKC*

osewood Canterbury, with
ee divisions and a frieze
wer, 19¾ in. (50 cm.) wide, c.
0. **£300-350**   *SB*

A birds eye maple Canterbury,
c. 1830, 22 in. high. **£525-560**
NC

A George IV mahogany four
division Canterbury, fitted
drawer, 1 ft. 7½ in. (49.5 cm.)
high by 1 ft. 6½ in. (47 cm.) wide,
c. 1825. **£320-380**   *SKC*

A late Regency mahogany
Canterbury, inlaid with ebony
lines throughout, early 19th C.
£1,000-1,200   *SBA*

An early 19th C. Canterbury, 2
drawer, with carrying handle
(casters not original). **£650-
775**   *NC*

A William IV rosewood folio
rack, with a removable
rectangular top, height 42 in.,
width 28 in., c. 1830. **£840-
1,000**   *SBe*

William IV folio stand, with
inged sides, 34 in. (86 cm.)
ide. **£850-1,050**   *C*

A Victorian mulberry veneered folio cabinet, the glazed doors with velvet-lined interior and opposing dummy doors, 2 ft. 7½ in. high by 2 ft. 4½ in. wide, c. 1855. **£1,300-1,500** *SKC*

A Victorian inlaid walnut Canterbury/whatnot, with 3 music divisions, 24 by 16 in. **£450-550** *BW*

A Regency rosewood reading pedestal bookcase, with an adjustable ratcheted top, on plinth base, 64 cm. **£1,100-1,300** *P*

A rosewood what not, c. 1840, 24 in. wide by 16½ in. deep by 32½ in. high. **£270-310** *PAM*

A Victorian mahogany Canterbury/whatnot with a drawer in the frieze, 23 by 15 in. **£330-450** *BW*

A burr-walnut whatnot white ceramic castors, 38 in., c. 1860. **£300-350** *S*

A Victorian what not, 38 in. high. **£120-140** *LL*

A William IV mahogany whatnot, the base inset with a single drawer, 42½ by 24 in., c. 1835. **£700-900** *SB*

A Victorian rosewood what not c. 1850, 33 in. high. **£125-150** *MAT*

Victorian ebonised and marquetry etagere, 16 in. £230-**Hy.D

A 19th C. rosewood whatnot, 36 in. wide. **£230-300** *Ch*

One of a pair of Regency rosewood four-tier whatnots, 20 in. wide. **£2,300-2,500** the pair *C*

late 18th C. 2-tier mahogany dumb waiter, 28 in. high. **£625-NC**

A French ormolu-mounted kingwood two-tier centre table, in the style of P. Sormani, 39 in. (99 cm.) wide. **£1,500-1,800** *C*

A Victorian 3 tier etagere, with floral marquetry and rosewood crossbanding, height 2 ft 7 in. by 1 ft. 6 in. wide. **£160-200** *WHL*

19th C. oak dumb waiter, 31 high. **£180-280** *RDv*

A Georgian mahogany two tier dumb waiter, 26 in. diam., 38 in. high. **£550-650** *L*

An 18th C. mahogany three-tier dumb waiter, 43 in. high. **£540-600** *WR*

An early George III mahogany three-tier dumb waiter, 45 in. high. **£300-380** *DWB*

DUMB WAITERS

made throughout the Georgian period — from 1714–1830

they seem to have always been almost solely made of mahogany

any examples from the first half of the 18th C. are extremely scarce

during Chippendale period supports often carved with foliage, acanthus leaves, broken scrolls etc.

- Robert Adam's neo-classical style radically changed the design
- the pillars now tended to become plainly cylindrical with turned collars at top and bottom
- the late 18th C. and early 19th C. saw the introduction of pierced galleries often made of brass
- during the Regency period some dumb waiters made from rosewood

A marquetry and satinwood cellaret on stand, the sides crossbanded, reconstructed and inlaid late 19th C., 25 by 15¾ in. (63.5 by 40 cm.). **£265-300** *C*

A George III satinwood and mahogany cellaret, the made-up supports with castors, 1 ft. 7¾ in. (50 cm.) high by 1 ft. 5 in. (43 cm.) wide, c. 1790. **£350-420** *SKC*

A George III mahogany cellaret, enclosing twelve partitions, brass carrying handles, 36 cm. wide. **£37 430** *Bon*

An early Victorian mahogany wine cooler, enclosing a zinc lined interior, c. 1840, 29 in. wide. **£350-400** *SBe*

A late George III mahogany wine cooler, with lead lined interior, 24 by 18 by 20 in. **£390-450** *ELR*

A Victorian 25½ in. rectangula tapered wine cooler, 2 ft. 6 in. high. **£370-420** *AG*

A Sheraton mahogany wine cooler, inlaid with a marquetry panel, with an ivory escutcheon, on cast gilt metal legs, 69 cm. **£590-650** *P*

A Regency mahogany wine bin, 29 in. **£370-420** *Hy.D*

A Victorian mahogany cellaret, 32 by 20 in. **£180-250** *PSH*

A good early George III mahogany wine cooler, brass bound, the lead lined interior with 7 partitions, 50 cm. wide. **£1,200-1,400** *Bon*

A Regency mahogany cellaret, 2 ft. 4 in. wide, c. 1810. **£350-400** *S*

A good George III mahogan; wine cooler, with brass carryi handles and bandings and enclosing a zinc-lined interio stamped with the maker's ma 'I.S.', c. 1780, width 19 in. **£1,200-1,500** *SBe*

One of a pair of George III style Cocobolo oval wine coolers, with brass bands, side handles and zinc liners, 600 cm. wide. **£900-1,100** the pair   *PJ*

George III brass bound ahogany wine cooler, lead ned, 28 in. across, 23¼ in. high. **560-680**   *TW*

A George III brass-bound mahogany wine cooler, the top crossbanded, lead-lined and with a drainage tap, 2 ft. 1 in. high by 2 ft. 1 in. wide, c. 1780. **£900-1.200**   *S*

A late 18th C. birch candle stand, top 14 in. diam., 30 in. high. **£190-225**   *NC*

A William IV rosewood teapoy, c. 1835, width 16 in. **£350-400**   *SBe*

William IV brass inlaid sewood teapoy (slight faults). 90-450   *RG*

A Regency rosewood and satinwood banded teapoy, the interior comprising 4 canisters and 2 mixing bowls, 2 ft. 5 in. high by 1 ft. 4½ in. wide, c. 1815. **£430-480**   *SKC*

n Empire mahogany lamp ble, the gilt metalled galleried op with inset mirror. **£300-** 60   *MMB*

An unusual 19th C. mahogany reading stand. **£170-220** *Max*

A late 18th C. mahogany candlestand, 27 in. high (with minor repairs). **£300-350** *B.M*

An early Victorian tea poy, converted to a workbox, c. 1840, 30 in. high by 16 in. wide by 13 in. deep. **£280-330**   *JGM*

An 18th C. mahogany andlestand, c. 1770, 30 in. igh. **£500-600**   *RD*

A Swiss carved bear umbrella stand, 3 ft. 4 in. (102 cm.) high, c. 1870. **£380-430**   *SKC*

A Japanese bronze umbrella stand, 19th C., 23½ in. high. **£190-210**   *SV*

A Victorian brass-bound oak umbrella stand, 26 in. high. **£90-105**   *SV*

An early Victorian mahogan washstand (unconverted), 22 in. wide by 18 in. deep by 34 i high, c. 1840. £100-130 PA

A George III inlaid mahogany corner washstand, fitted with a Masons 11½ in. ironstone bowl, a 9 in. ewer and two soap holders, 2 ft. £350-420 AG

A late 18th C. wash-stand, 12 in. wide by 32 in. high. £260-290 NC

A George III mahogany washstand, 32 in., partly 18th C. £220-250 SBA

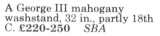

A kingwood jardiniere, with a lid above a zinc-line container, 30 by 26 in., 1850's. £390-430 SB

One of a pair of cream-painted plant stands, superstructure enclosing a netted compartment for flowers, possibly Scandinavian, 36 by 39½ in. (92.5 by 100 cm.), mid-19th C. £800-1,000 pr. SB

A Georgian mahogany basir stand, the circular top above small drawer, 34 in. £200-250 RMcT

A Chinese rosewood and marble inlaid urn stand, 81 cm., Guangxu. £140-180 SB

A pair of walnut and marquetry jardinieres, with an inlaid drop-in top, with gilt-bronze mounts, 30 by 27 in. (76 by 68.5 cm.), c. 1870. £1,800-2,000 SB

A French marquetry jardiniere, with a removable lid within a strapwork border, and kingwood veneered frieze, c. 1880, width 23 in. £320-400 SBe

A Charles II ornately carved cabinet stand, with a later top, 17th C., 47 in. wide, 32 in. high, 23 in. deep. £260-320 L

A giltmetal-mounted mahogany gueridon, with white marble to mid 19th C., 22½ in. (5 cm.) diam. £800-1,000 C

stained hardwood urn stand,
ith a marble inset top,
uangxu, 80 cm. £300-350
B

A Chinese rosewood urn stand,
with a marble inset top, 56 cm.,
Guangxu. £240-300   SB

An oriental hardwood carved
stand. £165-180   LAC

Victorian walnut jardiniere,
e lobed top centred by a
sebowl, c. 1860, 30 in. high.
60-320   L

A pair of George III cream-
painted and gilded tripod
torcheres, with later coronas,
redecorated, bearing labels for
'World Refugee Exhibition of
Treasures, No. 218', 61½ in.
high. £2,200-2,600   C

An Edwardian mahogany
jardiniere, inlaid, with brass
liner, 36 in. high. £100-140
PAM

One of a pair of Oriental
rosewood jardiniere stands,
with inset pink marble, 16 in.
diam. £350-400 the pair   Ch

pair of ormolu-mounted
ony and boulle pedestals, 56
. high. £2,200-2,500   C

A parquetry occasional table,
stamped 011919, late 19th C.,
31¾ by 14 in. (80.5 by 36 cm.).
£160-200   SB

An 18th C. urn stand, c. 1790
(with some warpage), 27 in.
high. £425-460   EAN

A Chinese vase stand, c. 1855,
32 in. high. £150-175   MAT

A George III mahogany and brass bound plate bucket, with brass swing handle, 16 in. high. **£350-450** *DWB*

A Georgian brass-bound mahogany bucket, 14 in. high. **£480-525** *SV*

A 19th C. mahogany urn stand with brass gallery, 25 in. high. **£90-100** *B.M*

One of a pair of Padouk Oriental stands, 19th C., 32 16 by 12 in. **£400-465** pr.

An 18th C. French walnut dole cupboard, 34 in. wide. **£400-500** *B*

An ivory cabinet, with two cupboard doors and thirteen small drawers, engraved and stained, engraved kanagu (tiny piece missing), signed Hojitsusai Mitsuaki (or Komei), late 19th C., 23.6 cm. high. **£650-750** *C*

A small silver-mounted gold lacquer cabinet (damaged), signed Mitsumasa koku, late 19th C., 33 cm. high. **£1,100-1,400** *C*

One of a pair of George III brass-bound plate buckets, in. diam. **£1,600-1,900** the pair *C*

An elm dough-bin, with two separate compartments (slight woodworm), c. 1800, 43 by 19 by 32 in. **£176-200** *OB*

A late 17th C. spice cupboard and cutlery box, English, c. 1680, 14 in. wide. **£500-560** *A.E.F.*

A Roiro-Nuri shodana, the ba with 2 sliding doors, in gold an silver hiramakie, engraved kanagu (old damages), late 18th/early 19th C., 112.3 by 102.8 by 46.5 cm. **£2,200-2,500** *C*

A William IV mahogany and parcel-gilt standing bookshelf, the sides with giltmetal trellis-pattern grilles, 51 in. (130 cm.) wide. **£750-880** *C*

A late 18th C. elm dough bin or stand. **£190-260** *Max*

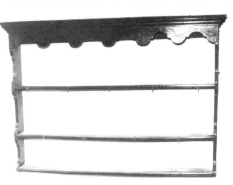

A miniature inlaid revolving bookcase, 14 in. high, c. 1900. **£35-50** *SV*

George III satinwood and ahogany open bookcase, laid with ebonised lines, 48 in. 22 cm.) wide. **£880-980** *C*

An oak Delft rack, c. 1740. **£225-260** *DEB*

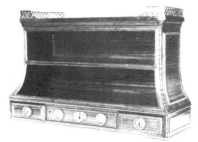

19th C. Chippendale-style ookshelf, with fretwork sides, 7 in. wide, 33½ in. high. **£225-75** *B.M*

A Louis XVI bois Satine cartonnier, attributed to J. H. Riesener, 35 in. (89 cm.) wide. **£4,200-4,800** *C*

Rare mid 17th C. oak hanging shelves, 27 in. wide, 34 in. high. **£2,000-2,500** *TJ*

A set of 19th C. mahogany shelves, 42 in. wide. **£300-325** *W*

mahogany clothes stand, late th C., 25 in. high by 27 in. ide. **£30-40** *PAM*

One of a pair of George III giltwood pelmets, 76 in. wide. **£550-650** the pair *C*

A Florentine doorframe and door, of Renaissance style, blue painted and gilded, the frame, 68 in. wide, 106 in. high; the door, 34 in. wide, 89 in. high. **£2,300-3,600** *C*

Chinese lacquer shrine, with vo cupboard doors, each with a arved and gilt panel, and ainted panels, the interior also arved and gilt, 112 by 88 cm., uangxu. **£250-300** *SB*

A kidney shape mahogany marquetry tray, 27 in. wide, c. 1800. **£250-300** *LAC*

An Italian oak screen, two panelled doors, flanked by linenfold panels, partly 17th C., 103½ in. (263 cm.) wide. **£1,600-1,800** *C*

A late Victorian mahogany inlaid tray, c. 1900, 2 ft. 2 in. wide. **£100-160** *SKC*

A Sheraton mahogany small oval tray with shell motif, c. 1810, 14½ in. wide. **£120-140** *AD*

One of a pair of silver-mount Lac Burgaute oval trays, 13 in. wide, late 18th C., the silv bearing late 19th C. Dutch control marks. **£1,800-2,10(** the pair *C*

A late 18th C. decorated papier maché tray, c. 1790, 28 in. across. **£180-220** *JGM*

A Sorrento marquetry reversible tray and games tabl the other side with a chess board, signed A. Gargiulo, Sorrento, c. 1900. **£280-360** *SB*

A George IV mahogany spinning wheel, 3 ft. 1½ in. (95 cm.) high, c. 1825. **£280-330** *SKC*

A late 18th C. satinwood spinning wheel, with a detachable top, fitted with a drawer, 1.16 m. high. **£550-650** *P*

A late 18th C. mahogany spinning wheel, with brass mechanism and wheel, Sheffield plate label inscribed S. Thorp, Abberley, Invd., 16 in. long by 19¾ in. wide by 35 in. high. **£1,600-1,800** *Hy.D*

A miniature Regency fruitwood stool, c. 1810, 6¼ in. high. **£85-95.** *McH*

A Spanish walnut vargueno, the fall with velvet-backed pierced iron lockplates, enclosing a well-fitted interio on later stand, 41¾ in. wide, early 17th C. **£2,500-3,000**

A late Georgian mahogany tall library steps, 105½ in. high, 23¼ in. wide. **£2,500-2,800** *C*

A 19th C. elm miniature table, c. 1850, 4½ in. high. **£65-75** *McH*

A kingwood and marquetry miniature writing-table, with drawer fitted for writing, wit foliate ormolu plaques, handle and lock-plates, 51¼ in. (54 cm wide. **£550-600** *C*

A Victorian miniature oak dining room suite, comprising sideboard, dining table and 6 dining chairs. £70-120   *WW*

Dutch mahogany and marquetry miniature chest of drawers, 17 in. £180-240 *Ty.D*

A Dutch colonial miniature lignum vitae and walnut lowboy, 17½ in. wide, 18th C. £220-270   *SKC*

An early 19th C. miniature bureau money box, c. 1820, 6½ in. wide by 4½ in. deep by 6½ in. high. £30-45   *JGM*

A Dutch oak and marquetry miniature bureau-cabinet, with a single panelled cupboard door, sloping flap and 3 long drawers, 16 in. wide, 25½ in. high. £900-1,100   *C*

URNITURE APPENDIX

dam, Robert (1782-92)
rchitect and furniture designer,
partnership with his brothers
ohn, James and William, he
esigned complete schemes for
ouse interiors. Summarised his
ew of the Neoclassical as 'all
elicacy, gaiety, grace and
eauty'.

maranth
alisander or purple wood.

rmoire (Fr.)
French name for a press, clothes
upboard or any large cupboard.

umbrey
15th and 16th C. term for a
omestic or ecclesiastical
upboard with doors, used as a
afe, armoury and food cupboard

achelor's Chest
small low chest of drawers with
folding top which converts into a
ble, made from the early 1700's
nwards.

ergere (Fr.)
n armchair, originally
pholstered, now also used to
escribe a chair with carved sides
nd back.

**iedermeier Style (1820's-
0's)**
amed after a character in the
ournal 'Fliegende Blätter', it was
n Austro-German caricature of
rench Empire Baroque style
urniture.

onheur du Jour (Fr.)
small writing table, introduced
France in the second half of the
8th C., it was sometimes
urmounted by a cupboard.

ugatti, Carlo (1855-1940)
talian furniture designer, father
f car designer Ettore and sculptor
embrandt Bugatti, was very
terested in Japanese art, and
his influenced his furniture
esigns, which involved the use of
ellum covered wood and pewter
lay.

Bureau Mazarin
A type of flat-topped writing table,
standing on eight legs.

Bureau Plat (Fr.)
A flat-topped writing table.

Calamander wood
A hard cabinet wood, brownish
with black stripes, used in
furniture manufacture in the late
18th and early 19th C. Also known
as coromandel wood.

Campaign Furniture
Cased furniture made especially
for the Peninsular and Crimean
Wars, e.g. Campaign Chest.

Carlton House Desk
A writing table which has a low
superstructure with drawers at the
back and sides of the writing case.

Chauffeuse (Fr.)
A low fireside chair.

Chiffonier
A low cupboard or side cupboard.
Originally in 18th C. with solid
doors these were replaced during
the Regency with brass lattice
doors and by glass or wood doors
in the Victorian period.

**Chippendale, Thomas (1718-
79)**
Cabinet maker, published a book
of designs 'The Gentleman and
Cabinet Makers Directory' in
1754, 1755 and 1762. After his
death, the company (Chippendale,
Haig & Co. until 1896) continued
under the direction of his son
Thomas (1749-1822).

Coaching Table
A small table, on X-shaped legs,
the top of which has central
hinges so that it can be closed up
like a book.

Cock Bead
A round mould used on the edges
of drawers from c. 1730 onwards.

Coromandel
See Calamander wood.

Cricket Table
A small plain three-legged table
made throughout the 17th C. It is
unclear how the name was
derived. It may have been a
development of the term 'cricket'
used to describe a plain stool.
Alternatively it may have arisen
because the three legs resembled
the three stumps in a game of
cricket, or it may be so called
because it was arguably designed
to stand steady on hearthstones,
the haunt of crickets.

Credence Table
A type of late 16th and early 17th
C. domestic flap table which when
closed is either semi-circular or
has a three-sided front. Originally
a credence table was a small table
at the side of an Altar on which the
bread and wine were placed before
they were consecrated,
additionally it was in early times a
type of side table or buffet where
the meats were tasted prior to
serving to guests.

Deudarn
A Welsh name for a press or hall cupboard with a two-tier superstructure.

Dole Cupboard
An early hanging cupboard with ventilated doors, used to distribute bread amongst the poor.

Encoignure
A French corner cupboard, normally made to stand on the floor and of table height.

Escritoire
A cabinet with a fall front which lowers to form a flat writing surface. Made as a tall cabinets from c. 1760.

Etagere
The French equivalent of a Whatnot. A stand with tiers of shelves supported by corner posts.

Fauteuil
An upholstered armchair with open sides and padded elbows. The term became popular in England and America in the mid-19th C.

Gainsborough Chair
A modern term used to describe an open-sided armchair, otherwise known as a French Chair.

Gillow
Furniture manufacturers, founded in Lancaster in 1695 by Robert Gillow. A London branch of the firm was opened in 1761. The original site in Oxford Street is still occupied by Waring & Gillow Ltd.

Gueridon
A stand for a candlestick or lamp.

Harewood
Sycamore dyed a greyish-green colour, much used in late 18th C. as a decorative veneer.

Hepplewhite, George
Cabinet maker and owner of small business in London. Influenced furniture designs when his book 'The Cabinet Maker and Upholsterer's Guide' was published in 1788, two years after his death.

Liberty & Co.
Business set up in 1875 by Sir Arthur Lasenby Liberty (1843-1917) in Regent St. London. The Company specialised at first in selling Oriental silks, but soon added other items to their stock including Tudric pewter,

metalware, furniture, etc.

Lignum Vitae
A dark brown hardwood. Used from the 17th C. onwards.

Loo Table
A circular card table, specifically designed in the early 19th C. for the card game known as 'Lanterloo'.

Mendlesham Chair
Low backed 19th C. variant of the Windsor style chair. The back was made up of square cut rather than turned batons and the cross rails were often separated by a row of small balls.

Monk's Bench
Otherwise known as a chair-table, table-chaire or table-chairwise; the back is hinged to swing up and form a table.

Mule Chest
A large chest with two or three drawers in the base, made from the 17th C. onwards.

Padouk
Hard, heavy purplish red wood, used from mid-18th C.

Palisander
A type of rosewood.

Patera
A rosette-like ornamental disc, carved, inlaid or painted, used to decorate furniture during the late 18th C. From the early 19th C. paterae of cast brass were applied to furniture.

Prie-dieu Chair
An upholstered high back single chair originally used for praying.

Pugin, Augustus Welby Northmore (1812-52)
Architect designer and champion of the Victorian Gothic revival. He published illustrated works on his designs, Contrasts (1836); The True Principles of Pointed or Christian Architecture (1841); and An Apology for the Revival of Christian Architecture in England (1843).

Secretaire Capucin
A table which converts into a writing table with an extending leaf and a rising flight of drawers.

Sheraton, Thomas (1751-1806)
Cabinet maker and designer. Influenced furniture design with his publications: The Cabinet Maker and Upholsterer's Drawing

Book (1791-4), Cabinet Directory (1803) and Cabinet Maker, Upholsterer and Genera Artists' Encyclopaedia (1805). H designs were light, Neo classica and emphasised vertical straigh lines, dainty details and ingeniou contrivances. It is doubtful whether he actually had a workshop in London.

Table a Ouvrage
A worktable.

Table de Toilette (Fr.)
Dressing table.

Thuya Wood
A warm golden brown wood from a North African tree. The curly figure and spotted markings of this wood made it a popular choic for decorative veneers from the 18th C. onwards.

Tricoteuse (Fr.)
A small work table with a galler

Tridarn
Welsh name for a press or hall cupboard developed in the mid-17th C., characterised by a thre tiered superstructure.

Vargueno
A Spanish cabinet or desk with fall front originally made at Vargas (Bargas) near Toledo.

Vernis Martin
A type of imitation lacquer patented by the brothers Martin for furniture decoration.

Verre Eglomise
Glass decorated or engraved through gold or silver leaf and backed with red, blue, green or black pigment. A method of decoration very much in fashion 1700 and also in the Regency.

Wainscot
A term derived from the Dutch word 'wagenschot' to describe th two oak planks cut from the centr of a log. From the 14th to the ear part of the 17th C. wainscot mean oak and later on it was used to describe any piece of furniture solid wooden construction, e.g. Wainscot Chair, Wainscot Bed.

Wellington Chest
A tall chest with 6 to 8 drawers designed to take collections of coins or other small articles. Th hinged right hand side overlap the drawer edges and is secured b a single lock, thus locking the whole cabinet.

Zebra Wood
A striped brown wood. Used as veneer from the late 18th C.

GUIDE TO STYLES

Dates	Monarch	Period	Woods
1603-1625	James I	Jacobean	
1625-1649	Charles I	Carolean	Oak period
1649-1660	Commonwealth	Cromwellian	up to c. 1670
1660-1685	Charles II	Restoration	
1685-1689	James II	Restoration	
1689-1694	William and Mary	William and Mary	
1694-1702	William III	William III	Walnut period
1702-1714	Anne	Queen Anne	1670-1735
1714-1727	George I	Early Georgian	
1727-1760	George II	Early Georgian	Early mahogany period
1760-1811	George III	Late Georgian	1735-1770
1812-1820	George III	Regency	Late mahogany period
1820-1830	George IV	Regency	1770-1810
1830-1837	William IV	William IV	
1837-1901	Victoria	Victorian	
1901-1910	Edward VII	Edwardian	

Until quite recently, pine was held to be a cheap, useful timber, regarded disparagingly by 'real' furniture dealers. How often have we heard 'The pine boom is over', 'Pine prices can't increase any more'? However it isn't and they have. Now people are realising that there are some very high quality pine pieces especially from the 18th C. The old adage of 'If it's pine, strip it', has thankfully if slightly tardily, been replaced with an appreciation of the early painted pieces. The signs are that the upward trend will continue.

An early 19th C. Irish pine dresser with breakfront cornice and cotton-reel moulding to sides, 6 ft. 3 in. high, 4 ft. 6 in. wide. **£500-550** *PF*

A very ornate 19th C. pine breakfront German dresser, 59 in. wide, 23 in. deep, 90 in. high. **£815-845** *PC*

A 19th C. Devonshire glazed pitch pine dresser with quadriform moulding and fielded panelled drawers, 52 in. wide, 82 in. high, 19 in. deep. **£595-620** *PC*

19th C. pine bookcase on upboard, typical marriage of vo pieces of furniture, 51 in. ide, 74 in. high. **£185-195** *SP*

19th C. pine glazed bureau okcase, with six interior awers and two drawers low, 7 ft. 3 in. high, 3 ft. 6 in. de, 19 in. deep. **£650-700** *C*

A 19th C. Scottish pine dresser with applied bullseye moulding on the pediment and a bevelled mirror on the centre cupboard, 51 in. wide, 20 in. deep, 85 in. high. **£375-395** *PC*

A 19th C. pine West Country small cottage glazed dresser with cupboards below and applied split mouldings, 6 ft. 3 in. high, 4 ft. wide, 18 in. deep. **£248-278** *CC*

unusual Victorian pine pboard, with brushing slide er fitted two door cupboard, th hinged lid-enclosed awers, 40 in. long, 32 in. high, in. deep. **£215-245** *OA*

A Georgian opened top pine corner cupboard with fluted sides and shaped shelves, 82 in. high, 44 in. wide. **£300-320** *PC*

A 19th C. pine mule chest with hinged top and two drawers beneath, 3 ft. wide, 18 in. deep, 2 ft. 2 in. high. **£85-95** *CC*

A 19th C. pine corner cupboard with semi-arched moulded panelled doors, 31 in. wide, 44 in. high. **£200-250**   *OA*

A 19th C. pitch pine coffer, with interior candle box, 19 in. high, 36 in. wide. **£45-50**   *SSP*

A Georgian pine corner cupboard, with shaped shel inside, 41 in. high. **£145-17** *AL*

A small Victorian pine cupboard on stand, 19 in. wide, 17 in. deep, 29 in. high. **£40-50**   *AL*

A Victorian pine corner cab 25 in. wide, 33 in. high, 16 deep. **£95-110**   *AL*

A Victorian pine corner cabinet, with single locking door, 18 in. high, 12 in. deep, 18 in. wide. **£40-50**   *AL*

A Victorian painted pine box/chest, with original decoration, 37 in. wide, 17 in. deep, 18½ in high. **£40-50**   *AL*

A 19th C. pine corner washstand with a shaped base, 2 ft. 6 in. wide, 3 ft. 2 in. high. **£40-50**   *CC*

A Victorian pine chest, 36 i wide, 20½ in. deep, 17½ in. hi **£55-65**   *AL*

An 18th C. domed marine chest in pine with oak legs and original spearhead hinges, 4 ft. 6 in. wide, 2 ft. deep, 34 in. high. **£220-240**   *CC*

A mid 19th C. pine coffer w fielded panels and flat bun fe 54 in. wide, 24 in. deep, 27 i high. **£110-120**   *PC*

An early 18th C. deed box (date on exterior added later, three earlier dates inside), original iron handles and spearhead hinges, with pegged sides to lid. **£85-95**   *PF*

cottish pine chest of drawers
h one deep top drawer made
ppear as five small drawers,
. 8 in. wide, 3 ft. 10 in. high.
30-200   *PF*

A 19th C. pine chest of drawers,
with three drawers and
mahogany handles, 30 in. high,
40 in. wide. **£90-110**   *PD*

A 19th C. Scandinavian pitch
pine chest with split turned
decorations to side and original
small brass handles, 3 ft. wide,
19 in. deep. **£110-130**   *CC*

pair of Victorian pine chests
drawers, one on legs, 44 in.
de, 20 in. deep, 42 in. high.
200-230 the pair   *AL*

A Georgian pine chest of
drawers, 42 in. wide, 18½ in.
deep, 41½ in. high. **£95-110**
AL

A late 19th C. Serpentine-
fronted chest of drawers, with
splashback and applied split
turnings, 39 in. wide, 48 in.
high. **£150-200**   *PF*

Victorian pine bed cupboard,
th dummy chest of drawers
nt, 21½ in. deep, 47 in. wide,
in. high. **£130-150**   *AL*

A Victorian pine buffet, on 5
legs, fitted with 7 drawers, 71 in.
wide, 21 in. deep, 35½ in. high.
£260-300   *AL*

A Lincolnshire pine dresser
with carved back board, 60 in.
wide, 22 in. deep, 66 in. high.
£300-330   *PC*

Victorian pine dressing table,
ith new handles, 42½ in. long,
2 in. deep, 65 in. high. **£120-**
40   *AL*

A Victorian pine dressing table,
42 in. wide, 18 in. deep, 62½ in.
high. **£100-120**   *AL*

A 19th C. small plain pine
dressing chest with mahogany
handles, 3 ft. 3 in. wide, 4 ft. 6 in.
high, 18 in. deep. **£95-120**   *CC*

A late 19th C. pine dressing chest, with bevelled glass and porcelain handles, 42 in. wide, 64 in. high, 18 in. deep. **£125-135** *AL*

A Victorian pine wash stand, with a marble top, the superstructure with 3 tiles, 30 in. wide, 17 in. deep, 39 in. high. **£50-60** *AL*

One of a pair of 20th C. pine bedside cupboards with one drawer and cupboard below, 34 in. high, 24 in. wide, 18 in. deep. **£130-150 pair** *PC*

A 19th C. pitch pine dressing chest, with carved mirror supports and shaped brackets below, 3 ft. wide, 6 ft. high. **£140-150** *PF*

A 19th C. Scandinavian pine wardrobe with two fielded panelled doors, interior fitted with swivel pegs and a drop well in the base, 6 ft. 7 in. high, 3 ft. 2 in. wide, 17 in. deep. **£260-290** *CC*

An Irish pine food cupboard, with panelled doors and sides and fantail moulding to cupboard doors, c. 1850, 6 ft. 6 in. high, 5 ft. wide, 24 in. deep. **£450-500** *CC*

A 19th C. pine wardrobe and washstand, with two drawers and cupboard with panelled doors, 77 in. high, 43 in. wide, 1 in. deep. **£250-290** *AL*

A 19th C. Scandinavian seven piece pine wardrobe with panelled doors, with one drawer in base and standing on bun feet, 6 ft. 4 in. high, 3 ft. 9 in. wide, 21 in. deep. **£200-250** *CC*

A 19th C. pine sideboard, with beaded and panelled doors and carved side pillars, 49 in. long, 38 in. high, 20 in. deep. **£230-270** *MS*

An Edwardian pitch pine wardrobe, with deep drawer to base and porcelain handles, 32 in. wide, 78 in. high. **£85-95** *MM*

Victorian pine desk, 24 in.
ep, 47 in. wide, 35 in. high.
00-360   *AL*

A late 19th C. pine pedestal desk
with nine drawers, 4 in. wide, 2
ft. 2 in. deep, 31 in. high. £300-
350   *PC*

A late 19th C. pine table, with
concealed drawer at one end, 38
by 41 in. (open), 29 in. high.
£70-90   *AL*

Edwardian pine table and
ht of drawers married to
ke desk, 43 in. wide, 21 in.
p, 35 in. high. £135-145

A 19th C. Devonshire pine
table, with tapered legs and
shaped top rail, 9 ft. long, 3 ft. 3
in. wide, 30 in. high. £380-
400   *CC*

A small Georgian pine side
table, on tapering legs, 23 in.
wide, 30 in. high, 19 in. deep.
£145-185   *OA*

9th C. small pine side table,
th fine turned tapering legs
d black porcelain handles, 35
wide, 28 in. high, 17 in. deep.
5-95   *OA*

A chunky 19th C. pine dairy
table, with new handles, 30 in.
high, 22 in. wide, 15 in. deep.
£50-55   *AL*

A Welsh pine drop leaf table,
with one drawer and ogee scroll
each end, 30 in. wide, 33 in.
extended. £95-115   *PF*

small Spanish table, with
aped side rails and one deep
awer, 24 in. high, 24 in. wide,
in. deep. £90-120   *SM*

A Victorian pine tripod table, 33
in. diam. £110-120   *OA*

A 19th C. pine side table, with
one drawer and porcelain
handles, 36 in. wide, 24 in. deep.
£45-50   *AL*

A 19th C. pine bench table, 84 in. long, 23 in. deep. **£120-130** *MS*

A large Victorian pine desk, with mahogany top and 3 frieze drawers, 80 in. wide, 29 in. deep, 33 in. high. **£150-180** *AL*

A 19th C. pine work table, with applewood top, 78 in. long, 24 in. wide. **£130-160** *AL*

An Irish pine country table, with double rail, c. 1850, 4 ft in. long, 25 in. wide. **£110-150** *CC*

A 19th C. butter churn on stand, end over end, made by Lister & Co., Darsley, Yorks., 12 gallon capacity, 4 in. high. **£80-90** *PF*

A 19th C. pitch pine desk, with side flap and two porcelain ink-wells, 36 in. high, 33 in. wide, 24 in. deep. **£100-110** *AL*

A Victorian pine table, with t drawers, 46½ in. wide, 30 in deep, 31 in. high. **£130-150** *AL*

An early 19th C. pine spit rack, unpolished, 54 in. high, 60 in. wide. **£250-300** *CC*

An Edwardian pine coal box, with iron carrying handle and brass side handles, 17 in. wide, 18 in. high. **£85-125** *OA*

A Victorian pine fire surrou 40 in. wide, 48 in. high. **£3C 40** *AL*

A Victorian pine four-tiered buffet, with two drawers, 48 in. wide, 57 in. high. **£215-245** *OA*

An 18th C. pine and oak peg joined cradle, 39 in. long, 19 in. wide. **£125-150** *CC*

A 19th C. hoop towel rail, w barley twist ends. **£25-30**

Victorian pine spice cabinet, h fifteen various sized wers with brass handles maged, woodworm in back), by 18 by 28 in. **£85-100**

A 19th C. flight of cobblers drawers, with original mahogany handles, 21 in. high, 25 in. wide, 10 in. deep. **£90-95**   *AL*

A 19th C. pine overmantel mirror, with scratch carving, 34 in. high, 48 in. wide. **£40-45**   *AL*

A 19th C. pine curd strainer. **£12-14**   *PF*

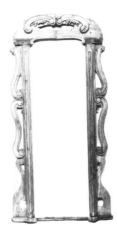

wedish pine box bed, with als and turned arms, c. 1850-6 ft. 4 in. long, 3 ft. 8 in. high, n. deep. **£300-400**   *CC*

A 19th C. child's high chair which converts into a low rocking chair. **£75-85**   *PF*

A Victorian carved pine rococo mirror, 56 in. high, 26 in. wide. **£185-225**   *OA*

omerset settle with boards in the back, c. 1840, 5 in. wide, 5 ft. 10 in. high, 21 deep. **£590-610**   *CC*

A Victorian pine bench, 38 in. wide, 12 in. deep, 16 in. high. **£35-40**   *AL*

A pine Victorian bed with oak posts and legs and close boarded base, c. 1850, 6 ft. 6 in. long, 4 ft. 6 in. wide. **£250-300**   *CC*

A 19th C. Welsh spinning stool, 24 in. high. **£25-35**   *PF*

A Victorian pine stool, 20 in. high, 12 in. square. **£15-20**   *AL*

ictorian pine dressing ror, with oval box in base, 15 wide, 19 in. high. **£40-50**

An 18th C. pine Welsh lambing chair, **£500-550**   *CC*

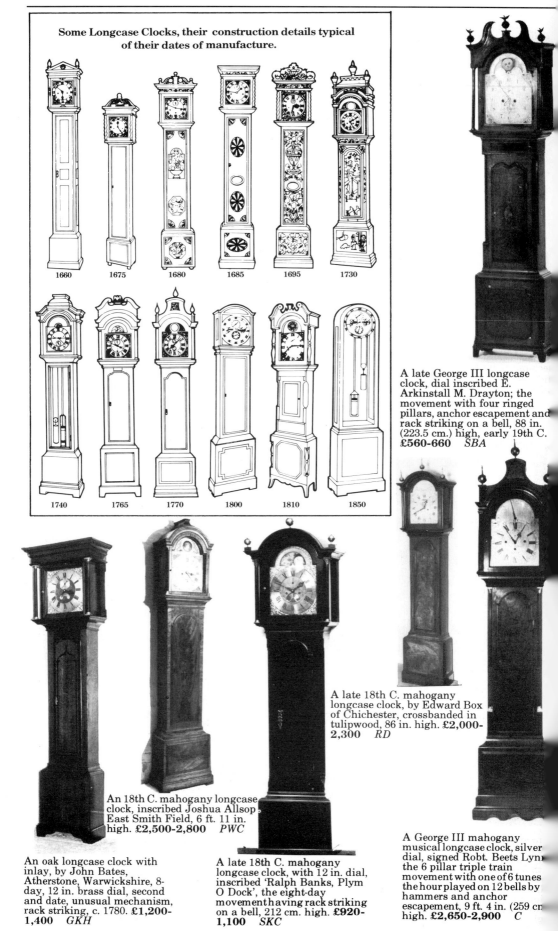

Some Longcase Clocks, their construction details typical of their dates of manufacture.

1660   1675   1680   1685   1695   1730

1740   1765   1770   1800   1810   1850

A late George III longcase clock, dial inscribed E. Arkinstall M. Drayton; the movement with four ringed pillars, anchor escapement and rack striking on a bell, 88 in. (223.5 cm.) high, early 19th C. **£560-660**   *SBA*

A late 18th C. mahogany longcase clock, by Edward Box of Chichester, crossbanded in tulipwood, 86 in. high. **£2,000-2,300**   *RD*

An 18th C. mahogany longcase clock, inscribed Joshua Allsop, East Smith Field, 6 ft. 11 in. high. **£2,500-2,800**   *PWC*

An oak longcase clock with inlay, by John Bates, Atherstone, Warwickshire, 8-day, 12 in. brass dial, second and date, unusual mechanism, rack striking, c. 1780. **£1,200-1,400**   *GKH*

A late 18th C. mahogany longcase clock, with 12 in. dial, inscribed 'Ralph Banks, Plym O Dock', the eight-day movement having rack striking on a bell, 212 cm. high. **£920-1,100**   *SKC*

A George III mahogany musical longcase clock, silver dial, signed Robt. Beets Lyn, the 6 pillar triple train movement with one of 6 tunes the hour played on 12 bells by hammers and anchor escapement, 9 ft. 4 in. (259 cm high. **£2,650-2,900**   *C*

oak and mahogany 8 day
gcase clock, brass dial with
tre date and moon
chanism, by Brandreth,
ddlewich, c. 1770. **£1,450-**
50   *Tr*

An oak longcase clock,
crossbanded in mahogany,
having eight day movement,
brass and silvered dial, by
Joshua Brown, Liverpool,
height 7 ft. 1½ in. **£900-
1,200**   *OL*

A Scottish 8-day longcase clock,
the dial inscribed 'Blackett
Wallace, Brampton', with
subsidiary seconds dial with
date aperture, gong/eight bells
and chime/silent, 96½ in.
£700-800   *SBe*

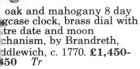

A Dutch inlaid walnut musical
longcase clock, signed Gerrit
Braber Amsterdam, the
movement with shaped plates,
seven pillars, three trains,
anchor escapement, rack Dutch
strike and playing 6 tunes on 15
bells by 29 hammers from an 8½
in. pinned cylinder, 19th C., 10
ft. high. **£3,400-4,000**   *C*

A Scottish eight-day longcase
clock, inscribed 'Dan Brown,
Glasgow', 22 in. wide, 86 in.
high. **£1,200-1,500**   *SBe*

mahogany longcase clock,
e 10½ in. dial signed Bayley &
john London, the movement
th 5 pillars and deadbeat
capement, the pendulum with
ler suspension, bimetallic
idiron rod and numbered
ew adjustments, 6 ft. 1 in.
gh. **£1,700-2,000**   *S*

A mahogany longcase clock,
the 13 in. dial inscribed 'Alexr.
Brown Coatbridge', the
movement with anchor
escapement and rack-striking
on a bell, 82½ in. (210 cm.), mid-
19th C. **£450-550**   *SBA*

An 18th C. oak longcase clock,
the 8 day striking movement
with brass square dial, Geo.
Brownless, Staindrop, 86 in.
high. **£580-640**   *TW*

333

A late 18th C. mahogany
longcase clock, the 12 in. brass
dial signed 'John Buckingham,
Plymouth Dock', the 8-day
anchor movement having rack
striking on a bell. **£800-880**
SKC

An early 19th C. mahogany
longcase clock, the 12 in. dial
signed Carter, Tooley Street,
Southwark, 6 ft. 5 in. (196 cm.)
high. **£880-1,000**   *SKC*

An 18th C. eight-day longcase
clock, inscribed 'Chater and
Sons, London', seconds dial
with maker's name and date
aperture below, 19 in. wide, 96½
in. high. **£770-900**   *SBe*

A Provincial oak longcase clock
with 8-day movement, by Mich
E. Coles, Scarborough, the
movement has 4 pillars and
rack, hour strike, with steel
pendulum rod and contemp.
lead weights, 84 in. high.
£1,200-1,700   *GKH*

A late 18th C. longcase clock,
with eight-day striking
movement, inscribed 'Thomas
Collier, Chapel en Le Frith'.
£400-600   *WHL*

A good late 18th C. long case
clock, by Caleb Evans, Bristol,
with 4 pillar movement and
anchor escapement, height 7 ft.
9 in. **£1,400-1,600**   *OT*

An antique 8-day grandfather
clock, by Thomas Spence
Dysart. **£890-1,000**   *BW*

A longcase clock, inset second
moon phases and date apertur
8-day movement, by David
Collier, Gatley, c. 1760. **£1,30**
1,600   *PW*

Some typical Longcase Clock faces with their approximate dates of manufacture.

1665   1685

1725   1750

1760   1775

1810   1825

Embellishment details and their approximate dates.

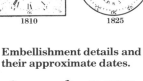

1670   1680   1705

1730   1760   1735

An 18th C. long case clock, John Flook, Bristol, with four pillar movement with anchor escapement striking on one bell. **£1,700-2,000**   *OT*

oak longcase clock, the 12 in. l inscribed Finney erpool; the movement with hor escapement rack king on a bell, on later cket feet (with restorations), n., mid-18th C. **£440-520** A

oak longcase clock, the 12 in. ass dial signed 'John Fox antham', the movement with hor escapement, ringed lars and chiming (bell king), 100 in. (254 cm.) erall, the case 19th C. stored). **£460-540**   *SBA*

An oak longcase clock, the 13½ in. brass dial signed 'Chas. Edwd. Gillett, Manchester', the movement with anchor escapement and rack striking on a bell, 96 in. (224 cm.), late 18th/early 19th C. **£950-1,250**   *SBA*

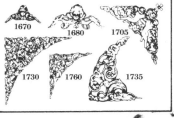

An 8 day rack striking longcase clock, with 14 in. square dial, inscribed B. Furnival, Oldham. **£450-550**   *SR*

A George III mahogany longcase clock, dial signed by John Gale London, rack-striking movement with anchor escapement. **£2,400-2,600**   *C*

An early 18th C. black lacquer longcase clock, by James Goodyer of Guildford, with 8-day movement, 7 ft. 11 in. high. **£960-1,200** *MMB*

A George I seaweed marquetry month duration longcase clock, the 12 in. brass dial signed Peter Garon London, the month-duration 5-pillar movement with anchor escapement and strike on bell, 9 ft. 4 in. (285 cm.) high. **£5,000-6,000** *C*

An Edwardian mahogany longcase clock, with 17 in. brass dial, signed, Goldsmith's Company, London, the three train movement, chiming the quarters, with semi dead-beat escapement and maintaining power, 2.45 m. **£2,600-3,000** *P*

A fine William and Mary marquetry longcase clock, 11 in. brass dial signed Chr Gould Londini fecit, the movement with anchor escapement and countwheel strike on bell, 6 ft. 9 in. (206 c high. **£6,900-7,500** *C*

A late Victorian striking and chiming 8-day longcase clock, brass dial inscribed 'R. H. Halford & Sons, London', striking and chiming on 9 chromium-plated tubular gongs (pendulum mercury lacking), height 110 in. **£2,300-2,500** *SBe*

An Edwardian muscial long cased clock, with Westminster and Whittington chimes, mercury pendulum and cylindrical brass weights, by Harrison & Son, Darlington, overall height 8 ft. 6 in. **£1,900-2,300** *M*

A George II walnut longcase clock, 8 day quarter striking movement, 8 bells, by Richard Grant of Fleet Street, c. 1755, 8 in. high, 2nd and 3rd train of later date. **£4,000-4,500** *JGM*

A late 17th C. seaweed marquetry longcase clock, 11 in. square dial, signed Cha Gretton London, rack-striking movement with anchor escapement, 7 ft. 7 in. (232 cm high. **£2,650-2,900** *C*

A longcase clock, by John
Hocker, Reading, with 8-day
chiming movement, 98 in. high.
£2,100-2,600   DSH

mahogany longcase clock, by
Clare Hatton, with 14 in.
uare brass dial; the
ovement with anchor
capement and rack striking
a bell, 84 in. (312 cm), early
th C. £390-450   SBA

A rare George II burr yew
musical longcase clock, with
age and phase of moon, six-tune
selector, signed Robt.
Henderson London, three-train
movement with anchor
escapement chiming on 10 bells
by 19 hammers, 8 ft. (244 cm.)
high. £7,000-8,000   C

An 18th C. Dutch walnut
marquetry alarum longcase
clock, the 13 in. dial signed Jan
Henkels Amsterdam, the
movement with Dutch striking,
8 ft. 9 in. high. £4,200-4,600
S

*Miller's Antiques Price Guide
builds up year by year to
form the most comprehensive
photo-reference system
available. The first three
volumes contain over 20,000
completely different
photographs.*

walnut musical longcase
ck, the 11 in. dial inscribed
hd. Houton Oversley Green;
three-train movement with
chor escapement, the
sical train playing on 8 bells
trolled by a pin wheel and
side governor (the case
onstructed and reveneered),
in. £1,300-1,500   SBA

A George III mahogany
chiming longcase clock, the 12
in. dial signed Willm. Hughes
High Holborn London, the
movement chiming the
quarters on eight bells, 7 ft 9 in.
high. £3,300-4,000   S

A 19th C. mahogany and inlaid
longcase clock, by Hughes of
Llangollen, with Tunbridge-
ware inlay, recoil movement, 26
in. £500-800   PS

A late 18th/early 19th C. 8-day
longcase clock, the 11 in. brass
dial inscribed 'Benj. Jacob,
London', with seconds dial and
date aperture (fully restored),
height 8 ft. 2 in. £2,700-
3,300   SBe

A George III longcase clock William Moon, London, eig[ht] day movement with anchor escapement, rack striking o[n] bell. **£1,000-1,300**   *OT*

An 8-day longcase clock, with 9½ in. square brass dial, inscribed Joseph Knibb, Londini fecit. **£3,800-4,200**   *BW*

An early 18th C. Dutch marquetry longcase clock, signed Preter Kloch, Amsterdam, movement with four ringed latched pillars, anchor escapement and internal countwheel strike on bell, 7 ft. 4 in. (224 cm.) high. **£5,000-6,000**   *C*

An Edwardian long case clock, fitted with Westminster, Whittington and St. Michael chimes, by William Lister & Sons, Newcastle upon Tyne, 7 ft. 5 in. high. **£1,500-1,600**   *AG*

An 18th C. longcase clock, Thomas Richardson of Weaveram, with eight-day striking movement. **£550-600**   *WHL*

An oak longcase clock, the 12 in. brass dial signed James Pain, London; the movement with ringed pillars and anchor escapement chiming on a bell (dial and movement altered), 82½ in. (210 cm.), late 18th C. **£430-500**   *SBA*

An early 19th C. long case clock, William Newby, Kendal, with four pillar movement striking on one bell with anchor escapement, height 8 ft. 6 in. **£2,400-2,700**   *OT*

A Charles II style simulated tortoiseshell 'grandmother' longcase clock, with 7¾ in. square dial signed Thos. Rapson, rack-striking weight driven movement with anchor escapement, 6 ft. high. **£1,800-2,200**   *C*

An oak cased 30-hour clock by Sidwell of Nuneaton, 11½ in. dial (replaced hour and minute hands), c. 1813, 6 ft. 6 in. tall. **£545-600** *GKH*

Georgian mahogany ngcase clock, with 16 in. brass l, the twin train movement th anchor escapement, by ancis Robotham, mpstead, 2.34 m. overall. ,700-3,100 *P*

A George III quarter striking, chiming, calendar mahogany longcase clock, the brass dial with age and phase of moon, signed Shakeshalft Preston with tune selector, the movement with four trains for anchor escapement, hour countwheel strike and chime on 11 graduated bells, 8 ft. (250 cm.) high. **£3,000-3,500** *C*

A late 17th C. walnut and marquetry longcase clock, the 11 in. square dial signed Thos. Speakman Londini Fecit, the later dial feet connecting to a four pillar movement with rack strike and anchor escapement, 6 ft. 7½ in. high. **£3,500-4,200** *C*

A George III mahogany longcase clock, by Thomas Wallace of Brampton, with brass dial, date aperture, phases of the sun and moon and 8-day movement, 8 ft. 4 in. high. **£850-1,000** *MMB*

A George III longcase clock, with engraved brass and silvered dial, 88 in. **£1,400-,700** *Hy.D*

A mahogany longcase clock, with painted dial and moving swan, by Taylor, Bridgewater, 8 day, c. 1840. **£875-975** *Tr*

LONGCASE CLOCKS
Case Finish

Ebony veneer	up to c. 1725	Carolean to early Georgian
Walnut veneer	from c. 1670 to c. 1770	Carolean to mid-Georgian
Lacquer	from c. 1700 to c. 1755	Queen Anne to mid-Georgian
Mahogany	from 1730	from early Georgian
Softwood	from c. 1760	from mid-Georgian
Mahogany inlay	from c. 1795	from mid-Georgian
Marquetry	from c. 1680 to c. 1760	from Carolean to mid-Georgian
Oak	always	

A George III oak longcase clock, the 14 in. brass dial inscribed Tempus Fugit, the movement with anchor escapement and rack striking on a bell, 88 in. (224 cm.), late 18th/early 19th C. **£490-550** *SBA*

| LONGCASE CLOCKS | | |
Dials		
8 in. square	to c. 1669	Carolean
10 in. square	from c. 1665-1695	
11 in. square	from c. 1690-1700	
12 in. square	from c. 1700	from Queen Anne
14 in. square	from c. 1740	from early Georgian
Broken-arch dial	from c. 1715	from early Georgian
Round dial	from c. 1760	from early Georgian
Silvered dial	from c. 1760	from early Georgian
Painted dial	from c. 1760	from early Georgian
Hour hand only	to c. 1680	
Minute hand introduced	c. 1663	
Second hand	from c. 1675	post-Restoration
Matching hands	from c. 1775	George III or later

A George III lacquered musical longcase clock, the brass dial with six-tune selector to the arch, the three-train movement with anchor escapement, chiming on 11 bells by 25 hammers, 8 ft. 3 in. (252 cm.) high. £2,600-3,000   C

An 18th C. grandmother clock with 8-day movement. £34 400   DA

A late-Georgian 8-day longcase clock. £450-550   WY

A 19th C. French boulle comptoise clock, the three train movement with petite sonnerie strike, the movement of iron frame with pin wheel escapement, 2.20 m. £2,800-3,200   P

A mahogany longcase clock, the dial signed, 95 in., on later bracket feet, mid-19th C. £400-480   SB

A George III North Country mahogany longcase clock, 8-day striking, with moon phase aperture, inscribed John Smith Chester, 8 ft. 2 in. £1,550-1,850   WW

A late 19th C. longcase clock, with 8-day movement, striking and chiming on brass chimes 8 or 4 tunes. £2,500-3,000   LT

BRACKET CLOCKS		
Dials		
Square dial	to c. 1770	pre-George III
Broken arch dial	from c. 1720	George I or later
Round/painted/silvered	from c. 1760	George III or later

egency brass-inlaid
hogany bracket clock, the 8
dial signed Benjn. Russell
wich, the repeating
vement with anchor
pement and later gong
king, 22½ in. high. £460-
S

A large Regency lancet bracket
clock, mahogany case with
inlay and stringing and with
painted dial, Perigal &
Duterrau, London, 19 in. high.
£600-1,000   KA

A Regency lancet
bracket clock by
Suggatt, Halesworth,
in ebonised case with
silvered dial, 16 in.
high. £500-800   KA

A Regency mahogany bracket
clock, with repeat, the white
painted dial inscribed
'Nathaniel Hedge, Bath', with
two train fusee movement with
anchor escapement and hour
striking on a bell, height 20 in.
£300-350   SBe

Regency lancet clock, in
hogany case with a silvered
l and a circular double fusee
vement, signed Barraud,
ndon, 17½ in. high. £800-
100   KA

A rare late 18th C. mahogany
alarm bracket clock, dial signed
Eardley Norton London, the
movement reconverted to verge
escapement with double fusee
and chain, backplate numbered
2183, 12 in. (30.5 cm.) high.
£3,900-4,300   C

A late 18th C. ebonised quarter
repeating bracket clock, signed
Willm, Harrison, London, the
movement converted to anchor
escapement with pull quarter
repeat on six bells, 13 in. (33
cm.) high. £1,300-1,500   C

n 18th C. bracket clock, with
own wheel escapement,
graved John Kay, London, in
ahogany case, 15 in. high.
1,000-1,200   RBB

An 18th C. striking and
chiming bracket clock, three
train fusee movement, quarter
chiming on eight bells and
striking on a larger bell, width
12¼ in., height 19 in. £800-
900   SBe

A George III striking bracket
clock, inscribed on the
backplate Ellicott & Taylor,
London, 12 by 8 by 18 in. high.
£750-850   AG

341

A George III bracket clock, with brass dial (8 in. diam.), signed 'Mark Rogers, Ringwood', the double fusee movement with anchor escapement striking on a bell, 49 cm. high. **£850-950** *SKC*

A George III mahogany hooded bracket clock, signed John Ellicott London, the movement with anchor escapement, double fusee and strike on bell, 33 in. (84 cm.) high. **£3,700-4,300** *C*

An oak cased bracket clock inscribed Benet Fink & Co. Cheapside, three train movement with Whittington and Cambridge chimes on bells and a wire gong, 30 in. high. **£500-600** *PWC*

A mahogany broken arch top bracket clock, engraved back plate, verge escapement, porcelain dial, c. 1780, 14 in. high. **£3,000-4,000** *KA*

A George III bracket clock, the striking movement by Sly, Weymouth, 16 in. high. **£800-900** *Hy.D*

A walnut and bronze bracket clock, the German movement with quarter-striking on 2 gongs, with a presentation plaque, 14½ in. (37 cm.), late 19th C. **£180-240** *SBA*

A George III period mahogany bracket clock, the eight day striking movement with anchor escapement, inscribed Geo. Younge, Strand, London, 18¼ in. high (pendulum a.f.). **£740-860** *GC*

A William IV bracket clock with rosewood case, double fusee movement and painted dial, 17 in. high. **£300-600** *KA*

An early 19th C. mahogany day striking bracket clock, the fusee movement having strike/silent mechanism, dial inscribed William Hanson Windsor, c. 1810, 16 in. **£1,500-1,700** *WW*

BRACKET CLOCKS Case Finish		
Ebony veneer	from c. 1660 to c. 1850	Carolean to mid-Victorian
Walnut	from c. 1670 to c. 1795	Carolean to mid-Georgian
Marquetry	from c. 1680 to c. 1740	Carolean to early Georgian
Rosewood	from c. 1790	from mid-Georgian
Lacquered	from c. 1700 to c. 1760	Queen Anne to early Georgian
Mahogany	from c. 1730	from early Georgian

A walnut bracket clock, now
with a German movement, 15½
in. (39.5 cm.), C. 1870. **£390-
420** *SB*

A bracket clock, fitted
Whittington and Cambridge
chimes, 14¾ by 9¼ by 24½ in.
high. **£890-1,000** *AG*

mahogany chiming bracket
ock, striking the quarters on 5
d gongs and 8 bells, 31½ in., 3
ys and pendulum, c. 1880.
990-1,100 *SB*

An early Louis XV ormolu-
mounted bracket clock, with
enamel-set chased dial, the
striking movement signed Hory
a Paris, 45 in. (114 cm.) high.
£1,400-1,600 *C*

An ebonised bracket clock, with
quarter-hour striking on 5
gongs and 8 bells, signed
Marshall & Sons, 87 George St,
Edinburgh, 23½ in. (60 cm.), c.
1870. **£900-1,200** *SB*

Louis XV boulle bracket
ock, the glazed dial with
triking movement, 45½ in. (105
m.) high. **£2,000-2,200** *C*

A Louis XIV contre partie
boulle bracket clock and
bracket, with striking
movement, signed on the face
Roquelon a Paris and engraved
on the backplate Rabby a Paris.
57 in. (145 cm.) high. **£1,450-
1,750** *C*

A boulle bracket clock, 19 in., c.
1880. **£200-240** *SB*

A Louis XV style bracket clock
with eight day movement and
ormolu face, in Buhl green
tortoiseshell and brass
scrollwork rococo case, 22 in.
high. **£450-520** *CDC*

19th C. Boulle bracket clock,
f Louis XIV design, the brass
ial inscribed Leroy a Paris, 42
n. high, together with
natching bracket. **£1,215-
,400** *PK*

A Louis XV Vernis Martin
bracket clock, the enamel dial
signed Courrieult a Paris, the
movement with outside
countwheel strike, 50½ in. (128
cm.) high. **£2,200-2,500** *C*

An early 18th C. ebonised striking bracket clock, dial with regulation ring, silvered chapter-ring, matted centre with false pendulum and date apertures quarter-repeating on six bells, now with deadbeat escapement, 15¼ in. (39 cm.) high. **£880-1,000** *C*

A Louis XIV Boulle Pendule Religieuse, now with deadbeat pin wheel escapement, external countwheel strike on bell, with pierced blue gate, signed I. Thuret a Paris, velvet-covered dial with applied chapter-ring, 23 in. (58 cm.) high. **£1,300-1,500** *C*

A Boulle bracket clock, with outside countwheel inscribed Souvenir from His Late Messmates of the Princess Royal, 1852, 12½ in., mid-19th C. **£280-340** *SB*

A Louis XIV bracket clock an bracket, with 8-day striking movement by Francois Gilber of Paris, in brass and tortoiseshell case, height 43 in excluding bracket. **£1,200-1,500** *LT*

An early 18th C. ebony striking bracket clock, the movement reconverted to verge escapement with six fine ringed pillars, internal rack strike on bell, signed John Barnett Londini fecit, 13 in. (33 cm.) high, dial 6½ in. diam. **£3,700-4,000** *C*

A George III ebonised striking bracket clock, the dial signed Richard Holmes, London, with strike/silent and regulation rings, the movement with verge escapement, 18 in. (46 cm.) diam. **£1,600-1,800** *C*

An early 18th C. ebony strikin bracket clock, with 6 in. brass dial, the movement reconverte to verge escapement, with internal rack strike on bell, signed Robert Williamson London, lacking repeat work, 12½ in. (32 cm.) high. **£2,600 2,800** *C*

An early 18th C. style English bracket clock, with three train movement, having quarter chime on eight bells and striking on a gong, engraved backplate and pendulum, 5¾ in., width 10¾ in., height 15¼ in. **£800-1,100** *SBe*

An early 18th C. ebonised striking bracket clock, with 7 in. brass dial, silvered chapter-ring and matted centre, movement backplate engraved and signed on a plaque Isaac Papavoine Londini fecit, reconverted to verge escapement, 13¾ in. (35 cm.) high. **£2,600-2,800** *C*

A mid-Georgian ebonised striking bracket clock, silvered chapter-ring matted centre with false pendulum, signed Edw. Faulkner, London, movement mounted with pull-wind springs for alarm (defective) and quarter-repeat on six bells, converted anchor escapement, 20½ in. (52 cm.) high. **£1,300-1,600**   *C*

A late George II bracket clock, the 8 in. dial signed A. M. Cressener London; the ringed four-pillar movement with anchor escapement and pin-wheel striking on a bell, 20 in. (51 cm.), mid-19th C. **£1,000-1,200**   *SBA*

A George II ebonised striking bracket clock, dial with false-pendulum and calendar apertures, signed Jno. Startridge, Lymington, the movement converted to anchor escapement, 19½ in. high. **£1,000-1,300**   *C*

George III mahogany striking bracket clock, signed James Forsyth London (date ring lacking hand), the movement with verge escapement, 18 in. high. **£1,400-1,750**   *C*

An early 18th C. bracket clock, by William Webster, Exchange Alley, London, with 8-day striking verge movement, signed by the maker, 18 in. high. **£2,500-3,000**   *B*

An 18th C. mahogany double-fusee striking bracket clock, by Abel Panchand, Oxford Street, London, 15 in. high. **£1,100-1,400**   *Lan*

An early George III ebonised quarter-striking bracket clock, the dial signed Cha. Cabrier, London, with strike/silent and regulation rings, false pendulum and date aperture, three-train movement with verge escapement, 19 in. (49 cm.) high. **£2,200-2,600**   *C*

An 18th C. red lacquered case bracket clock, by Jno. Crucifix, London, the 8-day movement with bob pendulum, 20 in. high, 11½ in. wide, 6 in. deep, the dial 7½ by 7½ in. wide, c. 1730. **£3,100-3,600**   *Win*

A quarter repeating mahogany bracket clock, striking on 5 rod gongs, signed Reid & Sons, Newcastle on Tyne, with a presentation plaque, 17 in., German, c. 1890. **£290-330**   *SB*

A mid-18th C. bracket clock, with maker's plaque inscribed 'T. Dicker, Silchester', having 8 in. square brass dial, two train fusee movement with anchor escapement, width 11½ in., height 17½ in. **£700-1,000**   *SBe*

A Victorian ebonised chiming bracket clock, signed John H. Bell Elm Street London, the triple chain-fusee movement with anchor escapement, 20½ in. high. **£700-830** *C*

An Edwardian 8-day striking bracket clock, by Moore & Co. of Dublin, 28 in. overall. **£290-350** *Ch*

A late Victorian chiming bracket clock, chime/silent regulator and chime on eight bells/Westminster setting dials, the three train moveme. striking on a gong, height 28 i. **£1,000-1,200** *SBe*

An early 19th C. mahogany bracket clock, with double fusee movement and musical chime, by Viner, London. **£770-900** *BW*

A Louis XIII ebonised striking bracket clock, black velvet-covered dial signed Du Hamel a Paris, movement with dual geared spring barrel, verge escapement and countwheel strike on bell, 16½ in. (42 cm.) high. **£2,300-2,800** *C*

An ebonised bracket clock, th. in. dial signed Henry Massy London, the five pillar movement with repeating a. strike/silent mechanism lacking and later anchor escapement, 14 in. high. **£88. 1,000** *S*

A mahogany bracket clock, the movement with turned pillars and double fusee, 19½ in., 1840's. **£300-350** *SB*

A 19th C. bracket timepiece, the 6 in. diam. dial inscribed Whytock & Sons ? Dundee, fusee movement, 13½ in. **£180-260** *A*

Some typical clock hands with their approximate dates.

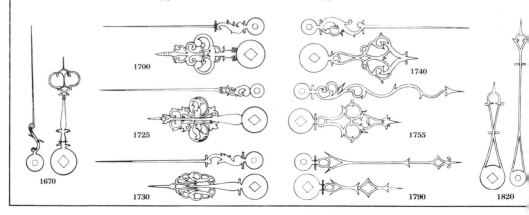

1700
1740
1725
1755
1670
1730
1790
1820

William IV bracket clock, dial Gravell & Son, London (no. 17). **£600-720** *BW*

An ornate 19th C. 8-day striking and chiming bracket clock, contained in a 'Victorian Gothic' walnutwood 'cathedral' case, 36 in. **£530-650** *Ch*

An 8 day chiming bracket clock, the movement with fusee drive chiming on eight bells with hour gong strike, 20 in. **£550-650** *WW*

n unusual gilt-metal porcelain nelled striking carriage ock, movement with lever atform, strike and repeat, 6¼ . (16 cm.) high. **£800-900** *C*

A carriage clock, the repeating lever movement with gong striking, 5¾ in. high, with a leather travelling case. **£500-600** *S*

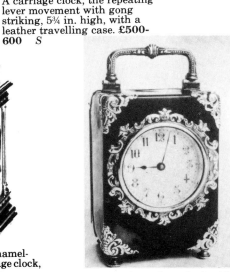

A 19th C. brass carriage clock, with striking movement. **£530-700** *BW*

An unusual gilt-metal grande sonnerie bottom wind carriage clock, movement with lever platform, signed Leroy & Fils., Patent No. 9501, 7 in. (17.5 cm.) high. **£2,200-2,500** *C*

A quarter-repeating enamel-mounted alarum carriage clock, ver escapement with ompensation balance, jewelled allets, and quarter striking on gongs, Chaude 36 Palais oyal Paris, 8¾ in., c. 1880. **3,800-4,200** *SB*

A French carriage clock with lever escapement, the tortoiseshell case ornately silver mounted hallmarked London 1897, 4½ in. **£380-420** *WHL*

A lacquered brass and porcelain striking carriage clock, movement with lever platform, strike, repeat and alarm on gong, 6½ in. (16.5 cm.) high. **£900-1,000** *C*

A brass carriage clock, hourly repeater, c. 1880, 5½ in. plus handle. **£450-650** *MB*

A brass alarum carriage clock with half-hour striking, hour-repeating, signed Henry Capt Geneve, and Henry Capt Ls. Gallopin et Cie. Succrs., with a leather case and key, 4½ in., late 19th C. **£760-860** *SB*

A rare ormolu miniature carriage clock, movement with lever platform and ivorine chapter-ring dial, 2¾ in. (7 cm.) high. **£770-900** *C*

A lacquered brass miniature carriage clock, movement with lever platform, 3¾ in. (10 cm.) high. **£330-390** *C*

A miniature gilt-metal carriage clock, movement with cylinder platform, case of oval form, 3¾ in. (9.5 cm.) high. **£650-750** *C*

A very small lacquered brass and enamel carriage clock, nickel-plated movement with vertical cylinder escapement 2¼ in. (5.75 cm.) high. **£450-550** *C*

A lacquered brass porcelain-mounted carriage clock, the movement stamped AM with lever platform, strike/repeat/alarm on gong, by Margaine, 7 in. high. **£770-900** *C*

A lacquered brass miniature carriage clock, movement with lever platform, 3½ in. (9 cm.) high. **£350-420** *C*

A French carriage clock, the eight-day strike repeating movement has alarm with original platform jewelled lever escapement, dial inscribed 'Examd. by Dent, 28 Cockspur St., London', 17 cm. high. **£560-620** *SKC*

brass carriage clock, by
harles Frodsham, London,
ith repeater movement and
ngraved dial plate, 6¾ in.
520-620   *A*

A rare gilt-metal grande
sonnerie calendar carriage
clock, movement with lever
platform strike, repeat and
alarm, dial signed L. Leroy &
Cie 13.15 Palais Royal Paris,
subsidiary dials for day, date
and alarm, 6¾ in. (17 cm.) high.
£2,600-3,000   *C*

A French gilt metal striking
carriage clock, with lever
platform and strike/repeat on
bell, 4½ in. high. **£990-1,200**
C

n English rosewood striking
rriage clock, signed Blundell
ondon No. 2686, movement
ith chain fusees, plain gilt
lance to the platform with
raight line escapement, 10¼
. high. **£2,700-3,200**   *C*

A French striking carriage
clock, with repeat, No. 1934,
having white enamel dial, hour
and half-hour striking on a
gong, 8 in. **£490-560**   *SBe*

A gilt metal porcelain-mounted
striking carriage clock, with
lever platform,
repeating/alarm on gong,
porcelain dial with
Watteauesque figures, 6 in.
high. **£950-1,200**   *C*

lacquered brass miniature
arm carriage clock,
ovement with cylinder
atform, alarm on underslung
ong, 3⅛ in. (8 cm.) high. **£290-**
50   *C*

A gilt-metal and porcelain
striking carriage clock,
movement with lever platform
with strike and repeat on gong,
with travelling case, 7 in. (18
cm.) high. **£800-900**   *C*

A gilt-metal and enamel
miniature carriage clock,
movement with lever platform,
case with champleve enamel
decoration, 3¼ in. (8.5 cm.) high.
£550-650   *C*

A brass oval carriage clock, with lever platform, repeating/strike, travelling case, 5½ in. (14 cm.) high. **£540-620** *C*

A grande sonnerie carriage clock, the repeating movement with alarm and coil strike, 7¾ in. **£990-1,200** *Hy.D*

A rare porcelain-mounted oval striking clock, movement with lever platform, repeat/alarm or gong, dial of blue ground 'Sevres' porcelain, 6 in. (15 cm. high. **£1,400-1,600** *C*

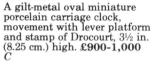

A gilt-metal oval miniature porcelain carriage clock, movement with lever platform and stamp of Drocourt, 3½ in. (8.25 cm.) high. **£900-1,000** *C*

A round French carriage timepiece, made in Paris, 4½ in. high, 3½ in. diam., c. 1890. **£200-300** *KA*

A French carriage strike and alarm clock, made for Chinese market with centre seconds, c. 1880. **£800-1,000** *KA*

An engraved gilt-bronze oval cased hour repeating carriage clock, the platform lever escapement striking on a spiral gong, 6 in., 1880's. **£400-500** *SB*

A lacquered brass striking carriage clock, stamped G.L., with lever platform, half-hour striking, hour repeat, five minute repeat with star wheel, by Gay, Lamaille & Co., 5⅞ in. (15 cm.) high. **£880-1,000** *C*

A gilt-metal quarter-striking carriage clock, stamped H.J., with lever platform repeating on two gongs, by Jacot, 5¾ in. (14.7 cm.) high. **£800-880** *C*

A French three train chiming carriage clock, stamped R. & C., with silvered lever platform, the indirectly wound third barrel geared to a pinned drum for the quarters on four bells in the base, by Richard & Co., travelling case, 7 in. (18 cm.) high. **£2,000-2,200** *C*

A brass carriage clock, striking hours and half-hours. **£330-380** *MB*

A 19th C. brass carriage clock, with circular enamel dial. **£200-260** *BW*

A brass carriage clock with engraved case and porcelain dial, quarter repeater and alarm, 6¾ in. high. **£900-1,000** *MB*

A 19th C. brass carriage clock. **£120-140** *MB*

n English brass 'Grande onnerie' carriage clock by mp and Sons, 7¼ in. high, c. 60. **£1,500-1,650** *MB*

A brass carriage clock, a strike repeater, 6 in. high. **£450-550** *MB*

A late 19th C. French ormolu ased carriage clock, with larm and repeating works, triking movement, by Foldsmith's Company, 6½ in. igh. **£990-1,200** *Lan*

A brass carriage clock by Couaillet of Paris, hourly repeater, 7¾ in. high, c. 1890. **£650-750** *MB*

A brass carriage clock, a quarter repeater on bell, c. 1880, 6½ in. high. **£900-1,000** *MB*

A gilt-brass grand sonnerie carriage clock, with a lever movement, quarter-repeating key and leather case, 7½ in. (19 cm.), c. 1900. **£600-900** *SB*

Make the most of Miller's
Look for the code letters in italic type following each caption.
Check these against the list of contributors on page 10 to identify the source of any illustration.
Remember — valuations may vary according to locality; use of the codes can allow this to be taken into account.

rare ormolu musical and utomaton carriage clock, the hovement stamped Japy 'reres, with lever platform, trike, repeat and alarm on bell, he mechanically separate husical box in the base onnected to dancing tight-rope valker, 11¾ in. (30 cm.) high. **4,800-5,300** *C*

A French repeater carriage clock, with painted china dial and side panels, signed L. Simmonet. **£1,000-1,200** *RMcT*

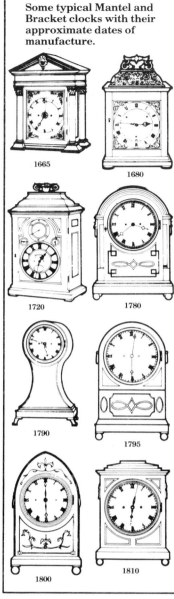

Some typical Mantel and
Bracket clocks with their
approximate dates of
manufacture.

1665

1680

1720

1780

1790

1795

1800

1810

A French gilt metal four-glass
clock, with perpetual calendar,
the rectangular movement
signed LeRoy & Fils A Paris No.
7483, with strike on bell and
visible coup perdu escapement,
18½ in. high. **£2,300-2,600**
C

A Louis XVI ormolu regulator
clock, the enamel dial signed
Lepaute a Paris, the movement
with outside countwheel strike,
18½ in. (47 cm.) high. **£3,300-
3,700**   *C*

A brass mantel clock, with
glazed sides, having enamel
dial by Marc, Paris. **£240-
300**   *BW*

An English 'four glass' chain
fusee clock, in light oak case,
1850, 17 in. high, 12½ in. wide
£400-600   *KA*

A 19th C. French four-glass
type mantel clock, by Japy
Freres, No. 705748, inscribed
Edward and Sons, Glasgow,
hour and half-hour striking,
mercury compensated
pendulum, height 14½ in.
£380-450   *SBe*

A gilt bronze mantel timepiece
and barometer, the anchor
escapement with an unusual
balancing ball pendulum,
signed Brevete 9623, 15 in., c.
1870. **£600-700**   *SB*

An unusual French
400-day timepiece,
glass style case, 1
in. high. **£200-
300**   *KA*

A 19th C. regulator mantel
clock, signed 'Boxell, Brighton',
the movement inscribed
'Medaille de Bronze', with
Brocot escapement and a gridiron style pendulum has rack
striking, 48 cm. high. **£990-
1,100**   *SKC*

French gilt-metal four glass calendar mantel clock, with visible Brocot's escapement, movement striking on bell, stamped C.R., 14½ in. (37 cm.) h. **£1,600-1,800**   *C*

A late Georgian mantel timepiece, with silvered dial inscribed 'G. & W. Yonge, Strand, London', single train fusee with anchor escapement, height 13 in. **£380-440**   *SBe*

An 18th C. mantel clock, with repeat, dial inscribed 'Thomas Hunter, London', the two train fusee movement with verge escapement, bob pendulum, hour striking on a bell, width 11½ in., height 20½ in. **£800-880**   *SBe*

late 19th C. black marble mantel clock by Wm. Gibson and Co., Paris and Belfast, with brass dial, 11 in. high. **£30-0**   *KA*

A Regency ebonised mantel clock, by Whitehurst of Derby, c. 1820, 11 in. high. **£1,200-1,400**   *JGM*

A 19th C. mantel clock, by 'Frodsham, Gracechurch Street, London', inscribed, the two train fusee movement with anchor escapement, hour and half-hour striking on a gong, 9¼ in. **£1,500-1,700**   *SBe*

A small Regency timepiece, in ebonised case by Roskell of Liverpool, 10 in. high. **£350-500**   *KA*

early 20th C. mantel clock, mahogany case with French movement, 13 in. high. **£120-0**   *KA*

An 18th C. balloon mantel clock, with eight day striking movement by William Ward of Bloomsbury, London, verge movement, 17¼ in. high. **£1,000- 1,300**   *LT*

Left

An early Victorian burr walnut drum shaped mantel clock, with white dial and fusee movement, by Blundell, London, 17½ in. high, 15 in. wide. **£300-500** *KA*

A brass case French clock, 11 in. high, c. 1840. **£250-400**   *KA*

A mahogany alarum mantel clock, of Capucine type, the movement with silk suspension and Morbier striking with outside star wheel and rack, 12 in. high, Jura, early 19th C. **£640-760**   *S*

A gilt bronze and champleve mantel clock, 17 in., c. 1870. **£680-780**   *SB*

A bronze and champleve enamel mantel clock, with simulated mercury compensated pendulum, 14¼ in. with key, late 19th **£360-430**   *SB*

A late 19th C. oak cased quarter chiming mantel clock, three chain fusee movement with silent and chime action on either 'Eight Bells' or 'Cambridge Chimes', 14½ in. high, 9½ in. long, 7 in. wide. **£620-680**   *DDM*

Miller's Antiques Price Guide builds up year by year to form the most comprehensive photo-reference system available. The first three volumes contain over 20,000 completely different photographs.

An F. Rzebitschek musical mantel clock, striking in quarters, with a small cylinder musical movement in the base, 23½ in. (60 cm.) high, Austrian, c. 1860. **£400-500**   *SB*

A Louis XVI ormolu and alabaster mantel clock, the circular movement with silk suspended pendulum and ra striking work planted on th backplate for the Dutch stri on two bells with trip repea signed D. F. Dubois a Paris, in. (43 cm.) high. **£2,100-2,500**   *C*

A Louis XVI French mantel clock, with silk suspension and count-wheel striking on a bell, signed 'Rouviere a Paris', 50 cm. high. **£450-520**   *SKC*

A Louis XV Ormolu mantel clock, with glazed dial signed Blondel a Paris, the movement with outside countwheel strike, 19½ in. (49.5 cm.) high. **£2,000-2,200**   *C*

A Louis XV ormolu mantel clock, by Artus a Alencon, w striking mechanism, 19 in. high. **£720-950**   *Mlms*

A Victorian mantel clock, with cast brass case, enamelled face and striking movement. **£160-220**   *ELR*

A musical mantel clock, two-train movement, with carved wood cuckoo and mechanical two-note bird song, late 19th C., probably Swiss, 15 in. (38 cm.) high. **£190-220**   *SB*

A Regency mahogany mantel clock, with striking movement, by Chadwick of Liverpool, 16 in. high. **£320-410**   *Mlms*

A quarter-striking oak mantel clock, with Westminster chimes on 5 rod gongs, 19¾ in., two keys and pendulum, c. 1900. **£380-420**   *SB*

Louis XVI ormolu mantel clock, with glazed dial signed epaute Rue Belle Fontaine a aris', the movement with utside countwheel strike, 15 in. 8 cm.) high. **£880-1,000**   *C*

A Louis XVI-style ormolu and white marble mantel clock, 15 in. (38 cm.) high. **£440-500**   *SKC*

A late 19th C. French brass and blue enamel mantel clock, 15½ in. high, 9½ in. wide. **£500-700**   *KA*

19th C. French striking antel clock, with exposed ovement, mercurial endulum, 15 in. high. **£310-80**   *A*

A marble and gilt-bronze mantel clock by Gavelle le Paria, with 5½ in. enamel dial, the movement with outside countwheel and silk suspension, late 18th/early 19th C. **£400-500**   *SBA*

A French striking mantel clock, with cloisonne enamel columns and bands. **£280-350**   *RMcT*

A French bronze mantel clock, dial signed 'Pre Leurtier a Paris', 22 in. (56 cm.) high. **£800-950** *C*

A gilt bronze mantel clock, 19 in., with a stand and a dome, c. 1860. **£770-900** *SB*

A gilt-bronze mantel clock, w twin fusee movement and h hour striking, signed Jame McCabe, London, 30¾ in. (4 cm.), mid-19th C. **£900-1,000** *SB*

A 19th C. French mantel clock, the eight-day movement having rack striking on a bell, 40 cm. high. **£600-700** *SKC*

A good 18th C. mantel clock, having a three train quarter chiming movement, Gaudron, Paris, 85 cm. high. **£3,300-3,800** *P*

A late 19th C. French mant clock, inscribed 'Chas. Frodsham, Clockmaker to t Queen, Paris', No. 28818, in green boulle case, under gla dome, height 18½ in. **£460-600** *SBe*

A gilt-bronze mantel clock, 18½ in., c. 1870. **£110-150** *SB*

A late 19th C. French porcelain mounted ormolu mantel clock, white enamel dial, bell striking eight day movement by Roblin & Fils Freres a Paris, glass dome, 19 in. high overall. **£290-350** *PWC*

Right
A 19th C. French ormolu and champlevé enamel mantel clock, 34.5 cm. high. **£630-750** *P*

A small mantel timepiece, with Lenzkirch movement, in French style, 11 in. **£90-120** *A*

A gilt bronze and porcelain mantel clock, 12¾ in. with a plinth, c. 1880. **£440-540** *S*

Boulle mantel clock, 14 in., c.
70. **£480-580**   *SB*

A Paris porcelain-mounted gilt-
bronze mantel clock, 14½ in., c.
1880. **£300-350**   *SB*

A gilt-metal mantel timepiece,
Vulliamy No. 1453, signed
Vulliamy London, the
movement with chain fusee and
anchor escapement, 11 in. high.
£990-1,200   *S*

South German brass
mepiece, the movement with
rrow plates, swelling pillars
d verge escapement with
ible pendulum, 13 in. high, c.
50. **£770-900**   *S*

An ormolu-mounted mantel
clock, the dial signed Furet a
Paris, the drum movement
supported on addorsed eagle's
heads, 17 in., key and
pendulum, c. 1870. **£680-800**
SB

An ormolu and 'Sevres'
porcelain mounted clock, the
Japy Freres movement
numbered R512, 21¼ in., key
and pendulum, c. 1860. **£990-
1,100**   *SB*

'Jewelled Sevres' mantel
ck, 17 in., with key and
ndulum, c. 1880. **£600-700**

An Empire ormolu mantel
clock, with striking movement,
signed at the left Frep Lurasco a
Amsterdam, 25½ in. (64 cm.)
wide; 27 in. (68.5 cm.) high.
£1,800-2,200   *C*

A Louis XVI bronze and ormolu
mantel clock, the glazed dial
signed 'Causard Her Du Roy a
Paris', with later striking
movement, 13 in. (33 cm.) high.
£900-1,000   *C*

A Louis XVI ormolu and white
marble mantel clock, the glazed
dial signed 'Kinable a Paris',
the movement with outside
countwheel strike, 15 in. (38
cm.) high. **£1,200-1,400**   *C*

A Charles X gilt bronze mantel
clock, 19 in., c. 1830. **£520-
620**   *SB*

A 19th C. French ormolu mantel
clock, inset with a Sevres
porcelain panel, painted with
figures of flowers, Raingo
Freres, Paris, 40 cm. high.
£570-700   *P*

A 19th C. French mantel clo
with porcelain panels and d
in the Sevres style, hour an
half-hour striking on a bell,
height 20¾ in. **£350-420**   *S*

A mahogany automaton
mantel clock, the dial with two
cherubs, one beating an anvil,
the other sharpening an arrow,
27 in. (movement replaced),
probably Vienna, early 19th C.
£280-320   *SB*

A carved wood mantel clock, 21
in., probably Austrian, c. 1870.
£750-900   *SB*

A grey marble mantel cloc
with ormolu decoration, Fr
19th C., 16 in. wide, 9 in. h
£80-140   *KA*

An Empire bronze and orm
mantel clock, the dial inscri
Wv. Overklift, WZ, a Dordre
40 cm. high. **£830-1,000**

A Restoration ormolu, bronze
and steel mantel clock, dial with
a plaque of Apollo, the
movement with outside
countwheel strike, 22¾ in. (58
cm.) high. **£1,200-1,300**   *C*

An Empire ormolu mantel
clock, the movement with
outside countwheel strike, 16
(41 cm.) high. **£680-780**   *(*

ilt bronze and white marble
ck garniture, 11 in., the
ndlesticks, 9 in., c. 1870.
70-420   *SB*

white marble and gilt-bronze
ck garniture, signed R. W.
max Manchester, 20 in.,
nked by a pair of vases, 15½
, c. 1880. **£200-260**   *SB*

gilt bronze and blue enamel
ck garniture, the dial signed
nables, Made in Paris, 14 in.,
nked by a pair of candelabra,
¼ in., c. 1900. **£2,200-**
500   *SB*

French garniture de
eminee, comprising 8-day
antel clock in heavy gilt brass
d porcelain case, and a pair of
branch, 5-light candelabra, 26
. **£3,000-3,500**   *RG*

A gilt-bronze and 'Sevres' clock
garniture, the clock 16½ in., the
candelabra, each with four
scrolling candle-arms, 19½ in.,
c. 1880. **£880-1,000**   *SB*

A 19th C. French 3-piece clock
garniture, the mantel clock by
Japy Freres, with hour and
half-hour striking on a bell, 16½
in., and a pair of matching side
urns, 12¼ in. **£270-340**   *SBe*

An Act of Parliament clock,
with chinoiserie decoration by
Henry Wilkes, Bristol, 47 in.
long. **£1,200-1,800**   *KA*

An 'Act of Parliament' wall
clock, having a 17 in. painted
dial, the single weight-driven
movement with an anchor
escapement, 124 cm. high.
£490-550   *SKC*

359

A late 19th C. Vienna 'Regulator', with spring driven movement, 42 in. high. **£200-300** *KA*

WALL CLOCKS
Case Finish

Ebony veneer	to c. 1690	to William and Mary
Marquetry	from c. 1680 to c. 1695	from Carolean to William and Mary
Mahogany	from c. 1740	from early Georgian
Oak	always	

A walnut wall timepiece, the movement with a chain fusee, 20½ by 16 in. (52 by 41 cm.), on a conforming bracket 8½ in. (21.5 cm.), c. 1850. **£180-220** *SB*

An American burr walnut striking drop dial wall clock, c. 1860, 26 in. high. **£200-300** *KA*

An early Victorian masonic clock, the enamelled dial displaying painted figures, with fusee movement. **£360-430** *BW*

An 18th C. English wall clock by James Foy, Taunton, anch escapement, single weight drive, dial 12 in. diam., total height 56½ in. **£650-800** *S*

A French 15½ in. square kitchen clock, hour and half-hour gong striking, with glass dial, of 8 day duration, c. 1890. **£145-170** *GKH*

Some typical Wall Clocks with their approximate dates of manufacture.

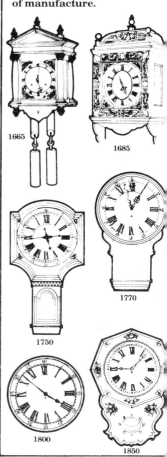

1665

1685

1750

1770

1800

1850

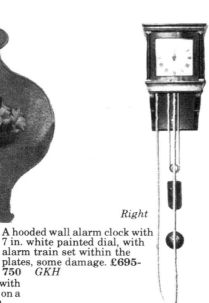

Right

A hooded wall alarm clock with 7 in. white painted dial, with alarm train set within the plates, some damage. **£695-750** *GKH*

A Black Forest wall clock, with French movement, striking on a bell, 36 in. long. **£150-220** *EEW*

ALL CLOCKS
ials

quare	to c. 1755	George II or later
roken arch	from c. 1720	
	to c. 1805	early to late Georgian
ainted/round	from c. 1740	George II or later
ilvered	from c. 1760	George III or later

An electric wall timepiece, with a 6 in. dial signed Ateliers Vaucanson Paris, movement with Hipp-type impulse mechanism and circular magnet, 20½ in. high. £1,080-1,300 *S*

A Louis XVI ormolu cartel clock, with glazed dial signed Atoine Coliau Rue de Mail, the movement with outside countwheel strike signed Coliau a Paris, 38 in. (96.5 cm.) high. **£3,700-4,200** *C*

2 train, spring driven cuckoo ock, fusee, the fully automated ckoo with moving head, ngs, tongue, with original ndulum bob, c. 1860. **£190-0** *GKH*

A Louis XV ormolu cartel clock, with enamelled dial, signed Dupont a Paris, 28 in. (71 cm.) high. **£900-1,200** *C*

A French striking Cartel clock, 12 in. by 21 in. high. **£240-300** *AG*

n Empire ormolu cartel clock, ith bridge-cock verge novement and an engine-urned gold dial, inscribed Breguet et fils', 13 in. (33 cm.) igh. **£1,600-2,000** *C*

A mid-Georgian giltwood cartel clock, signed Stepn Thorogood London, 34½ in. high. **£1,200-1,400** *C*

A late 18th C. cartel clock, with eight day movement, marked Bennett 65, Cheapside, makers to the Royal Observatory, length 43 in. **£320-400** *JF*

Miller's Antiques Price Guide builds up year by year to form the most comprehensive photo-reference system available. The first three volumes contain over 20,000 completely different photographs.

A French bronze cartel clock, with striking movement, the case edged with ormolu, signed 'E. de Labroue Fbt a Paris', late 19th C., 16 in. (40.5 cm.) diam. **£350-450** *C*

A walnut cuckoo clock, 40 in., Austrian, late 19th C. **£500-700** *SB*

A late 19th C. fusee English made lantern clock, 14 in. high. £450-500   KA

A 17th C. wing lantern clock, the movement with verge escapement and countwheel strike, 41 cm. high. £1,250-1,500   P

A 17th C. brass lantern clock, the movement with an anchor escapement, John Pennock, cm. high, and with an oak bracket. £900-1,100   P

A 17th C. single hand lantern clock, by William Rayment, Stow Market, rope and weight drive with anchor escapement, long pendulum and outside countwheel (case in need of attention), 13¼ in. £1,000-1,300   SBe

An English brass lantern clock, the dial plate signed Nicholas Coxeter in Long Lane Londini Fecit, the posted-framed movement with reconverted balance wheel verge escapement, countwheel strike and alarm, 15¼ in. high. £2,000-2,500   C

A brass lantern clock, the movement with chain fusee and hour-striking, 15½ in., late 19th C., pendulum and key. £300-500   SB

A brass lantern clock, the movement with twin chain fusee and pendulum locking, 15¾ in., late 19th C., key and pendulum. £350-550   SB

A Louis XV alarum lantern timepiece, the movement with verge escapement, 8½ in. high. £740-860   S

An English brass lantern clock, the dial plate signed Windmills, London, the posted framed movement with verge escapement, centre swinging short bob pendulum and countwheel strike on bell above, 15½ in. high. £1,400-1,800   C

An unusual skeleton clock, anchor escapement, fusee and chain imparting power to centre arbor, third wheel runner off epicyclic teeth of centre wheel, brass base signed Brookhouse Derby Wm. Strutt inv., under glass dome, 9¼ in. (23.5 cm.) high. £1,000-1,100   *C*

A Directoire ormolu skeleton clock, the dial signed by Le Roy a Paris, the movement with outside countwheel strike, 15½ in. (39 cm.) high. £480-600   *C*

brass skeleton clock with ngle train, steel wire fusee ovement and silvered dial, th glass dome, 15 in., c. 1825. 280-380   *RJG*

A 19th C. brass skeleton clock, with striking movement. £250-300   *MAI*

19th C. Skeleton clock, with see movement under glass ome, 1 ft. 4 in. high. £350-20   *WHL*

A French skeleton clock, 'Great Exhibition' type, timepiece alarm, with glass dome, 11½ in. high. £250-300   *KA*

An antique brass skeleton clock, with 8-day striking movement, on white marble base with dust cover. £440-550   *RRB*

late 19th C. cathedral keleton clock, with hour triking and repeat, two train usee movement striking on a ong, total height 21¾ in. 790-880   *SBe*

An English lacquered brass striking skeleton clock, with chain fusee, six-spoke wheels, rack strike on bell above and anchor escapement, signed Norman Sherborne, 14½ in. high. £1,800-2,100   *C*

A brass cathedral skeleton clock, the movement with a chain fusee, striking on a central bell and a gong, signed 'Vaughan Newport', on a white marble plinth, 21 in. £540-640   *SKC*

A French silver-gilt mounted desk-clock, the frame set with four cabochon sapphires, 19th C., 3⅜ in. (86 mm.) diam. £200-230   *C*

A desk clock by Charles Frodsham, No. 2075, with lever escapement, in silver heart form case. £350-400   *WHL*

A French 8-day cast brass Victorian clock, 12 in. high, 8 i wide. £60-100   *KA*

A table timepiece, with lozenge dial flanked by blue enamelled and engine-turned panels, on a lapis lazuli base, 8.50 cm. square. £440-600   *P*

A French mahogany regulateur de table, the circular going barrel movement with countwheel strike on bell, anchor escapement and gridiron pendulum, 21 in. high. £420-500   *C*

A black enamelled timepiece, with a quarter push-repeat movement, the silver case stamped 925 and with Swiss poincons, 6 cm. high. £250-350   *P*

A black marble and green ony desk strut clock, dial signed Cartier, with lever movement on folding ormolu leg signed Cartier 2198; folding gilt tool leather case, 6½ in. (17 cm.) high. £1,800-2,200   *C*

An ormolu-mounted malachite vase clock, of Louis XVI design, with enamel-set horizontal band dial, 11 in. high. £900-1,100   *C*

A Louis XVI Ormolu and Sevres Bleu Lapis porcelain tripod vase clock, the movement contained in the tapering body with two enamel-set concentric dials, 12 in. (30.5 cm.) high. £2,600-3,000   *C*

A French Empire Burr Maple regulateur de table, dial signe Lepaute Hr. de l'Empr. & Roy Place du Palais Royal, with countwheel strike on bell and deadbeat pin wheel escapement, gridiron pendulum with knife edge balance, 17½ in (44 cm.) high. £1,750-1,950 *C*

French striking clock, dated
uly, 1835, modelled from the
'. Front of Reims Cathedral,
e countwheel circular
ovement with silk suspended
endulum and countwheel
trike on a gong in the wooden
ase, 22½ in. (57 cm.) high.
400-460 *C*

A 'boudoir' timepiece, the fusee
verge movement signed by 'Jne.
Tarault a Paris', 16 cm. high.
£850-1,000 *SKC*

A D. Allard & Cie. musical
apostle clock, with a cylinder
musical movement playing 6
airs, early 20th C., Swiss, 40 in.
(102 cm.) high. **£520-600** *SB*

n oak hall clock, with anchor
capement, triple chain fusee
d quarter-hour striking on 9
bular bells, with an
scription dated 1897, 96 by 56
21 in., c. 1891. **£1,300-
500** *SB*

An 18th C. ship's
hour glass, 8 in.
£300-345 *TJ*

A Symphonion clock, with 11⅞
in. disc movement, clock
movement with locking-plate
striking, 78½ in. high, with 10
discs. **£2,000-2,500** *CSK*

A Creil et Montereau easel
clock, damaged, 46 cm. overall,
printed mark, c. 1880. **£170-
260** *SBe*

A red marble and bronzed
mystery clock, the drum
movement with countwheel
strike on gong, 32 in. high.
£1,000-1,300 *C*

late 19th C. French calendar
ock, with brocot
scapement, hour and half-hour
triking, with moon phase, day,
ate, month and leap year dials,
½ in. **£360-460** *SBe*

A 19th C. French travelling
clock, with striking and silk
suspension movement, by
Varques & Marchand, 8¾ in.
£190-210 *A*

An early French 8-day alarm
clock, in cast brass case, Maviez
of Paris, 6 in. high, c. 1830.
£300-400 *KA*

A two day marine chronometer
by H. G. Blair, makers to the
Admiralty, in a brass bound
coromandel box, c. 1870. **£400-
600**   *AM*

A two-day marine chronometer,
the movement with going
barrel, spring detent
escapement, Guillaume
balance, spiral steel spring with
terminal curve, the dial plate
signed 'Paul Ditisheim, Central
Second Marine Chronometer,
Seven Swiss Patents', diam. of
bezel 123 mm. **£1,900-2,300**
S

A two day marine chronomet
by John Poole, maker to the
Admiralty, with brass gimba
and mahogany case with flus
handles, c. 1855-75. **£400-
650**   *AM*

An 18 ct. gold lever keyless
watch, by J. W. Benson, the
three-quarter-plate movement
inscribed The Ludgate Best
London Make, bi-metallic
compensated balance with
blued spring, 52 mm.,
hallmarked London 1912.
£350-420   *SBA*

An 18 ct. gold keyless lever
watch, by J. W. Benson,
Ludgate Hill, 'The Field', no.
A4871, the three-quarter plate
movement with compensation
balance and gold cuvette,
hallmarked 1912, 51 mm. **£260-
320**   *SB*

A gold quarter-repeating
cylinder watch, the movemen
with plain three-arm balance,
parachute and compensation
curb repeating on gongs, gilt
cuvette signed Breguet No.
2647, 57 mm. diam. **£6,600-
7,600**   *C*

Left
An early silver pair-cased verge
watch, signed Nat.
Chamberlaine London, with
pierced cock and foot with
regulation work, outer case
horn covered with silver pique
(damage to horn, decoration
rubbed), 54 mm. diam. **£500-
620**   *C*

A Swiss gold dual-time cylinder
watch, with independent
seconds, Lepine-calibre
movement with standing
barrels and compensation curb,
inscribed Breguet a Paris, 60
mm. diam. **£2,400-2,700**   *C*

An 18 ct. gold lever watch, by
Campbell & Company, Belfast,
no. 53450, the three-quarter
plate movement with
compensation balance, 56 mm.,
hallmarked indistinctly 1893.
£500-550   *SB*

A gold Repousse pair-cased
Verge watch, signed Jno. Berry
Manchester, gold champleve
dial also signed, case embossed
with Rebecca at the Well, 60
mm. diam. **£2,800-3,200**   *C*

An 18 ct. gold hunting-cased ever watch, by E. J. Dent, no. 2031, the full-plate movement ith chain fusee and diamond ndstone, 49 mm., hallmarked 854. **£420-480** *SB*

A gilt-metal pair-cased verge watch, movement signed Delahoyde Dublin 825, unusually pierced cock, 54 mm. diam. **£150-190** *C*

A gold pair-cased cylinder watch, plain three-arm steel balance, gold 'scape wheel, cock signed Berkeley Square, dust cover Dwerrihouse Carter & Son, London, 1812, 54 mm. diam. **£460-520** *C*

gold freesprung lever keyless atch, ¾-plate movement gned Kew Certificate Class A .6 Marks No. 14768 Cahoon ros. 16 & 18 Castle Place elfast, freesprung with ercoil repeating on gongs, ld cuvette, dial signed Golay ondon 1886, maker's mark S) on case, 53 mm. diam. **,300-3,600** *C*

An 18 ct. gold keyless lever watch, by Halford & Sons, 43 Fenchurch Street, London, no. 2356, the three-quarter plate movement with compensation balance and gold cuvette, hallmarked 1902, 50 mm. **£280-350** *SB*

A silver pair cased pocket watch (hallmarked 1803), with fusee verge movement, signed 'Jn. Eginton, Coventry, No. 3288'. **£240-300** *SKC*

gold pair-cased cylinder atch, movement signed Tho. udge W. Dutton London 1400, graved half-plate foot, steel cape wheel and three-arm alance, cases plain London, 789. **£600-700** *C*

An 18 ct. gold lever watch, by Lowe & Sons, Chester, no. 1528 35544, the three-quarter plate movement with compensation balance and gold cuvette, 53 mm., hallmarked 1873. **£330-390** *SB*

An 18 ct. gold hunting cased keyless lever watch, by J. Hargreaves, no. 53066, the three-quarter plate movement with compensation balance and gold cuvette, hallmarked 1892, 57 mm. **£350-400** *SB*

A Swiss gold keyless lever watch, movement repeating on gongs, gold cuvette, dial signed Manoah Rhodes & Sons, Limited Bradford, case with monogram, 53 mm. diam. **£1,200-1,400** *C*

A mid-Victorian 18 ct. gold cased pocket watch, with keywound jewelled three-quarter plate fusee, English lever movement signed 'Manoah Rhodes and Sons, Bradford, No. 85370'. **£400-470** *SKC*

An 18 ct. gold keyless lever fob watch, by Thos. Russell and Son, the movement with bi-metallic compensated balance and inscribed Russell's machine made lever Gold Medal Paris 1878, 38 mm., hallmarked Chester 1880. **£230-300** *SBA*

A 22 ct. gold hunter-cased keyless pocket chronometer, ¾ plate movement signed James Richardson & Son Coventry & London 77598, Earnshaw's spring detent escapement, gold cuvette, Chester 1895, 54 mm. diam. **£1,000-1,200** *C*

An 18 ct. gold lever watch, b Thomas Russell & Sons, Liverpool, no. 97710, the thre quarter plate movement with compensation balance and go cuvette, with a gold chain, 5 mm., hallmarked 1898. **£600 650** *SB*

A gold hunter-cased keyless lever chronograph, ¾ plate movement signed T. R. Russell, 18 Church St. Liverpool No. 87844, overcoil to blued spring, gold cuvette, London 1833, 54 mm. diam. **£690-800** *C*

An 18 ct. gold three-quarter plate pocket watch, with jewelled English lever fusee movement, inscribed 'Straub and Hebting, 38, Blackman Street, Southwark — No. 02386' **£220-260** *SKC*

A gold quarter-repeating duple watch, the movement signed Vulliamy London aaai, plain three arm steel balance, unusual pierced foot, signed cuvette (London 1835), 47 mm diam. **£850-1,000** *C*

A French gold quarter-repeating and musical watch, converted to lever escapement repeating on gongs, music played by a pinned disc on 27 combs, gilt cuvette, enamel dial, 57 mm. diam. **£1,500-1,700** *C*

A French gold quarter-repeating and musical cylinder watch, music played by a pinned disc on 27 combs, gilt cuvette, 58 mm. diam. **£2,200-2,400** *C*

An 18 ct. gold hunting-cased keyless lever watch, by Nathaniel Wegg London, no 19245, the three-quarter plat movement with compensatic balance and gold cuvette, hallmarked 1882. **£350-420** *SB*

An 18 ct. gold half-hunting cased keyless lever watch, th Swiss movement with compensation balance, 48 mm hallmarked 1885. **£360-420** *SB*

A gold minute repeating keyless lever watch, with compensation balance and gold cuvette, 50 mm. **£770-880** *SB*

A French gold quarter-repeating cylinder watch, Lepine-calibre movement with compensation curb, plain three arm balance, standing barrel, repeating on gongs, gilt cuvette, 52 mm. diam. **£660-760** *C*

A Swiss gold minute-repeating keyless lever watch, fully-jewelled nickel-finished movement repeating on gongs, gold cuvette and enamel dial, 53 mm. diam. **£1,300-1,500** *C*

A French gold quarter-repeating musical cylinder watch, skeletonised backplate, plain three arm balance, the music played by a pinned disc on 27 combs, gilt cuvette signed Prevost freres a Toulouse, 59 mm. diam. **£2,600-2,800** *C*

A gold keyless lever watch, no. 27448, the three-quarter plate movement with compensation balance, hallmarked 1909, 50 mm. **£190-230** *SB*

An 18 ct. gold keyless Hunter pocket watch, quarter repeating with chronograph, Swiss fully jewelled lever movement, and repeat on two gongs. **£1800-2,000** *SKC*

Swiss gold and enamel cylinder watch, Lepine-calibre movement with plain three-arm gold balance, gold cuvette (damaged), 37 mm. diam. **£720-820** *C*

A French gold and enamel cylinder dress watch, Lepine calibre movement with gold cuvette, the case with black champleve enamel of a hunting scene, 39 mm. diam. **£520-650** *C*

A Swiss gold and enamel cylinder watch, bar movement, gold cuvette, 35 mm. diam. **£330-400** *C*

Left
A continental silver Jacquemart Verge watch, bridge-cock quarter-repeating movement, engine-turned silvered dial, 55 mm. diam. **£770-870** *C*

Swiss gold and enamel keyless lever watch, nickel-plated bar movement, gold cuvette, the case with enamel garden scene of a couple (chipped), 30 mm. diam. **£420-500** *C*

A Swiss gold and enamel hunter-cased keyless lever watch, with gold cuvette, 35 mm. diam. **£240-300** *C*

Right
A Swiss gold Jacquemart Verge watch, movement repeating on gongs with skeletonised backplate, glazed cuvette, 57 mm. diam. **£2,600-2,800** *C*

Left
An early silver form-watch case, lacking movement, later pendant, early 17th C., 32 mm. over pendant. **£800-1,000** *C*

CLOCKS APPENDIX

Barlow, Edward (1636-1716) (Booth)
Inventor of the rack repeating striking work for clocks, he also invented the cylinder escapement and patented it with William Houghton and Thomas Tompion in 1695.

Boulle, Andre Charles (1642-1723)
French cabinet maker, chaser and inlayer who invented a style of decoration using tortoiseshell, brass, silver and ivory; a Boulle clock refers to a clock which has a case veneered with this type of decoration. Boulle clocks were made throughout the life of Boulle and reproductions were made in the 19th C.

Breguet, Abraham Louis (1747-1823)
Prolific French clock and watch designer, invented a 'synchroniser', which was a device for setting watches right, and made many other developments; succeeded in business by his son Louis Antoine, retired 1833; Louis successor to L.A., b. 1804, d. 1883.

Brocot, Achille (1817-1878)
Paris, important French clockmaker, inventor of the Brocot escapement (which is a form of dead beat escapement) and the pin pallet escapement for pendulum clocks. He also designed and made perpetual calendar clocks.

Bull, Randulph
Important 16th C. English clockmaker, also keeper of the Westminster Great Clock.

Dent, E. J. (1790-1853)
English horologist of commanding ability, various premises in London, made the 'Westminster Clock' (Big Ben) following designs by Lord Grimthorpe. Succeeded by stepson Frederick who died in 1860.

Ellicot, John (1706-1772)
One of the foremost English clockmakers, invented the compensation pendulum, apprenticed to John Waters, 1687, Clockmakers' Company 1696, All Hallows, London Wall, 1696-1733.

Frodsham & Company, Charles (1810-71)
London, descended from a long line of horologists, makers of fine quality clocks, took over the business of Vulliamy in 1854. The company is still in existence.

Gaudron, P.
Paris 1690-1730, important French clock and watch maker.

Graham, George (1673-1731)
From 1695 worked with Thomas Thompion, to whom he was related. Invented dead-beat escapement and mercurial pendulum, also improved the cylinder escapement invented by Edward Barlow.

Gravell, William & Son
1820, 49 St. John Street, and until 1850, 29 Charterhouse Square, well known clockmakers, watches were wrapped in paper with equations of time.

Hocker, John
Reading, Apprenticed to John

Martin (White Gate Alley, admitted to the Clockmakers' Company in 1679 threatened by them in 1682 with prosecution for undue taking of apprentices), Hocker then apprenticed to Edward Josslin, admitted to the Clockmakers' Company 1729.

Hooke, Dr. Robert (1635-1703)
Academic, discovered the resilience of a spring is proportionate to the angle through which it has been wound, invented a timekeeper for finding the longitude at sea, a machine for wheel cutting, the anchor escapement and many other discoveries.

Huygen, Christian (1629-1695)
Mathematician and clock designer, designed a pendulum clock and a system of maintaining power; 1674 constructed a marine timekeeper.

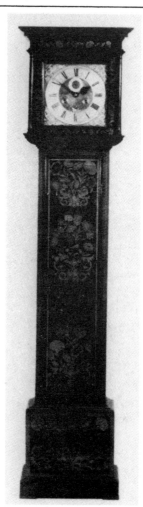

A William and Mary marquetry month duration Longcase clock, with 10½ in. square brass dial, the twin train movement with 6 pillars, outside countwheel strike and anchor escapement, Edward Burgis, London, c. 1690, 2.08 m.
£5,000-6,500   *P*

Japy, Frederic (1749-1812)
Beaucourt, France, 1799 patented clock mechanism part making machine.

Jump, Richard Thomas
London, joined Vulliamy in 1812; Joseph, his son, joined B. L. Vulliamy as an apprentice in 1827, died 1899.

Knibb, Joseph
Important British clockmaker, admitted to Clockmakers' Company, 1670, mention as of Oxon. 1677 made a turret clock for the state entrance to Windsor Castle which did service until 1829, it was one of the earliest turret clocks with brass wheels.

Lepaute, Jean, Andre (working 1748-74)
Eminent French clockmaker, improved the pin wheel escapement and made many unusual clocks, amongst these is a turret clock in the Louvre wound by an air current turning a fan.

Leroy, Chas.
Paris 1765, succeeded by Cachard 1808, signed clocks Leroy & Fils. Care must be taken not to confuse the clocks of Leroy & Fils with those of Le Roy.

Le Roy, Julien, (1686-1759)
Le Roy. Pierre,(1717-1785)
Son of Julien, eminent French clockmaker invented the duplex escapement and chronometer escapement.

Norton, Eardley
49 St. John St., Clerkenwell, maker of musical and astronomical clocks and watches. In 1771 he patented a striking mechanism.

Perigal & Duterrau
62 New Bond St., 1810-40 'Watchmaker to His Majesty'.

Poole, John (1818-67)
Chronometer maker and inventor of the auxiliary compensation.

Quare, Daniel (1648-1724)
17th C. English horologist of outstanding ability. He designed many of his own clocks and watches, patented a repeating device in 1687 and a portable weather glass in 1695.

Rayment, Richard
St. Edmunds Bury, c. 1700, noted for the Lantern clocks he made.

Tompion, Thomas (1639-1713)
Extremely important English maker of watches and clocks. He numbered all of his clocks from 1 to 542. Leading watchmaker in the court of Charles II and made some of the finest clocks in the World.

Vaucanson (b. 1709)
Noted for the automatic movements he built.

Vulliamy
Important English clockmakers. Justin: Pall Mall, 1730-75. Benjamin: son of Justin, Pall Mall, 1775-1820. Benjamin Lewis: son of Benjamin, 68 Pall Mall, an important clockmaker 1810-54.

Webster
Several generations of Websters produced clocks in London from 1675 onwards.

A Louis XVI giltwood barometer, with circular dial signed L'Ingenieur Godchaux a Paris Rue de Rivoli, the base with later mirror plate, 41 in. (104 cm.) high. **£600-720** *C*

A mahogany barometer, signed V. Alnino, Bourton on the Water, 36 in., mid 19th C. **£220-260** *SB*

mahogany clock barometer ith original pendulum ovement and silk suspension, 1840. **£1,700-1,900** *NC*

A satinwood wheel barometer by Amadio, c. 1840. **£675-725** *NC*

A rosewood wheel barometer by Balerna, Dundee with 8 in. dial, c. 1840. **£250-300** *NC*

A mahogany cased 19th C. mercurial banjo wheel barometer, the 8 in. silvered dial signed G. Broggi, warranted, with alcohol tubed thermometer. **£260-350** *SKC*

mahogany wheel barometer, e 8 in. dial inscribed D. ilesio, Kendall, the case inlaid ith rosettes and shell paterae, in. **£200-250** *SBA*

A late 18th C. wheel barometer, marked Guanziroli, Hatton Garden, length 44 in. **£310-400** *JF*

A 19th C. banjo mercurial barometer, with an 8 in. silvered dial signed 'Dom k Poneia, Aylesbury', with alcohol tubed thermometer. **£230-290** *SKC*

A 19th C. mercurial banjo barometer, the 8 in. dial is signed 'A. Guyeri, 74, Leather Lane, Holborn, London', with alcohol tubed thermometer in trunk of case. **£200-250** *SKC*

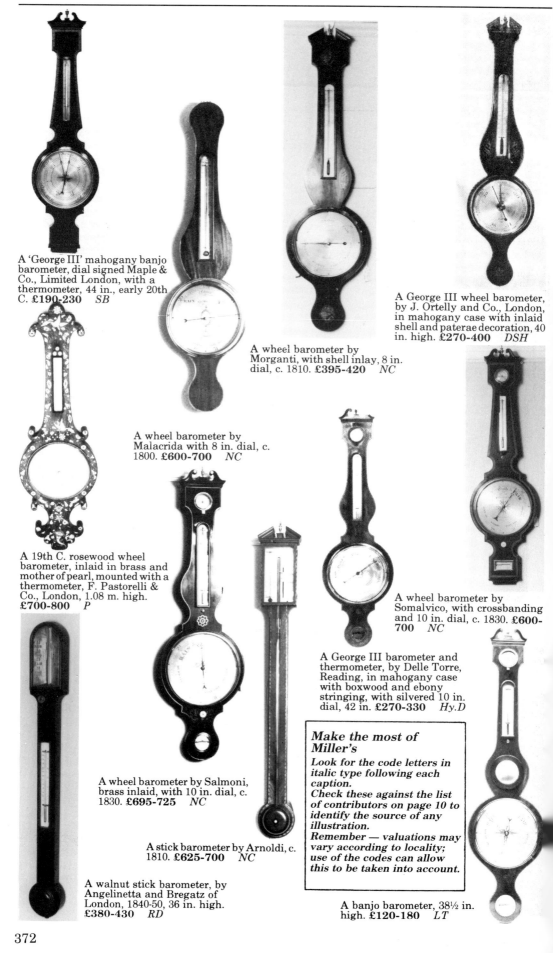

A 'George III' mahogany banjo barometer, dial signed Maple & Co., Limited London, with a thermometer, 44 in., early 20th C. **£190-230** *SB*

A George III wheel barometer, by J. Ortelly and Co., London, in mahogany case with inlaid shell and paterae decoration, 40 in. high. **£270-400** *DSH*

A wheel barometer by Morganti, with shell inlay, 8 in. dial, c. 1810. **£395-420** *NC*

A wheel barometer by Malacrida with 8 in. dial, c. 1800. **£600-700** *NC*

A 19th C. rosewood wheel barometer, inlaid in brass and mother of pearl, mounted with a thermometer, F. Pastorelli & Co., London, 1.08 m. high. **£700-800** *P*

A wheel barometer by Somalvico, with crossbanding and 10 in. dial, c. 1830. **£600-700** *NC*

A George III barometer and thermometer, by Delle Torre, Reading, in mahogany case with boxwood and ebony stringing, with silvered 10 in. dial, 42 in. **£270-330** *Hy.D*

A wheel barometer by Salmoni, brass inlaid, with 10 in. dial, c. 1830. **£695-725** *NC*

A stick barometer by Arnoldi, c. 1810. **£625-700** *NC*

A walnut stick barometer, by Angelinetta and Bregatz of London, 1840-50, 36 in. high. **£380-430** *RD*

A banjo barometer, 38½ in. high. **£120-180** *LT*

> ### Make the most of Miller's
> *Look for the code letters in italic type following each caption.*
> *Check these against the list of contributors on page 10 to identify the source of any illustration.*
> *Remember — valuations may vary according to locality; use of the codes can allow this to be taken into account.*

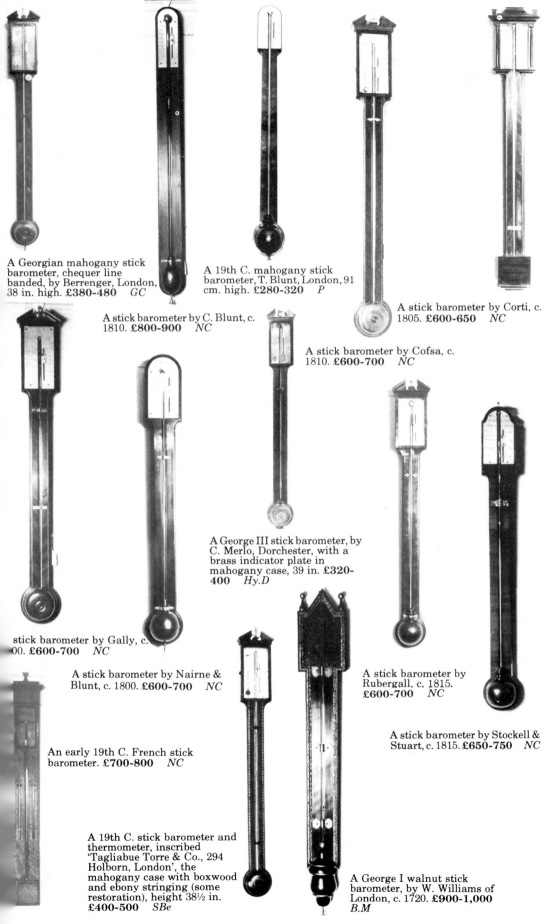

A Georgian mahogany stick barometer, chequer line banded, by Berrenger, London, 38 in. high. **£380-480** *GC*

A 19th C. mahogany stick barometer, T. Blunt, London, 91 cm. high. **£280-320** *P*

A stick barometer by C. Blunt, c. 1810. **£800-900** *NC*

A stick barometer by Corti, c. 1805. **£600-650** *NC*

A stick barometer by Cofsa, c. 1810. **£600-700** *NC*

A George III stick barometer, by C. Merlo, Dorchester, with a brass indicator plate in mahogany case, 39 in. **£320-400** *Hy.D*

stick barometer by Gally, c. 00. **£600-700** *NC*

A stick barometer by Nairne & Blunt, c. 1800. **£600-700** *NC*

A stick barometer by Rubergall, c. 1815. **£600-700** *NC*

A stick barometer by Stockell & Stuart, c. 1815. **£650-750** *NC*

An early 19th C. French stick barometer. **£700-800** *NC*

A 19th C. stick barometer and thermometer, inscribed 'Tagliabue Torre & Co., 294 Holborn, London', the mahogany case with boxwood and ebony stringing (some restoration), height 38½ in. **£400-500** *SBe*

A George I walnut stick barometer, by W. Williams of London, c. 1720. **£900-1,000** *B.M*

An octagonal slate sundial, by R. Melvin, London, 16 in. diam. **£80-120** *AM*

A brass universal equinoctial ring dial, signed E. Culpeper Fecit, 6 in. diam., c. 1730. **£1,550-1,700** *CSK*

A Butterfield dial, the folding bird gnomon with adjustable scale, inset compass (the glass replaced), with a list of towns and latitudes, signed Butterfield A Paris, 3 in. wide. **£600-700** *SBA*

A universal equinoctial sundial, by Herbert and Co., London, with silvered compass and chapter ring, with three levelling screws and quadrant, 5 in. diam., c. 1840-50. **£300-400** *AM*

A late 18th C./early 19th C. compass dial by Lietner and Heinemann, 6 in., with box, c. 1800. **£800-900** *FA*

A pocket sun dial, dated 1692 **£600-675** *A.E.F.*

Make the most of Miller's

Miller's is a price GUIDE Not a price LIST.

The price ranges given reflect the average price a purchaser should pay for similar items. Condition, rarity of design or pattern, size, colour, pedigree, restoration and many other factors must be taken into account when assessing values.

Miller's Antiques Price Guide builds up year by year to form the most comprehensive photo-reference system available. The first three volumes contain over 20,000 completely different photographs.

An 18th C. German pine diptych dial, by Stockert à Bavaria, printed scales and string gnomon, 8 cm. long. **£88-100** *P*

An Elliott Brothers brass equinoctial dial, the 1¾ in. diam. compass rose mounted on a brass platform, 3 in. wide, in shaped leather case, English, mid 19th C. **£280-320** *SB*

A J. Hicks oxidised brass universal equinoctial dial, 2½ in. diam., in black leather case, English, c. 1890's. **£250-350** *SB*

A brass miner's dial, the 5½ in. diam. compass rose inscribed Davis & Son, Derby No. 216, 11¾ in. wide, in mahogany box with leather case, English, late 19th C. **£180-260** *SB*

ebony-framed octant, with
ry scales and brass fittings,
Cameron of Liverpool, 12 in.
lius, c. 1830-40. **£140-180**
M

An early 19th C. brass and
ebony octant, by Cail,
Newcastle, with ivory scale,
vernier and nameplate, a set of
coloured filters and peephole
sight, 9 in. radius. **£270-320**
AG

An ebony octant, fitted with
bone scale and vernier, and
brass index arm and vane, in
mahogany case with three
coloured filters, English, late
19th C. **£200-280**   *SB*

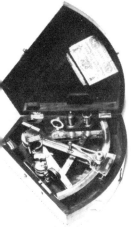

double-framed brass sextant,
th silver scale and vernier by
G. Blair and Co.., Cardiff
d Barr, in original shaped
se. **£200-300**   *AM*

A J. Coombes brass sextant,
with fruitwood handle and two
sets of coloured filters, 6½ in., in
mahogany case with three
telescopes and an N.P.L.
certificate, English, early 20th
C. **£180-240**   *SB*

A rare English boxwood
quadrant, Gunter type horary
quadrant, with a revolving
brass disc engraved with
months and five major
constellations, pin-hole sights,
c. 1700, 140 mm. radius.
£2,200-2,400   *C*

boxed Stella sextant, by
ughes & Son Ltd., last tested
24. **£300-350**   *Cas*

A brass bell-framed sextant,
with silver scale by Heath and
Co., complete with every
accessory, c. 1880. **£250-300**
AM

A good quality brass sextant, in
original condition, by Smith of
London, maker to the Royal
Naval College, Greenwich, with
platinum scale and gold
vernier, with original brass
bound mahogany case with
accessories, c. 1870. **£350-
400**   *AM*

brass pocket sextant by
roughton & Simms, London,
.2 cm. diam., inscribed Walter
ing from Charles Neale, Spril
852, with a leather case. **£220-
60**   *P*

A pocket sextant, with silver
scale by Troughton and Simms,
in original condition, c. 1860.
£60-100   *AM*

A combined miner's dial and theodolite, by Negretti & Zambra, with alternative cross-sights and altitude scale with telescope and level. **£330-390** *CSK*

A large brass theodolite by Troughton and Simms, London, c. 1870-80. **£200-300** *AM*

A Troughton & Simms 'Y' brass theodolite, 11½ in. high, in mahogany case, English, late 19th C. **£360-440** *SB*

A mid-19th C. 2¾ in. brass refracting telescope, signed Dollond, London, with rack-and-pinion focusing, with extension tube, three eye-pieces, and two filters, 43 in., English. **£600-700** *SB*

A Troughton & Simms theodolite, with oxidised brass sighting telescope, 10½ in. long, in mahogany case, English, early 20th C. **£300-380** *SB*

A complex hand held clinometer and compass by Elliott. **£40-60** *AM*

A 3 in. Negretti & Zambra refracting telescope on stand, length of tube 44½ in., in wooden case, English, mid-19th C. **£800-900** *SB*

A 3 in. J. Lizars brass refracting telescope, 37 in. long, with sighting telescope, in wooden carrying case, and extra eye-piece with solar filter, Scottish, early 20th C. **£350-420** *SB*

A 2½ in. refracting brass telescope, by Powell & Lealand No. 170 Euston Road, London with five eyepieces, tube lengt 30 in. **£390-450** *CSK*

A good 19th C. brass three-inc refracting terrestrial telescop by W. Watson & Sons of Holborn, main tube 42 in. **£440-600** *PS*

A 3 in. brass refracting telescope, the brass tube 42½ in. long, focusing by rack and pinion with sighting telescope mounted at side, 48 in. high, English, mid-19th C. **£690-800** *SB*

A late 18th C. brass reflecting telescope, in original condition. **£350-500** *AM*

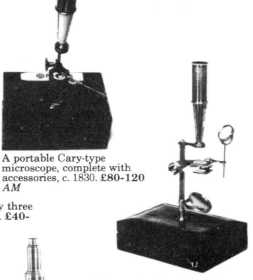

2¼ in. brass refracting table
escope, with rack and pinion
cusing, extended length 39
, with two tubes and two
ises, English, c. 1860-1870
30-430   *SBe*

A small brass and ivory three
draw telescope. (closed). £40-
50   *AM*

A portable Cary-type
microscope, complete with
accessories, c. 1830. £80-120
AM

six-draw monocular, with an
ory outer tube, 4.5 cm. diam.,
a red leather case. £77-100

A Cuff-type microscope, by
Dollond, London, with 6
objectives (one incomplete),
ocular, screw fine focusing,
bullseye, and sub-stage mirror.
£1,600-1,900   *CSK*

A Carpenter 'Cary Type' brass
pocket microscope, signed
Carpenter, 24 Regent Str.,
London, with mahogany case
containing various accessories,
English, early 19th C. £200-
300   *SB*

A Culpeper-type lacquered
brass microscope, with 5
objectives, one ocular and other
accessories. £880-1,000
CSK

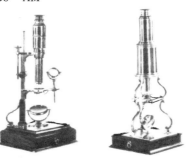

late Victorian brass drum
croscope engraved 'L.Simon,
uth Shields', 10 in. high,
ntained in 11 in. mahogany
x with accessories. £100-
0   *AG*

A vertical portable microscope,
with dividing objective, ocular,
focusing stage and leather-
covered case. £290-350   *CSK*

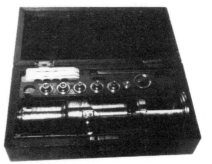

A Martin-type microscope, with
rack and pinion focusing and
ivory slides, c. 1830-40. £80-
120   *AM*

A large folding microscope, by
C. W. Dixey, New Bond Street,
with seven objectives, one
ocular and mahogany case.
£460-530   *CSK*

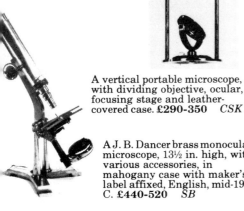

A J. B. Dancer brass monocular
microscope, 13½ in. high, with
various accessories, in
mahogany case with maker's
label affixed, English, mid-19th
C. £440-520   *SB*

A Dollond brass monocular
microscope, of bar-limb
construction, 13½ in. high, with
various accessories, in
mahogany case, English, mid-
19th C. £170-250   *SB*

A Leitz microscope, No. 271977, with monocular and binocular body, four objectives and six other objectives, seven eyepieces and two condensers, in wood case. £670-770   *CSK*

A Powell & Lealand brass monocular microscope, signed Powell & Lealand, 170 Euston Road, London, 1860, 14 in. high, with mahogany box of accessories, English, c. 1860. £1,100-1,300   *SB*

A brass monocular microscope, 14 in. high, with three oculars, two objectives, live box and stage forceps, in mahogany case, English, late 19th C. £180-240   *SB*

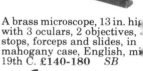

A brass microscope, 13 in. hig with 3 oculars, 2 objectives, stops, forceps and slides, in mahogany case, English, mi 19th C. £140-180   *SB*

A Ross brass field monocular microscope, No. 4090, 13 in. high, in mahogany case with eyepiece, 2 objectives, bench condenser and stage forceps, English, late 19th C. £200-250   *SB*

A Boettger brass binocular microscope, 14 in. high, one pair of oculars, one objective, polariser and live box in mahogany case, with two boxes of slides, Australian, c. 1880's. £200-240   *SB*

A binocular microscope, signe Smith & Beck London and dated 1851, complete with original case and accessories. £350-450   *AM*

A J. Swift brass binocular microscope, 16 in. high, in a mahogany case containing a set of accessories, English, late 19th C. £550-650   *SB*

A J. Swift & Son binocular microscope, 13½ in. high, with one pair of oculars, one ocular with cross-hairs, 4 objectives and polariser, in mahogany case, English, late 19th C. £380-430   *SB*

A Swift & Son brass binocular microscope, 13 in., in oak case with 2 eye-pieces, sub-stage condenser with patch stops, tweezers, bench condenser and polariser, English, late 19th C. £200-250   *SB*

A Watson's royal binocular and monocular microscope, with 8 objectives, two pairs of coulars, polariser and analyser, lucida attachment, nosepiece illuminator and other accessories, in mahogany case. £600-700   *CSK*

An early 19th C. microsco lamp, with blue glass filte with box, 12 in. high. £90 120   *FA*

microscope lamp, with
ndenser and blue filter, in
oden carrying case, English,
te 19th C. **£120-170** *SB*

A Beck brass dissecting
microscope, 19 cm. square, in a
case. **£180-220** *P*

A microscope lamp, on a brass
stand by R. & J. Beck, London,
with bull's-eye condenser.
£120-150 *P*

Bockett microscope lamp, by
llins, London, on a brass
se, with a glass shade and
lector, in a case. **£100-130**

A Malby's terrestrial globe,
with a steel support and
enclosed by a band, dated
Dublin, 1895, 18 by 16 in. (46 by
41 cm.). **£150-250** *SB*

A small size celestial globe by
John Lothian, St. Andrews Sq.,
Edinburgh, dated 1828, 10 in.
diam., in good condition. **£250-
350** *AM*

Left
An early miniature terrestrial
globe signed 'A New Globe of
the Earth by L. Cushee,' mid-
18th C., 7 cm. diam. **£650-
750** *C*

mid-19th C. Fletchers
restrial globe, by 'W. & A. K.
hnston, Geographers to the
een, Edinburgh', 18 in.
am., 12 in. **£300-370** *DWB*

A Victorian celestial globe,
inscribed 'published by J. Wyld,
Charing Cross, East, next door
to the post office, London', 24 in.
diam. **£500-620** *WW*

A pair of miniature terrestrial
and celestial globes signed Bale
and Woodward, 7.5 cm. diam.
£750-900 *C*

An early 19th C. pocket globe, inscribed 'Lane's Improved Globe, London', in a wooden outer case lined with a constellation 'Map of the Heavens'. **£300-350**   *SKC*

A pocket globe by Lane, London, in original conditio 1807. **£300-350**   *AM*

A 20 in. globe, painted with the names of oceans, continents and mountain ranges represented in relief, in brass mounting, 32 in. high, probably French, 20th C. **£250-350**   *SB*

A very early 19th C. orrery, showing the different phases the moon as it orbits round th earth by W. J. Shaw, 6¾ in. base. **£550-650**   *FA*

A Parkes and Hadley's patent orrery, the cast base divided into seasons and months, 9¾ in. diam., English, c. 1900. **£160-220**   *SB*

An early 19th C. paste board armillary sphere, inscribed a Paris chez Fz. Delamarche et Chles. Dien rue du Jardinet No. 13, 52 cm. high. **£680-740**   *P*

An A. T. Harris barograph, th fine stylus recording on clockwork drum, with thermometer at side and drawe below, 15 in. long, English, early 20th C. **£180-250**   *SB*

Vernier calipers in brass and steel, by Troughton and Simms, London. **£50-80**   *AM*

A mahogany waywiser, with iron-banded wheel, signed G. Adams Inst. Maker to His Majesty, Fleet St., London. **£950-1,100**   *CSK*

An early 19th C. gyroscope with glass dome, 12 in. hig **£380-440**   *FA*

A rosewood backstaff with fruitwood scales by Gabriel Stokes, Dublin, 23 in. high, c. 1730-40. **£1,500-1,800**   *AM*

Right
A mariner's circle, with four eyepieces, filters, scaled microscope, two alternative handles and fitted case, the dial engraved C. West, 5 Cursitor Street, Chancery Lane, radius 4½ in. **£1,200-1,500**   *CSK*

Right
A lacquered bronze ellipsograph, inscribed Farey Invt., London, in fitted sharkskin case. **£470-550** *CSK*

mid 19th C. brass sighting
strument, for taking bearings
ships in convoy, with box.
270-300 *FA*

mid 19th C. case of steel
putating instruments with
ny handles, including saws,
ves and scalpels, bone
ters, tourniquet and curved
dles and silk thread, the case
mahogany and lined with
e silk velvet, 18 in. long.
0-120 *AM*

MEDICAL INSTRUMENTS

Of all medical instruments, the
most sought after are the cased
sets, and the earlier the better.
18th and early 19th Century
instruments tend to have ivory
handles and the bleeding knives
have tortoiseshell cases. During
the middle of the 19th Century
they were changed to plain ebony
handles which were then
chequered (like a gun stock) to
stop the surgeon's hand from
slipping.

Instruments for post-mortem
operations are not as sought after
since the interest is on instruments
for operating on the living, not the
dead. Early para-medical
accessories such as ear-trumpets,
artificial limbs and false teeth,
early stethoscopes, medicine
spoons, pap boats — in silver,
plate, pewter, brass, porcelain,
wood, ivory, etc., etc., are also
collected.

Professor Lister's pronouncement
in 1872, that all instruments
should be sterilised before
operating, spelled the end of
decorative ivory or wood handles,
since these cannot be properly
sterilised, and from that time on
they were made with chrome-plated
handles. These are nowadays
greeted with stifled yawns by
collectors, but almost anything
else which is pre-1870 is of
interest.

For further information read
'Antique Medical Instruments' by
Elizabeth Bennion, Sotheby
Parke-Bernet Publications, £28.00,
available from Arthur Middleton
Ltd., 12 New Row, Covent Garden,
London WC2N 4LF.

A John Browning brass
spectroscope, with two prisms,
collimator with adjustable slit
width, 12 in. high, and two eye-
pieces, English, late 19th C.
£280-320 *SB*

A large and comprehensive
mahogany chest containing 3
tiers of surgeons instruments
for amputation, trepanning,
blood transfusion, etc., a plaque
on the lid inscribed 'Presented
to Dr. Williamson, in memory of
Mrs. Greenwood, his patient for
many years, 1896', by Arnold &
Sons, London, brass-bound box
is 18 by 11½ by 5¼ in. £250-
350 *AM*

small leather-bound case of 6
ory handled scalpels, by
eiss, London, 6 in. long, c.
860. £25-35 *AM*

A leather case containing ivory
handled eye-surgeon's
instruments, fine needles and
thread, scissors etc., by Weiss,
London, 8¾ by 4¾ in., c. 1880-90.
£30-40 *AM*

A doctor's leather wallet or
pocket set of small instruments
(some silver or tortoiseshell),
including scalpels, tweezers,
probes, guide, needles and silk
thread, folded length 5½ in., c.
1870. £35-45 *AM*

Georgian velvet lined
ahogany case containing
ony and ivory handled
panning instruments, the
se closed is 9 by 7½ in., c. 1820.
50-200 *AM*

A small Georgian mahogany
cased set of instruments for
minor surgery with
tortoiseshell bleeding knives,
ivory handled scalpels, etc.,
case 7¾ by 3¼ in., 1820. £50-
60 *AM*

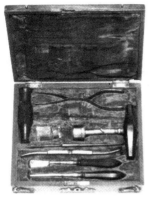

A trephining set, with ebony handles, contained in a velvet lined mahogany case, the perforator missing, 22 cm. wide. **£300-330**   *P*

A late Victorian fitted leather case containing drainage instruments (trocars and canulas), in silver, steel and ebony, case measures 9 by 3¾ in., c. 1870-80. **£25-35**   *AM*

A 19th C. rosewood and br inlaid case of drawing instruments, with an ivory r 26 cm. wide. **£44-60**   *P*

A 1905 pattern field surgeon's wicker panier, fitted with a set of instruments by Mayer & Meltzer, a folding lamp, silk and gut containers, syringes, etc., 77 by 34 cm. **£250-300**   *P*

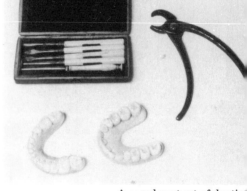

A cased part set of dentist knives, a set of carved ivo dentures and a pair of ste extracting pincers, c. 1820 **£290-340**   *Bon*

A set of dental scaling instruments, the 6 assorted scrapers screw into a turned ivory handle; early 19th C., the box 3 by 2½ in. **£60-70**   *AM*

An early ophthalmoscope, with an ivory handle, in a velvet lined leather case, length of case 4¾ in., length of assembled instrument 8 in., c. 1880. **£20-25**   *AM*

A small brass enema pump w fittings, in mahogany case, in. long, late 19th C. **£20-2** *AM*

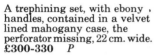

A brass enema or douche pump, with turned wood handle, by Arnold & Sons, London, 14 in. long, c. 1860-70. **£20-25**   *AM*

An early 19th C. cupping and bleeding set, the inside lined with red velvet and containing 6 assorted cupping glasses, lamp and scarifier, box 11½ by 6¾ by 4 in. **£100-150**   *AM*

polychromed European
ence barber-surgeon's bowl,
d 19th C., 9 in. diam., 3½ in.
ep. **£60-80**   *AM*

A cupping and bleeding set in a
silk-lined leather case, with
cupping glass, spirit bottle and
lamp and 12 bladed scarifier, by
'Coxetter University College,
London', in original condition,
c. 1870-80. **£80-120**   *AM*

A large English oval brass
barber-surgeon's shaving or
bleeding basin, with the
original owner's coat of arms
inscribed on one side, late 17th
or early 18th C. **£200-250**
AM

Three early 19th C. brass
scarifiers. **£50-65** each   *FA*

A decorated pottery inhaler,
transfer printed 'Maws Double
Valved Earthenware Inhaler',
10 in. high, 1890. **£15-20**   *AM*

ate 19th C. French-made
ray or inhaler, of chrome
ted brass with a porcelain
tainer and interchangeable
ry nozzles, height 18 in. **£80-
0**   *AM*

Mid 19th C. steel and brass
trephine, with a chequered
ebony handle, 5 in. high (a hand
turned instrument for drilling a
hole in the skull). **£20-25**   *AM*

A 12 bladed brass-cased spring-
loaded scarifier (or
scarificator), with quick-release
knob and trigger action, and
with adjustable depth for the
blades, box 2 in. square by 3 in.
high, mid 19th C. **£30-40**   *AM*

A mid 19th C. dental extraction
instrument, a steel shank and
hook with an ebony handle,
commonly known as a 'key', 6.
in. long. **£30-35**   *AM*

o Liston-type amputating
ves, with ebony handles, c.
0. **£10-15** each   *AM*

An early 19th C. surgeon's saw,
with carved ebony handle,
length 15 in. **£75-100**   *AM*

selection of 19th C. surgeon's
ws. **£20-40** each   *MA*

A 19th C. vaginal speculum in
wood and steel. **£150-180**
MA

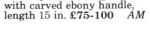

17th C. French steel
repanning elevator, 7 in. long.
80-120**   *RM*

A mid 19th C. staghorn-bound
vet's pocket knife, the back of
the main blade stamped 'To
Strike Fire', and with 2 other
phleams (or bleeding knives),
by Thomas Turner & Co.,
Sheffield, 4½ in. long. **£40-50**
AM

A phrenology pottery head, c.
1870, 10 in. high. **£50-60**   *FA*

A small silver plated ear trumpet or hearing aid, 4 in. high, mid 19th C. £30-35   *AM*

A Gibson pewter medicine spoon, c. 1850, 5 in. long. £4 58   *MA*

CAMERAS

Although the first fixed photographic image was achieved in 1816 the first cameras of general collecting interest are the 'wet-plate' cameras of 1840-1880. Cameras have seen a dramatic upsurge of collecting interest, with much interest being paid to the early Leica, Zeiss, Contax and Rollei. This era, 1920-1950, was the period of great, technical development, and interesting and unusual features always add to value.

Two 19th C. ebonised stethoscopes, 7 in. high. £30 each   *MA*

A Gandolfi Universal 5 by 4 hand-and-stand camera, with Tessar 16.5 cm. lens in Compur shutter. £130-190   *CSK*

A Georgian ivory handled tortoiseshell strap tongue scraper, 8 in., and another of silver coloured metal 5¼ in. £70-90 the pair   *Bon*

Left

A wet-plate camera, 4 by 5 in., with single element lens inscribed C. Shepherd, 97 Farringdon St., London, 4280, English, c. 1860. £670-800 *SB*

An Ottewill wet-plate slidi box camera, c. 1845. £600 800   *VC*

A fine Dallmeyer Tailboard wetplate camera, 4½ in. by 7¼ in., with Ross No. 2 Symmetrical 4 in. f16 lens, English, c. 1870. £350-450 *SB*

A Dallmeyer 3¼ by 6½ slidi box stereoscopic/mono wet-plate camera, with Dallmey brass-bound portrait lens wi Waterhouse stops (lacks ste lenses), 1860's. £2,200-2,400   *CSK*

A 5 by 4 sliding-box wet-plate camera, Ross Petsval-type brass-bound portrait lens No. 10626, with rack focusing and detachable plate storage compartment containing three d.d.s. £880-980   *CSK*

A Soho Tropical reflex ¼ plate camera, c. 1910. £500-1,000 dependent on condition, size, etc.   *VC*

An Ica Bebe camera, 6 by 9 cm. plate format, c. 1910. £70-100   *VC*

fine Zeiss Ikon Adoro 230/3
ropical folding plate camera,
d four single plate holders in
iginal box, German, c. 1936.
50-350   *SB*

A tropical folding plate camera,
6.5 by 9 cm., with Ruo-Optik
Iricentor 12 cm., f6.8 lens.
Probably Austrian, c. 1920.
£120-150   *SB*

A Gandolfi 2¼ by 3¼ tropical
hand-and-stand camera, with
Dallmeyer Stigmatic lens in
Compur shutter and Dallmeyer
wide-angle Anastigmat 3¼ in.
f 6.5 lens with panel. **£380-440**   *CSK*

Compass miniature plate
mera by Le Coultre, c. 1937.
50-500   *VC*

A quarter-plate tropical
Sanderson camera, with Ross
homocentric 5 in. f 6.3 lens in
Ilex shutter, film-pack adapter,
three d.d.s and instructions.
£260-320   *CSK*

A Una quarter-plate hand-and-
stand camera, by James A.
Sinclair & Co., London, with
Goerlitz Doppel Anastigmat
150 mm. f5.4 lens. **£660-760**
CSK

Left
An Ernemann folding reflex
camera, with Tessar 16.5 cm.
f 4.5 lens and focal-plane
shutter, 9 by 12 cm. **£100-150**   *CSK*

Marion postcard size reflex
mera, c. 1925. **£80-100**   *VC*

A 2 by 2 Dubroni hand camera
and printing frame containing
one glass negative and paper
contact print and instructions.
£1,100-1,300   *CSK*

A quarter-plate Artist twin-lens
reflex camera, by The London
Stereoscopic Co. with Ross
Zeiss Patent Anastigmat 150
mm. lens in Bausch & Lomb
aluminium pneumatic shutter.
£220-280   *CSK*

A quarter-plate Ensign folding
reflex camera, Model D with
Ross Xpres 5½ in. lens. **£160-220**   *CSK*

R

A perfect Detective falling-plate camera, by Photo-Hall, Paris, in carrying-case disguised as hand luggage (lacks lens). £70-100 *CSK*

A rare 3¼ by 3¼ Rouch's Eure Detective camera, with iris. diaphragm, sliding box focusing and changing back £330-430 *CSK*

A Newman & Guardia 5 by 4 special twin-lens reflex camera, with Anastigmatlinse 285 mm. taking-lens in N&G pneumatically controlled string-cocked shutter. £270-330 *CSK*

A forward half-plate mahog: stereo camera, Patent No. 21 with Lancaster stereo landscape lenses. £220-32(
CSK

A Welta Superfekta folding twin-lens reflex camera, with Tessar 10.5 cm. f 3.8 taking-lens. £70-80 *CSK*

A Newman and Guardia Nydia folding magazine plate camera, c. 1900. £250-350 *VC*

A Sanger-Shepherd 'The Myrioscope' stereoscopic camera, by Gaumont, and tw twelve plate push-pull magazines, in original leath: case, French, c. 1900. £100-120 *SB*

'The Kodak', a first-model Kodak factory-load box camera, No. 1156, with string-cocked barrel shutter. £1,100-1,300 *CSK*

A Royal Mail 15 exposure mahogany copying camera, by W. Butcher & Sons, London. £550-650 *CSK*

Left An early sliding box camera, 4¾ in. by 6½ in., with Imbert et Maunoury 'Vallantin' lens, 7¾ by 9¾ by 16¼ in., 19.7 by 25 by 41.5 cm., probably French, mid 19th C. £450-550 *SB*

A Kodak No. 1 factory-load box camera, No. 18931 with string-cocked sector shutter. £600-700 *CSK*

London Stereoscopic
mpany's postcard-size
g's own tropical roll-film
nera, Goerz Syntor 150 mm.
8 lens in Bausch & Lomb
ute shutter. **£330-400**
K

A Jeanneret Monobloc
stereoscopic camera, 6 cm. by 12
cm., with twin Krauss-Zeiss
Tessar 8.5 cm. f4.5 lenses with
two six plate push-pull
magazines and nine plate
holders, all in original leather
case, French, c. 1920. **£100-
140** *SB*

A Bellieni Stereo Jumelle
camera, 8 by 9 cm. for 24 single
of 12 stereo exposures, with
twin Zeiss Protar 110 mm. f8
lenses, French, 1900. **£160-
210** *SB*

An Ernemann stereo camera, c.
1910. **£60-80** *VC*

Luzo camera, 1st English roll
n camera, c. 1896. **£700-
)00** *VC*

A Richard's Homeos, the 1st 35
mm. stereo camera, c. 1913.
£750-1,000 *VC*

An Ensignette folding roll film
camera, made by Houghtons,
London, c. 1912. **£15-20** *VC*

Van Albada stereo camera, c.
)0. **£300-400** *VC*

Lizars Challenge dayspool
ding roll-film camera, with
ck symmetrical lens in Ilex
utter. **£160-220** *CSK*

A Kodak Panoram No. 1
camera, c. 1901. **£80-120** *VC*

A Lizars Challenge camera, for
roll film or plates, c. 1905. **£50-
100** *VC*

A Sinclair Tropical Una
camera, 6 by 9 cm. format, c.
1910. **£400-800** *VC*

A Maximar camera, 6 by 9 cm format, c. 1925. **£20-40**   *V*

A tropical Contessa Nettel postcard-size focal-plane camera, with Tessar 21 cm. f 4.5 lens in compound shutter. **£240-340**   *CSK*

A Kodak 3a autographic special camera, the first camera made with coupled range finder, c. 1920. **£25-30**   *VC*

A No. 3B quick focus Kodak camera, Model A by The Eastman Kodak Company, Rochester, N.Y., with pre-set focusing dial. **£95-130**   *CSK*

A Rodenstock 4 by 3 cm. roll-film camera, with Trinar-Anastigmat 5 cm. f 2.9 lens in rim-set Compur shutter. **£75-95**   *CSK*

An original model Rolliflex, c. 1929. **£25-40**   *VC*

A Newman & Guardia Sib Excelsior folding roll-film camera, with Ross Xpres 1 mm. f 4.5 lens. **£130-160**   *CSK*

A Leica II black camera, with f11 summar lens, c. 1930. **£80-150**   *VC*

A Butcher's reflex Corbine camera, a roll film reflex camera, c. 1910. **£25-40**   *VC*

An Ertel 35 mm. cine camera, c. 1920. **£200-300**   *VC*

A Zeiss Contax One camera (Zeiss equivalent of Leica), c. 1932. **£100-150**   *VC*

PHOTOGRAPHS

Although we do not attempt to illustrate photographs in this volume of Miller's it is worth noting the tremendous interest in this area of collecting. Prior to 1870 the main interest in photographs is their technical, rather than artistic, merit. The main problem here is the taking of new prints from old negatives. After the introduction of dry plates in the 1870's the subject matter, be it artistic quality or an identifiable subject become the main criteria. It is worth mentioning that Julia Margaret Cameron, for example, could not possibly have taken all the photographs ascribed to her — hence caution is required. The late 19th C. and early 20th C. saw a massive explosion in the number of photographs, hence in this period the main areas of collecting are famous subjects. Landscape studies, except if quite spectacular, command little interest.

There is also a large demand for limited editions of the work of living photograpers, particularly in America. This is an area where a discerning collector can build up a valuable collection by anticipating the popularity of a photographer.

A walnut table stereoscope, by
the London Stereoscopic &
Photographic Co., with rack
focusing, 16½ in. high. **£180-
220** *CSK*

A burr walnut Negretti &
Zambra magic table model
pedestal stereoscope, on
telescopic stand, 19 in. high,
and a quantity of stereoscopic
diapositives (some cracked).
£1,400-1,600 *CSK*

An antique Zograscope, c. 1810,
26 in. high. **£285-300** *EAN*

*Miller's Antiques Price Guide
builds up year by year to
form the most comprehensive
photo-reference system
available. The first three
volumes contain over 20,000
completely different
photographs.*

A Kinora moving picture
viewer, 12 in., 30 cm. high, with
fourteen reels depicting dogs,
clowns and comic scenes,
English, c. 1905. **£300-350**
SB

A Kinora viewer, with
magnifier focusing on to reel of
still photographs which give an
illusion of movement when
revolved by handle below, 12½
in.; 32 cm. long, with twenty-one
reels of photographs and
original box, English, c. 1910.
£330-350 *SB*

An oak Kinora folding
animated picture reel viewer,
with hand cranked mechanism.
£160-200 *CSK*

A Lapierre lampascope slide
projector (lacks reflector).
£100-150 *CSK*

A mahogany Zograscope, with
height adjustment, 23 in. high,
English, mid-19th C. **£130-
160** *SB*

A pontioscopic viewer, the
walnut graphoscope mounted
on rectangular pivoted base, 23
in.; 58.5 cm. long, Italian, c.
1870. **£120-180** *SB*

SCIENTIFIC INSTRUMENTS APPENDIX

Armillary Sphere
An instrument for demonstrating cosmological theory.

Back Staff
An early navigational instrument invented about 1590 by Captain Davies, used for taking the altitude of the sun at sea, so named because the observer used it with his back to the sun.

Butterfield Dial
Named after Michael Butterfield; a sundial, consists of an engraved base plate with adjustable gnomon and compass, reasonably accurate; most desirable are these with an octagonal base plate, silver or with the gnomon in the form of a bird.

Cary, William
Set up instrument making business in London in early 18th C.

Clinometer
An instrument for measuring slope or incline.

Daguerrotype
First photographic process available to the general public. A direct-positive process by which

only one photograph can be obtained; named after Louis Daguerre (1789-1851) who invented it c. 1830. Process superseded in 1850's by negative-positive process.

Diptych Dial
A portable folding sundial, mostly made in Germany.

Dollond
Important English instrument makers. John Dollond introduced achromatic lens for telescopes in 1758 which permitted shorter refracting telescopes. John Dollond died 1761. Peter and John, his sons, formed instrument making business in 1766, telescopes, microscopes, etc.

Equinoctial Dial
A dial whose hour scale is set parallel to the plane of the equator.

Orrery
Clockwork 18th C. successor to the armillary sphere made by George Graham for Charles Boyle, Earl of Orrery.

Scarifier
A small instrument containing a number of spring-mounted blades which, released by a trigger,

lacerate the skin for medical purposes.

Spectroscope
c. 1861 Instrument designed to examine spectra, made up of a collimator, prism and a telescop

Stereoscope 1850's-1860's
Entertainment device. Two pictures of a scene taken from slightly different angles were inserted into the viewer and whe looked at through the eye pieces the picture appeared to be three dimensional. Renewed interest i this form of entertainment in 1890's.

Trephine
An instrument for boring a hole i the skull.

Troughton and Simms
Foremost English instrument makers, theodolites, surveying instruments, telescopes, etc. Troughton brothers producing telescopes from 1782. Edward Troughton joined William Simms in partnership 1826.

Waywiser
A distance measuring device.

SILVER

The silver section remains one of the major problem areas for compilers of antiques price guides. Silver, being tied as it is to the world commodity and futures markets, tends to fluctuate quite significantly within a year. We report the state of the antique market shortly before going to press and perhaps the only consolation is that after crests and troughs the prices tend to re-establish at a fair median. The tragedy of such crests is that some antique silver is melted down to provide the raw material, which has to be sheer madness. One also hopes to show comparative prices of silver.

Small silver collectables have always been at a premium, although the prices of the more ordinary vinaigrettes, snuff boxes and caddy spoons have remained

reasonably static of late. In a recession one always finds people reassess what they are willing to pay and in this, as many other fields, the lesser quality end suffers.

It is also worthy of note that although famous makers do continue to hold their own in terms of price — some pieces now seem unreasonably high, in comparison to other contemporary pieces. I'm sure no one would argue that everything made by Hester Bateman or Paul Storr was of excellent quality. But names are certainly collectable. It would be wise to look at lesser known makers, if one is looking for a 'better' buy. However if security of investment is looked for, the famous names do seem a safe bet.

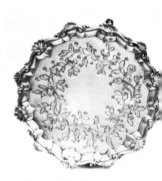

A George III silver salver, by John Carter, London, 1771, 7¼ in. (18.5 cm.) diam., 8½ oz. **£190-250**   *SBe*

An early George II Irish silver waiter, hallmarked Dublin 1777, max. diam. 7½ in. (19 cm.). **£190-220**   *SKC*

A silver George III waiter, on three hoof supports, by Richard Rugg, London, 1769, 6¼ in. (16 cm.) diam., 7½ oz. **£270-330** *SBe*

A George III circular waiter, by Hester Bateman, 6 in. diam., maker's mark, London, 1784, 155 gm. (5 oz.). **£300-400**   *SB*

A shaped circular Salver, 42.7
cm. diam., makers' mark of
Francis Dexter, London, 1840,
1,590 gm. (51.1 oz.). **£500-
700** *SB*

A pair of George III Irish
Salvers, 6½ in., possibly by
William Townsend, Dublin, c.
1760, 496 gm. (15.9 oz.). **£500-
700** *SBe*

A Queen Anne Salver on foot,
6¼ in. diam. by John Bache,
London, 1705, 231 gm. (7.4 oz.).
£400-500 *SBe*

A Victorian silver salver,
maker's marks E.K.R., London,
1873, 15½ in. (39 cm.) diam.
£450-550 *SBe*

A shaped circular salver, 40.5
cm. diam., maker's mark of D. &
C. Houle, London, 1852, 1,745
gm. (56.1 oz.). **£500-700** *SB*

A silver dessert stand, on
knopped trumpet base, 10 in.
diam., by Smith and Nicholson,
London, 1859, 20 oz. 2 dwt.
£220-300 *SBA*

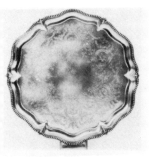

A shaped circular salver, on
three claw-and-ball supports,
36.3 cm. diam., maker's mark of
Thomas Smily, London, 1875,
engraved with a P.O.D.R. mark
for 26 November, 1867 (8),
stamped: 7868, 1,356 gm. (43.5
oz.). **£450-500** *SB*

A shaped circular Salver, 31 cm.
diam., makers' mark of William
Smiley for A.B. Savory & Sons,
London, 1859, also with the
partially erased stamp of A.B.
Savory & Sons, London, 939
gm. (30.1 oz.). **£300-440** *SB*

A Victorian silver salver, raised
on three feet, engraved with a
crest and motto, 1867, by
Stephen Smith and stamped
Goldsmith's Alliance Limited,
Cornhill, London, 11 in., 24 oz.
£200-340 *L*

Right
A two-handled tea-tray,
engraved with a cartouche, 74
cm., makers' mark of Walker &
Hall, Sheffield, 1908, stamped:
53429, 3,916 gm. (125.1 oz.).
£1,100-1,400 *SB*

Left
A George III tea tray, by
William Stud, London, 1810,
26½ in. (67 cm.), 3,313 gms.
(106.7 oz.) **£1,200-2,000** *SBe*

A George IV silver tea tray, by William Bruce, London, 1821, 27¼ in. (69 cm.), 3,203 gms. (103.2 oz.). **£1,600-2,200** *SBe*

A George III two-handled oval Tray by John Crouch II, 1808, 24 in. long, 140 oz. **£2,000-3,000** *C*

An oval two-handled tea tray, 70.5 cm. over handles, maker' mark of Frederick Elkington c Elkington & Co., Birmingham 1887, 4,257 gm. (136.8 oz.). **£900-1,500** *SB*

A Victorian silver tea tray, engraved in the centre with a crest, by Martin Hall and Company, London, 1888, 25 in. (63.5 cm.), 2,865 gms. (92.3 oz.). **£750-1,250** *SBe*

A Victorian silver tray, London, 1893, 7 oz., 10 in. wide. **£70-100** *SV*

A silver tea tray, the centre engraved with B, Edinburgh, 1910, by Hamilton & Inches, 27½ in. across handles, 120 o: **£800-900** *L*

A silver George III cake basket, 12 in. (30.5 cm.) wide, by ?, R. Gardner, London 1771, 10 oz. **£380-420** *SKC*

A silver card tray, Birmingham 1917, 5½ in. wide. **£45-55** *SV*

A silver Dutch sweetmeat basket, by Jan Buysen, Amsterdam, 1781 (the handle with later control mark), 6½ i (17 cm.) wide, 6 oz., 8 dwt. **£300 400** *SBA*

A George II shaped cake basket, with swing handle, engraved with later coat of arms, by S. Herbert & Co., 1759, 14¼ in. long, 37 oz. **£1,700-2,000** *C*

A German basket, pierced with scallework below a scroll foliage band, Augsburg 1815 (Rosenberg 306), maker's mark GCN (Rosenberg 1054), 5 in. across. **£220-280** *L*

A George III silver cake basket, by William Plummer, London, 1778, 13¾ in. (35 cm.) wide, 33 oz. **£1,100-1,400** *SBe*

A pair of silver baskets, London, 1850, 4¾ in. **£180-200** pair *MB*

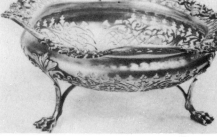

A silver fruit basket, 23 oz. by The Goldsmiths' and Silversmiths' Co. Ltd., London 1911. **£280-350** *SKC*

A two-handled circular tazza, 32.8 cm. over handles, maker's mark of Stephen Smith for Stephen Smith & Son, London, 1869, stamped: 433, 989 gm. (31.8 oz.). **£250-300**   *SB*

Miller's is a price GUIDE Not a price LIST.
The price ranges given reflect the average price a purchaser should pay for similar items. Condition, rarity of design or pattern, size, colour, pedigree, restoration and many other factors must be taken into account when assessing values.

An English openwork oval two-handled cake basket, in late 18th C. Dutch style, 33 cm. over handles, maker's mark overstruck by that of D. & J. Wellby, London, 1902, 710 gm. (22.8 oz.). **£300-400**   *SB*

A silver sweetmeat dish, Birmingham, 1912, 3½ in. high. **£30-32**   *Gs*

A shaped oval Cake Basket, 29 cm. long, maker's mark of West & Son of Dublin, Sheffield, 1910, stamped; 8459, 570 gm. (18.3 oz.). **£250-300**   *SB*

A small shaped oval Cake Basket, 28 cm. long, makers' mark of Harry Atkin for Atkin Brothers, Sheffield, 1886, 628 gm. (20.1 oz.). **£200-250**   *SB*

A pair of George III silver coasters, with turned hardwood bases, 1810, by Thomas Hayter, 12½ in. **£500-600**   *L*

A Cake Basket, 26.5 cm. diam., maker's mark Barker Brothers & Sons Ltd., Birmingham 1929, 548 gm. (17.6 oz.). **£100-150** *SB*

A small pierced epergne, 28.8 cm. high, maker's mark of Mappin & Webb, Sheffield, 1912, 965 gm. (31 oz.). **£150-200**   *SB*

An openwork oval Epergne, 49.5 cm. overall length, maker's mark of James Dixon & Sons Ltd., Sheffield, 1899, 1,433 gm. (46.3 oz.). **£500-550**   *SB*

An Edward VII silver epergne, by R. F. Mosley and Company Limited, Sheffield, 1908, 13¼ in. (34 cm.) high, 1,337 gms. (43 oz.). **£300-350**   *SBe*

An Edward VII silver-mounted cut-glass biscuit barrel, overlaid in green, by William Hutton and Sons Ltd., London, 1904, 7 in. (18 cm.). **£100-150** *SBe*

One of a pair of late-Victorian silver fruit stands, London, 1876, by F. B. Thomas of Bond Street, 154 oz. **£2,000-3,000** pr.   *PK*

A silver bowl, 3¾ in., 1881, 4 oz. **£40-60**   *MB*

A silver plate and ivory
Humidor, c. 1900, 6½ by 4¾ in.
£100-150

A circular Monteith Rose Bowl,
25 cm. diam., maker's mark of
Edward Barnard & Sons Ltd.,
London 1919, stamped, 409, 913
gm. (29.3 oz.). **£300-400**   *SB*

A Victorian parcel gilt dessert
stand, with shaped circular
frosted glass dish, by Elkington
& Co., Birmingham, 1868, 9½
in. high, 32 oz., 7 dwt.
(excluding glass). **£420-500**
SBA

A pair of Victorian silver bon
bon dishes, London, 1900, by
Hutton and Sons. **£40-60**
pair   *Gs*

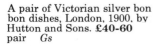

A silver bowl, probably
Portuguese, engraved with
script initials, unmarked, 18th
C., 12½ in., 15.8 oz. **£100-150**
L

One of a pair of silver bon-bon
dishes, London, 1896, 6 oz. **£60-
80 the pair**   *SV*

A pair of silver bon-bon dishes,
Birmingham, 1897. **£50-70**
SV

A pair of silver salts, slight
dent, 1784. **£80-90**   *SV*

(l) A silver trinket box, 1910, 2¼
in. diam. **£45-55**   *ST*
(r) A silver dish, Birmingham,
1919, 4 in. diam. **£25-35**   *ST*

A Japanese silver bowl, 25 cm.,
stamped mark, late 19th C.,
1,076 gm. **£300-330**   *SB*

A pair of silver salts, London,
1869. **£95-105**   *ST*

A pair of silver gilt salts,
London, 1871. **£70-80**   *SV*

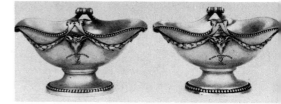

A pair of silver George III
pedestal salts, with a crest and
motto, 1775 maker's mark P.D.,
presumably an unregistered
mark of Peter Desvignes, 5¼ in.,
15.6 oz. **£450-650**   *L*

A boxed set of silver salts and spoons; salts, London, 1898; spoons, London, 1897. **£130-150** *ST*

A silver sauce tureen, by Thomas Robins, London, 1807, 9½ in. wide, 33 oz. **£500-700** *EAN*

A set of 4 silver salts and spoons, Birmingham, 1898, 5½ oz., in box. **£95-105** *SV*

A pair of foreign silver gilt salt cellars, also included are two salt spoons, 12 by 5 cm., 17 oz. **£150-200** *SKC*

A George III entree dish and cover, fully marked by William Fountain, London, 1812, the handle by another maker, 60 oz., 11¼ in. (28.5 cm.) wide. **£500-800** *SKC*

Left

An entree dish and cover, 14 in. (35 cm.) wide, by Henry Wilkinson and Co., Sheffield 1850, 52 oz. **£550-650** *SKC*

A George I silver sugar caster, engraved with armorials, marked on base and cover, by Isaac Liger, London, 1722, 8¼ in. (21 cm.) high, 420 gms. (13.5 oz.), scratch weight 14=1. **£1,000-1,500** *SBe*

A pair of silver-plated Victorian sauce tureens, by Martin Hall & Co., 9½ in. wide. **£200-250** *L*

A pair of silver George III entree dishes and covers, by William Sumner, London, 1804, 15 in. (38 cm.), 74 oz. **£1,300-1,500** *SBe*

A silver George III soup tureen, a shield of arms engraved to either side, 1816, by Benjamin Smith II and Benjamin Smith Jnr., 14½ in. across handles, 131 oz. **£3,000-3,200** *L*

A gadroon bordered oblong entree dish, cover and handle, 27 cm. long, maker's mark of Elkington & Co. Ltd., Birmgingham, 1907, the handle unmarked, 1,636 gm. (52.5 oz.). **£300-400** *SB*

A George II baluster caster, 6½ in. high, marked on base and cover, by Charles Hatfield, London 1731, 260 gm. (8.3 oz.). **£350-450** *SBe*

A set of 3 Victorian 10¾ in. oval silver entree dishes, Birmingham 1862, makers Elkington & Co., 137 oz. **£1,200-1,500** *PWC*

A pair of George II baluster shaped castors, London, 1743, by Samuel Wood, 5¾ in., 10 oz. **£500-600**   *DWB*

A silver pepperette, by R. Peaston, London, 1780, 5½ in. high. **£125-175**   *EAN*

A silver pepper pot, Birmingham, 1922, 2½ in. high. **£20-25**   *EAN*

A silver pepper pot, Birmingham, 1928, 3 in. high **£30-35**   *EAN*

A George III sugar basket, with gilt interior, Peter and Anne Bateman, London, 1775, 7.75 oz. **£300-400**   *WW*

A silver sugar basket by William Abdy, London, 1798, 6 in. wide. **£600-750**   *EAN*

A George III octagonal sugar basket, 5¾ in. wide, marked o base and swing handle, by William Frisbee, London, 179 271 gm. (8.7 oz.). **£300-380**   *SBe*

A Maltese silver sugar bowl and cover, 4 marks on base: M crowned, an eagle displayed, a diamond crowned, and AT above a turret, c. 1770, 5 in. high. **£410-490**   *L*

A silver sugar basin, Birmingham, 1913, 5½ oz. **£65-70**   *SV*

A Maltese silver sugar bowl and cover, 3 marks; an open hand, an M and a maker's mark GC for Guiseppe Cousin, c. 1790, 5½ in. high. **£500-700**   *L*

A George II silver mug, later embossed, 3½ in. high. **£145-175**   *EAN*

A Georgian silver christening mug, London, 1805, by C. Barnes, 3 in. high. **£125-150**   *ST*

A silver half pint mug, London, 1823, probably George Knight, 4¼ in. **£150-250**   *EAN*

A silver child's mug, London, 1869, Hands & Son, 3½ in. high. **£100-135** *EAN*

A silver child's mug, London, 1836, by J. Angell, 3½ in. **£180-220** *EAN*

silver embossed mug, ndon, 1873, Robert Harper, in. high. **£100-150** *EAN*

A Victorian silver mug, with gilt interior, maker's mark G.M.J., London, 1888, 6½ in. high, 18½ oz. **£330-360** *SBe*

A silver Christening mug, Birmingham, 1903. **£45-50** *SV*

ilver tankard by Thomas son, with Britannia ndard, 1720, 4¼ in. high. 0-320 *MB*

An early George II Scottish silver tankard, engraved with inscription, hallmarked Edinburgh, 1737, height 4 in. (10 cm.). **£220-250** *SKC*

A George II baluster mug, inscribed 'I.B. Sept. 7, 1747', by John Elston, Exeter, 1747, 4 in. (10 cm.) high, 5½ oz. **£270-330** *SBe*

silver mug, Birmingham, 18, 4 in. high. **£50-60** *EAN*

silver banded tankard, ndon, 1788, by R.W., 6 in. gh, 23½ oz. **£500-600** *EAN*

A Queen Anne tankard, inscribed E.P.A.H., 1713, the shaped terminal later initialled H.T.A., 6¾ in. high, by Humphrey Payne, London, 1706, 623 gm. (20 oz.). **£1,500-2,000** *SBe*

A Queen Anne tankard, by Colin McKenzie, Edinburgh, 1711, Assay Master Edward Penman, 8½ in. high, 40 oz. **£5,500-7,000** *C*

A George III cylindrical Tankard, 7½ in. high, by John Langlands, Newcastle, 1803, 707 gm. (22.7 oz.). **£500-800** *SBe*

A George II Baluster Tankard, 7¾ in. high, by William Shaw and William Priest, London, 1754, 692 gm. (22.3 oz.). **£850-1,050** *SBe*

A George II Baluster Tankar by John Payne, London, 175 799 gm. (25.7 oz.). **£850-1,050** *SBe*

A silver George III tankard, marked on base and cover, by John King, London, 1781, 7¾ in. high, 24 oz., 13 dwt. **£800-1,000** *SBA*

A George II provincial two-handled porringer, initialled M.S., corded handles, 3¼ in. high, by John Elston Junior, Exeter, 1731, 104 gm. (3.3 oz.). **£300-400** *SBe*

A George II silver baluster tankard and cover, later chas and embossed, and with a la spout, maker possibly John Jones I, height 21 cm., weight oz., London, 1742. **£400-50** *SKC*

A silver George I porringer, by Petley Lay, London, 1715, 4½ in. diam., 8 oz., 6 dwt. **£220-260** *SBA*

An early George III tankard, the body later embossed and engraved, hallmarked London 1764, makers Thomas Whipham and Charles Wright, height 20 cm., weight 30 oz. **£500-600** *SKC*

A silver lidded tankard by Joh Langlands of Newcastle, 7¼ i high. **£600-800** *MB*

A silver replica of the Warwick Vase, by Walker and Hall, Chester, 1906, 10½ in. high, 106 oz., 17 dwt. **£1,200-1,500** *SBA*

A George III silver-gilt cup and cover, bearing later presentation inscription, by John Wakefield, London, 1817, 9 in. (23 cm.) high, 25 oz. **£300-380** *SBe*

A George III silver tankard a cover, by Peter and Ann Bateman, later embossed, engraved inscription, height cm., weight 24 oz., hallmark London, 1791. **£500-700** *SKC*

A parcel gilt silver thistle form trophy cup, 14 oz. troy by R. Pearce and G. Burrows, London 1829. **£200-300** *SKC*

A 17th C. German silver wine cup, marked on bowl and foot with Augsburg pineapple for 1645-50 and maker's mark (Rosenberg 152 and 554), 6 in., 6.1 oz. **£900-1,200** *L*

...ictorian silver cup and ...er, by J. B. Hennell, London, ..., 22½ in. high, 74 oz., 1 dwt. ...0-1,200 *SBA*

A set of 6 Russian small silver-gilt and niello vodka goblets, unidentified workmaster AK, each 4 in. high, Moscow, 1841. **£400-600** *C*

A pair of George III goblets, 7¾ in. high, by Robert Hennell II, London, 1807, 698 gm. (22.4 oz.). **£500-700** *SBe*

...eorge III goblet, inscribed at ...ater date, 7 in. high, by ...bert and David Hennell, ...ndon, 1800, 308 gm. (9.9 oz.). ...00-300 *SBe*

A silver memorial chalice, in early 16th C. style, Birmingham 1902 maker's mark HP and Co, not traced but presumably relating to John Hardman & Co., 7¼ in., 13.2 oz. **£130-160** *L*

Two Victorian large sauce boats, by James Garrard, 1895, 59 oz. **£450-550** *C*

...Russian small silver-gilt and ...llo beaker, on three ball feet, ... in. high, Moscow, 1864. ...00-370 *C*

A Continental silver beaker. **£350-420** *RMcT*

A pair of oval sauce boats, 9¼ in., by John Wilme, Dublin, c. 1760, 49 oz. 2 dwt. **£4,000-5,000** *S*

A heavy pair of oval Sauce Boats, 16.5 cm. long, makers' mark overstruck by that of D. & J. Wellby, London, 1909, 947 gm. (30.4 oz.). **£300-400** *SB*

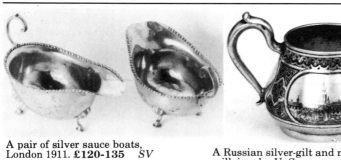

A pair of silver sauce boats,
London 1911. **£120-135** *SV*

A Russian silver-gilt and niello
milk-jug, by V. Semenov, the
jug 2⅛ in. high, Moscow, 1870.
£240-320 *C*

A silver cream jug, Londor
1897, 4 oz., 3 in. **£55-60**

A continental silver cow
creamer, import marks for
London 1903, weight 6 oz.,
length 5½ in., height 4 in. **£300-
360** *SKC*

A silver cream jug and sugar
basin, London, 1805.
£200-250 *EAN*

A silver George III cream ev
the front engraved with scr
initials, 1795, maker's mark
George Gray overstriking th
of Peter and Anne Batemar
in. high. **£150-200** *L*

A Georgian silver cream jug, by
Thos. Smith, London, 1778, 4½
in. **£100-150** *ST*

A silver cream jug, London,
1807, 3¼ in. high. **£100-130**
EAN

> **Miller's is a price GUIDE Not
> a price LIST.**
> **The price ranges given
> reflect the average price a
> purchaser should pay for
> similar items.** Condition,
>
> rarity of design or pattern,
> size, colour, pedigree,
> restoration and many other
> factors must be taken into
> account when assessing
> values.

A silver cream jug, Londor
1785, by George Smith, 5 i
high. **£100-150** *EAN*

A silver cream jug, London,
1791, 5½ in. high. **£130-160**
EAN

A silver cream jug,
Birmingham, 1906, 3 in. **£50-
60** *ST*

A silver cream jug, Lond
1794, 5 in. high. **£250-3**
EAN

A silver gilt wine ewer in the tyle Guiseppe Similioh, 15 in. igh, by Thomas Halford, 1817. 2,500-3,500 *MB*

A 'Cellini' pattern ewer, 30 cm. high, maker's mark of James Willis Dixon for James Dixon & Sons of Sheffield, London, 1875, 726 gm. (23.3 oz.) (all in). £500-600 *SB*

A silver William IV wine ewer, inscribed below the spout, 11¾ in. high, fully marked by the Barnard brothers, London, 1836, 30 oz. 2 dwt. £770-850 *SBA*

silver gilt helmet-shaped wer, by Wakely and Wheeler, ondon, 1926, 9 in. high, 20 oz., 2 dwt. £440-490 *SBA*

A Burmese silver ewer and cover, 31 cm., stamped peacock mark, c. 1880, 2,475 gm. £400-600 *SB*

A Victorian silver-mounted glass claret jug, the glass engraved and etched, by William and George Sissons, Sheffield, 10¾ in., 1878. £400-500 *SBe*

A silver-gilt mounted clear-glass claret jug, 25.4 cm. high, the mount unmarked, the cover struck only with the Edinburgh town mark and duty stamp, 1880's. £250-300 *SB*

A silver-mounted Glass Claret Jug, the mounts chased with figures after Teniers, makers' mark of John Newton Mappin for Mappin & Webb, London, 1885, possibly Thomas Webb & Sons, 25.7 cm. high. £300-360 *SB*

An Edward VII silver-mounted glass claret jug, by Elkington and Co., Birmingham, 1903. 12 in. (30.5 cm.) high. £300-400 *SBe*

A rare George II hot milk jug, by James Ker, Assay Master Edward Penman, Edinburgh, 1729, 4 in. high, 6 oz., 13 dwt. £420-500 *SBA*

A Victorian baluster jug, in 17th C. Scandinavian taste, 11 in. high, by C. T. and G. Fox, London, 1853, 1,476 gm. (47.5 oz.), Britannia Standard. **£700-800** *SBe*

A George III silver jug, later chased, London, 1809, by Emes and Barnard, 25 oz., 9 in. high. **£300-450** *A*

A hot water Jug, 27.4 cm. high makers' mark of R. Martin & E Hall for Martin Hall & Co. Ltd. London, 1875, stamped 1920, 743 gm. (23.8 oz.) (all in). **£300-450** *SB*

A Victorian baluster shaped hot water jug with cover, London, 1884, by R. Hennell, 9 in., 22 oz. **£550-650** *DWB*

A plain Baluster Hot-water Jug, in early 18th C. taste, 22 cm. high, maker's mark of C. S. Harris for C. S. Harris & Sons Ltd., London 1901, 654 gm. (21 oz.). **£250-300** *SB*

A Liberty & Co. 'Cymric' silve hot water jug, designed by Archibald Knox, with an ivor strap handle, 20 cm. high, 10 oz., stamped L & Co. 'Cymric' and hallmarks for Birminghan 1904. **£300-400** *P*

A silver coffee pot, London, 1795, R. & D. Hennell. **£700-900** *EAN*

A silver George II coffee pot, marked on body and lid, by Ayme Videau, London, 1744, 8 in. high, 19 oz., 7 dwt. **£1,200-1,500** *SBA*

A monster silver coffee pot and hot-milk jug on double lampstand, 33.4 cm. high, the stand 44 cm. wide, maker's mark of J. B. Carrington of Carrington & Co., London, 1900, 5,793 gm. (186.2 oz.) (all in). **£2,300-2,500** *SB*

A silver coffee pot, London, 1741, 26 oz. (marks rubbed). **£500-700** *SKC*

A Norwegian small pear-shaped coffee pot, by Joha Helmich Hoff, Bergen, 177 month-mark for December Warden's mark of Jens or Dithmar Kahrs, 5½ in. hig (gross 8 oz. 9 dwts.) **£550-6** *C*

A George IV silver coffee pot, 1822, by Richard Pearce, 8 in., 23.3 oz. **£330-400** *L*

A George III vase-shaped coffee pot, 11½ in. high, marked on base and cover, by Robert Gaze, London, 1796, 905 gm. (29.1 oz.) (all in). **£750-950** *SBe*

A William IV coffee pot, fully marked, by Joseph and John Angell, London, 1836, 9¼ in. high, 29 oz., 7 dwt. **£440-520** *SBA*

A Victorian coffee or hot water pot (handle slightly twisted), Sheffield, 1850, by Walter, Knowles & Co., 10 in., 29 oz. **£400-500** *L*

A plain tapering circular Coffee Pot, 24.7 cm. high. maker's mark of Hayne & Cater, London 1839, stamped: 8295, 921 gm. (29.6 oz.). **£400-500** *SB*

A George III silver teapot, London 1813, weight 20 oz., no engraving. **£220-280** *SKC*

A teapot and coffee pot, maker's mark of Robert Hennell, London, 1858-60, the first stamped: 'Turner's/New Bond St., 1,580 gm. (50 oz) (all in), the teapot repaired. **£400-500**

A George III silver teapot, maker's mark 'W.C.' (engraved initials), 26 by 13 cm. **£210-260** *SKC*

A silver coffee pot, by Rebecca Emes and Edward Barnard, 31 oz. troy, London, 1828. **£500-560** *SKC*

A compressed circular silver tea pot, 12.3 cm. high, maker's mark of J. & A. Savory of A. B. Savory & Sons, London, 1845, 614 gm. (19.7 oz.) (all in). **£260-300** *SB*

A George III silver teapot, hallmarked London, 1817, maker William J. Edwards, weight 25 oz. **£200-350** *SKC*

A Victorian silver teapot, by Edward, Edward Jnr., John and William Barnard, marked base, handle, cover and separate finial (crested), max. height 18 cm., weight 24 oz., London, 1842. **£400-500** *SKC*

An Edward Barnard & Sons compressed circular silver tea pot, 11.6 cm. high, maker's mark of E., E., J. & W. Barnard, London, 1845, stamped: 781/P, 578 gm. (18.5 oz.). **£200-300** *SB*

403

A good early Victorian tea pot, 1839, by John James Keith, 6¾ in. high, 27 oz. **£320-400** *L*

A William IV tea pot, 1835 George Hunter II, the finial slightly earlier by Emes & Barnard, 6 in. high, 23 oz. **£240-300** *L*

A silver teapot, London, 1894, 11 oz. **£110-120** *SV*

A silver continental 'bullet' teapot, 11 oz. troy, 10 cm. high, 11 cm. diam., marked 930, London import mark for 1898. **£150-200** *SKC*

A pair of oblong Tea Pots, 25.2 and 23.3 cm. long, makers' mark F & F, Sheffield, 1925/27, 1,106 gm. (35.5 oz.). **£280-360** *SB*

A melon-shaped Tea Pot, maker's mark of William Hunter, London, 1858, 806 gm. (25.9 oz.) (all in). **£280-360** *SB*

A large Sheffield Plate Tea Kettle on Lampstand, comp with Burner, 44 cm. height unmarked, c. 1850 **£150-20** *SB*

A silver tea kettle with spirit burner, Sheffield 1921. **£380-420** *WHL*

A compressed spherical Tea Kettle on lampstand (no burner), 34.5 cm. high, maker's mark of Richard Martin & Ebenezer Hall for Martin, Hall & Co. Ltd., London, 1885, 1,650 gm. (53 oz.) (all in). **£450-550** *SB*

A plain octagonal Tea Kettle Lampstand, complete with detachable Burner, 34.3 cm. high, makers' mark of the Goldsmiths & Silversmiths Ltd., London, 1926, 1,874 g (60.2 oz.). **£480-580** *SB*

A George III silver tea caddy, by Daniel Smith and Robert Sharp, London, 1765, 5¾ in. (14.5 cm.) high, 8 oz. **£350-400** *SBe*

A George III vase-shaped tea urn, 16½ in. high, by William Frisbee, London, 1804, 3,062 gm. (97.5 oz.) (all in). **£900-1,100** *SBe*

A George III Drum Tea Caddy, 3½ in. high, by Joseph Preedy, London, 1775, 320 gm. (10.3 oz.). **£800-1,200** *SBe*

A George III shaped oval twin tea caddy, 6½ in. wide, by Henry Nutting, London, 1783, 720 gm. (23.1 oz.), complete with silver-mounted key (locks in working order). **£1,000-1,200** *SBe*

A silver tea caddy, London, 1797, maker S.H., 5½ in. high. **£800-1,050** *EAN*

An unusual George III tea caddy, 6½ in. high, by Thomas Hemming, London, 1783, 404 gm. (13 oz.). **£1,200-1,500** *SBe*

Make the most of Miller's

Every care has been taken to ensure the accuracy of descriptions and estimated valuations.

Where an attribution is made within inverted commas (e.g. 'Chippendale') or is followed by the word 'style' (e.g. early Georgian style) it is intended to convey that, in the opinion of the publishers, the piece concerned is a later — though probably still antique — reproduction of the style so designated.

Unless otherwise stated, any description which refers to 'a set' or 'a pair' includes a valuation for the entire set or the pair, even though the illustration may show only a single item.

Continental silver tea caddy, import mark for London, 1893 (possibly French), height 5½ in. (14 cm.). **£190-220** *SKC*

A silver tea caddy, Birmingham, 1899, 5 oz. **£70-100** *SV*

A Russian nielloed silver tea-caddy, workmaster's initials M.G., Moscow, late 19th C., and a caddy-spoon, the caddy 3½ in. high. **£550-650** *C*

A silver tea caddy, 1897, Lee & Wigfull, 3 in. high. **£65-75** *ST*

405

A Victorian four piece silver tea and coffee set (cream jug not matching), three pieces London 1843, makers J. & A. Savory, the milk jug London 1839, maker's mark JT, 64¼ oz. **£900-1,100** *PWC*

A William IV three-piece sil tea set (some feet with splits a one foot repaired), by E.E., J W. Barnard, London 1832, 52 **£770-900** *O*

A three-piece silver tea set, maker's mark of Charles Reily & George Storer of Reily & Storer, London, 1839, the sugar basin stamped: 507, 1,658 gm. (53.3 oz.). **£600-700** *SB*

A German 4-piece silver te service, with carved ivory handles, Berlin, c. 1845, maker's mark of G Hossa (Rosenberg 1224), 115 oz. **£1,500-1,700** *L*

A fine George III silver four piece tea set, by Duncan Urquhart and Napthali Hart, with later sugar bowl, in a fitted oak case, hallmarked London 1804 and 1911. **£1,300-1,600** *SKC*

An Indian silver-coloured-metal tea set comprising: t pot, milk jug, sugar basin tray, 1,284 gm., late 19th C **£250-350** *SB*

A Victorian 4-piece silver tea and coffee set, fully marked, by Gibson and Langman for the Goldsmiths and Silversmiths Co. Ltd., Sheffield, 1862, 45 oz. all in. **£500-700** *SBe*

A Victorian four-piece tea service, tea and hot water pot by 'W.H.', London, 1865, the remainder by Robinson Edkins and Aston, 1844 & 1846, 63 oz. **£720-850** *SKC*

A small three-piece Tea Set, chased in the Aesthetic Movement taste, the tea pot 13.3 cm. high, maker's mark SGG in shaped rectangle Edinburgh, 1879, 587 gm. (18.8 oz.) (all in). **£400-500** *SB*

A three-piece tea set, maker's mark of George Angell, Londo 1851-53, all stamped: 21, 1,52 gm.; 49.1 oz. (all in). **£600-800** *SB*

three-piece silver tea set,
aker's mark of Elkington &
o. Ltd., London, 1897-98/1900,
666 gm. (53.5 oz.). **£550-**
30   *SB*

A Victorian three-piece tea
service, by 'C.B.', London, 1897-
98, 40 oz. **£350-420**   *SKC*

Japanese three piece silver-
oloured-metal coffee set,
omprising coffee pot, cream
g and sucrier, 18 cm., stamped
iragana mark, crane and
& K, c. 1900. **£140-180**   *SB*

An Edwardian 4-piece silver tea
and coffee service, by Elkington
& Co., Birmingham, 1901, 88 oz.
£980-1,200   *M*

n oval three-piece tea service,
apot with wood handle (knob
issing), London, 1904. **£400-**
0   *DWB*

A 3-piece silver tea service,
London, 1924, 32 oz. **£290-**
350   *BW*

A Victorian silver miniature
offee set, Henry Archer,
Sheffield, 1882, total weight 50
z., max. height of kettle, 8¾ in.
£670-800   *SKC*

A Victorian silver chocolate
pot, hallmarked London, 1887,
height 8 in. (20 cm.), weight 11
oz. **£220-260**   *SKC*

A pair of silver Queen Anne-
style pillar candlesticks
(weighted). **£185-220**   *RG*

A Victorian silver gravy argyle
y Robert Garrard, London,
844, 4½ in. high. **£500-700**
AN

A pair of William III silver table
candlesticks, later engraved
with armorials, marked on
bases and sconces, by Joseph
Bird, London, 1701, 5¾ in. high,
14 oz., 17 dwt. **£1,500-2,000**
SBA

A George II Taperstick, 5 in. high, by William Gould, London, 1747, 197 gm. (6.3 oz.), excluding later nozzle, unmarked. £400-500 *SBe*

A set of 4 George II silver table candlesticks, fitted with detachable nozzles, 9½ in. high, London, 1748, wt. 104 oz., probable maker Thomas Gilpin. £4,000-5,000 *MMB*

A silver taperstick by J Jacobs, c. 1750, 7 in. hi, £500-600 *EAN*

A pair of silver George II table candlesticks, with detachable nozzles, marked on bases, sconces and a nozzle, by William Cafe, London, 1759, 9¾ in., 43 oz., 18 dwt. £1,300-1,500· *SBA*

A pair of George III silver candlesticks, London, 1763/75, 10 in. high. £800-1,000 *EAN*

A set of 4 George III candlesticks, by John Wak and William Taylor, the fo filled by a turned wooded former, height 27 cm., hallmarked London 1782. £3,000-3,800 *SKC*

A pair of Georgian silver candlesticks, hallmarked Sheffield, 1819, maker S. C. Young & Co., height 11¾ in. (30 cm.) (filled). £700-800 *SKC*

A pair of early George III table candlesticks, with detachable nozzles, by Ebenezer Coker, London, 1767-68, 28 oz., 10 dwt., 8¾ in. (23 cm.) high. £800-1,200 *SKC*

A pair of silver table candlesticks, with detach nozzles, 29 cm. high, ma mark of Henry Wilkinson Sheffield, 1851, stamped: loaded. £300-500 *SB*

A set of four table candlesticks, 28 cm. high, maker's mark of Henry Wilkinson & Co. Ltd., London, 1891-92, also struck with their 'crossed keys' trademark, and stamped: 1567, loaded. £500-700 *SB*

A pair of George III silver candlesticks, Sheffield 1786-92, John Parsons & Co., 12 in. £500-600 *RMcT*

Right
A pair of silver Victorian Scottish table candlesticks, with detachable nozzles, marked on bases and nozzles, by Brook and Son, Edinburgh, 1893, 8 in. (20.5 cm.) high, 945 gms. (30.4 oz.). £340-400 *SBe*

A pair of Corinthian-styled candlesticks, hallmarked Sheffield, 1893, height 9 in. (23 cm.), maker 'W.G. and L.' (filled). £260-300 *SKC*

pair of Victorian
ndlesticks, 1892 by Martin,
all & Co., 7½ in. high, loaded.
00-300   *L*

A pair of George III two-light
Candelabra, the tapering stem
with vase-shaped socket, with 6
detachable nozzles, Matthew
Boulton, Birmingham, 1792,
16½ in. high. **£2,900-3,400**
C

A pair of Victorian silver
tapersticks, Birmingham, 1895,
maker's marks poorly struck,
J.W. ?, 3¼ in. high. **£120-160**
L

Victorian 5-light silver
andelabrum centrepiece, with
presentation inscriptions, by
lkington & Co., Birmingham,
862, 31½ in. high. **£1,550-
,800**   *SBA*

A pair of octagonal table
candlesticks, 21.4 cm. high,
maker's mark of Hawksworth,
Eyre & Co. Ltd., Sheffield, 1898,
stamped: 11163/3, loaded.
£200-400   *SB*

A pair of Regency three-light
Candelabra, by T. & J. Settle,
Sheffield, 1816, 21¾ in. high,
(weight of branches 80 oz.).
£3,000-4,000   *C*

silver chamberstick and
nuffer by Paul Storr, London,
814, 15½ oz. **£1,200-1,500**
MB

A silver Victorian chamber
candlestick, in the late 17th C.
style, maker's mark J.A., J.S.
London, 1882, 8½ in. (22 cm.)
long, 199 gms. (6.4 oz.). **£130-
160**   *SBe*

A pair of four-light candelabra,
49.4 cm. high, maker's mark of
Stephen Smith for S. Smith &
Son, London, 1886, stamped:
8596, 3,242 gm. (104.2 oz.).
£1,200-1,500   *SB*

A George III silver cruet frame,
with 6 cut-glass bottles, maker
J. W. Story and William Elliott,
length 25 cm., width 16 cm.,
height 22 cm., weight of silver
21 oz., hallmarked London
1809. **£440-520**   *SKC*

A George III silver cruet stand,
with 7 silver mounted cut-glass
bottles, London, 1800, maker's
mark CC. **£330-400**   *PWC*

A George III silver cruet stand,
with 2 cut-glass mustard pots,
four cut-glass bottles, London,
1807, maker Robert Henell; and
two English silver mustard
spoons, London, 1863, maker
George Angell. **£390-450**
PWC

A Cruet Frame, in mid 18th C. taste, 18 cm. wide, maker's mark of C.T. & G. Fox, London, 1845; and an Onslow pattern Salt Spoon, London, 1896, 409 gm. (13.1 oz.) of silver. **£200-300**   *SB*

A George IV silver cruet, containing 6 bottles and a mustard pot, London, 1825, maker's mark WB; and a silver mustard spoon, London 1824. **£300-400**   *PWC*

A cruet frame, 19th C. style, 25 c long, Robert Pringle, London, 19 876 gm. (28.1 oz.). **£300-360**

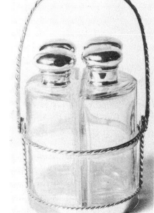

A silver inkstand by Chas. Aldridge and Henry Green, London 1774, 10½ in. wide. **£900-1,100**   *EAN*

A silver egg cruet, London, 1932, 8 in. high, 28½ oz. **£35 450**   *EAN*

Four silver topped scent bottles, in silver stand, 1904. **£107-130**   *ST*

A silver inkstand, by John & Thomas Settle, Sheffield, 1825, 10½ in. wide. **£800-1,300**   *EAN*

A silver inkstand, Sheffield, 1900, 16 oz., 8 in. long. **,190-210**   *SV*

A Victorian gadrooned inkstand, with two moulded glass pots, London, 1844, by R. Garrard II, engraved on base, 'Leuchars, London', 13 in. **£600-700**   *DWB*

A Victorian inkstand, with two cut glass pots with pierced holders and silver lids and central taper stick with snuffer, London, 1894, by Chas. Stuart Harris, 10½ in., 27 oz. **£400-500**   *DWB*

Left
A Victorian silver standish, by Barnard, hallmarked London 1849-50, all pieces marked, 41 by 29 by 24 cm. max. measurements, total weight 78 oz. **£1,300-1,500**   *SKC*

Right
A silver inkstand, London, 1899, 4½ in. wide. **£65-75**   *ST*

ne of a set of 6 silver forks,
ondon, 1845, 18 oz. **£200-250**
e set   *SV*

A silver bread fork, with ivory
andle, 1908. **£20-25**

set of six Victorian silver
ssert forks, London, 1882.
00-115   *Gs*

Twelve pairs of Victorian silver
gilt dessert knives and forks, in
fitted mahogany case from
Hunt and Roskell Ltd., 1874 by
Francis Higgins, 64 oz. **£1,000-
1,200**   *L*

A set of 3 George III silver table
forks, by Richard Cooke,
London, 1806. **£100-130**   *ST*

A unique silver gilt christening
set, by Thomas Heming, c. 1740,
carrying the garter arms.
£270-300   *MB*

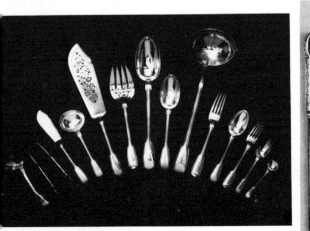

Victorian fiddle and thread
ttern silver table service, 73
ces, London 1878/9/80,
aker Francis Higgins, 168½
with fitted oak canteen case.
,500-3,000   *PWC*

A boxed set of silver spoons and
tongs, Birmingham, 1910. **£38-
45**   *ST*

A German early silver-mounted
bone-handled fork and skewer,
the fork with initials and date
1603, the skewer with later
mounts, the fork 7¼ in. long.
£440-560   *C*

A Georgian silver sugar sifter
spoon. **£30-40**

A silver sugar sifter spoon,
London, 1853. **£60-65**

A Sheffield silver sugar sifter
spoon, with gilded bowl,
marked HW Ltd, 1910. **£25-30**

A Georgian silver salt sifter
spoon, 1790. **£70-80**

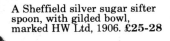

A Sheffield silver sugar sifter
spoon, with gilded bowl,
marked HW Ltd, 1906. **£25-28**

A George V silver sugar sifter
spoon, London 1910. **£15-20**

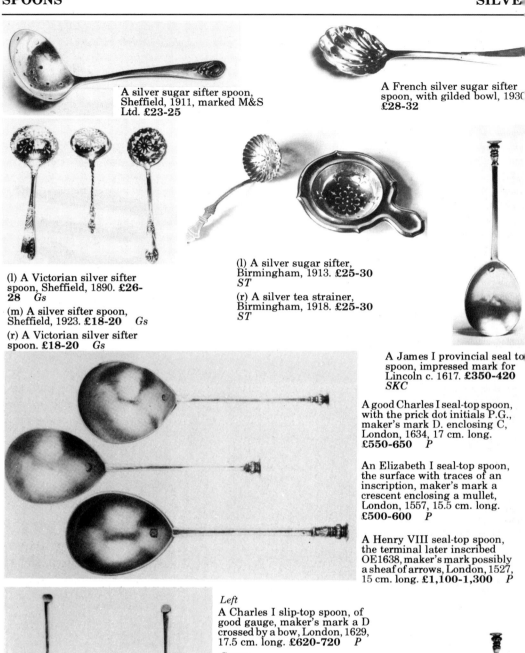

A silver sugar sifter spoon, Sheffield, 1911, marked M&S Ltd. £23-25

A French silver sugar sifter spoon, with gilded bowl, 1930 £28-32

(l) A Victorian silver sifter spoon, Sheffield, 1890. £26-28 *Gs*

(m) A silver sifter spoon, Sheffield, 1923. £18-20 *Gs*

(r) A Victorian silver sifter spoon. £18-20 *Gs*

(l) A silver sugar sifter, Birmingham, 1913. £25-30 *ST*

(r) A silver tea strainer, Birmingham, 1918. £25-30 *ST*

A James I provincial seal to spoon, impressed mark for Lincoln c. 1617. £350-420 *SKC*

A good Charles I seal-top spoon, with the prick dot initials P.G., maker's mark D. enclosing C, London, 1634, 17 cm. long. £550-650 *P*

An Elizabeth I seal-top spoon, the surface with traces of an inscription, maker's mark a crescent enclosing a mullet, London, 1557, 15.5 cm. long. £500-600 *P*

A Henry VIII seal-top spoon, the terminal later inscribed OE1638, maker's mark possibly a sheaf of arrows, London, 1527, 15 cm. long. £1,100-1,300 *P*

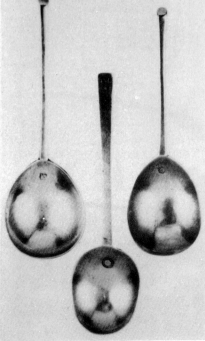

Left
A Charles I slip-top spoon, of good gauge, maker's mark a D crossed by a bow, London, 1629, 17.5 cm. long. £620-720 *P*

Centre
A Charles II provincial puritan spoon, prick dot engraved on the back TG1668, with the mark of a rayed sun within a dotted circle, c. 1665, 17 cm. long. £200-400 *P*

Right
A Charles I slip-top spoon, of good gauge, maker's mark a W over M, 16.5 cm. long. £390-430 *P*

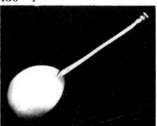

Charles I silver seal top spoon, London 1634, maker's mark 'C' with a 'D'. £380-450 *Win*

A Charles I seal top spoon, pricked initials, maker Charle Punge, impressed marks to bowl and stem, length 17.5 cm. London 1637. £210-250 *SK(*

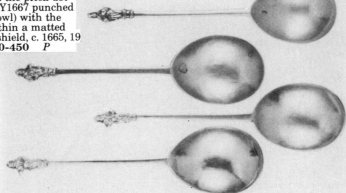

A Charles II unascribed provincial Apostle spoon, St. Matthew, with the prick dot inscription IGY1667 punched only (in the bowl) with the initials RP within a matted heart-shaped shield, c. 1665, 19 cm. long. **£380-450** *P*

A seal top spoon from the Commonwealth period, possibly by William Rawson, with pricked initials, length 18 cm., c. 1650. **£370-420** *SKC*

Centre

A rare Mary I Apostle spoon, St. Matthew, maker's mark RI conjoined, London, 1557, 19 cm. long. **£1,400-1,600** *P*

Bottom

A pair of Charles II unascribed provincial Apostle spoons, St. Matthew, each spoon engraved with prick dot initials HRA, unmarked, c. 1665, 19 cm. long. **£750-850** *P*

A cased set of silver George III table spoons and a Victorian sifter spoon, later embossed and engraved, hallmarked London 1801, the sifter spoon London 1842, makers Christopher and Thomas W. Barker and William Eaton. **£130-200** *SKC*

Six silver tablespoons, Newcastle, 1796. **£180-200** *ST*

A George III silver serving spoon, London, 1798, by George Smith, 11½ in. long. **£60-70** *Gs*

A Charles II Provincial-Exeter trefid spoon, of thick gauge, with pricked initials I.D. 1693, and with Exeter crown and X mark, 8 in. long, c. 1670. **£300-350** *P*

A silver Queen Anne dognose basting spoon, by Thomas Spackman, London, 1709, 13 in. (33 cm.) long, 4½ oz. **£350-400** *SBe*

A pair of silver serving spoons, London, 1807, 10½ oz. **£130-160** *SV*

A George IV silver serving spoon, by William Eaton, London, 1826, 12 in. long. **£60-65** *Gs*

A Queen Anne dog-nose spoon, engraved on the back with the prick-dot initials E.B. by W. Scarlett, London, 1705, 19.5 cm. long. **£100-130** *P*

A presentation fruit dessert service, by Francis Higgins, comprising 4 fruit spoons, 21.5 cm. long, 1887, and a sugar sifter, 15.5 cm. long, 1883, in fitted case, 13.5 oz. **£150-250** *P*

One of a set of 6 silver spoons, London, 1845, 16 oz. **£160-180** the set *SV*

A set of six silver picture-back spoons by Wm. Soames, Exeter, 1740. **£200-230** *MB*

A Georgian silver jam spoon, 1798. **£40-45**

A silver punch ladle, c. 1750, 14 in. long. **£80-120** *EAN*

A Georgian silver ladle, turned into an indented berry sugar sifter spoon in mid-1900's, marked TW JH. **£40-45**

A silver soup ladle, London, 1774, by Walter Tweedie. **£100-160** *EAN*

Two of a set of 4 George III toddy ladles, each engraved with a crest and baron's coronet, by James Erskine, Aberdeen, 1800, 3.75 oz. **£170-210** the set *P*

A pair of Victorian silver salt spoons, fiddle and thread pattern, London, 1885. **£16-18** *Gs*

One of a pair of George III fiddle pattern toddy ladles, with initials, maker's mark W.L. (William Law?), Dundee, c. 1815, 2.5 oz. **£140-180** the pair *SB*

A set of six Victorian silver dessert spoons, London, 1898. **£90-100** *Gs*

A set of 12 Guild of Handicraft silver coffee spoons, each with a turquoise or green stone cabochon, hammered, maker's mark London, 1906, 11.5 cm. **£200-300** *SB*

A Dutch silver gravy/cream skimmer spoon, c. 1920-30. **£40-50**

An early George III Onslow pattern sauce ladle, by Paul Callard, 1765, 2 oz. **£60-100** *P*

Three small silver ladles, London, 1807, 6 oz. **£80-120** *SV*

A silver George III Old English pattern soup ladle, the terminal engraved with a crest, 1781, by Hester Bateman, 5.4 oz. **£280-320** *L*

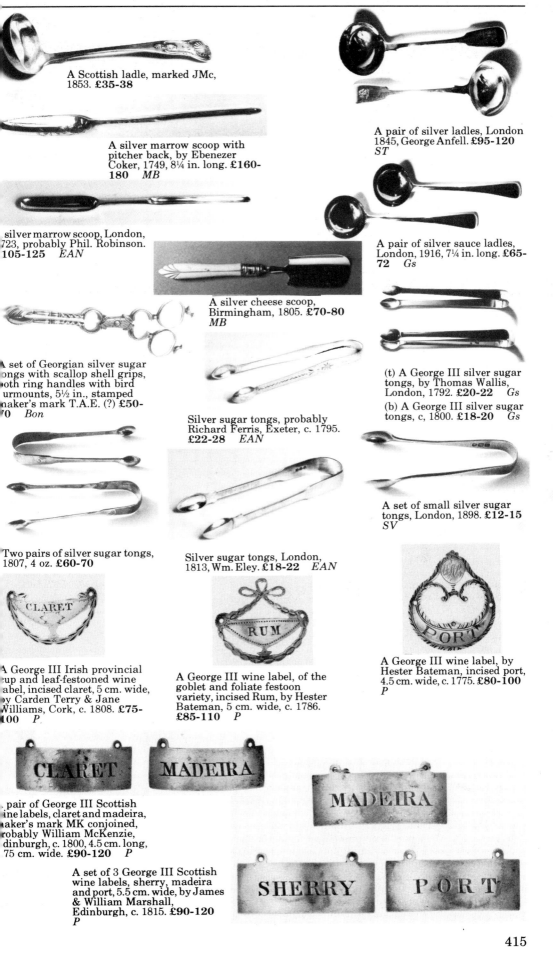

A Scottish ladle, marked JMc, 1853. **£35-38**

A silver marrow scoop with pitcher back, by Ebenezer Coker, 1749, 8¼ in. long. **£160-180**   *MB*

silver marrow scoop, London, 723, probably Phil. Robinson. **105-125**   *EAN*

A set of Georgian silver sugar ongs with scallop shell grips, oth ring handles with bird urmounts, 5½ in., stamped naker's mark T.A.E. (?) **£50-70**   *Bon*

Silver sugar tongs, probably Richard Ferris, Exeter, c. 1795. **£22-28**   *EAN*

Two pairs of silver sugar tongs, 1807, 4 oz. **£60-70**

Silver sugar tongs, London, 1813, Wm. Eley. **£18-22**   *EAN*

A pair of silver ladles, London 1845, George Anfell. **£95-120**   *ST*

A pair of silver sauce ladles, London, 1916, 7¼ in. long. **£65-72**   *Gs*

A silver cheese scoop, Birmingham, 1805. **£70-80**   *MB*

(t) A George III silver sugar tongs, by Thomas Wallis, London, 1792. **£20-22**   *Gs*
(b) A George III silver sugar tongs, c, 1800. **£18-20**   *Gs*

A set of small silver sugar tongs, London, 1898. **£12-15**   *SV*

A George III Irish provincial up and leaf-festooned wine abel, incised claret, 5 cm. wide, by Carden Terry & Jane Williams, Cork, c. 1808. **£75-100**   *P*

A George III wine label, of the goblet and foliate festoon variety, incised Rum, by Hester Bateman, 5 cm. wide, c. 1786. **£85-110**   *P*

A George III wine label, by Hester Bateman, incised port, 4.5 cm. wide, c. 1775. **£80-100**   *P*

pair of George III Scottish ine labels, claret and madeira, aker's mark MK conjoined, robably William McKenzie, dinburgh, c. 1800, 4.5 cm. long, 75 cm. wide. **£90-120**   *P*

A set of 3 George III Scottish wine labels, sherry, madeira and port, 5.5 cm. wide, by James & William Marshall, Edinburgh, c. 1815. **£90-120**   *P*

A matching set of 3 George III Scottish wine labels, rum, by Thomas Ross, brandy and whisky by J. & W. Marshall, 3.5 cm. wide, Edinburgh, c. 1816. **£80-110** *P*

A set of 4 George III wine labels, port, claret, madeira and sherry, 4.5 cm. wide, by J. Kay & Co., Sheffield, 1813. **£120-160** *P*

A rare George III Irish bacchanal wine label incised 'Whiskey', (sic.), 6 cm. wide, by John Townsend, Dublin, 1818. **£55-75** *P*

A set of 4 George III Scottish wine labels, incised gin, brandy, whisky and rum, 4.5 cm. wide, by W. & P. Cunningham, Edinburgh, 1814. **£140-180** *P*

A good pair of Victorian cast wine labels, by Paul Storr, pierced Ordinaire, and a third, matching, incised Harvey, 1835, 6 cm. wide. **£1,050-1,200** *P*

A pair of George IV treble vine-leaf wine labels, pierced sherry and port, 8.5 cm. wide, by Ledsam, Vale and Wheeler, Birmingham, 1826-29. **£88-110** *P*

A pair of George III neck rings, with unusual tongue and groove fastenings, madeira and port, 7.5 cm. wide, by William Bateman, 1808. **£200-250** *P*

A pair of early 19th C. 'barrel' wine labels, inscribed 'Whiskey' (sic.) and 'Sherry', 6 cm. wide, 5 cm. high, unmarked, c. 1830, 1.5 oz. **£160-200** *P*

An Early Victorian silver gilt mounted glass perfume bottle, 6½ in. high, by Charles Rawlins and William Summers, London, 1842. **£100-150** *SBe*

A George III silver wine funnel, with detachable strainer, by Peter and Anne Bateman, London, 1795, 5¾ in. (14.5 cm.) high, 4 oz. **£150-200** *SBe*

A silver wine funnel, maker H.B. London, 1790, 5 in. high. **£200-265** *EAN* if Hester Bateman. **£300-400**

A George III Wine Funnel, by Solomon Hougham, London, 1809, 165 gm. (5.3 oz.). **£200-250** *SBe*

A George III silver tray, with pair of snuffers, the tray 9 in. (23 cm.) wide, by Thomas Streetin, the snuffer by Wilkes Booth, both London, 1791, 214 gm. (6.8 oz.) all in. **£550-650** *SBe*

Victorian silver dressing
ble mirror, 53.5 by 38 cm.
x., hallmarked London 1871.
0-700   SKC

A silver-mounted velvet-
covered heart-shaped Mirror, 44
cm. high, makers' mark of
William Comyns, London, 1892.
£200-300   SB

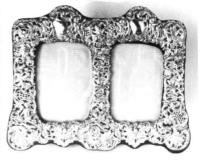

A silver double photo frame,
Chester, 1899, 9½ in. high.
£100-150   SV

Victorian silver dressing
ble mirror, inscribed 'Nina',
William Comyns and Sons,
ondon, 1897, 20 in. (51 cm.)
gh. £200-300   SBe

A silver photo frame, early 20th
C., 8¼ in. high. £65-70   SV

A silver-mounted Mirror, 45 cm.
high, maker's mark of the
Goldsmiths & Silversmiths Co.
Ltd., London, 1901, P.O.D.R.
number 324950. £80-120   SB

A Dublin hallmarked dish ring,
y Joseph Jackson, with glass
iner, 20 cm. max. diam., height
cm., c. 1780. £700-900   SKC
SKC

A boxed silver desk set,
Birmingham, 1928. £30-60
ST

One of two silver coolers, by
Goldsmiths and Silversmiths
Co. Ltd., London, 1932, 6¾ in.
and 5 in. high, 39 oz., 16 dwt.
£350-420 pr.   SBA

A French silver-gilt and
aroque pearl centrepiece
modelled as Jael, wife of Heber,
reparing to kill Sisera (few
ieces missing), 19th C., 8¼ in.
210 mm.) length. £440-500

A hinged silver reliquary,
formed as the head and
shoulders of a medieval king,
set with coloured stones, 9¾ in.,
late 19th C. £700-1,000   C

A large Nepalese repousse gilt
tara, with stone-encrusted body
ornaments, on a later double
lotus base, 18th C., 18 in. (46
cm.) high. £1,400-1,700   C

An Irish silver dish ring, 9 in. diam., Dublin, 1913, 13 oz. **£200-300** *V*

A silver-mounted Meerschaum pipe, with a monogram and crest inscribed 'in fumo vivimus', probably by John Hilsby of Liverpool, Chester, 1843, fitted wooden case, 7 in. wide. **£80-120** *SBA*

A silver table spirit lighter, depicting a fire imp, c. 1898. **£80-100**

A late Victorian silver buckle. **£26-30** *SV*

A silver wax jack by Henry Chawner, 1792, 6½ in. high. **£440-490** *MB*

A pair of silver napkin rings, Birmingham, 1883 and 1884. **£10-20** *ST*

A Victorian silver-mounted horn flagon, by William Frederick Wolstenholm, London, 1877, 10½ in. (26.5 cm.) high. **£280-330** *SBe*

A George III silver gilt mustard pot, London, 1819, by Joseph Wilson, 3½ in. high. **£400-520** *EAN*

A silver ashtray, Birmingham, 1907. **£16-19** *SV*

A Sheffield silver 'apostle' tea strainer, with gilded bowl, marked BM EH, 1892. **£15-30**

A Russian kovsh, cloisonne enamelled with flowers, 13½ in. wide, 1899-1908, 27 oz. **£3,300-3,600** by Faberge, otherwise **£1,000-1,500** *N*

A Victorian silver travelling candle lamp, with adjustable candle slide, John Newton Mappin, wt. 16 oz., London, 1885. **£180-220** *RMcT*

A 19th C. Dutch silver decanter, with double pourer, the glass finely etched, 11 in. high. **£180-220** *MB*

A silver mustard pot and spoon, London, 1897. £50-70 *EAN*

A silver mesh purse, with cast flowers, 1799. £165-185 *MB*

A silver mustard pot, Sheffield, 1851, 3 in. high. £80-120 *ST*

A silver-lidded cut glass pot, Chester, 1909, 3 in. £20-25 *SV*

A pair of silver salt cellars, with blue glass liners, Birmingham, 1912. £40-60 *SV*

A George IV mustard pot by Matthew Boulton, 1825. £70-80 *MB*

A silver and ivory cake knife, Sheffield, 1903. £20-30 *SV*

A silver fish slice, Edinburgh, 1834, marked J.A. £65-75 *ST*

A late Victorian silver vase, Sheffield, 1892, 4½ in. £85-95 *SV*

A silver confectionery slice, London 1853. £40-45

Royal. A silver Victorian presentation trowel, with carved and turned ivory handle, maker's mark T.W., Birmingham, 1887. £230-300 *SBe*

A Victorian silver butter knife, Sheffield, 1900. £9-11 *Gs*

(t) A silver butter knife, Birmingham, 1906, marked HM. £8-10

(b) A silver butter knife, Sheffield, 1911. £8-10

(l) A silver caddy spoon, Exeter, 1836, by John Stone. £20-30 *ST*

(r) A sterling silver tea strainer. £25-30 *ST*

A William IV silver toast rack, London, 1831, 9½ oz. £180-220 *SV*

419

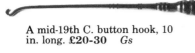

A mid-19th C. button hook, 10 in. long. £20-30   Gs

A silver backed clothes brush, Chester, 1916. £8-10   Gs

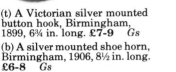

(t) A Victorian silver mounted button hook, Birmingham, 1899, 6¾ in. long. £7-9   Gs

(b) A silver mounted shoe horn, Birmingham, 1906, 8½ in. long. £6-8   Gs

A silver flask, Sheffield 1905. £58-65   ST

A silver pomander holder, 1¾ in. diam., c. 1862. £30-50   BY

(l) A mother of pearl fruit knife with silver blade, Sheffield, 1906. £10-12   Gs

(cl) A mother of pearl fruit knife with silver blade, Sheffield, 1912. £8-10   Gs

(cr) A silver pencil by S. Mordan, Chester, 1911. £12-14   Gs

(r) A silver penknife, London, 1901. £9-11   Gs

(l) A silver button hook, Sheffield, 1908. £10-12   ST

(m) A silver trump marker, Birmingham, 1904. £22-25 ST

(r) A silver fruit knife, Sheffield, 1909. £11-13   ST

A Continental silver scen† bottle and lipstick holder leather case, c. 1920's. £5£ 65   ST

A pair of late 18th C. razors, each side mounted in silver gilt, the blades stamped Moss, 200 Fleet Street, the mounts North German, c. 1775-80, with Dutch control marks, 1813-1893. £520-620   L

A boxed set of 6 liqueur glasses in silver stands, Birmingham, 1902. £85-95   ST

A silver lemon strainer, London, 1768, by Chas. Aldridge and Henry Green, 11½ in. across handles. £300-380 EAN

A fine George 1II silver Stilto† cheese scoop, with ivory handl† and sprung server, c. 1810. £80-120   EA

(l) A silver rattle, 1903. £35-40   ST

(r) An unusual 20th C. silver napkin ring, 1937. £45-50   ST

A 19th C. silver seal, initials 'AM'. £20-25   SV

A silver cigar cutter, Londor 1909. £23-28   SV

A silver pen container, with pen, Chester, 1907. £45-50 *SV*

A Georgian silver gilt child's combined rattle and whistle with coral teether, 4 in. £55-70 *Bon*

A silver shaving brush in case, London, 1819, 3 in. long. £100-150 *EAN*

A pair of George III silver framed spectacles, by Joseph Taylor, Birmingham, 1811. £20-50 *SBe*

VINAIGRETTES

- the first known use of the term 'vinaigrette' was in 1811, but 'spunge-boxes' and 'smelling bottles' had been popular in 18th C.
- the art of the 'toymen' was carried on in Birmingham, where Pemberton, Willmore & Mills perfected the repoussé view and topographical subject
- 'castle tops' made about 1830 — many of these fetch higher prices than some gold vinaigrettes
- many novelty shaped vinaigrettes
- there are almost as many different varieties of pierced grilles as there are vinaigrettes
- from 1815–1850 a great number of souvenir vinaigrettes, of such figures as Nelson, Wellington and famous buildings and events
- the die-stamping techniques employed by the Birmingham silversmiths meant that they could virtually mass-produce vinaigrettes

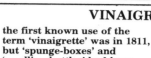

A silver and tortoiseshell tortoise pin box, with hinged lid, 14.3 cm. long, maker's mark of Thomas Johnson, London, 1881, engraved: 'Habermann/5 Avenue de L'Opéra, Paris. £300-400 *SB*

A Continental silver cigarette box, the lid enamelled, London import mark, 1928, possibly Austrian, wood lined, 4½ in. (11.2 cm.) wide. £200-250 *SBe*

A silver on copper small jewel case, with original velvet lining, 3¾ in., c. 1820. £30-35 *BY*

A silver box by Mathew Linwood, Birmingham, 1876, 3¼ in. wide. £80-120 *ST*

A German ornamental silver box and cover, chased with a 16th C. maritime battle (hinge defective), import marks 1903, 4¾ in. diam. £80-120 *L*

A Continental silver-gilt musical box, the cover enamelled with the Lake of Geneva, 19th C., 4⅛ in. (105 mm.) long. £700-900 *C*

A Japanese silver cigarette box, 15.5 cm., stamped Jungin, late 19th C., 481 gm. £60-80 *SB*

An Oval spicebox, the base and lid attractively engraved and initialled AW, 2¼ in. wide, maker's mark EH only, 1690. £450-550 *S*

A shaped rectangular card case, 9 cm. high, maker's mark of Nathaniel Mills, Birmingham, 1841. **£200-250** *SB*

A George IV table snuff box, with a contemporary presentation inscription, 1823 by William Elliott, 3¾ in. **£180-250** *L*

A silver and Oriental porcelain snuff-box, with engraved initials (lid cracked), early 18th C., 3 in. (76 mm.) long. **£260-320** *C*

A silver-gilt snuff-box, by Ledsam Vale and Wheeler, Birmingham, 1827, 3 in. (77 mm.) long. **£300-400** *C*

A Scottish curved snuff box, with presentation inscription, c. 1800. **£200-300** *PK*

A snuff box, 6.2 cm. long, maker's mark of Edward Smith, Birmingham, 1844. **£100-140** *SB*

A large snuff box, 9.8 cm. long, maker's mark of Hilliard & Thomason, Birmingham, 1856. **£200-260** *SB*

A silver snuff box by T.S., 1831. **£100-150** *MB*

(m) A silver snuff box, Birmingham, 1876. **£60-80** *MB*

(r) A silver snuff box by I.B., Birmingham, 1822. **£100-130** *MB*

A rectangular silver-gilt snuff box, 7.8 cm. long, maker's mark of T. Edwards, London, 1839. **£200-300** *SB*

A silver snuff-box, by John Lawrence & Co., Birmingham, 1824, 3 in. (76 mm.) long. **£130-160** *C*

A George IV silver-gilt snuff-box, with initials G.M., by Nathaniel Mills, Birmingham, 1827, 3¼ in. (83 mm.). **£200-350** *C*

A George IV oblong snuff box, gilt interior, 3 in. wide, marked Thomas Shaw, Birmingham, 1824. **£200-300** *S*

A George III silver snuff box, initialled J.D., with gilt interior, by John Shaw, Birmingham, 1810, a.f., 2¼ in. (5.7 cm.) wide. **£55-75** *SBe*

A silver 'Castletop' snuff-box, chased with a view of Colchester Old Town Hall, with inscription, dated 1844, by Nathaniel Mills, Birmingham, 1844. **£440-520** *P*

A silver snuff-box, the cover pierced and engraved, possibly German, early 18th C., 3¼ in. (84 mm.) long. **£450-550** *C*

A shaped rectangular
vinaigrette, 4.2 cm. long,
maker's mark of Edward Smith,
Birmingham, 1852. **£90-110**
SB

A Louis XV silver snuff-box, the
body chased and engraved,
maker's mark indistinct, Paris,
1763, 3½ in. (90 mm.) long.
£750-900   *C*

ilver-gilt vinaigrette, by
n Bettridge, Birmingham,
9, 1½ in. (39 mm.) long.
0-160   *C*

ilver vinaigrette, the lid set
h a die-stamped view of
wstead Abbey, maker's mark
Nathaniel Mills for N. Mills
ion, Birmingham, 3.6 cm.
g, 1838. **£330-400**   *SB*

(l) A silver vinaigrette by Ed.
Shaw, Birmingham, 1846.
£125-150   *MB*

(r) A 22 ct. gold vinaigrette,
French, c. 1830. **£320-360**
MB

(m) A silver vinaigrette by W.S.,
Birmingham, 1833. **£80-100**
MB

ilver vinaigrette, the cover
h a raised view of St. Paul's
hedral, 4.1 cm. long,
ker's mark of Joseph
lmore, Birmingham, 1842,
cm. long. **£500-600**   *SB*

A Victorian ceramic
scent bottle, in the form
of a thrush's egg with
silver cap by Sampson
Mordan, 1885. **£88-
130**   *P*

A late Victorian vesta case,
modelled as a horse's hoof, by
Jane Brownett, 1885, 6 cm.
high, 2.25 oz. **£100-200**   *P*

A vinaigrette and scent bottle,
gilded box and top, all
hallmarked London, 1865,
maker S. Mordan, 4 in. **£100-
150**   *ST*

A silver vinaigrette by Wm.
arpe, 1841. **£140-160**   *MB*

(r) A silver vinaigrette, 1824.
£80-120   *MB*

) A plain silver box by S.
mberton, Birmingham, 1801.
0-60   *MB*

A silver vesta, Birmingham,
98. **£20-25**   *ST*

l) A silver cheroot piercer,
rmingham, 1899. **£25-30**

(mr) A sovereign and half
sovereign case, Birmingham,
1909. **£20-30**   *ST*

(r) A silver vesta, Chester, 1905.
£25-30   *ST*

An unusual Victorian vesta
case, modelled as a lady's leg
wearing a boot, maker Charles
Cheshire, Birmingham, 1886,
6.75 cm. high. **£150-200**   *P*

An oval double pen-knife vesta box, 5.6 cm. long, maker's mark of S. Mordan & Co., London, 1891. **£80-90** *SB*

VESTA BOX

- In 1830's the wax match introduced, called a 'Vesta'
- they rapidly took over from tinder boxes
- some early boxes also contained a cutter
- in 1860's instead of the flat lid opening — exposing the highly dangerous phosphorous vestas to the air — the lid was moved to the end of the box
- at the same time an interior spring was added — check that this is still in place
- interior almost always gilded

- the height of popularity was the end of the 19th C. when corners were normally rounded off
- the early boxes tended to be made in London, after about 1890, Birmingham took over until the vesta box ceased to be made after the First World War
- some Birmingham boxes have the assay mark of Chester as Birmingham had a bad reputation for making cheap silver
- vesta boxes bearing marks of other assay houses are very desirable

An American shaped oblong vesta case, 6.7 cm. high, by R. Wallace & Sons Manufacturing Co., Wallingford, Connecticut: silver-coloured metal, c. 1895-1905. **£40-50** *SB*

A shaped rectangular vesta case, 7.2 cm. high, silver-coloured metal, unmarked, probably U.S.A., early 20th C. **£50-70** *SB*

An American rectangular vesta case die-stamped on reverse with a schoolboy caddie carrying a bag of golf clubs, 5.8 cm. high, importer's mark of D. & G. Edward for Edward & Sons, Glasgow, 1903. **£30-50** *SB*

An American vesta case, 6.8 cm. high, silver-coloured metal, maker's mark of William B. Kerr & Co Newark, New Jersey, stamped: 1824, early 20th C. **£40-50** *SB*

A vesta case, 'Patent/8189/London', 3.8 cm. high, maker's mark MW, London, 1889. **£55-65** *SB*

A vesta case, 4.6 cm. diam., maker's mark J.F., Birmingham, 1907. **£100-150** *SB*

An engine-turned kidney bean vesta case, 4.1 cm. long, maker's mark of Saunders & Shepherd, badly struck, Birmingham, 1900. **£50-60** *SB*

An American oblong vesta case, 61.5 cm. long, silver-coloured metal, c. 1900. **£60-80** *SB*

A plain kidney bean vesta c 5.4 cm. high, maker's mark George Unite, Birmingham 1906. **£60-80** *SB*

A square vesta case, 5 cm. high, maker's mark of Henry Matthews, Birmingham, 1906. **£60-70** *SB*

A vesta case/cigar cutter, 5.5 cm. high, maker's mark of Horton & Allday, Birmingham, 1897, stamped: 'The Unity Patent', P.O.D.R. number: 161636. **£50-60** *SB*

An engraved oblong vesta case, 4.8 cm. high, maker's mark WHH, Birmingham, 1907. **£45-55** *SB*

Right
A rectangular 'Royal Exchange Assurance' vesta case, 5 cm. high, maker's mark BC incuse, Birmingham, 1909. **£90-110** *SB*

A French vesta case, with poppies in Art Nouveau st maker's mark of Emile Puiforcat, 5 cm. high, silv coloured metal, c. 1900. **£ 60** *SB*

A gold-mounted Cairngorm vinaigrette, the cover and base set with turquoise beads, c. 1830, 1¾ in. (45 mm.) long. £2,000-2,300   C

A Russian vari-coloured gold snuff-box (split to rear wall), early 19th C., interior stamped label, red leather case (defective), 3¼ in. (83 mm.) long. £1,000-1,200   C

A gold-mounted Cairngorm desk seal, with revolving triple seal (blind), c. 1830, 4¼ in. (108 mm.) long. £800-1,000   C

A Swiss gold snuff-box, engraved with St. George and the Dragon, interior with later initials and date, early 19th C., 3⅝ in. (92 mm.) long. £1,150-1,300   C

A vari-coloured gold vinaigrette, early 19th C., probably Swiss, 1¾ in. (45 mm.) wide. £1,100-1,300   C

Left
A gold-mounted smoky quartz vinaigrette, the cover with cabochon crystal (hinge defective), c. 1840, 2¼ in. (56 mm.) long. £300-360   C

An engine-turned gold double snuff-box, with diagonally hinged covers, early 19th C., fitted red leather case, 4 in. (100 mm.) long. £1,100-1,300   C

A gold vinaigrette, the cover inscribed 'Emma', 19th C., 1⅜ (35 mm.) wide. £420-500

A French engine-turned gold snuff-box, edged in deep blue enamel, 19th C., 3½ in. (89 mm.) long. £2,200-2,600   C

A George II mocha-agate snuff-box, with chased cagework mounts, c. 1755, 3¼ in. (83 mm.) long. £2,100-2,400   C

A Swiss vari-coloured gold snuff-box, early 19th C., maker's initials CCS, fitted red leather case, 3⅜ in. (85 mm.). £1,000-1,200   C

An engine-turned gold snuff-box, the cover engraved with inscription and with small hair compartment, 18 ct., by John Linnit, London, 1828, 2½ in. (63 mm.) long. £1,500-1,700   C

A gold-mounted ivory snuff-box, carved with head of Medusa and the interior with miniature portrait of Mary, Queen of Scots, early 18th C., in. (85 mm.) long. £1,200-400   C

A Swiss gold snuff-box, early th C., maker's initials GT use, 3⅜ in. (85 mm.) long. £1,100-1,500   C

An octagonal gold snuff-box, with green-gold foliage borders, c. 1800, 2⅜ in. (60 mm.) long. £1,300-1,500   C

425

An engine-turned gold snuff-box, with Coronation medal of George II, and with portrait of Queen Caroline, 18 ct., by A. J. Strachan, London, 1807, 3 in. (75 mm.) long. **£800-900** *C*

A gold snuff-box, the cover with jasper panel, c. 1840, unmarked, 3⅛ in. (80 mm.) long. **£800-900** *C*

A vari-coloured gold vinaigrette, the covers bold chased in four colour gold, w short suspension chain, probably Swiss, 19th C., 1¼ (32 mm.) long. **£800-900**

A French engine-turned snuff-box, of concave section, early 19th C. with maker's initials J.F.M. and squirrel above, 3⅛ in. (80 mm.) long. **£1,450-1,600** *C*

A small rectangular gold musical snuff box (mechanism defective), French or Swiss, with key, early 19th C., 2¼ in. (57 mm.) long. **£2,500-3,000** *C*

A Swiss enamelled gold snu box, with painted views of t Lake of Geneva (chips overa maker's mark crowned, IC(? fitted case, 3⅛ in. long, c. 18: **£1,300-1,600** *C*

A French engine-turned gold snuff-box, of concave section, 19th C., 3¾ in. (95 mm.) long. **£1,600-2,000** *C*

A Swiss gold snuff-box (two dents to base rim), maker's initials MC incuse, 2⅞ in. long, c. 1800. **£1,000-1,600** *C*

A French engine-turned gol snuff-box, 3⅜ in. (86 mm.) lo **£1,000-1,200** *C*

A French gold snuff-box, 19th C., 3½ in. (89 mm.) long. **£1,600-1,900** *C*

A French gold-mounted tortoiseshell snuff-box, with an Italian micro-mosaic of a chaffinch, gold lining, Paris, 2⅝ in. diam., early 19th C. **£530-650** *C*

An Italian gold-mounted green porphyry-box, the cover set with an onyx cameo (hairline cracks), 2⅝ in. diam., the cameo early 18th C., the box 19th C. **£500-600** *C*

An Alfred Clark 18 ct. gold-mounted clear-glass powder box, lid engraved in intaglio and set with red gemstones, 1 cm. long, maker's mark, London 1901, engraved, 'Cla 33 New Bond Street', **£600-720** *SB*

A gold-mounted Cairngorm paper-knife, c. 1830, 115 mm. long. **£440-500** *C*

A vari-coloured gold sealing wax case, of oval section, probably Swiss, possibly by Johann Jakob II Handema 1790, 5⅛ in. (132 mm.) long **£550-650** *C*

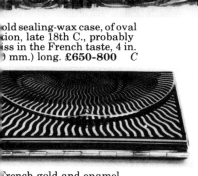

...old sealing-wax case, of oval ...tion, late 18th C., probably ...ass in the French taste, 4 in. ...0 mm.) long. **£650-800** *C*

...French gold and enamel ...mpact, by Van Cleef et ...els, Paris, with velvet slip ...e, 3⅛ in. (80 mm.) long. ...00-1,100 *C*

A small gold-mounted ivory card-case, the cover inscribed 'Souvenir D'Amitie', late 18th C., 2½ in. (60 mm.) high. **£420-500** *C*

A Faberge kovsh, the detachable rim and handle with applied seed-pearl decoration on a pinkish-brown ground, 84 standard, Moscow, 1908-17, 7⅝ in. (194 mm.) diam. **£1,600-1,900** *C*

...Iexican vari-coloured gold ...eroot-case, in green and red ...l, c. 1830, bearing ...aymaster's marks, 2⅜ in. (60 ...) long. **£1,100-1,300** *C*

A George III gold-mounted bloodstone egg bonbonniere, the cover with white enamel band inscribed 'l'amour surmonte tout obstacle' (small repair), c. 1765, 1⅞ in. (48 mm.) high. **£1,000-1,300** *C*

A George III gold-mounted green jasper etui, containing knife, scissors, combined file and tweezers and pencil holder, the case with later gold strengthening straps (stone cracked), mid-18th C., 3⅜ in. (86 mm.) high. **£700-800** *C*

A George II gold-mounted bloodstone etui, with diamond-set pushpiece (some damage to mounts), c. 1750, original fish-skin case, 4 in. (100 mm.) long. **£380-430** *C*

...George III gold-mounted ...odstone scent-flask, c. 1765, ...h French restricted ...rranty mark, 2¾ in. (70 mm.) ...h. **£400-450** *C*

A gold-mounted cut-glass scent bottle, 18th C., 3¼ in. (83 mm.) high. **£350-400** *C*

A gold and jasper table-seal, 1⅝ in. (41 mm.) high. **£500-600** *C*

...Louis XV vari-coloured gold ...it-knife, with one gold and ...e silver blade, in original ...agreen case (slightly ...maged), by Mathieu Coiny, ...ris, 1761, 4⅝ in. (117 mm.) ...g. **£1,700-2,000** *C*

Miller's Antiques Price Guide builds up year by year to form the most comprehensive photo-reference system available. The first three volumes contain over 20,000 completely different photographs.

A George III gold-mounted shagreen etui, containing fruit knife, scissors, ivory slip and pencil (two pieces missing), 3⅞ in. high, c. 1760. **£380-460** *C*

A rare old Sheffield snuff box, c. 1820. **£80-120**   *EAN*

A late Victorian silver plat sugar sifter spoon, marked & S. **£7-10**

An E.P.N.S. silver plate su sifter spoon, marked AT & **£3-5**

A silver-plated forward leaning figure of a winged nymph, 10 in. (25.5 cm.) high. **£100-120** *CSK*

An electroplated Britannia metal Nautilus cup, in the form of a Cupid, probably WMF, Germany, c. 1905, 47.5 cm. high. **£200-250**   *SB*

A Mappin silver plate sugar sifter spoon, with gilded bowl in mint condition, c. 1850. **£12-15**

A pair of Sheffield three light candelabra, with double sun mark of The Mathew Boulton Plate Co., 15 in. overall height. **£240-300**   *L*

A pair of Victorian silver plate berry sugar sifter spoons, marked Potter. **£11-13**

An early 20th C. silver p sugar sifter spoon. **£4-6**

A pair of old Sheffield plate candlesticks, mark of Blagden, Hodgson & Son, 9 in. high, c. 1820. **£95-135**   *EAN*

A pair of old Sheffield plate candlesticks, c. 1790, 6½ in. high. **£140-180**   *EAN*

A pair of silver plate George I style candlesticks, by Elkington, c. 1860, 9 in. high. **£125-150**   *BTH*

A Sheffield silver-plated 6-li candelabrum, with lobed ed detachable nozzles, no mak mark, c. 1850. **£250-290**

Sheffield silver-plated 6-light adelabrum, 32¾ in. **£250-** 0   *L*

Sheffield plate chamberstick th candlesnuffer and mmer, c. 1800. **£30-35** VG

n old Sheffield plate snuffer ay, c. 1790, 9½ in. long. **£30-**)   *EAN*

Sheffield silver-plated soup reen, cover and stand, graved with a coat of arms d a crest, cross keys mark of nry Wilkinson & Co., pre-50, 22 in. **£200-300**   *L*

A Heatmaster Easi-nest electroplated stacking tea service, comprising tea pot, hot-water jug, sugar basin and milk jug, stamped trade marks, Reg. Des. No. 853938, 1930's, 30.25 cm. stacked height. **£95-150**   *SB*

An old Sheffield plate snuffer tray, 9 in. long. **£30-60**   *EAN*

An old Sheffield plate chamber stick, c. 1840, 7 in. wide. **£30-60** *EAN*

An electroplate ewer and basin, probably French, c. 1880, 21 in. (53.5 cm.) wide, 26 in. (66 cm.) high. **£200-300**   *SBe*

A silver-plate tureen, c. 1820, 16 by 11 by 12 in. **£200-300** *ELR*

An English electroplated 3-piece tea set and tray, engraved in the Japanese taste, the tray 28.2 cm. wide, unmarked, c. 1885 (case). **£150-200**   *SB*

A pair of George III Sheffield plate 3-branch candelabra, 20 in. high. **£200-300**   *DSH*

A pair of five-light Candelabra, 56.5 cm. high, low-grade silver-coloured metal, German, early 20th C., 1779 gm. (57.2 oz.) (excluding the base). **£500-700**   *SB*

A 19th C. Sheffield plate helmet creamer, 6 in. high. **£35-40** *EA*

A Hukin and Heath electroplated sauce-tureen, cover and ladle, designed by Christopher Dresser, on three spike feet, H. & H. marks, 2188, 28th July 1880, 14.5 cm. diam. **£300-400**   *C*

An old Sheffield plate tea
caddy, 4½ in. **£45-50**   *EAN*

A Victorian electroplated
presentation tea and coffee
service and tray, engraved with
a monogram, the tray with a
presentation inscription, by
Elkington & Co., in oak case, c.
1880-1885. **£200-250**   *L*

A James Dixon and Sons
electroplate tea urn, with
presentation inscription,
maker's mark, c. 1878, 22 in.
cm.) high. **£200-300**   *SBe*

A pair of 18th C. old Sheffield
plate coasters, c. 1790, 6 in.
diam. **£210-270**   *JGM*

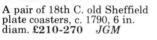

A set of four late 18th C. oil and
vinegar Sheffield plate
coasters. **£62-70** set   *EA*

An electroplated tea-urn, the
interior fittings intact, 21½ in.
£180-230   *L*

A pair of old Sheffield pla
goblets, c. 1820, 6¼ in. hi
£130-160 pair *EAN*

A fine pair of 19th C. Sheffield
plate wine coasters. **£165-185**
pair   *EA*

A rare old Sheffield plate sugar
basket. c. 1780. 4½ in. wide.
£50-80   *EAN*

A silver-plate bowl, height 2
cm., diam. 31 cm., weight 53 o
hallmarked Birmingham 19
£560-650   *SKC*

A 19th C. Sheffield plate
samovar, 15½ in. high. **£245-
285**   *EA*

A 19th C. silver-plated inkwell,
11¾ in. wide. **£40-60**   *SV*

An old Sheffield plate wi
cooler, c. 1800. **£150-20**
EAN

ated 58th Squadron desk
ament, bearing squadron
nber and motto, 14 cm. high,
t label of Goldsmiths' and
ersmiths' Company,
don. **£105-130** *SKC*

electroplated Table
trepiece. supporting a clear-
ss dish, 66 cm. height,
lish, c. 1860, patch. **£200-**
SB

The town of Chester has long been associated with gold and silver working, moneyers being recorded there from Saxon times, and goldsmiths from the thirteenth century. Nevertheless, there were no Assay Office marks relating to the town until 1686 and, although makers' marks are found of much earlier date, no sequence of date-letters occurred here until 1701. The Act of 1701 also marked the beginning of sequential date-letters from Exeter where goldsmiths had been working since at least the fourteenth century.

York, being the nation's Second City during the Middle Ages is believed to have established a date-letter sequence as early as 1559, and had a town mark in 1411. The office at York closed in 1857, that at Exeter closing 25 years later, in 1882.

Chester

	A	B	C	D	E	F	G	H	I	J	K
A	1701	1726	1751	1776	1797	1818	1839	1864	1884	1901	1926
B	1702	1727	1752	1777	1798	1819	1840	1865	1885	1902	1927
C	1703	1728	1753	1778	1799	1820	1841	1866	1886	1903	1928
D	1704	1729	1754	1779	1800	1821–2	1842	1867	1887	1904	1929
E	1705	1730	1755	1780	1801	1823	1843	1868	1888	1905	1930
F	1706	1731	1756	1781	1802	1824	1844	1869	1889	1906	1931
G	1707	1732	1757	1782	1803	1825	1845	1870	1890[1]	1907	1932
H	1708	1733	1758	1783	1804	1826	1846	1871	1891	1908	1933
I	1709	1734	1759	1784[1]	1805	1827	1847	1872	1892	1909	1934
K	1710	1735	1760	1785	1806	1828	1848	1873	1893	1910	1935
L	1711	1736	1761	1786	1807	1829	1849	1874	1894	1911	1936
M	1712	1737	1762	1787	1808	1830	1850	1875	1895	1912	1937
N	1713	1738	1763	1788	1809	1831	1851	1876	1896	1913	1938
O	1714	1739	1764	1789	1810	1832	1852	1877	1897	1914	1939
P	1715	1740	1765	1790	1811	1833	1853	1878	1898	1915	1940
Q	1716	1741	1766	1791	1812	1834	1854	1879	1899	1916	1941
R	1717	1742	1767	1792	1813	1835	1855	1880	1900	1917	1942
S	1718	1743	1768	1793	1814	1836	1856	1881	——	1918	1943
T	1719	1744	1769	1794	1815	1837	1857	1882	——	1919	1944
U	1720	1745	1770	1795	1816	1838	1858	1883	——	1920	1945
V	1721	1746	1771	1796	1817	——	1859	——	——	1921	1946
W	1722	1747	1772			——	1860	——	——	1922	1947
X	1723	1748	1773	——	——	——	1861	——	——	1923	1948
Y	1724	1749	1774	——	——	——	1862	——	——	1924	1949
Z	1725	1750	(1775)	——	——	——	1863	——	——	1925	1950

1. The *Sovereign's Head* mark was added on 1 December 1784 to show the payment of duty and continued until 30 April 1890.

Exeter

1701	1725	1749	1773	1797	1817	1837	1857	1877	
1702	1726	1750	1774	1798	1818	1838	1858	1878	
1703	1727	1751	1775	1799	1819	1839	1859	1879	
1704	1728	1752	1776	1800	1820	1840	1860	1880	
1705	1729	1753	1777	1801	1821	1841	1861	1881	
1706	1730	1754	1778	1802	1822	1842	1862	1882	
1707	1731	1755	1779	1803	1823	1843	1863		
1708	1732	1756	1780	1804	1824	1844	1864		
1709	1733	1757	1781–2	1805	1825	1845	1865		
1710	1734	1758	1783	1806	1826	1846	1866		
1711	1735	1759	1784[1]	1807	1827	1847	1867		
1712	1736	1760	1785	1808	1828	1848	1868		
1713	1737	1761	1786	1809	1829	1849	1869		
1714	1738	1762	1787	1810	1830	1850	1870		
1715	1739	1763	1788	1811	1831	1851	1871		
1716	1740	1764	1789	1812	1832	1852	1872		
1717	1741	1765	1790	1813	1833	1853	1873		
1718	1742	1766	1791	1814	1834	1854	1874		
1719	1743	1767	1792	1815	1835	1855	1875		
——	1744	1768	1793	1816	1836	1856	1876		
1720									
1721	1745	1769	1794	——	——				
1722	1746	1770	1795	——	——				
1723	1747	1771	1796	——	——				
1724	1748	1772	——	——					

York

	A	B	C	D	E	F	G	H	I
A	1631	1657	1682	1700	(1776)	1787	1812	1837	
B	1632	1658	1683	1701	(1777)	1788	1813	1838	
C	1633	1659	1684	1702	1778	1789	1814	1839	
D	1634	1660	1685	1703	1779	1790	1815	1840	
E	1635	1661	1686	(1704)	1780	1791	1816	1841	
F	1636	1662	1687	1705	1781	1792	1817	1842	
G	1637	1663	1688	1706	1782	1793	1818	1843	
H	1638	1664	1689	——	1783	1794	1819	1844	
I	1639	1665	1690	——		1795	1820	1845	
J	(1640)				1784	——			
K	1641	1666	1691	——	1785	1796	1821	1846	
L	1642	1667	1692	——	1786	1797	1822	1847	
M	1643	1668	1693	——		1798	1823	1848	
N	1644	1669	1694	——		1799	1824	1849	
O	1645	1670	1695	——	——	1800	1825	1850	
P	1646	1671	1696	——	——	1801	1826	1851	
Q	1647	1672	1697	——	——	1802	1827	1852	
R	1648	1673	1698	——	——	1803	1828	1853	
S	1649	1674	1699	——	——	1804	1829	1854	
T	1650	1675	——	——	——	1805	1830	1855	
U	1651	1676	——	——	——	1806	1831	——	
V	1652	1677	——	——	——	1807	1832	1856	
W	1653	1678	——	——	——	1808	1833		
X	1654	1679	——	——	——	1809	1834		
Y	1655	1680	——	——	——	1810	1835		
Z	1656	1681	——	——	——	1811	1836		

Former Assay Office Marks. Several of the larger provincial cities had Assay Offices which are now closed. Each had its distinctive mark, some of the mor important of which are shown below. There is also an Assay Office in Dublin and marks struck there before 1st April 1923 are recognised as approved British hallmarks. The Dublin mark is a figure of Hibernia.

Exeter

Glasgow

Newcastle

Chester

Dublir

London

gold & Sterling silver | Britannia silver

London		Exeter/cont								
1678	a	1712		1744		1780	e	1815	U	1850
1679	b	1713		1745	k	1781	f	1816	a	1851
1680	c	1714		1746	l	1782	g	1817	b	1852
1681	d	1715		1747	m	1783	h	1818	C	1853
1682	e	1716	A	1748	n			1819	d	1854
1683	f	1717	B	1749	O	1784	i	1820	e	1855
1684	g	1718	C	1750	P	1785	k	1821	f	1856
1685	h	1719	D	1751	q			1822	g	1857
1686	i	1720	E	1752	r	1786	l	1823	h	1858
1687	k	1721	F	1753	I	1787	m	1824	i	1859
1688	l	1722	G	1754	t	1788	n	1825	k	1860
1689	m	1723	H	1755	U	1789	O	1826	l	1861
1690	n	1724	I	1756	A	1790	P	1827	m	1862
1691	o			1757	B	1791	q	1828	n	1863
1692	p	1725	K	1758	C	1792	r	1829	o	1864
1693	q	1726	L	1759	D	1793	s	1830	p	1865
1694	r	1727	M	1760	C	1794	u	1831	q	1866
1695	s	1728	N	1761	f	1795	u	1832	r	1867
1696	t			1762	G	1796	A	1833	s	1868
		1729	O	1763	H	1797	B			1869
1697	a/b	1730	P	1764	J	1798	C	1834	t	1870
1698	c	1731	Q	1765	T	1799	D	1835	u	1871
1699	d	1732	R	1766	Z	1800	E	1836	A	1872
1700	e	1733	S	1767	m	1801	F	1837	B	1873
1701	ff	1734	T	1768	n	1802	G			1874
1702	g	1735	V	1769	O	1803	H	1838	C	1875
1703	h	1736	a	1770	P	1804	I	1839	D	1876
1704	i	1737	b	1771	Q	1805	K	1840	E	1877
1705	k	1738	C	1772	R	1806	L	1841	F	
1706	l	1739	d	1773	S	1807	M	1842	G	
1707	m			1774	T	1808	N	1843	H	
1708	n	1739	d	1775	U	1809	O	1844	J	
1709	o	1740	e	1776	a	1810	P	1845	K	
1710	p	1741	f	1777	b	1811	Q	1846	L	
1711	q	1742	g	1778	C	1812	R	1847	M	
		1743	h	1779	d	1813	S	1848	N	
						1814	T	1849	O	

Chester		Dublin	
1878	C	1904	
1879	D	1905	
1880	E	1906	
1881	F	1907	
1882	G	1908	
1883	H	1909	
1884	I	1910	
1885	K	1911	
1886	L	1912	
1887	M	1913	
1888	N	1914	
1889	O	1915	
1890	P	1916	
1891	Q	1917	
1892	R	1918	
1893	S	1919	
1894	T	1920	
1895	U	1921	
		1922	
1896	a	1923	
1897	b	1924	
1898	c	1925	
1899	d	1926	
1900	e	1927	
1901	f	1928	
1902	g	1929	
1903	h		

Birmingham

Birmingham			
1773	A	1778	F
1774	B	1779	G
1775	C	1780	H
1776	D	1781	I
1777	E	1782	K
		1783	L
		1784	
		1785	
		1786	
		1787	

Sterling silver
Marked in England

 Marked in Scotland

gold   silver   gold   silver

Birmingham   Sheffield

Birmingham

Year	Letter
1788	Q
1789	R
1790	S
1791	T
1792	U
1793	V
1794	W
1795	X
1796	Y
1797	Z
1798	a
1799	b
1800	c
1801	d
1802	e
1803	f
1804	g
1805	h
1806	i
1807	j
1808	k
1809	l
1810	m
1811	n
1812	o
1813	p
1814	q
1815	r
1816	s
1817	t
1818	u
1819	v
1820	w
1821	x
1822	y
1823	Z
1824	A
1825	B
1826	C
1827	D
1828	E
1829	F
1830	G
1831	H
1832	J
1833	K
1834	L
1835	M
1836	N
1837	O
1838	P
1839	Q
1840	R
1841	S
1842	T
1843	U
1844	V
1845	W
1846	X
1847	Y
1848	Z
1849	A
1850	B
1851	C
1852	D
1853	E
1854	F
1855	G
1856	H
1857	I
1858	J
1859	K
1860	L
1861	M
1862	N
1863	O
1864	P
1865	Q
1866	R
1867	S
1868	T
1869	U
1870	V
1871	W
1872	X
1873	Y
1874	Z
1875	a
1876	b
1877	c
1878	d
1879	e
1880	f
1881	g
1882	h
1883	i
1884	k
1885	l
1886	m
1887	n
1888	o
1889	p
1890	q
1891	r
1892	s
1893	t
1894	u
1895	v
1896	w
1897	x
1898	y
1899	z
1900	a
1901	b
1902	c
1903	d
1904	e
1905	f
1906	g
1907	h
1908	i
1909	j
1910	k
1911	l
1912	m
1913	n
1914	o
1915	p
1916	q
1917	r
1918	s
1919	t
1920	u
1921	v
1922	w
1923	x
1924	y
1925	z
1926	A
1927	B
1928	C
1929	D

Sheffield

Year	Letter
1773	E
1774	F
1775	H
1776	R
1777	h
1778	S
1779	A
1780	Z
1781	D
1782	G
1783	B
1784	I
1785	V
1786	k
1787	L
1788	m
1789	M
1790	L
1791	P
1792	U
1793	q
1794	m
1795	q
1796	Z
1797	X
1798	V
1799	E
1800	N
1801	H
1802	M
1803	F
1804	G
1805	B
1806	A
1807	S
1808	P
1809	K
1810	L
1811	C
1812	D
1813	R
1814	W
1815	O
1816	T
1817	X
1818	I
1819	V
1820	Q
1821	Y
1822	Z
1823	U
1824	a
1825	b
1826	c
1827	d
1828	e
1829	f
1830	g
1831	h
1832	k
1833	l
1834	m
1835	p
1836	q
1837	r
1838	S
1839	t
1840	u
1841	V
1842	X
1843	Z
1844	A
1845	B
1846	C
1847	D
1848	E
1849	F
1850	G
1851	H
1852	I
1853	K
1854	L
1855	M
1856	N
1857	O
1858	P
1859	R
1860	S
1861	T
1862	U
1863	V
1864	W
1865	X
1866	Y
1867	Z
1868	A
1869	B
1870	C
1871	D
1872	E
1873	F
1874	G
1875	H
1876	J
1877	K
1878	L
1879	M
1880	N
1881	O
1882	P
1883	Q
1884	R
1885	S
1886	T
1887	U
1888	V
1889	W
1890	X
1891	Y
1892	Z
1893	a
1894	b
1895	c
1896	d
1897	e
1898	f
1899	g
1900	h
1901	i
1902	k
1903	l
1904	m
1905	n
1906	o
1907	p
1908	q
1909	r
1910	s
1911	t
1912	u

Duty Marks. Between 1784 and 1890 an excise duty on gold and silver articles was collected by the Assay Offices and a mark depicting the Sovereign's head was struck to show that it had been paid. These are two examples.

gold & silver

George III

Victoria

Edinburgh

Year	Mark	Year	Mark	Year	Mark	Year	Mark	Year	Mark	Year	Mark
(castle)		1741	M	1777	A	1812	g	1847	A	1884	c
1705	A	1742	N	1778	Z	1813	h	1848	R	1885	d
1706	B	1743	O	1779	A	1814	i	1849	S	1886	e
1707	C	1744	P	1780	A	1815	j	1850	T	1887	f
1708	D	1745	Q	1781	B	1816	k	1851	H	1888	g
1709	E	1746	R	1782	C	1817	l	1852	U	1889	h
1710	F	1747	S	1783	D	1818	m	1853	W	1890	i
1711	G	1748	T	(castle/thistle/head) 1819	n	1854	X	(castle/thistle) 1891	k
1712	H	1749	U	1784	E			1855	Y	1892	l
1713	I	1750	V	1785	F	1820	o	1856	Z	1893	m
1714	K	1751	W	(castle/thistle/head) 1821	p	1857	A	1894	n
1715	L	1752	X	1786	G	1822	q	1858	B	1895	o
1716	M	1753	Y	1787	G	1823	r	1859	C	1896	p
1717	N	1754	Z	1788	H	1824	s	1860	D	1897	q
1718	O	1755	A	1789	I J	1825	t	1861	E	1898	r
1719	P	1756	B	1790	K	1826	u	1862	F	1899	s
1720	Q	1757	C	1791	L	1827	v	1863	G	1900	t
1721	R	1758	D	1792	M	1828	w	1864	H	1901	u
1722	S	(castle/thistle)		1793		1829	x	1865	I	1902	w
1723	T	1759	E	1794	N	1830	y	1866	K	1903	x
1724	U	1760	F	1795	P	1831	z	1867	L	1904	y
1725	V	1761	G	1796	Q	1832	A	1868	M	1905	z
1726	W	1762	H	1797	R	1833	S	1869	N	1906	A
1727	X	1763	I	1798	S	1834	C	1870	O	1907	B
1728	Y	1764	K	1799	T	1835	D	1871	P	1908	C
1729	Z	1765	L	1800	U	1836	E	1872	Q	1909	D
1730	A	1766	M	1801	V	1837	F	1873	R	1910	E
1731	B	1767	N	1802	W	1838	G	1874	S	1911	F
1732	C	1768	O	1803	X	1839	J	1875	T	1912	G
1733	D	1769	P	1804	Y	1840	J	1876	U	1913	H
1734	E	1770	Q	(castle/thistle/head) 1805	Z	(castle/thistle/head) 1877	V	1914	I
1735	F	1771	R	1806	a	1841	K	1878	W	1915	K
1736	G	1772	S	1807	b	1842	L	1879	X	1916	L
1737	H	1773	T	1808	c	1843	M	1880	Y	1917	M
1738	I	1774	U	1809	d	1844	N	1881	Z	1918	N
1739	K	1775	V	1810	e	1845	O	1882	a	1919	O
1740	L	1776	X	1811	f	1846	P	1883	b		

ENGLISH DRINKING GLASSES

l 18th century glasses should
ve a pontil mark under the foot,
ept that some faceted stem
sses had the pontil mark
und out during cutting of the
m. The presence of a pontil
rk does not, however, prove
at a glass is 18th century. Pontil
rks were left on some genuine
rly 19th century glasses, and are
be found on later glasses,
luding reproductions.

l feet and bowls of 18th century
sses should show striations
d tooling marks. A clear foot
th a smooth undersurface
licates a late 19th or 20th
tury glass. (A knowledge of the
nufacturing methods and the
ls used will assist in any
sessment of the marks found in
d on an 18th and early 19th
tury glass.)

nerally speaking, the diameter
the foot should be greater than
at of the bowl. However this is
t necessarily so on some late
th and early 19th century
mmers and later glasses with
dimentary stems.

tting was introduced on
glish glass sometime between
09-1719, and there is little
idence to support cutting on
nking glasses before 1750.

amond point engraving is found
an occasional early 18th
tury glass and the 'Amen'
cobite glasses and, in the former
se, if contemporary, is rare.
eel engraving was introduced
out 1725. Much commemorative

and Jacobite glass has been later
engraved. The quality of the
engraving is not always a reliable
guide.

The colour of an 18th and early
19th century glass is important,
but too much emphasis should not
be placed on this point, as so many
factors in the manufacturing
process could affect the eventual
colour. Some late 17th century
balusters had a greeny tint which
changed to a dark greyish and
then black tint in the early 18th
century. After the Balustroid
period glasses got progressively
clearer and brighter owing to
improvements, both in the
ingredients used and the
manufacturing processes.

A number of soda glasses are to be
found. There is nothing wrong
with these; they were a cheap
substitute for the lead glasses, but
are of little interest to collectors of
English glass. Size for size with
lead glasses, they are much
lighter, the metal hasn't the
brilliance of lead glass, and the
presence of a large number of
minute air bubbles (seed) often
helps these glasses to be
identified.

Poorly made 18th and early 19th
century glasses were not
uncommon, therefore, examples
made with good 'metal', with good
proportions and workmanship,
will always command a premium
over lesser examples.
Discrimination is necessary.

Dating of 18th & Early 19th Century English Drinking Glasses

Baluster stems	1685-1725
Moulded pedestal stems	1715-65
(Sweetmeats went on later)	
Balustroid stems	1725-60
Lightbalusters (including Newcastles)	1735-65
Composite stems	1745-75
Plain stems	1730-75
Air twist stems	1745-70
Incised twist stems	1750-70
Hollow stems	1750-60
Opaque white stems	1755-80
Mixed twist stems	1755-75
Colour twist stems	1755-75
Faceted stems	1760-1810
Rudimentary stems	Throughout the 18th & early 19th century

A pedestal — stemmed wine
glass, straight sided funnel
bowl set on octagonally
moulded tapering stem, c. 1730,
14 cm. high. **£400-500** *C*

our-sided pedestal-stemmed
e-glass, thistle-shaped bowl,
shoulder to the stem with a
wn at each angle and with
rs between, and enclosing an
ngated tear, folded foot, c.
5, 15.5 cm. high. **£800-
)** *C*

A pedestal-stemmed wine-
glass, funnel bowl with solid
lower part, tapering
octagonally-moulded stem,
folded conical foot, c. 1715, 15.5
cm. high. **£260-300** *C*

A four-sided pedestal stemmed
wine-glass, bell bowl, the
tapering square stem with stars
at the angles enclosing an
elongated tear, folded conical
foot, c. 1720, 15.5 cm. high.
£270-330 *C*

A pedestal-stemmed
champagne-glass, cup-topped
bowl on an annular knop,
hexagonally-moulded stem,
domed and folded foot, c. 1745,
17 cm. high. **£350-400** *C*

435

A pedestal-stemmed champagne-glass, rounded bowl, spirally-moulded octagonal stem, domed and folded foot, c. 1745, 17 cm. high. **£65-100** *C*

A baluster wine-glass, straight-sided funnel bowl with a solid lower part, inverted baluster stem with a large tear, folded foot, c. 1700, 15.5 cm. high. **£400-460** *C*

A baluster wine-glass, the funnel bowl with a tear to the solid lower part, on an inverted baluster section with an elongated tear above a folded conical foot, c. 1700, 14 cm. high. **£280-330** *C*

A baluster wine-glass, funn bowl with a solid lower part an inverted baluster stem enclosing a small tear abov base knob, domed and folde foot, c. 1705, 16 cm. high. **£2 280** *C*

A baluster wine-glass, flared funnel bowl with solid lower part, inverted baluster stem and base knob, folded conical foot, c. 1715, 14.5 cm. high. **£180-220** *C*

A baluster wine-glass, bell bowl on a cushion knop above an inverted baluster section and triple annulated base knob, domed foot, c. 1720, 16.5 cm. high. **£170-220** *C*

A baluster wine-glass, funnel bowl with a tear to the solid lower part, on an annulated knop, above an inverted baluster section and base knob, domed and folded foot, c. 1720, 17 cm. high. **£450-520** *C*

A baluster wine-glass, funn bowl on a baluster knop and inverted baluster knop divi by an annular knop, domed a folded foot, c. 1720, 13.5 cm. high. **£200-260** *C*

A baluster wine-glass, bell bowl, inverted baluster stem enclosing a tear above a base knob, folded conical foot, c. 1730, 16 cm. high. **£140-180** *C*

A 'kit-kat' style wine glass, with ogee bowl, inverted baluster at base of stem, c. 1740, 6½ in. high. **£240-280** *AA*

A baluster wine-glass, bell bowl with a tear to the solid lower part, inverted baluster stem enclosing a tear, domed foot, c. 1730, 16 cm. high. **£220-280** *C*

Right
A balustroid wine-glass of drawn-trumpet shape, the stem enclosing an elongated tear, supported on a triple collar above an inverted baluster section and base knob, domed foot, c. 1735, 19 cm. high. **£180-220** *C*

'Kit-Kat' wine-glass of drawn-trumpet shape, the stem enclosing a tear on a slender inverted baluster section, plain foot, (small chip to underside of foot), c. 1745, 17.5 cm. high. £120-140   C

A 'Kit-Kat' wine-glass of drawn-trumpet shape, the stem with an elongated tear above an inverted baluster section, on conical folded foot, c. 1750, 16 cm. high. £130-160   C

A light baluster wine-glass, trumpet shaped bowl on a cushion knop above an inverted acorn knop, plain section, inverted baluster knop and base knob, plain foot, Newcastle, c. 1740, 18 cm. high. £170-215 C

A wine-glass, bell bowl on a beaded knop above an inverted baluster section enclosing a tear, folded conical foot, c. 1750, 16.5 cm. high. £120-150   C

A baluster wine-glass, slender bell bowl, on a triple annulated knop above an inverted baluster section and base knob, conical foot, c. 1715, 21 cm. high. £400-460   C

A Newcastle baluster wine-glass, trumpet-shaped bowl on a ball knop above a beaded acorn knop, inverted baluster section enclosing a tear and base knob, plain foot, c. 1750, 18.5 cm. high. £350-400   C

A balustroid wine-glass, bowl of trumpet shape with solid lower part, wide stem tapering towards the base, plain foot, c. 1740, 16.5 cm. high. £100-130   C

A Newcastle wine-glass with funnel bowl, the stem with a drop-knop, cushion and beaded knops above inverted baluster section, on a folded foot, c. 1750, 16.5 cm. high. £200-250   C

A Dutch-engraved Newcastle wine-glass, funnel bowl engraved and inscribed above 'Fructus Amoris', on a triple annulated knop above slender inverted baluster section and base knob, conical foot, c. 1750, 18 cm. high. £800-950   C

A baluster wine-glass, funnel bowl with a small tear on an acorn knop above a base knob, folded conical foot, c. 1700, 14.5 cm. high. £750-850   C

A baluster wine-glass, the straight-sided funnel bowl with solid lower part on a mushroom knop with a tear above a plain section and base knob, folded conical foot, c. 1700, 16 cm. high. £600-700   C

A baluster wine-glass, funnel bowl on a cyst above an acorn knop and base knob, folded foot, c. 1710, 13.5 cm. high. **£550-650** *C*

A Newcastle wine glass, the round funnel bowl engraved with coat of arms on Newcastle stem, plain conical foot, 7½ in., c. 1750. **£800-900** *Som*

A rare fluted bowl wine glas with tear and collar knop on swollen stem (with second tea folded foot, c. 1710. **£590-65(** *AA*

A light-baluster Jacobite wine-glass, bell bowl engraved with a six-petalled rose and a bud, supported on a cushion and beaded knops above a swelling waist and base knob, domed foot, c. 1750, 17 cm. high. **£550-650** *C*

A baluster wine-glass, funnel bowl with a tear to the solid lower part, on a triple annulated knop above a plain section and base knob with an elongated tear, domed foot, c. 1715, 15 cm. high. **£300-360** *C*

A heavy baluster wine glass, the conical bowl with deep solid base and air tear on a stem with a conical knop and air tear on domed folded foot, c. 1710, 5⅝ in. **£550-650** *Som*

A baluster wine-glass, bell bowl on a knop above a drop knop, true baluster knop and base knob, high domed foot, c. 1720, 14 cm high. **£160-200** *C*

A baluster wine-glass, the funnel bowl with a small tea on a triple annulated knop enclosing a tear above a pla section and base knob, high domed foot, c. 1720, 15.5 cm. high. **£260-300** *C*

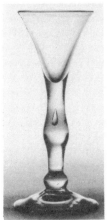

A baluster wine-glass, waisted bowl with solid lower part, on a wide collar above a plain stem with swelling waist knop, plain foot (two chips to foot rim and a small bruise to rim), c. 1725, 16 cm. high. **£100-150** *C*

A balustroid wine-glass of drawn-trumpet shape, the stem with swelling waist knop, with a small tear with base knob and conical foot, c. 1725, 16.5 cm. high. **£100-130** *C*

A baluster wine-glass, bell bowl supported on a triple-ringed collar above a true baluster section and base knob, folded foot, c. 1720, 16 cm. high. **£450-520** *C*

A baluster wine-glass, trumpe shaped bowl with a tear to th solid lower part on a triple colla above a cushion knop and tru baluster section, folded conica foot, c. 1725, 16.5 cm. high. **£200-250** *C*

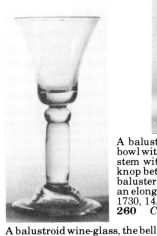

A baluster wine-glass, funnel bowl with a solid lower part, the stem with a central annular knop between inverted and true baluster knops and enclosing an elongated tear, domed foot, c. 1730, 14.5 cm. high. **£220-260** *C*

A balustroid wine-glass, the bell bowl with solid lower part on a cushion knop, above plain section and a domed foot, c. 1730, 17 cm. high. **£120-160** *C*

A 6 in. balustroid wine glass, with waisted bowl engraved with fruiting vine, baluster stem with annulated knop and small top knop, on domed and folded foot, c. 1730. **£220-260** *AG*

A bell bowl wine glass on baluster stem with central swelling, c. 1730, 6 in. high. **£170-190** *AA*

A baluster wine-glass, bell bowl on a drop knop above a beaded ball knop, plain section and base knob, domed foot, c. 1750, 18 cm. high. **£220-260** *C*

An early Victorian small fluted wine glass, on unusually knopped stem, c. 1840, 4½ in. high. **£15-20** *AA*

An engraved light baluster wine-glass, trumpet-shaped bowl, beaded shoulder-knopped stem with swelling waist knop, plain foot, Newcastle, c. 1750, 18.5 cm. high. **£320-360** *C*

A Georgian wine glass, with ogee bowl, the stem having medial as well as base knops, both teared, on folded foot, c. 1740-50, 6½ in. high. **£280-340** *AA*

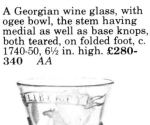

A composite-stemmed wine-glass, bell bowl, the stem filled with airtwist spirals set into a beaded inverted baluster knop, conical foot, c. 1750, 17 cm. high. **£170-200** *C*

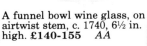

A funnel bowl wine glass, on airtwist stem, c. 1740, 6½ in. high. **£140-155** *AA*

A large conical wine glass on knopped stem, c. 1890, 6¾ in. high. **£10-15** *AA*

An airtwist wine-glass, the funnel bowl engraved and inscribed 'Liberty', on a double-knopped stem filled with airtwist spirals, conical foot (two chips to foot rim), c. 1750, 16 cm. high. **£500-600** *C*

439

An airtwist wine-glass, bell bowl, double-knopped stem filled with spirals, conical foot, c. 1750, 16 cm. high. **£90-120** *C*

An airtwist wine-glass, bell bowl, stem applied with a central coil collar and filled with spirals merging into the base of the bowl, conical foot, c. 1750, 18.5 cm. high. **£180-220** *C*

An airtwist wine-glass, funnel bowl, double-knopped stem filled with spirals, conical foot, c. 1750, 17.5 cm. high. **£140-180** *C*

An airtwist wine-glass, pan-topped bowl, stem with swelling waist knop filled with airtwist spirals, conical foot, (minute chip to underside of foot), c. 1750, 15 cm. high. **£65-115** *C*

A bell bowl wine glass, on airtwist stem, with vermicular collar, c. 1750, 6½ in. high. **£230-260** *AA*

An unusual wine glass, round funnel bowl, multi-series air twist stem with shoulder and central knops, 14.5 cm. **£180-220** *P*

An airtwist wine-glass with engraved funnel bowl, on a stem with a spiral core within a five-ply spiral, c. 1750, 15 cm. high. **£100-130** *C*

An early airtwist stem wine glass with conical bowl, c. 1750, 6½ in. high. **£130-160** *AA*

A Hurdels Verk engraved airtwist wine-glass, funnel bowl inscribed 'U. C. Lange' and F. Lange', the stem with a single spiral thread, conical foot (small chip to rim), c. 1780, 17 cm. high, **£200-250** *C*

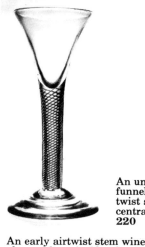

A wine glass on airtwist stem with honeycomb moulding on bowl, c. 1785, 5½ in. high. **£165-195** *AA*

A round funnel bowl wine glass on multiple spiral airtwist stem, c. 1760, 6 in. **£120-150** *AA*

An engraved airtwist wine-glass, pan-topped bowl, stem filled with spirals, plain foot (chip to underside of foot rim), c. 1750, 17 cm. high. **£65-110** *C*

A composite-stemmed wine-glass of drawn-trumpet shape, the bowl set into a double-knopped stem filled with airtwist spirals, domed foot, c. 1750, 17 cm. high. **£140-180** *C*

A composite-stemmed wine-glass, bell bowl, the stem filled with airtwist spirals merging into the base of the bowl, set into a beaded inverted baluster knop, folded conical foot, c. 1750, 17.5 cm. high. **£200-260** *C*

A bell bowl wine glass on double knop airtwist stem, with conical foot, c. 1750, 6½ in. high. **£200-250** *AA*

A composite-stemmed wine-glass, the solid lower part to the bell bowl filled with airtwist spirals, on a shoulder-knopped stem filled with spirals, and a domed foot, c. 1750, 17 cm. high. **£100-130** *C*

An airtwist Jacobite wine-glass, the trumpet-shaped bowl engraved with a seven-petalled rose and a bud, on a triple collar above a double-knopped stem filled with spirals, conical foot, c. 1750, 17 cm. high. **£450-600** *C*

A Jacobite wine glass, engraved with rose, two buds, reverse star, on multi spiral airtwist stem, c. 1750, 6½ in. **£450-500** *Som*

An airtwist Jacobite wine-glass, the funnel bowl engraved with a six-petalled rose, bud and a moth, the stem with a three-ply spiral about a central twisted core, conical foot, c. 1755, 15.5 cm. high. **£280-350** *C*

An airtwist Jacobite wine-glass, the funnel bowl engraved with a six-petalled rose, a bud, a half-opened rose, an oak leaf and a sun, supported on a shoulder-knopped stem filled with spirals conical foot (slight chips to foot rim) c. 1750, 16 cm. high. **£150-250** *C*

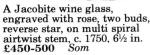

n airtwist Jacobite ine-glass, the bell owl engraved with a x-petalled rose, a bud, half-opened flower, a oth and a grub, the em applied with a ermicular collar and lled with spirals, nical foot, c. 1750, 16 n. high. **£750-900**

An airtwist Jacobite wine-glass, the funnel bowl engraved with a crown, flanked by a six petalled rose and bud, on a double-knopped stem filled with spirals, conical foot, c. 1750, 16 cm. high. **£900-1,100** *C*

A wine-glass of Jacobite significance with a funnel bowl, on a stem with airtwist spirals, on a conical foot, c. 1750, 15 cm. high. **£130-180** *C*

A wine glass, with pan-top bowl, on single series opaque twist stem, folded foot, c. 1755, 5⅞ in. **£140-160** *Som*

A wine glass with ribbed funnel bowl, wrythen at base, on triple opaque twist stem, c. 1750, 5¼ in. high. **£130-150** *AA*

A fine double-series opaque twist wine glass, with honeycomb moulded bowl, c 1760, 5¾ in. **£180-210** *So*

An airtwist Jacobite wine-glass with engraved bell bowl, on a stem filled with airtwist spirals and applied with a vermicular collar, on a conical foot, c. 1750, 16.5 cm. high. **£220-250** *C*

A Beilby wine glass, the bowl with band of fruiting vine in white enamel, on double series opaque twist stem, 1765, 5½ in. **£750-850** *Som*

A Lynn wine glass, the round funnel bowl with three radial ribs at base, on an opaque twist stem, c. 1760, 6¼ in. **£240-270** *Som*

An opaque-twist wine-glass, t funnel bowl enamelled in whi and a gilt rim, the stem with entwined thread core within nine-ply spiral, conical foot, 1770, 15 cm. high. **£500-560** *C*

A bucket-bowl wine glass, on triple series opaque twist stem, c. 1760, 6 in. **£160-180** *AA*

A sporting opaque-twist wine-glass with an engraved ogee bowl, on a stem with two entwined threads within a multi-ply spiral, terminating on a conical foot (chip to foot), c. 1770, 15 cm. high. **£200-250** *C*

A funnel bowl wine glass, on double series opaque twist stem, 6 in., c. 1770. **£95-105** *AA*

An ovoid bowl wine glass, on multiple opaque twist stem, 5 in. high., c. 1770. **£80-90** *AA*

An opaque-twist wine-glass, funnel bowl enamelled in whi by a member of the Beilby family with a gilt rim, the ste with a gauze corkscrew core within two spiral threads, conical foot, c. 1770, 15 cm. high. **£1,600-1,900** *C*

n opaque-twist wine-glass, funnel bowl enamelled in white at the Beilby atelier, the stem with an entwined double-thread core within a multi-ply spiral, c. 1775, 15 cm. high. **£750-950**

A wine-flute of trumpet shape, the stem with opaque gauze core entwined by two airtwist spirals, on a plain foot, c. 1760, 19 cm. high. **£120-150** *C*

A mixed-twist wine-glass, with funnel bowl, stem with a multi-ply airtwist cable entwined by a single opaque thread, conical foot, c. 1760, 16 cm. high. **£160-200** *C*

A colour-twist wine glass with ogee bowl, the stem with multiply spiral threads in opaque, translucent turquoise and chocolate brown (two minute chips to foot rim), c. 1760, 14.5 cm. high. **£420-460** *C*

A mixed-twist wine-glass, funnel bowl, stem with a multi-ply airtwist cable entwined by a single opaque thread and parts of an airtwist thread, conical foot (slight chips to foot rim), c. 1760, 16.5 cm. high. **£100-120** *C*

An opaque-twist shipping wine-glass, the rounded bowl inscribed 'Succefs to ye Good Intent Jas. Brooks Comr', stem with a central double-thread core within two flat ribbon spirals, conical foot (chip to foot), c. 1781, 14.5 cm. high. **£2,400-2,700** *C*

A colour-twist wine-glass with bell bowl, the stem with an airtwist spiral core entwined by a single cobalt-blue thread, conical foot, c. 1760, 17.5 cm. high. **£550-630** *C*

A colour twist wine glass, the moulded ogee bowl on a stem with opaque corkscrew twist edged with brown, c. 1770, 5½ in. **£650-700** *Som*

Make the most of Miller's
Look for the code letters in italic type following each caption.
Check these against the list of contributors on page 10 to identify the source of any illustration.
Remember — valuations may vary according to locality; use of the codes can allow this to be taken into account.

A colour-twist wine-glass, waisted bucket bowl, the stem with central blue gauze core within two opaque spiral threads, conical foot, (chips to foot rim), c. 1770, 17.5 cm. high. **£320-380** *C*

A colour twist wine glass, the ogee bowl on a stem with turquoise, brick red and opaque white twists, c. 1770, 5⅝ in. **£650-750** *Som*

A tartan-twist wine-glass with bell bowl, the stem with opaque laminated corkscrew core edged in translucent green within brick-red and opaque-white spirals, conical foot, c. 1770, 17 cm. high. **£480-550** *C*

443

A colour-twist wine-glass, bell bowl, the central core of entwined translucent blue, brown and opaque threads within four-ply spirals, plain foot, c. 1770, 17 cm. high. **£400-470** *C*

A colour-twist wine-glass of drawn-trumpet shape, the stem with cobalt-blue twisted core within a pair of opaque corkscrew spirals edged in blue, conical foot, (chips to foot), c. 1770, 18 cm. high. **£500-580** *C*

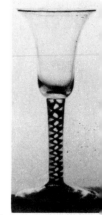

A colour-twist wine-glass with bell bowl, the stem with an opaque gauze spiral entwined with an opaque flat ribbon spiral edged in translucent brick-red and green, conical foot, c. 1770, 6.5 cm. high. **£550-630** *C*

A colour-twist wine-glass with bell bowl, shoulder knopped stem with opaque laminated corkscrew spiral edged in red about a central translucent green thread, conical foot, (chips to foot rim), c. 1770, 17 cm. high. **£180-220** *C*

A colour-twist wine-glass, ogee bowl with hammered flutes, the stem with translucent cobalt-blue core with opaque multi-ply spirals, conical foot, c. 1770, 15 cm. high. **£450-500** *C*

A colour-twist wine-glass with funnel bowl, the stem with opaque corkscrew core entwined with translucent pink and cobalt-blue threads, conical foot, c. 1770, 15 cm. high. **£550-630** *C*

A fine colour twist wine glass bowl base moulded with pair of blue spirals inside a single opaque white spiral, 5⅝ in. **£700-800** *Som*

A dated colour-twist wine-glass, ogee bowl inscribed 'U. C. Lange 1779' and 'J. Lange', stem with two entwined yellow threads within an opaque eight-ply spiral, conical foot, Hurdels Verk, c. 1779, 18 cm. high. **£420-500** *C*

An incised twist glass with ovoid bowl on folded foot, c 1750, 5½ in. high. **£300-35(** *AA*

An incised-twist wine-glass, funnel bowl with honeycomb-moulded lower part, incised-twist stem, conical foot, c. 1755, 15.5 cm. high. **£220-280** *C*

A wine glass, with pan top bowl on mercury corkscrew airtwist stem, c. 1745, 6⅜ in. **£130-160** *Som*

A mercury-twist wine-glass, pan-topped bowl, stem with two entwined corkscrew spirals, conical foot, (slight chip to underside of foot), c. 1750, 16.5 cm. high. **£50-80** *C*

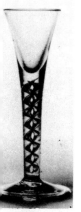

mercury-twist wine-glass, of
awn-trumpet shape, stem
th two entwined corkscrew
irals, conical foot, (chip to
n), c. 1750, 17 cm. high. **£110-
0**   *C*

A mercury-twist wine-glass,
funnel bowl with a solid lower
part, stem with two entwined
corkscrew spirals, domed foot,
c. 1750, 17 cm. high. **£150-
170**   *C*

A facet-stemmed wine-glass,
the rounded bowl engraved and
inscribed 'Liberty and Wilkes',
the stem cut with hexagonal
facets, on a conical foot, c. 1770,
14 cm. high. **£400-450**   *C*

A wine glass, the round funnel
bowl with chinoiserie
engraving on a centre knopped
diamond faceted stem, c. 1770,
6¼ in. **£225-275**   *Som*

stipple engraved wine glass
th 3 putti playing lyre and
mbourine, on faceted stem, c.
80, 5½ in. **£600-650**   *Som*

A wine glass, the ogee bowl on a
drawn faceted stem on
hexagonal faceted firing foot,
the bowl engraved with looped
stars and printies, c. 1775,
6¼ in. **£150-180**   *Som*

A fine Jacobite glass, the bowl
engraved with bee and crown
imperial, on faceted stem, c.
1770, 5¾ in. **£325-365**   *AA*

A Jacobite wine glass with
engraved funnel bowl, on an
hexagonally faceted stem, a
domed foot, c. 1780, 15 cm. high.
£200-220   *C*

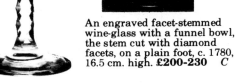

rare facet stem wine glass
th round funnel bowl and
usual scalloped foot, c. 1780,
in. **£255-285**   *AA*

A faceted stem wine glass
hammered on base of bowl and
the rim decorated with
engraving, c. 1780, 5 in. high.
£85-95   *AA*

An engraved facet-stemmed
wine-glass with a funnel bowl,
the stem cut with diamond
facets, on a plain foot, c. 1780,
16.5 cm. high. **£200-230**   *C*

A faceted stem wine glass with
engraved decoration around the
rim, c. 1780, 5 in. high. **£80-
90**   *AA*

One of a pair of ogee bowl wine glasses, on diamond faceted stems and faceted feet, the bowls engraved with fantasy landscapes, c. 1790, 5⅞ in. **£350-450** the pair *Som*

A Williamite wine glass, the trumpet bowl on plain draw stem, the bowl engraved wit 'the glorious memory of Kir William' within a laurel wrea 6¼ in., c. 1740. **£650-750** *Som*

An engraved facet-stemmed wine-glass with a funnel bowl, the stem cut with hexagonal facets, on a conical foot, c. 1780, 16 cm. high. **£300-350** *C*

A rare bell bowl wine glass on faceted stem with unusual heavy foot (from the Oppenheim collection), c. 1790, 6½ in. **£170-200** *AA*

A fine early engraved wine glass, c. 1790, 4 in. high. **£45-55** *AA*

A plain-stemmed Jacobite wine-glass of drawn-trumpet shape, the bowl engraved with a six-petalled rose, conical foot, c. 1745, 16 cm. high. **£440-500** *C*

A wine-glass of drawn-trum shape, the bowl with a sing raspberry-prunt, on folded f c. 1740, 17.5 cm. high. **£12(180** *C*

A flared bell bowl wine glass, teared on plain stem foot, c. 1740. **£80-90** *AA*

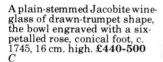

An armorial wine glass of drawn trumpet shape, c. 1745, 18 cm. high. **£200-300** *C*

A two piece wine glass, with Jacobite engraving, c. 1790, 4¾ in. high. **£85-90** *AA*

A plain-stemmed Jacobite wine-glass of drawn-trumpet shape, the bowl engraved with an eight-petalled rose, conical foot, c. 1745, 18 cm. high. **£320-380** *C*

A conical wine glass, with engraved rim, on plain foot, 1790, 4½ in. **£20-25** *AA*

double bowled dram glass,
in., c. 1750. **£150-160**
m

A very rare green wine glass,
with vertically ribbed ogee
bowl, on double series airtwist
stem, c. 1750. **£700-800**   *Som*

A Bristol green wine glass with
cup bowl on hollow wrythen
stem and domed foot with
applied trailing, c. 1790, 5 in.
£250-295   *Som*

A pair of Bristol green Georgian
wine glasses, on drawn stems, c.
1810, 5½ in. **£70-90** pair   *AA*

ne of a set of eight Bristol
een knopped wine glasses, c.
30, 5 in. high. **£285-300** set
A

A set of eight Bristol green wine
glasses, c. 1820. **£300-350** set
AA

One of a set of six green wine
glasses, c. 1840, 5 in. wide.
£175-200 the set   *AA*

One of a set of four green wine
glasses, c. 1820, 5 in. high. **£75-
90** set   *AA*

e of a set of six Victorian
en wine glasses, on crystal
ms, c. 1880, 5¼ in. high. **£55-
** set   *AA*

A cordial glass, the bell bowl on
a centre swelling knop stem
with large elongated air tear, c.
1740, 6 in. **£350-400**   *Som*

One of a set of six cranberry
wine glasses, c. 1880, 5 in. high.
£70-80 set   *AA*

A baluster cordial-glass, bell
bowl, the stem with a swelling
waist knop, shoulder knop and
base knob and with a tear, plain
foot, c. 1720, 16.5 cm. high.
£300-350   *C*

A baluster cordial-glass, bell
bowl on an annular knop, the
stem with swelling waist knop
and base knob enclosing a large
elongated tear, plain foot, c.
1745, 15.5 cm. high. **£300-
400**   *C*

A cordial glass with balustroid
stem on folded foot, c. 1750, 5¾
in. high. **£160-185**   *AA*

A double ogee bowl cordial glass, on balustroid stem with folded foot, c. 1750, 5¾ in. high. **£220-260** *AA*

An unusual Georgian cordial glass, the engraved bowl on faceted stem with knop, c. 1770, 6 in. **£295-350** *AA*

An Irish engraved cordial-glass, the funnel bowl inscri 'Eviry (sic) Man His Wish', plain stem, conical foot, c. 1 16.5 cm. high. **£220-260**

An engraved plain-stemmed cordial-glass of drawn-trumpet shape, the stem enclosing a small tear, domed foot, Irish, c. 1745, 18 cm. high. **£200-240** *C*

A cordial wine glass, the bowl engraved with bird and stylised rose motif, with a drawn tapering stem on folded foot, c. 1765, 5 in. high. **£75-85** *AA*

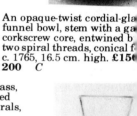

An opaque-twist cordial-gla funnel bowl, stem with a ga corkscrew core, entwined b two spiral threads, conical f c. 1765, 16.5 cm. high. **£15(200** *C*

A Williamite plain-stemmed cordial-glass, the bucket bowl engraved with a bust portrait of King William and inscribed 'The Immortal Memory', plain foot, c. 1750, 16.5 cm. high. **£2,500-3,000** *C*

An opaque-twist cordial-glass, funnel bowl, double-knopped stem filled with opaque spirals, conical foot (slight chip to underside of foot rim), c. 1765, 18 cm. high. **£120-160** *C*

An engraved opaque-twist cordial-glass, funnel bowl, stem with a gauze corkscrew spiral within two spiral threads, domed foot (very slight chip to foot rim), c. 1765, 18 cm. high. **£220-260** *C*

A mercury-twist cordial-gla funnel bowl, stem with fou spiral threads about a cent core, conical foot, c. 1750, cm. high. **£170-220** *C*

An opaque-twist cordial-glass, funnel bowl with hammered flutes, the stem with a gauze core entwined by two spiral threads, conical foot, c. 1765, 16.5 cm. high. **£150-200** *C*

An engraved opaque-twist cordial-glass, funnel bowl, stem with a double-thread core within an eight-ply spiral, conical foot, c. 1770, 17.5 cm. high. **£220-250** *C*

unusual ale glass, with deep isted round funnel bowl on wn multi spiral airtwist m, c. 1745, 7¾ in. **£150-** 0   *Som*

An opaque-twist engraved ale-glass, ogee bowl, the stem with a laminated corkscrew core within two spiral threads, conical foot (slight chip to foot), c. 1765, 19 cm. high. **£100-150**   *C*

One of a pair of fine ale glasses, with deep round funnel bowl engraved with hops and barley, on double series airtwist stem and thick conical foot, 7¼ in. **£450-500** the pair   *Som*

An electioneering opaque-twist ale-glass, funnel bowl inscribed 'Lowther and Upton Huzza' the stem with a gauze core entwined by two spiral threads, conical foot, c. 1761, 20 cm. high. **£380-420**   *C*

n engraved opaque-twist ale- ass, funnel bowl, stem with twined double thread core thin a multi-ply spiral, nical foot, c. 1775, 18.5 cm. gh. **£150-200**   *C*

An engraved plain-stemmed ale-glass of Jacobite significance, slender ogee bowl, folded conical foot, c. 1750, 18 cm. high. **£60-80**   *C*

An engraved plain-stemmed ale-glass, funnel bowl, on plain stem, conical foot, c. 1745, 18 cm. high. **£80-120**   *C*

An ale glass, decorated with hops and barley engraving, c. 1820. **£25-30**   *AA*

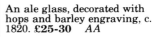

alustroid ale-flute, slender l bowl on a five-ringed nulated knop above a short in section and base knob, ded conical foot, c. 1730, 18.5 high. **£550-650**   *C*

One of a set of four early fluted ale glasses, on knopped stems, c. 1800, 5¼ in. high. **£85-95** the set   *AA*

One of a pair of tall ale glasses, with faceted bowls, on knopped stems with wide feet, c. 1825, 7¼ in. high. **£50-55** pair   *AA*

An ale glass, engraved with hops and barley, with knopped stem, c. 1820, 5¼ in. high. **£40-50**   *AA*

A wrythen ale glass, on pi
moulded foot, c. 1790, 4 in.
40   *AA*

Three wrythen ale glasses, on
knopped stems and pinch
moulded feet, c. 1780, 5 in.
£100-120 set   *AA*

An early ale glass, on pinch
moulded foot, c. 1780, 5 in. high.
£40-45   *AA*

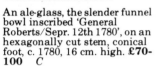

An ale-glass, the slender funnel
bowl inscribed 'General
Roberts/Sepr. 12th 1780', on an
hexagonally cut stem, conical
foot, c. 1780, 16 cm. high. **£70-
100**   *C*

A wrythen ale glass, on
knopped stem, with folded foot,
c. 1790, 4⅜ in. **£45-50**   *AA*

An early Victorian ale glass
with part wrythen bowl on ball-
knop stem, c. 1840, 6¼ in. high.
£30-40   *AA*

One of a pair of cut glass
Victorian flutes, on baluste
stems, c. 1850, 6¼ in. **£30-
pair   *AA*

An ale glass, with semi-
wrythen graded bowl, c. 1800,
4½ in. **£40-45**   *AA*

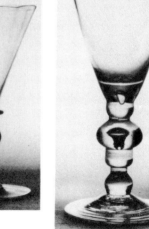

One of a set of three Victorian
flute glasses, on knopped stems,
c. 1850, 5¼ in. high. **£45-50**
set   *AA*

A Venetian goblet, funnel bowl
with flared everted rim, on a
merese above a small hollow
knop and slender inverted
baluster stem, conical foot, 16th
C., 14.5 cm. high. **£800-950**   *C*

A pair of Venetian goblets,
flared hexagonal bowls, on a
merese above a fluted knop and
wrythen-moulded inverted
baluster section, 17th C., 16 cm.
high. **£550-650**   *C*

A baluster goblet, funnel bow
with a tear on a cyst above
mushroom knop and base kno
folded conical foot, c. 1700, 1
cm. high. **£1,500-2,000**   *C*

...eavy baluster goblet, funnel ...l with a tear to the solid ...er part, on a cyst above a ...knop and short plain ...tion with a tear, folded ...ical foot, c. 1700, 17 cm. ...h. **£280-330** *C*

A baluster goblet, flared funnel bowl with a small tear to the solid lower part, on a small cyst above an acorn knop with a tear and base knob, folded conical foot, c. 1700, 21 cm. high. **£1,000-1,200** *C*

A baluster goblet, funnel bowl with solid lower part, on an annular knop and base knob with elongated tear, folded conical foot, c. 1700, 18 cm. high. **£550-650** *C*

A heavy baluster deceptive goblet, straight-sided funnel bowl of unusually thick metal, inverted stem with a large tear, thick folded foot, c. 1700, 16.5 cm. high. **£400-460** *C*

...aluster goblet, round funnel ...l on two ball knops ...losing a large and small ...r, folded conical foot, c. 1700, ...cm. high. **£350-400** *C*

A baluster goblet, slender bell bowl on an annulated knop above a true baluster section, conical foot (small chip to foot rim), c. 1715, 21 cm. high. **£280-320** *C*

A baluster goblet, the flared funnel bowl with solid lower part supported on a wide angular knop with an elongated tear above a base knob and conical foot (flash to foot rim), c. 1705, 18 cm. high. **£200-240** *C*

A baluster goblet, the flared funnel bowl with a small tear to the solid lower part, on a cyst above a cone knop, short plain section and a base knob with a tear, domed and folded foot, c. 1710, 19 cm. high. **£800-1,000** *C*

...otsdam armorial goblet, the ...nel bowl engraved, on ...ttened knop above inverted ...tion with base knop and ...cular foot, c. 1720, 17 cm. ...h. **£900-1,000** *C*

A baluster goblet, bucket bowl, on a triple annulated knop above a plain section with an elongated tear and base knob, folded conical foot, c. 1725, 17.5 cm. high. **£380-420** *C*

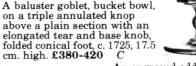

An engraved oddfellow goblet on ball-knop stem, c. 1835, 7½ in. high. **£85-100** *AA*

...baluster goblet, tulip-shaped ...wl with solid lower part, on a ...op knop enclosing a tear ...ove a short plain section, ...gh folded conical foot, c. 1725, ...cm. high. **£220-280** *C*

451

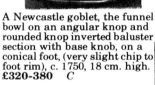

A baluster goblet, funnel bowl with a tear to the solid lower part, on a triple annulated knop above a plain section and base knob enclosing an elongated tear, domed and folded foot, c. 1725, 24 cm. high. **£750-850** *C*

A flute moulded goblet on baluster stem, 5½ in., c. 1840. **£15-20** *AA*

A Newcastle goblet, the funnel bowl on an angular knop and rounded knop inverted baluster section with base knob, on a conical foot, (very slight chip to foot rim), c. 1750, 18 cm. high. **£320-380** *C*

A baluster goblet, bell bowl, the stem with a beaded ball knop between true baluster and cushion knops above a plain section and base knob, domed foot, c. 1750, 23 cm. high. **£18 220** *C*

A pair of fluted-moulded goblets, on wrythen stems, c. 1790, 4⅜ in. **£60-65** pair *AA*

A Dutch-engraved Newcastle goblet, the funnel bowl engraved and inscribed above 'Apres Les Peines Les Plaisirs', on two graduated drop knops above true baluster section, on a domed foot, c. 1750, 8.5 cm. high. **£480-550** *C*

A goblet, the cup-shaped bowl with gadrooned lower part, on a triple annulated knop above a plain section and base knob and with two tears, folded conical foot, c. 1770, 22 cm. high. **£650-750** *C*

A plain-stemmed Jacobite goblet, the bucket bowl engraved with a seven-petal rose, folded conical foot, c. 17 17 cm. high. **£480-550** *C*

An engraved Georgian goblet, 4½ in., c. 1800. **£30-35** *AA*

A Georgian goblet, c. 1800, 4¾ in. high. **£25-30** *AA*

One of a set of four Georgia moulded goblets, c. 1815, 5⅞ high. **£125-130** set *AA*

late Georgian cut-glass
blet, on a pedestal stem, c.
25, 5 in. high. **£25-30**   *AA*

A large Victorian goblet, c.
1840, 6 in. high. **£30-40**   *AA*

One of a set of four finely cut
Victorian goblets on pedestal
stems, c. 1870, 5½ in. high. **£75-
90** set   *AA*

e of a set of five knopped
blets, with barrel bowls, 5 in.
gh, c. 1880. **£70-80** the set
4

One of a set of four wide
Victorian goblets, with flute-cut
bowls and inverted baluster
stems, c. 1880, 5¾ in. high.
£110-125 set   *AA*

A pedestal-stemmed goblet, the
funnel bowl supported on a
knop and folded foot, c. 1730, 18
cm. high. **£110-150**   *C*

pedestal-stemmed goblet,
anel-moulded waisted ogee
wl, hexagonally-moulded
em, folded conical foot, c.
745, 19 cm. high. **£240-280**

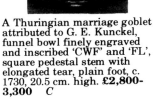

One of a set of four goblets with
hollow stems, c. 1840, 6¼ in.
£135-165 set   *AA*

A Thuringian marriage goblet
attributed to G. E. Kunckel,
funnel bowl finely engraved
and inscribed 'CWF' and 'FL',
square pedestal stem with
elongated tear, plain foot, c.
1730, 20.5 cm. high. **£2,800-
3,300**   *C*

A pedestal-stemmed goblet, the
flared trumpet bowl with solid
lower part, on a folded conical
foot, c. 1745, 18 cm. high. **£200-
250**   *C*

A set of nine slice cut goblets, on hollow stems, c. 1870, 7 in. high. **£175-195** *AA*

An airtwist goblet, ogee bowl, double-knopped stem filled with spirals, conical foot, (slight chip to underside of foot rim), c. 1750, 17 cm. high. **£65-140** *C*

An airtwist goblet, flared ogee bowl, stem enclosing a single multi-ply spiral cable, plain foot, c. 1750, 18.5 cm. high. **£65-100** *C*

An airtwist goblet, slightly waisted bucket bowl, stem w: a single multi-ply spiral cab conical foot, c. 1750, 20 cm. high. **£90-120** *C*

An early goblet on faceted stem, the bowl engraved with swags, c. 1810, 6 in. high, 3½ in. diam. **£90-110** *AA*

An opaque-twist goblet, the ogee bowl inscribed 'A Health To The King Of Prussia', the stem with twisted gauze core within a three-ply spiral, on a conical foot, c. 1765, 18 cm. high. **£200-250** *C*

An opaque-twist goblet, bucket bowl, stem with two spiral threads enclosing a gauze corkscrew core, conical foot (minute chip to foot rim), c. 1765, 18.5 cm. high. **£150-190** *C*

An Irish goblet with flute c bowl, cut knopped stem, th bowl engraved with the 8t] Royal Veteran Battalion, 5 in., c. 1820. **£125-175** *Sc*

A Victorian cut glass goblet, c. 1850, 6¼ in. high. **£15-18** *AA*

A German goblet and cover, funnel bowl on three mereses, on an inverted baluster stem with a tear, folded conical foot, Saxon, c. 1740, 31 cm. high. **£350-400** *C*

A goblet, faceted at the base bowl, and on slice-cut stem, 6 in., c. 1835. **£40-50** *AA*

A German armorial goblet and a cover, the funnel bowl engraved, facet-cut inverted stem with a plain foot cut with ovals, the goblet, c. 1770, overall height 26 cm. **£600-800** *C*

BOHEMIAN GLASS

- from 1800-c. 1830 — the Empire period — still influenced by classical movement
- from c. 1820-c. 1850 the Biedermeier movement influenced by Romantic movement
- after 1815 much coloured glass produced, firstly in ruby-red then green, blue and amethyst
- a true black opaque glass — hyalith glass — was produced in 1817
- hyalith glass was frequently gilded with classical motifs
- it was very brittle and lost popularity by 1840
- Egermann's red marbled lithyalin glass preceded a wealth of other colours, a patent was granted in 1828 although obviously he was experimenting for several years before this

- most of Egermann's lithyalin glass was produced from 1828-1840
- Egermann continued to perfect other colours, firstly c. 1820 red and yellow, then c. 1828 a light yellow and c. 1835 his gold-topaz
- in the early 1840's Egermann's secret techniques were stolen and the use of his colours became widespread, very rarely matching his quality
- in 1830's and 1840's yellow and green fluorescent glass was produced
- white opaque glass was popular throughout the period, as was enamel glass
- during the 19th C. the new white produced was used in excess in various overlay techniques
- much red glass with white overlay is produced in 19th C. taste, in the Soviet Union today

A Bohemian colour-twist goblet and cover, fluted funnel bowl, faceted inverted baluster stem and spire finial filled with translucent red and gilt spirals, plain foot, c. 1760, 29 cm. high. **£250-300** *C*

A Bohemian green glass goblet, the bowl of hexagonal section, on a multi-knopped stem, painted in bright colours and gold (slight chipping), 23.1 cm., mid-19th C. **£220-300** *SBe*

Bohemian armorial colourist goblet and a cover, the nnel bowl engraved, faceted verted baluster stem with nslucent red and gilt spirals, a plain foot, the spirally ulded finial enclosing a gle dark red thread, c. 1745, erall height 25 cm. **£530-0** *C*

A Bohemian gilt glass goblet, with straight-sided bowl, and faceted knop and red-and-white-twist stem, 42.2 cm., c. 1850. **£270-340** *SBe*

A Bohemian 'zwischengoldglas' fluted tumbler and a cover, painted in colours on silver, the spire finial with translucent ruby and gilt inclusions, c. 1745, 16 cm. high. **£1,100-1,400** *C*

Bohemian amber-flash ansparentemail beaker, inted with 'The Three races', the lower part cut with utes and on sunray base, late th C., 13 cm. high. **£800-0** *C*

A 19th C. red Bohemian glass lidded goblet, 10½ in. high. **£70-85** *SV*

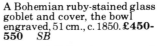

A Bohemian ruby-stained glass goblet and cover, the bowl engraved, 51 cm., c. 1850. **£450-550** *SB*

A Bohemian engraved colour-twist goblet and a cover on an inverted baluster stem filled with translucent red spirals, the spire finial filled with red and gilt threads, plain foot, c. 1750, the goblet 18 cm. high. **£370-430** *C*

A Bohemian goblet, the hexagonal bowl engraved in the manner of Hofmann and painted in transparent email colours, spreading hexagonal stem, c. 1845, 12.5 cm. high **£600-680** *C*

A glass goblet of dark emerald-green tint, with cup shaped bowl on a plain stem and conical foot, c. 1760, 13.5 cm. high. **£140-180** *C*

A Bohemian ruby-flash gobl the waisted hexagonal bowl engraved in the manner of Hofmann, on hexagonal ste and spreading foot with castellated rim, c. 1850, 19 c high. **£700-780** *C*

One of a set of six moulded and engraved sherry glasses, c. 1880, 4¼ in. high. **£75-85** set *AA*

Two matching silvered glass goblets with amethyst cut overlay marked underneath, London Varnish & Co. patent, 1850, 7½ in. **£350-395** *Som*

One of a set of four cut she glasses, c. 1890, 4½ in. high **£20-30** set *AA*

An early Victorian sherry glass on hollow faceted stem with knop, c. 1840, 4½ in. high. **£15-20** *AA*

A Georgian rummer, with moulded bowl, c. 1790, 5⅛ in. high. **£30-35** *AA*

An early rummer, on ball k stem, c. 1810, 5 in. high. **£2 30** *AA*

A Georgian rummer, pedestal stem, 4½ in., c. 1800. **£25-30** *AA*

A Georgian moulded rummer, c. 1790, 5½ in. **£45-50** *AA*

A Rummer, bucket bowl engraved and inscribed in diamond point 'St. Nicholas Church, Old Castle & Co. Court, Newcastle', and the initials CG, on capstan stem and plain foot, early 19th C. 14 cm. high. **£360-420**   *C*

n early moulded rummer, on rythen stem, c. 1800, 4½ in. 30-35 *AA*

One of a set of four Georgian rummers with ball knop stems, c. 1800, 5½ in. high. **£135-145** the set *AA*

A large Georgian rummer, c. 1810, 5½ in. high. **£30-40** *AA*

A rummer, the bucket bowl on a knife edge knop stem, the bowl ngraved with a bridge and loops and wooden houses, the everse with the Union flowers, c. 1810, 5⅜ in. **£180-210** *Som*

A Georgian rummer, c. 1810, 5¼ in. high. **£35-40** *AA*

A Georgian moulded bucket rummer, on knopped stem, c. 1815, 5½ in. high. **£20-25** *AA*

One of a pair of balloon rummers, on pedestal stems, c. 820, 5½ in. **£50-55** pair *AA*

A Georgian rummer, c. 1820, 5½ in. **£25-28** *AA*

A Georgian rummer, on edestal stem, c. 1820, 5⅛ in. igh. **£25-28** *AA*

A bucket rummer, on knopped stem, c. 1820, 5¾ in. **£25-28** *AA*

A pub rummer on knopped stem, c. 1825, 4¾ in. high. **£16-20** *AA*

A rummer, the bucket bowl on capstan stem, the bowl engraved with monogram within a floral cartouche flanked by barley ears, reverse with flowers of the Union, c. 1825, 5¼ in. £150-200 *Som*

An engraved coin-rummer, the bucket bowl engraved and inscribed with the initials 'JP' the hollow-knopped stem containing a George II two-shilling piece dated 1758, on plain foot, c. 1830, 14.5 cm. high. £400-480 *C*

'Speed the plough', a large rummer, the bucket bowl on a cushion knopped stem, the bowl engraved with the farmer's arms, the reverse with a horseman, c. 1825, 7½ in. £300 400 *Som*

A Georgian rummer, c. 1835, 5½ in. £20-30 *AA*

A pair of late Georgian bucket rummers, with fluted bowls and knopped stems, 5⅛ in. high. £45-50 pair *AA*

One of a set of three early Victorian heavy rummers, wi moulded decoration, pedesta stems, c. 1840, 5 in. £50-55 set *AA*

An early Victorian pub rummer, c. 1850, 5⅛ in. £15-20 *AA*

A late Georgian bucket rummer, flute cut on knopped stem, 6 in. high. £25-30 *AA*

A small pub rummer, c. 1860, 4 in. high. £7-10 *AA*

A Victorian flute-cut pub rummer, 1870, 6 in. high. £1 14 *AA*

A small Victorian pub rummer, with fine striations, 3¾ in. high. £10-15 *AA*

A Victorian rummer, c. 1880, 4⅜ in. **£8-10**   *AA*

Victorian pub rummer, on ce cut stem, c. 1880, 5¾ in. **£8-** *AA*

A Victorian rummer on slice-cut stem, c. 1890, 5⅞ in. high. **£8-12**   *AA*

A Victorian pub rummer, c. 1890, 5½ in. high. **£8-10**   *AA*

An early plain-stemmed dram glass, the ogee bowl lightly ribbed, on folded foot, c. 1745, 4 in. high. **£75-85**   *AA*

masonic dram glass, the umpet bowl with a base air ar on a heavy firing foot, the wl engraved with masonic mbol inside a floral rtouche, with traces of lding, c. 1740, 4⅛ in. **£125-** 5   *Som*

A Jacobite dram glass, the trumpet bowl with air tear in base and cushion knop, terraced firing foot, the bowl engraved with Jacobite rose and two buds, reverse with star, c. 1750, 3¾ in. **£700-800**   *Som*

A Jacobite dram glass, the drawn trumpet bowl on a conical foot, the bowl engraved 'the friendly hunt' and a Jacob's ladder sprig, c. 1760, 3½ in. **£125-165**   *Som*

One of a pair of engraved dram glasses, each having folded foot, 3½ in., c. 1790. **£80-90** pair   *AA*

A dram glass, on turned foot, c. 1820, 2¾ in. **£30-35**   *AA*

A German small glass beaker, enamelled with a flowering plant in a pot, with an inscription Meine Liebe bluht wie diese Blumen, and dated 1721, 2¾ in. **£220-300**   *L*

nasonic dram glass, on a mentary stem, the bowl raved with swags and ious masonic symbols, c. 0, 3⅜ in. **£125-165**   *Som*

tumbler, the body engraved he Ship Flint Club' with a oral cartouche, the reverse ith a monogram, 4 in., c. 1790. 100-130   *Som*

A Georgian pint glass tumbler, engraved with a coach and four, 'The Defiance', and monogram F.J., 4 in. **£400-480**   *L*

A Sunderland bridge beaker, with sailing boat and name George Thomas, the reverse with monogram and floral cartouche, c. 1820, 3½ in. **£135-165** *Som*

A Bohemian tumbler, of thistle shape, 16.4 cm., c. 1850. **£55-75** *SB*

One of a set of four Victorian faceted tumblers, c. 1880, 3½ in. high. **£25-30** set *AA*

A pair of Bohemian green glass tumblers, silvered and gilt with flowers, 13.6 cm., c. 1840. **£300-360** *SBe*

A Bohemian glass tumbler, in white overlaid in purple, with panels enamelled and gilt, the base with initials, 12.2 cm., c. 1850. **£190-240** *SBe*

A French heavily enamelled and gilded glass beaker, 3¾ in. c. 1870. **£45-50** *MT*

One of eight cranberry pony glasses, c. 1870, 3⅜ in. high. **£60-65** the set *AA*

A late 19th C lime green Mary Gregory pony glass, 4¼ in. **£30-40** *MT*

A cider glass, the deep round funnel bowl on a plain drawn stem with air tear, the bowl engraved 'cyder' and with apple spray, c. 1740, 6⅛ in. **£700-800** *Som*

A glass with double ogee bowl, on hexagonal silesian stem with domed foot, c. 1740, 5¾ in. high. **£185-200** *AA*

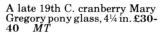

A late 19th C. cranberry Mary Gregory pony glass, 4¼ in. **£30-40** *MT*

A Bute glass, the bowl with simulated turnover boot, the reverse with a monogram within floral sprays, 3¼ in., c. 1810. **£50-60** *Som*

A 19th C. ogee glass, c. 1820, 4¾ in. £25-30 *AA*

A bucket bowl port glass, flute cut, on knopped stem, c. 1830, 4½ in. high. £5-10 *AA*

A double ogee glass, with ring knop on stem, and heavy foot, 5 in., c. 1830. £65-70 *AA*

baluster toastmaster's glass, onical bowl on quadruple nnulated knop above an verted baluster section nclosing a tear and base knob, lain foot (slight chip to rim), c. 725, 13.5 cm. high. £180-20 *C*

A Saxon dated Preisflote, the funnel bowl inscribed 'Ordens Schiessen zu Dresden, d. 3 Aug 1763', the lower parts cut with facets, conical foot, c. 1763, 26 cm. high. £850-1,050 *C*

A masonic firing glass, the round funnel bowl on a short stem with heavy firing foot, the bowl engraved with armorial arms of Chester and masonic symbols, 4 in., c. 1740. £280-320 *Som*

A toasting-glass of slender drawn-trumpet shape on a conical foot, c. 1750, 21.5 cm. high. £180-220 *C*

An opaque-twist firing-glass, double-ogee bowl, with gauze corkscrew core within a ten-ply spiral, terraced foot, c. 1765, 10 cm. high. £150-200 *C*

An engraved water-glass of drawn-trumpet shape, the bowl inscribed 'Sober Club, 1758' on a plain stem and conical foot, c. 1758, 15.5 cm. high. £300-380 *C*

A mead-glass, with cup shaped bowl, on a lightly wrythen-moulded stem with a honeycomb-moulded conical foot, c. 1730, 11 cm. high. £90-120 *C*

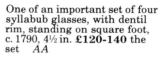

A set of 6 19th C. Cranberry glasses, 5 in. high. £45-55 *SV*

A set of 6 Victorian green glasses, 4¾ in. high. £50-60 *SV*

An early 'Tat' glass with knopped stem and folded foot, c. 1810, 3¾ in. high. £30-35 *AA*

One of an important set of four syllabub glasses, with dentil rim, standing on square foot, c. 1790, 4½ in. £120-140 the set *AA*

A Victorian jelly glass, with wrythen bowl and pinch moulded foot, c. 1830, 4 in. high £25-30 *AA*

One of a set of four cut jelly glasses, on knopped stems, c. 1840, 4½ in. high. £35-40 the set *AA*

A Victorian jelly glass, c. 1860, 4 in. high. £5-10 *AA*

A celery glass with strawberry diamond and flute cutting on a knopped stem and circular star cut foot, c. 1820, 7⅝ in. £110-130 *Som*

One of a set of three slice-cut jelly glasses, c. 1860, 3¾ in. high. £10-15 set *AA*

A baluster sweetmeat-glass, with double-ogee bowl set into a bowl shaped knop, on three cushion knops, domed and folded foot, c. 1725, 10 cm. high. £360-420 *C*

A small early sweetmeat-glass, the shallow bowl with gadrooned lower part, shoulder-knopped stem, folded conical foot, c. 1690, 10 cm. high. £70-120 *C*

An early sweetmeat, with the moulded bowl gadrooned at the base and a folded everted rim, on a bobbin knopped stem, with folded foot, c. 1700, 3¼ in. £225-250 *Som*

A sweetmeat-glass with double-ogee bowl on a domed and folded foot, c. 1740, 8 cm. high. £120-150 *C*

, pedestal-stemmed
weetmeat-glass, double-ogee
owl with vertical ribbing on a
mall annular knop,
ctagonally-moulded stem,
omed and ribbed foot, (small
hip to foot rim), c. 1740, 12 cm.
igh. **£80-120**   *C*

A pedestal-stemmed
sweetmeat-glass, double-ogee
bowl with vertical ribbing,
octagonally-moulded stem
enclosing an elongated tear,
domed and ribbed foot, (very
slight chip to underside of foot
rim), c. 1745, 14.5 cm. high. **£90-
120**   *C*

A sweetmeat, the ogee bowl and
domed folded foot similarly
ribbed, on a stem with inverted
baluster and base knop, c. 1750,
5¾ in. **£80-120**   *Som*

A sweetmeat-glass, the double-
gee bowl with a band of
ozenge below a bevelled
calloped border, octagonally-
noulded pedestal stem, domed
ctagonal foot (chip to foot rim),
. 1770, 15.5 cm. high. **£20-40**

A cut-glass sweetmeat-glass,
the double-ogee bowl with a
band of oval within lozenge
cutting and a bevelled scalloped
rim, octagonally-moulded
pedestal stem, faceted domed
foot with waved rim (two chips
to underside of foot rim), c. 1770,
15 cm. high. **£30-60**   *C*

A sweetmeat-glass, the bowl
with deeply gadrooned lower
part and folded rim, on a plain
stem and a folded foot, late 17th
C., 9.5 cm. high. **£110-150**   *C*

A sweetmeat-glass, the double-
ogee bowl with waved everted
rim cut with bands of ovals and
facets, on a beaded knop above
a fluted inverted baluster
section, facet-cut domed foot, c.
1775, 15.5 cm. high. **£40-80**   *C*

A taper stick, with knopped and
diamond faceted stem, domed
faceted foot with scalloped
edge, c. 1770, 6½ in. **£250-
300**   *Som*

A Victorian deep bowled
sweetmeat dish, on capstan
stem, c. 1860, 4½ in. high, 4⅝ in.
diam. **£15-20**   *AA*

A sweetmeat-glass, the bowl
with gadrooned lower part and
folded everted rim, on a plain
stem and a folded conical foot,
late 17th C., 9 cm. high. **£80-
120**   *C*

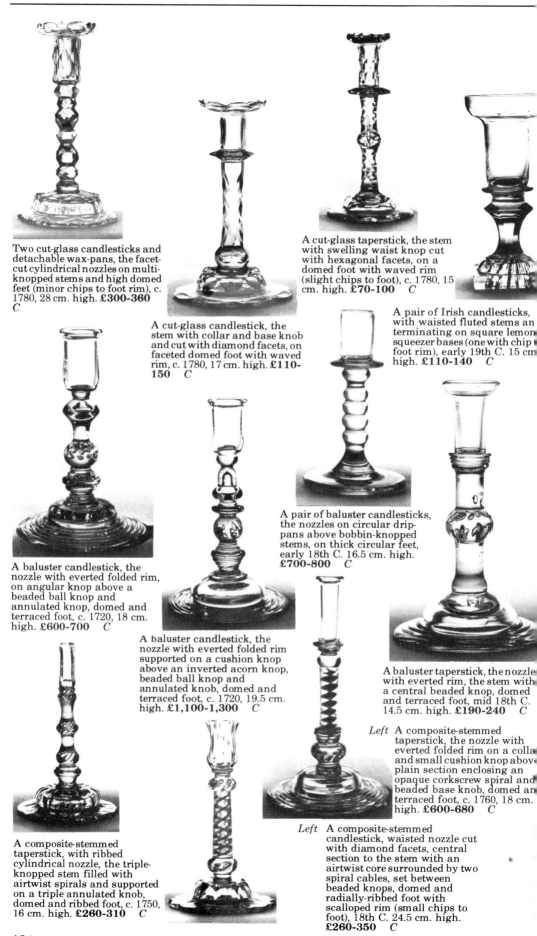

Two cut-glass candlesticks and detachable wax-pans, the facet-cut cylindrical nozzles on multi-knopped stems and high domed feet (minor chips to foot rim), c. 1780, 28 cm. high. **£300-360** *C*

A cut-glass candlestick, the stem with collar and base knob and cut with diamond facets, on faceted domed foot with waved rim, c. 1780, 17 cm. high. **£110-150** *C*

A cut-glass taperstick, the stem with swelling waist knop cut with hexagonal facets, on a domed foot with waved rim (slight chips to foot), c. 1780, 15 cm. high. **£70-100** *C*

A pair of Irish candlesticks, with waisted fluted stems an terminating on square lemon squeezer bases (one with chip foot rim), early 19th C. 15 cm high. **£110-140** *C*

A baluster candlestick, the nozzle with everted folded rim, on angular knop above a beaded ball knop and annulated knop, domed and terraced foot, c. 1720, 18 cm. high. **£600-700** *C*

A baluster candlestick, the nozzle with everted folded rim supported on a cushion knop above an inverted acorn knop, beaded ball knop and annulated knob, domed and terraced foot, c. 1720, 19.5 cm. high. **£1,100-1,300** *C*

A pair of baluster candlesticks, the nozzles on circular drip-pans above bobbin-knopped stems, on thick circular feet, early 18th C. 16.5 cm. high. **£700-800** *C*

A baluster taperstick, the nozzle with everted rim, the stem with a central beaded knop, domed and terraced foot, mid 18th C. 14.5 cm. high. **£190-240** *C*

Left A composite-stemmed taperstick, the nozzle with everted folded rim on a colla and small cushion knop abov plain section enclosing an opaque corkscrew spiral and beaded base knob, domed an terraced foot, c. 1760, 18 cm. high. **£600-680** *C*

A composite-stemmed taperstick, with ribbed cylindrical nozzle, the triple-knopped stem filled with airtwist spirals and supported on a triple annulated knob, domed and ribbed foot, c. 1750, 16 cm. high. **£260-310** *C*

Left A composite-stemmed candlestick, waisted nozzle cut with diamond facets, central section to the stem with an airtwist core surrounded by two spiral cables, set between beaded knops, domed and radially-ribbed foot with scalloped rim (small chips to foot), 18th C. 24.5 cm. high. **£260-350** *C*

A glass pedestal-stemmed candlestick with ribbed cylindrical nozzle on an octagonally moulded stem with stars at the shoulder, a domed and ribbed foot, c. 1750, 22 cm. high. **£190-240** *C*

A pair of composite-stemmed candlesticks, the nozzles with everted rims supported on beaded knops above octagonally-moulded pedestal sections and beaded base knobs, high domed and lightly terraced feet, c. 1750, 22 cm. high. **£750-850** *C*

A pair of composite-stemmed candlesticks, the ribbed nozzles on beaded inverted baluster knops above octagonally-moulded pedestal sections and beaded baluster base knobs, high domed feet with waved rims (small chips to foot rim), c. 1750, 24 cm. high. **£950-1,100** *C*

composite-stemmed
perstick, the nozzle with
erted rim, the stem with an
aque laminated corkscrew
iral between two beaded
ops, domed and terraced foot,
1760, 20 cm. high. **£750-**
0 *C*

A pair of cut-glass two-light candelabra (one finial restored, one foliate wax pan cracked, minor chips), c. 1780, 71 cm. high. **£1,400-1,600** *C*

A pair of Regency cut-glass and giltmetal candelabra, with hobnail-cut shafts and scrolled faceted branches, hung with pendant drops, 13½ in. high. **£1,000-1,300** *C*

pair of composite-stemmed
apersticks, the ribbed nozzles
upported on beaded ball knops
bove octagonally-moulded
edestal sections and base
nobs, domed and lightly
bbed feet, c. 1760, 16.5 cm.
igh. **£550-700** *C*

A pair of moulded glass chandeliers, 43 by 36 in., sold with packing crates, mid-19th C. **£700-800** *SB*

A pair of cut and moulded candelabra, 63.4 cm., late 19th C. **£350-420** *SBe*

A gilt-brass and opaque and etched glass chandelier fitted for 18 lights, 39½ in. (100 cm.), late 19th C. **£580-650** *SB*

A Baccarat pink dog-rose weight, 7 cm. diam. £400-500   *C*

A Baccarat pink pompom weight, 6.8 cm. diam. £300-350   *C*

A Baccarat two-coloured double-clematis weight, 6.7 cm. diam. £460-560   *C*

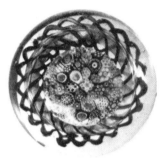

A Baccarat mushroom weight, on star-cut base, 8 cm. diam. £300-370   *C*

A Baccarat blue primrose weight, in blue, white and green, on star-cut base, 6 cm. diam. £400-480   *C*

A Baccarat turquoise-overlay patterned millefiori weight, cut with top and six side printies and on star-cut base, 8 cm. diam. £770-870   *C*

A Baccarat patterned millefiori paperweight, 7.5 cm. £240-280   *P*

A Baccarat dated close millefiori weight, with silhouettes of a squirrel, a horse, a cockerel, a goat and the date 1849, 6.5 cm. diam. £300-360   *C*

A Baccarat pansy paperweight, with star cut base, c. 1860. £550-600   *MB*

A Baccarat pansy paperweight, c. 1860. £450-580   *MB*

A Baccarat facet cut paperweight, with star cut base, c. 1860. £700-800   *MB*

A Baccarat pansy paperweight with a bud, with star cut base, c. 1860. £550-600   *MB*

A Clichy swirl weight, with lime-green and opaque white staves radiating from a central purple, green and white setup, 7.5 cm. diam. £400-480   *C*

A Baccarat faceted pansy weight, cut with a window and two rows of printies, on star-cut base, 7.3 cm. diam. £440-540 C

A Clichy swirl weight, with alternate mauve and opaque-white staves radiating from a large central green and white setup, 7.5 cm. diam. £500-600   C

A Clichy garlanded posy weight, 7.2 cm. diam. £880-1,000   C

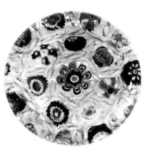

A Clichy turquoise 'Barber's Pole' concentric millefiori weight, in pink, turquoise and white, 7.2 cm. diam. £600-700   C

A Clichy patterned millefiori weight, in turquoise, white, pink, cobalt-blue, green and pink, 6.5 cm. diam. £500-590 C

A Clichy faceted patterned millefiori weight, cut with a window and five printies, 8 cm. diam. £500-600   C

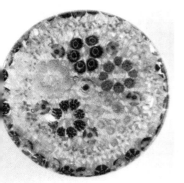

A Clichy patterned millefiori weight, in pale blue, red, white, green and pink, 8.7 cm. diam. £770-900   C

A Clichy faceted scattered millefiori weight, cut with a window and four side printies divided by flutes, 7.2 cm. diam. £450-550   C

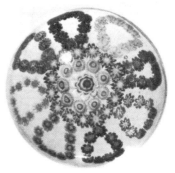

A Clichy patterned millefiori weight, in red, blue, green, pink, white, claret and purple, 8 cm. diam. £170-250   C

A Nailsea paper-weight, c. 1840, 4 in. £45-55   AA

A St. Louis blue double-clematis weight, 6.3 cm. diam. £240-300   C

A St. Louis paperweight, Latticino ground, with printies, circle of canes with central bouquets, c. 1860. £900-1,000   MB

A green paper-weight with branching foliage (Nailsea), c. 1830, 4 in. high. £40-45   AA

467

A St. Louis fruit weight, with a ripe pear and unripe pear, a peach and three cherries, 6 cm. diam. £300-360 *C*

A St. Louis single pear paperweight, the clear glass set with a fruit in yellow, the base star-cut, 7 cm. £440-500 *P*

A St. Louis signed and dated mushroom weight, including the date 1848 and the initials SL, on star-cut base, 7.3 cm. diam. £880-1,000 *C*

A St. Louis concentric millefiori mushroom weight, in blue, pink, white, green and salmon-pink, on star-cut base, 7.5 cm. diam. £400-480 *C*

Make the most of Miller's

When buying or selling, it must always be remembered that prices can be greatly affected by the condition of any piece.

Unless otherwise stated, all goods shown in Miller's are of good merchantable quality, and the valuations given reflect this fact.

Pieces offered for sale in exceptionally fine condition or in poor condition may reasonably be expected to be priced considerably higher or lower respectively than the estimates given herein.

A St. Louis close concentric millefiori weight, in shades of pale blue, pink, blue, green, white, salmon-pink and claret 7.5 cm. diam. £300-360 *C*

A scent bottle with scale cut blue overlay and silver top, 1850, 5 in. £100-130 *Som*

A Webb cameo scent flask with hinged silver cover, with amber glass overlaid in opaque white, Rd 11109 marks, the silver Birmingham, c. 1884, 23 cm. long. £450-520 *C*

(l) A Victorian green glass double scent bottle with silver/gilt mounts. £30-33 *Gs*

(r) A Victorian red glass double scent bottle. £40-48 *Gs*

A large dark green cornucopia scent bottle with silver finger ring and mounts, c. 1860, 3 in. £130-170 *Som*

A green double ended faceted scent bottle with vinaigrette end, silver gilt mounts, c. 1860 3⅜ in. £155-180 *Som*

Nine various late 18th/early 19th C. scent bottles, including a Victorian ruby glass double-ended scent bottle, the others enamel gilt. £10-25 each *Bon*

A flat oval cut scent bottle with silver top, c. 1780, 5 in. £38-48 *Som*

A Bristol blue scent bottle, of vase shape with gilt decoration and monogram in fitted shagreen case, c. 1780, 3 in. £170-200 *Som*

A Bristol flat scent bottle, facet cup with gilt decoration, c. 1790, 4⅜ in. **£170-200** *Som*

A small Bristol blue scent bottle with silver lattice framework in fitted shagreen case, c. 1775, 2½ in. **£200-260** *Som*

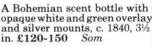

A Wrockwardine scent flask of green bottle glass, with opaque white and colour splashes, c. 1800, 3¾ in. **£75-95** *Som*

A Bohemian lithyalin glass scent bottle with silver gilt mount, c. 1840, 2½ in. **£140-180** *Som*

A Bohemian scent bottle with opaque white and green overlay and silver mounts, c. 1840, 3½ in. **£120-150** *Som*

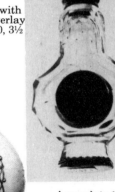

A Cameo amber scent bottle with opaque white decoration on amber body, silver gilt mount, c. 1880, 4⅜ in. **£300-360** *Som*

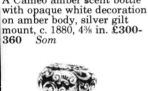

A Burmese glass scent bottle, in pink with pale blue, thickly gilt, the silver screw cap marked London, 1885, 13 cm. **£140-170** *SB*

A rare late 17th C./early 18th C. scent bottle with facet cutting and circular recesses either side of the body for solid perfume, silver mounts, 3¼ in. **£300-350** *Som*

A red rectangular scent bottle with silver medallion of Queen Victoria and silver crown stopper, c. 1886, 3¼ in. **£180-210** *Som*

A ruby cameo glass scent bottle, overlaid in white, the silver hinged lid by Horton & Allday embossed and marked Birmingham, 1887, clear glass stopper, 11.8 cm. **£550-650** *SB*

A pair of blue glass retrievers by John Derbyshire, Manchester, c. 1870. **£60-66** *Gs*

A rare pair of 18th C. scent bottles of French origin, in ormolu carriages, 7 in. high, c. 1780. **£195-215** pair *EA*

A Bohemian transparentemail hexagonal scent-bottle and stopper, c. 1840, 16 cm. high. **£180-220** *C*

A pair of early 19th C. glass 'Nailsea' fireplace ornaments of retrievers, 7 in. wide. **£54-60** *Gs*

A pair of green glass lions by John Derbyshire, c. 1870. **£60-66** *Gs*

A Vaseline glass perfume bottle and stopper, 7 in., c. 1880's. **£40-50** *MT*

An early 19th C. 'Nailsea' bottle glass ornament, 6 in. high. **£32-38** *Gs*

A frosted glass lion by John Derbyshire, c. 1870. **£30-34** *Gs*

A polychrome leaded glass panel, in an oval mahogany frame, possibly German, c. 1880, 65 by 35 in. (165 by 89 cm.). **£440-500** *SB*

A Bohemian Zwischengoldglas oval plaque by Hoxparth, (slight chip to rim), signed Hoxparth Fecit, c. 1790, with Lithyalin frame of marbled red/brown colour, 15 cm. long. **£190-230** *C*

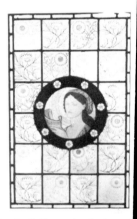

A Morris & Co. stained glass panel of Saint Cecilia, designed by Sir Edward Burne-Jones for Onecote Vicarage, inscribed Sancta Cecilia, c. 1863, 29½ by 18¼ in. (75 by 46 cm.). **£500-570** *SB*

A stained glass roundel, painted with the head of a young woman, 31 cm. diam., lead border, 1880-1900. **£100-200** *SB*

An 'Arts and Crafts' stair glass panel, c. 1900, 24 by 32 in. **£45-50** *F*

A Bristol blue rolling pin, c. 1840, 15 in. long. **£30-40** *AA*

A lace-maker's lamp, the spherical bowl on a hollow multi-knopped stem and conical folded foot, late 18th/early 19th C. 23.5 cm. high. **£150-200** *C*

A large opaque milk glass
rolling pin, c. 1850, 28 in. long.
£60-70 *AA*

An opaline rolling pin, c. 1840,
18 in. long. **£30-40** *AA*

English glass lacemaker's
np, 5½ in. high, c. 1760.
30-145 *A.E.F.*

A Burmese glass large night
light, with applied wishbone
feet with Burmese night light
cup, signed Thomas Webb, c.
1880, 6¾ in. **£400-450** *MT*

A glass oil lamp with three
curved spouts, late 17th C., 11
m. wide. **£80-120** *C*

A Burmese small size night
light and posy holder, signed
Thomas Webb, with applied
fern leaf, also signed Clark's
Fairy night light, 5½ in., c. 1880.
£260-285 *MT*

An amethyst wine bottle with
wrythen moulding, c. 1810, 11¾
in. **£120-145** *Som*

A serving bottle with square
body, c. 1740, 18 cm. high.
£350-420 *C*

Cranberry glass 4 branch
pergne, in the form of an iris
ower, 23¼ in. high. **£145-**
00 *PSH*

A pair of cranberry glass
Victorian lustres, 11 in. high.
£100-125 pair *E.E*

ive Victorian amethyst glass
rs and stoppers, 16 and 17 in.
240-320 *Hy.D*

A pair of Bohemian enamelled
ruby glass bottles and stoppers,
24.5 cm., c. 1850. **£80-130** *SB*

471

One of a set of twelve ruby glass
custard cups, c. 1860. **£70-80**
set   *MT*

A small Irish pap boat, with
turnover rim and sparrow bea
c. 1780, 2⅜ in. **£90-110**   *So*

A blue opaline glass casket, gilt
with fruiting vine, gilt-metal
mounts and loop handles, 11.4
cm., c. 1850. **£330-400**   *SBe*

A mid-18th C. Spanish glass
posset pot and cover, made at
La Granta de san il de Fonso,
Royal Glass factory. **£400-
520**   *WW*

A fine pair of Georgian sa
cellars, with crenellated ri
cut bowls and rhomboidal
bases, c. 1795, 3¼ in. **£75-**
AA

A small baluster Tazza, the flat
circular tray on two cushion
knops above a short plain
section and base knob and
enclosing two tears, domed and
folded foot, c. 1730, 11 cm. diam.
£90-120   *C*

A globular teapot and cover
(chip to rim of cover), c. 1725, 15
cm. wide. **£300-380**   *C*

A posset-glass with slender b
bowl, on a circular foot, c. 172
10 cm. high. **£100-140**   *C*

An early Nailsea hat, with
opaque white looping, c. 1810,
3½ in. **£55-65**   *Som*

A pair of 'opale' opaline bell-
shaped tumblers, painted by
J. B. Desvignes in colours,
enriched in gilding, c. 1825.
£600-800   *C*

An opaque white glass bell w
coloured trailing and knopp
wrythen handle, c. 1860, 12¼
£130-165   *Som*

An early Nailsea hat, with turn
up rim, c. 1800, 4 in. **£35-45**
Som

An English four bottle
condiment set, cut glass with
green shading to clear,
probably Stourbridge, 8 in.
high, c. 1860. **£170-190**   *MT*

ANTIQUITIES

lass was known in the Near Last from as early as 1500 B.C. However, it would have been a uxury item then and due to his initial rarity, the passage f time and the fragility of the naterial a collector would be ll advised to search out examples! In the 1st century B.C. a method of glass blowing was discovered. This brought about virtual mass production of glass items and accounts for the large number and diversity of styles available today. Many flasks have been found in tombs and can still be purchased for under £300. Repaired flasks and forgeries abound — intact glass has an accustomed clear ring.

core-fashioned balt blue glass abastron, with aque yellow and ite marvered zig- g design, 4⅛ in. .4 cm.) long, 5th- n C. B.C. £550- 0   *C*

A pale green glass feeder, with encrustation and iridescence, 4½ in. high, 6th C. A.D. £150-220   *C*

A pale green glass flask, a funnel-shaped collared rim slots into the neck, 7 in. high, 3rd C. A.D. £330-400   *C*

A pale blue translucent glass flask, 9½ in. (24.1 cm.) high, c. 4th C. A.D. £550-650   *C*

A green translucent glass flask, 9 in. (22.8 cm.) high, 3rd-4th C. A.D. £240-300   *C*

A translucent green glass flask, 7 in. high, c. 4th C. A.D. £270-320   *C*

A pale green translucent glass flask, 4½ in. high, 3rd-4th C. A.D. £120-180   *C*

A pale green translucent glass flask, 9½ in. (24.1 cm.) high, 3rd-4th C. A.D. £200-250   *C*

pair of translucent pale green ass flasks, 12 in. and 9¼ in. gh, 3rd-4th C. A.D. £350- 0   *C*

A brown glass Janus-headed flask, 3¼ in. (11.5 cm.) high, c. 3rd C. A.D. £370-430   *C*

A green translucent glass flask, slight iridescence, 5½ in. high, c. 4th C. A.D. £150-220   *C*

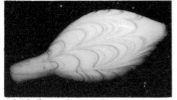

A Nailsea gimmel flask in pink and white, c. 1820, 6 in. long. £70-85   *AA*

A late 19th C. rare cranberry Mary Gregory hip flask, 3¾ in. £85-100   *MT*

A Nailsea gimmel flask, c. 1830, 8 in. high, 4 in. wide. £65-70   *AA*

A Nailsea type flask, with translucent blue looping, c. 1850, 10 in. £75-90   *Som*

A Victorian pilgrim vase, on black ground, with bright flowers, 8¾ in. high. £40-50   *SV*

An engraved glass pilgrim flask, with flattened ovoid body, short neck and two applied loop handles, elaborately engraved and inscribed YE MEN-AT-ARM 29 cm., set on a wooden base 1860. £140-160   *SB*

A Bohemian Lithyalin flask and stopper, of marbled red/brown glass enriched with a gilt band, perhaps Riesengebirge, c. 1840, 33 cm. high. £220-260   *C*

A pair of Bristol amethyst decanters with gilt wine labels for rum and brandy, c. 1790, 8½ in. £400-500 pair   *Som*

An engraved decanter and stopper of mallet shape, engraved and cut with a branch of trailing fruit vine, with facet cut spire stopper, c. 1765, 29 cm. high. £200-250   *C*

A Lynn decanter of club shape, c. 1770, 22.5 cm. high. £200-240   *C*

A pair of green glass decanters, inscribed in gold 'Rum' and 'Shrub', mid/late 18th C., 31 cm. £320-380   *SBe*

A Lynn bottle-decanter, c. 1770, 18.5 cm. high. £160-200   *C*

...are Bristol blue decanter of ...uldered shape with three ...k rings and target stopper, c. ...0, 11 in. **£250-300** *Som*

An Irish decanter, with moulded base and vesica cutting, with three annulated neck rings, and moulded mushroom stopper, the base moulded 'Waterloo Cork', c. 1800, 10 in. **£225-265** *Som*

An Irish decanter with three feathered neck rings and moulded target stopper, impressed mark the Cork Glass Co., the body engraved 'The land we live in', the monogram and floral spray on reverse, c. 1800, 10¾ in. **£500-585** *Som*

A square spirit bottle with flute cutting and band of diamonds, the body engraved 'Nectar for the God of War, victorious Nelson', cut mushroom stopper, 8 in., c. 1810. **£280-320** *Som*

...three-quarter size ...orgian decanter, ...h three ringed neck ...d correct stopper, ...20, 9½ in. high. **£30-** *AA*

An early 19th C. cut glass decanter, with correct stopper, 11½ in. **£50-60** *AA*

An early Victorian green decanter with flute and diamond cutting and acorn stopper, c. 1840, 13¾ in. **£90-110** *Som*

A pair of Victorian green glass decanters and stoppers, slight damage to one stopper, 14¾ in. high. **£125-135** *SV*

...e of a pair of thumb cut ...anters, with spine stoppers, ...860, 11 in. high. **£55-65** ...r *AA*

A cut glass decanter with silver top, Sheffield, 1910, 12½ in. high. **£72-82** *ST*

A pair of finely-cut Georgian decanters, with correct numbered stoppers, c. 1830, 10 in. high. **£225-250** pair *AA*

Four oval cut spirit bottles, the stoppers engraved with initials H.R.S.B. standing for Hollands, Rum, Shrub and Brandy, and with oval cut bowl for ratafia, chips. In Sheffield plated stand on turntable, c. 1810, 11 in. **£400-480** *Som*

A set of three Bristol blue decanters with gilt labels Brandy, Rum, Hollands in black lacquer stand, c. 1790, 10¼ in. **£400-480** *Som*

A William IV glass claret j with stopper, heavily cut, 1 **£110-180** *WW*

A pear shaped cream-jug, early 18th C., 9 cm. high. **£120-150** *C*

A Victorian claret jug with plated top, 8 in. high. **£87-97** *ST*

An early cream-jug of wrythen-moulded bell shape (small chip), late 17th C., 9 cm. high. **£120-140** *C*

A Victorian claret jug, with faceted neck and and radial bowl, correct numbered an faceted stop, c. 1875, 12 in. h **£45-55** *AA*

A cream-jug with wrythen-moulded lower part, c. 1720, 10 cm. high. **£140-180** *C*

An engraved silver-mounted claret jug, possibly engraved by Franz Tieze, cover with London hallmark for 1888, 25 cm. **£290-330** *P*

A Victorian cut glass claret with plated top, 11 in. **£98-110** *ST*

water jug with sprig and star
tting and looped panels of
monds, strap handle, 6 in., c.
10. **£85-100**   *Som*

A clear glass cream jug, with
moulded body and blue
turnover rim, wrythen moulded
body, c. 1800, 3½ in. **£125-
165**   *Som*

A large baluster jug, 10 in.,
English, c. 1745-50. **£165-
200**   *L*

Victorian coloured glass jug,
1850, 8 in. high. **£50-60**   *AA*

A cut glass Irish water jug, c.
1870, 5¾ in. high. **£35-45**   *AA*

A heavily cut water jug, c. 1870,
7 in. high. **£15-25**   *AA*

late 19th C. cranberry Mary
regory cream jug, 3½ in.
100-130   *MT*

A dark green cream jug, the
pear shaped body on a capstan
stem, c. 1800, 6 in. **£200-235**
Som

A crackle ware Amberina jug,
with applied celery handle, 8
in., c. 1870. **£150-180**   *MT*

Nailsea bottle green glass jug
ith applied opaque white
ailing round rim, c. 1800, 9 in.
220-260   *Som*

A small Nailsea cream jug in
bottle green glass, c. 1800, 4 in.
£115-145   *Som*

A Nailsea baluster shaped jug,
green bottle glass with opaque
white inclusions, c. 1800, 7¾ in.
£150-180   *Som*

A Wrockwardine bottle green glass jug, with opaque white, blue, yellow and red inclusions, c. 1800, 7¾ in. **£200-260**   *Som*

A mug, the bulbous lower part moulded with 'nipt diamond waies', on circular foot, c. 1730, 9.5 cm. high. **£120-150**   *C*

A Nailsea cream jug, bottle green glass with white and opaque splashes, c. 1800, 5½ in. **£120-160**   *Som*

A mug, bell shape with gadrooned lower part and on circular foot, c. 1730, 10.5 cm. high. **£60-100**   *C*

A tankard of bell shape, with wrythen-moulded lower part, on circular terraced foot, mid 18th C., 15 cm. high. **£220-260**   *C*

A glass mug of bell shape, on circular foot, c. 1760, 11.5 cm. high. **£60-80**   *C*

A tankard of bell shape, with wrythen-moulded lower part on circular terraced foot, small rim chip, c. 1760, 20 cm. high. **£50-80**   *C*

A rare Victorian stemmed tankard, the stem with hollow central knop, containing a Victorian silver three-penny piece, 10 in., 1883. **£90-110**   *AA*

A late Georgian finely-cut Irish rosebowl on knopped pedestal stem and circular foot, 8 in. high, 9½ in. diam. **£90-110**   *AA*

A deep bowl, the lower part moulded with 'nipt diamond waies' and supported on a high conical foot with folded rim, c. 1690, 20.5 cm. diam. **£900-1,400**   *C*

One of a set of four green cooler bowls, c. 1830, 4 in. high, 5 in. diam. **£110-130** the set   *AA*

One of a pair of Victorian finger bowls, with radial cut bases, c. 1870, 3¼ in. high. **£15-20** the pair   *AA*

e of a set of six Bristol
nethyst cooler bowls, c. 1840,
in. high, 4½ in. diam. £275-
5 set   AA

One of a set of four Bristol
amethyst two-lip cooler bowls,
c. 1820, 3½ in. high, 4 in. diam.
£185-200 set   AA

A Bristol blue wine cooler bowl,
c. 1840, 3½ in. high, 4½ in. diam.
£25-30   AA

satin glass bowl, interior
ue, exterior pink combed in
rple and white, 14 cm.,
arked PATENT 12285, late
th C. £400-500   SB

A rare Nailsea bowl and cover
of rich amethyst applied white
looping, c. 1810, 7 in. £250-
300   Som

A Venetian 'Chalcedony' bowl,
the exterior with swirling olive-
green, yellow and brown
striations, the interior
marblised in blue/brown, 16th
C., 12.5 cm. diam. £260-300
C

footed glass bowl, in ruby and
hite, the flared bowl on short
nopped stem and tall pedestal
ase, enamelled with gilt, 34.8
n., c. 1850. £360-400   SB

A pair of cameo glass bowls,
each ruby ground overlaid in
white, 10 cm. diam., 1880's.
£800-950   SBe

A cameo glass bowl, of globular
form in frosted glass overlaid in
pink and white, 7.3 cm., 1880's.
£280-320   SB

Facon-de-Venise kottrolf, of
llowish metal, with kick-in
se, South German or
etherlandish, 17th C., 18 cm.
gh. £150-200   C

A Queen's Burmese ware posy
bowl, with five petal flower
decoration, 3 in. high, c. 1880.
£90-100   MT

An early Victorian celery vase,
engraved with grapes and vine
leaves on square base, c. 1840, 8
in. high. £45-50   AA

479

A 19th C. green Bohemian overlay vase, 7½ in. high. **£100-125**   *SV*

A Bohemian amber vase, with hexagonal bowl, on short baluster stem and petal-cut foot, 8 in. **£130-190**   *L*

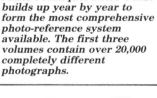

A Bohemian 'Ruby Flash' vase and cover, 17 in., second half 19th C. **£320-420**   *SBA*

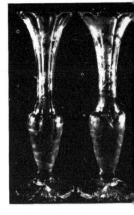

A pair of Bohemian engra vases, deeply engraved wi deer in a wooded landscap 44.8 cm., c. 1850. **£330-40** *SBe*

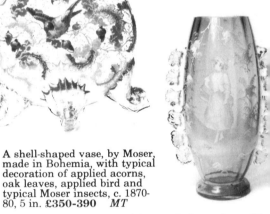

A shell-shaped vase, by Moser, made in Bohemia, with typical decoration of applied acorns, oak leaves, applied bird and typical Moser insects, c. 1870-80, 5 in. **£350-390**   *MT*

A Clutha vase, designed by Christopher Dresser, of olive green glass, 15½ in. marked Clutha designed C.D. registered. **£280-360**   *L*

A late 19th C. cranberry Ma Gregory vase, with applied shell decoration on sides, 9 i **£150-170**   *MT*

A Clutha glass vase, attributed to Christopher Dresser, dimpled into five sides, in bubbled green glass with trails of white and gold inclusions, 51.7 cm., c. 1885. **£400-500**   *SB*

Miller's Antiques Price Guide builds up year by year to form the most comprehensive photo-reference system available. The first three volumes contain over 20,000 completely different photographs.

A pair of Egermann Lithyalin ormolu-mounted oviform vases, in brown and olive-green colours, c. 1834, 43 cm. high. **£1,200-1,400**   *C*

A pair of late 19th C. ruby Mary Gregory bottle-shape vases, 9½ in. **£290-320**   *MT*

A Mammoth enamelled opal glass vase, 50.1 cm., mid-19th **£170-220**   *SBe*

French opaline vase, with
reen base and white fluted top
ith gold decoration, c. 1850, 11
. £175-195   MT

A pair of 19th C. pink opaline
vases, 12¾ in. high. £60-70
SV

A 19th C. opaline vase on
paque white ground, 6 in. high.
55-65   SV

A pair of 19th C. pink vases,
with overlay cherubs, 9½ in.
high. £45-55   SV

A tall opaline glass vase
enamelled by Maxant, signed,
54.6 cm., c. 1850. £330-400
SBe

A Thomas Webb peachblow
three footed glass vase, with
applied decoration with deep
lemon lining, c. 1870, 6 in. high.
£300-400   MT

pair of ruby portrait overlay
ass vases, 36.8 cm., c. 1850.
330-400   SBe

A pair of green overlay glass
vases, 30 cm., c. 1850. £200-
250   SBe

A glass vase, the blue glass
overlaid in white and gilt,
carved with trefoils, quatrefoils
and shaped panels, 39.5 cm., c.
1850   SB

A pair of green overlay vases,
the body enamelled with sprays
of lily of the valley and gilt, 45
cm., c. 1860. £650-750   SB

A small vase, unusual three
coloured blue, white on acid
yellow by Thomas Webb, c.
1880, 3 in. £400-450   MT

An early 20th C. white satin glass vase, 8 in. high. **£25-30** *SV*

A Victorian overlay vase, with slight rubbing, 5¾ in. high. **£60-70** *SV*

A Thomas Webb spill vase, with deep ruby stem, with a clear glass ruffled base, 8½ in., c. 1870. **£40-45** *MT*

A pair of St. Louis overlay gla macedoine vases, overlaid i opaque white and pink, 14 c high. **£170-210** *C*

A ruby cameo glass vase, of shouldered form with flared cylindrical neck, decorated in white flowers, possibly by Webb, 17 cm., c. 1880. **£580-620** *SB*

A Webb ruby cameo vase, dated 1895, the ovoid body overlaid in white and carved, 13.2 cm., the base etched Webb, 1895. **£500-600** *SB*

A vaseline blue glass spill vase, c. 1800, 8½ in. high. **£35-40** *AA*

A Stevens & Williams 'Silver two handled glass vase, decorated in pink, yellow an purple on a silvered ground, 1890, 34 cm. high. **£350-420** *C*

A 19th C. blue glass vase, with fluted rim and gilding, 10½ in. high. **£50-60** *SV*

A green glass vase, probably French, with 3 opaque white portrait medallions, late 19th C., 41 cm. **£85-100** *SBe*

A pair of 19th C. opaque green glass vases, 9½ in. high. **£50-60** *SV*

A ruby glass vase and cover decorated all over in white enamel and gold, c. 1850, 25 **£880-980** *L*

GLASS APPENDIX

abastron
vessel for holding ointments
ed by the ancients. Named after
abastron, a town in which there
s a manufactory of small
ssels.

ilby, William (1740-1819)
d Mary (1749-1797)
mous English glass enamellers
m Newcastle upon Tyne.
lliam started in Birmingham as
maker of enamel boxes, but was
corating glasses in Newcastle
1762. Mary decorating glasses
m 1767 onwards.

ristol
rst mention of glass
anufacture in Bristol was made
1696. During the 18th C. Bristol
came a famous glass making
ntre, noted for the coloured glass
oduced there. (A lot of coloured
ass has been erroneously
tributed to Bristol in the past).
ne peak of the coloured glass
aking period was 1790-1820. The
ost popular colour was blue and
nethyst; red was also used, as
as green especially after 1850.

ute Glass
amed after the unpopular
itish Prime Minister Lord Bute
ho was forced to resign in 1763.
e was commemorated with the
ite or Boot Glass.

lutha Glass
spired by old Roman glass,
signed by Christopher Dresser
d made by James Couper and
n, Glasgow, who patented it in
1890. Reputedly named after the

cloudy River Clyde, the metal is
clouded, streaked and bubbled.

Cork Glass Company
Opened in 1783 by Hayes Burnett
and Rowe. It survived until 1818
when it was succeeded by the
Waterloo Glass Company which
lasted until 1836.

Egermann, Frederick (1777-1864)
Bohemian glass decorator,
invented Lithyalin in 1828; he also
introduced yellow and red flashed
glass in 1820 and 1840.

Hurdels Verk
18th C. Scandinavian glass
making factory. Used coloured as
well as clear glass. Blue glass used
quite extensively from 1780.
Factory closed down in 1809.

'Kit Kat'
A type of drinking glass so called
because of a painting by Sir
Godfrey Kneller in the National
Portrait Gallery showing
members of the 'Kit Kat' Club
using similar shaped vessels. The
Kit Kat Club was a London Whig
Literary Club, c. 1690-1720, which
met for a time in the pie shop of
Christopher Cat or Catling.

Lithyalin
Name for valuable coloured
opaque glass invented by
Egermann (1777-1864) of
Blottendorf in 1828. It resembles a
semi-precious stone in appearance
and was much imitated in
Bohemia and Silesia.

'Mary Gregory' Glass
Glass items decorated in white

enamels with Victorian children
at play by Hahn of Galonz in
Bohemia from 1850 onwards. So
called because an American, Mary
Gregory, copied the designs on the
Bohemian glass whilst working in
Boston.

Millefiori
Ornamental glass made by fusing
coloured canes together, used from
1840's in paperweights where the
canes were enveloped in clear flint
glass.

Nailsea
Glass factory established 1788 by
John Robert Lucas. Used cheap
non-lead glass to make bottles and
crown window glass. Benefitted in
1793 from the tax which burdened
the makers of lead glass. Lucas
later went into partnership with
Edward Homer. Produced objects
decorated with white enamel,
probably obtained from Bristol. A
great deal of coloured glass was
supposed to have been made at
Nailsea, but there is no evidence to
support this. The Nailsea factory
closed in the 1870's. A lot of
Nailsea-type glass was made in
other parts of the country and has
been reproduced.

Opaline Glass
Semi-opaque ornamental glass
used in Victorian times, could not
be cut.

Printie
Small wheel ground circular
hollow cut in glass, more heavily
cut in Victorian times.

Vaseline Glass
So called because of the greenish
yellow tone of the glass
resembling the colour of vaseline
ointment introduced in 1878.

ART NOUVEAU AND ART DECO

t Nouveau and Art Deco are two
ite separate styles
compassing the period between
e 1880's and the late 1930's.
t Nouveau grew out of the Arts
d Crafts Movement of the late
th century. It is generally
cepted that it began in the early
ars of the 1880's, (although its
ots were evident in the decade
fore). It reached its peak of
pularity around 1900 and was
led off, quite literally, in the
rst World War.
he style is characterised by
wing lines and curves and a
ore feminine approach and feel
design. As the style progressed
became more ornate, to the point
here the decoration seemed to
ke over entirely.
ne of the most successful areas in
th Art Nouveau and Art Deco
as glass manufacture. The glass
akers inspired by Gallé and the
ancy School, developed a new
eedom which was almost
irrealist in concept. Art Glass
as collected at the time and is
ghly sought after now. Glass
as to be in prime condition to be
prime collecting interest. This
as encouraged many modern
kes and signature faking in
articular has flourished in
rance. Cabochons have been
lded to disguise imperfections
d synthetic glass pastes have
en used to hide cracks and chips.

One area in particular to watch is
Loetz glass vases from Austria.
Very few of these vases were
originally signed, only in fact,
those which were exported. Due to
the collector's mania for signed
pieces and devout belief in the
authenticity of any that are, many
now appear with the
characteristic 'Loetz, Austria'
engraved mark. Some of these are
extremely crude examples which
would never have been produced
by the factory.
'Art Déco' came into being after
the First World War and can be
seen as a reaction against some of
the more romantic notions of Art
Nouveau. The French call 'Art
Deco' the 25-style after the 'Paris
Exposition Internationale des
Arts Decoratifs et Industriels
Modernes', which was held in
1925. One of the main influences
in the Art world was the Cubist
Piet Mondrian. Art Deco is a
difficult style to pin down as it
displayed strong national
characteristics. In Germany the
Bauhaus developed quite
separately from the French
exponents. Art Deco tends to rely
heavily on machine-like forms,
with straight lines, chrome,
geometric patterns, particularly
zig-zags, and strident colours. Art
Deco bronze and ivory figures,
especially by Chiparus and Preiss,
have been faked in quite large

quantities and this has had a
levelling off effect on prices.
Another major problem is that
since both styles have become so
collectable, anything made
between 1880 and 1940 is
immediately categorised as Art
Nouveau or Art Deco. This has the
effect of debasing the actual
styles.

A Galle cameo glass
vase, in green
overlaid with
deeper green and
etched with ferns,
cameo mark 'Galle',
32.5 cm., c. 1900.
£660-800 *SB*

A two colour
layer cameo
glass vase by
Galle, 14¾ in.
high. **£450-650** *G*

A Galle cameo glass vase, in grey glass tinted pink, overlaid in white, deep purple and dark green, 25.75 cm., cameo mark 'Galle' with a star, after 1904. **£380-440**   *SB*

A three colour layer cameo glass vase, by Galle, c. 1900, 11¾ in. **£400-600**   *G*

An overlaid spill vase, on yellow oil ground with mau rose decoration, by Galle, 15 high. **£680-750**   *Lan*

A Galle cameo glass vase, in pink-tinted grey glass overlaid with purple, 60.25 cm., cameo mark 'Galle', c. 1900. **£1,000-1,100**   *SB*

A two colour layer cameo glass vase, by Galle, c. 1900, 9½ in. high. **£300-400**   *G*

A Galle cameo landscape glass vase, overlaid with brown and lilac glass and acid etched, signed in cameo Galle, 30 cm. high. **£880-1,000**   *P*

A fine two colour layer cam glass vase, by Galle, c. 190 11½ in. high. **£500-700**

A Galle cameo glass vase, in pinkish-grey glass, overlaid with clear amber/green, 35 cm. height, incised mark 'Galle', c. 1900. **£600-700**   *SB*

A Galle cameo glass vase, the greyish body overlaid with orange and deep ruby glass, acid etched and polished, signed 'E. Galle', 45 cm. high. **£2,200-2,600**   *P*

A small Galle carved cameo glass vase, in opaque milky-green glass, 9.5 cm., underside with impressed mark 'Galle modele et decors deposes', c. 1900. **£440-520**   *SB*

A fine three colour layer cameo glass vase by Galle, c. 1900, 10 in. high. **£600-800**   *G*

An early Galle enamelled gla vase, with an inscription in g 'Lien d'Amour', signed in reli 'Galle', 16.5 cm. high. **£460-565**   *P*

A Galle cameo glass vase, in grey glass tinted pink at the base, overlaid in white lilac and green, 27 cm., cameo mark 'Galle', c. 1900. **£360-420** *SB*

A three coloured layer mould blown 'Souffle' vase, of Japanese inspiration, by Galle, c. 1900, 9½ in. high. **£2,000-3,000** *G*

A fine three colour layer cameo glass vase, by Galle, 9½ in. high. **£700-900** *G*

A three colour layer cameo glass vase by Galle, c. 1900, 8½ in. high. **£450-650** *G*

EMILE GALLE (1846-1904)

Emile Gallé was born at Nancy, the provincial capital of Lorraine, the son of Charles Gallé a glass faience retailer. Emile studied in Nancy and at the Weimar Art School. He was apprenticed at the Meisenthal glasshouse, 1866-67. By the early 1870's he had set up his own workshop. He concentrated mainly on glass and furniture, although he did produce some faience.

By the 1890's he was turning out a large number of glass items. Initially everything was on a reasonably small scale. The fine quality of his moulded or blown glass, cased with layers of differently coloured glass, cut through to form the design, was never surpassed. Eventually, however, this had to be done on a more commercial level, unwanted glass was removed by hydrofluoric acid. These lost some of the quality and are not as desirable to collectors. Gallé reached the height of his fame by 1900 and tragically died of leukaemia in 1904. The factory continued after his death to produce work in his style until it closed in 1914. Every piece was then marked with a star beside the name Gallé.

A Galle cameo glass vase, in grey glass tinted pink, overlaid in white and green, cameo mark 'Galle', 30 cm., c. 1900. **£550-650** *SB*

Galle etched and enamelled vase, in pale green glass overlaid in milky-green glass, heightened with gilding, 9 cm., cameo mark 'Galle', c. 1900. **£260-320** *SB*

A Galle cameo glass flask, the greyish body overlaid with orange and ruby glass, signed 'Galle' on a four-leaved clover, 12.50 cm. high. **£380-500** *P*

Left
A three colour cameo glass vase designed with Japanese inspiration by Galle, c. 1900, 10½ in. diam. **£1,200-1,500** *G*

A fine three colour layer cameo glass vase, by Galle, 5¼ in. high. **£400-600** *G*

Right
A Galle purple glass flask, streaked internally with yellow/grey, 13 cm. body with incised signature, 'Galle', c. 1900. **£500-600** *SB*

A Galle cameo vase and cover, the greyish body rose and green tinted and overlaid with pale and deep brown glass, signed in cameo Galle, 14.50 cm. high. **£900-1,100** *P*

A miniature Daum etched and enamelled bottle and stopper, engraved mark 'Daum Nancy', 6.25 cm., c. 1900. **£120-180** *SB*

A Daum etched glass vase, in clear turquoise glass, the ground acid textured, engraved mark 'Daum Nancy France', 19.75 cm., 1920's. **£330-390** *SB*

A Daum cameo glass vase, in grey glass streaked with red, overlaid in mottled red/orange and yellow/green, 40 cm., cameo mark 'Daum Nancy', c. 1900. **£550-650** *SB*

A Daum etched and enamelled glass bowl, in yellow glass streaked with purple, gilt mark 'Daum Nancy', 12 cm. wide, c. 1900. **£250-320** *SB*

A Daum etched and enamelled vase, overlaid and painted in shades of yellow and green with mottled amber ground, enamelled signature Daum Nancy, France, 18.5 cm. high. **£360-420** *C*

A Daum etched and enamelled cameo glass vase, of oval section, the pale pink ground overlaid and painted in realistic colours, base enamelled Daum Nancy, 23 cm. high. **£580-680** *C*

An Art Deco glass bowl by Daum, with gold foil inclusions, wrought iron mounts by Majorelle, 10 in. diam. **£150-300** *G*

An Art Deco amber etched glass vase by Daum, 8¾ in. high. **£100-250** *G*

An Art Nouveau iridescent glass vase, by Victor Durand with heart and clinging vine decoration, 6 in. **£300-500** *G*

A Lalique glass vase, traces of blue staining, 16.5 cm., engraved mark 'R. Lalique France', 1930's. **£140-150** *SB*

A late Art Nouveau iridescent glass vase by Victor Durand, with heart and clinging vine decoration, c. 1920, 6½ in. high. **£300-500** *G*

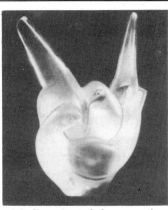

Lalique glass vase, traces of
lue staining, 15.75 cm.,
ngraved mark 'R. Lalique
rance', 1930's. £140-160
B

A Lalique frosted glass vase, in
the form of two doves, 9½ in.
high, signed Lalique, France,
1930's. £300-500   N

'Ceylan' a Lalique opalescent
glass vase, moulded with four
pairs of budgerigars, engraved
in block letters R. Lalique,
France, 24 cm. high. £360-
500   P

Lalique frosted glass
istletoe vase, 7 in., c. 1930.
280-330   MT

Gui, a Lalique frosted glass
vase, script R. Lalique, France,
6¼ in. high. £130-190   CSK

A Lalique opalescent glass
vase, in milky glass with
turquoise staining, 23.25 cm.,
lightly engraved mark
'Lalique', 1920's. £240-280
SB

Chasseurs, a Lalique glass
vase, 27 cm. height, engraved
mark 'R. Lalique France, No
893', 1920's. £400-440   SB

Esterel: A grey-stained frosted
glass vase, wheel engraved R.
Lalique, France, moulded R.
Lalique, 15.5 cm. high. £150-
190   C

A Lalique frosted glass thistle
vase, 8½ in., c. 1930. £200-
250   MT

A Lalique opalescent glass
vase, 18 cm., engraved mark 'R.
Lalique France', 1920's. £190-
240   SB

Poissons', a Lalique opalescent
lass vase, detailed with green
tain, 23.7 cm., base with
noulded mark, 'R. Lalique',
920's. £370-420   SB

A 'Druids' opalescent glass jar,
in pale matt blue staining, 19
cm. diam., incised 'R. Lalique,
France, No. 937'. £300-350
SKC

A brown-stained frosted glass vase, printed etched R. Lalique, France, 18.5 cm. high. **£115-140**   *C*

'Ormeaux', a Lalique green opalescent glass vase, signed R. Lalique, France, No. 984, 17 cm. high. **£550-700**   *P*

A Lalique vase, stained i green, 16 cm., engraved ' Lalique'. **£140-180**   *SK*

A Legras 'Indiana' glass vase, decorated internally in natural colours with cameo clear glass relief and gilt borders, unmarked, 32 cm. high. **£330-415**   *P*

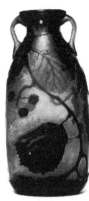

A Legras cameo glass vase, in grey/green overlaid in dark and lighter shades of green, 24.5 cm., cameo mark 'Legras', c. 1900. **£330-400**   *SB*

A Loetz iridescent glass vase, pink/brown glass, 24 cm., engraved mark, 'Loetz Austria c. 1900. **£850-950**   *SB*

A green iridescent glass vase, in the style of Loetz, highlighted in blue, green and golden iridescence, 7¼ in. high. **£200-280**   *CSK*

An iridescent glass spill vase, in metallic pink shading to gold, 34.25 cm., vase engraved 'L.C.T. Favrile', stamped 'L.C. Tiffany Furnaces Inc 151' and with company trade mark, c. 1900. **£380-420**   *SB*

An iridescent glass vase, attributed to Loetz, in red, cm., c. 1900. **£340-400**   *S*

One of a pair of Loetz glass vases, 24 cm. high. **£200-280** the pair   *P*

A Loetz iridescent glass vase, decorated with pale peacock/gold lustre, 24 cm., c. 1900. **£400-500**   *SB*

A Tiffany iridescent glass vase, overall pink/gold lustre, crackled at the rim, 45.5 cm. max height, engraved mark 'L.C.T. 9583A', affixed manufacturers' paper label, 1906. **£880-1,080**   *SB*

A Loetz 'Phenomenon' glass vase, the green glass body with a pale peacock-blue iridescence, 16 cm. high. **£70-110**   *P*

iridescent cobalt bottle,
ributed to Loetz, decorated
th greenish-gold pulled
read design, 28.5 cm. high.
80-800   *C*

A Loetz cameo glass vase, the
milky-white ground overlaid
and etched in shades of blue,
relief signature, 39 cm. high.
£580-640   *C*

A Loetz cameo glass vase and
cover, in yellow glass overlaid
with brown and etched with
leaves, cameo mark 'Loetz', 23.5
cm., c. 1900. **£250-300**   *SB*

A Loetz iridescent glass vase,
10.5 cm. high. **£150-210**   *P*

One of a pair of Loetz glass
vases, each enclosed within a
'Juventa' pewter mount, 31 cm.
high. **460-560** the pair   *P*

'Jack in the Pulpit' iridescent
ase, attributed to Loetz, with
reen glass body, 23 cm. high.
260-400   *P*

A Walter pate-de-verre vase, in
yellow glass streaked with
amber, detailed in red, purple
and green, incised mark 'A.
Walter Nancy', 16.75 cm.,
1920's. **£500-600**   *SB*

A pate de verre vase, in black,
orange and green, 14.75 cm.,
incised mark 'A Walter Nancy',
1920's. **£590-660**   *SB*

A Brocard vase, enamelled in
red, blue and grey, enriched
with gilding, retailer's paper
label, 39.5 cm. high. **£280-
320**   *C*

. Degue cameo vase, the
reyish body overlaid with
pple green shading to deep
ue, signed Degue, 50 cm. high.
250-400   *P*

A pair of Limoges enamelled
vases, by Sarlandie, 23.7 cm.
and 24 cm., gilded marks
'Sarlandie Limoges', and one
with paper label marked 'No
212/4 Groseilles givrees',
1920's. **£180-220**   *SB*

An Austrian iridescent glass
vase, in violet, gold and blue,
possibly Kralik, 20 cm. high.
£110-190   *P*

A Limoges enamelled vase, by
Camille Faure, in turquoise,
green, blue and yellow, gilded
mark 'C. Faure Limoges', 19.2
cm., 1920's. **£420-520**   *SB*

A Val St. Lambert cut and
etched cameo glass vase,
overlaid in blue, cameo mark
'Val St. Lambert', 25.5 cm., c.
1906. **£300-400**   *SB*

489

A Sabino opalescent heavy glass vase, early 20th C., moulded mark 'Sabino, Paris' (slight chip to foot rim), height 17.2 cm. **£150-200** *SBe*

(l) A French frosted glass vase, 1930's, 8 in. high. **£40-50** *F*

(r) An Art Deco Czechoslovakian glass vase, 6 in. high. **£65-75** *F*

A Loetz iridescent glass vase, the body of deep ruby tone, with exhibiting externally peacock blue iridescent feathering with shades of gold and violet, 19 cm high, signed 'Loetz', Austria. **£550-650** *P*

An Art Nouveau enamelled glass vase, in clear lime-green glass mounted with a bronzed metal fairy seated in gilt flowers, 18.5 cm., c. 1900. **£110-130** *SB*

One of a pair of iridescent glass vases, the pale green-lemon body having irregular green horizontal banding, enclosed in a twin-handled pewter mount, 17 cm. high. **£160-230** the pair *P*

A pair of Art Nouveau vases with green glass and plated brass bases, 12 in. high, c. 19[ ] **£25-30** *F*

A De Vez cameo vase, the slightly opalescent body overlaid with ruby and deep green glass, 40 cm. high, signed in script 'de Vez'. **£550-650** *P*

An unusual internally decorated and cut Galle glass bowl, the underside with engraved mark 'E. Galle', 12.5 cm., c. 1885. **£820-950** *SB*

A Galle fire-polished overlay cache-pot, sea-green and milk white, signature Emile Galle within a vine leaf, Nancy, models et decor deposes (small chip to rim), 15.5 cm. **£550-650** *C*

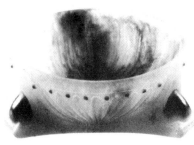

A Walter pate-de-verre shallow dish, modelled by Henri Berge, 6½ in. wide, moulded mark A. Walter Nancy Berge, S.C. **£660-800** *CSK*

'Nemours', a Lalique circular bowl, heightened with pale brown staining, moulded R. Lalique, France, 25.50 cm. diam. **£200-350** *P*

A Lalique jardiniere 'Luxembourg', stencilled mark, Lalique Crystal, France, 9 in. (22.8 cm.), c. 1926. **£230-300** *SBA*

Pallme Konig iridescent glass
wl, the neck with three
aidens in bronzed metal, 15
n. high. **£220-300** *P*

A Wiener Werkstatte blue glass
dish, designed by Josef
Hoffmann, etched Wiener
Werkstatte mark, 12 cm., c.
1910. **£300-360** *SB*

A lime green glass turkey bon-
bon dish, c. 1930, 8 in. high.
£25-30 *F*

A Daum silver-mounted glass
ewer, signed Daum Nancy, 11
cm. high. **£460-580** *P*

A Lalique glass perfume bottle
and stopper, 12.5 cm., moulded
mark 'R. Lalique', 1920's. **£220-
280** *SB*

A WMF silvered pewter
mounted green glass decanter,
6.5 cm., WMF marks, c. 1900.
420-480 *SB*

A Daum green scent bottle, in
cameo glass, 6½ in. high. **£225-
250** *LEX*

Left

A Lalique large size frosted
glass dahlia perfume bottle, 7
in., c. 1930. **£200-250** *MT*

Right

A Lalique glass perfume bottle
and stopper, for 'Cyclamen', by
Coty, with six flower fairies,
13.5 cm., incised mark 'R.
Lalique', 1920's. **£480-520**
SB

A Tiffany iridescent glass
perfume bottle and stopper, in
pale gold lustre and green, 11.5
cm., c. 1900. **£330-400** *SB*

An Art Deco scent bottle with
black glass lid, 2½ in. high.
£12-18 *LEX*

n Art Deco Marcel Franck
cent bottle, 4 in. high. **£10-
2** *LEX*

A silver and enamel on glass
scent bottle, hallmarked
London 1919, 6½ in. high. **£40-
48** *LEX*

A Societe des Artistes Verriers
internally decorated glass
bottle and stopper, 13 cm.
height, underside with
engraved mark 'SAV 281 Aa',
1920's. **£170-220** *SB*

491

A fine Art Deco cut glass scent
bottle, with blue silk tassle.
£48-55   *LEX*

A fine Art Deco scent bottle on
bakelite stand, 4 in. high. £50-
60   *LEX*

An Art Deco (turquoise) cut
glass bottle, 9½ in. high. £2
30   *LEX*

A Walter pate-de-verre glass
paperweight, modelled by
Henri Berge, signed A. Walter
Nancy and Berge, 4 cm. high.
£250-330   *P*

'Perruches', a Lalique frosted
glass seal, moulded as two
budgerigars, heightened with
grey staining, signed 'R.
Lalique', 5.5 cm. high. £180-
240   *P*

'Hirondelles', a Lalique froste
glass seal, moulded with three
swallows, signed 'R. Lalique',
cm. high. £280-400   *P*

'Figurine Se Balancant', a
Lalique glass seal, intaglio
moulded with a winged maiden,
signed 'Lalique', 7 cm. high.
£280-340   *P*

Grand Libellule: presse-papier,
moulded in glass with
dragonfly, moulded R. Lalique,
inscribed R. Lalique, France, 21
cm. high. £800-1,000   *C*

A Lalique glass seal, intagli
moulded with a budgerigar
perched on the letters MN,
signed 'Lalique', 6 cm. high.
£180-240   *P*

'Suzanne au bain', a Lalique
frosted glass figure, 22.5 cm.,
engraved mark 'R. Lalique
France No 833', 1920's. £1,000-
1,200   *SB*

A pair of Lalique glass
bookends, brown staining,
19.25 cm., each with engraved
mark 'R. Lalique', 1920's. £770-
870   *SB*

A Lalique box and cover,
heightened with green stainin
with a finial in the form of
naked girl, marked R. Laliq
France, 16 cm. high. £200-
250   *P*

Galle etched and enamelled glass casket, in clear amber glass, detailed in naturalistic enamels and gilding, 15.5 cm., 1890's. **£2,800-3,200** *SB*

An Art Deco wall mirror, flanked by two Lalique panels, each well moulded with a jackdaw, 91 cm. across. **£600-800** *P*

'Souris', a Lalique smoky grey glass ashtray, centred with the crouching model of a mouse, signed R. Lalique, France, 7 cm. high. **£120-220** *P*

An Etling frosted glass lamp, on chromed metal base, fitted for electric light, 26.5 cm., moulded mark 'Etling France 86', 1920's. **£570-670** *SB*

A bronze table lamp, with leaded glass shade, in reds, greens and cream, 58 cm., base stamped 'Gorham Co. QV293', c. 1900. **£1,300-1,500** *SB*

A Lalique glass powder box and cover, with traces of green staining, moulded mark 'R. Lalique Made in France', 1920's. **£140-200** *SB*

'Mures', a Lalique glass inkwell, moulded on the underside with fruiting brambles, 16 cm. diam., engraved mark 'R. Lalique France No 431', 1920's. **£66-90** *SB*

An Art Deco crackle glass egg, containing decanter and liqueur glasses, 11½ in. high. **£45-55** *LEX*

A Monart art glass lamp, in green and gold, Scottish with original label, c. 1920, 15 in. high. **£90-100** *F*

A Lalique frosted glass clock, 11.5 cm., moulded mark 'R. Lalique', 1920's. **£330-400** *SB*

An Art Deco hand painted Cranberry glass Easter egg, 6 in. high. **£15-18** *LEX*

A fine Galle acid etched table lamp and shade, signed, mounted in bronze, with electric light fittings, 40 cm. high. **£1,100-1,400** *HSS*

A French Art Deco table lamp and shade, with landscape decoration, by Le Gros, 15 in. high. **£420-540** *Lan*

493

A bronze patinated metal and painted glass table lamp, 53 cm., shade signed 'Handel 7203', base with affixed woven silk label 'Handel', c. 1910. **£440-500** *SB*

A bronzed and leaded glass table-lamp, probably by Handel Co. Inc., 62 cm. high. **£780-900** *C*

An Art Nouveau fine two colou layer cameo glass lamp, by Galle, 20½ in. high. **£4,500-6,500**

An Art Nouveau lamp, with a Tiffany style shade, 2 ft. 9 in. high. **£550-700** *PW*

A Tiffany Studios gilt-bronze, glass and abalone table lamp, 42.5 cm., stamped 'Tiffany Studios New York', 1910/20. **£440-540** *SB*

An Austrian Art Nouveau lamp, c. 1910, 25 in. high. **£12 150** *F*

An American lamp in spelter and bronze, with stained glass, 16 in. high, mid-1930's. **£220-250** *F*

A Tiffany-style table lamp, leaded shade with panels of apple green and emerald gre on a green patinated metal column, American, 6.5 cm. high. **£400-490** *P*

A bronze Art Nouveau lamp, the shade mounted with green and opalescent glass, 52 cm. high, c. 1900-10. **£350-450** *SKC*

A Hunebelle opalescent glass chromed metal mounted table lamp, moulded mark 'A. Hunebelle France', 38 cm., 1930's. **£420-480** *SB*

A Lalique opalescent glass lamp, in a chromed metal support, engraved mark on glass 'R. Lalique France No. 320', 29.5 cm., 1930's. **£350-420** *SB*

'Roitelets', a pair of Lalique frosted glass lamps, the 'U' shaped stems moulded in relief with wrens in flight, marked R. Lalique, France, 22 cm. high. **£250-350** *P*

A Sabino glass wall light, moulded mark internally 'Sabino No. 4684 Paris Depose', 5.75 cm., c. 1930's. **£300-360** *SB*

A Lalique glass hanging shade, with six pointed shades attached to central hexagonal body, 78.5 cm. max. width, stencilled mark 'R. Lalique', 1920's. **£740-820** *SB*

A Quezal iridescent glass shade, with feathered panels of blue and gold lustre against a white lustre ground, engraved mark 'Quezal', 15.25 cm., c. 1910. **£130-170** *SB*

n Art Deco lamp, partly ilded, with a spelter figure, 24 . high, 1930's. **£175-200** *F*

An Arts and Crafts copper hanging lantern, by the March Brothers, 39 cm. high. **£75-150** *P*

An Art Deco lamp, with pewter base and hessian covered in plastic shade, 24 in. high. **£65-85** *LEX*

An 'Art Deco' brass and ivory lampstand, 60.5 cm., 1930's. **£880-1,000** *SKC*

A decorative bronze table lamp, with beaten copper shade, 58 cm., c. 1900. **£400-460** *SB*

An alabaster, marble and spelter Art Deco lamp, 15 in. tall, 1930's. **£95-105** *F*

An Art Nouveau bronze lamp, 47.5 cm., c. 1900. **£1,200-1,500** *SB*

A bronze and glass lamp, the shade signed Arsoli, the bronze signed Zach, 76 cm., fitted for electricity, c. 1910. **£500-800** *SB*

A Lalique amber glass chandelier, moulded with stylised flower-heads, with four original cords, moulded mark R. Lalique, 12 in. diam. **£90-150** *CSK*

A Maignan gilt bronze lamp, signed in the maquette, foundry mark 'Eug. Blot Paris', 34 cm. high, c. 1900. **£420-500** *SB*

495

'Stella', a Nelson gold-painted-metal Art Nouveau lamp, 67 cm., marked 'Ant Nelson', applied title plaque, c. 1900. **£280-330**　*SB*

A chrome and glass Art Deco lamp, with a stag, 11 by 9 in. **£55-65**　*LEX*

A Wahliss turn glaze earthenware lamp, printed factory mark stamped 'Made in Austria' '4822 22', 52 cm., c. 1900. **£990-1,200**　*SB*

An Art Deco table light with chrome base and green lamp, 18½ in. high. **£50-60**　*LEX*

A pair of small celluloid table lamps with silk shades, 14½ in. high. **£35-45**　*LEX*

A grape lamp, c. 1915, 22 in. **£300-350**　*F*

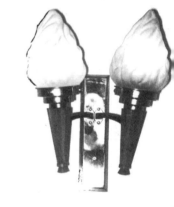

One of a pair of Art Deco wall lights. **£45-50 pair**　*F*

A bronze and ivory figure of a dancing girl, by Henry Fugere, signed, on alabaster plinth, 17 in. high. **£510-650**　*M*

An Alonzo gilt-bronze and ivory figure of a female warrior, signed in the maquette 'V. Alonzo', 33 cm., c. 1920. **£520-620**　*SB*

A green patinated wrought-iron Art Deco standard lamp, attributed to Edgar Brandt, 183 cm., 1920's. **£300-360**　*SB*

A bronze and ivory figure of young girl, in blue and gold dress, 24.75 cm., marble base with engraved mark 'D. Chiparus', 1920's. **£600-700**　*SB*

Salome: a cold painted bronze and ivory figure, by Henri Fugere, on rectangular onyx base, signed Fugere 5140, the base, Fabrication Francais Paris G.-M. (restoration), 42 cm. high. **£1,600-1,800**　*C*

A Colinet gilt-bronze and ivory dancing girl, 53 cm., base marked 'C.J.R. Colinet', 1920's. **£990-1,100**　*SB*

gilt-bronze and ivory figure of dancing girl, signed Joe escomps, on a marble socle, .5 cm., 1920's. £375-425 B

A Harders painted bronze and ivory figure, modelled as an Oriental maiden wearing a pale green kimono, signed 'Harders R.u.M.', 42 cm. high. £850-1,000 P

A Lorenzl Art Deco ivory and bronze figure, 1920's-30's, 11 in. high. £170-230 LEX

A Lorenzl painted bronze and ivory figure of a girl, wearing a silvered-brown dress, on onyx base, inscribed Lorenzl, 34 cm. high. £230-300 P

Lorenzl painted bronze and ory figure of a girl wearing a reen dress, on octagonal onyx ase, inscribed Lorenzl, 36.5 n. high. £380-450 P

A Philippe painted bronze and ivory figure, modelled as a girl wearing a pink-tinted tunic, signed 'P. Philippe R.u.M.'. £1,050-1,300 P

'The Butterfly Girls', a Poertzel bronze and ivory group, on green marble pedestal, 42.5 cm., base marked 'Prof. Poertzel', 1930's. £2,800-3,200 SB

A Lorenzl painted bronze and ivory figure of a lady, wearing a green skirt with a gilt tunic, on an onyx base, inscribed Lorenzl, 34 cm. high. £450-550 P

Prof. Poertzel painted bronze d ivory group, on an onyx se, signed 'Poertzel', 19.5 cm. 00-620 P

'The Hoop Girl', a Preiss painted bronze and ivory figure, on a brown onyx base, 21 cm. high. £570-680 P

A Preiss bronze and ivory figure, of a maiden, wearing a gilt and green dress, on onyx base, inscribed F. Preiss, 18 cm. high. £440-550 P

A Preiss painted bronze and ivory figure of a young girl, in a pink floral dress, onyx base, inscribed F. Preiss, 25 cm. high. £800-950 P

A Preiss painted bronze and ivory figure of a young lady, on a green onyx base, inscribed F. Preiss on base, 25.25 cm. high. **£1,450-1,700** *P*

'The Flame Leaper', a painted bronze and ivory figure by Preiss, modelled as a girl, the stepped marble base with a circular mirror, inscribed F. Preiss, 36 cm. high. **£3,900-4,300** *P*

ART DECO BRONZE AND IVORY FIGURES

- produced in large quantities in the 1920's and 1930's
- many made in Vienna and Paris
- bronze frequently cold-painted; ivory mainly hand carved and hence no two figures absolutely identical
- figures in other cheaper materials such as spelter and plaster were mass-produced and many of these are of poor quality
- F. Preiss works are highly collectable, especially for his fine ivory carving of children and classical nudes
- D. Chiparus and C. Colinet were both known for their nudes but also for highly theatrical figures
- Bruno Zach has become associated with figures of a decidedly erotic nature, girls with whips and tight-fitting garments
- many fakes have appeared on the market — watch crudely carved ivory faces and hands; the bronze is often cast in original moulds but fakers find the join to the ivory difficult to make smooth and flowing
- discolouration and cracks on the ivory can detract seriously from value, particularly on the face

'The Sunshade Girl', a Preiss painted bronze and ivory figure, on a marble base, unmarked, 22 cm. high. **£1,100-1,400** *P*

A Preiss painted bronze and ivory figure, modelled as a young girl, on a marble base, inscribed F. Preiss, 17.5 cm. high. **£630-750** *P*

F. Preiss. An Art Deco painted bronze and ivory figure of a huntress, on a green onyx base, signed, 16½ in. **£4,000-4,400** *Hy.D*

Left

After Frederick Preiss. A cold-painted bronze and ivory figure of a young girl, signed F Preiss and stamped with the KP monogram, German, 13 in. (33 cm.) overall, early 20th C. **£550-650** *SBA*

'Aphrodite with a Tazza of Fruit', a Preiss gilt bronze and ivory figure, modelled as a classical maiden, unmarked, 22 cm. high. **£550-650** *P*

Con Brio: a bronze and ivory figure, within a circular green onyx dish, signed in bronze F. Preiss (restoration and cracked), 32.5 cm. high. **£1,500-1,700** *C* *Left*

A Preiss painted bronze and ivory figure of a schoolboy, on a brown onyx base, inscribed F. Preiss, 21 cm. high. **£400-500** *P*

An Aichele bronze nude study, on rough granite base, signed in the maquette 'Aichele', 13.25 cm., c. 1920. **£520-630** *SB*

Amazon: a Marcel Bouraine bronze figure of a javelin thrower, signed H. Bouraine Etling Paris, 63.5 cm. wide. **£1,150-1,350** *C*

bronze and ivory ballet ncer, on green marble base, 26 cm., 1920's. **£570-700**

A Colinet bronze figure, on circular marble base, signed Cl. J. R. Colinet, 35.5 cm. high. **£280-340** *P*

A green patinated bronzed figure, 29 in. long, etched on base D.H. Chiparus. **£220-260** *CSK*

bronze bust, on giltwood inth, inscribed Raoul Larche, under's seal Silot Decauville, aris, serial no. 973K, 44.5 cm. igh. **£1,100-1,300** *C*

A small Muller bronze bust, igned in the maquette 'H. Muller', 12.5 cm., c. 1900. **£330-400** *SB*

A Kelety bronze group, on mottled gray marble base, engraved mark 'Kelety', 39.5 cm., 1920's. **£600-720** *SB*

A good bronze group of two lovers, signed Jean Descomps, epreuve 1, and with Paris Foundry seal, 29.5 cm., rubbed brown/green patination, dated 1934. **£500-600** *SB*

y, a Lorenzl patinated ze and silvered figure of an ant young woman, on an x base, 9½ in. high, signed nzl. **£150-220** *CSK*

An Art Deco gilt bronze semi-nude female figure, signed Lorenzl, on a green marble plinth and base, 11⅛ in. high, some damage to base. **£100-150** *GC*

A pair of silvered and gilt painted bronze figures by Lorenzl, on orange veined green onyx base, 10½ in. high, signed Lorenzl. **£300-400** *CSK*

A bronze figure of a spearman, in Art Deco style, on a marble base, 48 cm. by 60 cm., rubbed brown patination, 1930's. **£200-230** *SB*

A Zach silvered bronze figur marked 'Bruno Zach', 68.5 cr high excluding base, 1920's. **£1,000-1,300** *SB*

After Bruno Zach. A gilt-bronze figure of a young woman, signed Bruno Zach, on a marble plinth, 47 cm., c. 1920's. **£320-380** *SB*

A bronze figure of a naked girl, 28 cm., monogrammed 'J.D.', 1920's. **£200-240** *SB*

An Art Deco bronze figure of a woman, having ivory face and hands, inscribed 'Chant de la Fileuse par Mce. Gt. Favre', 17 in. high. **£540-660** *Ch*

An Art Deco nude in a hoop, 12 in. high, 1930's. **£25-30** *F*

A Simon gilt-bronze nude tambourine dancer, on mottl green/black marble base, marked 'Simon 14', 45.75 cm 1930's. **£270-320** *SB*

A spelter Art Deco figurine, on wooden base, signed Lorenzl, 8½ in. high. **£40-60** *LEX*

An Art Deco spelter and marb figure, 22 in. wide. **£110-130** *F*

A pair of chrome Art Deco figures, on marble bases, 11 in. high. **£30-35 pair** *LEX*

An Art Deco figurine of a dancer, in spelter, on a marble base, 6½ in. **£45-55** *LEX*

A Dauvergne silvered and gilt-metal group of a huntress and hind, engraved mark 'J. Dauvergne', 49 cm. max. height, 1930's. **£110-170** *SB*

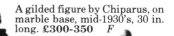

plaster Art Deco figure of
iana, 20 in. long. **£60-70**
EX

A gilded figure by Chiparus, on
marble base, mid-1930's, 30 in.
long. **£300-350**   *F*

gilded plaster figure, c. 1930's,
in. long. **£65-70**   *F*

A gilded plaster nude figure, c.
1930's, 30 in. high. **£20-30**   *F*

Two Art Deco figures, 8 in. high,
mid-c. 1930's. **£15-20 each**   *F*

A Galle faience cat, yellow with
blue hearts and spots, 34 cm.,
enamelled mark 'E. Galle
Nancy', 1880's. **£500-580**   *SB*

A crackle glazed group of a
crouching woman and two
greyhounds, 54 cm. max.
length, indistinct moulded
mark, impressed 'Made in ...',
1920's. **£80-120**   *SB*

Quimper black glazed
arthenware falcon, 35 cm.,
nderside with painted mark
Quimper Giot' monogrammed
IB', 1920's. **£120-160**   *SB*

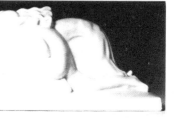

An art deco terracotta group,
incised Gennarelli, 82 cm. wide.
£260-300   *C*

A Zsolnay lustre glazed
earthenware figure of a young
woman weeping, brilliant
green/gold lustre, lustre mark
'Zsolnay Pecs.', 14.5 cm., c.
1900. **£200-260**   *SB*

n Art Deco porcelain figure of
n elf, by Wade, 4 in. **£12-15**
EX

A Goldscheider cold painted
earthenware bust of a young
woman, moulded factory
plaque, impressed
'Reproduction Reserve',
numbered '1994 401 34', 63 cm.,
c. 1900. **£300-370**   *SB*

An Art Deco porcelain figure of
green buffalo, 7 in. long. **£20-
26**   *LEX*

An Andre Fau crackle glaze earthenware figure, 27 cm., impressed facsimile signature 'Andre Fau', impressed mark 'Made in France Boulogne', 1920's. £100-130 *SB*

An Art Deco plaster lady, 11 in. high. £35-40 *LEX*

A Liberty and Co. 'Tudric' pewter clock, designed by Archibald Knox, 14 cm., stamped 'Made in England Tudric Pewter 0106 Rd 46801⁅ c. 1903. £580-650 *SB*

A Liberty & Co. pewter clock, designed by Archibald Knox, 20.5 cm., stamped 'English Pewter made by Liberty & Co. 0609 Rd 469010', c. 1903. £980-1,200 *SB*

A 'Tudric' pewter timepiece, stamped and numbered 0382, 25 cm. high. £200-250 *P*

A 'Tudric' pewter timepiece with copper face, 17 cm. hi⁅ stamped 0629. £190-250

A 'Tudric' pewter timepiece, the blue and green enamelled dial with a copper chapter ring, 23 cm. high, stamped and numbered 0371. £170-220 *P*

A pewter clock, with landscape enamelled plaques on the case, with copper dial, incised on reverse 'March Bros., 1905', 33.50 cm. high. £300-400 *P*

A Liberty & Co. 'Cymric' silv⁅ timepiece, set with two turquoise matrix cabochons, the dial with legend 'Festina Lente', 10 cm. high, maker's marks for Birmingham 1905 £200-250 *P*

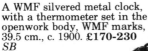

A WMF silvered metal clock, with a thermometer set in the openwork body, WMF marks, 39.5 cm., c. 1900. £170-230 *SB*

A massive bronze clock, part-polished, part-silvered, part-verdigris patinated, 31.5 cm., signed in the maquette 'R. Lamourdedieu', founder's mark 'La Stele', numbered '8', 1920's. £300-350 *SB*

copper-cased Art Nouveau
mepiece, the design attributed
George Walton, 21 cm. high.
200-300 *P*

A simulated ivory and white
metal mantel clock, by Geo.
Maxim, the body in black and
beige marble, 25 in. long,
impressed signature. **£180-250** *CSK*

An Art Deco marble clock, 12 in.
tall. **£65-75** *F*

n Art Nouveau metal clock,
signed by Jules Brateau, with
blue enamelled face with gilt
merals, inscribed on the
nels Jules Brateau, 35 cm.
gh. **£1,050-1,200** *P*

An Art Deco mantel clock, with
green enamel dial, the
movement Swiss, in a green
leather case from J. C. Vickery,
Regent Street. **£110-150** *L*

An art deco Lapis Lazuli and
Aventurine mantel clock, the
square case with white onyx
centre, Swiss lever movement,
28.5 cm. wide. **£1,150-1,400**
C

n art nouveau bronze tray,
robably by Raoul Larche, 50
m. wide. **£650-800** *C*

A French clock, c. 1930's, 19 in.
long. **£30-35** *F*

A Jouant patinated metal dish,
cast in low relief with a nymph
riding a seahorse, marked
'Jouant', 68 cm. wide, c. 1900.
£120-160 *SB*

A W.M.F. Art Nouveau sweet
dish, with glass lining, 11 in.
long. **£55-65** *LEX*

WMF

The Württembergishe
Metalwaren Fabrik operated
in Württemberg between the
1890's and the early 1920's
producing metalware in the
Art Nouveau taste. Of
particular interest is the fine
quality of the pewter and
silver-wares.

A W.M.F. Art Nouveau fruit
bowl, 10 in. diam. **£45-50**
LEX

A Hannig silvered metal vase,
marked 'J. R. Hannig', 46 cm., c.
1900. **£150-200** *SB*

A Jean Dunand wrought-metal vase, inlaid in contrasting metals, 17 cm., marked 'Jean Dunand 1913'. **£170-220** *SB*

A Linossier patinated metal vase, with mottled brown red patination, 24 cm., stamped 'Linossier', 1920's. **£200-260** *SB*

An Art Nouveau brass and copper vase, by Fisher Stran in. high. **£15-20** *KNG*

A pair of Art Deco pottery vases by Sylvac, 7 in. high. **£12-15** *LEX*

An Art Nouveau porcelain vase. **£18-22** *LEX*

A pair of Ernst Wahliss porcelain figural vases, in p and cream, 12½ in. high, sta marks. **£260-360** *CSK*

A WMF pewter centrepiece, in the form of an Art Nouveau maiden, her dress flowing outwards to form 4 dishes, stamped marks, 25.5 cm. high. **£315-395** *P*

An Art Nouveau pewter sweet-meat centre piece, 8½ in. long. **£200-215** *LEX*

An Art Deco china vase, 7¹⁄ high. **£15-20** *LEX*

A WMF silvered pewter dish, 22.5 cm., WMF marks, c. 1900. **£260-300** *SB*

An Art Nouveau porcelain centre-piece, 12 in. high. **£120-200** *CSK*

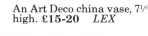

An Art Deco cake stand, wi celluloid plate and chrome stand. **£15-18** *LEX*

A pair of W.M.F. pewter and brass two-branch candelabra, stamped marks, 26.5 cm. high. **£850-950** *C*

A W.M.F. silvered Britannia metal candelabrum, with two candle sconces and drip pans, 0¼ in. high, stamp marks. **£320-400** *CSK*

An Amphora centrepiece, silver, gold and grey lustre glaze, 47 cm., impressed factory mark 'Imperial Amphora Turn Amphora Austria 747 20', c. 1900. **£190-240** *SB*

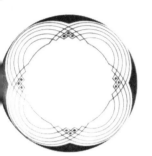

A Bauscher decorated porcelain plate, designed by Peter Behrens for the Games Room in the Behrens House at Darmstadt, green on white, 20 cm. diam., impressed factory mark 'Bauscher Weiden' and stencilled monogram 'B', 1901. **£330-400** *SB*

One of a pair of four-light candelabra, designed by Otto Prutscher, stamped 'Etnw. Prof. Otto Prutscher', stamped 800, maker's mark 'M & C', 1910/20, 14.25 cm. **£2,000-2,300** the pair *SB*

A pair of small German bronze Art Nouveau candlesticks, each in the form of a naked nymph, each stamped 'Geschch 5070', 21.5 cm., c. 1900. **£300-380** *SB*

A Clarice Cliff tureen and cover, designed by Laura Knight, 19.5 cm. height, printed factory mark and designer's facsimile signature, first edition, 1934. **£260-350** *SB*

An Art Nouveau mother of pearl ashtray, 7½ in. wide. **£20-25** *F*

Two Clarice Cliff plates, designed by Laura Knight, 25.25 cm. approx. diam., each with printed factory mark and designer's facsimile signature, first edition, 1934. **£270-330** *SB*

An Art Deco ashtray on marble base, with gilded figure, 6½ in. long. **£25-30** *F*

Art Deco chrome lighters, c. 1930's. **£10-12, £45-55, £15-20** *F*

An Art Deco table lighter, in silver plate with devil decoration, 10 in. high. **£60-68** *LEX*

An Art Deco bakelite cigarette box, with spring loaded action, 4 in. long, 3½ in. wide. **£10-12** *LEX*

A celluloid Art Nouveau box, coloured cream with pink buttons on lid, 2¾ in. diam., 2¾ in. high. **£12-15** *LEX*

An Art Nouveau W.M.F. trinket box from the Gaiety Theatre presented to Frances Fowler, in. long. **£30-40** *LEX*

A solid silver Art Deco powder compact, 1930's, 3½ in. diam. **£30-35** *LEX*

An Art Deco chrome kettle, 10 in. high. **£10-12** *LEX*

An Edward Barnard & Son Lt silver kettle, stand and spirit burner, maker's mark, Londo 1911, 43 oz., 31.5 cm. high. **£680-800** *C*

A Boucheron stamped stoneware jug, with creamy glaze speckled with blue body, 27 cm., underside marked 'Boucheron Paris London', c. 1900. **£500-550** *SB*

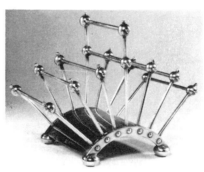

A Heath and Middleton silver toast rack, designed by Christopher Dresser, 12.5 cm., makers' marks for Hukin and Heath, P.O.D.R. mark, London 1881. **£440-500** *SB*

An Art Nouveau silver caddy spoon, by Liberty & Co., Birmingham, 1911. **£85-105** *SBe*

An Art Deco cocktail shaker and tray with glasses. **£35-45** *LEX*

A Guild of Handicrafts silver chalice and cover, designed by C. R. Ashbee, maker's mark, London 1901 (finial loose), 32.5 cm. high. **£430-500** *C*

A pair of Liberty's Tudric pewter Art Nouveau bon bon dishes, 1912, 5½ in. high. **£8** 110 *LEX*

A Charpentier square bronze medallion, inscribed 'Societe des Amis de la medaille francais Fondee Le 28 Fevrier 1899'. £90-130   P

An Austrian bronze mirror, signed B. Butzke, 42.5 cm. high. £1,100-1,300   C

An Arts and Crafts pewter faced picture frame, by the March Brothers, 26 cm. high. £80-150   P

A selection of 1920-30 wall masks. £10-25   LEX

A rare Art Deco pin cushion lady. £25-35   LEX

An Art Nouveau pewter frame, 9 by 6 in. £25-30   LEX

An Art Deco electric fire, 1930's. £45-50   F

An Art Deco chrome trolley with peach glass mirror trays, 2 in. high, 20 in. long. £160-180   LEX

An Art Nouveau burnished metal fire grate and surround, c. 1920, 46½ in. high. £240-255 LAC

Part of an Art Deco suite, comprising: 3-seater settee, 2 armchairs, 2 tub chairs and a pouffe, 1930's. £750-950 suite   F

A fine Art Deco dressing case, 17 in. long. £75-88   LEX

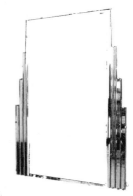

An Art Deco mirror, c. 1930's, 35 by 25 in. £35-40   F

507

FRENCH BRONZE FIGURES

- much of the French sculpting of the 19th C. was in the classical style
- as sculptors had to rely on public commissions they had to stay well within the prevailing trends
- one of the most successful bronze sculptors was the 'Animalier' A. L. Barye (1795-1875)
- much of the neo-classical sculpting was technically excellent but often lacked true originality and vitality
- A. E. Carrier-Belleuse (1824-1887) although basically a revivalist still managed to break away from the flat neo-classical style
- there were many mass-produced bronzes, tending to be of a more sentimental nature

- sculptors like Moreau (1822-1912) made vast numbers of such bronzes, which were cast by commercial founders like Barbedienne
- with the coming of the Second Empire there was a new direction and verve, with sculptors such as J. B. Carpeaux (1827-1875)
- the late 19th C. symbolist style grew out of this era and was certainly influenced by David d'Angers (1788-1856) and Francois Rude (1784-1855)
- it is worth noting that only the early casts of the 19th C. bronzes have the original quality and many bronzes are cast on old moulds right up to the present day

A parcel-gilt figure of a strutting pheasant, signed L. Bureau, 27.3 cm. on a verde antico plinth, c. 1900. **£200-250** *SB*

A Rare Peyrol Bronze Group, signed I. Bonheur, with Peyrol founders stamp, 30 by 20 cm., rubbed light/brown patination, probably c. 1870. **£520-580** *SB*

A bronze figure of a bull, signed Rosa B, rubbed dark brown patination, c. 1860's. **£350-400** *SB*

A 19th C. French bronze group of a mounted postillion with two carriage horses, after Isidore Jules Bonheur, inscribed I. BONHEUR, 35 cm. high. **£800-1,000** *C*

A bronze group of a carthorse and a man, signed E. Drouot, 39 by 74 cm., green and light brown patination, c. 1900. **£520-590** *SB*

A bronze group of an animal circus act, titled Cr. Du Pajaga on an ebonised oval base, 12¾ in. (21 cm.), rich dark brown patination, mid 19th C. **£400-450** *SB*

A large bronze group, signed Barye Fils, 51 by 38.4 cm., rubbed brown/gilt patination, c. 1870's. **£900-1,100** *SB*

A bronze figure of a bull, signed Fratin, 40.3 cm., rich light and dark brown patination, on a black marble plinth, c. 1860. **£410-480** *SB*

A pair of bronze Marly horses, after Coustou, late 19th C., 50 cm. **£580-660** *SB*

pair of Bergman cold painted
ronze camelier groups, with
e Bergman seal and stamped
eschutz, 20.5 cm., Austrian, c.
900. **£600-700** *SB*

A 19th C. Hungarian bronze
group of a crusading knight on
horseback overcoming a
dismounted infidel, after
Kolozsvary brothers, inscribed
Kolzsvary Test, 35 cm. high.
£650-750 *C*

A 19th C. English bronze
statuette of the Duke of
Wellington on horseback, after
Baron Carlo Marochetti,
inscribed C.M., and FONDU
PAR MOREL ET Cie A
LONDRES and 16, 45 by 43 cm.
£600-750 *C*

Mathias Gonzales bronze
anther, on mottled black
arble base, signed in the
aquette 'Mathias Gonzales',
tamped 'Bronze', 25 cm. high,
920's. **£180-250** *SB*

A 19th C. Russian bronze group
of a peasant woman and her
child on horseback, after
Ievgueni Lanceray, inscribed in
Russian E. LANCERAY, 1884,
and founder's inscription F.
CHOPIN, 31.5 cm. high.
£1,200-1,500 *C*

G. Garrard, a bronze study of a
stallion, signed and dated 1821,
9¼ in. high. **£270-330** *SKC*

19th C. Russian bronze group
f a Mongolian warrior on
orseback, after Ievgueni
anceray, inscribed in Russian
LEXEI E. LANCERAY, 48
m. high. **£800-1,000** *C*

A bronze group of a
thoroughbred and a dog,
entitled Angelo and signed P.
Lenordez and V. Boyden, 28
cm., rich slightly rubbed dark
brown patination, c. 1870.
£1,100-1,400 *SB*

A 19th C. Russian bronze group
of a Cossack and a pack horse,
signed Lepilye Lanceray, 17 in.
£1,350-1,650 *RG*

bronze group of a wolf
ttacking a stallion, signed
. J. Mene, 16.2 cm., slightly
ubbed green/dark brown
atination, c. 1860. **£300-**
60 *SB*

A gilt-bronze group of a
cockerel, signed F. Pautrot, 20
cm., c. 1860. **£560-650** *SB*

A bronze group of a lion and an
antelope, stamped Fratin, 35
cm., rich brown patination, c.
1860. **£500-600** *SB*

After Pierre Jules Mene. A bronze figure of an Arab stallion, signed P. J. Mene, entitled Arabe, 20.5 by 22.8 cm., rubbed brown/black patination, c. 1870. **£400-450** *SB*

Ferdinand Pautrot: A macaw, signed, 11½ in. **£330-400** *L*

After Pierre Jules Mene. A bronze group, signed P. J. Mene, 10.5 by 14 cm., gilt and brown patination, c. 1860. **£300-350** *SB*

An Austrian cold painted bronze group of a Bedouin, seated on a camel, 8 in. high. **£160-200** *SR*

A Russian bronze group, signed Gratchev, founder's mark C.F. Woerffel, St. Petersburg, 9 in. **£400-480** *Hy.D*

A large bronze group of King Charles spaniels, signed G. Valton, 18 in. **£340-400** *BW*

A bronze equestrian hunting group, 49 by 47 cm., rubbed green/brown patination, c. 1860. **£410-470** *SB*

A 19th C. French bronze group of Theseus slaying the minotaur, after Antoine Louis Barye, inscribed BARYE and F BARBEDIENNE FONDEUR PARIS and underneath 16.21 and S, 44.5 cm. high. **£800-1,000** *C*

After Bruno Zach. A gilt-bronze group of two polo players, signed Zach on an onyx base, 25 cm., German, c. 1920. **£180-220** *SB*

Left
One of a pair of 19th C. French bronze groups, after the models by Boizot, 44 cm. and 46 cm. high, raised on chased ormolu scroll bases. **£900-1,200** the pair *P*

A bronze figure of The Dying Gaul, from the foundry of F. Barbedienne. **£130-160** *MA*

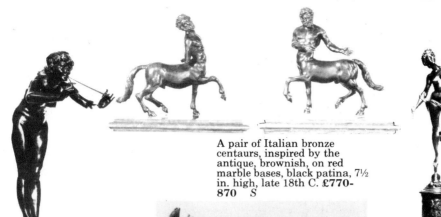

A pair of Italian bronze centaurs, inspired by the antique, brownish, on red marble bases, black patina, 7½ in. high, late 18th C. **£770-870** *S*

After Bologna. A pair of bronze figures of Mercury and Fortune, dark brown patination, 34 in. (87 cm.), late 19th C. **£290-350** *SBA*

A large bronze figure of a young girl, signed Beguine, 81 cm., dark black/green patination, c. 1900. **£800-900** *SB*

A bronze group, modelled as Lucifer with a Bacchante, overall pale green patina, 88 cm. long, inscribed R. Carvinin? and dated 1889. **£580-700** *P*

A bronze group of an Indian squaw, signed Cumberworth Sculpeteur Vittoz Ciseleur, 52 cm., rich light-brown patination, c. 1850. **£700-800** *SB*

Left

A 19th C. French bronze statue of Amphitrite after Valentin Eugene Deplechin, inscribed AMPHITRITE and E. Deplechin and serial no. 58842 35, 51 cm. high. **£660-800** *C*

A 19th C. French bronze statue of a naked young woman, known as 'Dans Les Roseaux', after Edouard Drouot, inscribed E. Drouot, 53.5 cm. high. **£550-650** *C*

A 19th C. French bronze fountain figure of a nymph with an upturned vase resting on her head, after Felix Maurice Charpentier, inscribed F. Charpentier and RENE FULDA, Fondeur, Paris, 102 cm. high. **£1,800-2,000** *C*

A gilt-bronze group of Leda and the swan, signed Emm. Fontaine, on a marble socle, 37.5 cm., c. 1900. **£220-250** *SB*

Barbedienne bronze figure, signed P. Dubois 186? F. Barbedienne Foudeur and with the Reduction Mechanique A. Collas seal, 38 cm., rich light brown patination, c. 1860's. **£260-300** *SB*

After Jean-Jacques Feuchere. A bronze figure of Psyche, signed 'J Feuchere Scpt' and inscribed Vittoz Bronzier, dark red-brown patination, 18 in. (46 cm.), late 19th C. **£280-320** *SBA*

After Etienne-Henry Dumaige. A group of two dancing girls, signed Dumaige Sculp, rubbed gilt-brown patination, 20½ in. (52 cm.), mid-19th C. **£460-520** *SBA*

After Anatole Guillot. A pair of bronze figures of huntsmen, rich dark brown patination, 18 in. (46 cm.), late 19th C. **£440-520**   *SBA*

After Houdon. A bronze bust of Diana, signed Diane de Houdon, Musée du Louvre, 49 cm., green/brown patination, c. 1880. **£250-300**   *SB*

After Houdon. A bronze bust of Voltaire, 32 cm., rich dark brown patination, mid 19th C. **£110-140**   *SB*

Paul Maximillien Landowski. A large allegorical bronze figure of Perseus, weathered patination, 168 cm., late 1930's. **£1,600-1,900**   *SB*

Ernest Shore Jones, a bronze bust of a negress, signed, 29 in. high. **£700-800**   *SKC*

A 19th C. German bronze statuette of Eve, after Conrad Meit, 32 cm. high. **£400-500**   *C*

A 19th C. Franco-Polish bronze statuette of a fisherwoman, after Henryk Kossowski the Younger, inscribed Kossowski Eleve de Math MOREAU, 81.5 cm. high. **£1,300-1,600**   *C*

A 19th C. Belgian bronze statuette of a miner, after Meunier, inscribed C. MEUNIER (circular marble plinth), 42 cm. high. **£200-270**   *C*

A 19th C. Belgian bronze statuette of a workman drinking, after Constantin Emile Meunier, inscribed C. Meunier and J. PETERMANN. FONDEUR. BRUXELLES, 50 cm. high. **£1,000-1,300**   *C*

A Seifert patinated bronze figure, modelled as a man, inscribed F. Seifert, 27 cm. high. **£240-300**   *P*

Henry Weekes, R. A. an Elkington silver-plated bronze figure, signed H. Weekes Sc, Elkington & Co. Founders, 49 cm., 1860's. **£420-480**   *SB*

A 19th C. French bronze statuette of 'The grief of Orpheus', after Charles Raoul Verlet, inscribed Raoul Verlet, 83.5 cm. high. **£1,900-2,100**   *C*

After Bruno Zach. A gilt-bronze group of a young couple, signed Bruno Zach, on a marble plinth, .5 cm., German, c. 1920. 300-360 *SB*

A pair of Louis XVI bronze putti, on ormolu socles, the bases not fitting, 11½ in. (29 cm.) high. **£770-900** *C*

An Austrian cold painted bronze figure of a Nubian, 7½ in. high. **£130-180** *SR*

bronzed metal figure of a egro boy seated on a bamboo ool with a basket on his knee, 2 in. high. **£1,100-1,500** *H B*

A 19th C. French gilt-bronze statuette of Bacchus (bowl replaced), on a stepped marble base with ormolu trimming, 33 cm. high. **£220-300** *C*

A 19th C. bronze standing nude female figure, on a square green variegated marble base, 22¾ in. high. **£270-350** *GC*

A 19th C. French gilt bronze statuette of an enthroned Roman emperor (moulded wooden base), 29 cm. high. **£350-420** *C*

A pair of Flemish bronze pricket candlesticks, 11 in. (26 cm.) high, 17th C. **£450-550** *C*

A bronze figure of Nelson, 38 cm., red/brown patination, 1870's. **£160-190** *SB*

A pair of 'Louis XVI' gilt-bronze and marble candelabra, c. 1870, 12½ in. (32 cm.). **£200-230** *SB*

One of a pair of gilt bronze *SB* andelabra, each with 7 crolling candle-arms, 20 in., he base engraved with a crest, . 1880. **£390-450** the pair *SB*

A pair of Regency bronze and ormolu candelabra, 28½ in. (72.5 cm.) high. **£900-1,100** *C*

A parcel-gilt bronze group of a cherub and a putto, 41.5 cm., c. 1860. **£450-500** *SB*

A pair of parcel gilt-bronze and white marble candelabra, each with a putto after Clodion, 20 in. (51 cm.), c. 1860. **£550-650** *SB*

A pair of Barbedienne bronze and gilt bronze candelabra, each with 5 candle-arms, 27½ in., signed Henry Cahieux and F. Barbedienne Fondeur, 1870's. **£230-300** *SB*

One of a set of 4 gilt bronze wa lights, 22 in., fitted for electricity, mid-19th C. **£500-600** the set *SB*

One of a pair of bronze and gilt-bronze bras d'applique, 20½ in., 1860's. **£600-700** the pair *SB*

One of a set of 6 'Louis XV' gilt-bronze bras d'applique, fitted for electricity, each stamped F & S with a number, 16 in., c. 1900. **£350-450** the set *SB*

A gilt-bronze chandelier, wit six scrolling candle-arms ea supporting four lights, fitted f electricity, 1840-1860, 41 by 4 in. (104 by 107 cm.). **£280-320** *SB*

A pair of bronze campana urns, cast in bas-relief, 13⅜ in. (34 cm.), c. 1850. **£300-350** *SB*

A 16th C. bronze mortar, with medallions each bearing two crowns inscribed 'Duble Cro---rash', 7¼ in. (18.5 cm.) diam. **£170-220** *SKC*

A pair of French bronze urn cast in high relief, on marbl plinth, 12 in. high, c. 1880. **£440-540** *L*

An early 18th C. bronze mortar and pestle, c. 1720, 6 in. diam. **£120-140** *McH*

An unusual Barbedienne gilt-bronze-mounted ostrich egg, the shell Japanese gold-lacquered, 23 cm., signed F. Barbedienne, c. 1870, fitted case. **£200-250** *SB*

A pair of gilt-bronze mounted porcelain ewers, 19¼ in., late 19th C. **£350-400**   *SB*

A Marrionet patinated bronze dish, marked 'A. Marrionet', 38.5 cm., c. 1900. **£200-260** *SB*

An 18th C. bronze chalice, 6 in. high. **£68-78**   *McH*

gilt-bronze and porcelain mp, fitted for electricity, 19 ., c. 1860. **£240-300**   *SB*

A Siot gilt-bronze table garniture, comprising four 'woven' baskets, 6½ by 11½ in., signed Raoul Larche and Siot, Paris, impressed numbers, 1890's. **£1,500-1,800**   *SB*

A Thai bronze Buddha, perspex block base, 14th/15th C., 10½ in. (26.5 cm.) high. **£300-330** *C*

bronze and Porta Santa Rara arble fountain, 30 in. (76 cm.) iam. **£1,600-2,000**   *C*

Make the most of Miller's

Look for the code letters in italic type following each caption.
Check these against the list of contributors on page 10 to identify the source of any illustration.
Remember — valuations may vary according to locality; use of the codes can allow this to be taken into account.

Miller's is a price GUIDE Not a price LIST.

The price ranges given reflect the average price a purchaser should pay for similar items. Condition, rarity of design or pattern, size, colour, pedigree, restoration and many other factors must be taken into account when assessing values.

A Thai gilded bronze figure of the Buddha, 14th C., 12 in. (30.5 cm.) high. **£1,600-1,800**   *C*

Chola bronze group of Uma-Iaheshvara, Chamba, 1th/12th C., 4¾ in. (9.5 cm.) igh. **£1,200-1,400**   *C*

A repousse bronze group of Vishnu and Lakshmi-Narayana, on a circular metal-tiered base, 12th C., 18 in. (46 cm.) high. **£1,500-1,700**   *C*

A Chola miniature bronze figure of Krishna, 10th C., 4 in. (10 cm.) high. **£660-760**   *C*

A Nepalese gilt bronze figure of Indra, 15th C., 5¼ in. (13.5 cm.) high. **£1,300-1,500** *C*

A large antique Benin bronze head, 15 in. high. **£280-340** *B*

A Tibetan bronze group of Sambara, 17th C., 17 in. (43 cm high. **£900-1,000** *C*

A Sukothai bronze head, with perspex base (back of head missing), 17th C., 10 in. (25.5 cm.) high. **£1,000-1,200** *C*

A Sino-Tibetan bronze figure of a portrait monk, 17th C., 13 in. (33 cm.) high. **£1,900-2,200** *C*

A Sino-Tibetan bronze figure Na-Ro-Kha-Cho-Ma, late 17th C., 7 in. (18 cm.) high. **£440-540** *C*

A large Tibetan gilt bronze repousse figure of Manjusri, originally holding sword and inset with turquoise and coloured stones, sealed, 17th/18th C. **£900-1,100** *C*

A Sino-Tibetan gilt bronze figure of Gautama, with semi-precious stone urna, on a separately cast double lotus base, 17th/18th C., 12 in. (30 cm.) high. **£1,000-1,200** *C*

A Tibetan bronze group of Achila and Sakti, 18th C., 4¼ (11 cm.) high. **£330-360** *C*

A bronze figure of a Buddha, late Ming/early Qing Dynasty, 10½ in. (27 cm.) high. **£350-450** *C*

A Tibetan bronze figure of Maitreya, the eyes inlaid with silver, late 18th C., 10 in. (25.5 cm.) high. **£1,000-1,200** *C*

Sino-Tibetan gilt bronze figure of Na-Ro-Kha-Cho-Ma, c. 1900, 9 in. (23 cm.) high. **£600-800** *C*

A Tibetan gilt bronze repousse figure of Marpa, 18th C., 16½ in. (42 cm.) high. **£800-1,200** *C*

A Japanese bronze and soft-metal group of Oni Nembutsu, Meiji period, with wood stand, 23.2 cm. high. **£270-320** *C*

A West Tibetan bronze figure of White Tara (crown missing), 19th C., 11½ in. (28 cm.) high. **£250-350** *C*

A Miyao bronze group of a monkey trainer, 18.5 cm., incised Miyao, c. 1900. **£420-480** *SB*

A Japanese bronze figure of a seated young lady, signed Takahashi Royoun, Meiji period, with wood base, 39.2 cm. high. **£380-450** *C*

A bronze figure of a Samurai, supporting four foliate candle nozzles (slightly damaged), 19th C., 106.5 cm. high. **£900-1,100** *C*

A pair of Hidenao bronze cranes, 34.5 and 25 cm., signed Hidenao, c. 1900. **£450-520** *SB*

A Seiya bronze group of an elephant attacked by two tigers, ivory tusks, 27 cm., cast Seiya saku, c. 1900. **£300-360** *SB*

A Japanese silvered bronze figure of an eagle, perched on a gnarled tree-stump, 19.5 cm., incised and applied mark, c. 1900. **£130-170** *SB*

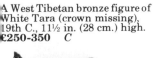

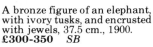

A Japanese articulated bronze cray fish, 73 cm. overall, c. 1900, wood stand. **£720-820** *SB*

A bronze figure of an elephant, with ivory tusks, and encrusted with jewels, 37.5 cm., 1900. **£300-350** *SB*

517

A Chinese bronze figure of Jackdaw, with detachable backplate, 12 in. high, 15 in. wide. **£190-250** *VV*

A bronze group of three stags and two does (tip of one antler missing), signed Genryukei Seiya zo, Meiji period, 37.5 cm. long. **£600-700** *C*

A pair of Japanese bronze vases, each decorated in iroe hirazogan and takazogan, signed Akiyoshi sei, late 19th C., 29.9 cm. high. **£500-600**

A pair of Japanese bronze vases, inlaid with silver and gold decorations, 20.5 cm., engraved mark, c. 1900. **£250-300** *SB*

A pair of bronze vases, 30 cm., c. 1880. **£270-300** *SB*

A Ryuki bronze vase, 43.5 cm cast Ryuki chu, c. 1900. **£200-250** *SB*

A pair of inlaid Hattori bronze vases, engraved factory mark, 27 cm. **£300-360** *SKC*

A pair of inlaid bronze vases, 17 cm., signed in hiragana, c. 1900. **£250-300** *SB*

A pair of Japanese bronze vases, each cast in relief, 26.5 cm., early 20th C. **£110-150** *SB*

A Japanese 8¼ in. bronze bowl and cover, engraved and inlaid in gold, 12½ in. high. **£330-400** *PWC*

A bronze globular Censer and cover, dated Daoguang jiachen year (1844 A.D.) and of the period, 15½ in. (39.5 cm.) high. **£120-200** *C*

518

An Ichijoken Joun bronze koro and cover, cast Ichijoken Joun o, 56 cm., mid-19th C. **£750-850** *SB*

A Japanese bronze incense burner and cover, decorated in silver and gold, 16 cm., incised mark and inlaid reversed, 'e', late 19th C. **£130-160** *SB*

A Chinese bronze incense burner and cover, inlaid and applied with gold and silver, on three curved legs, 30.5 cm., Daoguang. **£310-360** *SB*

Japanese inlaid bronze laque, decorated and highlighted in gold, 36.5 cm., two incised seals, c. 1900. **£280-330** *SB*

An inlaid bronze kogo and cover, 14 cm., c. 1900. **£200-250** *SB*

A pair of bronze vases and covers, 40 cm., c. 1900. **£225-250** *SB*

A Luristan bronze pin, 8¾ in. high, 8th-7th C. B.C. **£40-70** *C*

A Sino-Shan bronze drum, with three frogs at each of the compass points and one side with a descending procession of three elephants (minor damage), 26¾ in. (68 cm.) high. **£500-600** *C*

A Luristan bronze fork, 4¼ in. high, 8th-7th C. B.C. **£50-100** *C*

Luristan bronze fibula, with pin and catch-plate, 3⅛ in. wide, 800 B.C. **£100-150** *C*

An Egyptian bronze figure of Isis suckling Harpocrates, 7½ in. (19.2 cm.) high, Dynasty XXX-early Ptolemaic. **£2,000-2,500** *C*

An Egyptian bronze mirror, the bronze disc inserted into a wooden handle, 11½ in. high, dynasty XVIII. **£460-600** *C*

An Etruscan bronze mirror, with a scene of a lasa (repaired with minor restoration), 10⅛ in. high, c. 3rd C. B.C. **£260-350** *C*

519

An Egyptian bronze figure of a standing falcon, wearing a double crown (plinth partly corroded away), 7¾ in. (19.6 cm.) high, Ptolemaic, 4th-2nd C. B.C. **£880-950**   *C*

A Roman bronze cauldron, 7 in. (17.8 cm.) high, c. 1st C. B.C./A.D. **£150-200**   *C*

Miller's is a price GUIDE Not a price LIST.
The price ranges given reflect the average price a purchaser should pay for similar items. Condition, rarity of design or pattern, size, colour, pedigree, restoration and many other factors must be taken into account when assessing values.

An Etruscan bronze beaked Oinochoe (base slightly damaged), 8¼ in. (21 cm.) high c. 4th C. B.C. **£400-500**   *C*

A Roman bronze Olpe, 9 in. (22.8 cm.) high, c. 1st C. A.D. **£1,700-2,000**   *C*

An ormolu chandelier, of Regence style, supporting four foliate branches ending in drippans and candle-nozzles dividing four branches each with two nozzles, 34 in., c. 1830. **£1,100-1,300**   *C*

An Italian Empire ormolu 12 light chandelier, fitted for electricity, 36 in. diam. **£990 1,150**   *C*

A pair of early Louis XV Ormolu wall-lights, 16¼ in. (41 cm.) high. **£1,950-2,250**   *C*

A set of 4 Italian painted and gilded wall-sconces, supporting two later giltmetal candlebranches, fitted for electricity, 35½ in. high, 18th C. **£1,600-1,800**   *C*

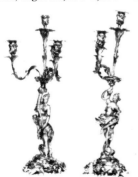

A pair of ormolu table candelabra, each of 4 lights, 21 in., c. 1840. **£280-340**   *SB*

A pair of ormolu table candelabra, each for two lights, 14 in., 1840-60. **£500-600**   *SB*

A pair of Ormolu wall-light fitted for electricity, possibl German, 23 in. (58 cm.) hig **£2,000-2,200**   *C*

A pair of Louis XV ormolu chenets, in the manner of Caffieri, 18½ in. (47 cm.) high. **£3,000-3,200**   *C*

A pair of early George III giltwood wall-brackets, 15 in. high. **£2,900-3,400**   *C*

A pair of ormolu and bronze candelabra, 17¼ in., mid-19th C.   *SB*

A pair of ormolu models of Sphinxes, on Porta Santa Rara marble bases, 11¾ in. (30 cm.) high. **£800-1,000**   *C*

A pair of French ormolu and bronze chenets, 28 cm. high. **£350-430**   *P*

An ormolu tazza, with lift-out liner, the body inset with four cameo panels, on grey fossil marble plinth, early 18th C., 9 in. (25 cm.) high. **£880-1,000** *C*

An ormolu Athenienne, with red lacquered bowl, tasselled drapery and ending in paw feet, 17½ in. (44 cm.) diam., 32 in. (81 cm.) high. **£1,600-1,900**   *C*

A pair of 18th C. ormolu ewers, 28 cm. high. **£960-1,100**   *P*

A rare Venetian brass candlestick, early 16th C., 11 in. (28 cm.) high. **£1,500-1,700**

A 17th C. single brass candlestick, 7½ in. high. **£130-150**   *KNG*

BRASS CANDLESTICKS

- difficult to date: designs used over long periods, no makers' marks
- sockets first appeared on domestic candlesticks in the late 13th C.
- 14th C. sockets are polygonal and have two holes for removing the stub
- smaller holes used to end of 15th C.
- mid 17th C. the drip pan tended to move further from the foot
- from the early 18th C. unpierced sockets were the norm
- after this time brass candlesticks were greatly influenced by silver styles
- 1700 saw the introduction of the hollow cast stem, this allowed a development of the faceted stem
- by the 1720's a plainer base returned
- in the 1750's the rococo style was produced, this also saw the introduction of drip-pans fixed to the nozzle
- during the 1780's stems were cast in one piece rather than two
- from this time on there was a tremendous variety of forms, styles and decoration

Two Dutch brass candlesticks known as a 'Heemskerks' mid-drip pan, 1600-1700, c. 1650, 7¾ in. high. **£530-600** *JC*

A brass candlestick/oil lamp (unscrews — made in two halves) possibly Spanish, 9½ in., 18th C. **£150-180** *JC*

A pair of mediaeval brass pricket candlesticks, the knopped stems spreading at the base, each with lion sejant supporters, North European, c. 1500. **£3,000-3,400** *Bon*

A pair of French brass candlesticks, c. 1766, 5 in. high. **£90-120** pair *KNG*

A seamed French brass candlestick, pre-1750, 7 in. high. **£50-60** *KNG*

A single brass Adams-style candlestick, of unusual shape, in. high, c. 1790. **£18-24** *DE*

A single brass candlestick, late 16th C., probably French, 9¼ in. high. **£240-280** *JC*

An early 18th C. pair of brass candlesticks, with petal bases, 8 in. high. **£275-300** *Cl.A*

A pair of brass candlesticks, c. 1780. **£50-70** *KNG*

A pair of George I brass candlesticks, c. 1720, 7 in. high. **£200-230** *DEB*

A pair of French brass candlesticks with good faceted stem, c. 1700, 6 in. **£240-270** pair *JC*

An 18th C. English brass candlestick, almost petal base, seamed column, c. 1740, 7 in. high. **£50-80** *JC*

A Spanish brass candlestick with claw feet, late 17th C., 6 in. high. **£120-140** *JC*

A pair of brass candlesticks, 19th C., 9 in. high. **£65-95** *O*

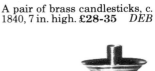

A pair of brass candlesticks, 9½ in. high, c. 1840. **£30-35** *DEB*

A pair of brass George III candlesticks, c. 1810, 8½ in. high. **£79-89** *McH*

A pair of brass candlesticks, c. 1840, 7 in. high. **£28-35** *DEB*

pair of brass candlesticks, c. ⁷60, 9 in. high. **£45-50** *DEB*

A pair of Victorian brass candlesticks, with screw ejectors and founders mark, c. 1850, 8 in. high. **£65-75** *JC*

A pair of brass candlesticks, c. 1840, 9 in. high. **£35-40** *DEB*

A pair of 19th C. Continental brass church candlesticks, 6½ in. high. **£40-45** *DEB*

pair of brass candlesticks, c. ⁸40. **£35-40** *KNG*

An early 18th C. pair of brass candlesticks, with ejectors, 8 in. **£185-200** *Cl.A*

A pair of 18th C. brass candlesticks, c. 1760, 7 in. high. **£180-200** *McH*

A pair of 18th C. petal base brass ejector candlesticks, c. 1730, 8 in. high. **£170-210** *JGM*

brass George I candlestick ᵥith side ejector, c. 1720, 8 in. ᵢgh. **£55-62** *DEB*

A 17th C. brass chamberstick, with makers mark, 8 in. long. **£125-135** *KNG*

A brass Great Exhibition patent candlestick, 1851, with maker's nameplate, 8 in. high. **£35-40** *DEB*

A pair of Regency brass column taper sticks, c. 1815, 7 in. high. **£120-140** *McH*

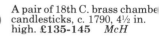

A rare 17th C. German brass chamberstick, with makers mark, 7½ in. long. **£150-170** *KNG*

A pair of 18th C. brass chambe candlesticks, c. 1790, 4½ in. high. **£135-145** *McH*

An early 18th C. brass chamber stick. **£35-40** *Cl.A*

An early 19th C. brass chamber stick. **£35-40** *Cl.A*

A 19th C. brass chamberstic by Henry Loveridge. **£25-3** *KNG*

A 19th C. 12 light Dutch brass chandelier, c. 1830, approx. 29 in. across. **£700-900** *JGM*

An early 19th C. two-tier chandelier, the brass frame mounted with four candle branches, 50 in. high. **£480-580** *SBe*

One of a pair of Georgian bras wall lights, with three candl holders. **£200-250** pair *JC*

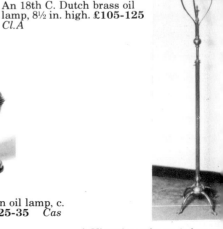

An 18th C. Dutch brass oil lamp, 8½ in. high. **£105-125** *Cl.A*

One of a pair of brass lamps, some parts replaced, fitted for electricity, 43 in., 1880's. **£360-430** the pair *SB*

A brass Aladdin oil lamp, c. 1940's, 20 in. **£25-35** *Cas*

A brass students' lamp, c. 1860-70, 13½ in. high. **£45-50** *DEB*

A Victorian telescopic brass standard oil lamp, 68 in. hig **£120-150** *PAM*

HORSE BRASSES

18th C. horse brasses are very rare — made from a brass called latten, have hammer marks on the backs (but watch reproductions which are much lighter and thinner)

did not really become popular in Britain until after the Napoleonic wars

tremendous variety of styles

there are many commemorative brasses

c. 1835 cast brasses appeared — the earliest form was calamine brass which is of particularly coarse feel with pitting

c. 1870-1900 machine-stamped brasses appeared, made from iron-rolled spelter brass

main value points
- any pre-1815 examples
- piercing
- unusual shape
- commemorative
- raised boss

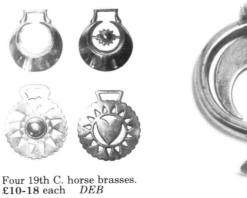

Four 19th C. horse brasses. £10-18 each *DEB*

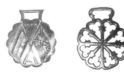

A 19th C. horse brass swinger. £15-20 *KNG*

Four 19th C. horse brasses (rare). £20-30 each *DEB*

Four 19th C. horse brasses. £16-30 each *DEB*

18th C. Continental brass stirrups. £20-25 *KNG*

19th C. horse brass swinger. 5-20 *KNG*

An 18th C. cast brass Irish fender, 3 ft. 5 in. long, 7 in. deep. £200-240 *JCr*

A small Victorian brass round end fender, 2 ft. 3 in. long. £30-40 *JCr*

A brass and cast iron Victorian fender, 4 ft long, 1 ft. 2 in. wide. £200-230 *JCr*

Barnard, Bishop & Barnard st brass fireplace surround, signed by Thomas Jeckyll, .3 cm. height, 45.2 cm. width, th trade mark and gistration mark for ovember 1873. £100-200

Two martingales with 19th C. horse brasses. £150-175 each *DEB*

A Georgian serpentine fender, 44 in. long. £400-460 *JCr*

A 19th C. brass and iron fan guard, with wide mesh, 17 in. high, 25 in. wide. £85-90   *JCr*

A pair of Georgian steel and brass fire iron rests, 9 in. long, 12 in. high. £110-120   *JCr*

An early Victorian brass fire dog, 2 in. high. £310-340   *JC*

A 19th C. French Rococo brass sparkguard, 32 in. high, 28 in. wide. £300-345   *JCr*

A Victorian copper and brass fire screen, 2 ft. 5 in. high, 1 ft. 11 in. wide. £155-175   *JCr*

A 19th C. brass chestnut roaster, 20 in. long. £65-75   *Cl.A*

A brass lead panelled fire screen, 30 in. high. £150-18 *JCr*

A late 17th C./early 18th C. Dutch brass warming pan, with repousse work, with Adam and Eve, 40 in. long. £250-380   *JC*

A French brass pre-war spark screen, 30 in. high, 27 in. wide. £300-330   *JCr*

An early 19th C. brass skimmer 20 in. long. £85-95   *Cl.A*

A set of steel and brass Georgian fire irons, £150-165   *JCr*

A set of Georgian fire irons, with unusual handles. £145-165   *JCr*

An 18th C. brass skimmer, 24 in. long. £45-50   *KNG*

An 18th C. brass tinder box.
£115-135   Cl.A

A brass roaster, 18 in. long, c.
1790. £170-185   A.E.F.

A pair of brass horse chimney
ornaments, c. 1840, 6¼ in. high.
£85-95   McH

A Regency brass claw/feather
doorstop, c. 1820, with natural
patination, 15 in. high. £80-
90   McH

An 18th C. brass cat trivet.
105-125   Cl.A

A 19th C. brass doorstop, c.
1860, 14 in. high. £77-87
McH

A 19th C. gilded brass mantel
ornament of George IV, 7 in.
high. £15-20   KNG

A green painted brass figure of
Sadi, inscribed M. le Verrier, 5½
in. (14 cm.) high, on square onyx
base. £66-86   CSK

brass purdonium, complete
with shovel. £150-200   SKC

A 19th C. brass mantel
ornament of a mythical figure, 5
in. high. £15-20   KNG

A 19th C. brass table bell, 5½ in.
high. £9-14   MA

19th C. brass mantel
rnament of a jockey, 3½ in.
igh. £7-10   KNG

Three 19th C. brass and wood
hand school or fire bells, 12 in.
high, 9 in. high. £20-40 each
MA

A 19th C. brass desk bell, 8½ in.
high. £30-35   MA

19th C. Indian brass
rticulated fish, 10 in. long.
30-45   KNG

A 19th C. brass trivet, c. 1870, 9 in. long. £25-30 *BTH*

A late 18th C. brass iron stan
7½ in. long. £15-20 *KNG*

A late 19th C. brass iron sta
9¼ in. wide. £18-20 *Gs*

A 19th C. brass hand bell of seried tone, 10 in. long. £50-60 *MA*

A brass and copper kettle, early 19th C., 12 in. high. £48-60 *OB*

A 19th C. brass trivet 10½ by in. £20-25 *KNG*

A brass and copper kettle, early 19th C., 11 in. high. £44-60 *OB*

A brass tea kettle with porcelain handle, c. 1840, 8½ in. high. £90-100 *McH*

An early 18th C. pestle an mortar, 6 in. high. £60-7 *KNG*

A late 18th C. brass jug, 7 in. high. £25-30 *KNG*

An 18th C. brass lidded flagon, 11 in. high. £195-205 *Cl.A*

An 18th C. brass muffineer, 3 in. high. £95-105 *Cl.A*

A pair of 19th C. Persian brass bowls, decorated with birds, 6 in. high. £30-35 pair *KNG*

A 19th C. brass ½ gill measur
2½ in. high. £25-28 *LAC*

An 18th C. brass flour dredger, 4 in. high. **£65-75**   *KNG*

An 18th C. brass nutcracker of simple wing nut and screw type, 4 in. **£55-70**   *Bon*

An 18th C. brass pepperpot, 3½ in. high. **£65-75**   *KNG*

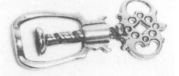

18th C. brass nutcrackers, 3 in. **£145-165**   *TJ*

A brass oak letter rack, c. 1860, 6½ in. wide. **£55-65**   *McH*

A 19th C. French brass letter rack. **£30-35**   *KNG*

A Regency brass letter stand, c. 1820, 5½ in. wide. **£88-98** *McH*

n 18th C. brass church ardens clay pipe holder, 10 in. ng. **£40-50**   *KNG*

A brass letter clip, c. 1850, 5 in. long. **£15-20**   *KNG*

(l) A 19th C. brass letter clip. **£12-15**   *KNG*

(r) A 19th C. gilded French brass letter clip. **£12-15**   *KNG*

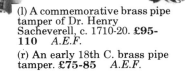

n early Victorian brass watch and, c. 1856, 10 in. high. **£58- 8**   *McH*

(l) A commemorative brass pipe tamper of Dr. Henry Sacheverell, c. 1710-20. **£95- 110**   *A.E.F.*

(r) An early 18th C. brass pipe tamper. **£75-85**   *A.E.F.*

An early 18th C. Dutch brass alms dish with Adam and Eve, with fine patination, with inscription, 1st quarter of 18th C., 22 in. wide. **£300-400**   *JC*

A brass honour box, c, 1800.
£230-280 *Cl.A*

A 19th C. brass ship's officer
box commode, 11 in. square.
£60-70 *MB*

An 18th C. Dutch brass tobacco
box, 5¼ in. **£270-300** *A.E.F.*

An Empire gilt and bronzed
brass inkstand, the cover in t
form of a plumed helmet, 5½ i
£460-550 *Hv.D*

A rare George II brass tobacco
box, with original lead weight,
c. 1750, 9 in. high. **£185-195**
BTH

(l) An 18th C. Indian betel-nut
brass box. **£40-50** *KNG*
(r) A 19th C. Indian betel-nut
brass box, 2 in. diam. **£20-30**
KNG

A rare brass egg cup stand,
English, c. 1790, 8 in. **£650**
725 *A.E.F.*

An 18th C. brass coaster, 5 in.
diam. **£65-75** *Cl.A*

A Georgian brass shoe horn.
£35-40 *Cl.A*

An 18th C. brass footman, 10 in.
high. **£65-70** *Cl.A*

A 19th C. brass cribbage board,
8 in. long. **£40-45** *Cl.A*

A copper Meteorite navigati
lamp, with flat back, 15 in. hi
£90-100 *Cas*

A rare brass fireman's badge
for the West of England
Insurance Company, 5½ in. (14
cm.) high. **£150-200** *C*

Three 19th C. miniature brass
pieces, table **£20-25**, chair
£20-25, fender **£4-6** *Cl.A*

A set of 3 copper double
navigation lamps (2 large, 1
small), early 20th C., large one
23 in., small one 18 in. **£370-**
400 set *Cas*

A mid 19th C. mahogany ship's wheel, with brass rim, 36 in. wheel. **£250-280**   *Cas*

A copper and brass paraffin port navigation lamp, 18 in. high. **£80-90**   *Cas*

An early 20th C. steel paraffin lamp with copper struts, made n Birmingham, 18 in. tall. **£65-70**   *Cas*

A late 19th C. Swedish brass ship's telegraph, on brass stand, 37 in. high. **£300-350**   *Cas*

A brass porthole with opening atch, early 20th C., 15 in. diam. **£80-90**   *Cas*

A naval copper and brass anchor lamp, c. 1947-48, 10 in. tall. **£40-44**   *Cas*

A 20th C. aneroid brass barometer, from the Ministry of Defence, 4½ in. diam. **£35-40**   *Cas*

A late 19th C. solid brass steam whistle, 30 in. high. **£160-180**   *Cas*

A 20th C. bronze propeller, 13 in. diam. **£35-40**   *Cas*

Left
A 20th C. brass life raft beacon, triggered by mercury, 13 in. long. **£15-20**   *Cas*

A late 19th C. Siebe Gorman iver's helmet, good quality, 20 n. high. **£600-750;** eproduction **£350-400**   *Cas*

An early 20th C. copper and brass electric navigation lamp, 12 in. high. **£80-90**   *Cas*

An early 20th C. brass porthole, 5 in. diam. **£40-45**   *Cas*

A late 19th C. brass ship's telegraph repeater, made by A. Robinson & Co., 13 in. diam. **£80-90**   *Cas*

An early 20th C. brass binnacle, with oil light on one side, electric on other, 14 in. high. **£115-125**   *Cas*

A copper prophylactic amulet ('zmeevik' in Russian), on one side the head of Medusa, on the reverse the Eleusa Virgin, Byzantine (of Russian provenance), probably 13th/14th C., 7 cm. diam. **£540-620** *C*

A copper wall sconce, Newlyn Studio Arts and Crafts movement, c. 1880, 12¼ in. high, 6 in. wide. **£35-40** *KNG*

A George I copper tea kettle, c 1720, 13 in. high. **£275-300** *McH*

A fine copper tea tasters kettle, c. 1850, 8¾ in. high. **£120-140** *McH*

A late 19th C. copper kitchen kettle, with brass knop, 12 in. high. **£40-50** *Cas*

A Victorian copper kettle, 9½ in. diam., 13 in. high. **£50-70** *PAM*

An antique hot water urn £100-140 *Max*

An early Victorian pedestal hot water urn. **£140-220** *Max*

15 tin-lined copper saucepans and skillets, with armorial crest and Temple and Crook stamp, the largest 12 in. diam., English, mid-19th C. **£250-350** *SB*

A set of five early 19th C. copper harvest measures. **£250-330** *SBe*

An antique copper coffee urn. **£70-130** *Max*

A copper tea urn, with brass tap, c. 1940's, 16 in. high. £4 50 *Cas*

A Georgian copper ale warmer, with iron handle, 4 in. high. **£30-40** *KNG*

A circular copper jardiniere, with flared rim, 11 in. **£20-40** *DDM*

A large copper jug, 21½ in. high. **£130-160** *SKC*

Three copper rum measures, the largest 12 in. (30.5 cm.) high, late 19th C. **£200-300** *SB*

A Victorian copper coal scuttle, 18 in. high. **£40-60** *PAM*

A copper funnel, 23 in. high. **£40-60** *PAM*

A copper and brass two handled vase, of the Arts and Crafts Movement, c. 1880, 8½ in. high. **£20-25** *KNG*

One of a set of six 19th C. copper lids, 10-5½ in. diam. **£110-120** set *Cl.A*

A Georgian copper chocolate pot, with turned fruitwood side handle, 18 cm. high. **£120-160** *SKC*

An early 19th C. Dutch copper milk churn, with brass ring handles, rim and urn finial, 30 in. (76 cm.) high. **£460-560** *SKC*

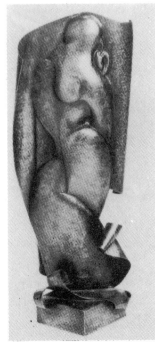

An abstract copper sculpture, 38 cm. high. **£75-130** *P*

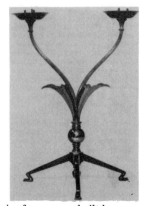

A pair of copper and gilt-bronze candlesticks, stamped W.A.S. Benson, 1890's, 14 in. (36 cm.). **£175-205** *SB*

18th-19th C. PEWTER

- plates one of the most common items of 18th C. pewter
- plain rim came in c. 1720
- the 'single reed' carried on until c. 1740
- c. 1760-1780 the Continental wavy-edge was popular
- the 17th C. triple reed plate gained popularity again in Queen Anne's reign
- the earlier plates have hall marks on front of rim
- styles of tankards tended to remain for long periods of time

- English lidded tankards started c. 1670 and it was not for another 100 years c. 1770 that the tankard without a lid became popular
- Irish flagons have cylindrical bodies with heavy domed lids and a large handle
- Scottish flagons have an almost flat lid
- Pewter suffered from the availability and popularity of other materials; pottery, porcelain, treen, iron and silver

- this led in the 19th C. to the alloying of tin with antimony — Britannia metal
- lead alloy pewter then became virtually solely for pub ware
- the Ale Standard in 1826, when a new standard measure was introduced, makes for a good break between pre-Imperial, and post-Imperial pewter
- Scottish measures are highly collectable as many of the best pewterers were Scottish

A Victorian pewter pint tankard, c. 1840, 4½ in. high. **£55-80**   *OB*

A Georgian pewter pint tankard, inscribed 'In Woodroff, Devonshire Arms, New Duke Street, Portman Square', c. 1780, 4¾ in. high. **£75-100**   *OB*

A George III pewter tankard, monogrammed J.M.G. and with crowned cross mark, 4½ in. high. **£44-64**   *OB*

A Victorian baluster ½ pint pewter tankard. **£20-25** *KNG*

A Victorian ½ pint pewter tankard by James Yates. **£15-20**   *KNG*

A Victorian 1 pint pewter tankard. **£25-30**   *KNG*

A German pewter flagon, engraved H.C. dated 1776 within a heart surrounded by flowering foliage, Waiblingen, late 18th C., 10¼ in. (26 cm.) high. **£400-500**   *C*

A George I Pewter Tankard, the scroll handle with double volute thumbpiece to the domed cover, 7 in. high. **£350-450**   *C*

A George II Pewter Tankard, the scrolled handle with shaped thumbpiece to the domed cover, 7 in. high. **£480-580**   *C*

A Swiss pewter humpen, Zurich, mid-18th C., cover repaired, 8 in. (20 cm.) high. £250-300 C

A George II Pewter Tankard, 7 in. high. £300-400 C

Right
A Swiss pewter bauchkanne stamped with the dates 1769 and 1787, engraved R.D.I.V. Vallais, mid 18th C., 8½ in. (21.5 cm.). £200-250 C

A Commonwealth Flagon, inscribed on handle PEIRs, 9½ in. high. £850-1,000 C

A Dutch Pewter Flagon, Amsterdam, 18th C., 9 in. high. £250-350 C

A Swiss Pewter Stitze, Freiburg, 18th C. 9½ in. high. £200-350 C

A French Pewter Pitcher, with double-acorn thumbpiece to the heart-shaped cover, inscribed on the neck with Jersey verification mark G.R., 18th C., 8¾ in. high. £150-250 C

A Commonwealth Pewter Flagon, with a twin cusped thumbpiece to the 'Beefeater' style cover, 8¾ in. high. £600-800 C

A Charles I Pewter Flagon, touch E.G., 10¼ in. high. £1,300-1,800 C

A Dutch flagon, touch D.K., late 18th C., 9 in. high. £300-360 C

A George III ale flagon, inscribed W. Hickford, Blue Boar Hotel, Malden, late 18th C., 8¾ in. high. £280-320 C

A Northern French flagon, 18th C., 8 in. high. £190-250 C

A Scottish pot-bellied Pewter Flagon, cover replaced, late 17th C., 9¾ in. high. £250-350 C

A fine George III Norwich Guild Pewter Flagon by Philip Mathews, inscribed Drinke Fare, Don't Sware, God Save ye King, October 6th, 1772, 8 in. high. **£800-900**   *C*

A Guernsey litre Pewter Flagon, the D-shaped handle with double-acorn thumbpiece to the heart-shaped cover, inscribed IrR, 18th C., 11½ in. high. **£300-450**   *C*

A Scottish Pewter pot-bellied Flagon, on splayed foot, bearing the touch W.I., late 17th C., 10 in. high. **£550-650**   *C*

A very fine James I Pewter Flagon, stamped on the handle with maker's touch I.F.W., 11½ in. high. **£1,300-2,000**   *C*

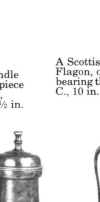

A George III flagon, 12¼ in. high. **£330-380**   *C*

A James I flagon, traces of touch on handle, hinge repaired, 14 in. high. **£1,400-1,600**   *C*

A Guernsey Pewter Flagon of quart capacity inscribed on lid C.D.G., 18th C., 8¾ in. high. **£200-300**   *C*

A Jersey Flagon of quart capacity by I.N., Jersey Verification mark GR, mid 18th C., 8¼ in. high. **£250-350**   *C*

An 18th C. pewter flagon, 8 in. **£66-110**   *Hy.D*

A pewter Commonwealth flagon, with double-volute thumbpiece to the circular cover, 11½ in. (29 cm.) high **£800-1,000**   *C*

A pair of pewter Scottish flagons, inscribed 'Free Church, Crailing, 1843', 19th C., 12 in. (30.5 cm.) high. **£200-300**   *C*

A matched set of four ½ pint pewter beakers, early 19th C., maker's stamp, Watson, all belong to White Hart, Newhaven — all have 1826 Imp. Portcullis stamp. **£120-150**   *JC*

A double decilitre French pewter measure, c. 1800. £65-70 *KNG*

An early Georgian pewter loving cup, 5¾ in. (14.5 cm.) high. £150-250 *C*

A Scottish uncrested Tappit Hen Pewter Measure of Imperial Pint capacity, late 18th C., 9 in. high. £180-220 *C*

A Scottish Crested Tappit Hen Pewter Measure, late 18th C., 12 in. high. £300-350 *C*

A Scottish Crested Tappit Hen Pewter Measure of Imperial Pint capacity, late 18th C., 9½ in. high. £300-350 *C*

A Scottish Crested Tappit Hen Measure, initialled on neck IB, MW, late 18th C., 12 in. high. £350-450 *C*

A Victorian pewter 1 gill measure. £15-20 *KNG*

A German pot-bellied Pewter Measure with scroll handle inscribed P. Wittorf, Holstein, 6½ in. high. £150-200 *C*

A rare Scottish Pewter pot-bellied Measure, late 17th C., 5¾ in. high. £300-400 *C*

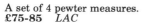

A set of 4 pewter measures. £75-85 *LAC*

An early 19th C. Irish half-pint pewter measure (without handle—Irish measures never had handles), c. 1840, 5 in. high. £20-40 *JC*

A pewter spouted pint measure, c. 1820-40, 4½ in. high. £28-35 *JC*

A Victorian pewter ½ gill measure. £15-18 *KNG*

537

An early 18th C. pewter teapot, with wood handle, maker's mark a stag and E.U.1722, possibly Edward Ubly, 5 in. £115-135   *Hy.D*

A George III Pewter Ale-Jug, the baluster body engraved with a monogram, the scroll handle with pierced thumbpiece to the domed cover and spout, 8¼ in. high. £200-250   *C*

A George III ale-jug, by William Wright, London, 8¼ in. high. £330-380   *C*

A rare narrow rimmed pewter dish by William Banckes, 12½ in. diam., c. 1690. £200-250 *JC*

A German Rosewater Pewter Dish in the manner of Caspar Enderlein, Nuremberg, early 16th C., damaged, 18 in. diam. £650-750   *C*

A French Rosewater Pewter Dish, after a design by Francois Broit, Montbeliard, early 16th C. the rim damaged. £1,200-1,400   *C*

A circular pewter charger, with reeded rim, touch A.D., impaled initials E.T. and S.T., early 18th C., 18½ in. diam. £150-200   *C*

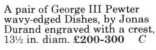

A pair of George III Pewter wavy-edged Dishes, by Jonas Durand engraved with a crest, 13½ in. diam. £200-300   *C*

A fine circular Pewter Charger by Thomas King, London, with triple-reeded rim, late 17th C., 15 in. diam. £600-700   *C*

A rare late 18th C. Venetian pewter plate with lion engraving, 9 in. diam. £50-60   *KNG*

A rare George II Pewter Bleeding Bowl, marked with cubic capacities, 5½ in. diam. £500-600   *C*

An 18th C. pewter dish, inscribed Burntisland Kirk and dated 1763, 18 in. diam. £240-280   *TJ*

538

An 18th C. pewter wavy edged plate, 10 in. diam. **£75-85**   *TJ*

A pewter inhaler, c. 1850, 5½ in. high. **£80-90**   *MA*

One of a set of 3 early 19th C. German pewter plates, 9½ in. diam. **£125-150** for 3   *KNG*

A William and Mary Pewter Porringer, 3 in. diam. **£200-250**   *C*

A pair of Charles II Pewter Porringers, touch HB on handles. **£300-450**   *C*

A pair of Pewter Porringers, late 17th C., 2¾ in. diam. **£520-620**   *C*

An 18th C. pewter wavy edged bowl with carrying handles, 10½ in. diam. **£275-375**   *TJ*

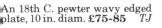

A pair of pewter tazza (footed plates) of nice small size, by William Shayler, in good condition, c. 1740, London, 7 in. diam. **£240-280**   *JC*

A pewter cake basket, with central sea blue/green enamel panel and loop handle, model No. 0357 — engraved presentation dated 1916, 12 in. **£30-60**   *RJG*

An early 19th C. pewter chamberstick, 5½ in. diam. **£25-30**   *KNG*

A mid-17th C. pewter slip-top spoon, bearing a rose within a beaded circular shield, English, c. 1645, 17 cm. long. **£50-70**   *P*

An early 19th C. pewter bedpan of typical shape, with screw on handle. **£60-80**   *Bon*

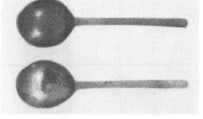

A pair of mid-17th C. pewter Puritan spoons, punched with the initials H.S.(?), English, c. 1660, 16.5 cm. long. **£50-70** *P*

A mid-17th C. North European pattern pine-cone or 'Fradlett' knop spoon, with touch-mark of three spoons in a circle, c. 1650, possibly Danish or Norwegian, 17 cm. long. **£50-60** *P*

An early 17th C. pewter acor knop spoon, with indistinct touchmark, English, c. 1620, 16.25 cm. long. **£50-65** *P*

A cast-iron and ceramic cooking range, with 4 hot plates, 2 ovens, burning box and ash drawer, 33 by 30½ in., probably Belgian, c. 1915. **£500-600** *SB*

A cast-iron stove, marked B V 1830 (Baerum Vaerk), with cast urn above (to hold perfumed water), Norwegian, c. 1830, 75 by 30 in. (190.5 by 76 cm.). **£650-750** *SB*

A Scandinavian cast-iron stove, marked Kvaerner Brug No. 41, with burning box at the base, and with three sections above, each holding a hot-plate, probably Norwegian, c. 1880, 25 by 75 in. (63.5 by 190.5 cm.). **£400-480** *SB*

The Resplendor, the cast-iron stove in black-leading, marked D. Cie (Deville & Cie), with fuel-loading beneath removable lid, c. 1910, 61 by 23½ in. **£450-510** *SB*

An early cast-iron stove, marked Eidsfos, with three croissant ovens above burning box, raised on wooden simulated brick base, Norwegian, c. 1780, 85 by 27 in. (216 by 68.5 cm.). **£2,000-2,500** *SB*

A cast-iron stove, marked Diosi (Drammens Jernstoberi), Norwegian, c. 1840, 53 by 32 in. (134.5 by 81 cm.). **£700-800** *SB*

ast-iron pot stove, marked
fos No. 194, finished in
ck-leading, with central
tif of Three Graces,
rwegian, c. 1880, 56 by 24 in.
50-900 *SB*

A Scandinavian cast-iron
stove, with burning box at the
base, and three pierced sections
above, each holding a hot-plate,
probably Norwegian, c. 1880's,
26 by 72 in. (66 by 183 cm.).
£400-450 *SB*

A Scandinavian cast-iron pot
stove, finished in black-leading,
probably Norwegian, c. 1910, 15
by 55 in. (38 by 140 cm.). **£120-
160** *SB*

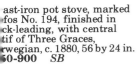

A Scandinavian cast-iron
stove, marked H. Rasmussen &
Co., Ödene 1918, finished in
black-leading, with door at the
front opening to reveal hot-
plate, c. 1918, 15 by 69½ in. (38
by 176.5 cm.). **£180-220** *SB*

Scandinavian cast-iron pot
ove, marked Jernstoberiet
odthab, probably Norwegian,
1910, 21 by 73 in. (53 by 180
n.). **£250-300** *SB*

Monopole 117 Roses, the large
cast-iron stove marked De Ville
et Cie C Charlesville, with fuel-
loading beneath hinged lid,
French, c. 1890, 18½ by 47 in. (47
by 119 cm.). **£280-320** *SB*

A cast-iron stove, finished in
hand-enamelled vitreous
enamel and nickel-plating by
C. F. Kuppersbush et Sohne,
with removable scalloped
hearth, German, c. 1910, 20 by
43½ in. (51 by 110.5 cm.).
£1,100-1,300 *SB*

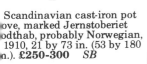

A small cast-iron pot stove,
bearing C.V. monogram, hot-
plate beneath removable lid,
raised on three feet, probably
Belgian, c. 1900, 14 by 36 in. (36
by 91.5 cm.). **£200-250** *SB*

Right
Blue Poppy, a cast-iron stove,
by Sougland, finished in hand
enamelling and blue vitreous
enamel, the pierced lid
revealing fuel-loading flap, c.
1918, 26¼ by 17 in. (67 by 43
cm.). **£420-480** *SB*

erby, a stove in green vitreous
namel, marked Nestor-Martin,
ith hot-plate beneath
movable pierced lid, standing
removable hearth, Belgian,
1910, 16 by 43 in. (41 by 109
n.). **£240-280** *SB*

Right
Godin, a cast-iron stove in
nickel-plating and brown,
pierced lid lifting to reveal fuel-
loading flap, French, c. 1910, 16
by 36½ in. (41 by 93 cm.). **£420-
480** *SB*

541

Chouberska Etincelants, a cast-iron bow-fronted stove finished in black-leading, by Societe Chouberskey, Paris, raised on wheels, French, c. 1880, 24 by 23 in. **£450-500** *SB*

An enamelled stove, Moblois no. 434, marked Pied-Celle Fumay, probably Belgian, c. 1925, 19 by 18 in. (48 by 46 cm.). **£60-100** *SB*

A pair of Adam-style cast-iron stoves, with fuel-loading through lid at the top, Scottish, earl 19th C., 37½ in. (95.5 cm.) high. **£250-300** *SB*

A 20th C. iron grate basket, 20 in. long, 10 in. wide, 14 in. high. **£60-70** *JCr*

Westminster, the cast-iron stove in green vitreous enamel, marked Les Fonderies Bruxelloises, standing on removable hearth, c. 1920, 27 by 27½ in. (68.5 by 70 cm.). **£300-350** *SB*

Dragonfly, by Sougland, the cast-iron stove in maroon vitreous enamel, upper flap with handle in the form of the body of a dragonfly, French, c. 1926, 26½ by 19¾ in. (67 by 50 cm.). **£220-280** *SB*

A cast-iron cooking range, marked L.Blton Perinster, finished in black-leading and ceramic tiles, Belgian, c. 1910, 35½ by 31 in. (90 by 79 cm.). **£350-400** *SB*

A small Georgian steel serpentine fender, 2 ft. 11 in. long, 6¾ in deep. **£120-130** *JCr*

Holiday cast-iron stove, finished in blue vitreous enam with black-leaded details, French, c. 1905, 26 by 19½ x 1 in. **£180-240** *SB*

A cast-iron cooking range, finished in blue vitreous enamel, each of the five acce doors decorated, 40 in. wide. **£280-320** *SB*

A pair of Victorian steel fi dogs, 25 in. high. **£155-18** *JCr*

A small 18th C. steel serpentin fender, 3 ft. 9 in. **£60-70** *JC*

A set of 3 19th C. steel fire irons, c. 1830, 30 in. high. **£50-70** *JGM*

George III steel serpentine asket grate, 44½ in. (113 cm.) ide. **£750-900** *C*

A pair of English pipe tongs, c. 1790, 14½ in. **£125-150** *A.E.F.*

A pair of 18th C. metal ember tongs, 20 in. long. **£200-225** *TJ*

An 18th C. English steel roaster, 29 in. high. **£220-250** *A.E.F.*

An 18th C. type wrought and sheet iron charcoal box brazier, 8 in. square. **£20-35** *Bon*

A George III brass and steel spit ack, the cog mechanism with ead weight and turned wooden back wheel, stamped P. Pearson, 11 in. high. **£650-750** *C*

An 18th C. Scottish steel roaster. **£450-500** *A.E.F.*

An English 18th C. steel roaster of superb quality. **£300-350** *A.E.F.*

A 19th C. tin chamber stick. **£7-10** *Cl.A*

A French metalware taper stick/candlestick, 7¼ in., c. 16th/17th C. **£350-400** *JH*

A 17th C. hearth lark spit, 14 in. wide. **£45-50** *Cl.A*

An 18th C. rush nip, 8 in. high. **£135-145** *A.E.F.*

An 18th C. type wrought iron spit jack, the reverse with bracket mounts, 15½ in. **£300-350** *Bon*

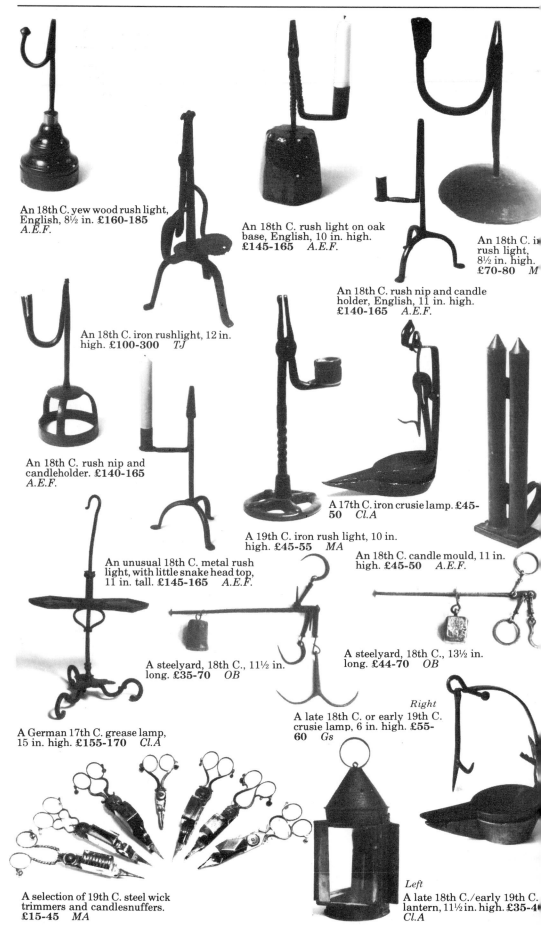

An 18th C. yew wood rush light, English, 8½ in. £160-185 *A.E.F.*

An 18th C. rush light on oak base, English, 10 in. high. £145-165   *A.E.F.*

An 18th C. ir rush light, 8½ in. high. £70-80   M

An 18th C. rush nip and candle holder, English, 11 in. high. £140-165   *A.E.F.*

An 18th C. iron rushlight, 12 in. high. £100-300   *TJ*

An 18th C. rush nip and candleholder. £140-165 *A.E.F.*

A 17th C. iron crusie lamp. £45-50   *Cl.A*

A 19th C. iron rush light, 10 in. high. £45-55   *MA*

An 18th C. candle mould, 11 in. high. £45-50   *A.E.F.*

An unusual 18th C. metal rush light, with little snake head top, 11 in. tall. £145-165   *A.E.F.*

A steelyard, 18th C., 13½ in. long. £44-70   *OB*

A steelyard, 18th C., 11½ in. long. £35-70   *OB*

Right
A late 18th C. or early 19th C. crusie lamp, 6 in. high. £55-60   *Gs*

A German 17th C. grease lamp, 15 in. high. £155-170   *Cl.A*

A selection of 19th C. steel wick trimmers and candlesnuffers. £15-45   *MA*

Left
A late 18th C./early 19th C. lantern, 11½ in. high. £35-4 *Cl.A*

544

Three 19th C. brass combination locks. £12-50 each   *MA*

Four 19th C. brass padlocks. £7-12 each   *MA*

Three 19th C. iron and brass padlocks. £12-48 each   *MA*

A large Wrought-Iron Key, with oval bow turned shank and notched bit, English, 18th C., 13 in. wide. £25-35   *C*

A French Steel Key, with pierced and scrolled bow, turned ferrule and notched hollow shank; late 17th/early 18th C. £30-50   *C*

A steel key, the loop pierced with a cross and scrollwork, turned ferrule and fluted shank, English, 18th C. £50-60   *C*

A Georgian iron doorkey, rare size, c. 1800, 10 in. long. £75-85   *McH*

A pair of late 17th C./early 18th C. scissors, 8½ in. long. £35-40   *Cl.A*

ate Gothic Wrought-Iron , with circular bow and rced bit, 7½ in. wide. £40- C

A pair of 18th C. iron dividers, 14 in. long. £75-85   *TJ*

A brass key, with coat of arms and surmounted by a crown, 7½ in. (19 cm.) long. £30-40   *SKC*

A pair of steel scissors, 12 in. long. £100-125   *TJ*

A selection of 18th and early 9th C. iron and steel keys. £12- 0 each   *MA*

A 17th/18th C. wrought iron scold's bridle with side chain and hinged side and top plates, 6½ in. **£100-125** *Bon*

A rare 18th C. wrought iron slavery belt with manacles, and a pair of leg irons with double ended key. **£120-150** *Bon*

An early 19th C. iron dog col with spikes. **£40-45** *MA*

An early 18th C. wrought iron bell pull of open twist type, 5½ in. **£30-40** *Bon*

A 17th C. metal gauntlet. **£100-125** *TJ*

An 18th C. steel 'Church Warden's' Pipe, 18½ in. long. **£200-225** *TJ*

Four 19th C. West Country Friendly Society polehead finials of turned cast, cut a pierced brass plate, two of th can be attributed to Ansfor and Ditcheat, formed 1878, dissolved 1924, and Stratton the Fosse. **£25-40** each *E*

Five early 19th C. boot hooks. **£3-5** each *Bon*

A 16th C. metal clock figure, 9 in. high. **£650-750** *TJ*

A 20th C. sand-blasted cast i shoe last. **£4-7** *Cas*

A bell metal miniature footman, c. 1810, 7¾ in. wide. **£89-99** *McH*

A pair of bell metal horse doorstops, c. 1840, 8½ in. high **£125-145** *McH*

A 19th C. North Country brass and iron money bank, c. 1850, 7 in. high. **£75-85** *McH*

A 'walnut' sovereign case, base metal, with a powder puff and mirror, c. 1900. **£55-60** *ST*

Four Victorian uncut figura seals cast in the form of sh bearing cherubs and postbc **£20-25** each *Bon*

German iron strong box, with
k-plates on 3 sides, 17th C.,
in. wide. **£600-680**   *C*

Right
One of a pair of Spelter figures
of Don Juan and Don Cesar, one
signed indistinctly Dev &
Leroy, 36½ in. and 35 in., c.
1890. **£600-700** the pair   *SB*

A Victorian lead garden
fountain, 27 in. high. **£110-
140**   *SKC*

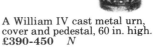

A William IV cast metal urn,
cover and pedestal, 60 in. high.
£390-450   *N*

n Edwardian tin gallon
easure, 7 in. diam., 8 in. high.
35-40   *AL*

A pair of black-painted cast iron
urns, 24 in. diam., 67 in. high.
£1,100-1,300   *C*

A Pontypool purdonium and
cover, painted with sprays of
flowers on a red ground, 20 in.
(51 cm.) wide. **£350-420**   *SKC*

lead insurance sign for the
n Insurance Company. **£20-
0**   *Bon*

An early Dutch tobacco jar (lid
missing), c. 1750, 5 in. long.
£12-20   *OB*

Three various lead insurance
signs including BATH-SUN-
FIRE. **£20-30** each   *Bon*

METALWARE APPENDIX

Amulet
Any small item worn by men
and his animals as protection
against evil.

Cat Trivet
Plate or Muffin warmer made in
the form of a double tripod so
that it would stand steady on
uneven hearthstones.

Chenet
An andiron, used to support the
end of a log in a fire.

Crusie Lamp
An open iron lamp, the oil filled
bowl supplies a rush wick which
is supported in the beak spout.

Humpen
A tall almost cylindrical
tankard of German origin.

Lark Spit
A spit used for roasting small
birds.

Oinochoe
A vessel used for dipping wine
from a crater and filling wine
cups.

Olpe
A Greek Jug.

Quaich
Derived from the Gaelic word
cruach meaning a cup.
Originally of staved wood with
two plain handles, one on either
side. From the 17th C. onwards
produced in silver and pewter.

Scolds Bridle
A device which was hinged and
clamped over the head, a small

plate projecting into the mouth
held the tongue down making
speech impossible; used as a
punishment for women found
guilty of nagging.

Spit Jack
Iron device for holding meat and
turning it as it roasts over a fire;
various forms: dog driven,
weight driven (16th C.); air-
driven (18th C. — hot air fan in
the chimney) and clockwork.

Tappit Hen
A Scottish measure vessel, the
term formerly indicated a
measure of three pint size, but is
now usually applied to all
capacities.

CHARACTER DOLLS

- in 1909 Kammer & Reinhardt introduced a large number of character dolls
- these were modelled from life, showing all the nuances of childish temperament
- a model was made and then a mould taken, which was used about fifty times
- Simon and Halbig cast and painted the heads for many other manufacturers, including Kammer & Reinhardt, such heads are marked K & R, Simon & Halbig, or K & R, S & H and the model number
- early K & R character dolls are of exceptional quality

- the French had remained supreme in the manufacture of dolls, in the 19th C. with Jumeau one of the main exponents
- however, from the 1890's the Germans had perfected equal skills
- after K & R introduced their characters many other makers followed: Heubach Armand Marseille, Bruno Schmidt, Kestner, and S.F.B.J. (the Societe Francaise de Fabrication de Bebes et Jouets)

- obviously these dolls were expensive and so they were hardly produced in large quantities
- K & R model 117 is usually considered to be one of the most desirable, in fact any 'pouty' doll is highly collectable
- the most common is model 126
- there are more Heubach characters than any other
- as one gets nearer to the First World War quality tends to decrease and character dolls produced after the war are, in many cases, poor quality

A bisque-headed doll, jointed composition body, AM 390, Armand Marseille, early 20th C., 23 in. high. £160-200 PAM

An Armand Marseille kid-bodied shoulder plate doll, with bisque lower arms, Mold 370. £240-260 HA

An Armand Marseille kid bodied doll, with original clothes, 15 in. long, c. 1900. £130-140 HA

An Armand Marseille 390 m doll, in original clothes, 18 i long, c. 1900. £100-115 H

An Armand Marseille toddler doll, Mold No. 995, with remade wig, 15 in. long, c. 1924. £100-120 HA

An Armand Marseille bisque-headed doll, the composition body with soundbox operated by pull cord, marked on head '1894 AM5 DEP Made in Germany', 48 cm. high. £280-340 SKC

Left

A rare Kammer and Reinhardt bisque head character doll, with short wig, blue eyes, closed mouth and jointed composition body, 19 cm., marked K R 11419. £440-540 P

An Armand Marseille 390 mo doll, in original clothing, wit retouched hands, c. 1900-10. in. long. £130-150 HA

A Victorian doll, the china head by S. Halbig, with wood joints and cream stucco body, 24 in. £110-160 RMcT

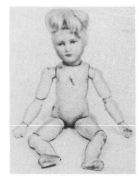

Right

A Simon & Halbig, Kämmer & Reinhardt doll, redressed, 23 in. long, c. 1890. £200-250 HA

Kämmer & Reinhardt
aracter doll, 17 in. long, c.
10. **£220-240** *HA*

A Simon & Halbig doll
(redressed), 1078 mold, 18 in.
long, c. 1890. **£200-250** *HA*

A Simon & Halbig, Kammer &
Reinhardt doll, 17½ in. long, c.
1908. **£225-250** *HA*

A small Simon & Halbig K Star
R doll, fair bisque in nice
condition, with original clothes,
14 in. long, c. 1890. **£170-220**
HA

Simon & Halbig, Kammer &
einhardt character doll, mold
o. 126, 17 in. long, c. 1920.
220-240** *HA*

A Bisque-headed baby doll,
with open mouth and having
composition body, marked 'K.
and R., Simon and Halbig 122,
32', 32 cm. high. **£210-280**
SKC

A Bebe Cosmopolite Japanese
girl doll, with Simon and
Halbig bisque head, impressed
1199, size 6, closing glass eyes,
open mouth, ball jointed
composition body dressed in
traditional costume, c. 1910, 17
in. **£570-650** *SBe*

A bisque-headed doll, with blue
sleeping eyes, and jointed body,
wearing embroidered dress,
marked Simon & Halbig S&H,
11¾ in. high. **£95-110** *CSK*

arge 'chunky' Jumeau, with
sed mouth and fixed
erweight eyes, with original
, size 12, c. 1880. **£1,200-
00** *HA*

Left

A bisque-headed bebe, with
closed mouth and composition
body, eyes operated by a lever,
23 in. high, stamped Depose
Tete Jumeau BTE 10 and with
sticker on the body reading
Bebe Jumeau Diplome
d'Honneur. **£600-700** *CSK*

Left

A French late 19th C. bisque-
headed doll by Jumeau, having
replacement wig and brown
fixed eyes, in original dress,
marked on head 'C' above 'EJ',
42 cm. high. **£1,100-1,400**
SKC

An early Emile Jumeau, of very
good quality porcelain, ball
jointed at shoulder and hip with
fixed wrists, marked on head
and body, with original clothes,
c. 1880. **£1,500-2,000** *HA*

549

A Jumeau doll, with bisque head, blue glass eyes, marked on the reverse with a rust coloured mark A (over) 8, and having ball jointed composition body (needs re-stringing), approx. 21 in. £680-780 *SBe*

A bisque-headed Bebe, with fixed blue eyes, and fixed wris composition body, marked Depose E7 J and stamped on t. body Jumeau Medaille d'Or, Paris, 16 in. high. £1,200-1,500 *CSK*

A bisque-headed bebe, with fixed blue eyes and jointed composition body, wearing underclothes and brown shoes, marked in red Tete Jumeau DEPOSE B te SGDG 4 and stamped in blue on the body Jumeau Medaille D'Or Paris, 13 in. high. £760-860 *CSK*

A Cuno & Otto Dressel poppy doll, with shoulder head on cloth body, and composition lower arms, c. 1912. £245-265 *HA*

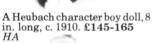

A Kestner character baby doll, 10½ in. long, c. 1910. £245-265 *HA*

A Kestner 136 doll, 2 in. long, c. 1900. £28 320 *HA*

A Heubach character boy doll, 8 in. long, c. 1910. £145-165 *HA*

An Einco character head boy doll, redressed in velvet outfit, 9 in. long, c. 1910. £140-160 *HA*

A Schoenau & Hoffmeister 'Hanna' character doll, 23 in. long, c. 1910. £240-260 *HA*

A bisque swivel-headed Parisienne, with closed mouth, fixed eyes, wool wig and kid body, 13 in. high, French, c. 1870. £340-400 *CSK*

A 'Melitta' character doll, size 12, dressed i sailor's uniform, c. 1910, 22 in. long. £200 250 *HA*

A bisque swivel-headed bebe, the closed mouth with slightly parted lips, fixed blue eyes and gussetted kid body with bisque arms, 10 in. high (one ear chipped). £1,650-1,850 *CSK*

A china shoulder-headed doll, with blue painted eyes and stuffed body with china limbs, mid-19th C., 16 in. high. £370-420 *CSK*

Thuringian bisque porcelain
-aded doll, with painted face,
ass eyes and cloth body, her
wer legs of porcelain, dressed
original bridal costume,
arked 270 DEP 2., 15 in., c.
70. **£300-380**   *WW*

A bisque-headed bebe, with
open-closed mouth, fixed blue
eyes and jointed wood and
composition body, French, c.
1878, 14 in. high. **£580-680**
CSK

A bisque-headed bebe, with
closed mouth, fixed blue eyes
and jointed composition body,
11 in. high, marked FG in a
cartouche. **£360-420**   *CSK*

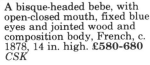

A talking doll, with china head,
dressed in a child's white silk
dress and bonnet, 21 in. high.
£160-190   *Lan*

bisque shoulder-headed folie,
ith fixed brown eyes and bone
histle handle with squeaker,
narked O French, with original
lothes, 13½ in. high. **£195-**
35   *CSK*

A walking bisque-headed doll,
jointed composition body
marked AB, made in Germany,
27 in. high, early 20th C. **£140-**
180   *PAM*

A Bisque-headed doll, with
brown sleeping eyes, open
mouth and pierced ears and
having composition body,
marked '191 17 (one leg and
head detached), 32 in. high.
£360-400   *SKC*

A wax-over-composition doll,
with fixed blue eyes, the stuffed
body wearing underclothes and
pink silk dress, 14½ in. high, c.
1815. **£140-180**   *CSK*

A Nymphenburg china doll,
shoulder head, the head 3½ in.
high, with Nymphenburg
mark. **£290-340**   *CSK*

An unusual wax over
composition Schmitt French
doll, all original, a little washed
on the face, 14 in., c. 1885. **£400-**
500   *HA*

A poured wax shoulder head
doll, with wax arms and legs, on
a cloth body, probably by
Pierotti with contemporary
clothes, c. 1880, 18 in. long.
£130-140   *HA*

he Schmitt shield
on body.

A bisque-headed character
child doll, with blue sleeping
eyes, and open-closed mouth,
jointed body, marked SFBJ 247
Paris, 18 in. high. **£750-950**
CSK

551

A wax-over-papier mache headed doll, with fixed blue eyes and wax-over-composition arm and legs, 17 in. high (only one hand), probably English, c. 1830. £70-100   *CSK*

A wax shoulder-headed doll, with jointed wooden body with wire for closing the dark glass eyes, wearing original white silk dress, c. 1845, 11½ in. high. £950-1,100   *CSK*

A wax-over-papier mache headed doll, with fixed brown eyes, the stuffed body in original Turkish costume, 14 in. high, c. 1830. £450-550   *CSK*

A Victorian poured shoulder wax doll, with glass eyes, inserted hair, the cloth body with poured wax limbs (one missing), in original dress, in. (38 cm.), c. 1870. £220-280 *SBA*

A painted wooden doll, 9 in. high. £220-280   *CSK*

A carved painted wooden doll, with inset enamel eyes, stitched brows and eyelashes, wearing remains of brown silk dress and hat trimmed with artificial flowers, c. 1785, 14 in. high. £490-600   *CSK*

A Victorian wax over composition shoulder head doll, with composition arms and legs, on a cloth body (some cracks on face), made in Germany, with original clothes, 14 in. long, c. 1900. £80-100 *HA*

A peg wooden doll, undressed 1890-1900. £40-60   *HA*

A French fashion doll, with shoulder plate swivel head, on kid body, 15 in. long, c. 1880. £450-550   *HA*

A French fashion doll, dressed by the English Augustinian Convent at Neuilly, Paris, with Bisque head and kid body, 14 in. long. £500-600   *HA*

A French fashion doll, with original sheepskin wig, gussetted kid body and original clothes, 32 cm. £390-430

An interesting solid-headed doll with painted eyes and closed mouth, with original clothes, 13 in. long, c. 1890. £60-80   *HA*

A two faced doll for pin cushion, the character face representing on one half-old age, the other half youth, 3 in. high, c. 1860. £200-220   *HA*

A Belton head doll, 10 in. long c. 1900. £145-165   *HA*

cloth toddler doll, with
ainted brown hair, blue eyes
nd stuffed body, 17 in. high, by
athy Kruse. **£290-350** *CSK*

A composition baby doll, with
painted features, and spring
joints at shoulder, neck and hip,
with a Schoenhut doll sticker,
patented January 17th 1911
U.S.A., 12 in. high. **£150-200**
CSK

A rare black papier mache-
headed doll, with brown
painted eyes, the kid body with
painted wooden limbs covered
at the joints with red paper
bands, wearing original
Turkish dress and turban, 13 in.
high, c. 1830. **£850-1,000**
CSK

n 18th C. Neapolitan crib
gure of an old woman,
earing a painted and silken
ostume, 13 in. (33 cm.) high.
70-85 *SKC*

A wicker doll's cradle (slightly
distressed), 15 in. long, c. 1900.
£15-30 *HA*

A Lioret Bebe Jumeau talking
doll, the bisque head with fixed
eyes and open mouth, with
'Merveilleux' phonograph
mechanism, 21½ in. high, with
two ¾ in. cylinders. **£2,300-
2,800** *CSK*

seated dandy musical
utomaton, probably by
ecamps, the figure re-painted
nd re-dressed (Now non-
nctional), French, 24 in. high,
1880's. **£580-640** *SB*

A bisque-headed walking doll,
turns head as walks, Simon
Halbig 403, 26 in. high. **£300-
350** *PAM*

A Victorian Heubach character
toy, character heads turn and
cry on pressing centre, 9 in.
long. **£275-300** *HA*

An E. Martin bisque-headed
'Swimming Doll' automaton,
stamped Gbr. 165 8/O K with
blue glass eyes and partly open
mouth with clockwork
mechanism (worn), French,
16½ in. long, late 19th C. **£360-
420** *SB*

A bisque-headed musical doll, in original costume and carrying a tortoiseshell guitar inlaid with ivory and mother of pearl, as the handle is wound the music is played and head and arm moves, 13 in. high. **£380-420** *CSK*

A pullalong toy of a bisque-headed doll, wearing original cut plum velvet suit, as the wheels move his right arm moves from side to side, 11½ in. high, probably lacks accordion. **£230-290** *CSK*

A Victorian bisque headed crown doll, with musical movement. **£90-130** *CDC*

An Automaton doll, head marked Tete Jumeau 4 and red check marks, damaged, redressed, 18 in. **£500-600** *SB*

TOYS

- musical automata were produced from the 18th C.
- some of the first were the singing birds
- 18th C. birds were enamelled with no feathers
- there has been a glut of reproductions in the last year
- 19th C. clockwork nursery pictures are now highly desirable — always more so if in working order
- many made in the 1880's and 1890's in tin
- wooden arks have been made from the middle of the 18th C.
- mass produced arks arrived in 1800
- the best period for the collector of arks is 1860's and 1870's
- German arks always the best
- many wooden, iron and papier-mache pull-along toys made especially in the 19th C.
- in the 19th C. many cheap wind-up toys were produced — the most collectable by Fernand Martin
- mechanical toy banks appeared in the 1870's mainly from America
- the most desirable being in cast iron with moving parts, worked by the coin
- many have a patent number

A mechanical bird automaton, with red feathers, 9 in. (23 cm.) high. **£120-160** *SKC*

A singing bird automaton, probably French, 18½ in. h c. 1895. **£370-420** *SB*

A singing bird in cage, with embossed brass label B. A. Bremond, Manufacturer, 16 in. high. **£680-780** *CSK*

A monkey fisherman automaton, head and arms move and fish swims (disconnected), with two-air musical movement, No. 138231, marked J. Phalibois, with glass dome, French, c. 1880's. **£1,300-1,500** *SB*

A bocage automaton, with automated and 3 stationar birds, 26 in. high, with gla dome. **£1,100-1,300** *CS*

A spice box automaton, probably by Nicholas Ingleheart, when desired action is selected the figure moves the lid to reveal the spice within, English, 13¾ in. wide, c. 1830's. **£330-400**   *SB*

A mechanical acrobatic teddy bear, the clockwork mechanism activating arms and head, 29 cm. high, probably of continental origin, c. 1900. **£260-310**   *SKC*

A cast-iron simulated organ bank, stamped 'Pat. June 13 1882' American, 7½ in. (19 cm.) high, late 19th C. **£130-160**   *SB*

A kicking mule cast-iron money bank, by J. & E. Stevens Co., stamped 'Always Did 'Spise A Mule', the base stamped 'Patd; Apr 22nd 1879', American, 9¾ in. (25 cm.) long, late 19th C. **£70-80**   *SB*

A German mechanical tinplate lithographed money bank, 6½ in. high. **£150-180**   *AK*

A Punch and Judy cast-iron money bank, by Shepard Hardware Co., the base stamped 'Buffalo NY USA Patd. in U.S. July 15.'84 and July 22.'84 Rd England' (re-painted), American, 7½ in. (19 cm.) high, late 19th C. **£88-100**   *SB*

A Lucie Atwell fairy tree biscuit money box, Crawfords Biscuits, 14 in., c. 1930's. **£45-50**   *PM*

A Chocolat Menier money box / chocolate dispenser, c. 1930's, French. **£30-35**   *PM*

A magic ball toy, based on an act by La Roche in Barnhams Circus, by Fernand Martin, c. 1902, 14 in. high. **£300-400**   *AK*

Left
An English baby toy by Green Monk Products, c. 1930, 4¼ in. high. **£9-11**   *Gs*

A tinplate mechanical hurdy gurdy called Pete and the Monkey by Distler, 1920's, 7½ in. high. **£350-400**   *AK*

A selection of Clicker toys, Germany, 1940's-1960's, probably by CKO. **£2-4**   *PM*

A Distler printed tinplate fire engine, clockwork-powered, with adjustable ladder, c. 1920, 11¼ in. long. **£120-150** *CSK*

A Distler Mickey Mouse tinplate organ-grinder, with clockwork mechanism playing simple tune (damaged), German, 8 in. (10.5 cm.) high, c. 1930. **£450-520** *SB*

A German tinplate hand painted parrot, by Gunthermann, c. 1890, 10 in. high. **£375-400** *AK*

A hand painted tinplate washerwoman, probably by Gunthermann, 5½ in. high. **£200-300** *AK*

A tin-plate Charlie Chaplin, not in working order, probably Schuco, 6½ in. high. **£110-130** in good order, motor working. **£200-230** *PM*

A Gunthermann tinplate roundabout with a musical movement, 1925-30, 8½ in. high. **£300-350** *AK*

A German tinplate clockwork mechanical billiard player, the figure hand painted and the table lithographed by Gunthermann, 5 in. high, 8 in. long. **£400-475** *AK*

A German felt-covered drumming pig, by Schuco, mid-1920's to late 1930's, 4½ in. high. **£25-35** *AK*

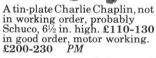

The Anxious Bride, a printed tinplate toy of a weeping woman, in a wheeled cart with clockwork motor, 9 in. long, by Lehmann, c. 1910. **£320-380** *CSK*

A good example of Lehmann's 'Paddy and the Pig', patent date 12 May 1903, tinplate with clockwork mechanism, 14 cm. long. **£220-280** *SKC*

A Schuco cloth and tinplate mechanical Donald Duck, c. 1930, 6 in. high. **£50-65** *AK*

(m) A Lehmann sea-lion, early 20th C., one reproduction flipper and whiskers. **£65-70** *PM*

(l) A Lehmann 'Stubborn Donkey' early 20th C. **£110-125** *PM*

(r) A Lehmann sea-lion 'Aha', c. 1910's. **£4-6** *PM*

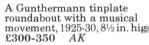

A Stock 'Paddy's Pride' tinplate toy, clockwork, German, 7½ in. (19 cm.) long, c. 1915. **£180-220**   *SB*

A Lehmann 'Oh-My' tinplate toy, No. 690, with clockwork mechanism, German, 10 in. (25.5 cm.) high, c. 1915. **£80-100**   *SB*

A 'Bucking Broncho' tinplate horse with cowboy rider, with clockwork mechanism, by Lehmann, 7½ in. long, c. 1910. **£130-180**   *CSK*

A drawing clown, made by Phillip Vielmetter, which works on a hand crank with changeable cams for different pictures, c. 1897, 5 in. high. **£800-900**   *AK*

A French hand painted Flywheel Clown and Drum with Goat probably by Rossignal, 5½ in. high. **£380-420**   *AK*

A Wells clockwork Father Christmas, 1930's/1940's, with original box, 5 in. **£18-20**   *CR*

A tin-plate Ferris wheel, possibly by Oro of Brandenburg, 6 in. high, 8 by 4½ in. base, c. 1920. **£70-80**   *PM*

A mechanical tinplate dancing couple, by F. Martin, c. 1915, 8 in. high. **£500-550**   *AK*

A German tin lighthouse, driven by internal candle, 1920's, 6½ in. **£12-15**   *CR*

A tinplate mechanical schoolmaster, by Kellerman, c. 1930, 5½ by 6 in. **£375-425**   *AK*

A tin drumming panda toy, 5 in. long. **£10-16**   *DO*

A Japanese 'Bandai' clockwork giraffe, made for African market, 8 in. high, late 1950's/1960's. **£25-30**   *CR*

A early post-war Japanese tinplate clockwork toy railroad car, 5¼ in. **£45-50**   *CR*

An early post-war Japanese celluloid and tin clockwork skipping elephant, 5½ in. long. **£30-35** *AK*

A battery operated performing clown, manufactured by Alps, Japan, 1960's, 10 in. high. **£35-45** *AK*

A French tinplate and wood radiquet steam boat, 21 in. long, dependent on size. **£700-2,000** *AK*

A Mettoy paddle boat, with box, 1940's, 10½ in. **£25-30** *PM*

A Bing tinplate torpedo boat, in scarlet, grey and black (lacking guns), with clockwork mechanism (partly re-touched), 14¾ in. long. **£450-550** *SB*

A Bing live steam spirit-fired ocean liner, in scarlet, white and navy blue with yellow trim, German, 2 ft. 1 in. (63.5 cm.) long, c. 1910. **£800-950** *SB*

A 1930 German tinplate clockwork plane, probably made by Tipp, bearing a Mickey Mouse mascot which belonged to the pilot Andre Galland, 14 in. wingspan. **£230-250** *AK*

A 1930's French Jep clockwork flying boat/seaplane, 13 in. long. **£180-200** *CR*

A Bing battleship, with grey tinplate hull, the superstructure (stamped with trademark) removable to give access to the clockwork motor, c. 1912 (partly repainted and funnels detached), 29 in. long, 6-inch beam. **£750-850** *CSK*

A clockwork and tinplate airliner, in red, white, blue and grey, British made, wingspan 53.5 cm., in original cardboard box, c. 1940. **£110-140** *SKC*

A tinplate Alfa-Romeo racing car, finished in scarlet, with clockwork mechanism (steering mechanism disconnected), German, c. 1925. **£220-260** *SB*

for better examples. **£300-600**

A Toonerville Trolley by Fischer, made in different sizes, 2 in. high. **£150-175** *AK*

A tinplate landaulette, probably by either Carette or Karl Bub (one headlamp missing), with clockwork mechanism, German, 11 in. long, c. 1912. **£400-450** *SB*

The largest tinplate clockwork airship, made by Tipp and Co., 25 in. long. **£750-850** *AK*

A Chad Valley printed tinplate delivery van, with opening rear door, all-metal wheels and clockwork motor, 10½ in. long, c. 1930. **£110-150** *CSK*

A C. R. Rossignol tin-plate Paris bus, 12 in. long, 1930's. **£160-180** *PM*

A German tinplate Hessmobile, mid-1930's, 8 in. long. **£225-275** *AK*

A Nifty main street tin-plate trolley, stops intermittently, door opens and bell rings, made in Germany, 9 in. c. 1930. **£80-90** *PM*

A Mettoy racing car, made in England, early 1950's (with original box), 9½ in. long. **£15-18** *PM*

(l) A Chinese tinplate motorcycle and sidecar, late 1960's, 7 in. long. **£18-20** *CR*

(r) A French tinplate motorcycle by Technofix, 1950's. **£20-24** *CR*

A tinplate Technofix clockwork 'Busy Diesel', 23 in. long, 1950's. **£30-35** *CR*

Two German cars by Arnold, 1950's, 10 in. wide. **£25-30** *CR*

A Technofix clockwork rocket express, 15 in. long, 1950's. **£30-35** *CR*

Left
A Japanese battery operated tinplate robot, imported to America under the name of Cragston, c. 1950's, 11 in. high. **£80-100** *AK*

A Japanese Alps friction tin-plate bulldozer and driver, 1960's, 9 in. long. **£25-30** *CR*

A Linemar Robotrac, battery operated, early 1960's, 10 in. wide. **£45-55** *CR*

A 1960's Japanese S. & E. battery operated pom pom tank, 12 in. long. **£50-55** *CR*

A Japanese tinplate robot bulldozer, mid-1960's, 9½ in. long. **£50-75** *AK*

Left
A Japanese tinplate flying saucer, imported by Cragston, early 1960's, 7 in. diam. **£40-60** *AK*

A Hungarian space vehicle, late
1960's, 13 in. **£25-30**   *PM*

An English Merit Dan Dare
gun, 1950's. **£8-10**   *CR*

Three Japanese robots, made
by S. & H., battery operated, 12
in. high, c. 1965-70. **£25-35**
each   *CR*

A Daiya Japanese super sonic
gun, with box, 1960's. **£8-10**
CR

A selection of small clockwork
robots and space craft, 1960's-
1970's. **£8-18**   *CR*

A Japanese super sonic gun,
late 1960's. **£6-8**   *CR*

(l) A Corgi Monkey mobile. **£3-
5**   *PM*

(r) A Husky Monkey mobile. **£1-
3**   *PM*

A Dinky toy motor truck, in re
and blue, 22 series, 1933. **£85
100**   *SB*

(l) A Dinky Jaguar XK120,
1950's. **£8-10**   *PM*

(m) A Corgi Aston DB4, 1960's.
£2-4   *PM*

(r) A Dinky Lamborghini
Marzal, 1970's. **£2-4**   *PM*

Dinky toy delivery van, 22
series, 1934. **£200-240**   *SB*

A Dinky pre-war royal airmail
car (paint good, some fatigue).
£80-120   *SKC*

A Dinky 24 Series sports coupe,
badge type radiator, no spare
wheel (slight damage). **£120-
160**   *SKC*

A Dinky pre-war 28 Series 2nd
type Osram van (fatigued,
slight chipping to paint). **£110-
150**   *SKC*

(l) A Dinky toy Austin taxi, 36G
1946-50. **£15-20**   *PM*

(r) A Dinky toy Foden flat truck,
1950. **£10-14**   *PM*

A Dinky 36 Series Salmson
four-seater tourer, complete
with original driver (near-side
rear wing missing). **£100-
140**   *SKC*

A Dinky pre-war 28 Series 2nd
type Swan Pens van (slight
fatigue and chipping to paint).
£120-160   *SKC*

A Dinky Bedford Heinz van
with advertising, with ketchup
bottle, late 1950's. **£60-70**
(version with can. **£15-20**)
PM

(l) A Dinky Bristol 450, 1950's.
£5-10   *PM*

(m) A Spot-on Jensen, early
1960's. £5-10   *PM*

(r) A Corgi Mangusta
Detomaso, 1970's. £2-4   *PM*

(l) A Memo, M.L. Paris 2 seater
racing car, c. 1930's, 10 in. £25-
30   *PM*

(r) A John Cobb 'Railton' record
car, 394.6 mph., made by Mini
Models, c. 1950, 10½ in. £30-
35   *PM*

A John Hill & Co. (no
trademark), silver bullet record
car, 17.5 cm. long (a.f.). £80-
120   *SKC*

Left

(l) A Minic clockwork steam
roller and box, 5 in. long, late
1940's. £12-15   *PM*

(c) A Minic Carter Paterson
delivery van, with advertising.
£24-30   *PM*

(r) A Minic Ford type. £15-20
PM

A Portuguese Buick, 1950's, 11
in. £10-20   *CR*

A Spot-on Routemaster bus,
early 1960's, 7½ in. wide. £60-
70   *PM*

Right

A Meccano constructional car,
runs 150 ft. on one winding, 13
in. long. £250-300   *AK*

A friction drive Express van, 3¼
in. possibly by G. E. Einfalt.
£18-20   *PM*

A clockwork Meccano sports
car, the blue body with outside
brake lever, on white rubber-
tyred wheels, the front wheels
steered from the cockpit, in
original box, 12 in. long. £400-
450   *CSK*

(l) A Schuco 3000 tele-steering
car, with box, 1930's. £25-30
PM

(r) A Schuco Kommando Anno
2,000, 1930's. £35-40   *PM*

American toys of the 1930's:
Tootsie toy fire pumper. £30-
35. U.S. Mail truck. £30-35.
Buck Rodgers battle cruiser.
£40-45. A Manoil coupé. £35-
40   *PM*

Right

A Japanese 'T.N.' police-jeep, 11
in. long, late 1950's. £35-40
CR

A Tippco tinplate fire engine,
made in Germany, full working
order, battery lights with water
pump on front bumper, 1930's,
18 in. long. £105-125
absolutely complete. £150-
175   *PM*

A Nervasport Renault racing
car, in metallic blue, with pre-
set steering and clockwork
motor, 14 in. long, c. 1930. £75-
100   *CSK*

Two Japanese Bandai battery operated cars, with horns and lights and gear system, 1960's, 11 in. long. **£25-35** each *CR*

A Frankonia 'James Bond' Aston Martin, Japan, friction drive with opening roof (called 711 to avoid copyright), with box, c. 1967, 12 in. wide. **£15-20** *PM*

Two German clockwork cars, by Prameta (British zone), 1950's, 5 in. wide. **£40-55** *CR*

Two 1960's Japanese friction station wagons, 12 in. long. **£15-18** *CR*

DIE-CAST MODELS

- 1870-1900 flat and semi-flat soldiers made by Germans
- Britains invented the hollow cast technique
- this led to wide range of military figures
- earliest had oval bases and paper labels — now rare
- farm items gaining popularity, but soldiers still most desirable, zoo animals still not so desirable
- original box adds substantially to value

Britain's 3rd Hussars, mounted with carbine, and officer on prancing horse, set no. 13, 5 figures. **£30-50** *SB*

Britain's Skinner's Horse (Duke of York's own cavalry), mounted with officer, set no. 47 **£20-30** *SB*

Britain's British Army tank, with personnel and machine-gun, set no. 1203. **£70-100** *SB*

A Marklin field gun, the weapon of cast-iron and cast-brass, finished in khaki with vertical adjustment by rack and worm at one side, 16 in. (40.5 cm.) long, German, c. 1905. **£110-140** *SB*

Britain's 4th Bombay Grenadiers, marching at slope, set no. 68, 14 figures. **£55-75** *SB*

Britain's covered lorry, with gun and limber, complete with short pole ammunition limber, set no. 1462. **£90-110** *SB*

Right
H.I.H. The Emperor of Germany, contained in original box, Britain's, c. 1895. **£100-150** *SB*

Britain's bi-plane, finished in silver, no. 1521. **£500-600** *SB*

562

Britain's Egyptian infantry, standing at attention, set no. 117. **£30-50**   *SB*

Britain's Devonshire Regiment, marching at trail, set no. 110, 8 figures. **£35-45**   *SB*

Britain's Hodson's Horse (4th Duke of Cambridge's Own Lancers), mounted with officer, and bugler, set no. 46, 4 figures. **£40-60**   *SB*

Britain's Prussian infantry, marching at slope, set no. 154, 8 figures. **£40-50**   *SB*

Britain's French Dragoons, mounted, with officer, set no. 140. **£50-60**   *SB*

Britain's Japanese cavalry, mounted with officer, set no. 135, 8 figures. **£45-65**   *SB*

Britain's Bulgarian infantry, marching at trail, with two officers, set no. 172, 11 figures. **£55-70**   *SB*

Britain's Queen's Own Royal West Kent Regiment, marching at slope, with officer, set no. 157. **£40-50**   *SB*

Britain's Sudanese infantry, marching at trail, set no. 116, set of 19. **£70-95**   *SB*

Britain's Boy Scouts with Scout-master, walking with stick in hand, from set no. 161, 17 figures. **£65-75**   *SB*

Britain's Austrian Dragoons, mounted, with trumpeter, set no. 176, 5 figures. **£50-70**   *SB*

Britain's West Point cadets, marching at slope, winter dress (16), set no. 226, together with West Point cadets marching at slope, summer dress (8), set no. 299. **£60-70**   *SB*

Britain's infantry, marching at slope, with officer, in tropical service dress, set no. 1294, 8 figures. **£35-45**   *SB*

Britain's United States aviation privates in peaked caps, no. 334, 8 figures. **£30-40**   *SB*

Britain's 3rd/12th (Sikh) Frontier Force Regiment, marching at slope, set no. 162? 16 figures. **£70-90**   *SB*

Britain's general staff officers, mounted, walking, on motorcycle, standing with binoculars and horse, all in service dress, set no. 1907, 7 figures. **£55-75** *SB*

Britain's Argentine infantry, marching at slope with officer, no. 1837, 6 figures. **£40-50**   *SB*

Britain's New Zealand infantry, marching at slope, with two officers, set no. 1542, 16 figures. **£35-45**   *SB*

Britain's Russian infantry, marching at slope with two officers, 16 figures. **£60-80** *SB*

Britain's Box No. 2077 'King's Troop R.H.A.': six-horse gun team (walking), limber and field gun. **£90-110**   *SKC*

Britain's collectors series, The Sussex Regiment, marching with sloped arms, with officer, 8 figures. **£30-40**   *SB*

Britain's United States Marines, marching at slope, in blue uniforms (8), marching at slope in active service dress (8). **£80-100**   *SB*

Britain's Green Howards, marching at slope, with two officers, standard-bearer, two trumpeters and drummer, set nos. 255 and 1595, 19 figures. **£160-200**   *SB*

Some English lead toys: A lead windmill. £4-6. A Taylor & Barrett 'Girl on Donkey', 1930's. £4-6. A Britain's Shetland pony with rider. £5-10. A Britain's blacksmith and anvil. £4-7. An F. G. Taylor haystack, late 1940's. £3-5 *PM*

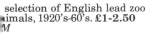

selection of English lead zoo imals, 1920's-60's. £1-2.50 *M*

impo lead 'Cowboys' by the res, 4 piece set, 1950's. £10-5 *PM*

A selection of English lead circus figures, 1930's-50's. £7-14 *PM*

A selection of English lead figures, 1930's-50's. £2-4 *PM*

A child's game of 'Mosaic in Colours', early 20th C. £3-4 *Gs*

An early 19th C. draughts set, 15½ in. square, draughtsmen of later date. **50-65** *JGM*

A Victorian boxed set of hildren's building blocks. £40-0 *MB*

The "ACE" FOOTBALL POOL GAME

The Ace Football Game, late 1930's. £10-16 *DO*

roulette game, box with ivisions of black, yellow, red, rey and bearing four coronet ymbols, 1 ft. 6½ in. wide, mid-9th C. £120-150 *SB*

A Hispano-Moresque parquetry gamesbox, inlaid in ivory and rosewood with chess squares, the interior with a backgammon board inlaid in tortoiseshell and mother of pearl, 17th C., 22½ in. (56.5 cm.) wide. £1,450-1,650 *C*

'etits Chevaux', an early 'rench horse racing gambling 'ame, in original case. £225-'60 *P*

A 19th C. wooden box with miniature wooden skittles. £20-25 *MA*

A 19th C. game of Spellicans.
£16-18   Gs

A 19th C. child's game, in a
wooden box, with bone letters.
£34-38   MA

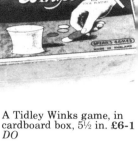

A Tidley Winks game, in
cardboard box, 5½ in. £6-1
DO

A 'Willy's Walk to see
Grandmamma' game, with
board 21½ by 24½ in., by A. M.
Myers & Co., 15 Berners Street,
c. 1869. £60-70   CSK

A word making and word
taking game. £5-8   DO

A 19th C. bone teetotum. £22-
25   MA

A word making and word
taking game, in cardboard box,
4½ in. long. £8-10   DO

A painted wooden Noah's Ark
and animals, with sliding panel
(broken) on one side, with
approx. 110 animals and birds
(damaged), c. 1910. £230-
260   SBA

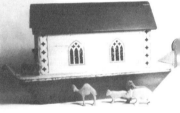

An early 20th C. Noah's Ark, 2
in. long. £90-110   Cl.A

A 19th C. wooden yo-yo. £20-
25   MA

A mid 19th C. carved wood
English butcher's shop, with
master butcher, butcher,
apprentice, shop cat and
accessories in a glazed case, 5
by 71 cm., with a printed bac:
drop. £790-900   P

Left
A late 19th C. stable and coach
house, with two skin covered
horses and metal-wheeled gig,
43 cm. wide by 50 cm. high.
£220-270   SKC

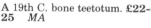

A. Barrett & Sons, Pixieland
Series No. 2, 'The Pixie Tea
Party', a midsummer night's
feast for a pixie king, in original
box. £140-220   P

A Victorian dolls washing-set, made of wood, consisting of washing bath, tub and board, the bath 6 in. long. £25-30 AL

A child's tinplate cooking range, together with copper utensils, probably French, 1 ft. 3½ in. (39.5 cm.) c. 1915. £180-210 SB

A child's tinplate cooking range, with 5 hot-plates, bain marie, flue, kettle, three pans and towel rail, probably French, 1 ft. 2 in. (35.5 cm.) wide, c. 1920. £150-200 SB

A Victorian dolls knife and fork, made of white metal, 4½ in. long. £1-2 AL

A German hand painted Marklin horse, 1903, 5 in. long. £180-220 AK

A Victorian 7-piece dolls dessert service, marked 'Best P&B' (Powell and Bishop Hanley, 1876-78). £20-25 AL

A wooden rocking horse, with mane and leather harness, later saddle and blanket, 43 by 57 in. (109 by 145 cm.), early 20th C. £220-300 SBA

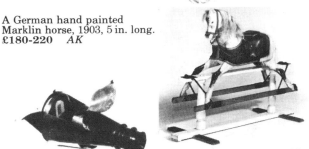

A Polyorama panoptique viewing device, with five diapositives, viewer 6¼ in. long, diapositives 3½ in. diam. £770-900 CSK

An American wooden struggling toy, 8 in. high. £85-100 DO

An 'Allwin' penny-in-the-slot machine (lacks back), 2 ft. 3 in. (68.5 cm.) high, c. 1920. £28-35 SB

An Edwardian child's tricycle, modelled as a running horse, 36 in. long, c. 1905. £250-300 CSK

A brass figure of a policeman, with nodding head and moveable helmet, by John Hassell, 4½ in. high. £180-280 CSK

A 'Ding-a-bell' penny-in-the-slot amusement machine, 1 ft. 6 in. (76 cm.), c. 1950. **£33-40** *SB*

A pussy shooting gallery penny-in-the-slot amusement machine, 6 ft. 5 in. (195.5 cm.) high, c. 1935. **£350-470** *SB*

A football penny-in-the-slot amusement machine (adapted to take 1p.), 3 ft. 7 in. (109.5 cm.), c. 1950. **£280-350** *SB*

A 9 in. gauge 2-2-2 live steam coal-fired locomotive, almost certainly built at the workshops of the Grand Junction Railway at Crewe, 3 ft. 3½ in. (99.6 cm.) long over buffers, 1 ft. 2 in. (35.5 cm.) wide, c. 1853-60. **£950-1,100** *SB*

A Bassett-Lowke 4-4-0 electric gauge 'O' Prince Charles locomotive and tender, 40 cm long. **£110-130** *SKC*

A Bassett-Lowke 2-6-0 electric gauge 'O' Mogul locomotive and tender, green livery, No. 866 (minor repainting), 45 cm. long. **£200-250** *SKC*

A Bassett-Lowke 0-6-0 electric gauge 'O' goods locomotive and tender (repainted black overall), 39 cm. long. **£60-80** *SKC*

A Marklin O-gauge clockwork tank locomotive, 'Stephenson' No. 329, with brake and reverse levers, 12½ in. long, with a length of track. **£800-900** *CSK*

A Marklin gauge 2 dining car, in LNWR livery, the hinged roof opening to reveal fitted interior. **£720-820** *CSK*

An Ernest Plank model steam plant, having whistle, pressure gauge, filler plug, drain cock, spirit burner and governor, 12½ in. **£115-145** *SBe*

A Hornby O-gauge electric 'Royal Scot', in LMS red livery, No. 6100, in original boxes. **£250-270** *CSK*

A Bing spirit-fired gauge 'one' 4-2-2 locomotive, No. 7094, the front wheels of tender detached, German, the whole 1 ft. 9½ in. (55.5 cm.) long, c. 1914. **£400-470** *SB*

A 2½ in. gauge 2-6-0 locomotive and tender 'Dyak', coal-fired copper boiler with all fittings, and twin outside cylinders with Walshaert's valve gear, length 31½ in. **£460-560** *SBe*

n '00' gauge 2-6-2 steam
comotive, finished in brass
nd painted green lined black,
¼ in. (18.5 cm.) long. **£85-**
00 *SB*   *Right*

A Bing stationary steam plant,
with dynamo supplying power
to light-bulb socket, German, 15
in. (38 cm.) long, c. 1915. **£150-**
180 *SB*

A 3½ in. gauge coal-fired 0–6–0
tank locomotive 'Rob Roy', sold
with set of drawings, water
pump handle, coal shute,
carrying case and section of
display track. **£660-720** *SBe*

A Bing gauge '2' clockwork
model of the L.S.W.R.
4-4-0, locomotive and tender, in
near mint original paintwork.
£900-1,000 *C*

A Stuart Turner steam
driven model beam engine,
he 6¾ in. spoked flywheel
with belt pulley, wooden
agged single cylinder with
in. stroke, slide valve,
rain cocks. displacement

lubricator and steam valve
with compressed air pipe
union, painted green and
mounted on polished
mahogany rectangular
base, 16½ in. **£250-350**
SBe

A Prince Albert Crimp Cut
Cigarette tobacco tin, 4½ in.
high. **£6-9** *DO*

TINS

- Huntley & Palmers were
  really the pioneers of the
  decorated biscuit tin
- the firm started in 1822 and
  by the 1840's they were
  packaging their biscuits in
  tins, often with labels glued
  to the outside
- by 1860's their attractively
  decorated tins were transfer-
  printed
- in 1870's Barclay and Fry
  developed a technique of
  offset lithography for colour
  printing on tins
- other firms including the Tin
  Plate Decorating Co. and
  Benjamin George were by
  now producing transfer
  printed tins
- Huntley, Boorne & Stevens,
  who made tins for Huntley &
  Palmers, had a virtual
  monopoly of the use of
  Barclay and Fry's colour
  printing method until 1889
- in the 1880's and 1890's many

firms sprang up making tins
and they developed a method
for printing on curved
surfaces — so shapes varied
enormously
- Peek Frean produced printed
  tins from 1880's
- people realised that attractive
  tins sold products, just as pot
  lids had sold their contents
- Hudson Scott of Carlisle
  earned a Royal Warrant from
  Queen Victoria
- at Christmas and public
  holidays, tins appeared of
  every description
- commemorative tins are also
  highly collectable, as are
  military tins
- the early 20th C. saw many
  novelty tins and between the
  wars these increased in
  quantity and outrageous
  forms
- after the Second World War
  tins became extremely boring

A Salmon and Gluckstein Ltd.
London Snake Charmer
cigarette tin, 1915. **£10-15**
DO

A Salmon and Gluckstein's
Dandy Fifth cigarette tin, 6½ in.
wide. **£8-12** *DO*

A Salmon and Gluckstein's
Gold Flake cigarette tin, 5½ in.
long, c. 1920's. **£8-14** *DO*

A Bond of Union smoking
mixture tin, 5 in. long, 1920's.
£12-18 *DO*

A Meadowland cigarette tin, 'The Co-operative Wholesale Society Ltd.', 4 in. long, 1920's. **£10-15** *DO*

A Clarke's Money Maker Flake tobacco tin, 6½ in. long, 1925, **£8-12** *DO*

A B. Morris and Sons Ltd. Gold Leaf Honey Dew Flake tobacco tin, 4 in. long, 1920. **£7-12** *DO*

A Walters 'Palm' fireside assortment tin, c. 1930's, 8 in. long, 4½ in. wide. **£10-18** *DO*

A Player's Medium Navy Cut tin, 3 in. long, 1930's. **£3-6** *DO*

A Murray's mellow smoking mixture tin, 4½ in. high, 1940's. **£4-8** *DO*

A Cadbury's commemorative chocolate tin, 5½ in. long. **£8-12** *DO*

A Parkinson's original Royal Doncaster butter-scotch tin, 1930's, 7½ in. long. **£15-22** *DO*

The 'Quorn' custard powder tin, 4 in. high, 1920's. **£12-18** *DO*

A set of seven American sweet tins, c. 1914, 3 in. long. **£30-40** for set of seven *DO*

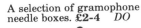

A Victorian tea tin, 4 in. lon[g] **£10-15** *DO*

A selection of gramophone needle boxes. **£2-4** *DO*

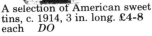

A Lyons Red Indian sweet tin, 11 in. high, 1930's. **£50-70** *DO*

A selection of American sweet tins, c. 1914, 3 in. long. **£4-8** each *DO*

A Lyons tea tin, with game in lid, 5½ in. high. **£25-30** *DO*

A tin change tray, Angel Verdeau and Company, 8½ in. long, c. 1915. **£13-18** *DO*

early Huntley & Palmer cuit tin, 7 in. long. **£10-18**

A carbolic tooth powder tin, 3 in. diam. **£3-6** *DO*

A decorative advertising mirror, framed in maple, 42 by 48 in. (107 by 122 cm.). **£120-150** *SB*

An exploding bottle of Mason's O.K. sauce, original label to exterior, the stopper removing with a 'bang' when primed, 6 in. high, c. 1910. **£90-120** *SB*

A Day and Martin's wax boot sample polish tin, 1½ in. diam., 1930. **£2-3** *DO*

honey box tin, 3 in. high. **£2-** *DO*

A Demon detective camera tin, manufactured by the American Camera Co., c. 1889. **£570-600** *P*

A selection of advertising pins and badges. **£3-7** *DO*

n 18th C. tobacconist's sign, the form of a blackamoor gure, 24 in. high. **£420-480**

A Victorian toy/display 'Swallow Bakery' barrow, 13 in. high. **£50-70** *PAM*

Wills' Gold Flake cigarettes ay, 12½ in. diam., c. 1920. **£7-** *AL*

A Schweppes lemon squash tray, metal (scratched), 12½ in. diam., c. 1920. **£7-9** *AL*

A 'Whitbread' tray, metal (scratched), 12½ in. diam., c. 1920. **£7-9** *AL*

A 'Dewars' White Label Whisky tray, metal (slight scratches), 12½ in. diam., c. 1920. **£7-9** *AL*

A Dr. Corry's Worm Powders show card, 10 in. high, c. 1915. **£10-16** *DO*

A Thermos Flask show card, 14½ in. high. **£20-26** *DO*

A Chivers' jam 1926 calendar, 5¼ in. high. **£4-5** *DO*

A Dee and Ess Cocoa Essence show card, late 1930's, 7 in. high. **£3-6** *DO*

A Komo Floor Polish show card 8 in. high. **£14-18** *DO*

A Mitchell's English Pea's show card, 11 in. high. **£10-14** *DO*

A Cunard Line shop card, 7 by 9 in. **£16-20** *DO*

A Joseph Bardou & Fils shop card, 12 by 8 in. **£16-20** *DO*

An Adkin's Nut Brown Tobacco show card, 15 in. high. **£16-20** *DO*

A State Express 333 show card 14 in. high. **£20-26** *DO*

A Red and White Cigarette show card, 9 in. **£5-8** *DO*

A smart Glove-Wear shop card, 10 by 12 in. **£10-14** *DO*

A Compass Cigarettes shop card, 15 by 10 in. £20-25 *DO*

Selo Films show cards, 11 in. high. £20-26 *DO*

A Banner Pyjamas show card, 11 in. high. £10-14 *DO*

'The People Popular Sunday Newspaper' metal advertising placard, 36 by 24 in. £35-40 *DO*

A Mansion Polish shop card, 7 by 9 in. £7-10 *DO*

A Tonette Boot Polish shop card, by Harry Rowntree, 10 by 7 in. £10-20 *DO*

'Lister Diesel Engines' metal advertising placard, 30 by 20 in. £60-75 *DO*

A 'Kayo Chocolate' metal advertising placard, 28 by 14 in. £20-26 *DO*

First World War Recruitment Posters, nine in all, various sizes. £140-190 *S*

nes (Willard Frederic) and ers. A series of 13 large torial posters with captions Charles Mather (four torn), 20 by 910 mm., Chicago ther & Co., c. 1929. £130-0 *S*

First World War Recruitment Posters, four letterpress posters issued by H.M.S.O., three lithographed pictorial posters issued by Parliamentary Recruiting Committee, No. 22, 121 and 122, a pictorial poster for War Bonds 'Our Aeroplanes: You Can Help' and another, various sizes. £150-200 *S*

Hassal (John) Veritas Mantels and Burners, 'Gosh! them Veritas beat all', 118 by 80. in. (300 by 200 cm.), late 19th C. £30-70 *S*

Wain (Louis) watercolour drawing for an advertisement for Capstan Cigarettes, signed, with three editorial comments below, framed and glazed, 254 by 383 mm. **£220-280**   *S*

A Fraser (Claud Lovat) Poster for 'The Beggars' Opera by Mr Gay, Lyric Theatre, Hammersmith, coloured lithograph, framed and glazed, 760 by 510 mm., c. 1920. **£110-150**   *S*

A 'Top Bronnen' metal advertising placard, 44 by 16 in. **£50-60**   *DO*

Paul Colin, 'Cie. Gle. Transatlantique', lithographic poster, 1,070 by 675 mm., signed in the block, framed and glazed, 1930's. **£370-430**   *SB*

A war savings campaign poster. **£6-10**   *DO*

Toulouse Lautrec, 'La Revue Blanche', 280 by 200 mm., pl. 82. **£50-70**   *SB*

Five fruit crate labels, the largest 11 in. (28 cm.) wide. **£30-50**   *S*

Charles Kiffer: 'Camille Vernades', chromolithograph poster, signed in black, Imp. Tolmer, linen-backed, 160 by 117 cm. **£260-325**   *P*

A James Haworth & Bro. sample book of commercial art, c. 1925-35. **£60-100**   *S*

Right

Will Bradley, 'Chap Book', 300 by 185 mm., pl. 136; and 'Women's Edition Buffalo Courier', 303 by 179 mm., pl. 60. **£30-50**   *SB*

Left

Eleven humorous music hall songs, all with pictorial covers incorporating portraits of the performers, 11 lithographed, by H. G. Banks, 7 coloured, complete with music, c. 1891-1904. **£75-120**   *S*

Eight music hall songs, all with pictorial covers, the music hall songs incorporating portraits of the performers, coloured lithographs, 5 by H. G. Banks, 4 by Stannard, complete with music, c. 1891-1904. **£100-150** *S*

Twelve humorous music hall songs, all with pictorial covers incorporating portraits of the performers, coloured lithographs, 10 by H. G. Banks, 2 by Stannard, complete with music. **£85-120** *S*

Twelve humorous music hall songs, all with pictorial covers incorporating portraits of the performers, coloured lithographs, 10 by H. G. Banks, one by Sidney Kent, complete with music, c. 1895-1900. **£95-120** *S*

'There's a man here who's very much struck by my Personality,' watercolours heightened with body colour, signed, framed and glazed, 9¾ by 7½ in. (24.5 by 19 cm). **£40-90** *S*

A collection of 230 European bookplates, including 63 etched examples and a number of woodcuts or wood-engravings, some printed in colour, by Bayros, Orlik, Schneider, 14 signed by the artist, the majority with identification on backs, c. 1895-1920. **£130-190** *S*

A pack of Victorian playing cards. **£18-20** *Gs*

An R. Caldecott picture book No. 2, 5½ in. high. **£7-9** *Gs*

A Kate Greenaway Almanack for 1885 (published by George Routledge & Sons). **£24-26** *Gs*

A Kate Greenaway Almanack for 1894 (published by George Routledge & Sons), 4 in. high. **£24-26** *Gs*

Make the most of Miller's

Every care has been taken to ensure the accuracy of descriptions and estimated valuations.

Where an attribution is made within inverted commas (e.g. 'Chippendale') or is followed by the word 'style' (e.g. early Georgian style) it is intended to convey that, in the opinion of the publishers, the piece concerned is a later — though probably still antique — reproduction of the style so designated.

Unless otherwise stated, any description which refers to 'a set' or 'a pair' includes a valuation for the entire set or the pair, even though the illustration may show only a single item.

Miller's Antiques Price Guide builds up year by year to form the most comprehensive photo-reference system available. The first three volumes contain over 20,000 completely different photographs.

A key-wound overture musical box, probably by Berens Blumberg & Co. (with 8 broken teeth), contained in walnut veneered case, Swiss, 19 in. wide, c. 1860. **£950-1,100**   *SB*

A Swiss musical box, the rosewood and boxwood case inlaid with floral marquetry, the single cylinder playing 8 airs, 24 in., 19th C. **£600-800** *CEd*

A Bremond piccolo cylinder musical box, No. 10988, contained in rosewood veneered case with ebony and mother of pearl banding, 31 in. wide, Swiss, c. 1880. **£1,200-1,400** *SB*

A Bremond interchangeable cylinder musical box on stand, No. 10404, in rosewood case, playing 6 airs on each cylinder, 36 by 30 by 22 in., Swiss, c. 1880. **£1,400-1,600** *SB*

A 19th C. gloria mandoline zither music box, now on a table stand, the 4 interchangeable cylinders (9 by 2 in. diam.) each play 6 tunes, no. 3371, the case 22 in. wide. **£900-1,200** *B*

A 'bells-in-sight' cylinder musical box, probably by B. H. Abrahams, the 32.2 cm. cylinder playing 12 airs, gamme number 32720, Swiss, 25½ in. wide, c. 1880's. **£660-760** *SBA*

A Swiss cylinder musical box with 8 in. cylinder, in a Louis XVI style painted work table having fitted interior, 25½ in. **£260-360** *SBe*

A Nicole Freres mandoline zither musical box, No. 46514, the 46 cm. cylinder playing 12 airs including Rossini, Brahms, Weber and Bach, 87 cm., Swiss, c. 1885. **£1,300-1,600**   *SB*

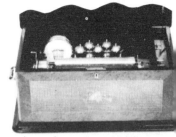

An orchestral musical box, playing 8 airs accompanied by 19-key organ, 7 engraved bells, drum and castanet, 28 in. wide, the cylinder 14 in. **£2,200-2,600** *CSK*

An interchangeable cylinder musical box, each of the three 28 cm. cylinders playing 8 airs, on a stand with cylinder storage drawer, Swiss, late 19th C., 37 in. (94 cm.) wide. **£1,200-1,500** *SB*

An interchangeable cylinder musical box, by Nicole Freres, No. 44475, with 12 cylinders playing 6 airs each, in rosewood veneered case on table with two cylinder drawers, 38 in. wide, the cylinders 13 in. **£2,900-3,300** *CSK*

Clariona paper-roll organette, with 14-note reed mechanism, together with four paper rolls, American, c. 1890, 12 in. (30.5 cm.) wide. **£200-220**   *SB*

A small barrel organ, the 12-note movement with wooden pipes and pinned wooden barrel, English, early 19th C., 12 in. (30.5 cm.) wide. **£330-380**   *SB*

A Peerless pneumatic organ paper-roll organette, with 20-note mechanism, with 6 paper rolls, late 19th C., 41 cm. wide. **£200-250**   *SB*

A Herophone organette, with square cardboard 'discs' and revolving keyframe and pressure bar, 18½ in. square, with eight 'discs'. **£550-650**   *CSK*

A Le Brestois spring-wound mandoline barrel piano, with 86 cm. pinned wooden barrel, the sides with handle, tune indicator and piano/mandoline control, French, early 20th C., 58 by 43 by 26 in. **£1,700-1,900**   *SB*

A 41-key street barrel piano, by the Dekleist Musical Instrument Mfg. Co., North Tonawanda, N.Y., U.S.A., playing eight airs — with spare barrel, 42 in. wide. **£4,000-4,500**   *CSK*

A late 19th C. German polyphon, with 21 discs, 32 in. **£3,000-3,300**   *WW*

A paper-roll mechanical zither, 19 in. (48 cm.) wide, together with 6 paper rolls, German, late 19th C. **£250-300**   *SB*

A 25¼-inch upright coin-in-slot Symphonium disc musical box, with duplex combs, stand with disc storage compartment, 85 in. high, and 13 discs. **£3,000-3,300**   *CSK*

A coin-slot gramophone, with 7 in. turntable, top-wind motor, needle bowl, coin-slot and (defective) mechanism, 26 in. wide, with Gramophone Co. and Angel transfers, 1899 (incomplete). **£780-880**   *CSK*

A prototype H.M.V. Lumiere pleated-diaphragm gramophone and radio, the 14 in. diaphragm mounted on double-joined arm, for use at an angle of 45 degrees, 16½ in. wide, c. 1924. **£700-800**   *CSK*

An H.M.V. Model No. 1 gramophone (1928) auto change, playing up to 20 records, with remote control consul, 41½ in. wide. **£400-450**   *YHA*

A Chippendale Console Edison Diamond Disc phonograph, official laboratory model, type CC32, 40½ in. wide, c. 1925, and 25 Edison discs. **£380-450**   *CSK*

A London Console Edison Diamond disc phonograph, type LC38, with Edison soundbox and arm for playing lateral records and mute in horn, 35 in. wide, c. 1925, and discs. **£250-300**   *CSK*

A Pathephone No. 44 enclosed-horn table machine, with Pathe Concert reproducer, 19 in. wide. **£320-360**   *CSK*

A Klingsor table grand gramophone, with Klingsor soundbox and internal horn enclosed by tuned strings and doors, 16 in. wide. **£85-120**   *CSK*

A Pathe Concert U horn talking machine, in cabinet with Pathe Concert reproducer, 36⅓ in. high. **£1,000-1,300**   *CSK*

A Nirona tinplate toy gramophone, with square green case and Nirona sound reflector, the case 7 in. square. **£60-110**   *CSK*

A Klingsor gramophone, with Klingsor soundbox, internal horn enclosed by strings, with bisque porcelain figure of a couple dancing, 38½ in. high **£1,400-1,600**   *CSK*

A Parlophon tin-plate gramophone, with 10 in. turntable, Parlophon Reform soundbox and Parlophon tone-arm, the horn 10¾ in. wide. **£220-280**   *CSK*

A basketwork gramophone, with Paillard Maestoso soundbox and small internal horn, 17 in. wide. **£200-260**   *CSK*

An Induphon 138 child's tinplate toy gramophone, 9½ in. diam. **£65-110**   *CSK*

An experimental H.M.V. Lumiere pleated diaphragm gramophone, the record played from underneath, 22½ in. wide, the diaphragm 12 in. diam., c. 1920. **£500-600**   *CSK*

An 11⅞ in. Symphonion disc musical box, No. 267094, the centre-drive movement with sublime harmonie comb arrangement, 18 in. wide, with 25 metal discs, German, c. 1900. **£350-400**   *SB*

A Style No. 2 gramophone mechanism (lacks turntable). **£300-350**   *CSK*

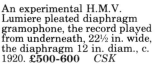

A Radior talking machine, with Diamond Hill-and-dale reproducer, 8 in. turntable, 15¼ in. wide. **£160-220**   *CSK*

A machine for demonstrating the principles of sound recording and reproduction, 6¾ in. wide, made by Augustus Stroh and used by W. H. Preece in 1878. **£2,500-2,700**   *CSK*

A rare tinfoil phonograph, weight-driven motor with centrifugal air-brake governor (mouthpiece damaged), 63 in. high, c. 1878, marked Edison's Phonograph, manufactured by The London Stereoscopic Company. **£8,500-9,500** *CSK*

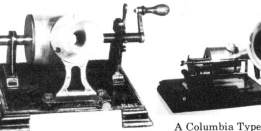

A cast-iron tinfoil phonograph, embossed Phonographe Edison B.S.G.D.G.E. Hardy a Paris, 142, 8¼ in. wide, the mandrel 2 by 5½ in. diam., 1878. **£2,300-2,500**   *CSK*

A tin-foil phonograph, with integral feed-screw on mandrel shaft, quick-release catch and turned boxwood mouthpiece, 8½ in. wide, the mandrel 2¾ by 2¾ in. diam., c. 1880. **£2,500-2,800**   *CSK*

A Columbia Type AB graphophone, with aluminium floating reproducer, standard and slip-on grand mandrels and aluminium witch's hat horn. **£900-1,100**   *CSK*

A Columbia AH disc graphophone, with 10 in. turntable, the conical horn with brass bell (carrier arm modern), American, c. 1904. **£330-400** *SB*

An Edison spring motor phonograph (lacks horn and lid), c. 1898. **£550-650**   *CSK*

A Home Grand graphophone, model HG No. S497, with six-spring motor, 5 in. mandrel and reproducer (lacks winder and horn, trunnion damaged). **£430-500**   *CSK*

An open-works phonograph of Pathe/Lioret type. **£370-450** *CSK*

A Columbia Type B graphophone, No. 411221, with aluminium floating reproducer. **£200-250** *CSK*

A Paillard Echophone phonograph, with floating reproducer, in carton and with modern aluminium horn, in 'reversible' walnut case. **£230-290** *CSK*

A Pathe Coquet phonograph, with key-wound two-minute mechanism, floating reproducer and spun aluminium horn, French, c. 1904. **£120-180** *SB*

A triple horn gramophone, with Goldring Special soundbox, the centre horn 15¾ in. diam., the two outer horns 9¾ in. diam., with plaque of the American Manufacturing Co. (of Hamburg). **£1,100-1,300** *CSK*

A rare Gramophone Company Auxetophone, compressed air gramophone with Auxetophone soundbox, gooseneck tone-arm with air-tube, air reservoir and triple-spring motor, 31 in. wide c. 1908 (lacks compressor). **£2,300-2,500** *CSK*

A Stollwerck chocolate disc phonograph, with Junghans key-wound motor, with one wax record, 3 3/16 in. diam., c. 1902 (lacks stylus). **£580-680** *CSK*

A style No. 6 gramophone, by the Gramophone & Typewriter Ltd., Maiden Lane, with 14 in. brass horn. **£660-800** *CSK*

An Edison home phonograph, model A, No. H54061, now with combination pulley and Diamond B reproducer (horn exterior repainted), with folding crane, c. 1903, modified, c. 1913. **£400-460** *CSK*

An Edison Triumph phonograph, model B No. 59056, now with combination pulley, model 0 combination reproducer, oak Music Master horn and crane, c. 1907, modified c. 1911. **£770-870** *CSK*

An Edison Standard phonograph, model 'B' No. 631526, now with two and four-minute gearing, model 'H' four-minute reproducer and 19 in. horn. **£280-340** *CSK*

A model 'B' Pathephone, with 10 in. turntable, nickel-plated reproducer and telescopic iron travelling arm, the base 11 in square, c. 1907 (diaphragm replaced). **£280-330** *CSK*

n H.M.V. New Melba
amophone, with mahogany
orn and triple-spring motor in
ahogany case (soundbox
placed, tone-arm modified).
380-440 *CSK*

A Lindstrom horn gramophone,
with Favrola soundbox, 18 in.
diam., with trade plaque of P.
Van Leeuwen & Zoon,
Amsterdam, c. 1908. **£360-
430** *CSK*

A mahogany horn
gramophone, patent number
25410-08, tapered tone arm and
double-spring motor, the horn
21½ in. diam., c. 1912. **£280-
400** *CSK*

n E.M.G. Mark XA
ramophone, with 12 in.
urntable, electric motor, and
apier mache horn (lacks
oundbox), English, c. 1932, 29
1. (73.5 cm.) diam. **£220-280**
B

A Peter Pan portable
gramophone, pocket model,
with Saturn (originally Peter
Pan) soundbox, c. 1926. **£120-
180** *CSK*

A Concert Automatique
Francais coin-slot talking
machine, of Pathe type with
Pathe Concert soundbox, 84 in.
high. **£1,000-1,200** *CSK*

A Symphonion horn
gramophone, in nickel-plated
case with Symphonion
soundbox, 9 in. diam., the horn
13 in. **£200-250** *CSK*

An E.M.G. Mark XB oversize
gramophone, with E.M.G. four-
spring soundbox, spring motor
and papier-mache horn, 33½ in.
diam., c. 1936 (horn cracked).
£660-760 *CSK*

A Continental singing bird box,
the bird with brightly coloured
plumage beneath an oval
hinged lid, 25½ in. **£500-620**
SBe

A Kalliope musical Christmas
tree stand, the movement with
centre drive, 9¼ in. diam. discs
playing on single comb and 6
bells, with 11 metal discs,
German, c. 1900, 23 in. (59 cm.)
wide. **£400-470** *SB*

APPENDIX

Mandoline Musical Box
Ranks amongst the rarer boxes.
The cylinder is pinned so that
the teeth are struck in quick
succession thus producing the
tremolo sound of a mandolin.

Nicole Frères
Important 19th C. Swiss
musical box manufacturer. One
of the best makers of musical
boxes, the products therefore
being amongst the more
expensive boxes today.

Overture Musical Box
A box playing a selection of

operatic overtures, the
reproduction being of
particularly high quality since it
has a combination of a large
diameter cylinder and fine teeth.
Highly prized amongst
collectors.

**Phonograph or
Graphophone**
Invented by Thomas Edison in
1876, it was a machine which
recorded sounds on to a tinfoil
cylinder and could also be used
to play back the recorded
material.

Symphonium and Polyphon
Musical boxes which play tunes
from perforated metal discs. The
disc musical box was first
manufactured by Ellis Parr and
Paul Lochmann in Leipzig, this
was the Symphonium. Five
years later, in 1890, two
employees of the Symphonium
factory started to produce the
Polyphon. Coin operated boxes
are generally more desirable
than hand operated ones.

An Amplion Concert Dragon Horn, loud speaker, type AR.23, all oak horn, 20 in. high, 14 in. diam., 1927. **£55-60** *YHA*

An S. G. Brown cow-horn speaker, type H3, mid 1920's, horn 9 in. diam. **£10-15** *YHA*

An Amplion 'Dragonfly' horn speaker, 1920's, 9 in. high. **£40-45** *YHA*

A small Reva phone horn speaker, horn 7 in. diam. 1920's. **£10-15** *YHA*

An Amplion speaker, late 1920's, 13 in. high. **£15-20** *YHA*

A lacquered papier mache 'Confucious' speaker by Andia, late 1920's, 13 in. high. **£35-40** *YHA*

A moving coil speaker, late 1920's, 12 in. diam. **£10-1** *YHA*

A Brown Junior extension speaker, 9 in. high, late 1920's/30's. **£10-15** *YHA*

A Gecophone early cone speaker type BC 1770, 1925, 1 in. wide. **£20-25** *YHA*

RADIOS

- in 1894 Branly and Lodge transmitted signals by Hertzian waves and the 'wireless' was born
- morse and speech transmitters were developed during the First World War
- commercial broadcasting began in the U.S.A. in 1920 and Britain in 1922
- the first mains radio set (the Radiola 17) was produced in America in 1925
- this is a fascinating field for the collector and has increased in popularity over the past few years. Sets should be in full working order. Novelty shapes are highly collectable as are any of the very early experimental sets

An Ediswan crystal set, Model No. 1924, P.O. registration No. 4385, 5 in. wide. **£25-30** *YHA*

A B.T.H. 'Bijou' wireless crystal receiver, (was supplied by Walter Simpson, Aberdeen), B.B.C. approved, 861, 2nd edition 1923, case 7 in. high. **£30-35** *YHA*

Auckland's crystal set,
B.C. approved P.O. Type No.
1, No. 80 1923/24, 5½ in. tall.
0-35   *YHA*

A Revophone II, 2V wireless set,
B.B.C. registration no. 2090,
case 13 by 11 in., mid 1920's.
£70-80   *YHA*

A W. H. Bailey crystal set, in
oak case, at 88 Oxford St.,
London, 1925, 8 in. wide. **£30-
35**   *YHA*

Brownie model No 2 crystal
, with moulded ebonite body,
25, 6 in. wide. **£30-35**   *YHA*

A Walters crystal set, with
single valve amplifier, 1922-24.
£65-75   *YHA*

A Gecophone crystal set, 6 by 8
in., early 1920's. **£20-25**   *YHA*

Gecophone Crystal set, Model
. BC1001, B.B.C. registration
. 102, 9 in. wide, early 1920's.
0-35   *YHA*

A Marconiphone 'Baby' crystal
set, B.B.C. registration No.
4215, 5½ in. wide, 1922. **£25-
30**   *YHA*

A Gecophone radio, B.B.C.
registration No. 2000, 1922, 17
in. high. **£150-180**   *YHA*

Marconiphone V2A, long
ange model, radio B.B.C.
gistration No. 0175, 1922, 12
. wide. **£250-300**   *YHA*

A Marconi bakelite wireless,
1920's to 1930's, 10 in. wide.
£30-40   *LEX*

A Marconi VI radio, 1923/24,
(single valve receiver), 7 in.
high. **£75-80**   *YHA*

A Marconi Model No.47 radio,
15 in. wide, c. 1928. **£85-100**
YHA

A selection of three radios of
early 1930's: battery Portadyne.
£10-12. A Cossor A.C. mains
'Melody Maker' model 40. **£15-
18.** An Alba mains operated
radio. **£10-12**   *YHA*

A Marconi Type 42 AC radio
1932, 17 in. tall. **£60-65**   *YH*

A Belmont radio (U.S.A.), 10 in.
wide, c 1932. **£20-25**   *YHA*

An Ekco AC 85 radio, 1930's,
in. wide. **£30-35**   *YHA*

A very rare CAV Baby Grand
battery radio, late 1920's, 29 in.
wide, 31 in. high, 22 in. deep.
£300-350   *YHA*

A Selector Cabinet Portable
radio, on swivel base, late
1920's with aerial and charging
dial in back, 17 in. high. **£35-
40**   *YHA*

An Ekco type AD.75 radio, 1
in. high. **£35-40**   *YHA*

An Ekco 312, 1930 AC 2V radio,
18 in wide. **£75-80**   *YHA*

An Osram Music Magnet 4, 4V
receiver, 1930, 18 in. wide. **£50-
60**   *YHA*

A 1933 Philips Model 834 radio,
in Philite case, 18 in. high. **£40-
45**   *YHA*

A Pye 4-valve portable radio, in
mahogany case, 17 in. high,
early 1930's. **£20-25**   *YHA*

A Pye 4-valve portable radio, in mahogany case, 17 in. high, early 1930's. **£20-25** *YHA*

A Bush type DAC 90 radio, 1939, 12 in. wide. **£15-20** *YHA*

An Electone radio time clock, (to switch radio on in the morning), 5 in. high, late 1920's-early 1930's. **£15-20** *YHA*

A Bowyer Lowe microphone, early 1920's, 10 in. high. **£15-20** *YHA*

A 1931 Philips Model 930.A radio, 18 in. high. **£40-45** *YHA*

A civilian wartime radio A.C. receiver, 1944, 14 in high. **£10-15** *YHA*

A W.W.II German Army field teleprinter. **£120-160** *SKC*

A morse code tapper, 1910-20. **£15-20** *YHA*

A morse code buzzer, 1910-20. **£20-25** *YHA*

A 1936 Philco 'Peoples Set' Model 444, 15 in. high. **£65-70** *YHA*

An Ever Ready Sky Casket radio, battery operated, 9 in. wide, 1950's. **£10-15** *YHA*

An 'Electromicro' microphone, with original box, late 1920's — early 1930's. **£10-12** *YHA*

An early Exide accumulator, 1920's-30's. **£4-6** *YHA*

A ship's magnetic detector, by Marconi's Wireless Telegraph Co Ltd., No. 93647, 18½ in. wide. **£700-1,000**   *CSK*

Two very early Marconi valves, V24's, 1916. **£10-15** each *YHA*

A selection of early radio valves, 1920's. **20-30p.** each *YHA*

An early spark coil, for early wireless transmitting experiments, 10 in. wide, early 1900's. **£25-30**   *YHA*

An Ami Continental 45-r.p.m. juke box, 64 in. (162 cm.) high, American, c. 1961. **£150-200** *SB*

A copy of the Radio Times, Vol. 1 No. 1, September 28th 1923. **£15-20**   *YHA*

Two books of cigarette cards of Radio Celebrities of the 1920's and 1930's. **£5-10** each   *YHA*

Right

A National cash register No. 741327, with decoratively cast chromed casting, 33 keys and paper receipt roll holder and drawer, 22 in. wide. **£80-120** *SBA*

A Rockola Hi-Fi 200 juke box, about 60 by 24 by 8 in. (152.5 by 81 by 20 cm.). **£50-70**   *SB*

A National cash register No. 271005, Last Patent Oct. 27th '96, with cast brass casing, 27 keys, paper roll receipt holder and drawer, 18 in. wide. **£100-140**   *SBA*

An Ami Model A juke box, 69 in. (175 cm.) high, American, c. 1947. **£800-1,000**   *SB*

A Bal-Ami 45-r.p.m. juke box, 52½ in. (133 cm.) high, c. 1965. **£90-110**   *SB*

n unusual table telephone, the ase with number index and elector, with nickel-plated bell nd support, 10 in. wide, robably French, c. 1910. **£160-10** *SB*

A decorative table telephone, marked G. Bailleux Ste Indlle des Telephones, 17 in. high, French, c. 1892. **£330-390** *SB*

A table telephone, marked Systeme Ader Socte Indlle des Telephones, mahogany and bakelite, 12 in. high, French, c. 1910. **£400-490** *SB*

A table telephone, marked 'Systeme Ader Ste Indlle des Telephones, G. Bailleux', with two ear-pieces and central mouthpiece, the bakelite base cracked, 16 in. high, French, c. 1892. **£300-370** *SB*

table telephone, marked Socte ndlle des Telephones, the mahogany base mounted on brass claw feet, with hand set and additional ear-piece, 16 in. high, French, c. 1910. **£280-350** *SB*

A table telephone, marked Ste Fse des Telephones Syst Berliner, with mouthpiece at the front and hook to one side supporting hand set, 13 in. high, French, c. 1904. **£380-450** *SB*

A mahogany table telephone, marked Maison Rouselle et Tournaire, two ear-pieces and central mouthpiece, 15 in. high, French, c. 1907. **£240-300** *SB*

A teak table telephone, marked Ch. Milde Fils & Cie, 13 in. high, French, c. 1892. **£450-580** *SB*

An early 20th C. Swedish telephone by Erickson. **£200-250** *FA*

A wall telephone, rewired, c. 1920. **£80-90** *FA*

TELEPHONES

Although Alexander Graham Bell is generally acknowledged as the inventor of the telephone, the actual story is somewhat more confused. Philip Reis developed his Fernsprecher in 1861. This, however, had many drawbacks, one of the major being that vowels could not be transmitted. Also in contention were Dolbear, Varley, Thomson, Edison and Gray. In fact Bell beat Elisha Gray to the patent office by a matter of hours. Between 1876 and the early 1880's there were many new designs. Bell and Edison both produced many commercial telephones in the '80's and '90's, usually in hardwood. The Swede Erickson developed the cradle telephone in the early 1890's. These were produced in large quantities and are often highly decorated. The patent plates add to the value and decorative issues tend to be more valuable than the standard ones.

An Edmondson's calculating machine, with brass centre display for up to 20 digits, in fitted mahogany case, English, late 19th C. **£490-600** *SB*

An early Daw and Tait typewriter, No. 77, contained in original mahogany carrying case, 8½ in. wide, English, c. 1886. **£3,300-3,600** *SB*

An Odell typewriter, bearing 'Perry & Co. Ltd.' plaque, in original oak carrying case, with glass bottle and accessories, 10¼ in wide, American, c. 1890. **£660-720** *SB*

An early Sholes and Clidden typewriter, manufactured by E. Remington & Sons, 15 in. (38 cm.) wide, American, c. 1878. Also a framed document, extolling the virtues of the Remington typewriter and a book of cuttings relating to the new era of the writing machine, including a letter addressed to Queen Victoria inviting her to inspect the machine. **£1,800-2,200** *SB*

A Sun typewriter, with linear index mechanism, stamped 1168, 12 in. long. **£950-1,100** *CSK*

A rare European sewing machine, by the Coventry Machinists Company. **£400-450** *CSK*

A Britannia lock-stitch sewing machine, of Wheeler and Wilson type, the stitch plate stamped 'The Britannia M'f'g. Company Colchester, England, dated 1st June 1867, No. 5997. **£550-650** *CSK*

An 18th C. oak and mahogany Braid loom, of 'torture bed' design, 38 cm. wide. **£55-70** *P*

A 19th C. wooden clamp, c. 1820-30. **£35-37** *SS*

An 18th C. mahogany Braid loom, of 'torture bed' design with a ratcheted wheel and mounted with spindles to one end, 30 cm. wide. **£50-70** *P*

(l) An early 19th C. ivory clamp. **£33-35** *SS*

(m) An 18th C. ivory clamp. **£25-27** *SS*

(r) An early 19th C. ivory clamp. **£22-25** *SS*

(l) An Italian 18th C. carved ivory needle case. **£20-25** *SS*

(m) An amethyst glass needle case, c. 1835. **£34-38** *SS*

(r) A coquilla needle case, c. 1835. **£60-65** *SS*

A tortoiseshell etui, inlaid with mother of pearl with gold-mounted instruments, c. 1840, 4 in. high. **£425-485** *EAN*

A 16th C. tooled leather etui in the form of a fish on a circular base, 12½ in. **£390-450** *Bon*

Right

(l) A painted treen fern pin cushion, c. 1860. **£10-12** *SS*

(m) A painted treen pin cushion, c. 1840. **£6-8** *SS*

(r) A lithographic pin cushion 'of Clevedon' (with mirror on back), c. 1860. **£13-15** *SS*

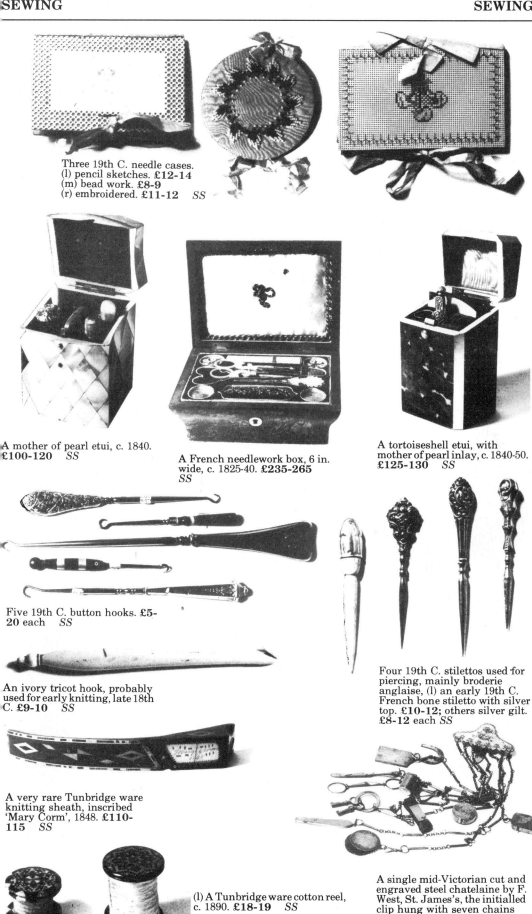

Three 19th C. needle cases.
(l) pencil sketches. **£12-14**
(m) bead work. **£8-9**
(r) embroidered. **£11-12**   *SS*

A mother of pearl etui, c. 1840.
£100-120   *SS*

A French needlework box, 6 in.
wide, c. 1825-40. **£235-265**
SS

A tortoiseshell etui, with
mother of pearl inlay, c. 1840-50.
£125-130   *SS*

Five 19th C. button hooks. **£5-
20** each   *SS*

An ivory tricot hook, probably
used for early knitting, late 18th
C. **£9-10**   *SS*

Four 19th C. stilettos used for
piercing, mainly broderie
anglaise, (l) an early 19th C.
French bone stiletto with silver
top. **£10-12**; others silver gilt.
£8-12 each *SS*

A very rare Tunbridge ware
knitting sheath, inscribed
'Mary Corm', 1848. **£110-
115**   *SS*

(l) A Tunbridge ware cotton reel,
c. 1890. **£18-19**   *SS*
(r) A Tunbridge ware cotton
reel, c. 1890. **£18-19**   *SS*

A single mid-Victorian cut and
engraved steel chatelaine by F.
West, St. James's, the initialled
clip hung with seven chains
each with numerous household
attachments. **£90-120**   *Bon*

A Tunbridge ware pin cushion, tape and waxer, 2 in. high, c. 1880. **£28-30** *SS*

Four 19th C. coquilla sewing tapes (vegetable ivory). £14-17 *SS*

A selection of thimbles:
1. An early 20th C. charm from child's bracelet. **£2-4** *SS*
2. A child's thimble, 19th C., 1870. **£7-9** *SS*
3. Advertising 'Sparva'. **£5-8** *SS*
4. A rare 19th C. coquilla thimble, c. 1830. **£48-53** *SS*
5. A 19th C. thimble with thread cutter. **£19-20** *SS*
6. A Georgian horn thimble, c. 1820. **£70-80** *SS*

A Georgian burr-yew oval 2-division tea caddy, with crossbanded top having marquetry decoration. **£180-260** *BW*

A George II burr-yew tea caddy, inlaid with silver strapwork lines, with three replacement plated caddies, 9 in. (23 cm.) wide. **£350-420** *SKC*

An unusual Adam-design rolled paper work caddy, c. 1800, 5 in. wide. **£220-260** *AD*

A George II laburnum-wood tea caddy, replacement interior with two lidded caddies flanking a glass mixing bowl, 10 in. (25 cm.) wide. **£100-130** *SKC*

A pair of George III satinwood tea-caddies, crossbanded and inlaid, 4¾ in. wide. **£450-550** *C*

A Georgian satinwood tea caddy, crossbanded in tulipwood with 2 marquetry oval panels. **£120-200** *BW*

A satinwood round top tea caddy with amboyna panels, c. 1800, 8 in. wide. **£140-150** *AD*

A rare oval inlaid tea caddy, c. 1790, 5½ in. wide. **£190-210** *AD*

A mahogany Sheraton caddy. **£130-150** *AD*

A rare Regency rosewood tea caddy, with all original interior, c. 1805, 12 in. long. **£400-450** *EAN*

A 19th C. hexagonal rolled paper tea caddy. **£220-280** BW

A birdseye maple two division caddy with glass liner, c. 1810, 12 in. wide. **£140-165** AD

An early 19th C. inlaid tea caddy, 7½ in. **£200-225**

A 19th C. mahogany tea caddy, 9 in. wide. **£40-50** SV

A 19th C. brass-bound tea caddy, with two lidded compartments, with brass fittings, 9 in. wide. **£100-115** SV

A Sheraton caddy of excellent quality, c. 1800, 13½ in. wide by 6¼ in. deep. **£85-95** LL

A Regency prisoner of war caddy, c. 1815, 7¼ in. wide. **£80-90** AD

A mahogany tea caddy, c. 1820, 12 in. wide. **£125-140** LAC

A mahogany square caddy, c. 1820, 4½ in. wide. **£90-100** AD

A George III satinwood cutlery-box, enclosing a velvet-lined interior, 7½ in. (19 cm.) wide. **£300-350** C

A pair of George III mahogany knife boxes, with satinwood crossbanding, 9 in. (23 cm.) wide, c. 1790. **£570-630** SKC

An 18th C. shagreen knife box, fitted with twenty-four steel-bladed knives, having stained ivory handles, 34 cm. high. **£300-400** P

A small mahogany knife box, with original interior, c. 1790, 13 in. high by 8½ in. wide. **£195-215** ST

A mahogany knife box, c. 1780, 17 in. long. £185-200 *EAN*

A Regency rosewood and brass inlaid decanter box, containing six glass decanters (the decanters replaced), 30 cm. wide. £350-400 *Bon*

A George III mahogany knife box, now a decanter case with satinwood shell and star inlay, with 3 decanters and 7 glasses, 9 in. wide, c. 1800. £270-330 *SKC*

A continental mid-19th C. amboyna and ebonised tantalus, applied with 4 bois durci panels, the interior with giltmetal lift-out stand fitted with 4 decanters and 10 glasses. £360-420 *PK*

A late 19th C. oak 3-bottle spirit tantalus, the hinged lid opens to reveal fitted compartments and secret drawer, 14 in. wide. £260-360 *PW*

An unusual tantalus, including drawers for cigarettes and playing cards, c. 1905, 16 in. wide. £325-355 *ST*

A 19th C. walnut box with three glass scent bottles, brass lock plate and shield, 7 by 3 by 4½ in. £110-120 *SV*

Make the most of Miller's

Every care has been taken to ensure the accuracy of descriptions and estimated valuations.
Where an attribution is made within inverted commas (e.g. 'Chippendale') or is followed by the word 'style' (e.g. early Georgian style) it is intended to convey that, in the opinion of the publishers, the piece concerned is a later — though probably still antique — reproduction of the style so designated.
Unless otherwise stated, any description which refers to 'a set' or 'a pair' includes a valuation for the entire set or the pair, even though the illustration may show only a single item.

A maplewood decanter box, with lined interior, with three cut glass bottles, 17 in. high, c. 1860. £265-285 *EA*

A coromandel-wood box, decorated with ivory, brass and mahogany and with three scent bottles, 5½ in. wide, c. 1870. £60-70 *EA*

An Austrian travelling liquor set, with 6 Bohemian glass flasks; 4 saucers; a funnel; and two pairs of Vienna porcelain liquor bowls, shield mark in underglaze blue, two incised '820', one '817' and the last '823', box 24 cm. wide, c. 1825-30. £550-650 *SKC*

A Georgian mahogany cased gentleman's shaving and toiletry box, swivel jointed to reveal three sections and including most of the original contents, 9 in. long. £90-110 *Bon*

An inlaid rosewood box, with original fittings inside, rosewood lids decorated with Sheffield knobs and silver inlay, 11 in. wide, c. 1800. £175-195 *EA*

A fitted box in coromandel, with solid silver fittings, including silver manicure set, hallmarked 1675, 14 in. wide. £365-385 *EA*

A mid-19th C. gentleman's toilet box, with silvered fittings and hidden drawer, 12 in. wide. £215-235 *BTH*

A walnutwood-cased travelling toilet box, fitted with concealed drawers and cut-glass bottles and other items, mounted in silver plate, mid-19th C. £230-300 *EEW*

A Victorian rosewood vanity box, with brass stringing, the interior fitted with full set of 11 original cut glass bottles and jars with silver lids hallmarked 1841, also with manicure set with carved mother of pearl handles, 12 in. wide. £385-400 *EA*

A fitted travelling box in rosewood inlaid with brass, containing bottles, jars, etc., the lid with a mirror. £135-145 *EA*

A brass-bound hardwood travelling dressing case, fitted with 11 silver-mounted cut-glass bottles or boxes, maker's mark T.W. London, 1876, also a mirror, 2 secret drawers and various steel and mother of pearl items. £300-380 *SB*

An inlaid coromandel dressing box, filled with bottles and lift out trays, lid inlaid with brass, mother of pearl and gold, c. 1870. £125-145 *EA*

A rosewood toilette box, with 11 silver-topped containers, a teaspoon, thimble, corkscrew, button hook, pencil, scissors, spatula, penknife and belt hook, hallmarked London, 1856, silver 18 oz. £300-360 *SKC*

A mahogany apothecary's chest, with 12 compound bottles (6 missing), a pallet, a balance with weights, a mortar and pestle, a measuring flask and five small bottles, 11½ in. wide, English, c. 1825. **£300-400** *SB*

An Asprey & Son travelling dressing case, the brass-bound and monogrammed hardwood case fitted with 11 cut-glass bottles or boxes and a hand mirror, London, 1880/81, also with various silver-gilt-metal items, the case 34.4 cm. wide, the lock removed. **£750-900** *SB*

A mahogany apothecary's chest, the fitted interior with compound bottles, a measuring flask, brass hanging balance and glass mortar and pestle, 8½ in. wide, English, c. 1830. **£280-330** *SB*

A mahogany apothecary's chest, with 15 bottles (some original), a balance and weights, pestle and mortar, zinc drug canisters and steel spatula, English, early 19th C. **£400-480** *SBA*

A mahogany apothecary's chest, inscribed 'from Apothecaries Hall', containing 18 glass bottles, 2 zinc containers, glass mortar and pestle, a booklet 'List of Medicines' and other items, 12 in., English, c. 1850. **£460-580** *SB*

An early 19th C. medicine chest, with glass bottles, mortar and pestle and scales, 8½ in. high, c. 1820. **£330-360** *Gs*

A good 19th C. mahogany domestic medicine chest, fitted with 23 bottles, with powder and other drawers, scales and weights, a pestle and mortar, etc., 39 cm. high. **£440-540** *P*

A G. Rowney & Co. porcelain and enamel painting box, c. 1860-70, 10 in. wide. **£50-55** *Gs*

A 17th C. Italian adige chest, the interior fitted with boxes and compartments, 2 ft. 5 in. by 1 ft. 3 in. by 1 ft. 5 in. **£630-730** *WHL*

A mahogany apothecary's chest, containing 4 miniature bottles, glass mortar and pestle, 4 large bottles, 6 small bottles and 4 zinc compound containers, when closed 9½ in. wide, English, mid-19th C. **£400-500** *SB*

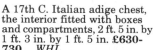

An unusual Victorian lacquered writing box, 11 in. **£104-114** *ST*

A Victorian miniature writing slope, 10 by 7 in. **£56-62**   *ST*

A Stanley architect's drawing instrument chest, containing compasses, dividers, ruling pens, wooden curves, ivory and wood rulers, paints, pallets, stencils and wooden triangles, English, c. 1875. **£450-550** *SB*

A small Victorian writing slope with ink well and ruler, 11 in. wide. **£45-55**   *ST*

A satinwood writing slope, c. 1800, 12 in. wide. **£240-260** *EAN*

A Victorian rosewood writing box, with leather writing inset and two ink bottles, 9½ in. deep by 14 in. wide by 5 in. high. **£50-70**   *PAM*

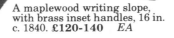

A maplewood writing slope, with brass inset handles, 16 in. c. 1840. **£120-140**   *EA*

An early Victorian stationery box, c. 1840. **£135-155**   *ST*

A mahogany military campaign box, brass bound corners with side handles, wooden fitted interior with stationery tray, 18 in. long, c. 1890. **£115-130**   *EA*

An octagonal Tunbridge workbox, c. 1800, 10 in. wide. **£175-195**   *AD*

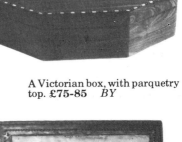

A Victorian box, with parquetry top. **£75-85**   *BY*

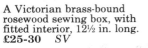

A Victorian brass-bound rosewood sewing box, with fitted interior, 12½ in. long. **£25-30**   *SV*

An English Regency ebonised jewel casket, with 4 drawers and a secret drawer, decorated all round. **£225-260**   *BY*

A Napoleonic prisoner of war straw work box, c. 1815, 12½ in. wide. **£100-120**   *Gs*

A late Victorian jewel box with
silver mounts, 1898, 10 in. wide.
£64-70   ST

A boulle casket, inlaid with
scrolling leaves and applied
with gilt-bronze leaf mounts, 4¾
by 12½ in., c. 1870. **£150-220
SB**

A late 19th C. jewel casket,
inlaid with ivory, ebony and
cherrywood, bordered with
mother of pearl, 13½ in. wide.
£50-60   EA

An oak bible box, with lock and
lined with Victorian (1867)
newspaper, late 17th C., 25 in.
wide. **£115-145   OB**

A William and Mary oyster
shell bible box, veneered in olive
wood, c. 1685, 19 in. wide. **£575-
675   BTH**

A wooden box with sliding top
and a coloured transfer print of
Brighton Pavilion, c. 1830, 10
in. wide. **£100-110   AD**

An early 18th C. oak box, with
original brass lock, hasp and
hinges, 13½ in. wide, c. 1710.
£95-105   BTH

An elm dome-top box, with lock,
18th C., 17 in. wide. **£44-64
OB**

A mid-19th C. domed
coromandel box, on gothic
lines, 9½ in. wide. **£65-75   EA**

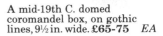

A 19th C. walnut coin cabinet,
designed after the Roman
temple of Antoninus and
Faustina, 69 cm. high, 60 cm.
wide. **£1,200-1,500   P**

A fine quality 19th C. walnut
box, overlaid with brass and
lined with original satin, four
corner pockets, 11 in. wide. **£55-
65   EA**

A Dutch colonial hardwood and
marquetry table cabinet, with
two small and one long drawer,
45 cm. wide. **£240-290   Bon**

Three 19th C. Tunbridge boxes,
2½, 3, 7 in. wide. **£20-50 each
MA**

An English oak pipe tray, c.
1760, 24½ in. long. **£230-250
A.E.F.**

A Spanish embossed leather
deed box, with wrought-iron
lock-plate, 17th C., 21 in. wide.
£450-620   C

An 18th C. English tinder box,
13 in. high. £100-125   A.E.F.

A late 17th C. church offertory
box, with iron hinge and lock,
12 in. £170-210   Bon

An 18th C. oak candle box, 13
in. high. £75-85   A.E.F.

An early 19th C. salt box, 13 in.
high. £55-60   Cl.A

A Scottish salt box, c. 1840,
combination oak, birch,
mahogany, 12 in. high. £82-
90   McH

A salt box, c. 1820, 11½ in. high.
£160-180   EAN

An 18th C. elm and pear wood
candlebox, 12 in. long, c. 1750.
£90-100   McH

A carved oak candlebox, 18 in.
high. £95-105   TJ

An 18th C. candlebox, 16 in.
high. £100-125   TJ

BOXES AND TREEN APPENDIX

Bilboquet
A game which consists of a cup on
a stem handle and a ball
connected by string, the object
being to catch the ball in the cup.

Campaign Furniture
Furniture made for use in the
Peninsular and Crimean Wars e.g.
Campaign box, campaign chest.

Cat
A device used for warming plates
or standing workboxes on. It was
made up of two inverted tripods set
into a central sphere so that it
would remain stable on uneven
hearthstones. So called because
however dropped to the ground, it
always lands on its feet.

Desk Sander
A small container with a pierced
top originally used to sprinkle
pumice on greasy vellum to make
it suitable for writing on. Later on
it was found that the pumice was
also ideal for drying wet ink.

Engine Turning
Intricate decoration engraved by a
lathe with an eccentric motion.

Lamhog or Piggin
Common drinking jugs of Irish
Taverns in mediaeval times. They
tend to be circular downward
tapering vessels which flare out at
the base, varying in size from ¾
pint to 3 pint capacity.

Lignum Vitae
A strong brown and greenish

black wood from the West Indies.
Used for fine wood-wares, such as
loving cups, from the 17th C.

Quaich
A Scottish drinking bowl which
was originally made of staved
wood with two plain handles, one
on either side. The name is derived
from the Gaelic word *cruach*
meaning a cup.

Straw Splitter
First used from 1800 onwards,
they are nearly all made from
mahogany and are pierced with a
number of circular windows into
which are inserted various wheels
with spoke blades, these are then
used to split straw into anything
from four to sixteen splints.

TREEN APPENDIX (*cont.*)

Tantalus
A mid 19th C. name for a case in which decanters are visible but locked up. The name was taken from Tantalus the son of Zeus who was punished for wronging the Gods by having to stand in water which ebbed away when he attempted to drink and with grapes above him which withdrew whenever he reached for them.

Trencher
Earliest style of plate. In Norman times meat was served on slices of bread or 'tranches', and the bread in turn was placed on flat trenchers. When eating habits changed and meat was no longer served on bread, a circular hollow was made in the trencher to contain the meat. In this way it is believed that the trencher

gradually evolved into the type of plate we know today. The most valuable are square trenchers with a hollow for salt.

Tunbridge Ware
Small souvenir wood-wares decorated with marquetry, parquetry and wood mosaics, produced in the Tunbridge Wells and Tonbridge area from 1660 onwards, although wood mosaics did not appear until 1827. The value and desirability of Tunbridge ware items is dependent on the intricacy and quality of decoration and condition — articles with small pieces of mosaic missing should not be purchased unless they are very rare as it is difficult to repair wood mosaic.

An English coconut cup, c. 1760, 6 in. high. **£200-225**   *A.E.F.*

A 17th C. engine turned cup, English. **£750-850**   *A.E.F.*

A very fine English 17th C. lignum vitae lobed cup with silver mounts, 5 in. diam., 4¼ in. high. **£1,500-1,750**   *A.E.F.*

A 17th C. lignum vitae loving cup, English, 9 in. high. **£680-750**   *A.E.F.*

A 17th C. cup and cover, English. **£1,000-1,250**   *A.E.F.*

A 17th C. Irish lamhog, 6 in. high. **£350-600**   *A.E.F.*

A pair of 19th C. wooden Continental brass bound beer tankards, 6 in. high. **£90-100** the pair   *MA*

A small 19th C. wooden Scandinavian beer tankard, 6½ in. high. **£50-60**   *MA*

An 18th C Scottish tankard, bound with patinated copper, 9 in. high. **£230-290**   *A.E.F.*

A pair of 18th C. Treen goblets, 6½ in. **£160-180**   *Cl.A*

A 19th C. Scandinavian beer tankard, with naive painted figures, 8½ in. high. **£35-40** *MA*

A standing mazer, a drinking bowl, used in monastic communities, c. 1600, 6 in. diam. **£1,350-1,500**   *A.E.F.*

A 17th C./18th C. Welsh food bowl. **£28-30**   *A.E.F.*

A 17th C. English lignum vitae wassail bowl, 10 in. **£750-850**   *A.E.F.*

A mediaeval English mazer, with silver mount, 4¼ in. diam., c. 1480. **£1,300-1,500**   *A.E.F.*

A mediaeval elm bowl, possibly for begging, to be hung from waist. **£100-125**   *A.E.F.*

An 18th C. lignum vitae pestle and mortar, 8 in. high. **£155-175**   *Cl.A*

A 19th C. Welsh food bowl, 7½ in. diam. **£35-45**   *A.E.F.*

An 18th C. Welsh porridge bowl and spoon, 5½ in. diam. **£100-125**   *A.E.F.*

An 18th C. English dairy bowl, 16 in. diam. **£95-110**   *A.E.F.* (Wood shrinks across grain. Objects tend to become oval with age.)

A Scottish quaich, c. 1790, 4½ in. across. **£200-225**   *A.E.F.*

A Scottish quaich, c. 1820, 4½ in. across. **£100-125**   *A.E.F.*

An 18th C. Scottish quaich, 4 in. wide. **£40-45**   *A.E.F.*

An 18th C. pair of English fruitwood salts, 3 in. **£65-75** pair   *A.E.F.*

A Scottish bicker (for drinking), with feathered work. **£50-55** *A.E.F.*

An early 17th C. treen table salt, 4¾ in. **£350-450**   *JH*

599

A coopered jug, 17 in. high.
£180-200   *TJ*

A wooden measure, 2 in. high.
£7-10   *LAC*

A set of three seed measures,
original polychrome finish,
impressed NR, impressed CH, c
1820. £95-105   *McH*

A rare 17th C. treen square
trencher, 8¼ in. square. £200-
250   *TJ*

An early 19th C. milk skimmer,
probably Welsh, 8 in. diam.
£30-35   *A.E.F.*

A ½ pint wooden measure,
carved from the solid, 5 in. high
£12-15   *LAC*

An 18th C. Treen eight-sided
coaster. £55-65   *Cl.A*

A 17th C. platter, 11 in. diam.
£85-95   *A.E.F.*

A 17th C./early 18th C. English
platter, 8½ in. diam. £70-75
A.E.F.

An 18th C. English oak coaster,
11¾ in. diam. £200-250
A.E.F.

A 17th C. oak trencher stand of
slender rectangular form,
raised on four short feet, 26 in.
long. £450-520 and four
17th/18th C. circular treen
platters, 9 in. diam. average.
£170-220   *Bon*
        Right
An old Shetland dish from the
Bateman collection, 10½ in.
wide. £55-65   *TJ*

A pair of late 18th C. mahogany
plate tilters, 7 in. £40-60   *Bon*

A mahogany cheese
slide/coaster, c. 1800, 17½ in.
wide. £150-175   *B.M*

An oak Stilton cheese coaster,
18 in. wide, c. 1780. £275-350
A.E.F.

A mahogany cheese coaster, c. 1800, 15 in. wide. **£125-150** *B.M*

An 18th C. walnut candlestick, c. 1780, 5 in. diam. **£65-75** *McH*

A fine pair of 18th C. yew wood candlesticks, 12 in. high, c. 1780. **£245-265** *McH*

A pair of 18th C. Treen candlesticks, 2 in. high. **£115-135** *Cl.A*

A mid-18th C. walnut adjustable candlestand, lead weighted underneath, some damage, restored foot, 10 in. high. **£65-80** *JC*

An English 18th C. adjustable treen candlestick, 8 in. high. **£350-450** *JH*

A pair of wooden candlesticks, c. 1800, 12 in. high. **£125-150** *A.E.F.*

A pair of 19th C. oak treen candlesticks, 10 in. high. **£40-60** *JC*

An 18th C. candle stand, 39 in. high. **£325-375** *A.E.F.*

An 18th C. ratchet floor standard. **£400-450** *A.E.F.*

An 18th C. spoon. **£10-12** *A.E.F.*

A 19th C. Welsh treen loving spoon, the splat form stem pierced and engraved with stylised floret medallions and heart forms, 10 in. **£60-80** *Bon*

An 18th C. Welsh Caernarfon spoon, for feeding a child, 6 in. **£25-30** *A.E.F.*

An 18th C. English ladle, 10½ in. long. **£200-225** *A.E.F.*

A 19th C. Welsh knitting sheath, the baton enclosing two balls and decorated with geometric surface decoration, 22½ in. **£50-65** *Bon*

An 18th C. wooden-base floor standard with bird top. **£600-650** *AEF*

A Welsh treen loving spoon, the stem pierced, carved and enclosing three balls, 9¼ in. **£90-110** *Bon*

A 19th C. Treen spice turret, 5½ in., c. 1840. **£55-60**   *AD*

A lignum vitae coffee and spice mill, c. 1760, 9 in. high. **£400-450**   *A.E.F.*

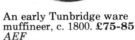

An early Tunbridge ware muffineer, c. 1800. **£75-85** *AEF*

Two 18th C. treen sugar castors with urn shape bodies and domed screw tops, 6 in. **£75-95** the two   *Bon*

Three 18th and 19th C. wooden desk sanders. **£15-35 each** *MA*

A 17th C. treen sander, 3¼ in. **£100-120**   *JH*

An 18th C. string barrel, 4 in. high. **£45-50**   *Cl.A*

Three 19th C. lignum vitae string boxes. **£25-35 each** *MA*

A 19th C. wooden barrel with wicker binding and brass padlock, 8 in. long. **£50-60** *MA*

A 19th C. lignum vitae string box, 5 in. high. **£45-48**   *Gs*

A carved coconut shell with pewter mouth and silver button on bottom, early 19th C. **£50-70**   *JC*

An early 19th C. carved coquilla nut snuff box in the form of a seated frog, silver hinged mounts, 3½ in. **£200-250** *Bon*

A carved and dated coconut shell, from Jamaica, 1829. **£100-200**   *JC*

A carved coconut shell, 5 in. long., c. 1700. **£100-125**   *F*

A 19th C. Coquilla nutme grater. **£27-30**   *Gs*

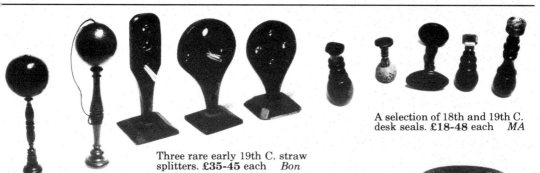

A selection of 18th and 19th C. desk seals. **£18-48** each   *MA*

Three rare early 19th C. straw splitters. **£35-45** each   *Bon*

Two 19th C. wooden bilboquets, 6½ in. high, 7½ in. high. **£30-40** each   *MA*

A mid-18th C. Continental box, 4¼ in. wide. **£400-500**   *A.E.F.*

A 17th C. lignum vitae tobacco or spice jar, with engine turning, 3¾ in. high. **£330-365**   *A.E.F.*

A late 17th C. Continental boxwood snuff box, c. 1680-90, 4 in. wide. **£400-450**   *A.E.F.*

A Tunbridge ware box, c. 1890. **£25-28**   *SS*

An 18th C. table miser's snuff box in burr yew, 6 in. diam. **£225-250**   *A.E.F.*

A small wooden snuff box carved by Thomas Foster, 1710, 3½ in. **£45-50**   *A.E.F.*

Two 17th C. wooden apple or cheese scoops. **£65-75**   *A.E.F.* (unusual in wood — common in bone)

A pair of 17th C. English nutcrackers, 6 in. long. **£180-195**   *A.E.F.*

A pair of 19th C. treen lemon press barrels with rod handles and turned base spouts, the upper sections beaded, 7 in. **£150-180**   *Bon*

18th C. rosewood sugar nips. **£70-80**   *Cl.A*

Two 18th C. treen Scottish oatmeal rollers, 8 in. **£20-30** each   *Bon*

A pair of 18th C. treen nutcrackers of crossover lever type, the handles stamped decoration and engraved with the date 1787, 5 in. **£70-95** *Bon*

An 18th C. Treen nutcracker.
£55-60   *Cl.A*

A Georgian decorated tip-staff,
c. 1820. **£45-50**   *McH*

A 17th C. Nuremburg chalice
case, to hold a turned chalice
with up to 80 cups inside,
complete, 10 in. high. **£750-
850;**   A.E.F.

A 19th C. lignum vitae school
rattle, 6 in. long. **£16-18**   *MA*

A late 18th C. wooden hearth
cat. **£38-42**   *Gs*

An English 18th C. fruitwood
nut cracker, for hazelnuts. **£35-
40**   *A.E.F.*

A Victorian policeman's turned
truncheon, 13½ in. long, c. 1860.
£16-18   *McH*

Five Georgian painted wooden
truncheons, including one
decorated with the Liverpool
crest, another with Royal
cypher, crown and arms, one
dated 1829 (the first year of the
Metropolitan Police), lengths
vary 20 in. to 12 in. **£20-30**
each   *Bon*

A large treen luggie. **£30-40**
Bon

A treen pencil box in the shape
of a book, 5 in. long, dated 1669.
£500-600   *JH*

A late 17th C. Dutch oak
footwarmer, 8 in. (20 cm.) wide.
£300-350   *SKC*

Four 19th C. wooden
mousetraps of various designs,
including one with enclosed
drowning chamber, and a
wooden rat trap of peg and
block construction. **£280-320**
(the five)   *Bon*

A 19th C. wooden Lumi Tsubos,
a Japanese 'ruler' 12½ in. long.
£80-90   *MA*

An English 18th C. mahogany
and mirror-panelled scissor
stand, raised on three ivory ball
feet, 12½ in. **£80-100**   *Bon*

A French spice cupboard with drawers, with fruitwood sides, c. 1800, 26 in. high, 16½ in. wide. **£300-380**   *A.E.F.*

An 18th C. wooden baby walker ring with hinged metal hook and mounts, 20 in. **£30-40**
Bon

MAUCHLINE WARE

- popular wooden souvenir ware, pioneered by A. & A. Smith in Ayrshire
- firm started in 1820, lasted until the late 1930's
- earliest boxes decorated by hand
- from 1850-1900 transfer printing was introduced
- most desirable are commemorative, pictures of America and Canada, any with pictures of Robert Burns or Scottish heroes
- not nearly so collectable are the German copies of Mauchline ware — these have transfer printed scenes on paper, stuck on and then varnished

An oak Welsh/English spoon rack, c. 1780, 24 in. high. **£350-375**   *A.E.F.*

A Mauchline ware needle-case, c. 1850-1876. Inverary Castle. **£16-18**

A Mauchline ware egg timer of 'Beachy Head, Lighthouse'. **£12-15**   *SS*

A Mauchline ware pail of Herstmonceux Castle, c. 1850-1870. **£10-12**   *SS*

(l) A Mauchline ware 'Go to Bed' of 'The Bay, Cliffs and Pier, Weymouth', c. 1850-1870. **£17-19**   *SS*

(r) A Mauchline ware 'Go to Bed' of Bournemouth looking West, c. 1850-1870. **£14-16**   *SS*

(l) A Mauchline ware thimble and needlecase of Kelso Abbey and Melrose Abbey, c. 1850-1870. **£24-26**   *SS*

(r) A Mauchline ware thimble case of Weymouth, c. 1850-1870. **£15-17**   *SS*

A Mauchline ware jewel box, c. 1850. **£60-65**   *AD*

A Mauchline ware postal ruler, c. 1850, 9¼ in. **£24-27**   *McH*

Three Mauchline ware pin cushions, c. 1850-1870,

(l) Hotel and Pier, Penmaenmawr. **£8-10**   *SS*

(m) Clifton Gardens, Folkestone. **£12-14**   *SS*

(r) Herne Bay looking east. **£19-21**   *SS*

A Mauchline ware thermometer of Paragons Fort Crescent, Margate, c. 1850-60, 6½ in. high. **£15-20**   *SS*

A Mauchline ware cradle of Bournemouth, c. 1850-70, 4½ in. **£20-25**   *SS*

A Mauchline ware spill holder 'The Beach, Minehead', 7½ in. high, c. 1850-70. **£15-18**   *SS*

An Egyptian gesso-painted wooden mask, with traces of green colour on the face, the false beard painted black, 18½ in. (47 cm.) high, Late Period. **£300-350**   *C*

A pair of marquetry panels, in various woods including tulip, coromandel, purpleheart, walnut and burr-maple, c. 1860, 26½ by 19¼ in. (67.5 by 49 cm.). **£500-560**   *SB*

An Egyptian wooden figure of Thoth as a baboon, seated on a tall shrine (worn), on wooden stand, 9½ in. high, Dynasty XXX. **£700-800**   *C*

An early Spanish carved wood polychrome figure of a monk, in 15th C. robe, 29½ in. **£580-700**   *DWB*

A large carved oak panel, Scandinavian, now in three parts, 1860-80, 43¼ by 74¾ in. **£550-650**   *SB*

A 15th C. carved wood roof boss, traces of gilding, 18 in., on later carved oak shield. **£820-1,000**   *L*

One of a set of 4 carved oak panels, each with scenes of Crusoe and Man Friday, by Thomas Tweedy, 3 framed, 24½ by 14½ in., c. 1862. **£990-1,100** the set   *SB*

A carved wooden ship's figurehead, with glass eyes, possibly from the barquentine 'Fra Benvolio', 30 in. (76 cm.) high, c. 1870-1875. **£800-1,000**   *SB*

An 18th C. Flemish oak statue of Christ the Good Shepherd, 155 cm. high. **£1,400-1,700**   *C*

An Elizabethan carved wooden griffin, 18 in. high. **£2,000-3,000**   *TJ*

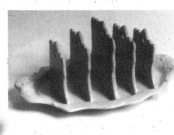

A Clarice Cliff pepper pot, 5½
£20-25   *Brit*

A Clarice Cliff pepper pot, 5½
£25-30   *Brit*

A Clarice Cliff pepper pot,
entitled 'My Garden', 5½ in.
£20-25   *Brit*

A Victorian china toast rack, in
blue, 8 in. long. £10-12   *AL*

A Mintons pepper pot, in bright
orange, green and yellow, 5 in.
£15-20   *Brit*

A Minton baking set, 6 pieces,
1912-1921, 5½ in. high (sugar
shaker). £5-6 each   *AL*

A 19th C. pewter toast rack, 6 in.
long. £10-15   *KNG*

A 'The Doctor's China Tea' tin
with hinged lid (scratched), 6¾
in. high, c. 1920's. £5-7   *AL*

A Victorian ground ginger jar
and cover (glaze cracked), 3¾ in.
high. £7-9   *AL*

An early Victorian spice tin,
with six spice compartments
inside (grater missing from lid),
½ by 4 by 3 in. £20-25   *AL*

A blue and white striped pottery
'Currants' jar and cover, the
bottom stamped 'Greens
Cornish Ware', 5½ in., c. 1920.
£7-10   *AL*

A blue and white striped 'Sauce'
bottle, marked 'Greens Cornish
Ware', 7½ in. £5-7   *AL*

An Edwardian ginger tin, 3 in.
high. £3-4   *AL*

607

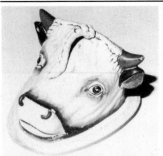

A Staffordshire cheese dish, c. 1850. **£95-105**   *LAC*

A Royal Winton hand-painted marmalade jar and cover, 4 in. tall. **£20-25**   *Brit*

A Mintons marmalade pot and cover, with blue pansies and butterfly finial, 5 in. **£20-25** *Brit*

A green Wedgwood cheese dish, pre-1871, 8 in. tall. **£200-230** *LAC*

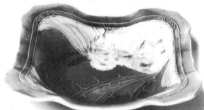

A Mintons dish, 8 in. wide. **£50-60**   *Brit*

A Carlton-ware small dish, 4 in. wide. **£5-10**   *Brit*

A Carlton-ware dish, 10 in. wide. **£15-20**   *Brit*

An Edwardian 'Brown and Poulson' shortbread mould, in. diam. **£14-16**   *AL*

A Victorian fire-proof pie dish, marked 'Hemmings, Abington St, Northampton' (rim chipped), 9 in. wide. **£5-7**   *AL*

A Whieldon-ware Staffordshire tureen game dish and cover, c. 1860, 12 in. wide. **£75-85** *LAC*

A Victorian pottery bread plate, the rim moulded with 'Give us our daily bread' and ears of wheat, highlighted with gilt, 12 in. **£16-20**   *AL*

A Cadburys' cocoa jug (glaz cracked), with tin cocoa measure, c. 1920s, 6 in. high. **£8-10**   *AL*

A Wedgwood game dish, 10 in. wide, c. 1860. **£75-83**   *LAC*

A Verwood pottery cheese strainer, early 19th C., 13 in. diam. **£10-15**   *Cl.A*

A Carlton-ware juice extractor and jug, in orange and yellow in. **£10-15**   *Brit*

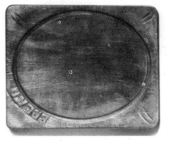

An Edwardian bread board, 8½ by 11 in. £7-8   AL

An Edwardian wooden butter knife and dish, with glass liner, knife 7 in. long, dish 7 in. diam. £6-8   AL

A Victorian terracotta cheese cover, 6¼ in. high. £5-7   AL

'The Adaptable Hot Water Bottle', Bed Warmer and a Pocket Warmer, made at the Old Fulham Pottery, c. 1910, 10½ in. high and 3½ in. high. £30-50 the pair   PAM

A 'Zerocool' butter cooler, terracotta with a pottery base, 11 by 4 in., c. 1920. £8-10   AL

A Victorian stone jar, bearing the inscription 'Crosse and Blackwell', Oilmen, 21 Soho Square, 9 in. high. £8-10   AL

A 'Gourmet' pie cup (glaze cracked), 3 in. £3-5   AL

(l) A Magic patent corkscrew, c. 1900. £18-22   MA

(r) A folding pocket corkscrew, c. 1900. £18-22   MA

A 'Gourmet' pie cup, 3 in. £4-6   AL

> *Miller's is a price GUIDE Not a price LIST.*
>
> *The price ranges given reflect the average price a purchaser should pay for similar items. Condition, rarity of design or pattern, size, colour, pedigree, restoration and many other factors must be taken into account when assessing values.*

A selection of 19th C. peg and worm pocket corkscrews. £15-25   MA

A Victorian pottery stoneware wine keg, 15 in. high. £15-20   AL

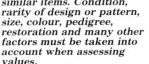

(l) A two pronged corkscrew in brass case, patent 1899. £20-25   MA

(r) A late 19th C. Champagne tap corkscrew, 6½ in. long. £22-25   MA

A late 19th C. corkscrew. £9-11   Gs

609

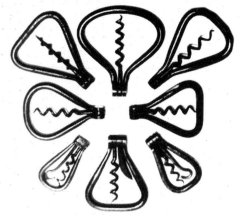

A selection of 19th C. harp pocket corkscrews. **£4-20** *MA*

(t) A Lund patent London rack corkscrew with bottle grasp, c. 1860, 9½ in. long. **£140-160** *MA*

(b) A Lund patent London rack corkscrew, c. 1860, 7½ in. long. **£28-35** *MA*

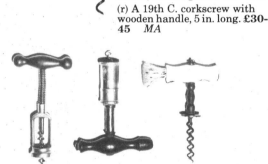

(l) A 19th C. bone and steel corkscrew with decorated shank, 6 in. long. **£30-45** *MA*

(r) A 19th C. corkscrew with wooden handle, 5 in. long. **£30-45** *MA*

A selection of French late 19th C. plated iron corkscrews. **£20-75** *MA*

Three 19th C. corkscrews. (l) c. 1830, **£25-28**; (m) c. 1870, **£20-23**; (r) c. 1900. **£9-12** *LAC*

A 19th C. four pillar king screw, **£95-120** *MA*

(t) A patent double action corkscrew by Thomason, c. 1802, 8½ in. long. **£95-120** *MA*

(b) An open barreled double action corkscrew, 10 in. long. **£95-120** *MA*

(l) An early 20th C. brass corkscrew, 5½ in. long. **£20-25** *MA*

(r) A late 19th C. Challenge steel corkscrew, 6 in. long. **£14-20** *MA*

(m) An early 19th C. brass Farrow and Jackson wingnut corkscrew, 6 in. long. **£48-58** *MA*

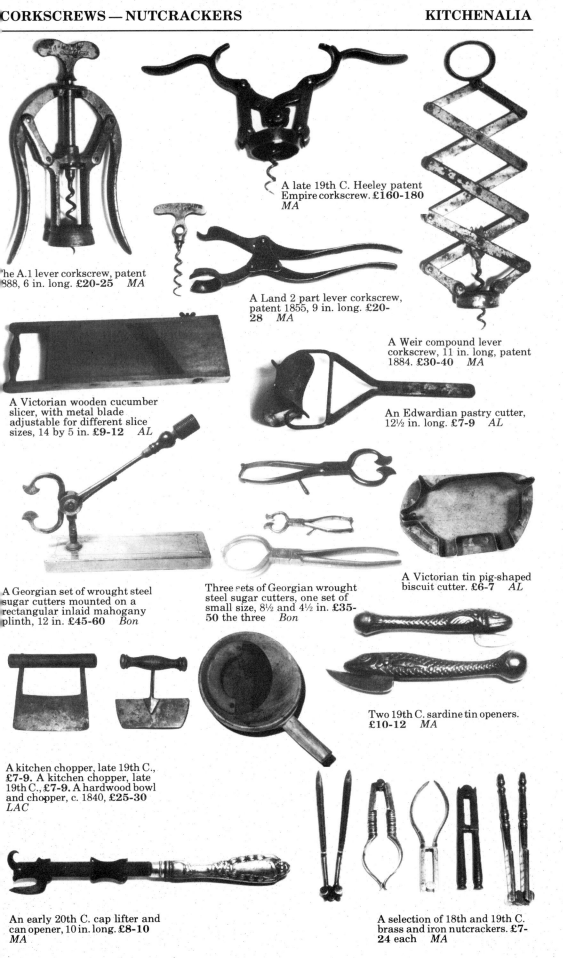

The A.1 lever corkscrew, patent 1888, 6 in. long. £20-25   MA

A late 19th C. Heeley patent Empire corkscrew. £160-180
MA

A Land 2 part lever corkscrew, patent 1855, 9 in. long. £20-28   MA

A Weir compound lever corkscrew, 11 in. long, patent 1884. £30-40   MA

A Victorian wooden cucumber slicer, with metal blade adjustable for different slice sizes, 14 by 5 in. £9-12   AL

An Edwardian pastry cutter, 12½ in. long. £7-9   AL

A Georgian set of wrought steel sugar cutters mounted on a rectangular inlaid mahogany plinth, 12 in. £45-60   Bon

Three sets of Georgian wrought steel sugar cutters, one set of small size, 8½ and 4½ in. £35-50 the three   Bon

A Victorian tin pig-shaped biscuit cutter. £6-7   AL

Two 19th C. sardine tin openers. £10-12   MA

A kitchen chopper, late 19th C., £7-9. A kitchen chopper, late 19th C., £7-9. A hardwood bowl and chopper, c. 1840, £25-30 LAC

An early 20th C. cap lifter and can opener, 10 in. long. £8-10 MA

A selection of 18th and 19th C. brass and iron nutcrackers. £7-24 each   MA

Two Victorian jelly moulds. £6
each   *AL*

Late 19th C. sugar nips, £12-
15. A saltglaze jelly mould,
early 19th C., £12-15. A small
white jelly mould, £8-10   *LAC*

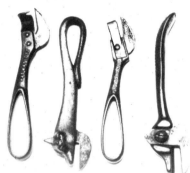

A selection of 19th C. tin
openers. £4-7   *MA*

A pair of butter stamps, 2 in.
and 3 in. £10-13 each   *AL*

A selection of 19th C. brass
pastry jiggers. £8-10   *MA*

A Victorian nutmeg grater,
with compartment for spare
nutmeg in the handle, 7½ in.
long. £12-14   *AL*

A 19th C. wooden Peugeot
coffee grinder. £24-28   *MA*

Three 18th C. treen
pastry/butter rolling moulds.
£20-30 each   *Bon*

An Edwardian cheese press, 12
in. high. £40-45   *AL*

A Victorian salad shaker, 10 in.
£9-11   *AL*

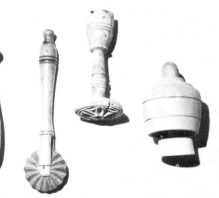

A Regency cane basket, 11 in.
£5-6   *AL*

A Victorian small wicker egg
basket, 8 in. diam. £5-6   *AL*

(l) A late 19th C. leather pricker. £6-8   *LAC*
(lm) A pastry marker, late 19th C. £3-5   *LAC*
(rm) A butter print. £10-12   *LAC*
(r) A butter print. £10-12   *LAC*

A Victorian plaited rush basket (woodworm in handle), 13 by 10 in. £6-8   *AL*

A Victorian wicker and rush egg basket, 13 in. wide. £4-6 *AL*

A Victorian wicker and plaited rush basket, 10 in. diam. £4-5 *AL*

A Victorian heavy wicker egg basket, 13 in. diam., 21 in. high. £10-12   *AL*

A Victorian wicker bread basket, 13 in. diam. £4-6   *AL*

A Victorian oval wicker shopping basket, 15 in. wide. £6-8   *AL*

A Victorian willow and wicker basket, 12 in. high, 9 in. diam. £5-7   *AL*

An oval Victorian wicker basket, 14 in. long, 12 in. high. £5-7   *AL*

A Victorian willow basket, 9½ in. high, 10½ in. diam. £5-7 *AL*

An early 19th C. ivory drinking vessel, 3¾ in. high. £16-18 *MA*

An oval Victorian wicker basket, 13 in. long, 11 in. high. £5-7   *AL*

A 'Bovril' mug, with gilt rim, 3½ in. high, c. 1920. £7-9   *AL*

A silver-plated 'Bovril' spoon, 6 in., c. 1920. £2-4   *AL*

A set of Victorian food weights, made of black glazed pottery, the largest 10 in. diam. £13-15   AL

A 19th C. pine spoon rack. £35-40   MAT

A miniature Victorian pine chest of 2 drawers, 12½ in. wide, 11½ in. deep, 9 in. high. £15-20   AL

A small Victorian pine chest of drawers, 17 in. wide, 12½ in. deep, 17 in. high. £45-50   AL

A Victorian pine cat box, 14 in. deep, 11 in. wide, 15½ in. high. £25-30   AL

A Guernsey cream can and cover, made of tin, the bottom impressed 'De La Rue, maker Guernsey', 8 in. high, c. 1880. £5-7   AL

An Edwardian tin string container, with cutter at side, 7 in. high. £7-9   AL

An Edwardian string holder, Sandows patent, 6½ in. wide. £5-7   AL

A Victorian pine fire screen, 26 in. high, 18 in. wide. £25-30   AL

A George V wooden gallon measure, with duty mark (woodworm in base), 5 in. high, 9½ in. diam. £20-25   AL

An Edwardian tea tin, 13 in. high. £9-12   AL

An Edwardian green painted tea tin, 15½ in. high. £20-25   AL

A large Edwardian string holder, 12½ in. wide. £10-13   AL

A miniature Victorian pine cupboard. £10-13   AL

IRONS

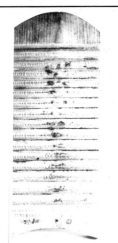

A Victorian pine wash-board, 23 by 9 in. **£5-7**   *AL*

It was not until the 16th C. that Europeans used a heated tool to smooth clothes. Earlier they used a mangle or rubbing devices to flatten cloth while it was damp.

It is not clear whether the idea of using a hot iron arose spontaneously in the West or whether it was introduced from the Orient. But probably the Dutch introduced ironing to add to the white woman's burden. And what a burden! So that the iron should retain its heat as long as possible, it was made as heavy as a woman could handle — often weighing 6 lb. or more.

At first there were two kinds of iron: the sad iron heated on the stove, and the box iron — hollow and kept hot by a pair of solid iron slugs heated in the fire and inserted alternately into its body.

The box iron was the aristocrat — often made of brass and elaborately embossed. The sad one, made of iron, was a functional, blacksmith-made affair, 'heavy, practical and ponderous' — in fact, the true middle-English meaning of the word 'sad'.

As use of the iron spread during the 17th and 18th C. the need for a self-heating iron became obvious. In the 19th C. designs appeared which allowed for a charcoal fire to burn inside the iron. These mainly originated in America and were immediately popular. The Bless and Drake foundry produced 100,000 of them in the year 1856 alone! Then came all sorts of variations including improvements in draught control so that charcoal or coke would burn more evenly. And there were methods of burning gas, paraffin, vegetable oil, petrol and methylated spirits.

In 1870, a certain Mrs. Potts, of Iowa, U.S.A., fed up with her old sad iron, decided to improve it. First, she designed one that was pointed at both ends for ironing into odd corners. Then she patented one with a detachable handle and two soles. The soles were heated on the stove and the handle attached alternatively to each so that it never got too hot.

Electricity came in the 1880's. The old-timers fought on well into the 20th C. but now a flex trails where once wafted smoke and fumes.

A mid 19th C. Carron No. 12 iron, 7½ in. long. **£8-10**   *FA*

A mid 19th C. tailor's iron by Levine & Sons, 35 Greenfield Street, London, E.1, 8 in. long. **£5-8**   *FA*

A late 19th C. toy iron, 3¾ in. long. **£10-15**   *FA*

An early 19th C. British cap iron, 4¾ in. long. **£20-24**   *FA*

A late 19th C. French flat iron, No. 5, 6 in. **£8-10**   *FA*

A late 19th C. Belgian flat iron, No. 4, 6½ in. long. **£7-10**   *FA*

A Kenrick No. 3 polisher iron, 4¾ in. long. **£10-14**   *FA*

A straight chimney charcoal iron, made in Hong Kong at the end of the war for the eastern market, 8 in. tall. **£30-35**   *FA*

A mid 19th C. Vulcan chimney iron, with vulcan head damper, 7 in. long. **£30-40**   *FA*

An early 19th C. British lace box iron, 3½ in. long. **£45-50** *FA*

A mid 19th C. British box iron, 6 in. long. **£15-20** *FA*

A mid 19th C. charcoal iron, 7 in. high. **£25-30** *FA*

Mid-19th C. Colebrookdale cold-handle sad irons (made to stack one on top of the other), 6 in. wide. **£25-30** *FA*

A late 19th C. American petrol iron, 9 in. wide. **£30-35** *FA*

A late 19th/early 20th C. small iron trivet, made in Japan, 3 in. long. **£2-3** *FA*

A late 18th C. miniature brass iron stand, 4 in. long. **£10-15** *KNG*

A set of five American stacking trivets. **£30-40** *FA*

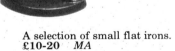

A late 19th C. Chinese brass pan iron, with ivory tao-tie handle, 10 in. long. **£45-55** *FA*

A selection of small flat irons. **£10-20** *MA*

An early 20th C. electric travelling iron, complete with box and accessories. **£3-5** *FA*

A mid 19th C. goffering iron, 6 in. high. **£5-8** *FA*

A Victorian cast-iron iron stand, 6 in. long. **£10-13** *AL*

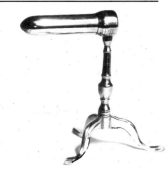

A pair of late 18th C. goffering tongs, 10½ in. long. **£5-7** *FA*

Miller's Antiques Price Guide builds up year by year to form the most comprehensive photo-reference system available. The first three volumes contain over 20,000 completely different photographs.

A Kenrick No. 10 goffering iron, 4½ in. high. **£25-30** *FA*

A brass goffering iron, c. 1730. **£80-90** *Cl.A*

Early 20th C. cast iron domestic scales, with brass fittings, 13 in. wide. **£30-40** *Cas*

An early 20th C. cast iron personal weighing machine, with enamel dial, used with reflecting fall front mirror, 8 in. high. **£55-65** *Cas*

An early 20th C. domestic kitchen-type spring balance, 12 in. high. **£18-22** *LAC*

Cast iron greengrocers' scales with copper pan, early 20th C., 20 in. wide. **£50-60** *Cas*

A brass and cast iron Salter spring balance kitchen scales, 1940, 17 in. high. **£45-50** *Cas*

A Victorian apothecary's beam scale, 11 in. wide by 12 in. high. **£58-64** *LAC*

A Victorian brass banking scales, 18 in. high. **£110-125** *Cas*

(l) A brass Winfield candlestick letter scale, c. 1870, 6½ in. high. **£38-45** *MA*

(r) A Joseph and Edmund Radcliffe candlestick letter scale, c. 1870, 5½ in. high. **£38-45** *MA*

An early 20th C. spring letter scale, 4 in. high. **£8-11** *LAC*

A 19th C. jewellers beam scale with weights, 19½ in. high. **£95-105** *LAC*

An early 20th C. spring letter scale, 3¼ in. high. **£9-12** *LAC*

A rare Victorian candlestick letter scale, 6½ in. tall. **£45-50** *LAC*

A 20th C. Royal Navy spring balance, with pan. **£20-25** *Cas*

Mordan pocket letter scales for India and England, 4½ in. long. **£40-45** *MA*

A 19th C. John Sheldon pocket postal scales and seal, in silver plate, 2½ in. long. **£55-60** *MA*

19th C. Chinese opium scales in wooden box with brass pans, 11 in. long. **£68-78** *MA*

Two brass Victorian sovereign scales. **£14-28 each** *MA*

A 17th C. lead weight. **£20-24** *LAC*

A Georgian shagreen cased part set of four weights, 1¾ in., and another 19th C. brass cased set of weights, the case of bucket shape (the smallest weight missing), 1¾ in. **£20-30 each** *Bon*

An early 19th C. folding Guinea scale, by Stephen Houghton & Son, Ormskirk, 11 in. long. **£58-68** *MA*

A drug (opium) scale from Northern Thailand, 6 in. wide. **£50-60** *LAC*

(l) A late 19th C. brass pocket coin scale, 3½ in. long. **£40-50** *MA*

(r) A 19th C. wooden pocket coin scale, 4¼ in. long. **£38-48** *MA*

An Avery guinea balance, 6 in. closed. **£55-65** *LAC*

TOOLS

A set of brass flat circular weights, 2 lb.–½ dram. £27-32 *LAC*

Corporation of Manchester metric carat weights 500 to 1005, dated 1914, 5 in. wide. £70-85 *LAC*

A compass plane no. 113, by Stanley Rule and Level Co., patented 1877, in near mint condition, 10 in. long. £40-50 *RM*

Tool collecting is still in its infancy and can only grow in interest. Prices have advanced, admittedly from a low base, greatly in the last five years. The price differential between the good and the mediocre or common will extend further as collectors become discriminating.

As far as planes are concerned, sometimes the maker's name is obscured by various owners' stamps (early examples often have no maker's name) so dating has to be done by observing the general characteristics of the plane. In essence, all moulding planes made after about 1810 are 9½ in. long and any moulding planes longer than this are older. Robert Wooding is one of the best known early makers (1710-1739) and his planes are about 10¼ in. long. The value of moulding planes varies immensely from about £1 to £100+ each, depending on condition, maker or rarity. Metal planes are, on the whole, more valuable and usually much younger, 18th C. or earlier are rarely found and the bulk are from about 1840 to 1930. The interest in metal planes lies in the quality of construction coupled with rarity. The most famous makers of metal planes were Spiers, Norris and Preston. Spiers originated the dovetailed steel range of planes which was copied by Norris and a few others. Smoothing, Shoulder and Rebate planes have survived in large quantities and prices range from about £10 to £100, condition being very important. The longer Panel and Try planes are rarer and more valuable — £80 plus. Mitre planes have not survived in any quantity and although originally cheaper to produce than Panel or even Smoothing planes, are now some of the most sought after, maybe selling for over £200 each.

Wooden braces have perhaps the most eye appeal of the smaller tools. In this case the type of wood is usually the important criterion in determining value, coupled with the maker. Beech is the most common, boxwood and rosewood the rarest. The Wm. Marples brass framed Ebony Ultimatum brace is most sought after by collectors. In unused condition it is worth nearly £200, if condition is poor the value can be £100 or less. The ordinary brass plated, as opposed to framed, braces have survived in abundance and are still cheap at around £15-£35 each.

Of the larger tools, lathes are the main ones to consider and the foot powered wooden frame examples can be attractive. Many are unnamed, but the finest were made by Holtzapffel or Evans, often with equipment for ornamental turning in ivory or ebony. The latter are rare, and if well equipped, can fetch thousands of pounds rather than hundreds.

Very few museums have comprehensive collections of Tools, but there are some very good ones. In England the Science Museum probably has the most interesting collection and it includes some very good lathes.

A 19th C. Portuguese rebate plane in ebony and mahogany, made in the form of a double barrel gun, 27 in. long. £100-200 *RM*

A beechwood plough plane by Stockoe, 10 in. long. £15-20 *RM*

A beech and fruitwood rebate plane, by D. Malloch, Perth, with 1¾ in. blade, 9½ in. long. £35-55 *DSH*

A no. 97 cabinet maker's edge plane, japanned with nickel plate trim and rosewood handle, made by Stanley, 10 in. long. £40-50 *RM*

A large French rebate plane, dated 1752, 45 in. long. £200-300 *RM*

A nickel plated steel side rebate plane by Edward Preston, c. 1890. £20-30 *RM*

A miniature beechwood smoothing plane, 4 in. long, with 1 in. blade, and a miniature beechwood rabbet plane with convex sole, 3⅛ in. long. **£20-40** *DSH*

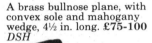

A double iron moulding plane, by Sinclair. **£10-15** *RM*

A beechwood and boxwood plough plane, by Summers Varvill, York, with adjustable fence and brass-mounted moving fillister, 8½ in. long. **£25-50** *DSH*

A brass bullnose plane, with convex sole and mahogany wedge, 4½ in. long. **£75-100** *DSH*

A boxwood thumb plane, 3 in. long. **£15-25** *RM*

A dovetailed steel mitre plane by Moon, 145 St. Martins Lane, c. 1840. **£200-300** *RM*

A unique sill plane, craftsman made in walnut and boxwood, 6½ in. long. **£20-30** *RM*

A 19th C. chamfer plane in beechwood, by Edward Preston, 5 in. long. **£20-30** *RM*

A nickel plated cast iron shoulder plane, by Edward Preston, c. 1900. **£30-40** *RM*

A late 19th C. violin maker's brass plane. **£50-60** *RM*

A steel and mahogany rabbet plane, 8 in. long. **£30-50** *DSH*

A late 19th C. cast iron spill plane, by Edward Preston, 7 in. long. **£30-40** *RM*

A late 19th C. nickel plated and cast iron spoke shave, by Edward Preston, 9½ in. long. **£10-15** *RM*

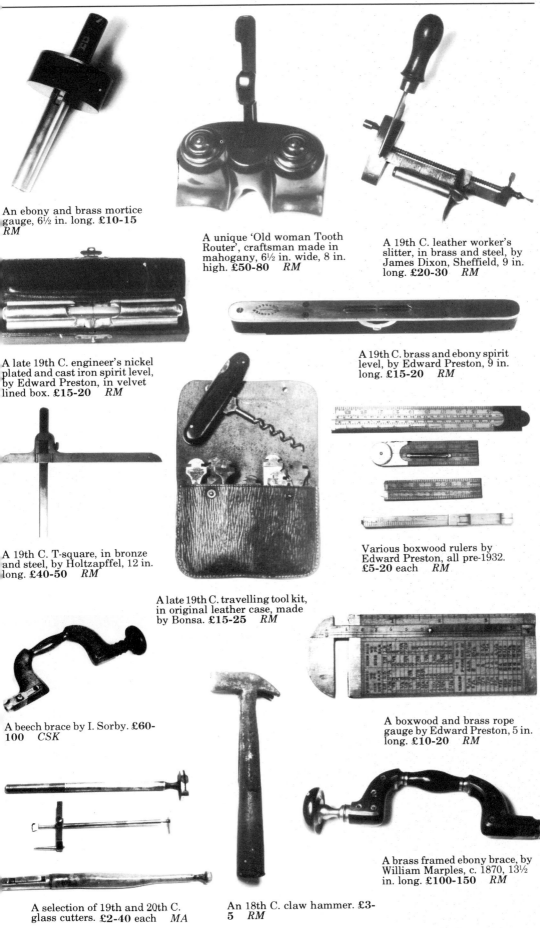

An ebony and brass mortice gauge, 6½ in. long. **£10-15** *RM*

A unique 'Old woman Tooth Router', craftsman made in mahogany, 6½ in. wide, 8 in. high. **£50-80**   *RM*

A 19th C. leather worker's slitter, in brass and steel, by James Dixon, Sheffield, 9 in. long. **£20-30**   *RM*

A late 19th C. engineer's nickel plated and cast iron spirit level, by Edward Preston, in velvet lined box. **£15-20**   *RM*

A 19th C. brass and ebony spirit level, by Edward Preston, 9 in. long. **£15-20**   *RM*

A 19th C. T-square, in bronze and steel, by Holtzapffel, 12 in. long. **£40-50**   *RM*

Various boxwood rulers by Edward Preston, all pre-1932. **£5-20** each   *RM*

A late 19th C. travelling tool kit, in original leather case, made by Bonsa. **£15-25**   *RM*

A beech brace by I. Sorby. **£60-100**   *CSK*

A boxwood and brass rope gauge by Edward Preston, 5 in. long. **£10-20**   *RM*

A brass framed ebony brace, by William Marples, c. 1870, 13½ in. long. **£100-150**   *RM*

A selection of 19th and 20th C. glass cutters. **£2-40** each   *MA*

An 18th C. claw hammer. **£3-5**   *RM*

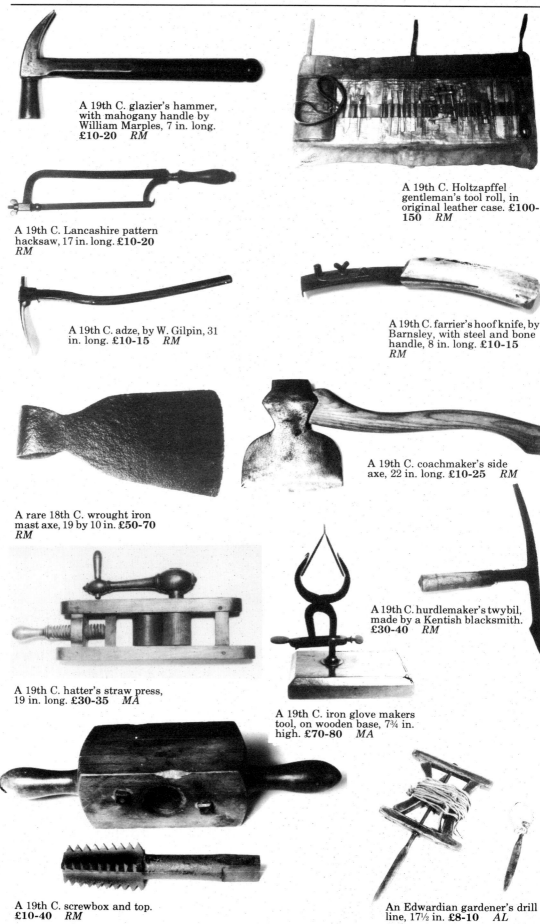

A 19th C. glazier's hammer, with mahogany handle by William Marples, 7 in. long. **£10-20** *RM*

A 19th C. Lancashire pattern hacksaw, 17 in. long. **£10-20** *RM*

A 19th C. adze, by W. Gilpin, 31 in. long. **£10-15** *RM*

A 19th C. Holtzapffel gentleman's tool roll, in original leather case. **£100-150** *RM*

A 19th C. farrier's hoof knife, by Barnsley, with steel and bone handle, 8 in. long. **£10-15** *RM*

A 19th C. coachmaker's side axe, 22 in. long. **£10-25** *RM*

A rare 18th C. wrought iron mast axe, 19 by 10 in. **£50-70** *RM*

A 19th C. hurdlemaker's twybil, made by a Kentish blacksmith. **£30-40** *RM*

A 19th C. hatter's straw press, 19 in. long. **£30-35** *MA*

A 19th C. iron glove makers tool, on wooden base, 7¾ in. high. **£70-80** *MA*

A 19th C. screwbox and top. **£10-40** *RM*

An Edwardian gardener's drill line, 17½ in. **£8-10** *AL*

A penny farthing, with repainted steel frame, front brake and solid rubber tyred wheels, front 54 in. diam., rear 15½ in. diam. **£700-850** *SKC*

A penny farthing, with unusual four tube forks, spoon type front brake and solid rubber tyres, 52 in. diam. wheel, c. 1885. **£750-900** *SKC*

A W.W.II B.S.A. folding pedal cycle, repainted olive drab. **£140-190** *SKC*

A bicycle, with 52 in. driving wheel, rubber tyres and brake, in need of restoration. **£800-1,000** *CSK*

A racing velocipede, c. 1880, with rubber tyres and rear brake. **£1,300-1,500** *CSK*

A tricycle, c. 1885, possibly by New Imperial, overall length 57 in., in good general order. **£1,100-1,300** *CSK*

A Coventry ordinary bicycle, club racing model, c. 1885, in good condition. **£1,100-1,300** *CSK*

A Velocipede, cast iron frame and wooden wheels with iron rims, c. 1867-69, 49 in. high. **£1,800-2,000** *CSK*

A 1900 Humber combination safety tandem bicycle, 96 in. long. **£480-600** *CSK*

An 1897 Dursley Pedersen gentleman's cycle, with cantilever frame, original saddle suspension and rod and caliper braking system. **£530-650** *PS*

A black-painted Velocipede bicycle, c. 1868, 52 in. high. **£400-450** *CSK*

A 1937 Royal Enfield Solo Motorcycle, 348 cc., Reg. No. CWL 517, Frame and Engine Nos. 3651, restoration necessary. **£450-600** *CSK*

A 1927 New Hudson 346 c.c. Model S2 solo motorcycle, reg. no. CF 8074, frame no. M12933, engine no. NF128, in good condition. **£550-650**   *CSK*

A 1926 Gnôme-Rhône 350 cc solo motorcycle, not registered, frame no. 16098, engine no. 6404, fully restored in very good condition. **£1,600-1,800**   *CSK*

A 1928 Ariel 557 c.c. Model A solo motorcycle, reg. no. SGF 806V (re-registered), frame no. W2685, engine no. W2025, in good condition. **£550-650**   *CSK*

A 1929 F.N. 350 c.c. solo motorcycle, reg. no. (France) 321 BA 89, frame no. 74543, engine no. 70003C, in good condition. **£550-650**   *CSK*

A 1929 Monet-Goon 147 c.c. solo motorcycle, not registered, fitted with M.A.G. engine, 3-speed gearbox, in running condition, some attention needed. **£400-500**   *CSK*

A 1922 F.N. 286 c.c. 'Lightweight' solo motorcycle, reg. no. ME 3365, frame no. 61015, single cylinder, 2 speed. **£1,100-1,300**   *CSK*

A 1930 Rudge Whitworth 499 c.c. racing motorcycle, reg. no. BJB 506, engine no. 63. **£1,900-2,300**   *CSK*

A 1926 Sunbeam 3-litre four-seater sports tourer, reg. no. BA 6104, chassis no. 4151 F, 6 cylinder, 2,916 c.c., 4 speed. **£17,000-20,000**   *CSK*

A 1921 Sunbeam 24 h.p. four-door limousine, reg. no. L 9897, coachwork by Cunard, London, chassis no. 24E/7052/21, engine no. 24/7500/21, 6 cylinder, 4,524 c.c., 4 speed. **£7,500-8,500**   *CSK*

A 1928 Morgan Aero 1,096 c.c. sports two-seater, reg. no. PH 8267, chassis no. 14695, engine no. 4/TOW/95096/3/W, vee-twin, 2 speed. **£3,000-3,300**   *CSK*

A 1932 De Soto SCX (Chrysler Mortlake Six), 19.8 h.p. two-seater convertible coupe, reg. no. YY 1232, chassis no. 6009912, engine no. SCX 1158, 6 cylinder, 2,794 c.c., 3 speed. **£4,000-6,000** *CSK*

A 1933 S.S. I 16 h.p. four-seater sports tourer, reg. no. MRG 634, chassis and engine nos. 136458, 6 cylinder, 2,054 c.c., 4 speed. **£11,000-15,000** *CSK*

A 1937 Bentley 4½-litre four-door sports saloon, reg. no. EU 6278, coachwork by Thrupp and Maberly, London, chassis no. B.19 JY, 6 cylinder, 4 speed. **£5,000-6,000** *CSK*

Right
A 1926 A.C. 12/24 h.p. Royal Model two-seater and dickey, reg. no. YP 8328, chassis no. 30912, engine no. 5764 E, 4 cylinder, 1,496 c.c., 3 speed gearbox. **£5,000-6,500** *CSK*

A 1936 Morris 8 h.p. Series I two-door de luxe saloon, reg. no. HV 6428, chassis no. S. 1E 77578, engine no. BE 190098, 4 cylinder, 918 c.c., 3 speed. **£1,000-1,300** *CSK*

A 1935 Alvis Speed Twenty sports saloon, reg. no. WS 7223, coachwork by Charlesworth, Coventry, chassis no. 17811, engine no. 14773, 6 cylinder, 4,387 c.c., 4 speed. **£7,000-8,000** *CSK*

A 1939 Lagonda LG6 4½-litre four-door sports saloon, engine 6 cylinder. **£6,000-7,000** *CSK*

A 1942 Willys M.B. ¼-ton 4 x 4 (Jeep), restored, taxed and M.O.T. **£2,550-2700** *SKC*

A 1942 Morris C.8 Mk. III field artillery tractor (restoration required to engine), with spare engine and gearbox. **£70-120** *SKC*

A 1948 Jaguar 3½-litre four-door sports saloon, reg. no. HWU 913, chassis no. 613332, engine no. S.4105, 6 cylinder, 3,485 c.c., 4 speed. **£2,000-3,200** *CSK*

A Lalique glass cockerel mascot, in clear lightly pink tinted glass, 20.25 cm., moulded mark 'R. Lalique France', 1920's. £440-540 *SB*

'The Spirit of the Wind', a Lalique glass car mascot, 26 cm. width, moulded mark 'R. Lalique France', metal mount with Breves Gallery mark and patent number, and with internal green filter, c. 1925. £1,700-1,900 *SB*

A Lalique glass hawk mascot, in pink-tinted glass, moulded mark 'R. Lalique', engraved 'France', mount with Breves Galleries details, 20 cm. high, 1920's. £440-550 *SB*

A decorative 'Angel' car mascot, in cast bronze, 7¼ in. (18.5 cm.) high, c. 1930. £60-90 *SB*

A mounted car mascot, 5 in. high, 1930's. £45-50 *F*

An unusual Bentley car mascot, signed Gordon Crosby, in the form of a stylised female Icarus, 5¾ in. high, mounted on mahogany base, English, c. 1927. £750-950 *SB*

A chromium-plated Rolls-Royce Spirit of Ecstasy, signed Charles Sykes, 1911, etched Reg. U.S. Pat. Off., 6½ in. high. £250-350 *CSK*

A chromium-plated Old Bill, inscribed Bruce Bairnsfather, Copyright, 4¼ in. high. £50-90 *CSK*

A brass standing figure of an elephant, inscribed A.E.L. R/D, 4 in. long, mounted on a radiator cap. £150-220 *CSK*

Telecote Pup: Bonzo, a plated metal mascot on base. £60-75 *P*

A chromed brass mascot of a running girl, the base inscribed M. Hiley, 19 cm. high, mounted on a radiator cap. £22-30 *P*

Mappin and Webb, a speed goddess, a chromed-plated brass mascot, with monogram mark, 20 cm. high, mounted on a radiator cap. £55-70 *P*

Rolls-Royce: Spirit of Ecstasy, Silver Ghost model, fully marked and very worn, nickel-plated brass. **£130-180**   *P*

A chromium-plated and enamelled British Racing Drivers' Club badge, inscribed H.R.H. Prince Chula Chakrabongse G.C.V.O., 512, 4½ in. (11.5 cm.) high. **£170-200**   *CSK*

A nickel-plated Royal Automobile Club badge, with a blue enamelled plaque inscribed Kent Automobile Club, N 73, 4½ in. high. **£80-140**   *CSK*

A nickel-plated F.N. badge, 4 in. high. **£180-260**   *CSK*

A Rover 12 h.p. motor car dashboard and registration plate CY 3551. **£60-100**   *CSK*

A nickel-plated Royal Automobile Club badge, inscribed D.117, 5¾ in. high. **£150-220**   *CSK*

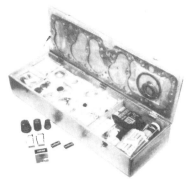

A late Victorian baby's perambulator, with spoked wheels, rear 58 cm. diam., front 42 cm., with original tyres, the wooden body with leather hood and brass stays, 118 cm. **£240-300**   *SKC*

A Rolls-Royce overseas touring spares kit, in fitted wooden box, 28 in. long. **£170-250**   *CSK*

Miller's is a price GUIDE Not a price LIST.

The price ranges given reflect the average price a purchaser should pay for similar items. Condition, rarity of design or pattern, size, colour, pedigree, restoration and many other factors must be taken into account when assessing values.

A vintage Bowser petrol pump with crank and dial enclosed by a revolving shutter, 81½ in. **£100-120**   *SBe*

An ivory brise fan, painted and gilt, 8½ in., c. 1730. **£500-600**   *CSK*

An ivory brise fan, painted and lacquered, 8½ in., c. 1730. **£380-430**   *CSK*

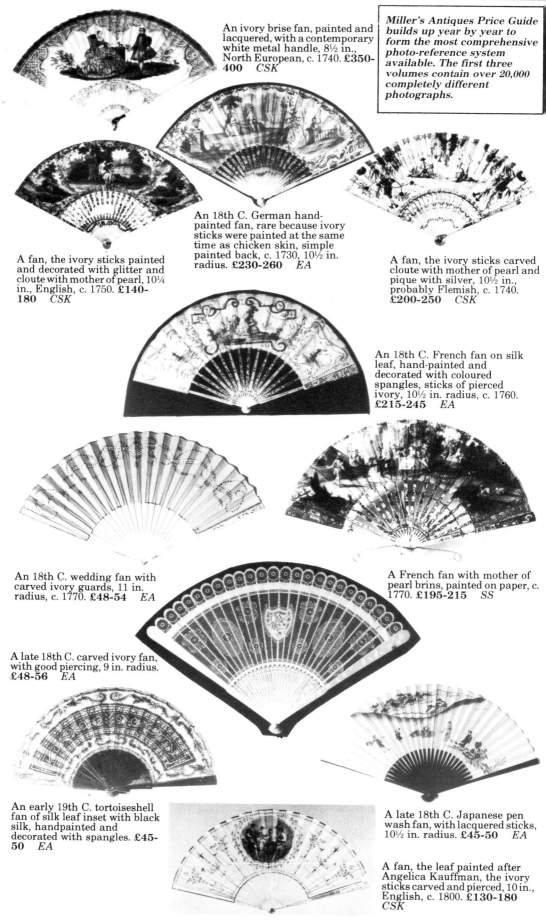

An ivory brise fan, painted and lacquered, with a contemporary white metal handle, 8½ in., North European, c. 1740. £350-400   *CSK*

An 18th C. German hand-painted fan, rare because ivory sticks were painted at the same time as chicken skin, simple painted back, c. 1730, 10½ in. radius. £230-260   *EA*

A fan, the ivory sticks painted and decorated with glitter and cloute with mother of pearl, 10¼ in., English, c. 1750. £140-180   *CSK*

A fan, the ivory sticks carved cloute with mother of pearl and pique with silver, 10½ in., probably Flemish, c. 1740. £200-250   *CSK*

An 18th C. French fan on silk leaf, hand-painted and decorated with coloured spangles, sticks of pierced ivory, 10½ in. radius, c. 1760. £215-245   *EA*

An 18th C. wedding fan with carved ivory guards, 11 in. radius, c. 1770. £48-54   *EA*

A French fan with mother of pearl brins, painted on paper, c. 1770. £195-215   *SS*

A late 18th C. carved ivory fan, with good piercing, 9 in. radius. £48-56   *EA*

An early 19th C. tortoiseshell fan of silk leaf inset with black silk, handpainted and decorated with spangles. £45-50   *EA*

A late 18th C. Japanese pen wash fan, with lacquered sticks, 10½ in. radius. £45-50   *EA*

A fan, the leaf painted after Angelica Kauffman, the ivory sticks carved and pierced, 10 in., English, c. 1800. £130-180   *CSK*

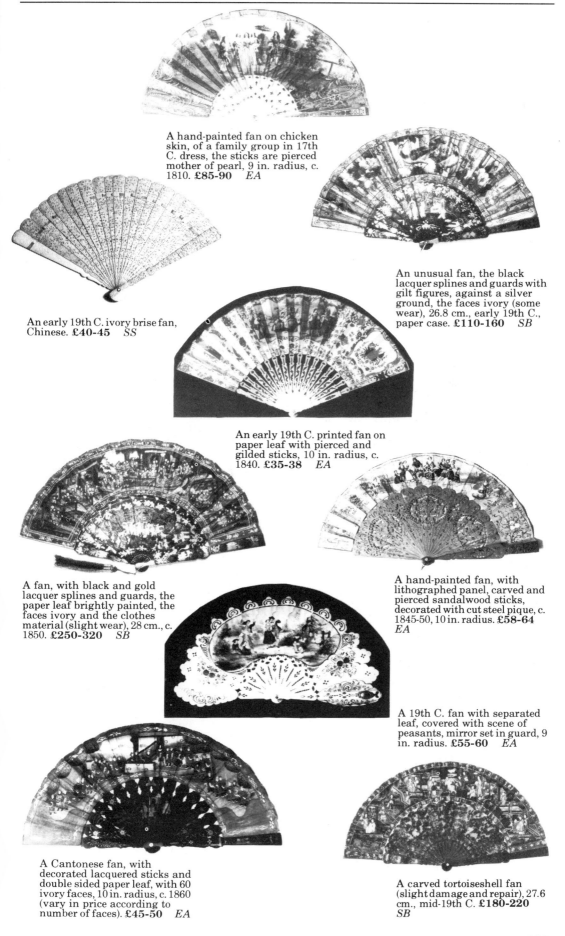

A hand-painted fan on chicken skin, of a family group in 17th C. dress, the sticks are pierced mother of pearl, 9 in. radius, c. 1810. **£85-90** *EA*

An early 19th C. ivory brise fan, Chinese. **£40-45** *SS*

An unusual fan, the black lacquer splines and guards with gilt figures, against a silver ground, the faces ivory (some wear), 26.8 cm., early 19th C., paper case. **£110-160** *SB*

An early 19th C. printed fan on paper leaf with pierced and gilded sticks, 10 in. radius, c. 1840. **£35-38** *EA*

A fan, with black and gold lacquer splines and guards, the paper leaf brightly painted, the faces ivory and the clothes material (slight wear), 28 cm., c. 1850. **£250-320** *SB*

A hand-painted fan, with lithographed panel, carved and pierced sandalwood sticks, decorated with cut steel pique, c. 1845-50, 10 in. radius. **£58-64** *EA*

A 19th C. fan with separated leaf, covered with scene of peasants, mirror set in guard, 9 in. radius. **£55-60** *EA*

A Cantonese fan, with decorated lacquered sticks and double sided paper leaf, with 60 ivory faces, 10 in. radius, c. 1860 (vary in price according to number of faces). **£45-50** *EA*

A carved tortoiseshell fan (slight damage and repair), 27.6 cm., mid-19th C. **£180-220** *SB*

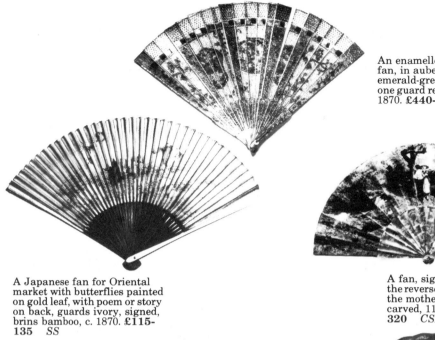

An enamelled and silver-gilt fan, in aubergine, blue and emerald-green (ribbon broken, one guard repaired), 18.8 cm., c. 1870. **£440-550** *SB*

A Japanese fan for Oriental market with butterflies painted on gold leaf, with poem or story on back, guards ivory, signed, brins bamboo, c. 1870. **£115-135** *SS*

A fan, signed E. Rudaux 1876, the reverse monogrammed F.B., the mother of pearl sticks carved, 11 in., 1876. **£280-320** *CSK*

A lacquer fan, in two tones of gold on black (slight wear), 28 cm., c. 1880. **£125-155** *SB*

A metal fan, enamelled blue and green (slight wear), 21.2 cm., c. 1880. **£150-200** *SB*

A Victorian wedding fan, with hand-painted leaf, and decorated pearl sticks, 9 in. **£48-52** *EA*

An attractive Victorian printed fan with paper leaf, embossed reverse, on pierced sticks, 10 in. radius. **£38-45** *EA*

A late 19th C. lace fan with oyster mother of pearl sticks (with box), 9½ in. radius. **£25-30** *EA*

A high Victorian fan on gauze, some damage. **£16-18** *SS*

An American mourning fan, Edwardian, with box. **£5-10** *SS*

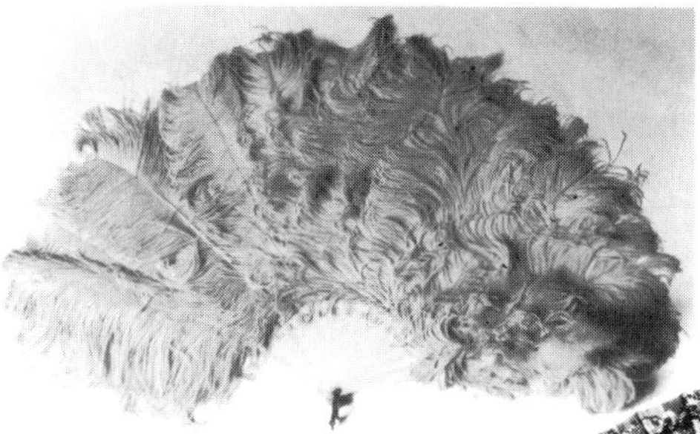

A white ostrich fan, with ivory sticks, 17 in. radius. **£28-32** *EA*

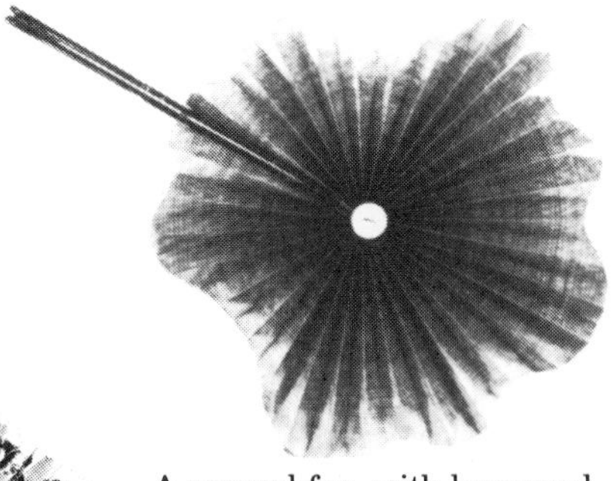

A parasol fan, with lacquered sticks and mother of pearl button, 11 in., c. 1795, contemporary case inscribed 'given to me by the Duchess of Devonshire'. **£85-110** *CSK*

A Japanese fan, c. 1910-1920. **£5-8** *SS*

LACQUER

- **lacquerwork was known in China from the 12th C. B.C.**
- **traders brought back examples from the late 17th C.**
- **many larger carved lacquer pieces e.g. screens made in the Ching (Qing) period 1644-1912 were exported to Europe**
- **Holland was probably one of the first European countries to employ a technique of lacquer work — in no way emulating the sheer lustre and brilliance of the early Chinese and Japanese**
- **in England the work was called japanning**
- **often as many as 30–35 coats were applied before the surface was ready for painting and gilding**
- **one point to note with lacquer is that the early pieces tend to have the correct number of layers, whereas in late 19th C. pieces, the quality dropped markedly. Once again quality and condition are crucial**
- **Japanese and Chinese lacquer until the end of the 19th C. tends to leave a smooth surface, whereas European lacquer has a tendency to craze**
- **much furniture in particular has been re-lacquered and particular attention should be paid to gilding — any which is too bright is suspicious**

A 19th C. papier mache box, with beautiful flower detail, 6½ in. square. **£130-240**

A 19th C. papier mache tea caddy, with two lidded interior, 8½ in. wide. **£200-225** *SV*

A Suzuribako, decorated in gold and silver hiramakie, okibirame, togidashi and heidatsu on a maki-bokashi ground (slight damage), 19th C., 25.6 by 24.2 cm. **£900-1,200** *C*

A large lacquer box, decorated in blue, green, red, puce and ochre, basketwork panels on the sides (restored), with a jian mark, 17th/18th C., 26¾ in. (68 cm.) wide. **£400-500** *C*

A 19th C. papier mache tea caddy, 4½ in. high. **£40-50** *SV*

A 19th C. papier mache card box, with four compartments, 6¼ in. wide. **£160-175** *SV*

A small Shukan inlaid lacquer box and cover, inlaid aogai seal, Japanese, 9 by 8 by 3 cm. **£650-750** *SKC*

A 19th C. papier mache snuff box, with Swiss scene, 3½ in. wide. **£75-85** *MB*

A gold lacquer box and cover, modelled as a seated boy, 19th C., 8.6 cm. high. **£550-650** *C*

A gold lacquer box and cover, modelled as a kneeling girl (kinutsa missing), signed on the nashiji base Jusansai, and kakihan, 19th C., 7.9 cm. high. **£450-500**   *C*

A lacquer sake bottle, decorated in gold and silver hiramakie with inlaid silver dew-drops (slight abrasions), unsigned, Momoyama style, early Edo period, 22 cm. high. **£350-420**   *C*

A pair of Japanese lacquer and Shibayama moon vases and covers, with ivory finials, 6 in. **£1,400-1,600**   *L*

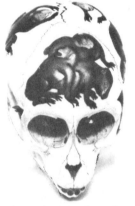

A rare lacquered monkey skull, 9 cm., mid-19th C. **£440-560** *SB*

A Japanese lacquered serving dish, modelled as a fish with one side detachable, details in gilt. **£700-800**   *SB*

A Japanese lacquered tree trunk vase, in brown and gold lacquer, 61 cm., mid 19th C. **£400-480**   *SB*

A Chinese export black and gold lacquer hanging lantern, with painted glass panels, 19th C., 22 in. (56 cm.) high. **£660-850**   *C*

A small gold lacquer model of a No mask, 19th C., 6 cm. high. **£150-200**   *C*

A red lacquer coffee set, each piece of sealing-wax red and silver and gold lacquered (some damage), 38 by 55 cm., c. 1880. **£220-290**   *SB*

A rare lacquer pillow, the central section in red lacquered basket-weave (chips and crack), 24.4 cm., mid-19th C. **£260-320**   *SB*

A Namiki lacquer plaque, a mirror black ground around silvery-grey bird with red flash, 37.5 cm., gilt Namiki kan (under direction of) and signature and kakihan, 37.5 cm., c. 1880. **£850-950**   *SB*

A lacquered ostrich egg on stand, decorated in gold, red and black, Japanese, 25.5 cm. **£320-380**   *SKC*

TORTOISESHELL

- not the shell of the tortoise, but of the hawksbill marine turtle
- first became popular in the 17th C.
- used to embellish furniture, particularly cabinets in mid to late 17th C.
- in the early 18th C. many snuff boxes, patchboxes and bonbonnieres were produced
- in the 18th C. the dark shell was the most popular
- during Regency tortoiseshell was used for combs and spectacle frames

- especially collectable are the carved 18th C. combs, rather than the moulded 19th C. variety
- during 19th C. the Italians became the great craftsmen working in tortoiseshell
- as with many other small decorative antiques the 1850's saw the production of an amazing number of moulded tortoiseshell pieces
- however in this period there are some very attractive boxes, etuis and combs with silver inlay

A tortoiseshell caddy, c. 1800, 7 in. wide. £275-325 *NC*

A tortoiseshell caddy, c. 1825, 6½ in. wide. £245-265 *NC*

A late 17th C. tortoiseshell Indo-Portuguese Box with silver mounts, 6½ in. wide. £450-550

A George III tortoiseshell tea caddy, with silver banding, central silver plaque and silver escutcheon, 7 in. (the interior partition lacking). £85-125 *L*

An early 19th C. tortoiseshell tea caddy, 7 in. wide. £220-250 *EAN*

A tortoiseshell shaped front tea caddy, 7 in., c. 1810. £130-150 *AD*

A 19th C. tortoiseshell tea caddy, 5 in. wide. £170-190 *SV*

A late 19th C. tortoiseshell silver gilt box, 7½ in. wide. £300-400

A pierced silver and tortoiseshell box, c. 1910, 3¼ by 4¾ in. £140-160

A 19th C. tortoiseshell tea caddy with internal lid and two compartments, 5 in. wide. £200-225 *SV*

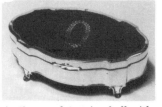

A silver and tortoiseshell with silver piqué medallion trinket box, c. 1920, 4 by 2½ in. £40-50

A gold-mounted tortoiseshell box (small chips to tortoiseshell), probably French, 18th C., 2½ in. (63 mm.) diam. £450-550 *C*

A late 19th C. small stationery box, in tortoiseshell and silver, 6 in. high. **£250-300**

(l.) A tortoiseshell and applied silver card case, c. 1860-1870, 4 by 3 in. **£60-80**

(r.) A tortoiseshell, silver and silver piqué card case, c. 1910, 4 by 3 in. **£80-120**

A late 19th C. heart shape box, in tortoiseshell and cast silver, 3 in. high. **£350-450**

A 19th C. dressing tray, in tortoiseshell and silver piqué, 9 in. long. **£100-150**

An Art Nouveau tortoiseshell and gold comb, c. 1900. **£60-90**

A selection of combs in tortoiseshell and piqué, c. 1840-90. **£60-100**

A tortoiseshell and silver dressing tray, with piqué medallion, early 20th C., 11½ in. long. **£100-150**

A tortoiseshell dressing tray, with gold, silver and mother of pearl piqué, c. 1840-50, 9½ in. long. **£150-350**

SCRIMSHAW

- a form of carving done by sailors particularly in the 19th C.
- the most popular medium was the tooth, jawbone or panbone of the sperm whale
- value really hinges on date, quality of carving plus the actual subject of the carving
- nautical and commemorative subjects command high prices
- freehand inscription is more desirable than copies of plates from books
- there are many fakes around, not to be confused with genuine modern Scrimshaw, 'plastic' ivory has not been kept exclusively for netsuke but has also been adapted to Scrimshaw

A pan-bone scrimshaw, 3¼ by 2¼ in. (8.3 by 5.8 cm.), late 19th C. **£75-100**   *SB*

A pan-bone scrimshaw, decorated, entitled 'Mary Lawson Miss Lamson's dismissal', 7½ by 6¾ in., late 19th C. **£200-300**   *SB*

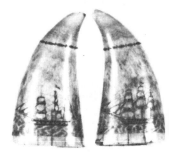

A large carved whale's tooth, decorated in relief with Andromeda and Perseus, 8 in. (20 cm.) long, English, late 19th C. **£160-220**   *SB*

A pair of whale's tooth scrimshaw, each with decorated base and mounted on wooden plinths, 5¾ in. high, probably American, mid-19th C. **£100-150**   *SB*

A pair of whale's tooth scrimshaw, 4½ in. (11.5 cm.) high, late 19th C. **£100-180** *SB*

A coral bottle, with matching stopper. **£180-220**   *C*

Two late 18th C. Scrimshaw commemorative horns, one with engraved decorations of serpents and a swan, the other with thistle, rose and shamrock. **£200-300**   *JC*

A pair of decorated dolphin jaws, each 19½ in. (49 cm.) long, late 19th C. **£100-150**   *SB*

A large pink coral carving, with wood stand, 46.3 cm. wide. **£3,300-3,600**   *C*

A mottled grey and black jade carving of a recumbent water-buffalo, on wood stand, 21.2 cm. long. **£880-1,000**   *C*

A coral group, of three girls (slight damage), on wood stand, 23 cm. high. **£2,000-2,200**   *C*

A mottled grey, pale and dark green jade carving of a water buffalo (one horn repaired), on wood stand, 27.5 cm. long. **£400-450**   *C*

A dark celadon and russet jade carving of a water buffalo, 17th C., 13.5 cm. long. **£1,600-1,800**   *C*

A mottled white jade carving of a female immortal, with wood stand, and fitted box, 23.2 cm. high. **£1,100-1,300**   *C*

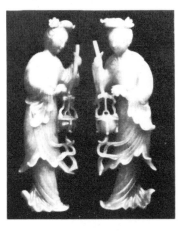

A mottled white, beige, russet and pale green jade carving of Guanyin, on wood stand, 33 cm. high. **£460-520**   *C*

A pair of mottled pale and dark green jade carvings, with wood stands, and fitted boxes, 22.9 cm. high. **£1,000-1,100**   *C*

A green jade incense burner, 18th/19th C., on wood stand, 18.8 cm. wide. **£1,600-1,900**   *C*

A mottled pale grey and light brown agate bottle, one side carved in relief using the white inclusions. **£260-290**   *C*

A jade vase and cover, white, russet, lavender and green; with wood stand and box, 28.3 cm. high. £1,100-1,300 *C*

A pale grey and russet jade bottle, green jade twig stopper, late 18th/early 19th C. £220-260 *C*

A white, lavender, emerald and dark green jade vase and cover, 22.3 cm. high. £3,500-4,000 *C*

A smoked crystal cylindrical brush pot, on separate stand (stand slightly damaged), 20 cm. high. £600-690 *C*

A pale celadon and beige jade vase and cover, carved and pierced (finial slightly repaired), 20.6 cm. high. £1,050-1,200 *C*

A pale grey and beige jade incense burner and cover, entirely carved and pierced, probably 18th C., on wood stand, 19 cm. wide. £3,500-4,000 *C*

A mottled celadon and grey jade incense burner and cover, 21.8 cm. wide. £500-600 *C*

A mottled russet, pale and dark apple-green jade vase and cover, carved and pierced on wood stand, 37.5 cm. high. £6,000-6,500 *C*

A green jade altar set, comprising two elephants with vases and an incense burner, all three inset with coral, turquoise and mother of pearl, the vases 27 cm. high, the incense burner 37 cm. high. £4,500-4,900 *C*

> **Make the most of Miller's**
> *When buying or selling, it must always be remembered that prices can be greatly affected by the condition of any piece.*
> *Unless otherwise stated, all goods shown in Miller's are of good merchantable quality, and the valuations given reflect this fact.*
> *Pieces offered for sale in exceptionally fine condition or in poor condition may reasonably be expected to be priced considerably higher or lower respectively than the estimates given herein.*

A pair of mottled spinach-green jade oval plaques, the reverse incised with two-line poems, 26.6 cm. high. £680-740 *C*

A Tibetan rock crystal snow-lion, and a later gilt-metal single lotus base (cracked, slight damage), probably 18th C., 3¼ in. (8 cm.) high. **£320-400** *C*

An alabaster bust, entitled Mignon, signed Prof. G. Besji, 37 cm., c. 1890. **£200-250** *SB*

A white marble bust of Queen Anne, signed J. E. Boehm Fecit, 93 cm., dated 1873. **£250-320** *SB*

A Tibetan solid rock crystal phur-pa, 19th C., 10¼ in. (26 cm.). **£600-700** *C*

A white marble bust of a young girl, signed Ettore Zocchi, 53.5 cm., 1870's. **£400-480** *SB*

A white marble figure of a young woman dancing, 102 cm., Italian, c. 1860. **£400-450** *SB*

A 19th C. French marble bust of a young woman, in the style of Boizot, 45 cm. high. **£300-380** *C*

A white marble group of two young lovers, signed L. Cigole Roma and dated 1867, 69 cm. **£320-360** *SB*

A 19th C. French terracotta bust of a Vendeen General, by Duchesse Castiglioni-Colonna, called Marcello, signed Marcello 96, 30.5 cm. high. **£350-420** *C*

A good white marble group of the bathers, signed C. L. Hartwell, 57 cm., 67 cm. with marble plinth, 1920's. **£410-460** *SB*

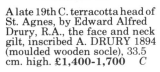

A late 19th C. terracotta head of St. Agnes, by Edward Alfred Drury, R.A., the face and neck gilt, inscribed A. DRURY 1894 (moulded wooden socle), 33.5 cm. high. **£1,400-1,700** *C*

A grey-veined white marble pedestal, applied with gilt-bronze cherub mounts, 109 by 27 cm., c. 1900. **£500-600** *SB*

A 19th C. English marble bust of a man, by Edward Hodges Baily, inscribed E.H. Baily R.A., Sculpt. London 1838, 73.5 cm. high. **£500-600** *C*

A pair of ormolu-mounted marble urns and covers, late 18th C., 14 in. (36 cm.) high. **£300-400** *C*

A solid porphyry urn, on turned socle and moulded circular base, early 19th C., 9 in. (23 cm.) high. **£270-330** *C*

A South Arabian alabaster funerary plaque, 6½ in. (16.5 cm.) high, 1st C. B.C./A.D. **£230-280** *C*

A pair of ormolu-mounted granite pot-pourri vases, 19th C., fitted for electricity, 24 in. (61 cm.) high. **£1,000-1,200** *C*

A pair of ormolu mounted marble urns, 13¼ in. (33.6 cm.), c. 1900. **£330-400** *SB*

A Kashan mottled red sandstone head of a male figure (face extensively rubbed), on a metal block base, 13½ in. (34 cm.) high. **£700-900** *C*

A blackstone Bengal group of Uma Mahesvara, on a steel base, 16th C., 25 in. (63.5 cm.) high. **£1,300-1,500** *C*

A Khmer sandstone figure of a saint, 12th C., 21 in. (53 cm.). **£1,900-2,200** *C*

A Jain Alabaster figure of a seated Tirtankhara, 17th/18th C., 18 in. (46 cm.) high. **£1,600-1,800** *C*

A Syrian painted stucco bust of a woman, hollow moulded, 10¾ in. (27.3 cm.) high, c. 3rd-4th C. A.D. **£380-420** *C*

An ivory stele, 25.6 cm., late 19th C. **£125-175** *SB*

A Chinese ivory carving of a scholar, wood stand with cloisonne enamel borders, 26.8 cm. high. **£280-320** *C*

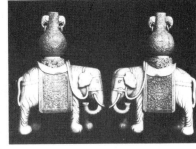

An ivory model of Amida (piece missing), 19th C., 38.6 cm. high. **£2,000-2,200** *C*

A pair of Chinese ivory carvings of standing saddled elephants, 19th C., 23.2 cm. high. **£800-1,000** *C*

An ivory Immortal, 20 cm., mid-19th C., with wood stand. **£120-150** *SB*

An ivory Buddha, 21.5 cm., mid-19th C. **£120-160** *SB*

Make the most of Miller's
Look for the code letters in italic type following each caption.
Check these against the list of contributors on page 10 to identify the source of any illustration.
Remember — valuations may vary according to locality; use of the codes can allow this to be taken into account.

A sea ivory group of Eibisu, black detail, engraved Ikko, 23 cm., c. 1900. **£340-480** *SB*

A sea ivory group, engraved Rishi, 32.8 cm., c. 1900. **£200-250** *SB*

A large ivory figure of Kannon (head-dress damaged), signed Gyokumin, Meiji period, 52.1 cm. high. **£900-1,200** *C*

A sea ivory Kwannon, engraved Masayuki, 32.2 cm., c. 1900. **£180-220** *SB*

A well-carved ivory group, signed Chikaaki, Meiji period, 59.8 cm. high. **£1,600-1,900** *C*

A well carved ivory group, signed on green tablet Masakaze, Meiji period, 41.6 cm. high. **£1,500-2,000** *C*

A coloured sea ivory Handaka Sonja (tail chipped), red engraved Kogetsu, 28.5 cm., c. 1900. **£300-350** *SB*

An ivory carving of Gama Sennin, with details engraved and stained light brown, signed Muneharu, Meiji period, 42.2 cm. high. **£500-600** *C*

A coloured ivory Gama Sennin, coloured in red and gold, signed Gyokumin, 14.5 cm., c. 1880. **£180-220** *SB*

An ivory butal, with grey detail, 29 cm., four character mark, c. 1900. **£420-480** *SB*

An ivory group (damaged)
engraved Masaaki, c. 19
18 cm. **£250-300** *SB*

An ivory traveller, signed
Komin on a reserve, 16 cm., c.
1900. **£250-280** *SB*

An ivory group (foot repaired),
fixed wood stand, inlaid Japan
and CH Mark, 23 cm., c. 1900.
£250-300 *SB*

A sea ivory
immortal, engraved
Koichi, 29 cm., c.
1900. **£130-160**
SB

An ivory carving of
a Chinese sage,
engraved and
stained detail,
signed on red tablet,
Gyokuzan, late 19th
C., 37.1 cm. high.
£500-600 *C*

An ivory armourer, the detail
well engraved, textured and
black filled (small piece
missing), signed Shimin on a
lacquer reserve, 9 cm., 19th C.
£700-850 *SB*

An ivory carving of an old
woman and three small
children, signed Hozui, late
19th C., 14.1 cm. high. **£850-
950** *C*

An ivory group (part of rod
missing), signed Harutake, 1
cm., c. 1900. **£300-360** *SB*

A set of 3 ivory carvings (two
slightly damaged), one signed
Yukihiro, late 19th C., the
tallest 20.1 cm. **£1,600-
1,800** *C*

An ivory basket-seller (one
basket with infill missing),
signed Hyoitsu, with wood
stand, 17 cm., c. 1900. **£850-
1,050** *SB*

An ivory woodsman
(chipped), 38 cm., c.
1900. **£800-900**
SB

An ivory and lacquered wood
Sarumawashi, wood stand,
signed Ho-min, 30 cm. **£550-
650** *SKC*

An ivory group (small piece
missing), engraved red
Tamayuki, 19 cm., c. 1900.
£520-600 *SB*

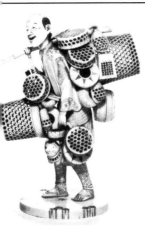

An ivory basket-seller, details inlaid in lacquer, stained ivory and mother of pearl (chip on one leg), signed Yoshiishi, 19 cm., c. 1900, wood stand. **£780-880** *B*

A lacquered ivory peasant, signed Shosai, 17.2 cm., early 20th C. **£380-435** *SB*

An ivory fisherman, signed Muneyasu on a lacquer reserve, 15 cm., c. 1900. **£200-250** *SB*

A large ivory carving of an ancient warrior, eyes inlaid in shell, signed on red tablet Seiko, Meiji period, 54.8 cm. high. **£1,300-1,500** *C*

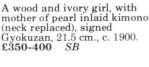

A group of bone birds, on a wood stump, the eyes inlaid or black filled, 32.4 cm. overall, c. 1900. **£170-200** *SB*

A wood and ivory girl, with mother of pearl inlaid kimono (neck replaced), signed Gyokuzan, 21.5 cm., c. 1900. **£350-400** *SB*

An ivory 'Netsuke' of the Takarabune, sepia stain, engraved Komin, c. 1900, 5.5 cm. **£135-170** *SB*

An ivory Netsuke, engraved Masakazu, 7 cm., c. 1880. **£170-250** *SB*

An ivory 'Netsuke', carved with Shoki playing a samisen, engraved Yanatake, 5.3 cm., c. 1900. **£200-250** *SB*

An ivory Netsuke, 3.5 cm., c. 1880. **£170-220** *SB*

A fine large ivory netsuke of a rakan, his eye pupils inlaid in black horn, unsigned, late 18th C. **£900-1,100** *C*

A finely carved ivory netsuke of a Manzai dancer, signed Seiwa, late 19th C. **£300-350** *C*

Right
An ivory Netsuke, with black engraved details (eyes missing), 6.5 cm., engraved Tomotada, c. 1880. **£140-180** *SB*

A wood and ivory netsuke of Fukurokuju (one foot replaced), signed Hirotada, late 19th C. **£600-700** *C*

An ivory netsuke of a rat,
signed Homin, probably late
18th C. **£280-350**   *C*

A well-patinated ivory netsuke
of an ox, eyes inlaid in black
horn, originally inscribed
Tomotada, the characters
defaced, 18th C. **£500-600**   *C*

A well-modelled ivory netsuke
of a persimmon (age crack),
signed Mitsuhiro (Ohara),
Osaka school (1810-1875).
£450-500   *C*

A finely carved ivory netsuke of
a group of 9 masks, signed
Ryomin, 19th C. **£350-400**   *C*

A well patinated ivory netsuke
of a squirrel, inlaid eyes,
unsigned, c. 1800. **£300-400**
C

An ivory netsuke of a running
boar, the eye pupils inlaid in
black horn (age cracks),
unsigned, 18th-19th C. **£300-
400**   *C*

A Narwhal ivory model of a
kirin, the eye pupils inlaid in
black horn, unsigned, early
19th C. **£650-750**   *C*

A well carved ivory netsuke of a
seated oni, eye pupils inlaid in
dark horn, the details engraved
and stained brown, signed
Tomomasa, 19th C. **£500-
600**   *C*

An ivory netsuke of a hare, its
eyes inlaid in pale horn, mid-
19th C., with added signature
Keifu. **£400-450**   *C*

A fine ivory netsuke of
Tadamori, signed Shuosai, mid-
19th C. **£400-500**   *C*

An ivory netsuke of Ono no
Komachi, signed Masatoshi,
early 19th C. **£220-280**   *C*

An ivory Manju Netsuke, 4.2
cm., late 19th C. **£120-160**
SB

An ivory netsuke of Omori
Hikohichi, signed Shuzan
(Ranrinsai Shuzan), 19th C.
£750-850   *C*

Left
A Shizumo ivory shell dream,
engraved black Shizumo, 7.5
cm., c. 1900. **£50-80**   *SB*

An ivory Okimono of a group of six rats, their eyes inlaid, 8 cm., c. 1900. **£130-180**   *SB*

A marine ivory carving of 2 skeletons, details engraved and stained red and black, late 19th C., 15.9 cm. high. **£750-850**   *C*

A pale boxwood netsuke of a dragon, the eye pupils inlaid in black horn, inscribed Tomokazu, 19th C. **£400-450**   *C*

An ivory Okimono (damaged), signed Shuchi on a lacquer reserve, 7.5 cm., c. 1900. **£460-650**   *SB*

Right   A Mingyoku ivory Okimono, engraved Mingyoku, 8.2 cm., c. 1900. **£120-150**   *SB*

An ivory Okimono of an ape riding a horse, 11 cm., late 19th C. **£230-270**   *SB*

A set of three ivory masks, each of a Buddhist deity, 15.2 to 15.5 cm., c. 1900. **£120-150**   *SB*

An ivory orange (minute chip), 5.5 cm., c. 1900. **£200-280**   *SB*

An ivory grotesque (one neck and arm repaired), engraved red Shokwasai Juzan, Mon (pupil), 6.8 cm., c. 1870. **£300-350**   *SB*

A Gyokubun ivory okimono (lacks knop), signed Gyokubun on a lacquered reverse, 6.5 cm., c. 1900. **£270-330**   *SB*

An articulated ivory crayfish (some pieces replaced), 39 cm. extended, c. 1900. **£330-380**   *SB*

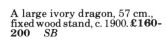

A composite ivory cart box, distressed, 21 by 29 by 38 cm., mainly late 19th C. **£290-350**   *SB*

A large ivory dragon, 57 cm., fixed wood stand, c. 1900. **£160-200**   *SB*

An Okawa Shizutada model of a rickshaw, the carriage set with soft-metal wheels, signed, 15 cm. long. **£500-600**   *SKC*

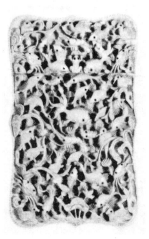

An ivory card case, carved with a profusion of sea creatures and birds, the eyes inlaid, 10.5 cm., c. 1900. **£130-170** *SB*

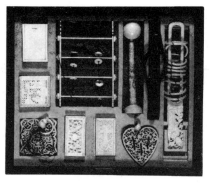

A set of Chinese ivory puzzles, including ball and strings, tangrams, trellis and rings, within a black lacquer box, c. 1870. **£230-280** *SB*

An ivory card case, of shield form, 10.5 cm., c. 1870. **£120-150** *SB*

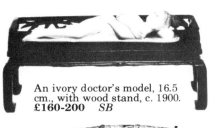

An ivory doctor's model, 16.5 cm., with wood stand, c. 1900. **£160-200** *SB*

A large ivory sword sheath, details coloured black and red, 100.5 cm., c. 1880. **£900-1,100** *SB*

A Japanese stained ivory bottle, carved in relief with Hotei, Ebisu and Fukurokuju. **£260-290** *C*

An inlaid bone Aikuchi sheath, in mother of pearl and horn, slight inlay missing, altered?, 30.5 cm., c. 1900. **£200-250** *SB*

An ivory shrine, containing Buddha and an altar behind pierced doors, door knobs missing, 24 cm., fixed wood stand, c. 1880. **£160-220** *SB*

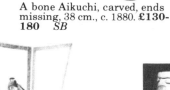

A bone Aikuchi, carved, ends missing, 38 cm., c. 1880. **£130-180** *SB*

A stained ivory snuff bottle and stopper, 9.5 cm., c. 1900. **£120-160** *SB*

An ivory box and cover, carved overall, knob repaired, 11 cm., c. 1900, with stand. **£400-500** *SB*

An Hosensai Rinho lacquered ivory brush pot (damaged), lacquered Henensai Rinho, 29 cm., c. 1870. **£850-950** *SB*

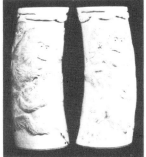

A pair of ivory tusk vases, finely carved, inlaid with ebony (one slightly cracked, bases missing), one with square seal late 19th C., 30 cm. high. **£1,000-1,300** *C*

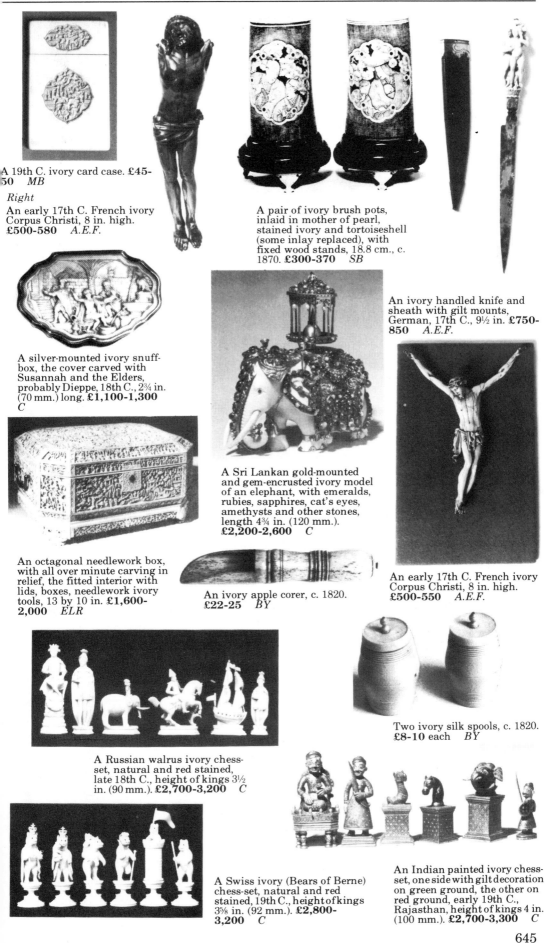

A 19th C. ivory card case. **£45-50**   *MB*

Right
An early 17th C. French ivory Corpus Christi, 8 in. high. **£500-580**   *A.E.F.*

A pair of ivory brush pots, inlaid in mother of pearl, stained ivory and tortoiseshell (some inlay replaced), with fixed wood stands, 18.8 cm., c. 1870. **£300-370**   *SB*

An ivory handled knife and sheath with gilt mounts, German, 17th C., 9½ in. **£750-850**   *A.E.F.*

A silver-mounted ivory snuff-box, the cover carved with Susannah and the Elders, probably Dieppe, 18th C., 2¾ in. (70 mm.) long. **£1,100-1,300**   *C*

A Sri Lankan gold-mounted and gem-encrusted ivory model of an elephant, with emeralds, rubies, sapphires, cat's eyes, amethysts and other stones, length 4¾ in. (120 mm.). **£2,200-2,600**   *C*

An octagonal needlework box, with all over minute carving in relief, the fitted interior with lids, boxes, needlework ivory tools, 13 by 10 in. **£1,600-2,000**   *ELR*

An ivory apple corer, c. 1820. **£22-25**   *BY*

An early 17th C. French ivory Corpus Christi, 8 in. high. **£500-550**   *A.E.F.*

Two ivory silk spools, c. 1820. **£8-10** each   *BY*

A Russian walrus ivory chess-set, natural and red stained, late 18th C., height of kings 3½ in. (90 mm.). **£2,700-3,200**   *C*

A Swiss ivory (Bears of Berne) chess-set, natural and red stained, 19th C., height of kings 3⅝ in. (92 mm.). **£2,800-3,200**   *C*

An Indian painted ivory chess-set, one side with gilt decoration on green ground, the other on red ground, early 19th C., Rajasthan, height of kings 4 in. (100 mm.). **£2,700-3,300**   *C*

A Meissen porcelain chess-set, modelled as frogs, in green or grey, the bases marked, height of kings 3¼ in. (80 mm.). **£2,700-3,300**   *C*

A Chinese ivory chess-set, natural and red stained (few pieces damaged), with folding lacquered board, gilt and inlaid mother of pearl, c. 1820, height of kings 5¼ in. (132 mm.). **£660-760**   *C*

An enamel snuff-box, transfer-printed in black ink, with original gilt-metal mounts, 18th C., probably Birmingham, 3¾ in. (96 mm.) long. **£280-340**   *C*

A Staffordshire enamel patch box, inscribed 'Wherever I be I'll think of Thee'. **£30-40**   *Bon*

A transfer printed patch box, the lid with an altar and inscribed 'Always the Same', cracked. **£30-40**   *Bon*

A Staffordshire enamel patch box, inscribed 'The Gift of a Friend', pale blue sides. **£30-40**   *Bon*

A Staffordshire enamel patch box, inscribed 'Hail gentle peace to Britain's shore, O dwell with us nor leave us more', some damage. **£30-40**   *Bon*

A Samson enamel patch box, transfer printed with a rustic scene and motto. **£30-40**   *Bon*

A silver-mounted French enamel snuff-box, 9 cm., mid-19th C. **£240-300**   *SKC*

A Bilston enamel snuff-box, with hinged back, c. 1765, 3 in. (75 mm.) high. **£700-800**   *C*

A Continental boite-a-portrait, 2½ in. **£65-100**   *Bon*

A Viennese enamel snuff box, painted with Venus and Acteon, the base with a grisaille landscape, silver-gilt mounts, 2¾ in., mid 19th C. **£280-330**   *Bon*

A Continental enamel snuff box, gilt mounts. **£45-60**   *Bon*

An enamelled cigarette case, 8.7 cm. long, silver-coloured metal, maker's mark of Max Fleischmann, Pforzheim, early 20th C. **£415-465**   *SB*

A pair of Barbedienne champleve enamel vases, now fitted as lamps for electricity, signed F. Barbedienne, 16 in., late 1870's. **£680-780** *SB*

An enamel box, mounted in ormolu, the jewelled lid painted in enamels, French, mid-19th C., 6 in. long. **£150-220** *EEW*

A Viennese enamel cornucopia, the curled horn enamelled, with silver gilt and enamelled jewelled bands, 15 in., mid 19th C. **£1,800-2,000** *Bon*

A pair of Battersea salts, with original liners, on pink and gilt ground, c. 1790. **£300-340** *MB*

A Continental blue ground enamel etui, decorated in Bilston style, gilt metal mounts, lacking interior fittings. **£85-100** *Bon*

An early 19th C. German enamel box with puce enamel, 8½ in. wide. **£900-975** *AD*

A Viennese enamel sedan chair, 3 in., some damage. 19th C. **£100-130** *Bon*

A Staffordshire enamel sander, painted with coloured bunches of flowers, with gilt-metal mounts, 18th C., 1¾ in. (45 mm.) high. **£170-230** *C*

A pair of French enamel candlesticks, painted en grisaille, enriched with gilding, 21 cm. high, late 19th C. **£325-375** *SB*

A pair of Champleve vases, each decorated with a band of taotie masks, stamped mark, 30 cm., late 19th C. **£240-300** *SB*

A Viennese silver-gilt and enamel jewel box, formed as a carriage, the panels painted with legendary heroes (few chips), 19th C., 5¼ in. (132 mm.) high. **£1,500-1,700** *C*

A pair of Cloisonne vases, 91 cm., c. 1900. **£620-690** *SB*

A pair of Cloisonne vases, each decorated on a midnight blue ground, 25 cm., c. 1900. **£250-420**   *SB*

A pair of 19th C. Japanese bright blue ground cloisonne vases (each with a small dent), 14 in. **£450-520**   *WW*

A Cloisonne vase, with silver wire decoration on a midnight blue ground, 46 cm., 1900, wood stand. **£260-320**   *SB*

A pair of cloisonne vases, each with silver wire decoration (slight crack beneath one lip), 15 cm., fitted wood box, c. 1900. **£200-260**   *SB*

A pair of cloisonne vases, each with silver wire decoration, 19 cm., wood stands, c. 1900. **£180-250**   *SB*

A pair of Japanese cloisonne vases, on a dark blue ground, 14 in. **£300-350**   *Hy.D*

A pair of cloisonne vases, with silver wire decoration on midnight-blue ground, 6.5 cm., c. 1900. **£160-190**   *SB*

A plique-a-jour cloisonne vase 13 cm., early 20th C. **£270-350**   *SB*

A Kawaguchi Gin Bari silver-mounted Cloisonne vase, engraved Kawa-gu-chi, 12 cm. **£520-600**   *SKC*

A cloisonne vase, with silver wire decoration thickly enamelled in the form of a Chinese cabbage, silver rim and base (slight crack), 23 cm., early 20th C. **£1,500-1,800**   *SB*

One of a pair of cloisonne enamel vases (one rim very slightly damaged), Meiji period, 17 cm. high. **£900-1,100 pr.**   *C*

A late 18th C. cloisonne koro and cover, with red, yellow and green flower and leaf pattern on pale turquoise ground, 28 in. wide, 27 in. high. **£5,100-5,900**   *DSH*

A cloisonne koro and cover, with wood stand, 9 cm., c. 1900. **£320-360**   *SB*

A cloisonne bowl and cover, 26 cm., c. 1900. **£720-820**   *SB*

A Cloisonne koro and cover, 9.5 cm., c. 1900. **£100-120**   *SB*

A cloisonne enamel bowl and cover, Meiji period, 18.6 cm. high. **£520-620**   *C*

A pair of large cloisonne dishes, in bright colours on a blue ground (both damaged on border), 76 cm., c. 1900. **£2,000-2,300**   *SB*

A pair of Cloisonne dishes, with a vivid sky-blue ground, 48 cm. diam. **£350-420**   *SKC*

An early Cloisonne dish, on a turquoise ground, 39 cm., mid 19th C. **£90-120**   *SB*

A Cloisonne plate, 30.5 cm., c. 1900. **£120-180**   *SB*

Two Cloisonne plates, 30.5 cm., c. 1900. **£250-300**   *SB*

A pair of Cloisonne plaques, each decorated on a black ground, 30.5 cm., c. 1900. **£160-200**   *SB*

A Cloisonne enamel double bottle, each decorated in colours, on a turquoise ground. **£240-280**   *C*

A cloisonne enamel plaque, with silver-coloured metal frame, 7.2 cm. diam., the reverse inscribed: 'Phoebe & Harold Stabler / London / 1923'. **£185-235**   *SB*

A circular cloisonne enamel plaque, with silver-coloured metal frame, 7.1 cm. diam., the reverse inscribed: 'Phoebe & Harold Stabler/London/1922'. **£140-190**   *SB*

Left
A Russian silver gilt and Cloisonne enamel spoon, St. Petersberg, maker 'N.C.'. **£230-270**   *SKC*

An antique Chinese silk and metal thread pictorial carpet, decorated with a series of five-clawed imperial dragons, inscribed Pao-ho Tien (Hall of Protecting Harmony), 11 ft. 9 in. by 9 ft. **£4,500-5,000** *C*

An antique Chinese silk and metal thread pictorial carpet, with a horse running through a stylised sea containing Buddhist emblems, inscribed Chung-ho Tien Pei-yung (Made for use in the Hall of Central Harmony), 11 ft. 11 in. by 9 ft. 3 in. **£3,300-3,600** *C*

An antique Chinese silk and metal thread pictorial carpet, one end inscribed T'ai-ho Tien Pei-yung (Made for use in the Hall of Supreme Harmony), probably Peking, 9 ft. 10 in. by 8 ft. 2 in. (299 by 248 cm.). **£3,600-4,200** *C*

An Iran village, probably Abadeh, rug, colours: white, two blues, brown-red, green, pink, pale orange and black, c. 1920, condition: good, 6 ft. 8½ in. by 5 ft. **£550-650** *L*

An Afshar rug, condition: fair, 6 ft. 3 in. by 4 ft. 2 in. **£220-280** *SBe*

An antique Belouch rug, in ivory, brown, blue, green, tan, brick-red and burgundy, 5 ft. 5 in. by 3 ft. 10 in. **£1,100-1,400** *C*

An Isfahan rug, in beige, burgundy and dark brown (one small area of moth damage), 7 ft. 5 in. by 4 ft. 9 in. (226 by 145 cm.). **£2,300-2,600** *C*

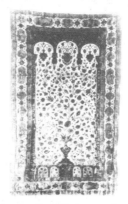

A very fine Kashan embossed silk prayer rug, on a gold and silver thread ground, and ice blue edging, 6 ft. 10 in. by 4 ft. 3 in. **£2,300-2,700** *GC*

A Kashan rug, in blue, yellow and ivory, with a stellar inscription lozenge in one corner, 7 ft. 9 in. by 5 ft. 9 in. (236 by 175 cm.). **£2,800-3,200** *C*

Left
A Garabagh pictorial rug, condition: fair, 7 ft. 6 in. by 4 ft. 10 in. **£500-600** *SBe*

Right
A Heriz carpet, in brick-red, indigo, pistachio-green, ivory and royal blue, 12 ft. by 8 ft. 3 in. (366 by 251 cm.). **£2,300-2,600** *C*

An antique Bordjalu Kazak rug, in mustard yellow and royal blue, with a short kilim strip at one end (area of slight wear), 6 ft. 7 in. by 4 ft. 9 in. **£3,300-3,600**   *C*

A Kazakh rug, condition: fair, brown, corroded, 8 ft. 11 in. by 3 ft. 9 in. **£450-550**   *SBe*

A Kazak Lenkoran rug, in sea-green, powder-blue, ivory and sand-yellow (slight overall wear, extreme corners rewoven), 6 ft. 10 in. by 4 ft. 3 in. **£1,600-1,900**   *C*

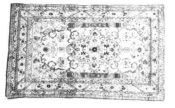

A set of two Kerman rugs, condition: fair, slight wear, 6 ft. 8 in. by 4 ft. 2 in., 6 ft. 8 in. by 4 ft. 1 in. **£610-720**   *SBe*

A Kerman carpet, condition: slight wear, 12 ft. 6 in. by 8 ft. 10 in. **£650-750**   *SBe*

A south-west Iran (probably Khamseh Confederation) rug, colours: blue, red, yellow, white, green, dark brown and black, c. 1910, condition: fair, 6 ft. 1½ in. by 4 ft. 1 in. **£330-400**   *L*

A Kurdish rug, colours: brown, red, blue, green, pink, yellow, white and black, c. 1900, condition: good, but for corrosion, 5 ft. 8½ in. by 3 ft. 11 in. **£260-320**   *L*

A Malayir rug, in indigo, blood-red, ivory and brick-red (slight overall wear), 6 ft. 6 in. by 3 ft. 10 in. (198 by 177 cm.). **£500-600**   *C*

A Marasali prayer rug, in ivory, royal blue, blood-red and dark brown (ends reduced, one area of damage and slight overall wear), 4 ft. 5 in. by 3 ft. 5 in. (135 by 104 cm.). **£1,400-1,700**   *C*

A Turkish, probably Mudjar, rug, colours: red, purple-red, blue, green, pale orange, yellow, brown and black, c. 1910, condition: good, 4 ft. 4½ in. by 2 ft. 11 in. **£220-260**   *L*

A Qashqai rug, in blood red, ivory and blue (slight overall wear, minor restoration), 7 ft. 6 in. by 5 ft. 3 in. **£1,100-1,400**   *C*

A Sarouk rug, in yellow, indigo, brick-red and ivory, 6 ft. 7 in. by 4 ft. 10 in. (201 by 147 cm.). **£2,600-3,000**   *C*

A Sileh rug, condition: fair, 9 ft.
9 in. by 5 ft. 10 in. **£300-380**
SBe

A Sarouk rug, in ivory, indigo,
brick-red, blue and lemon-
yellow, 7 ft. 3 in. by 4 ft. 6 in.
£2,000-2,200 *C*

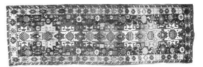

A Shirvan runner, condition:
fair, restored, 11 ft. by 3 ft. 8 in.
£400-520 *SBe*

A Shirvan rug, in dark blue,
brick red and ivory and signed
(small repairs), 9 ft. 10½ in. by 3
ft. 10½ in. **£1,000-1,100** *GC*

A Shirvan rug, with royal blue
field, dated at one end
AH1310/AD1892 in two places,
5 ft. 6 in. by 4 ft. 3 in. **£2,500-
3,000** *C*

A Tabriz prayer rug, in
raspberry-red, royal blue, sky-
blue, green and ivory, 6 ft. 6 in.
by 4 ft. 3 in. **£1,600-1,800** *C*

A Tabriz rug, condition: fair,
slight wear, 6 ft. 7 in. by 4 ft. 6 in.
£150-220 *SBe*

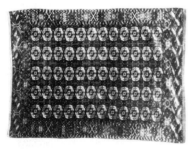

A fine antique Tekke Turkoman
carpet, the wine-red field with
five columns of linked Tekke
guls (small area of moth
damage, slightly dry), 8 ft. 11 in.
by 6 ft. 5 in. **£2,100-2,400** *C*

A Caucasian Kilim, in blood-
red, sea-green, indigo and
yellow, woven in two parts, 12
ft. 3 in. by 6 ft. 6 in. (373 by 198
cm.). **£400-450** *C*

A medallion Ushak carpet, in
blood-red, royal blue, pale
yellow and medium blue (slight
overall wear, restored and
minor damage), 11 ft. 8 in. by 6
ft. 6 in. (354 by 198 cm.).
£4,500-5,000 *C*

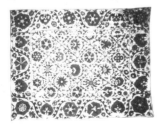

A Bokhara Suzani panel, in
cream, sky-blue, rust-red,
burgundy and sea-green, on
four panels, backed on linen, 5
ft. 1 in. by 3 ft. 11½ in. (155 by
121 cm.). **£1,000-1,200** *C*

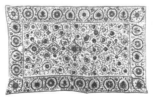

A Samarkand Suzani, on five
linen panels and backed with
linen (cut, restored and
stained), 8 ft. 9 in by 5 ft. 4in.
(266 by 163 cm.). **£650-750** *C*

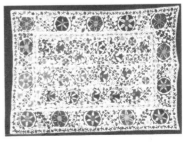

An Uzbek Bokhara Suzani,
with coloured silks on a natural
linen ground, 2.18 by 1.64 m.,
printed linen. **£350-400** *P*

A fragment of a border band, woven in bright colours, Peruvian, pre-Columbus, framed and glazed, 7 by 13¾ in. **£280-320** *CSK*

A Yomut azmalyk, condition: fair, 3 ft. 8 in. by 2 ft. 5 in. **£480-550** *SBe*

A Flemish feuille de choux tapestry fragment, early 17th C., the lower section rewoven, 6 ft. 8 in. by 3 ft. 8 in. **£3,400-3,800** *C*

A set of 12 carpet bowls, decorated in either blue, green or red against white, one plain white 'jack', 3¼ in. (8.2 cm.) diam., English, late 19th C. **£90-130** *SB*

An early Stuart petit point needlework panel, in silk, c. 1630, tortoiseshell veneered and ebonised frame, 9¾ in. by 12¾ in. **£880-1,080** *WW*

A burr-yew grand piano, the keyboard inscribed Patent Erard, London, 39 by 102 in., mid-19th C. **£2,500-3,000** *SB*

A rare William IV upright cabinet pianoforte, in brass and ebony inlaid mahogany case, dated approximately 1832, width 48½ in. **£220-300** *LT*

A Broadwood marquetry oak boudoir grand piano, the iron frame stamped Patent, with ivory accidentals, c. 1880. **£800-1,000** *SB*

A 19th C. boudoir upright pianoforte, the wood framed action by John Broadwood & Co. London, Pattern No. 1572, instrument no. 94246, in a satinwood veneered and marquetry case, 4 ft. 7 in. **£650-800** *WHL*

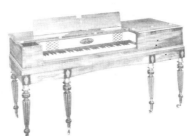

A mahogany and rosewood square piano, the satinwood nameboard painted and inscribed Patent Goulding, D'Almaine, Potter & Co., 20 Soho Square, London, bearing the serial no. G.W.D.N.2410, 66 by 24½ in. **£500-600** *L*

An 18th C. dress, of leaf-brown silk damask, the neck-line with a later border of Honiton lace. **£88-100** *L*

A George III mahogany square piano, by Thomas Haxby of York, with a satinwood name plate, named and dated 1776, 4 ft. 4 in. **£700-830** *WW*

A pair of blue and white pearlware shoe buckles, late 18th C. £55-65   *CSK*

A man's 18th C. coat, of purple cloth, the borders, neck, pocket flaps and cuffs finely embroidered in silks, with silk waistcoat. **£200-250**   *L*

An early 19th C. gentleman's hat wig with gathered plaits, ribboned tail and curled side pieces, rectangular tin case with interior compartments and a wooden barber's wig stand of disc shape, with clamp support. **£40-50**   *Bon*

A 16th/17th C. leather loving cup, 6 in. high. **£220-250** *A.E.F.*

A sandwich box and flask in leather case, c. 1900. **£55-60** *ST*

An 18th C. leather drinking vessel, 5 in. high. **£100-125** *TJ*

A 19th C. wooden leather bound water bottle, 12 in. high. **£50-60**   *MA*

A Victorian picnic basket, with padlock, containing three cups and saucers, a kettle, stand and burner, a fuel container and a sandwich box and three spoons, 11½ by 6½ by 7 in. **£45-50**   *AL*

Two 19th C. vesta case whistles. **£28-38**   *MA*

A selection of 19th and 20th C. named police whistles. **£6-12** *MA*

A selection of 19th C. lady's whistles, in agate, jet, silver and plate. **£10-35**   *MA*

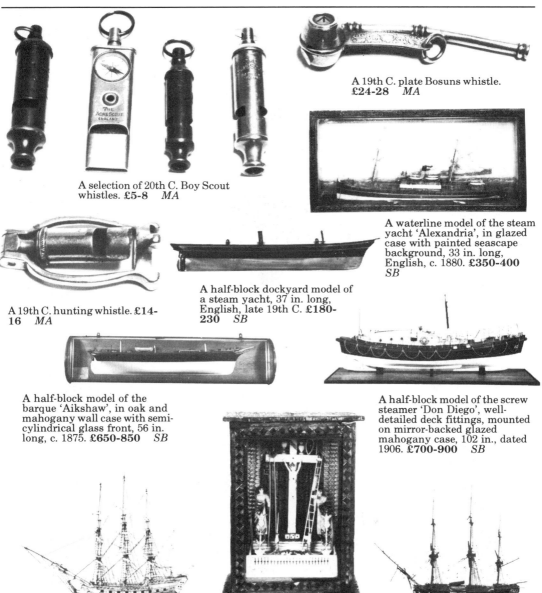

A 19th C. plate Bosuns whistle.
£24-28   *MA*

A selection of 20th C. Boy Scout
whistles. **£5-8**   *MA*

A waterline model of the steam
yacht 'Alexandria', in glazed
case with painted seascape
background, 33 in. long,
English, c. 1880. **£350-400**
SB

A 19th C. hunting whistle. **£14-
16**   *MA*

A half-block dockyard model of
a steam yacht, 37 in. long,
English, late 19th C. **£180-
230**   *SB*

A half-block model of the
barque 'Aikshaw', in oak and
mahogany wall case with semi-
cylindrical glass front, 56 in.
long, c. 1875. **£650-850**   *SB*

A half-block model of the screw
steamer 'Don Diego', well-
detailed deck fittings, mounted
on mirror-backed glazed
mahogany case, 102 in., dated
1906. **£700-900**   *SB*

A Napoleonic prisoner of war
bone and horn ship model, 30
cm. high, 37 cm. long, in case.
£800-950   *PK*

A Napoleonic prisoner-of-war
carved and painted bone group
of the Crucifixion, contained in
a straw work and glazed case,
25 cm. high. **£220-260**   *P*

A prisoner-of-war model of 'The
Victory', with 114 brass
cannons (many now missing), 9
by 10 in., contained in glazed
mahogany wall case, 12 by 15
in., French, c. 1810. **£2,500-
3,500**   *SB*

A French prisoner-of-war work
straw picture, framed and
glazed, 19¼ by 29 in., early 19th
C. **£350-450**   *SB*

An unusual miniature horse,
covered in hide, on mahogany
base, 17¼ in. (44 cm.) long, late
19th C. **£120-180**   *SB*

A model of a frigate, 17 by 26 in.,
on two turned brass columns
above walnut base, English,
20th C. **£150-250**   *SB*

A stuffed long-eared owl, within glazed case, 17½ in. high. **£80-120**   *SB*

A stuffed tawny owl, within glazed case, 22 in. (56 cm.) high. **£70-120**   *SB*

Stuffed exotic birds, on ebonised base, under glass dome, 26 in. (66 cm.) high, late 19th C. **£120-150**   *SB*

An enamel and gilt-metal desk set, comprising: a single-well inkstand, a pen rest and a blotter, painted in bright colours, probably French, 20th C. **£375-425**   *SB*

A boulle desk set, with two cut-glass inkwells and covers, frieze with drawer, 6 by 15¾ in., c. 1860. **£200-250**   *SB*

An early 19th C. tortoiseshell and mother of pearl inkstand, 13½ in. wide. **£345-385**   *EAN*

A Jennens and Bettridge papier mache inkwell set and pen tray, 12 in. wide. **£40-45**   *EA*

A mediaeval French comb, c. 1480, in boxwood and bone (in perfect condition). **£2,500+** A.E.F.

A pair of Burmese giltwood figures, inset with coloured stones and glass, 65 cm., c. 1900. **£550-700**   *SB*

A Regence giltwood wall-bracket, possibly German, 22 in. (56 cm.) wide. **£500-600**   *C*

Right
An Italian mosaic panel, in bright colours, 19th C., 9¼ in. (23.5 cm.) wide. **£1,100-1,300**   *C*

Left
An early 20th C. Crown violet scent in original leather box, 5 in. wide. **£20-25**   *EA*

Two late 19th C. ear trumpets in composition material, 10 in. long, 7 in. long. **£30-35** each *MA*

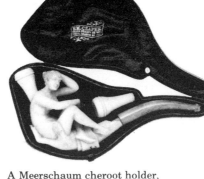

A Meerschaum cheroot holder, engraved 'Alex' with spare nozzle, 14.5 cm. long, probably Austrian, late 19th/early 20th C., in case with label: 'E.M. Czapek/Prana Prikopy 85 Nov/Praq. Graben 85 Neu', the bowl chipped. **£170-190** *SB*

A pair of ormolu bras d'applique, each with three candle arms, c. 1860, 25 in. (63.5 cm.) with wall brackets. **£240-300** *SB*

An early 19th C. brown stoneware phallus, moulded with a satire mask head and realistically rendered, 11 in. **£90-110** *Bon*

A Victorian mechanical bellows, 19 in., 19th C. **£100-140** *RMcT*

A pair of Regency lights, 11½ in. high. **£600-650** *NC*

A Georgian brass cased centrifugal hand blower with pierced drive wheel, 23 cm. **£200-250** *Bon*

A mother of pearl model of Aston Hall, on ebonised base, the glazed case with mirrored back, 18th C. **£1,100-1,300** *C*

A fine quality 18th C. powder flask, Moghul work from Mysore, 7 in. overall width. **£300-380** *A.E.F.*

Early 19th C. Irish peat bellows, 20 in. long. **£120-140** *Gs*

A horn snuff mull, c. 1820. **£48-56** *BY*

(t) An enamel and gold pencil with magnifying glass in top, c. 1890. **£40-45** *LAC*

(m) A 15 ct. gold pencil, c. 1880. **£30-35** *LAC*

(b) A 15 ct. gold pencil. **£25-30** *LAC*

A Victorian viewer, 10½ in. long. **£6-8** *AL*

(t) Victorian lorgnettes, c. 1890. **£35-40** *LAC*

(c) Edwardian silver tooth pick, c. 1910. **£10-13** *LAC*

(b) Edwardian tooth pick, c. 1910. **£10-13** *LAC*

A 19th C. French hatters head-measuring device, 12 in. long, 8 in. high. **£100-120**   *MA*

Five 15 ct. gold watch keys. 1, **£25-30** enamelled; 2, **£15-20**; 3, **£20-25**; 4, **£40-45** enamelled (moving centre); 5, **£25-30** *LAC*

A 19th C. mother of pearl aide memoire. **£14-16**   *SS*

A 19th C. bone aide memoire. **£20-30**   *SS*

An early James Watt duplicating machine, in mahogany box, with wetting book, leaves of tissue papers, bottles, packets of compounds and instructions, English, 17½ in. wide, c. 1825. **£200-300** *SB*

A 6-case inro (some restoration), signed Hasegawa Kyosensai Shigeyoshi saku, and red tsubo seal, late 18th/early 19th C. **£400-450**   *C*

An 18th C. tinder pistol in steel, brass and wood, 5½ in. long. **£200-240**   *MA*

A Protecto shield 'for reading and sun-glare', with box. **£7-9**   *PM*

A Nemmoto Shibayama tsuba, of notched oval section, the details in mother of pearl, stained ivory and horn, on a well-lacquered ground (some inlay missing, chips to lacquer at rim), 11.5 cm., relief silver Nemmoto and tsukuru on pads, late 19th C. **£450-530**   *SB*

An iron tsuba, yosukashi and nikubori, with slight gilt detail, unsigned, Bushu School, 19th C., 7.7 cm. **£85-120**   *C*

An etched glass scent bottle, 1920's, 8½ in. high. **£25-30** *LEX*

A fine four-case inro (very slightly damaged), signed Jokasai, late 18th/early 19th C., with attached coral bead ojime and ivory netsuke, signed Tsuneyuki, late 19th C. with wood box. **£700-800**   *C*

INDEX

This index is cross-referenced. However if a word does not appear under the category e.g. 'porcelain, tyg', it will be found under its initial letter i.e. 'tyg'. All pointer information is indexed in italics.

668

BACK ISSUES

Each edition of Miller's Antiques Price Guide and Professional Handbook is a complete and valuable reference work, but each is unique in that it contains an entirely different selection of photographs, descriptions, valuations and specialist information from any other.

Back Issues Order Form

Please send me the following copies of Miller's Antiques Price Guide and Professional Handbook;

1980 [ ]   1981 [ ]

I understand that the cost is £8.95 for a single volume or £15.00 for two, and enclose my cheque to cover the cost of all volumes ordered.
Please debit my Access/Barclaycard account number.

NAME _____

ADDRESS _____

_____

_____ SIGNATURE _____